Bloom's Classic Critical Views

MARK TWAIN

Bloom's Classic Critical Views

Bloom's Classic Critical Views

MARK TWAIN

Edited and with an Introduction by
Harold Bloom
Sterling Professor of the Humanities
Yale University

BLOOM'S
LITERARY CRITICISM
An imprint of Infobase Publishing

Bloom's Classic Critical Views: Mark Twain

Copyright © 2009 Infobase Publishing

Introduction © 2009 by Harold Bloom

Bloom's Literary Criticism
An imprint of Infobase Publishing
132 West 31st Street
New York NY 10001

Library of Congress Cataloging-in-Publication Data
Mark Twain / edited and with an introduction by Harold Bloom.
    p. cm. — (Bloom's classic critical views)
  Includes bibliographical references and index.
  ISBN 978-1-60413-134-5 (acid-free paper) 1. Twain, Mark, 1835–1910—Criticism and interpretation. 2. Humorous stories, American—History and criticism. I. Bloom, Harold.
  PS1338.M273 2008
  818'.409—dc22

                        2008028105

Bloom's Literary Criticism books are available at special discounts when purchased in bulk quantities for businesses, associations, institutions, or sales promotions. Please call our Special Sales Department in New York at (212) 967-8800 or (800) 322-8755.

You can find Bloom's Literary Criticism on the World Wide Web at
http://www.chelseahouse.com

Contributing editor: Fabian Ironside
Series design by Erik Lindstrom
Cover design by Takeshi Takahashi
Printed in the United States of America
Bang EJB 10 9 8 7 6 5 4 3 2 1

This book is printed on acid-free paper.

Contents

Series Introduction

Bloom's Classic Critical Views is a new series presenting a selection of the most important older literary criticism on the greatest authors commonly read in high school and college classes today. Unlike the Bloom's Modern Critical Views series, which for more than 20 years has provided the best contemporary criticism on great authors, Bloom's Classic Critical Views attempts to present the authors in the context of their time and to provide criticism that has proved over the years to be the most valuable to readers and writers. Selections range from contemporary reviews in popular magazines, which demonstrate how a work was received in its own era, to profound essays by some of the strongest critics in the British and American tradition, including Henry James, G.K. Chesterton, Matthew Arnold, and many more.

Some of the critical essays and extracts presented here have appeared previously in other titles edited by Harold Bloom, such as the New Moulton's Library of Literary Criticism. Other selections appear here for the first time in any book by this publisher. All were selected under Harold Bloom's guidance.

In addition, each volume in this series contains a series of essays by a contemporary expert, who comments on the most important critical selections, putting them in context and suggesting how they might be used by a student writer to influence his or her own writing. This series is intended above all for students, to help them think more deeply and write more powerfully about great writers and their works.

Introduction by Harold Bloom

Everyone should read Mark Twain's sketch "Cannibalism in the Cars," where we are told of some two dozen travelers stranded by heavy snows when their St. Louis to Chicago train breaks down in December 1853. They are nowhere, and after a week's starvation they elect some of their number for breakfast, lunch, and dinner. Only a few other moments in American literature are as delicious as the remembrances of Twain's narrator after ending a week's hunger:

> We improvised tables by propping up the backs of car-seats, and sat down with hearts full of gratitude to the finest supper that had blessed our vision for seven torturing days. How changed we were from what we had been a few short hours before! Hopeless, sad-eyed misery, hunger, feverish anxiety, desperation, then—thankfulness, serenity, joy too deep for utterance now. That I know was the cheeriest hour of my eventful life. The wind howled, and blew the snow wildly about our prison-house, but they were powerless to distress us any more. I liked Harris. He might have been better done, perhaps, but I am free to say that no man ever agreed with me better than Harris, or afforded me so large a degree of satisfaction. Messick was very well, though rather high-flavored, but for genuine nutritiousness and delicacy of fiber, give me Harris. Messick had his good points—I will not attempt to deny it, nor do I wish to do it—but he was no more fitted for breakfast than a mummy would be, sir—not a bit. Lean?—why, bless me!—and tough? Ah, he was very tough! You could not imagine it—you could never imagine anything like it."

Exuberant always, Twain's humor has many modes, but this is one of my favorites in its wicked intensity. Bert Brecht's: "First comes eating, *then* comes morality" rarely is better conveyed. Even freer in Twain's humor is a vein in which ethics is irrelevant, as in the great sketch "Journalism in Tennessee." Twain, seeking a more healthful climate, arrives in Tennessee and is hired as associate editor of the *Morning Glory and Johnson County War-Whoop*. The chief editor, a man of armed gusto, soon is shooting it out in his office with a rival editor, Colonel Blatherskite Tecumseh. Caught in the crossfire, the bloodied Twain resigns in the accurate expectation that other enraged editors are en route:

> Take it altogether, I never had such a spirited time in all my life as I have had to-day. No; I like you, and I like your calm unruffled way of explaining things to the customers, but you see I am not used to it. The Southern heart is too impulsive; Southern hospitality is too lavish with the stranger. The paragraphs which I have written to-day, and into whose cold sentences your masterly hand has infused the fervent spirit of Tennessean journalism, will wake up another nest of hornets. All that mob of editors will come—and they will come hungry, too, and want somebody for breakfast. I shall have to bid you adieu. I decline to be present at these festivities. I came South for my health, I will go back on the same errand, and suddenly. Tennessean journalism is too stirring for me.

The comic genius of Mark Twain, skeptical and sublimely poised between ironical satire and American frontier extravagance, goes on defining his nation's most individual yet characteristic humor.

BIOGRAPHY

Mark Twain
(1835–1910)

The humorist, journalist, travel writer, novelist, and short story writer who took the name Mark Twain in Nevada in 1863 was born Samuel Langhorne Clemens in Florida, Missouri, in 1835. "I was born without teeth—and there Richard III had the advantage of me," he joked in "A Burlesque Biography" (1871), continuing:

> But I was born without a humpback, likewise, and there I had the advantage of *him*. My parents were neither very poor nor conspicuously honest.
>
> But now a thought occurs to me. My own history would really seem so tame compared with that of my ancestors that it is simply wisdom to leave it unwritten until I am hanged.

The family moved to Hannibal, Missouri, in 1839, which, renamed as "St. Petersburg," would provide the location for the novels *The Adventures of Tom Sawyer* and the early chapters of *The Adventures of Huckleberry Finn*.

Sam's father died when Sam was only eleven years old. The loss, according to the critic Van Wyck Brooks, set into motion an unresolved conflict that would blight Clemens as a writer. To support his family, he began taking work, in due course dropping out of school and working at various newspaper offices. He worked for his brother Orion's newspaper, which he ran when Orion's business matters drew him elsewhere. During his brother's leaves of absence, Sam would introduce satirical attacks on local dignitaries and celebrities into the paper, to Orion's great irritation. Even more goading for Orion was the fact that circulation improved under Sam's tutelage. After several arguments, Sam left Orion's newspaper and wandered east as a printer but returned to write for successive newspaper "concerns" (and failures) orchestrated by Orion.

Sam Clemens famously graduated to working on the riverboats that traveled the Mississippi River, rising to the hallowed position of a pilot. This, Clemens would later say, might have suited him forever had not the railroad risen to such prominence in those years, rendering the riverboats all but obsolete. Another great and insurmountable obstacle for the steamboats was the onset of the Civil War.

After an ill-starred and mainly farcical foray into warfare, nominally fighting on the Confederate side (recounted in "The Private History of a Campaign That Failed," 1885), Clemens abandoned the conflict and went to the West Coast on a commission as his brother's private secretary. Orion had been awarded the position of secretary of the new state of Nevada. How Sam came to Nevada and quickly switched vocations, first to silver miner, then to journalist, is recounted in his third book, *Roughing It* (1872).

In Virginia City, Nevada, Sam Clemens took his better-known *nom de plume* and as "Mark Twain" made a name for himself (or, at least, earned notoriety) on the West Coast. Through the interventions of eastern humorist Artemus Ward (whose actual name was Charles Farrar Browne), who was then touring parts of the West with his "burlesque lecture," Mark Twain was introduced to a New York readership (1865). His story of "Jim Smiley and His Jumping Frog" soon garnered international renown, to Twain's bemusement (and to some consternation). Twain's first book, titled after and centered on the jumping frog, followed, published in New York in 1867.

Mark Twain was then contracted to write letters from a cruise ship (the *Quaker City*) bound for Europe and the Holy Land. These letters gave rise to *The Innocents Abroad* (1869), from which his fortune and fame began to grow significantly. In England, particularly, unscrupulous publishers "pirated" all and any of Twain's newspaper work, even pieces that were not actually by Twain. From this imposition sprang Twain's obsession with international copyright law.

For his next project, Twain essayed a collaborative novel, *The Gilded Age*, in 1873, which was only compromised by the contributions of his staid collaborator, Charles Dudley Warner (a New England neighbor of Twain's). Twain's subsequent solo effort, *The Adventures of Tom Sawyer* (1876), fared better. A quick succession of books followed, with Twain going back and forth among genres, from travel writing and autobiography to historical fiction, then to autobiographical fiction, all the while continuing to produce humorous sketches and short stories: *A Tramp Abroad* (1880), *The Prince and the Pauper* (1881), *Life on the Mississippi* (1883), *The Adventures of Huckleberry Finn* (1884), *A Connecticut Yankee in King Arthur's Court* (1889), *The American Claimant* (1892), *Tom Sawyer Abroad* (1894), *The Tragedy of Pudd'nhead Wilson* (1894), *Personal Recollections of Joan of Arc* (1896), *Tom Sawyer, Detective* (1896), *Following the Equator* (1897), *The Man That Corrupted Hadleyburg and Other Stories and Essays* (1900), *Adam's Diary* (1904), *What Is Man?* (private printing, 1906), *Christian Science* (1907), *Captain Stormfield's Visit to Heaven* (1907), and *Is Shakespeare Dead?* (1909).

At times, Twain was working on several works simultaneously; a recurring criticism was that within any one work he veered inexplicably between different genres.

This confusion was mirrored in Twain's movements and the relocation of his household. First by necessity and later by habit, Mark Twain led a peripatetic existence for most of his life. As Tom Sawyer and Huckleberry Finn would be led on excursions outside St. Petersburg, "lighting out for the Territory," so it went for their author. A summary of Twain's complicated movements is given in Merle Johnson's *Bibliography* (New York: Harper and Brothers, 1910), pp. 149–150:

> Those who value Mr. Clemens' speeches and fugitive efforts will find use for the appended Chronology of his various residences and travels as an aid for search in newspaper files and other local sources.
>
> 1861–64, in Nevada; in summer of 1864 to San Francisco; 1865, in California; in 1866, a trip to Hawaii, then back to San Francisco; 1867, across the isthmus to New York, thence to Washington, back to New York, sailing in June on *Quaker City* trip to the Orient; 1868, in Washington, thence in March to San Francisco, and back in September to New York; in fall of 1869, to Buffalo, balancing between Buffalo and Elmira until the fall of 1870, removing to Hartford; in July, 1871, to England; most of 1872 and 1873 between London and Hartford; 1874 to 1877 in Hartford, with summers in Elmira; winter of 1877–78 in Chicago, then to Europe; 1879, in England, France, and Germany, until September, then back to U. S.; 1880, until 1890, mainly in Hartford, with summer changes, mostly to Elmira, home of Mrs. Clemens; most of 1891–92–93–94 in Europe, wintering in Aix-les-Bains, Berlin, Florence, and Paris in turn; 1895, to Europe, then back for lecture tour of U. S.; leaving Vancouver for 'round-the-world trip.

Twain's personal life was necessarily affected by this propensity to drift. His private life is best divided between his Jacksonian bachelor years spent along the Mississippi River and among the silver mines of Nevada and his Victorian life as a devoted husband and father, when he relocated to the civilized East Coast realms of New York State and Connecticut. Twain married Olivia Langdon, whom he had fallen in love with after first seeing her image in a locket (her brother's), while on the *Quaker City* cruise. They remained together until Livy's death in 1904 in an apparent state of domestic bliss (though recent studies find chinks in this guise, almost inevitably). Twain and Livy had a son who died at less than two years of age, a loss for which Twain characteristically blamed himself. Of three daughters, Twain outlived all but one of them. Domestic bliss, its crushing collapse, and the deep, furious cynicism that followed, characterized Twain's last years. His final project was an autobiography, vast and fluid, which he dictated to secretaries and which would be distinguished by its remarkable candor. So large and rambling are the manuscripts that they have never been satisfactorily ordered nor yet printed in their entirety.

Twain was a celebrity as much as he was a writer, and he enjoyed socializing and the limelight (unlike writers such as Nathaniel Hawthorne or Herman Melville). While notoriety brought him into contact, however fleeting, with the majority of his contemporaries in American (and English) literature, his fondness for publicity and a dynamic social life detracted somewhat from his writing. Even the novelist and critic William Dean Howells, who was Twain's foremost friend and champion, remarked that "I hate to have him eating so many dinners, and writing so few books." While Twain was popular with readers, he was a popular target for the critics. Twain addressed this problem in a letter to Andrew Lang in 1890, in which he argued that "I have never tried . . . to help cultivate the cultivated classes. . . . And I never had any ambition in that direction, but always hunted for bigger game—the masses." This state has been rectified, of course, but that rehabilitation was done mostly posthumously.

As can be seen from the accounts that follow, Twain aggravated and offended as much as he charmed and enchanted. His career veered and wobbled, both critically and financially. A characteristic behavior that would haunt Twain through the end of his life was an inveterate propensity to invest in crackpot patents that failed to turn a profit.

Mark Twain died, in 1910, at the age of seventy-four. He was survived by one daughter, Clara.

PERSONAL

"The first chapters are fascinating," Dwight Mcdonald writes of *The Adventures of Tom Sawyer*, "for here ... we see a mass-culture hero taking form." The same might be said of the earliest glimpses of Mark Twain, as he takes that name in Virginia City, Nevada, when he was writing for that city's *Enterprise* newspaper. Mark Twain's formative years as a writer—after he had served as a pilot on the Mississippi River and apprenticed for his brother's newspapers in Missouri and Iowa—were spent serving the mining communities on the frontier. This vital period of his life is potentially and frequently overshadowed by his later, international career. This "prehistory," which precedes his novels, romances, and travel books, his hobnobbing with millionaires and celebrities, and his acclaimed after-dinner speeches nevertheless saw the proper development of the "Mark Twain" persona. It was in this guise and under this name that Clemens earned notoriety, if not necessarily the sort of fame he would later seek.

Students may find it valuable to compare the earliest Twain—alternately called a "beef-eating, blear-eyed, hollow-headed, slab-sided ignoramus," a "pilfering reporter," and "a *liar*, a *poltroon* and a puppy"—to the "grampa" figure of Twain's final years (a façade, of course) or to the late twentieth century's critically rehabilitated and serious author. Can the author of *Personal Recollections of Joan of Arc* be detected in the blackguard of the mining camps?

One of the best sources to gauge Twain's metamorphosis is Ambrose Bierce, the acerbic author of the *Devil's Dictionary* (among other works), who lurks behind Twain's career as a sort of less successful doppelganger (in one late letter, he even remarks on their mutual resemblance). While Bierce stands for wit, as he says, Twain stands for humor, and, by popular standards, humor prevailed over wit. Increasingly overlooked and already bitter by nature (he was dubbed "Bitter Bierce," as well as "Dod Grile"—a flimsy anagram of "God Riled"), Bierce serves as a deflating Momus figure (the personification of censure and mockery in Greek mythology) for Twain, who was near (if not with) Twain from the early days, whether in San Francisco or London, and who observed him to the last.

For the most part, over time, personal estimates of Twain only increase in their warmth. By the end of his life, Twain was a well-established "clubbable man"; that is, a joiner of clubs. He was welcomed by elite groups of wealthy men or by confirmed literary successes. He was also a man of "the people," inasmuch as he liked to parade down Fifth Avenue on a Sunday morning as churchgoers were emerging from St. Patrick's Cathedral. Yet when approached by Theodore Dreiser—then an aspiring unknown—Twain is cagy and remote. Thus accounts of the man inevitably vary. The obvious question to be asked, which necessarily can not be answered, is, which was the real Twain? This query is asked more than once in the texts that follow. Dreiser's account gives us an interesting outsider's view. Henry W. Fisher's accounts have a certain level of intimacy but also contain an unusual level of candor, that cannot be found even in the memoirs of Twain's closest friend, William Dean Howells.

One might well ask, how are these snippets of information relevant? How should they be used as literary data? A good example, if perhaps excessive, is provided by Van Wyck Brooks in *The Ordeal of Mark Twain* (1920). Following the publication of Arthur Bigelow Paine's *Mark Twain: A Biography* (1912), critics were provided with a vast repository of data, which coincided—fortunately or unfortunately—with the advent of psychoanalysis. Private lives were henceforth fair game in literary (or indeed any form of) analysis. Even Brooks's toughest opponent, Bernard DeVoto, conceded that Brooks's "system" was "the most important critical idea of the last pre-war and first post-war decades." In rapid succession, the critical movement called New Criticism would challenge such methodology, with critics such as John Crowe Ransom, Allen Tate, and Cleanth Brooks insisting that the life of the author is of no relevance to the text, which is wholly separate and an independent entity. This argument continues, scarcely abated, to this day.

UNSIGNED "VIRGINIA AT MIDNIGHT" (1863)

The author of this short "item" tells first of how he climbed Mount Davidson at night to look over the city, at the summit "pulling out the comforter that Mark Twain had pressed upon us"—a bottle of gin. "And then—Mark Twain's bottle, never full, being empty—we slowly descended." The following description picks up the trail at the station house.

We found Jack Perry's Deputy, Mark Twain, expostulating with a newly arrested subject who insisted that Mark Twain had stolen his gin bottle and boots. We don't believe the latter accusation but for the former—there was a bottle in Mark's pocket in lieu of the one he gave us, and he told significantly when making the gift that he was going "prospecting" for another.

—Unsigned, Virginia City *Bulletin*,
"Virginia at Midnight," July 11, 1863

UNSIGNED "WHAT DOES IT MEAN?" (1863)

We have noticed several men on E Street today with red streaks on the right arms of their coats. Have we any secret society whose aims are bloody, or what else does this thing mean? Perhaps Mark Twain can enlighten us.

Mark Twain—We have always given you the credit of being the best-tempered and most amiable man under the sun, but we find we have been mistaken, for you came out this morning "barking with rage." We knew you had a splendid item written on those blood-red stains of which we made mention yesterday; but then we had a duty to perform, and for the sake of sparing you we could not allow a good opportunity to go by ourselves. Besides if you did lose one good item, did we not furnish you with a dozen better ones? The night we saw you coming from Chinatown with a "feather in your cap" we supposed you had turned Pah-Ute, but did not imagine you would so soon take to a scalping knife.

—Unsigned, Virginia City *Bulletin*,
"What Does It Mean?" July 24, 1863

Unsigned "Unhealthy" (1863)

At the solicitation of at least 1500 of our subscribers, we will refrain from again entering into a controversy with that beef-eating, blear-eyed, hollow-headed, slab-sided ignoramus—that pilfering reporter, Mark Twain.

> —Virginia City *Bulletin*, "Unhealthy,"
> August 5, 1863

Mark Twain (1863)

My dear Mother and Sister,—Ma, you have given my vanity a deadly thrust. Behold, I am prone to boast of having the widest reputation, as a local editor, of any man on the Pacific coast, and you gravely come forward and tell me "if I work hard and attend closely to my business, I may aspire to a place on a big San Francisco daily, some day." There's a comment on human vanity for you! Why, blast it, I was under the impression that I could get such a situation as that at any time I asked for it. But I don't want it. No paper in the United States can afford to pay me what my place on the "Enterprise" is worth. If I were not naturally a lazy, idle, good-for-nothing vagabond, I could make it pay me $20,000 a year. But I don't suppose I shall ever be any account. I lead an easy life, though, and I don't care a cent whether school keeps or not. Everybody knows me, and I fare like a prince wherever I go, be it on this side of the mountains or the other. And I am proud to say I am the most conceited ass in the Territory.

> — Mark Twain, letter to Mrs. Jane Clemens
> and Mrs. Moffett, August 19, 1863, from
> *Mark Twain's Letters*, Paine, ed., 1917, 1: 92

Unsigned "Worse and Worse" (1863)

The genius who hashes up the locals for the Enterprise, and who outraged the feelings of the whole community yesterday by publishing a really disgraceful sensation story, wholly without point, other than the giving expression to a sort of natural talent he possesses, this morning comes out in another article on the same subject even worse than that published yesterday. We say worse, because the fact of the almost universal condemnation of the story, when it was discovered to be an unmitigated falsehood, compelling its author to swallow his own words, and his doing so publicly, is even more injurious, or should be, to the reputation of an editor than the first promulgation of the untruth. The man who could pen such a story, with all its horrors depicted in such infernal detail, and which to our knowledge sent a pang of terror to the hearts of many persons, as a joke, in fun, can have but a very indefinite idea of the elements of a joke. Why, the editors of the Gold Hill News had their feelings worked up to fever heat by reading the harrowing details of the story, and it will without doubt be republished in all the California and Atlantic papers, and commented on as an incident of our Territorial social system. Is there any joke in this? Is it any joke for a newspaper heretofore of undoubted veracity and reliability permitting itself to spread a story broadcast through the land that disgraces and injured the reputation of the very community that sustains it? If this is a joke we can't see the point where the laugh comes in.

—Unsigned, Virginia City *Bulletin*,
"Worse and Worse," October 29, 1863

UNSIGNED (1863)

The horrible story of a "murder" which we yesterday copied in good faith from the *Enterprise* turns out to be a mere "witticism" of Mark Twain. In short, A LIE—utterly baseless, and without a shadow of foundation. The *Enterprise* is the pioneer newspaper of the Territory, is more widely known than any other, and having been ably and respectably conducted, has heretofore been considered a reliable medium of information. The terrible tale related in its columns yesterday, and copied into ours, was believed here, and will be believed elsewhere—wherever the *Enterprise* and the *News* are read. It will be read with sickening horror, and the already bloody reputation of our Territory will receive another smear.

—Unsigned, Gold Hill Daily *News*,
October 29, 1863

UNSIGNED (1863)

That fellow's heart must be as callous to all the nobler feelings of our nature, as the throat of a whiskey guzzler is to the sense of burning. No remorse for outraging a whole community! . . . It shows a very peculiar taste indeed in one whose feelings would appear to be seared as with a hot iron against all human sympathy, to appeal to those whom he has deceived by the allusion to those very feelings he is so evidently destitute of. For him to complain of having his deed published in "small caps" by a contemporary whom he fooled so badly as he did the Gold Hill *News*, is absurd, ridiculously absurd. . . . And it is an exhibition of even worse taste to suppose that because his contemporaries exposed the malicious hoax, that they did so to injure the *Enterprise* for their own advantage. . . . And it exhibits a peculiar taste to coin new terms to abuse those on whom his taunts fall as harmless as do minie balls on the towers of a monitor.

—Unsigned, Virginia City *Bulletin*,
October 30, 1863

UNSIGNED (1863)

MARK TWAIN.—This favorite writer is 'melancholy;' he has got the mulligrubs. "Where be his jibes, now? his gambols? his flashes of merriment that were wont to set Virginia in a roar? Not one now to mock his own grinning? Quite chop-fallen?" (Bully for Shakespeare.) We haven't had a good square joke out of poor Mark these four or five days. He sits behind *that* historic pine table morose and melancholy, and drinking mean whiskey to drown his misery. Cheer up, friend Mark; the courier brings the welcome news that all is quiet at Dutch Nick's, the 'bar' on Mrs. Hopkins' head is coming out like a new 'red' shoe-brush; the murderer has had *that* gash in his throat caulked and pitched, and the blood in *that* pine forest is not ankle deep. Awake, Mark! arise and toot your horn if you don't sell a clam.

—Unsigned, Gold Hill Daily *News*,
November 2, 1863

ARTEMUS WARD (1864)

Artemus Ward was the pen name of Charles Farrar Browne, the humorist born in Waterford, Maine, in 1834. Browne's biography mirrors that of Samuel Clemens in many ways. His father died young, and he and his elder brother, Cyrus, both went into the printer's trade to support their mother. Charles worked in Boston for a time, setting type for *The Carpet-Bag*, a humor journal that printed the first known Samuel Clemens story in the East. Browne, it can be conjectured, set the type for Clemens's words. Browne made quicker progress in the humor line than Clemens did, travelling south as far as Arkansas, working as a printer and a teacher at times before he wound up in Cleveland. Working at that city's principal newspaper, the *Plain Dealer*, Browne made his name, writing a local editor's daily column on whatever was happening at the time. This job left room for whimsy, and among Browne's many burlesques, hoaxes, and one-line squibs appeared a series of fake letters from an illiterate small-time showman who signed himself "Artemus Ward." Artemus fast became a national phenomenon and—in time—an international one. Browne was the first touring humorist, with his burlesque lectures that rambled and digressed from their attested subject. It is certain that his performances had a profound effect on Mark Twain's direction after he saw and met Browne in Nevada.

Charles Browne's fame was large enough that he traveled to England with his burlesque panorama show. He was at the height of popularity when he became ill in England, and he died there of tuberculosis in Southampton in 1867, at the age of thirty-three. Ironically, the two crossed paths once more when the ship returning to New York with the body of Artemus Ward passed the ship called the *Quaker City*, about to depart with Twain on board. At the time, Twain had been contracted to write the letters that would make up *The Innocents Abroad*.

The name of Artemus Ward will recur in a number of the critical extracts in this volume. Artemus Ward was at first a useful name for Mark Twain to cite in order to get ahead, particularly on the East Coast. As Twain's reputation spread nationally and then internationally, his continuing association with Artemus perhaps began to chafe. The works of Artemus remained in print for more than forty years after Charles Browne's death in 1867. Even in his last days, Twain had to contend with the comparisons. While many critics, following Bernard DeVoto, now minimize the influence, it cannot reasonably be underrated. Artemus Ward, contrary to popular belief, was not simply a dialect humorist or a misspeller. His newspaper work in Cleveland (little of which was ever published in book form) had a powerful influence and was syndicated across the United States. Mark Twain would have been entirely familiar with this work, as well as the Artemus Ward letters.

In this letter, which has been wilfully misread by a recent Twain biographer to signal some kind of romantic relationship between the two writers, Ward/Browne promises to get Twain published in the New York *Mercury*. Robert Henry Newell (a humorist himself, writing as Orpheus C. Kerr) was the literary editor of the Sunday edition. He was connected with the New York Bohemians and so with Artemus Ward. Ward's Bohemian connections would also lead to another early eastern appearance by

Mark Twain, in the *Saturday Press*, edited by Henry Clapp, Jr., who appears later in this section.

———∿∿— —∿∿— —∿∿—

AUSTIN, *Jan. 1, '64*

MY DEAREST LOVE,—I arrived here yesterday a.m. at 2 o'clock. It is a wild, untamable place, full of lion-hearted boys. I speak tonight. See small bills.

Why did you not go with me and save me that night?—I mean the night I left you after that dinner party. I went and got drunker, beating, I may say, Alexander the Great, in his most drinkinist days, and I blackened my face at the Melodeon, and made a gibbering, idiotic speech. God-dam it! I suppose the Union will have it. But let it go. I shall always remember Virginia as a bright spot in my existence, as all others must or rather cannot be, as it were.

Love to Jo, Goodman and Dan. I shall write soon, a powerfully convincing note to my friends of "The Mercury." Your notice, by the way, did much good here, as it doubtlessly will elsewhere. The miscreants of the Union will be batted in the snout if they ever dare pollute this rapidly rising city with their loathsome presence.

Some of the finest intellects in the world have been blunted by liquor.

Do not, sir—do not flatter yourself that you are the only chastely-humorous writer onto the Pacific slopes.

Good-bye, old boy—and God bless you! The matter of which I spoke to you so earnestly shall be just as earnestly attended to—and again with very many warm regards for Jo. and Dan., and regards to many of the good friends we met. I am Faithfully, gratefully yours,

ARTEMUS WARD.

—Artemus Ward, Charles Farrar Browne,
letter to Twain, January 1, 1864, from
Mark Twain's Letters, Arthur Bigelow Paine, ed.,
New York: Harper and Brothers, 1917, 1: 93–94

UNSIGNED (1864)

"Sammy Clemens' jokes are too bitter to be funny."

—Unsigned, *Virginia City Bulletin*,
April 1864, *Twainian* 8:2, p. 2

VARIOUS CORRESPONDENTS (1864)

ENTERPRISE OFFICE,
Saturday, *May 21, 1864*

JAMES LAIRD, ESQ.—*Sir*: In your paper of the present date appeared two anonymous articles, in which a series of insults were leveled at the writer of an editorial in Thursday's ENTERPRISE, headed "How is it?—How it is." I wrote that editorial.

Some time since it was stated in the Virginia *Union* that its proprietors were alone responsible for all articles published in its columns. You being the proper person, by seniority, to apply to in cases of this kind, I demand of you a public retraction of the insulting articles I have mentioned, or satisfaction. I require an immediate answer to this note. The bearer of this—Mr. Stephen Gillis—will receive any communication you may see fit to make.

SAM. L. CLEMENS

OFFICE OF THE VIRGINIA DAILY UNION
VIRGINIA, *May 21, 1864*

SAMUEL CLEMENS, ESQ.—Mr. James Laird has just handed me your note of this date. Permit me to say that I am the author of the article appearing in this morning's *Union*. I am responsible for it. I have nothing to retract. Respectfully,

J. W. WILMINGTON

ENTERPRISE OFFICE,
Saturday Evening, *May 21,1864*

JAMES LAIRD, ESQ.—*Sir*:—I wrote you a note this afternoon demanding a published retraction of insults that appeared in two articles in the *Union* of this morning—or satisfaction. I have since received what purports to be a reply, written by a person who signs himself "J. W. Wilmington," in which he assumes the authorship and responsibility of one of said infamous articles. Mr. Wilmington is a person entirely unknown to me in the matter, and has nothing to do with it. In the columns of your paper you have declared *your own* responsibility for *all* articles appearing in it, and any farther attempt to make a catspaw of any other individual and thus shirk a responsibility that you had previously assumed will show that *you* are a cowardly sneak. I now *peremptorily* demand of you the satisfaction due to a gentleman—without alternative.

SAM. L. CLEMENS

OFFICE OF THE VIRGINIA DAILY UNION,
VIRGINIA, Saturday Evening, *May 21st, 1864*

SAM'L. CLEMENS, ESQ.:—Your note of this evening is received. To the first portion of it I will briefly reply, that Mr. J. W. Wilmington, the avowed author of the article to which you object, is a gentleman now in the employ of the *Union* office. He formerly was one of the proprietors of the Cincinnati *Enquirer*. He was Captain of a Company in the Sixth Ohio Regiment, and fought at Shiloh. His responsibility and character can be vouched for to your abundant satisfaction.

For all editorials appearing in the *Union*, the proprietors are personally responsible; for communications, they hold themselves ready, when properly called upon, either to give the name and address of the author, or failing that, to be themselves responsible.

The editorial in the ENTERPRISE headed "How is it?" out of which this controversy grew, was an attack made upon the printers of the *Union*. It was replied to by a *Union* printer, and a representative of the printers, who in a communication denounced the writer of that article as a liar, a poltroon and a puppy. You announce yourself as the writer of the article which provoked this communication, and demand "satisfaction"—which satisfaction the writer informs you, over his own signature, he is quite ready to afford. I have no right, under the rulings of the code you have invoked, to step in and assume Mr. Wilmington's position, nor would he allow me to do so. You demand of me, in your last letter, the satisfaction due to a gentleman, and couple the demand with offensive remarks. When you have earned the right to the title by complying with the usual custom, I shall be most happy to afford you any satisfaction you desire at any time and in any place. In short, Mr. Wilmington has a prior claim upon your attention. When he is through with you, I shall be at your service. If you decline to meet him after challenging him, you will prove yourself to be what he has charged you with being: "a liar, a poltroon and a puppy," and as such, cannot of course be entitled to the consideration of a gentleman.

Respectfully,
JAMES L. LAIRD

ENTERPRISE OFFICE, VIRGINIA CITY
May 21, 1864—9 o'clock, P.M.

JAMES L. LAIRD, ESQ.—*Sir:* Your reply to my last note—in which I *peremptorily demanded satisfaction of you, without alternative*—is just received, and to my utter astonishment you still endeavor to shield your craven carcass behind the person of an individual who in spite of *your* introduction is entirely unknown to me, and upon whose shoulders you *cannot* throw the whole responsibility. You acknowledge and reaffirm in this note that "For all *editorials* appearing in the *Union*, the *proprietors are personally responsible.*" Now, sir, had there appeared no *editorial* on the subject endorsing and reiterating the slanderous and disgraceful insults heaped upon me in the "communication," I would have simply called upon you and demanded the name of its author, and upon your answer would have depended my farther action. But the "Editorial" alluded to was equally vile and slanderous as the "communication," and being an "Editorial" would naturally have more weight in the minds of readers. It was the following undignified and abominably insulting slander appearing in your "Editorial" headed "The 'How is it' issue," that occasioned my sending you first an *alternative* and then a *peremptory challenge*:

"Never before in a long period of newspaper intercourse—never before in any contact with a contemporary, however unprincipled he might have been, have we found an opponent in statement or in discussion, who had no gentlemanly sense of professional propriety, who conveyed in every word, and in every purpose of all his words, such a groveling disregard for truth, decency and courtesy as to seem to court the distinction, only, of being understood as a vulgar liar. Meeting one who prefers falsehood; whose instincts are all toward falsehood; whose thought is falsification; whose aim is vilification through insincere professions of honesty; one whose only merit is thus described, and who evidently desires to be thus known, the obstacles presented are entirely insurmountable, and whoever would touch them fully, should expect to be abominably defiled."—Union, *May 21*

You assume in your last note, that I "have challenged Mr. Wilmington," and that he has informed me "over his own signature," that he is quite ready to afford me "satisfaction." Both assumptions are utterly false. I have twice challenged *you*, and you have twice attempted to shirk the responsibility. *Mr. W's* note could not possibly be an answer to my demand of satisfaction from *you*; and besides, his note simply avowed authorship of a certain "communication" that appeared simultaneously with your libelous "editorial," and states that its author had "nothing to retract." For your gratification, however, I will remark that Mr. Wilmington's case *will be attended to in due time* by a distant acquaintance of his who is not willing to see him suffer in obscurity. In the meantime, if you do not wish yourself posted as a coward, you will *at once accept my peremptory challenge, which I now reiterate.*

SAM. L. CLEMENS

OFFICE TERRITORIAL ENTERPRISE
VIRGINIA, May 21, 1864

J. W. WILMINGTON—*Sir*: You are, perhaps, far from those who are wont to advise and care for you, else you would see the policy of minding your own business and letting that of other people alone. Under these circumstances, therefore, I take the liberty of suggesting that you are getting out of your sphere. A *contemptible ass and coward* like yourself should only meddle in the affairs of *gentlemen* when called upon to do so. I approve and endorse the course of my principal in this matter, and if your sensitive disposition is aroused by any proceeding of his, I have only to say that I can be found at the ENTERPRISE office, and always at your service.

S. E. GILLIS

[To the above, Mr. Wilmington gave a verbal reply to Mr. Millard—the gentleman through whom the note was conveyed to him—stating that he had no quarrel with Mr. Gillis; that he had written his communication only in defense of the craft, and did not desire a quarrel with a member of that craft; he showed Mr. G's note to Mr. Millard, who read it, but made no comments upon it.]

OFFICE OF THE VIRGINIA DAILY UNION,
Monday Morning, May 23, 1864

SAMUEL CLEMENS, ESQ.:—In reply to your lengthy communication, I have only to say that in your note opening this correspondence, you demanded satisfaction for a communication in the *Union* which branded the writer of an article in the ENTERPRISE as a *liar*, a *poltroon* and a puppy. You declare yourself to be the writer of the ENTERPRISE article, and the avowed author of the *Union* communication stands ready to afford satisfaction. Any attempt to evade a meeting with him and force one upon me will utterly fail, as I have no right under the rulings of the code, to meet or hold any communication with you in this connection. The *threat* of being posted as a coward cannot have the slightest effect upon the position I have assumed in the matter. If you think this correspondence reflects credit upon *you*, I advise you by all means to publish it; in the meantime you must excuse me from receiving any more long epistles from you.

JAMES L. LAIRD

I denounce Mr. Laird as an unmitigated liar, because he says I published an editorial in which I attacked the printers employed on the *Union*, whereas there is nothing in that editorial which can be so construed. Moreover, he is a liar on general principles, and from natural instinct. I denounce him as an abject coward, because it has been stated in his paper that its proprietors are responsible for all articles appearing in its columns, yet he backs down from that position; because he acknowledges the "code," but will not live up to it; because he says himself that he is responsible for all "editorials," and then backs down from that also; and because he insults me in his note marked "IV," and yet refuses to fight me. Finally, he is a fool, because he cannot understand that a publisher is bound to stand responsible for any and all articles printed by him, whether he wants to do it or not.

SAM. L. CLEMENS

—Various Correspondents, Virginia City
Territorial Enterprise, May 24, 1864

UNSIGNED EDITORIALS (1864)

HOITY! TOITY!!

The cross-firing that has been going on for a week past between the *Union* and the *Enterprise*, concerning a donation made by the employees of the former paper to the Sanitary Fund, has at last culminated in a serious row, and the bloody and barbarous code has been appealed to. Nearly a column of this morning's *Enterprise* is devoted to the publication of the correspondence between Sam Clemens (Mark Twain) and James L. Laird, and Mr. Wilmington, who comes in as an intervenor, and assumes the responsibility of the article for the publication of which Clemens holds Laird to an account. Laird declines to accede to the proposition of Clemens, and the latter proceeds to "post" him, with all those epithets in such case by the code made and provided. This is emphatically a bad egg. In the first place, the cause of the quarrel was not one calculated to enlist public sympathy; neither did the discussion of the question demand the use of the language which was resorted to. If the matter results in bloodshed, the victim will not be mourned as a martyr in a holy cause, nor the victor crowned with laurel as the champion of right. The sentiment of a civilized community revolts at the appeal to the bloody code on every trifling cause of offense. There is another reason, and that a very serious one, why we object to the code being called into requisition on slight occasions among the editorial fraternity. We have noticed that there is a proneness to fire at the legs, and that "there is a divinity that *un*-shapes our *ends*" to the extent that one of the parties is ever afterwards remarkable for the gait vulgarly styled the "step and go fetch it." We have, albeit living in a duelling community; lo! these many years, managed thus far to keep step with the balance of our fellow citizens; and have no fancy, now that we are passing into the "sere and yaller," to have every impudent scallawag on the street accosting us with, "How are you, old limpy?" This thing must be put stop [*sic*].

A FALSTAFFIAN DUEL

As we go to press, a rumor is rife in town that Pete Hopkins, of Carson, having heard that his friend Mark Twain was about to enter into a contract to be killed, has come to the rescue and assumed the dying part. Pete has had no rest since that terrible massacre at Dutch Nick's, and is desirous of dying a savage death; besides, he thinks he would make a better target than Mark, in which opinion we coincide. Blood, or *something else*, is likely to grow out of the difficulty, unless the parties can be made to believe, in the language of Bulwer, that "the pen is mightier than the sword." The duel will perhaps come off in the pine forest at Empire City. Horrible! most horrible!

—Unsigned Editorials, Gold Hill
Evening News, May 24, 1864

Henry Clapp, Jr. (1865)

In the annals of canonical American literature, Henry Clapp, Jr. made a lasting contribution in being an early friend, backer, and publisher of Walt Whitman. He also published Mark Twain's story "The Jumping Frog of Calaveras County" in his journal the *Saturday Press*, purely as a favor to Artemus Ward. Clapp, a former Massachusetts temperance lecturer and then—after a spell in Paris—a radical advocate of "free love," was also the leader of the group of Bohemians that met at Charles Pfaff's beer cellar on Broadway at Bleecker Street. Walt Whitman and Artemus Ward were also among the distinguished set that gathered at Pfaff's. Whitman brought Emerson to Pfaff's once, but he recoiled at the threshold.

This brief notice announces the appearance of the "Jumping Frog" story. The dialect humorist "Josh Billings" (Henry Wheeler Shaw) debuted in the same issue. Billings was, with Artemus Ward and Petroleum V. Nasby, another humorist with whom Twain would continue to be classed for the rest of his life, to the irritation of his supporters.

We give up the principal portion of our editorial space, to-day, to an exquisitely humorous sketch—"Jim Smiley and his Jumping Frog"—by Mark Twain, who will shortly become a regular contributor to our columns. Mark Twain is the assumed name of a writer in California who has long been a favourite contributor to the San Francisco press, from which his articles have been so extensively copied as to make him nearly as well known as Artemus Ward.

We have the pleasure also of introducing to our readers, this week, Mr. Josh Billings, whom we will leave to speak for himself.

—Henry Clapp, Jr., *Saturday Press*, vol. 4,
no. 16, November 18, 1865, p. 248

UNSIGNED (1866)

This legend of how Samuel Clemens got the name Mark Twain is less quaint than the one Mark Twain preferred—that he took the name from riverboat Captain Isaiah Sayers. For that reason, it might be true. Another legend, again relating to drinks rather than river navigation, was proposed by the Eureka *Sentinel* on May 8, 1877.

A Washoe genius thus explains the origin of the *nom de plume* "Mark Twain." "Wall now, d'ye see," says he, "'Mark'—that is Sam, 'ye see—used to take his regular drinks at Johnny Doyle's. Well, 'Mark' that is Sam, d'ye see, used to run his face, bein' short of legal tenders. Well, 'Mark, that is Sam, d'ye understand, always used to take two horns consecutive, one right after the other, and when he come in there and took them on tick, Johnny used to sing out to the barkeep, who carried a lump of chalk in his pocket and kept the score, 'mark twain,' whereupon the barkeep would score two drinks to Sam's account—and so it was, d'ye see, that he came to be called 'Mark Twain.'"

—Unsigned, Nevada City, California,
Transcript, February 22, 1866

Ambrose Bierce (1870)

Ambrose Bierce was the American short story writer and humorist who knew Mark Twain in San Francisco and then again in London. "'Dod Grile' (Mr. Bierce) is a personal friend of mine, I like him exceedingly," Twain wrote in a letter, before adding that "there is humor in Dod Grile, but for every laugh that is in his book there are five blushes, ten shudders and a vomit. The laugh is too expensive." Their "friendship," then, was not easy or unequivocal. Bierce's so-called "official" biographer, Walter Neale, claimed that Bierce "hated" Twain. Certainly there is a hint of bile about these pieces, early incarnations of literary gossip. Bierce was actually habitually acerbic, and he maintained that this was strictly business.

Students comparing these two major writers of American humor will find these brief articles of great value. No small amount of energy has been expended by critics in the last hundred years to try to solve the mystery of Mark Twain's marriage. It had the appearance of being a harmonious match, all the more reason for Dwight Mcdonald to doubt the supposed domestic bliss. Late in life, Twain was unusually receptive to a female advocate of "free love," while refusing absolutely to publicly endorse her views. To Theodore Dreiser, Twain claimed that "after the first few years of marriage, men don't love their wives, and they are not strictly faithful." Is there some truth to the theory that Twain was attracted to Livy for her respectability, if not for her money? Ambrose Bierce was probably the first person to voice such suspicions, and as such he is the father of a long-lived and still-vibrant critical tradition.

ON THE MARRIAGE OF MARK TWAIN

Mark Twain, who, whenever he has been long enough sober to permit an estimate, has been uniformly found to bear a spotless character, has got married. It was not the act of a desperate man—it was not committed while laboring under temporary insanity; his insanity is not of that type, nor does he ever labor—it was the cool, methodical, cumulative culmination of human nature, working in the breast of an orphan hankering for some one with a fortune to love—some one with a bank account to caress. For years he has felt this matrimony coming on. Ever since he left California there has been an undertone of despair running through all his letters like the subdued wail of a pig beneath a washtub. He felt that he was going, that no earthly power could save him, but as a concession to his weeping publishers he tried a change of climate by putting on a linen coat and writing letters from the West Indies.

Then he tried rhubarb, and during his latter months he was almost constantly under the influence of this powerful drug. But rhubarb, while it may give a fitful glitter to the eye and a deceitful ruddiness to the gills, cannot long delay the pangs of approaching marriage. Rhubarb was not what Mark wanted. Well, that genial spirit has passed away; that long, bright smile will no more greet the early bar-keeper, nor the old familiar "chalk it down" delight his ear. Poor Mark! he was a good scheme, but he couldn't be made to work.

PROMPT CONSEQUENCE OF MARK'S MARRIAGE

It is announced that Mark Twain, being above want, will lecture no more. We didn't think that of Mark; we supposed that after marrying a rich girl he would have decency enough to make a show of working for a year or two anyhow. But it seems his native laziness has wrecked his finer feelings, and he has abandoned himself to his natural vice with the stolid indifference of a pig at his ablutions. We have our own private opinion of a man who will do this kind of thing; we regard him as an abandoned wretch. We should like to be abandoned in that way.

MARK'S ROMANCE PANS OUT

Mark Twain's father-in-law is dead, and has left that youth's wife a quarter of a million dollars. At the time of Mark's marriage, a few months since, we expressed some doubt as to the propriety of the transaction. That doubt has been removed by death.

—Ambrose Bierce, *News Letter*, "On the Marriage of Mark Twain," February 19, 1870, "Prompt Consequence of Mark's Marriage," June 18, 1870, "Mark's Romance Pans Out," August 27, 1870

EDWARD PERON HINGSTON (1870)

Edward Peron Hingston was an impresario—a promoter and tour manager for stage performers. He promoted the Scottish magician John Henry Anderson, the "Wizard of the North," but his best-known work—at least to literary posterity—was his promotion of and tour with Charles Farrar Browne, the Maine humorist known as Artemus Ward.

Hingston emphasizes the frontier focus of Twain's position (writing from ten years later, when Twain's international fame was assured) and the remoteness and wildness of Twain's surroundings ("I might come to grief?"). This perspective is especially noteworthy since it is one of

the earliest English views of Mark Twain. As Hingston notes, he found
Twain when he had "scarcely rendered his name familiar to the public of
Boston or New York." Hingston saw, then, the process by which—through
Artemus Ward's eastern contacts, including Robert Henry Newell of the
Mercury and Henry Clapp, Jr. of the *Saturday Press*—a way was cleared for
Mark Twain's promotion in the East.

———————— ———————— ————————

"I might come to grief?"

"You might."

"Roll over a precipice perhaps, and break my neck?"

"Well; that's so. Your temper might be tried in that way. The roads over the
Sierra are pretty rough just now, and we are likely to have ugly weather."

"Then, I think the game is hardly worth the candle, my friend. No riding
over the mountains alone for me. Besides, what would there be to see when
I got to Nevada?"

"You would see the big silver mines."

"I have seen the Mexican ones. They were large enough for me. Is there
anything else to repay me for the journey?"

"Yes. You would see *Mark Twain*."

"Ah! I will go."

The foregoing is, as nearly as I can remember, an abstract of a conversation
with a literary friend in San Francisco, towards the close of the year 1863. I
knew that in a few months I should have to visit Nevada on business. Why not
avail myself of a leisure week and ride over the Sierra to see the wonders of
the new territory? A mountain summit 6000 feet high, snow, slippery paths,
and very rough roads were the hindrances. But when my friend mentioned
the name of Mark Twain the mountains grew less steep, the roads perfectly
practicable, and the snow became white roses. I had read many of Mark
Twain's contributions to the press of the Great West. I had heard numerous
reports of his talents, his jovial wit, his social singularities, and his extreme
good fellowship. In one of the papers I had seen him styled—"That moral
phenomenon, Mark Twain." Believing that a "moral phenomenon" would
be something to see, and that the conversation of a man who could write so
humorously would be worth listening to, I started for Nevada.

At the town of Placerville I came to a halt. My horse—a borrowed one—
did not at all care about seeing Mark Twain. He preferred to see a veterinary
doctor. The people of Placerville told me that I had better make the journey
in the stage-coach. I did so; but not till nearly two months later, when the

roads were in better condition. Then it was that I landed myself in Virginia City, a terraced town, built on the side of Mount Davidson; and there it was that I met Mark Twain.

"You will find him at the office of the *Territorial Enterprise*," was the direction I received.

Virginia City was but a few months old. The *Territorial Enterprise* was a daily paper, well edited, copious in its information, fortunate in its advertisements, of large dimensions, and published every morning, where a year or two previous, there had been the silence of the wilderness and the tents of the Indian savage.

The newspaper office was in C Street. Its foundations were of granite, its front of iron. In its basement was a saloon for drink, furnished with a piano, the use of which I was informed was "to tone down the troubled spirits of the visitors." Behind the drinking saloon were two of Hoe's cylinder steam-printing presses. On the first floor of the building were the offices of mining share-brokers, and a wholesale brandy store. On the second story were some more brokers and some attorneys, and on the third floor were the editorial offices of the paper. I asked for Mr. Mark Twain, and hearing his name mentioned, the gentleman of whom I was in quest called out to Mr. Wright, to whom I had addressed myself—

"Dan, pass the gentleman into my den. The noble animal is here."

A young man, strongly built, ruddy in complexion, his hair of a sunny hue, his eyes light and twinkling, in manner hearty, and nothing of the student about him, but very much of the miner—one who looked as if he could take his own part in a quarrel, strike a smart blow as readily as he could say a telling thing, bluffly jolly, brusquely cordial, off-handedly good-natured—such was the kind of man I found Mark Twain to be.

Let it be borne in mind that from the windows of the newspaper office the American desert was visible; that within a radius of ten miles Indians were encamping amongst the sage-brush; that the whole city was populated with miners, adventurers, Jew traders, gamblers, and all the rough-and-tumble class which a mining town in a new territory collects together, and it will be readily understood that a reporter for a daily paper in such a place must neither go about his duties wearing light kid gloves, nor be fastidious about having gilt edges to his note-books. In Mark Twain I found the very man I had expected to see—a flower of the wilderness, tinged with the colour of the soil, the man of thought and the man of action rolled into one, humorist and hard-worker, Momus in a felt hat and jack-boots. In the reporter of the *Territorial Enterprise* I became introduced to a Californian celebrity, rich in eccentricities of thought, lively in fancy, quaint in remark, whose residence upon the fringe of civilization had allowed his humour to develop without restraint, and his speech to be racily idiomatic.

The name of MARK TWAIN is a *nom de plume* for Mr. Samuel L. Clemens; whose [brother], Mr. Orion Clemens, held a high position in the territorial government of Nevada. Before visiting that territory Mark Twain had afforded evidence of his literary ability on the Californian side of the Sierra. At the time of my introduction to him his talents had scarcely rendered his name familiar to the public of Boston or New York, and he expressed to Artemus Ward and myself a very earnest desire to be better known in one or other of those cities. Artemus promised to get him appointed a contributor to the *New York Mercury*, a promise that I believe was faithfully kept.

Writing of himself and his friend Dan de Quille, his *collaborateur* on the Nevada paper in 1863, Mark Twain says, in an advertisement of the *Territorial Enterprise*—"Our duty is to keep the universe thoroughly posted concerning murders and street fights and balls and theatres, and pack-trains, and churches, and lectures, and school-houses, and city military affairs, and highway robberies, and Bible societies, and hay waggons, and the thousand other things which it is within the province of local reporters to keep track of and magnify into undue importance for the instruction of the readers of a great daily newspaper. Beyond this revelation everything connected with these two experiments of Providence must for ever remain an impenetrable mystery."

With the rapid development of a literature of its own, California offered Mark Twain increased scope for his talents. A series of remarkably original articles, abounding in drollery and grotesque humour, were contributed by him to various journals of San Francisco, among which were the *Golden Era*, *Californian*, and *Overland Monthly*, and he soon became transferred from the rough life of Nevada to undertake editorial duties in San Francisco. The tale of "The Jumping Frog," a capitally told and richly conceived humorous story of the California gold-mines, gave its author an immediate and widespread popularity. "The Jumping Frog" has been republished everywhere, and is as well known to the readers of Australia as it is to the literary public of London and New York. It has been highly praised by Mr. Tom Hood in the pages of *Fun*, and a friend of mine had it put into his hands by a Parsee merchant in Bombay, who assured him that it was the funniest thing he could read. . . .

I believe that Mark Twain has never visited England. Some time since he wrote to me asking my opinion relative to his giving an entertainment in London. He has appeared in New York, and elsewhere as a lecturer, and from his originality would, I have no doubt, be able to repeat his lectures with success were he to visit this country. But I never met him in the character of a public entertainer, and can only speak from experience of his remarkable talent as a humorous writer, and of his cordial frankness and jovial good-fellowship as a friend and companion.

—Edward Peron Hingston, "Introduction to
Hotten's *Choice Works of Mark Twain*," 1870

ATTRIBUTED TO EDWARD PERON HINGSTON (1873)

In this unsigned introduction to the pirated collection *Choice Works of Mark Twain* (London: John Camden Hotten, 1873), E.P. Hingston recalls events during time spent in Virginia City with Artemus Ward and Mark Twain. In an "author's copy" of the book, Mark Twain wrote in the margin: "All of this is untrue. S.L.C." However, directly underneath, scrawled out, is the additional remark that it "would be useless rubbish if true." Mark Twain wrote these comments for the publishers Chatto and Windus when they took over the accounts of John Camden Hotten after he died. What had been a pirated edition became, with Twain's consent and assistance, an official edition. "This is a well written biographical sketch," Twain wrote across the text. "If Hotten wrote it I wholly lay aside the ancient grudge I bore him."

However, this particular part was written by Hingston, not Hotten, and Twain excised it from the subsequent text. This, like several other remarks and gestures from Twain, points to an "anxiety of influence" with Artemus Ward. What else in this story might Twain have preferred not to be republished?

Virginia City was continually gay and festive, and as Artemus and his friend rambled through it in the evening they found innumerable dancehouses, wherein miners, in their red shirts, were footing it to the music of hurdy-gurdies, played by itinerant maidens. Dr Hingston, in his "Genial Showman," tells us that at Sutcliff's Melodeon a ball was taking place, and at the Niagara Concert Hall there were crowds assembled around the door, while from within came forth the sounds of negro minstrelsy, with the clash of bones and the twang of banjos. Artemus spent his time with Mark Twain, descending silver mines, and visiting the strange places of the city. Hingston drove round the neighbourhood, and made arrangements for lectures at Gold Hill, Silver City, and Dayton. An amusing adventure—or, rather, a practical joke—was played upon Artemus by Mark Twain, and as a then-resident of Virginia City has given us full particulars of the occurrence, we think we cannot do better than tell the story as he told it to us:—

"How are you off for fashionable society in this city?" asked Artemus of Mark Twain, when the two humourists met at the International Hotel in Virginia City, Nevada.

"Our bar-rooms are well attended in the evening, and we have some noble ball-rooms on the side streets, where the hurdy-gurdy girls provide the music, and a little shooting adds to the fun," replied Mark Twain.

"You must put me through to-night," said Artemus. "I am not heavy on the shoot; but my soul yearns towards hurdy-gurdy girls. We will go into society."

Virginia City at that time was one of the most extraordinary towns in the mining territories. Its streets were shelves cut out of the side of a high mountain, its population consisted of miners, teamsters, bar-keepers, speculators, gamblers, adventurers, and loafers; its soil was silver, and its surroundings sand, sage-brush, and savages. The Indian, with his scalping-knife in his girdle, and the white man with his pistol in his belt, passed one another on its planked footways, glowered at each other in its dreary suburbs. In the bars and dancing rooms might be met rough-clad men of all nationalities—American, English, German, French, Mexican, and Brazilian; all alike disposed to drink, dance, fight, play cards, or pop at one another with pistols, as circumstances might suggest, or fancy prompt. To see life in this strange city was Artemus Ward's wish, and he could have no better cicerone than Mark Twain, who, being then a reporter on the *Territorial Enterprise*—the oddly-named daily paper of the city—was specially well qualified to show him round.

Ward and Twain visited three dancing rooms in the course of the evening. In the third there was a very pretty German girl who played polkas on the hurdy-gurdy to the dancers, and who spoke a little broken English. She had a look of sadness about her. Artemus became interested in her appearance, and after having a dance, with Mark Twain for his partner, drew the hurdy-gurdy girl aside and entered into conversation.

The keeper of the saloon became impatient. His patrons wanted more dancing.

"Artemus," said Mark Twain, "leave the musical instrument alone, and let the sweet strains flow on."

"Do not come between two souls," replied Artemus, unwilling to break off his conversation with the fair-haired German.

Music was wanted, and there was no one but the hurdy-gurdy girl to supply it. The saloon-keeper spoke out in a voice of thunder; the hurdy-gurdy responded with a lively jig. To dance seemed to be the wish of every one except Artemus, whose attention was wholly directed towards the instrumentalist, and with whom he recommenced conversation at the end of the dance. Perceiving that the further stay of Artemus would be detrimental to the harmony of the evening, and probably lead to a quarrel, Mark Twain drew him away, and on gaining the street pleasantly reminded him that the frequenters of the saloon were disposed to object to any monopoly of their orchestra. "Besides," added Twain, "that young lady does not belong to one of our first families."

Artemus replied that he was very much struck with the appearance of the hurdy-gurdy girl, that she had told him a pitiful story of how she had been inveigled to leave her friends and take up with her present life, and that as she strongly desired to return to New York, he was half disposed to take her there. "I have an idea, too," he remarked, "that I could introduce that hurdy-gurdy into my lecture; I have never had a pianiste, but that young lady is an artist, and would do instead of one. She could play an obligato accompaniment to my sweet discourse."

Mark Twain enjoyed the drollery of the idea, but assured Artemus that he was deceived in his estimate of the German girl's character, and that from what he knew of her in the city, she was hardly worthy of sympathy or assistance. Artemus was not to be convinced, and challenged his friend with interested motives in dissuading him from running away with what he termed "the city orchestra." Two days afterwards Mark Twain arranged that Artemus and he should pay a visit to the great Gould and Curry Mine, a subterranean town burrowed into the sides of Mount Davidson, and out of which many thousand tons of silver have been taken. Some idea of its extent may be formed from the fact that it contains about five miles of tunnels, passages, and underground streets. Artemus knew that his friend Mark would prepare a reception for him in the mine, and therefore suggested that the hurdy-gurdy girl should be invited to give them a little music within the mountain.

"I have settled all that. Germania's child of music will be there," replied Mark Twain.

The way of descent into the Gould and Curry was by a tunnel or adit, down which a tramway led far into the mine. The proprietors and officials of the works were in readiness to receive their visitors and to lower them pleasantly in a handsome mahogany car. Arrived in the heart of the mountain, the various modes of mining for silver were exemplified and described to Artemus, who was also permitted to try his hand at mining, a spot being indicated to him whence in a very few minutes he was able to extract some fine specimens of silver ore. Whether the polite miners had courteously buried it there previous to his visit is not for me to say. The mine having been partially inspected, the party assembled in a subterranean restaurant, there to partake of champagne. After some dozen toasts had been duly honoured, the sound of a hurdy-gurdy was heard in the distance along one of the dimly-lit passages. Artemus started, and cried out,

"That's my German friend! Bring her here."

Instead of coming nearer, the music seemed to recede.

"Gentlemen, excuse me," said Artemus, "I want to speak to that young lady. She must come and have some champagne."

"We will go after her and fetch her," said Mark Twain. "Sweet music leads the way. Come on!"

From tunnel to tunnel, running all sorts of dangers, Artemus and his friend hurried along, the hurdy-gurdy still mysteriously keeping ahead. Mark Twain grew tired of the pursuit, and suggested the probabilities of falling down a shaft.

"I must find her," replied Artemus; "but it's no use calling out to her again. She's frightened, and making away from us. That's she. I see the light ahead. Now she's turned up another tunnel."

"Keep up the track then," said Twain, holding up a light he had borrowed from one of the miners. "But had you not better let the girl go?"

"No; come on. There's the hurdy-gurdy, louder and nearer. This way. Round this corner. Hi! Hurdy-gurdy! Music! Faderland! Gretchen—stop!"

Just then the music ceased, the distant light disappeared, a pistol shot resounded through the subterranean ways, and in a few seconds Artemus and Mark were confronted by two men, whose faces were so covered with dirt that in the gloom it was impossible to distinguish the countenance of either. One of them pointed a pistol towards Artemus, and roughly demanded, "Why are you following my wife?

"Is the young lady with the hurdy-gurdy your wife?" stammered Artemus.

"She is; if I have not killed her. And I'll blow you to eternal blazes for trying to steal her."

"She did not tell me she was married. She—"

"*She!* She's bad enough; but it's you—you pair of thieving loafers. Stand still and say your prayers before I put a bullet into both of you."

"Don't shoot us in the mine," expostulated Mark Twain. "Let us have a little fresh air to die in."

"My name is Slayful Jim. I have had a hundred men for breakfast—I have. Slayful Jim is not a man for palaver, nor to have his wife stolen from him. Say your prayers, and let me shoot."

The other man, who had hitherto kept silent, now interfered, saying that he knew Mark Twain, and did not believe him to be a villain.

"But who is the other loafer?"

"He is my friend, Artemus Ward, who lectured in Virginia last night. Haven't you heard of him?" replied Twain.

Slayful Jim was silent for a few seconds, and then said, "I guess I've never shot a lecturer yet. So I'll give you a fair chance. I'll stand here. Just you go back, both of you, down that tunnel as fast as you can, and when I've counted thirty, I'll fire. If I kill one of you I'm satisfied, and if I miss you both, Slayful Jim is a square man, and will let you off this time. Run. I'm on it—one—two—three—"

Artemus and Mark took to their heels.

"Thirty!" cried Slayful Jim, and off went the pistol.

Nobody was shot. Mark Twain hurried Artemus to the car; both shook hands hastily with the gentlemen of the mine, and ascended to daylight with all speed.

The next day Artemus left for Austin in the stage coach. Mark Twain was there to bid him "good-bye." So also was Dan de Quille, Twain's coadjutor on the *Enterprise* newspaper, and with him another gentleman of Virginia, whose humourous smile attracted Artemus's attention.

"Twain," said he, "I think I have seen that man's face before."

"Very likely, Mr. Ward."

"There's something in his voice too that reminds me of—of—Slayful Jim."

Mark Twain laughed immoderately. Just then Dan de Quille commenced playing a hurdy-gurdy, which hitherto he had kept concealed, while the gentleman of the humorous smile, producing a pistol, uttered the word "Thirty," in a voice not to be mistaken and fired the weapon into the air.

"Sold!" cried Artemus, throwing himself back in the coach to laugh, as to the music of the hurdy-gurdy the horses galloped off down Mount Davidson.

—Edward Peron Hingston, attributed, from the
"Introduction," *Choice Works of Mark Twain*,
London: John Camden Hotten, 1873

Ambrose Bierce "Letter from England" (1872)

I cannot say that I was much interested in Ann [Hathaway] and her affairs. The visitors' book here was very much more to my mind; and therein, among a multitude of famous autographs I found those of General Sherman and Mark Twain. I could not repress a smile as I read the name of the grim, heartless, and unimaginative warrior recorded at this shrine of pure sentiment—a sentiment, too, of the sicklier sort. From Mark something like this was to be expected. I had met him a few evenings before in London. We had dined together at one of the literary clubs, and in response to a toast Mark had given the company a touching narration of his sufferings in Central Africa in discovery of Dr. Livingstone! It was, therefore, not surprising that he should have penetrated as far as Shottery. He was probably looking for Sir John Franklin.

—Ambrose Bierce, "Letter from England,"
Daily Alta California, October 10, 1872

Anthony Trollope (1873)

Anthony Trollope was an esteemed English novelist. Joachim Miller was the "poet of the Sierras," a self-promoting extrovert who dressed the part of the "frontiersman" and entertained Victorian London literary society. He was in London at the same time as Ambrose Bierce and Mark Twain, and the three were acquainted. Twain and Bierce looked on Miller and his attention-grabbing stunts with distaste and—possibly—a little envy.

Two of the wildest of your countrymen—Joachim Miller and Mark Twain—dine with me at my club next week. Pity you have not established the rights of your sex, or you could come and meet them and be as jolly as men!

—Anthony Trollope, letter to Kate Field, July 1873

Ambrose Bierce (1873–74)

My Dear Stoddard,

I shall go on Tuesday next; naturally I have very little time at my command. But if Monday evening will be convenient I shall be very glad to dine with you and Clemens, as per kind invitation, but shall have to leave early. . . . My friendly regards to Mark. . . .

P.S. Mark will receive from Chatto—who hopes he does not inherit Hotten's feuds—a little book which I am authorized to say is intended as a peace offering.

I am very pleased that Mark likes my Fables, but your idea—that they ought to create a "furor"—I think that is the word—amuses me. I don't create furors. [. . .] If I had one of Mark's cocktails I would finish this letter; as it is I have not the spirit to get through it, and if anything else strikes me I'll telegraph.

—Ambrose Bierce, letters to Charles
Warren Stoddard, November 22, 1873,
and January 1874

Bret Harte (1876–77)

Francis Bret Harte was the author of countless popular short stories of the West, including "The Luck of Roaring Camp" and "The Outcasts of Poker Flat." He was the editor and founder of San Francisco's *Overland Monthly,* for which Mark Twain had also written.

This correspondence demonstrates how the spirit of frontier journalism and literature and the wild camaraderie and rough good will of the early days were exhausted by the 1870s. Former friends were reduced to cavilling over small details. It resembles rather the mining boom itself, in a sense, in which a democratic dream gives way to a stiff, industrial system.

Details of "Ah Sin," based on a dialect poem of the Californian mining community, became world famous. Hard up and looking to cash in, Harte proposed a collaboration with Twain that dramatized characters from both their works. Twain agreed. This was the deal that dissolved into acrimony and farce. Twain eventually rewrote much of Harte's work (leaving "hardly a foot-print of Harte in it anywhere," he told Howells), although many years later he conceded that Harte's "was the best part of it."

This selection serves to highlight two constants in Samuel Clemens's life: an attraction to business that necessitated his often blundering involvement in it—here the American Book Company—and then his rejection of close friends for slights imagined or otherwise. Twain went from warmth to almost vicious contempt for Bret Harte over this matter.

TO SAMUEL L. CLEMENS, 16 DECEMBER 1876

45 Fifth Avenue,
Decem. 16th/76

My dear Mark,

I got a short note from Parsloe yesterday, making an appointment to meet me at Dutton's at 10:30 to-day. I was there, waited an hour, but *he* didn't come. At about 3 P.M. he called on me here, where after some desultory talk I read him those portions of the 1st & 2d act that indicated his *role*, and he expressed himself satisfied with it, and competent to take it in hand. As nearly as I could judge he was pleased.

Of the contract, its nature, what would be his share of the profits, and generally what we should expect from him *I said nothing*. In fact I was only too glad to leave all that business with you. He talked,—a little prematurely I thought and with a certain egotism that I had noticed before—about his having made the fortunes already of certain people to whom he had been subordinate, and of his intention now of trying to make his own. He intimated that he was hereafter "going to look out for himself." To all of which I said nothing, and shall deliver him into your hands without committing you to even a single suggestion. He is to go with me to Hartford on such day as I may name early next week, and I shall give you notice by telegraph of our coming twelve hours before. You can, if you like, meet us at the station, and we can go to your lawyer's at once.

You will be surprised, I dare say, that with all my anxiety to push our play into print I am still halting and fussing over the manuscript. I've been revising the 1st and 2d Act—writing myself *up* and you down, that is trying to make myself more easily intelligible, and you not quite so *prononcé*. I find that Mrs H's opinion of the real Plunketts jumps with your wife's, and I think we'll have to modify Miss P. at least. I think that Mrs H. and Mrs C. represent fairly our feminine auditors, and as we are not constructing women "after our own image" or as we have seen them, I suppose we will have to defer to their ideas of what a woman ought to be. . . .

Remember me kindly to your wife, Mrs Langdon and Miss Hess. Tell Mrs Clemens that she must forgive me for my heterodoxy—that until she does I shall wear sackcloth (fashionably cut) and that I would put ashes on my head but that Nature has anticipated me, and that I feel her gentle protests to my awful opinions all the more remorsefully that I am away; say to Miss Hess she isn't from Boston, and that I always agreed with her about the natural infamy of Man; tell Mrs Langdon I forgive her for liking you so much, and her general disposition to weakly defer to your horrible egotism and stubbornness; and then kiss Susie for me, and implore "the Ba" on your bended knees, to add me to the Holy Family.

Always, dear old fellow,

Yours B.H.

TO SAMUEL L. CLEMENS, 1 MARCH 1877

713 Broadway, NY

Mar. 1st 77

My dear Clemens,

As I've been writing for my bread-and-butter for the last few days, and as your letter called for no answer except I should receive one from Ford, which I should have forwarded promptly, and as nothing has come from Ford, I have taken my own time to talk with you. Had I written the day after receiving your letter, I hardly think we would have had any further correspondence or business together. As it is I'm not anxious to write this. But there are a few things I must say to you.

First. As to the American Publishing Co.

If Mr. Bliss was a business man he would have sent *me* a statement of my a/c *when it was due*, and given me an opportunity of examining it—of knowing what he was doing and what he had done about my property, and what profit I was to expect from it. He would have exhibited his charge for "*interest on advances*"—a charge so preposterous and outrageous that if he will look at his contract he will see that it is so, and if he comes in contact with my lawyer he will know it is so.

Second—As to his sales of my book and the amount of copyright: *No publisher of any of my works, at any day, or time has done as badly as he has.* It is no answer to this to repeat your formula "that the hook was delayed by me, that my reputation had suffered by it, that I had lost my popularity &c. &c. &c." The only test is what other publishers are doing now, and since then, and at the time of Bliss' publication, with my *other* books. Mr. Osgood offered Robson $250 *advance* (without *interest*, of course,) on the sale of the much abused play of "Sandy Bar"—which he would offer to the trade at 65¢. Inside of a month, Osgood had credited me on account of "Thankful Blossom"—a book published originally in a daily newspaper and sold by Osgood for 60¢—with one half the amount of copyright that Bliss shows for his sales in 5 mos of a book that a magazine paid $6000 for, and which he sells for $3.50. In brief, Osgood has sold more copies of "Thankful Blossom" in a month, than Bliss has sold of "Gabriel Conroy" in five months,—and on looking over my copyright accounts, I find I have never in my literary experience sold less than four or five thousand copies in the first three months of publication. Either Bliss must confess that he runs his concern solely in *your* interest, *and* that he uses the names of other authors to keep that fact from the public, or else he is a fool. No sane business man would advance $6000 dollars on a book, of which in 5 mos he sold only 2000 copies, unless he had some other reason for it. I dont think his friendship for me goes as far as that. Possibly he may have carelessly made up his accounts. Ticknor of J. R. Osgood & Co, to whom I stated the case, tells me that from his experience of the dealings of the regular trade with subscription houses, that Bliss has probably already disposed of at least 2000 copies to the trade *alone*. Even Bliss' advances of $6,000 cannot cover the loss I shall have from respectable publishers by publishing with *him*. Now, this is somewhere wrong, Mark, and as my friend you should have looked into Bliss's books and Bliss's methods, quite as much with a desire of seeing justice done your friend, as with the desire of seeing what chance you had of recovering any possible advance of $500 on our mutual work, if it failed.

I have written this on a separate page that you might show the preceding ones to Bliss. I only add one other fact (*to yourself solely*) which *you* may have forgotten. I had forgotten it, until looking for my contract with Bliss I found a letter from you of the same date. You requested me to tell Bliss that his contract with me was of *your* making and out of your influence with me as a friend, and you afterwards admitted to me that a disputed question of one or two thousand dollars was settled in your favor by *virtue of that contract so made*. I am willing to admit that your loan of $750 wipes out that obligation,—nor should I have referred to it, but for the tenor of your letter the other day, which struck me as being inconsistent with the facts.

Now, as to "Ah Sin"! First:

Parsloe called here and showed me your letter. I dont object to San Francisco as the place of *début*, except that from my own knowledge they prefer something with an Eastern endorsement, and I really can't see how our main idea of bringing out the play in a small town so that we might be able to superintend rehearsals, is furthered by this.

Secondly.

If there is any one thing that we are *sure* about, regarding our play— anything that we do *know*, by actual experience, by general report, by universal criticism, by the consent and acknowledgement of the public—it is that Parsloe is a perfect Chinaman! Now to spend five or six hundred dollars to send him to San Francisco *to study Chinese character* is simply *preposterous*—so preposterous, that even the honest fellow himself saw it. Without waiting for my opinion, he told me he wouldn't do it. And in saying this to you I think I have overlooked your implied insult—an insult I admit I felt keenly when he showed me your letter—of your offering this actor, in a mere whim and idiotic impulse—the very sum you refused to advance your *collaborateur* who called that actor into life, who had given already four or five weeks of his time to you and whom you refused on the plea of *poverty*!

No, Mark, I do not think it advisable for us to write another play together. Your offer of "$25 per week and board"—is flattering I admit—but I think that if I accepted it, even you would despise me for it. I can make about $100 per week for a few weeks here at my desk—my only idea of asking you for an advance was to save me from the importunity of my creditors, and give me that quiet, which as a nervous man yourself, you ought to know is essential to composition. I had not the slightest idea of your speculating out of my poverty, but as a shrewd man, a careful man, a provident man, I think you will admit that in my circumstances the writing of plays with you is not profitable.

Allowing even that I came to you on a salary of $25 per week, as I could not, after your letter, break bread or eat salt with you—dont you see as an economic man, as a shrewd man, that my board at the cheapest hotel would cost me at least $7.50 per week and that I should have only $17.50 to support my wife and 4 children. I know it can be done cheaper than that, but I think I'll struggle on here on $100 per week—and not write any more plays with you.

As to the play, already written—except a protest against your marring it any more by alterations until it is rehearsed, and a special, and I think not improper request that you will try to allow me some understanding of the characters I have created, you can do with it, according to your business shrewdness and sagacity, as you may deem best for both of us—subject to my endorsement.

I think I object to San Francisco.

I have no answer from Ford. I shall telegraph him again tomorrow.

Yours, very respectfully,
Bret Harte

Mr. Saml. L. Clemens
Hartford.
P.S. I have kept a copy of this letter.

—Bret Harte, letters to Clemens,
December 16, 1876, and March 1, 1877

Unsigned (1877)

Like the legend published in the Nevada City *Transcript*, on February 22, 1866, this version of how Mark Twain took his name is less flattering to the author. When he was reinventing himself for a more genteel audience—a constant process for Mark Twain—it was always best to minimize such details as excessive drinking. The question remains: Which was the real source?

Coal Oil Tommy was a legendary profligate who inherited a fortune in oil and lost it through extravagant, ostentatious dissipation. He wound up, ironically, hauling oil for fifty cents a barrel.

—◈— —◈— —◈—

We knew Clemens in the early days and know . . . how he came to be dubbed "Mark Twain." John Piper's saloon . . . used to be the grand rendezvous for all . . . Virginia City Bohemians. Piper conducted a cash business and refused to keep any books. As a special favour . . . he would occasionally chalk down drinks to the boys on the wall back of bar. Sam Clemens, when localizing for the Enterprise, always had an account with the balance against him. Clemens was by no means a Coal Oil Tommy, he drank for the pure . . . love of the ardent. Most of his drinking was conducted in single-handed contests, but occasionally he would invite Dan De Quille, Charley Parker, Bob Lowery or Alf. Doten, never more than one of them . . . at a time, and whenever he did his invariable parting injunction was to "mark twain," meaning two chalk marks . . . in this way . . . he acquired the title which has since become famous wherever . . . English . . . is read or spoken.

—Unsigned, Eureka, Nevada, *Sentinel*,
May 8, 1877

Albert Bigelow Paine "The Whittier Birthday Speech" (1877)

While this account is from Paine's later biography, it is included here because it contains several vital documents within it, unavailable elsewhere, particularly Ellen Tucker Emerson's letter to Twain's wife.

This speech—which quickly became legend, as Paine recalls (and as is evidenced by Ambrose Bierce's reaction in the following entry)—is perhaps most interesting and important for showing most clearly how Mark Twain stood in the eyes of Boston's "Brahmin" society, how he tried so hard to be accepted but had that recalcitrant blundering "imp of the perverse" (as Paine has it). Most notable, arguably, is Ellen Tucker Emerson's response, telling us of Emerson's enjoyment of Mark Twain's work—scantly apparent otherwise. Thematically, in their later work, there is much that unites the two writers. Emerson began to reevaluate his earlier affirmations. His son's death was one of the main causes of his turn to doubt and uncertainty.

Mark Twain was forgiven by Emerson, and they met again, at another dinner where he redeemed himself with a more moderate speech for Oliver Wendell Holmes. Twain and Howells went to Concord, Massachusetts, to visit Emerson casually a few weeks before Emerson died. What they spoke of remains a mystery, perhaps their mutual dislike for the English pirate of their works, John Camden Hotten.

It is noteworthy that the forgiveness is directed by Emerson's daughter to Twain's wife, as though this was the gendered role.

— ⁓ — ⁓ — ⁓ —

It was the night of December 17, 1877, that Mark Twain made his unfortunate speech at the dinner given by the *Atlantic* staff to John G. Whittier on his seventieth birthday. Clemens had attended a number of the dinners which the *Atlantic* gave on one occasion or another, and had provided a part of the entertainment. It is only fair to say that his after-dinner speeches at such times had been regarded as very special events, genuine triumphs of humor and delivery. But on this particular occasion he determined to outdo himself, to prepare something unusual, startling, something altogether unheard of.

When Mark Twain had an impulse like that it was possible for it to result in something dangerous, especially in those earlier days. This time it produced a bombshell; not just an ordinary bombshell, or even a twelve-inch projectile, but a shell of planetary size. It was a sort of hoax—always a doubtful plaything—and in this case it brought even quicker and more terrible retribution than usual. It was an imaginary presentation of three disreputable frontier tramps who at some time had imposed themselves on a lonely miner as Longfellow, Emerson, and Holmes, quoting apposite selections from their verses to the accompaniment of cards and drink, and altogether conducting themselves in a most unsavory fashion. At the end came the enlightenment that these were not what they pretended to be, but only impostors—disgusting frauds. A feature like that would be a doubtful thing to try in any cultured atmosphere. The thought of associating, ever so remotely, those three old bummers which he had conjured up with the venerable and venerated Emerson, Longfellow, and Holmes, the Olympian trinity, seems ghastly enough to-day, and must have seemed even more so then. But Clemens, dazzled by the rainbow splendor of his conception, saw in it only a rare colossal humor, which would fairly lift and bear his hearers along on a tide of mirth. He did not show his effort to any one beforehand. He wanted its full beauty to burst upon the entire company as a surprise.

It did that. Howells was toastmaster, and when he came to present Clemens he took particular pains to introduce him as one of his foremost contributors and dearest friends. Here, he said, was "a humorist who never left you hanging your head for having enjoyed his joke."

Thirty years later Clemens himself wrote of his impressions as he rose to deliver his speech.

> I vaguely remember some of the details of that gathering: dimly I can see a hundred people—no, perhaps fifty—shadowy figures, sitting at tables feeding, ghosts now to me, and nameless forevermore. I don't know who they were, but I can very distinctly see, seated at the grand table and facing the rest of us, Mr. Emerson, supernaturally grave, unsmiling; Mr. Whittier, grave, lovely, his beautiful spirit shining out of his face; Mr. Longfellow, with his silken-white hair and his benignant face; Dr. Oliver Wendell Holmes, flashing smiles and affection and all good-fellowship everywhere, like a rose-diamond whose facets are being turned toward the light, first one way and then another—a charming man, and always fascinating, whether he was talking or whether he was sitting still (what he would call still, but what would be more or less motion to other people). I can see those figures with entire distinctness across this abyss of time.

William Winter, the poet, had just preceded him, and it seemed a moment aptly chosen for his so-different theme. "And then," to quote Howells, "the amazing mistake, the bewildering blunder, the cruel catastrophe was upon us."

After the first two or three hundred words, when the general plan and purpose of the burlesque had developed, when the names of Longfellow, Emerson, and Holmes began to be flung about by those bleary outcasts, and their verses given that sorry association, those *Atlantic* diners became petrified with amazement and horror. Too late, then, the speaker realized his mistake. He could not stop, he must go on to the ghastly end. And somehow he did it, while "there fell a silence weighing many tons to the square inch, which deepened from moment to moment, and was broken only by the hysterical and blood-curdling laughter of a single guest, whose name shall not be handed down to infamy."

Howells can remember little more than that, but Clemens recalls that one speaker made an effort to follow him—Bishop, the novelist, and that Bishop didn't last long.

> It was not many sentences after his first before he began to hesitate and break, and lose his grip, and totter and wobble, and at last he slumped down in a limp and mushy pile.

The next man had not strength to rise, and somehow the company broke up.

Howells's next recollection is of being in a room of the hotel, and of hearing Charles Dudley Warner saying in the gloom:

"Well, Mark, *you're* a funny fellow."

He remembers how, after a sleepless night, Clemens went out to buy some bric-à-brac, with a soul far from bric-à-brac, and returned to Hartford in a writhing agony of spirit. He believed that he was ruined forever, so far as his Boston associations were concerned; and when he confessed all the tragedy to Mrs. Clemens it seemed to her also that the mistake could never be wholly repaired. The fact that certain papers quoted the speech and spoke well of it, and certain readers who had not listened to it thought it enormously funny, gave very little comfort. But perhaps his chief concern was the ruin which he believed he had brought upon Howells. He put his heart into a brief letter:

> My Dear Howells,—My sense of disgrace does not abate. It grows. I see that it is going to add itself to my list of permanencies, a list of humiliations that extends back to when I was seven years old, and which keep on persecuting me regardless of my repentances.
>
> I feel that my misfortune has injured me all over the country; therefore it will be best that I retire from before the public at present. It will hurt the *Atlantic* for me to appear in its pages now. So it is my opinion, and my wife's, that the telephone story had better be suppressed. Will you return those proofs or revises to me, so that I can use the same on some future occasion?
>
> It seems as if I must have been insane when I wrote that speech and saw no harm in it, no disrespect toward those men whom I

reverenced so much. And what shame I brought upon you, after what you said in introducing me! It burns me like fire to think of it.

The whole matter is a dreadful subject. Let me drop it here—at least on paper.

Penitently yours,   MARK

So, all in a moment, his world had come to an end—as it seemed. But Howells's letter, which came rushing back by first mail, brought hope.

"It was a fatality," Howells said. "One of those sorrows into which a man walks with his eyes wide open, no one knows why."

Howells assured him that Longfellow, Emerson, and Holmes would so consider it, beyond doubt; that Charles Eliot Norton had already expressed himself exactly in the right spirit concerning it. Howells declared that there was no intention of dropping Mark Twain's work from the *Atlantic*.

> You are not going to be floored by it; there is more justice than that even in *this* world. Especially as regards *me*, just call the sore spot well. I can say more, and with better heart, in praise of your good feeling (which was what I always liked in you), since this thing happened than I could before.

It was agreed that he should at once write a letter to Longfellow, Emerson, and Holmes, and he did write, laying his heart bare to them. Longfellow and Holmes answered in a fine spirit of kindliness, and Miss Emerson wrote for her father in the same tone. Emerson had not been offended, for he had not heard the speech, having arrived even then at that stage of semi-oblivion as to immediate things which eventually so completely shut him away. Longfellow's letter made light of the whole matter. The newspapers, he said, had caused all the mischief.

> A bit of humor at a dinner-table talk is one thing; a report of it in the morning papers is another. One needs the lamplight and the scenery. These failing, what was meant in jest assumes a serious aspect.
>
> I do not believe that anybody was much hurt. Certainly I was not, and Holmes tells me that he was not. So I think you may dismiss the matter from your mind, without further remorse.
>
> It was a very pleasant dinner, and I think Whittier enjoyed it very much.

Holmes likewise referred to it as a trifle.

It never occurred to me for a moment to take offense, or to feel wounded by your playful use of my name. I have heard some mild questioning as to whether, even in fun, it was good taste to associate the names of the authors with the absurdly unlike personalities attributed to them, but it seems to be an open question. Two of my friends, gentlemen of education and the highest social standing, were infinitely amused by your speech, and stoutly defended it against the charge of impropriety. More than this, one of the cleverest and best-known ladies we have among us was highly delighted with it.

Miss Emerson's letter was to Mrs. Clemens and its homelike New England fashion did much to lift the gloom.

> DEAR MRS. CLEMENS,—At New Year's our family always meets, to spend two days together. To-day my father came last, and brought with him Mr. Clemens's letter, so that I read it to the assembled family, and I have come right up-stairs to write to you about it. My sister said, "Oh, let father write!" but my mother said, "No, don't wait for him. Go now; don't stop to pick that up. Go this minute and write. I think that is a noble letter. Tell them so." First let me say that no shadow of indignation has ever been in any of our minds. The night of the dinner, my father says, he did not hear Mr. Clemens's speech. He was too far off, and my mother says that when she read it to him the next day it amused him. But what you will want is to know, without any softening, how we did feel. We were disappointed. We have liked almost everything we have ever seen over Mark Twain's signature. It has made us like the man, and we have delighted in the fun. Father has often asked us to repeat certain passages of *The Innocents Abroad*, and of a speech at a London dinner in 1872, and we all expect both to approve and to enjoy when we see his name. Therefore, when we read this speech it was a real disappointment. I said to my brother that it didn't seem good or funny, and he said, "No, it was unfortunate. Still some of those quotations were very good"; and he gave them with relish and my father laughed, though never having seen a card in his life, he couldn't understand them like his children. My mother read it lightly and had hardly any second thoughts about it. To my father it is as if it had not been; he never quite heard, never quite understood it, and he forgets easily and entirely. I think it doubtful whether he writes to Mr. Clemens, for he is old and long ago gave up answering

letters, I think you can see just *how* bad, and how little bad, it was as far as we are concerned, and this lovely heartbreaking letter makes up for our disappointment in our much-liked author, and restores our former feeling about him.

ELLEN T. EMERSON.

The sorrow dulled a little as the days passed. Just after Christmas Clemens wrote to Howells:

I haven't done a stroke of work since the *Atlantic* dinner. But I'm going to try to-morrow. How could I ever—

Ah, well, I am a great and sublime fool. But then I am God's fool, and all his work must be contemplated with respect.

So long as that unfortunate speech is remembered there will be differences of opinion as to its merits and propriety. Clemens himself, reading it for the first time in nearly thirty years, said:

"I find it gross, coarse—well, I needn't go on with particulars. I don't like any part of it, from the beginning to the end. I find it always offensive and detestable. How do I account for this change of view? I don't know."

But almost immediately afterward he gave it another consideration and reversed his opinion completely. All the spirit and delight of his old first conception returned, and preparing it for publication[1] he wrote:

I have read it twice, and unless I am an idiot it hasn't a single defect in it, from the first word to the last. It is just as good as good can be. It is smart; it is saturated with humor. There isn't a suggestion of coarseness or vulgarity in it anywhere.

It was altogether like Mark Twain to have those two absolutely opposing opinions in that brief time; for, after all, it was only a question of the human point of view, and Mark Twain's points of view were likely to be as extremely human as they were varied.

Of course the first of these impressions, the verdict of the fresh mind uninfluenced by the old conception, was the more correct one. The speech was decidedly out of place in that company. The skit was harmless enough, but it was of the Comstock grain. It lacked refinement, and, what was still worse, it lacked humor, at least the humor of a kind suited to that long-ago company of listeners. It was another of those grievous mistakes which genius (and not talent) can make, for genius is a sort of possession. The individual is pervaded, dominated for a time by an angel or an imp, and he seldom, of himself, is able to discriminate between his controls. A literary imp was always lying in wait for Mark Twain; the imp of the burlesque, tempting him to do the *outre*, the outlandish, the shocking thing. It was this that Olivia Clemens had to labor hardest against: the cheapening of his own high purpose with an extravagant false note, at which sincerity, conviction, and artistic harmony took wings and fled away. Notably he did a good burlesque now and then, but his fame would not have suffered if he had been delivered altogether from his besetting temptation.

Note

1. *North American Review*, December, 1907, now with comment included in the volume of "Speeches." Also see Appendix O, at the end of last volume.

> —Albert Bigelow Paine, "The Whittier
> Birthday Speech," December 17, 1877,
> *Mark Twain: A Biography: The Personal
> and Literary Life of Samuel Langhorne
> Clemens*, New York: Harper and
> Brothers, 1912, vol. II, pp. 603–610

Ambrose Bierce
"Comment on a Famous Faux Pas" (1878)

This mocking voice from California reminds Twain, in his darkest moment, of what he used to be and what he is trying to forget—one lowdown and disliked by the police. Ambrose Bierce persists in Twain's biography as a reminder of how he was. However, Bierce also alters the facts. Twain's Whittier birthday speech described Emerson, Longfellow, and Oliver Wendell Holmes as tramps; it kept Whittier out of it.

Mark Twain's Boston speech, in which the great humorist's coltish imagination represented Longfellow, Emerson and Whittier engaged at a game of cards in the cabin of a California miner, is said to have so wrought upon the feelings of the "best literary society" in that city that the daring joker is in danger of lynching. I hope they won't lynch him; it would be irregular and illegal, however roughly just and publicly beneficial. Besides, it would rob many a worthy sheriff of an honourable ambition by dispelling the most bright and beautiful hope of his life.

> —Ambrose Bierce, "Comment on a Famous
> Faux Pas," The *Argonaut*, January 5, 1878

Joel Chandler Harris (1881)

At this time in 1881, Twain was gathering himself and others for a lecture tour with George Washington Cable. Joel Chandler Harris, the author of the "Uncle Remus" tales, was one of Twain's choices for a fellow lecturer, until Twain realized that he was intensely shy and that the project was thus impracticable.

The Constitution, Atlanta, Ga.
Editorial Rooms, 4 August, 1881

My dear Mr. clemens:—

You have pinned a proud feather in Uncle Remus's cap. I do not know what higher honor he could desire than to appear before the Hartford public arm-in-arm with Mark Twain. Everybody has been kind to the old man, but you have been kindest of all. I am perfectly well aware that my book has no basis of literary art to stand upon; I know it is the matter and not the manner that has attracted public attention and won the consideration of people of taste at the North; I understand that my relations toward Uncle Remus are similar to those that exist between an almanac-maker and the calendar; but at the same time I feel very grateful to those who have taken the old man under their wing.

The ghost story you spoke of is new to me, and if I dared to trouble you I would ask you to send me the outlines so that I might verify it here. I do not remember to have heard it, but I do not by any means depend upon my own memory in matters of this kind. It is easy to get a story from a negro by giving him a sympathetic cue, but without this it is a hopeless task. If you have the story in manuscript, I would be very grateful to you for a sight of it; if not, I will try and find it here in some shape or other.

While I am writing, I may as well use the gimlet vigorously.—I have a number of fables ready to be written up, but I don't want to push the public to the wall by printing them in the magazines without intermission. I must ask your advice. Would it be better to print the new fables in a volume by themselves, or would it be better to bring out a revised edition of Uncle Remus, adding the new matter and issuing the volume as a subscription book? I am puzzled and bothered about it.

Glancing back over these two sheets, I am compelled to admit that you have escaped lightly. Nevertheless, you cannot escape my gratitude for your kindness to Uncle Remus.

    Sincerely yours

    Joel Chandler Harris

In his reply, Mr. Clemens commented on his friend's modest estimate of his abilities:—

"You can argue *yourself* into the delusion that the principle of life is in the stories themselves and not in their setting, but you will save labor by stopping with that solitary convert, for he is the only intelligent one you will bag. In reality the stories are only alligator pears—one eats them merely for the sake of the dressing. 'Uncle Remus' is most deftly drawn and is a lovable and delightful creation; he and the little boy and their relations with each other are bright, fine literature, and worthy to live. . . . But I seem to be proving to the man that made the multiplication table that twice one is two."

Mr. Clemens offered some advice regarding the publishing of a second volume of tales and sent the outline of the "ghost story" (called in his version "The Golden Arm"), which had been told him in childhood by his "Uncle Dan'l," a slave of sixty years, before the flickering blaze of a kitchen fire. Father was familiar with a variant of this story and afterward developed it in the dramatic "Ghost Story" told by 'Tildy, and incorporated in "Nights with Uncle Remus." Mr. Clemens was anxious for father to appear with him in readings, and followed up this letter with a request that father meet him in New Orleans, where he was to stop for a few days in the course of a trip down the Mississippi River with Mr. Osgood, the publisher, to discuss this and other matters. Father replied:—

> I will gladly meet you in New Orleans unless some unforeseen contingency should arise. In regard to my diffidence, I will say that the ordeal of appearing on the stage would be a terrible one, but my experience is that when a diffident man does become familiar with his surroundings he has more impudence than his neighbors. Extremes meet. At any rate, your project is immensely flattering to me, and I am grateful to you for even connecting me with it in your mind. I appreciate the fact that, if successfully carried out, it would be the making of me in more ways than one. It would enable me, for one thing, to drop this grinding newspaper business and write some books I have in mind. I only hope you will see your way clear to including me in the scheme in some shape or fashion. A telegram three or four days in advance of your arrival in New Orleans will enable me to be on hand promptly; and you might mention the name of the hotel provided you settle that matter in advance also.
>
> Gratefully yours
> JOEL CHANDLER HARRIS

—Joel Chandler Harris,
letter to Clemens, August 4, 1881

AMBROSE BIERCE (1886)

In this article, Ambrose Bierce makes a sharp division between Mark Twain's early and later work. Bernard DeVoto would, in due course, come to a similar conclusion, finding that all of Mark Twain's best work had been produced by 1890.

Mark Twain has been a funny man in his day and though the humor that once set thousands in a roar has vanished with the poverty which Mark Twain joked away, a fond public is still unwilling to believe that the jester is no more. We are sorry for Mark the Jester and our grief is mingled with disgust for those who will not let the ashes of the dead clown be but persist in stirring them up in the vain hope of evolving a latent spark. Foremost among these desecrators of the tomb of Mark the Jester is Mark the Money-worm. Aided and abetted by the minions of the Associated Press, Mr. Samuel Clemens takes his spade and dark lantern, hies him to the burying ground and rattles the skeleton of poor Mark Twain. His last atrocious desecration was committed at the Typotheta dinner in New York one evening of this week. Here is what the Associated Press conspirators say of the infamy:

> At the Typotheta dinner last night Mark Twain made a long and humorous speech of which the following is a sample: "The chairman's historical reminiscences about Gutenberg and Caxton have cast me into the reminiscent mood. For I also in a small way am an antiquity. I was acquainted with the printer of the olden time. I swept out his office for him and carried his papers about for him. The carrier was then an object of interest to all the dogs in the town. If I had saved up all the bites I ever received I could keep M. Pasteur busy for a year."

"Of which the following is a sample." The irony of those rascals cannot be repressed. They telegraph this mournful specimen over three thousand miles as a sample. They should rather have called it an epitaph, an affidavit, an indisputable proof that Samuel Clemens, Esquire, of Hartford, Connecticut, was masquerading in the motley of Mark Twain, a humorist erst of the Pacific Coast, who departed this life some years back, and that S. Clemens, Esq., was making a mighty poor fist of the business.

—Ambrose Bierce, *The Wasp*,
January 23, 1886

Ambrose Bierce "Prattle" (1888)

I have been looking through Mark Twain's new Library of Humor and find that it justifies its title. Possibly I am a trifle prejudiced in its favour, for the very funniest thing in it, according to my notion of humor, is a brief biography of myself. It is as follows—barring the bracketed words—

> Ambrose Bierce, author of "Bierce's Fables" (I am not), was born in Akron, O. (I was not), in 1843 (I was not). He served as a soldier in the war, and in 1865 went to San Francisco (I did not), where he was engaged in newspaper work until 1872. Then he went to London, where he had great success (I had not), and published "Bierceiana" (I did not). With the younger Tom Hood he founded London *Fun* (I did not). He returned to California in 1877 (I did not) and is now an editor of the San Francisco EXAMINER (I am not).

That is just like Mark Twain: he will not publish another fellow's work without tacking on something of his own so confoundedly amusing that the other chap's reads, in the shadow of it, like a call to the unconverted, or a pen-picture of a dead Emperor in an advanced state of decomposition. I wish I had written my own biography and he the extracts from my work.

—Ambrose Bierce, "Prattle," *San Francisco Examiner*, August 2, 1888

Walt Whitman (1889)

Although there have been several attempts to compare Mark Twain, in his career and his works, to the poet Walt Whitman, the two had virtually no connection. Twain kindly made some charitable donations to Whitman when asked, but one wonders whether he ever read the poet. In a letter written to congratulate Whitman on his seventieth birthday, the critic Dwight Mcdonald notes that "instead of congratulating the age on Whitman, it congratulates Whitman on the age." Indeed, in the letter Twain rambles on about the industrial advances of the day. Edgar Lee Masters singled this letter out as evidence of Twain's overweening philistinism: "The poet, according to Twain, was to be congratulated for having lived in the age which had seen 'the amazing, infinitely varied and innumerable products of coal-tar.'"

What Whitman thought of Twain gradually emerged as the volumes making up Horace Traubel's *With Walt Whitman in Camden* began to be published (the nine volumes took ninety years to be published, starting in 1906). These texts, with Traubel recording verbatim Whitman's proverbial table talk, are the source of the following remarks. They are made off the cuff, and one suspects that Twain did not overly occupy Whitman's mind. Nevertheless, Whitman's comments are of course invaluable to any student writing a comparison of Whitman and Twain.

23 February 1889

I think he mainly misses fire: I think his life misses fire: he might have been something: he comes near to being something: but he never arrives.

20 March 1889

I have always regarded him as friendly, but not warm: not exactly against me: not for me either.

4 May 1889

Keep your eyes wide open—I need hardly advise you to do that— you do that anyhow: but I mean, describe what you see,—people, stands, stores, vehicles, shows, the human curios—and let the rest retell itself. It will! The French are uniquely gifted in that way—oh wonderfully—only with this drawback—a tendency I always dislike, never will accept—a superciliousness which seems to hold them from mixing with the event, the fact, they describe. It is a quality our own humorists have had—which is their weakness: Bret Harte, Mark Twain—the others, who fairly enough touch off the rude Western life, but always as though with the insinuation, "see how far we are removed from all that—we good gentlemen with our dress suits and parlor accompaniments!" W[hitman] criticised the want of truth in the magazine stories now vogued— "the stories of Western, South-Western, life. 'Hit' they will say for 'it,' for instance. That is news to me. If it has come into use, it has come lately—for in my time there was no such exaggerated emphasis. In fact, that is the prevailing error—an aggravation of the peculiarities of dialects. It spoils some of those very good stories in the magazines—stories excellent in themselves, but too apt to exceed the truth, perhaps to excite our interest, perhaps from defect of ear."

—Walt Whitman, 1889, from *With Walt Whitman in Camden*, Horace Traubel, 4: 208, 4: 390–391, 5: 131–132

Horace Traubel (1889)

I received a four-page note from Mark Twain, full of generalities with practically no word about W[alt]. W[hitman]. Have not yet referred to it in W[hitman]'s presence.

1 November 1889

I had letters from Mark Twain and Gilder.

Dear Gilder—

I shall not need to answer this letter, I suppose, since I can answer it through you. It seems to be an application for a contribution of from one to five dollars per month. I am quite willing to be put up on the list of two-dollar contributors, and I enclose five months contribution in advance herewith.

Yours sincerely,
SL Clemens.

Hartford
Oct 30th '89

55 Clinton Place
Oct 31, 1889,

My dear Mr. Traubel,

Enclosed please find $10 from me, & $10 from Mark Twain –(S.L. Clemens) for Walt Whitman.

I write from my bed. Where's the book?

Sincerely, R.W. Gilder

W[hitman] exclaimed: "The good Clemens!"

—Horace Traubel, *With Walt Whitman in Camden*, 5: 229, 6: 106-107

WILLIAM JAMES (1892–93)

William James was a considerable force in American philosophy and in the early study of psychology, authoring numerous works including *The Principles of Psychology* (1890) and *The Varieties of Religious Experience* (1902), as well as espousing the philosophy of pragmatism and coining the term "stream of consciousness." He taught philosophy and experimental psychology at Harvard, and at Radcliffe College he taught and significantly influenced Gertrude Stein. His brother was the novelist Henry James. While Henry made no great connection with Twain (although they were both American novelists living in England at the same time), William— somewhat surprisingly—formed a friendship with him.

Letter to Josiah Royce, December 18, 1892

> Mark Twain is here for the winter in a villa outside the town, hard at work writing something or other. I have seen him a couple of times—a fine, soft-fibred little fellow with the perversest twang and drawl, but very human and good. I should think that one might grow very fond of him, and wish he'd come and live in Cambridge.

Letter to Francis Boot, January 30, 1893

> Mark Twain dined with us last night, in company with the good Villari and the charming Mrs. Villari; but there was no chance then to ask him to sing Nora McCarty. He's a dear man, and there'll be a chance yet. He is in a delightful villa at Settignano, and he says he's written more in the past four months than he could have done in two years at Hartford . . .

> > —William James, letters to Josiah Royce
> > and Francis Boot, from *The Letters of*
> > *William James*, Boston, 1920, I: 333, I: 341–342

DAN DE QUILLE (1893)
"REPORTING WITH MARK TWAIN"

Dan De Quille, the "Washoe Giant," was the nom de plume of William Wright, an Ohioan who had left his wife and five children to seek silver in the Nevada mining hills. He fell into journalism, for which he had a greater aptitude, writing for the Virginia City *Enterprise*. When he went on leave to see his family, Samuel Clemens was brought in to replace him. He had contributed to the *Enterprise* under the name "Josh," and had suitably impressed the editor. On Dan's return, he and Clemens (now fatefully recast as Mark Twain) became close confederates. When asked, the perplexed colleagues of Twain and De Quille opined that they felt sure that Dan would enjoy the wider and greater success, not Mark. This was famously not the case.

After Twain left Nevada for good, the two fell out of contact until 1875, when, by chance, each man wrote to the other and their letters crossed in the mail. From this connection, De Quille visited Twain in Connecticut and stayed with him, writing *The Big Bonanza*, his history of the gold and silver rushes, for Twain's publishers. After this, De Quille drifted back to Nevada and out of Twain's interest. De Quille died in 1898.

Students interested in the development of the persona of "Mark Twain" will find an excellent account here of how the transformation was enacted. In other details De Quille is equally captivating, such as in his description of the slashed baize of the tabletop. When he visits Twain in Connecticut years after, De Quille looks for more such slashes in vain. What might such a peculiar yet authentic detail suggest about how Mark Twain himself had changed in that time? Clues to Twain's early identity are scattered through this article. While the recollections of William Gillis may be colored by the years and further biased by a raconteur's innate tendency to exaggerate, De Quille's account is reliable, with a reporter's keen eye for the unique and the significant.

It was in the early days of the Comstock, just when the great boom in silver mining had fairly commenced, that I first met Samuel L. Clemens, now better known as Mark Twain. It was in the days when Washoe was still the popular name of all the silver mining regions of Nevada. Mr. Clemens had been engaged in prospecting at Aurora, Esmeralda County (then a lively camp), whence he sent to the *Territorial Enterprise*, of Virginia City, some humorous letters signed "Josh." The *Enterprise* was then not only the leading paper of "Silverland," but also was one of the liveliest and most prosperous newspapers on the Pacific Coast.

I had been at work on the *Enterprise* about two years, when, in December, 1862, I concluded to take a trip to the States, whereupon the proprietors of the paper—J. T. Goodman and D. E. McCarthy—engaged Josh (Mr. Clemens) to come in from Aurora and take a position on their paper as reporter. I was absent from the Comstock about nine months—on the Plains and in the States—and when I returned, Mr. Clemens had shed his nom de plume of Josh and taken that which he still retains and has made famous. Mark did not much relish the work of writing reports of mines and mining affairs, and for that reason, and because of the boom in business and rush of events demanding reportorial notice, I was asked to return posthaste and resume work on the paper—everything being, as my letter of recall said, "red-hot."

I found things red-hot indeed. Reaching San Francisco in the evening after dark, the first news I heard, even before our steamer had reached the wharf, was that Virginia City was on fire and was being "wiped out." At once there was great excitement, for a score or more of Washoe people were on board the vessel. Upon landing, we rushed to the newspaper offices and there heard that the town was still burning. I also learned that there had been a big fight among the firemen and that some of my friends and acquaintances had been killed and wounded. It was midnight before we heard that the fire was under control, and I then ascertained, to my great relief, that the *Enterprise* office had escaped, while all about it had been destroyed.

Thus I resumed business at the old stand in the thick of red-hot times—in the midst of flames and war. It was also in the midst of the cutting and shooting days—the days of stage robberies, of mining fights, wonderful finds of ore, and all manner of excitements. As may be imagined, Mark and I had our hands full, and no grass grew under our feet. There was a constant rush of startling events; they came tumbling over one another as though playing at leapfrog. While a stage robbery was being written up, a shooting affray started; and perhaps before the pistol shots had ceased to echo among the surrounding hills, the firebells were banging out an alarm.

The crowding of the whole population into that part of the town which had escaped the fire led to many bloody battles. Fighters, sports, and adventurers, burned out of their old haunts, thronged the saloons and gaming houses remaining, where many of them were by no means welcome visitors; and, as in the case of cats in strange garrets, battles were of nightly occurrence. Everybody was armed, and no man threw away his life by making an attack with his fists.

Mark and I agreed well in our work, which we divided when there was a rush of events, but we often cruised in company—he taking the items of news he could best handle, and I such as I felt myself competent to work up. However, we wrote at the same table and frequently helped each other with such suggestions as occurred to us during the brief consultations we held in regard to the handling of any matters of importance. Never was there an angry word between us in all the time we worked together.

Mark Twain, as a reporter, was earnest and enthusiastic in such work as suited him—really industrious—but when it came to "cast-iron" items, he gave them a lick and a promise. He hated to have to do with figures, measurements, and solid facts, such as were called for in matters pertaining to mines and machinery.

Mark displayed a peculiarity when at work that was very detrimental to the integrity of office property. In case he wished to clip an item or a paragraph out of a paper, and could not at once lay his hand upon his scissors, he would cut out the required matter with his knife, at the same time slashing into the baize covering of the table. His end of the cover was so mutilated that little was left of the original cloth. In its place appeared what might have passed for a representation of the polar star, spiritedly darting forth a thousand rays. Some years ago, when at Mark's house in Hartford, I found myself almost unconsciously examining the top of the fine writing desk in his library for evidences of his old knife-slashing habit, but did not find so much as a scratch.

Mark Twain was pretty apt in sketching in a rude way, and when reporting meetings where there were long waits or uninteresting debates, he would cover the margins of his copy paper with drawings. When reporting the meetings of the Board of Aldermen, where there was often much tedious talk, he would frequently make sketches illustrative of the subjects under discussion. Some of his offhand sketches were very good—good in the same way that a pun is sometimes good, though farfetched and ridiculous. I have forgotten the subjects of most of these pencil sketches. I recall one, however, that might have been labeled "The Captured Menagerie." There had been some trouble about collecting city license from a menagerie (it had paid county license) and the matter came up before the Board of Aldermen. Mark was amused at the talk of what could be done and what would be done with the show and showmen if the license was not paid at once, and so he pictured it all out. He depicted the city marshal leading away the elephant by its trunk, and the mayor mounted upon a giraffe which he had captured, while one policeman had a lion by the tail, and another had captured a rhinoceros. Still others had shouldered kangaroos, strings of monkeys, and the like.

This was about his best effort, and after writing out his report of the meeting, he kept his sheets of notes for some time, working up and improving the several pictures. At his home in Hartford, Mark sometimes dabbles in oil colors, he having taken lessons in art since the Comstock days. He points with pride to the curly head of a dove-colored bull on an easel in his library, and hints that the best effects were all achieved without the assistance of his teacher.

Mark Twain was fond of manufacturing items of the horrible style, but on one occasion he overdid this business, and the disease worked its own cure. He wrote an account of a terrible murder, supposed to have occurred at Dutch Nick's, a station on the Carson River where Empire City now stands. He made a man cut his wife's throat and those of his nine children, after which diabolical deed the murderer mounted his horse, cut his own throat from ear to ear, rode to Carson City (a distance of three and a half miles), and fell dead in front of Pete Hopkins's saloon.

All the California papers copied the item, and several made editorial comment upon it as being the most shocking occurrence of the kind ever known on the Pacific Coast. Of course rival Virginia City papers at once denounced the item as a "cruel and idiotic hoax." They showed how the publication of such "shocking and reckless falsehoods" disgraced and injured the state, and they made it as sultry as possible for the *Enterprise* and its "fool reporter."

When the California papers saw all this and found they had been sold, there was a howl from Siskiyou to San Diego. Some papers demanded the immediate discharge of the author of the item by the *Enterprise* proprietors. They said they would never quote another line from that paper while the reporter who wrote the shocking item remained on its force. All this worried Mark as I had never seen him worried. Said he: "I am being burned alive on both sides of the mountains." We roomed together, and one night when the persecution was hottest, he was so distressed that he could not sleep. He tossed, tumbled, and groaned aloud. So I set to work to comfort him. "Mark," said I, "never mind this bit of a gale; it will soon blow itself out. This item of yours will be remembered and talked about when all your other work is forgotten. The murder at Dutch Nick's will be quoted years from now as the big sell of these times."

Said Mark: "I believe you are right; I remember I once did a thing at home in Missouri, was caught at it, and worried almost to death. I was a mere lad and was going to school in a little town where I had an uncle living. I at once left the town and did not return to it for three years. When I finally came back I found I was only remembered as 'the boy that played the trick on the schoolmaster.'"

Mark then told me the story, began to laugh over it, and from that moment ceased to groan. He was not discharged, and in less than a month people everywhere were laughing and joking about the "murder at Dutch Nick's."

When Mark wrote the item he read it over to me, and I asked him how he was going to wind it up so as to make it plain that it was a mere invention.

"Oh, it is wound up now," was the reply. "It is all plain enough. I have said that the family lived in a little cabin at the edge of the great pine forest near Dutch Nick's, when everybody knows there's not a pine tree within ten miles of Nick's. Then I make the man ride nearly four miles after he has cut his throat from ear to ear, when any fool must see that he would fall dead in a moment."

But the people were all so shocked at first with the wholesale throat-cutting that they did not stop to think of these points. Mark's whole object in writing the story was to make the murderer go to Pete Hopkins's saloon and fall dead in front of it—Pete having in some way offended him. I could never quite see how this was to hurt Pete Hopkins. Mark probably meant to insinuate that the murderer had been rendered insane by the kind of liquor sold over Hopkins's bar, or that he was one of Pete's bosom friends.

Today not one man in a hundred in Nevada can remember anything written by Mark Twain while he was connected with the *Enterprise*, except this one item in regard to the shocking murder at Dutch Nick's; all else is forgotten, even by his oldest and most intimate friends.

First and last, many newspapers, daily and weekly, have been published in Virginia City. The life of one of these was so short, however, that only a few persons are now aware that it ever had an existence. It opened its eyes to the light only to close them again forever. This was the *Occidental*, an eight-page weekly literary paper started by Honorable Tom Fitch, the "Silver-tongued Orator of Nevada." But one number of the paper was issued. The good die young—the *Occidental* was good. Why the paper died as soon as born I never exactly knew, but think it would be safe to say that all the "powder" in the magazine was used up in the first shot.

Twain and I were rooming together at the time in what was known as the Daggett building, a large brick structure where there were many lodgers. Tom Fitch and family were our across-the-hall neighbors. Of course we were informed in regard to Tom's newspaper venture and took a lively interest in all his literary plans. The paper was intended to constitute a sort of safety valve for the red-hot and hissing Comstock literary boiler. Writers on the other papers, and writers at large were to contribute to its columns.

In the number of this paper that was published, a romance was commenced that was to have been continued almost indefinitely. At least, in discussing the plan of it nothing was ever said about how it was to be ended, and had the story been carried forward in accordance with the original plan, it would have been one of the curiosities of literature, and probably running yet.

Honorable R. M. Daggett, late minister to the Hawaiian Islands, wrote the opening chapters of the story. A striking character in the story, as begun by Mr. Daggett, was an old hermit, "reported a Rosycrucian," who dwelt in a partially subterranean castle situated in a dark and secret mountain gorge where, "in the dead waist and middle of the night," smoke and flames were to be seen issuing from his chimneys while lights—red, blue, and green—flashed up in his heavily barred windows. The building had no visible door—all was solid masonry—and the person viewing it from the outside could only imagine a subterranean entrance, which no man could discover "for the dews that dripped all over."

The old white-haired alchemist had a pupil, of course, and this pupil was the hero of the romance, as it was begun by Mr. Daggett. In the great outside world dwelt the heroine, who started out—began business—as a very lovable young lady. The opening was full of mystery, and was very interesting. Mr. Daggett left the hero in a position of such peril that it seemed impossible he could be rescued, except through means and wisdom more than human.

Mrs. Tom Fitch was to have written the chapters for the next number of the paper; she would have been followed by Mark Twain, and he, in due course, by J. T. Goodman, Tom Fitch, and myself, when Mr. Daggett would again come in and take up the thread of the exciting tale.

Each person would have been obliged to extricate the hero, heroine (or any other useful character) from whatever sad predicament the writer preceding him might have devised, and would have aimed to puzzle the one who was to follow him. It would have been a sort of literary game of chess.

It was thought that Mrs. Fitch would respect Daggett's lovely heroine, and carry her along in unsullied beauty of both person and soul; but Mark Twain was sharpening his scalping knife for her. The old Rosycrucian was Daggett's pet. He wanted to carry the old fellow all through the story, but was afraid Mrs. Fitch would find him unmanageable and would roast him in one of his own furnaces. In case she did anything of the kind, Mr. Daggett was resolved to take a terrible revenge when he got hold of her pet character—he would do "a deed that the ibis and the crocodile would tremble at."

Although Mark and I had promised to let Mr. Daggett's old hermit live, we had secretly conjured up a demon fiddler who was to make his appearance in the mysterious barred castle at critical moments, and with rosined bow torment both the quivering string and the old alchemist. In case Daggett provided the old fellow with some spell sufficiently potent to "lay" the fiddler, we intended to introduce into the secret laboratory a spectral owl that should worry the occupant by watching his every movement; and following the owl we would send the whole progeny of devils—aerial, aquatic, and terrestrial— said to have been born of Adam's first wife, Lilith.

Mrs. Fitch and her lady friends and advisers doubtless had their plans for "warming" Mark and all the rest of us. However, with the death of the *Occidental*, all passed away into the realms of nothingness, "wie ein schatten vergehen"—as a shadow goes.

The story of the presentation to Mark Twain of a bogus meerschaum pipe has often been told, but in most instances without touching upon that which was the fine point of the whole affair. Major Steve Gillis, C. A. V. Putnam, D. E. McCarthy, and several other newspaper men put up a job to present Mark an imitation meerschaum pipe. They selected one they knew he would not like because of its shape, had its German silver mounting polished up, and on this the inscription, "To Mark Twain, from his Friends" was neatly engraved. A cherry stem about a yard long, with a genuine amber mouthpiece, was procured, and the present was ready. The presentation was to take place on a Saturday night, after the paper was up, at Harris's saloon, in Maguire's Opera House. Charley Pope, now proprietor of a theater in St. Louis, Missouri, was then playing at the Opera House, and he was engaged to make the presentation speech. All this being arranged, I said to Mark one night after we had gone to bed: "Mark, I don't know that I ought to tell you, but the boys are going to make you a present of a fine meerschaum pipe next Saturday night. Charley Pope is to make the presentation speech, and as it will doubtless be rather fine, I have thought it best to post you, in order that you may think up a suitable reply."

Mark thanked me most cordially for giving the business away—not once suspecting that the boys had made it my part to thus thoroughly post him, in order that we might all have the fun of watching him in his effort to convey the impression that the presentation was a genuine surprise.

This was really the point, and the big sell of the whole affair. Even Charley Pope was aware that Mark had been fully posted, therefore to us all it was deliciously ridiculous to observe Mark's pretended unawareness.

From the moment of our assembling until the ceremonies ended, every eye was fixed upon him, watching every shade of expression on his countenance.

Even with the enticing of Mark down to the Opera House saloon, the fun began, as he assumed a certain degree of coyness, pretending to hold back, and couldn't "see why we wanted him to go there." When our victim and all the conspirators had been assembled for some time round the center table in a private parlor of the saloon, Charley Pope made his appearance. Mark seemed surprised at seeing him enter the room.

Mr. Pope carried under his arm, wrapped in a newspaper, a bundle about a yard in length. Advancing to the table he proceeded to unroll the bundle, producing a ridiculous-looking pipe, with a straight bowl about five inches high, and about a yard of blue ribbon floating from the stem.

"That is a mighty fine pipe you have there, Charley," said Mark in an offhand, unconcerned tone of voice.

Mr. Pope made no reply, but throwing the newspapers upon the floor held the pipe aloft by the middle of the stem, as in the great paintings of the presentation of the Pipe of Peace, and began his speech with: "Mr. Clemens, on behalf of your friends and admirers, those you see here assembled and many others, I present you this magnificent meerschaum pipe as a slight," etc., etc.

Mr. Pope spoke about twenty minutes, making a really admirable speech. In parts it was very feeling, and again it was witty and jolly. Of course we applauded it from Alpha to Omega.

Then Mark Twain arose. In his hand he held the mighty calumet. He was sorry that he would be unable fittingly to reply to a speech so able and excellent as that of Mr. Pope—a speech that had touched his heart and stirred in his bosom feelings he could not find words to express. But the truth was that he had been taken by surprise. The presentation was a thing wholly unexpected.

He then launched forth into what we all knew was his prepared speech. He began with the introduction of tobacco into England by Sir Walter Raleigh, and wound up with George Washington. Just how he managed to bring in the father of his country I have forgotten; but he had him there in the wind-up, and showed him off to good advantage.

Often the thunders of applause brought him to a halt. He was made to feel that he was a success. Then he called for sparkling Moselle—no other wine would do him—and before the session was over six bottles, at five dollars a bottle, had vanished.

A day or two afterwards a printer let the cat out of the bag—told Mark his pipe was a "mere sham." Mark had suspected as much. Even on the night of the presentation, before we had consumed more than two of the six bottles of Moselle, I had detected him inspecting the bowl of the pipe with a sort of reproachful look in his eye.

I was alone in the "local room," one day, when Mark suddenly made his appearance with the pipe in his hand. He locked the door on the inside and put the key in his pocket. "I want to know from you, now," said he, "whether this pipe is bogus."

"It is just as bogus as they make 'em," said I.

"Did you know that when you capped me into preparing a speech?"

"Certainly. That was where the fun came in."

"'Et tu Brute!'" said Mark in a hollow voice; then he began to pace the room with his face on his breast.

I told Mark to take it easy and say nothing, as a really fine pipe—one that cost $45—was back of the bogus one and would be given him without ceremony or cost. Mark then subsided, but was by no means satisfied with the business. However, years after he told me that he thought more of the bogus pipe than he did of the genuine one. Like his Dutch Nick item, time ripened it.

At the time Mark Twain was on the *Enterprise* he wrote no long stories or sketches for that paper. Occasionally, however, he sent a sketch to the *Golden Era*, of San Francisco. After going to San Francisco he was for a time regularly employed on one or two papers, then wrote sketches and did piecework of various kinds. He did not much like reporting in the city by the sea. For a long time after going down to San Francisco, he wrote a weekly letter to the *Enterprise* in which he gave such chat as would not be sent by telegraph—chat made up in good part of personals in regard to the doings of Comstockers at the Bay, the humors of the stock market and the like.

In 1865, Mark Twain grew tired of a life of literary drudgery in San Francisco and went up into the mining regions of Calaveras County to rusticate and rejuvenate with some old friends—Steve, Billy, and Jim Gillis. The cabin of Jim Gillis is, and always has been, a friendly place of retreat in the mountain wilds for writers desirous of respite from the vanities and vexations of spirit incident to a life of literary labor in San Francisco. At his cabin the latchstring is always on the outside. Many are the well-known California writers who have at various times been sojourners in the hospitable mountain home of Jim Gillis. His cabin is a sort of Bohemian infirmary. There the sick are made well, and the well are made better—physically, mentally, and morally.

Mark Twain found life pleasant in this literary mountain retreat. He found the Bohemian style of mining practiced by the Gillis boys much more attractive than those more regular kinds which call for a large outlay of muscle. The business of the pocket miner is much like that of the bee hunter. The trail of the latter leads him to the tree stored with golden sweets, and that of the former ends in a pocket of sweetest gold.

Soon after Mark's arrival at the "Gillis Bohemian Infirmary," he and Jim Gillis took to the hills in search of golden pockets. They soon found and spent some days in working up the undisturbed trail of an undiscovered deposit. They were on the golden beeline, and stuck to it faithfully, though it was necessary to carry each sample of dirt a considerable distance to a small stream in the bed of a cañon in order to wash it. However, Mark hungered and thirsted to find a big, rich pocket, and he pitched in after the manner of Joe Bowers of old—just like a thousand of brick.

Each step made sure by the finding of golden grains, they at last came upon the pocket whence these grains had trailed out down the slope of the mountain. It was a cold, dreary, drizzling day when the home deposit was found. The first sample of dirt carried to the stream and washed out yielded only a few cents. Although the right vein had been discovered, they had as yet found only the tail end of the pocket.

Returning to the vein, they dug a sample of the decomposed ore from a new place and were about to carry it down to the ravine and test it, when the rain increased to a lively downpour. With chattering teeth, Mark declared he would remain no longer. He said there was no sense in freezing to death, as in a day or two when it was bright and warm they could return and pursue their investigations in comfort.

Yielding to Mark's entreaties, backed as they were by his blue nose, humped back, and generally miserable and dejected appearance, Jim Gillis emptied the sacks of dirt just dug upon the ground—first having hastily written and posted a notice claiming a certain number of feet on the vein, which notice would hold good for thirty days. This done they left the claim.

Angel's Camp being at no great distance from the spot, whereas their cabin was some miles away, Mark and Jim struck out for that place.

The only hotel in Angel's Camp was kept by Coon Drayton, an old Mississippi river pilot, and at his house the half-drowned pocket miners found shelter. Mark Twain having in his youthful days been a cub pilot on the Mississippi, he and Coon were soon great friends and swapped yarns by the dozen. It continued to rain for three days, and until the weather cleared up, Mark and Jim remained at Coon's hotel.

Among the stories told Mark by Coon during the three days' session was that of the "Jumping Frog," and it struck him as being so comical that he concluded to write it up. When he returned to the Gillis cabin, Mark set to work on the frog story. He also wrote some sketches of life in the mountains and the mines for some of the San Francisco papers.

Even after he had given it the finishing touches, Mark did not think much of the frog story. He gave the preference to some other sketches, and sent them to the papers for which he was writing. The frog story lay about the cabin for some time, when Steve Gillis told him it was the best thing he had written, and advised him to save it for a book of sketches he was talking of publishing.

A literary turn having thus been given to the thoughts of the inmates of the Gillis cabin, a month passed without a return to the business of pocket mining. While the days were passed by Mark and his friends in discussing the merits of the "Jumping Frog" and other literary matters, other prospectors were not idle. A trio of Austrian miners who were out in search of gold-bearing quartz happened upon the spot where Mark and Jim had dug into their ledge. It was but a few days after Twain and Gillis had retreated in a pouring rain. The Austrians were astonished at seeing the ground glittering with gold. Where the dirt emptied from the sacks had been dissolved away by the rain, lay over three ounces of bright quartz gold. The foreigners were not long in gathering this harvest, but soon discovering the notice posted on the claim, they dared not venture to delve in the deposit whence it came. They could only wait and watch and pray. Their hope was that the parties who had posted up the notice would not return while it held good.

The sun that rose on the day after the Twain-Gillis notice expired saw the Austrians in possession of the ground, with a notice of their own conspicuously and defiantly posted. The new owners soon cleaned out the pocket, obtaining from it in a few days a little over $7,500.

Had Mark Twain's backbone held out a few minutes longer, the sacks of dirt would have been panned out and the richness of the pocket discovered. He would not then have gone to Angel's Camp, and would probably never have heard or written the story of the "Jumping Frog," the story that gave him his first boost in the literary world, as the "Heathen Chinee" gave Bret Harte his first lift up the ladder of fame. Had Mark found the gold that was captured by the Austrians, he would have settled down as a pocket miner, and probably to this day would have been pounding quartz in a little cabin in the Sierras somewhere along about the snowline.

Returning to San Francisco from the mountains, Mark for a time resumed his literary hackwork. He then arranged to make a trip to the Hawaiian Islands, and wrote up the beauties and wonders thereof for the old Sacramento *Union*. While engaged in this work he conceived the idea of writing a lecture on the Sandwich Islands, wisely judging that he could in that way get more money out of a certain amount of writing than by toiling for the newspapers.

He delivered his lecture very successfully, both on the Pacific Coast and in the Atlantic States. On the Pacific Coast D. E. McCarthy, who had then sold his interest in the *Enterprise*, was with Mark as his agent. When they reached Nevada the lecture was first delivered in Virginia City. Next they went to Gold Hill, a mile south of Virginia City and just over a low ridge known as the Divide, a place noted in the annals of the Comstock for a thousand robberies by footpads.

A sham robbery was planned of which Mark was to be the victim. He was to be halted on the Divide as he was returning on foot from Gold Hill, and robbed of the proceeds of his lecture. Mark's agent, McCarthy, was in the plot, as also was his old friend Major Steve Gillis and other friends, with Captain Jack Perry, George Birdsall, and one or two other members of the police force. Twain and one or two friends (who were in the secret) were held up on a trail called the cut-off. The job was done in the regular road-agent style. The pretended robbers not only took the gripsack of coin—some $300—but also Mark's fine gold watch.

When he reached Virginia City, Mark was raging mad, as the watch taken from him was a present from a friend. He did not in the least doubt the genuineness of the robbery, and it so soured him against the Comstock that he determined to leave the next morning.

The robbery had been planned by Mark's old friends as a sort of advertising dodge. It was intended to create sympathy for him, and by having him deliver a second lecture in Virginia City afford the people an opportunity of redeeming the good name of the Comstock. He would have had a rousing benefit, and after all was over his agent would have returned him his watch and money. Of course, it would not have done to ask Mark to consent to be robbed for this purpose. His friends meant well, but like other schemes of mice and men this particular one failed to work. Mark was too hot to be handled, and when at last it was explained to him that the robbery was a sham affair he became still hotter—he boiled over with wrath.

His money and watch were returned to him after he had taken his seat in the stage, and his friends begged him to remain, but he refused to disembark. Upon observing some of his friends of the police force engaged in violent demonstrations of mirth, he turned his attention to them and fired at them a tremendous broadside of anathemas as the stage rolled away. Had he kept cool, he would have had a benefit that would have put at least a thousand dollars in his pocket, for the papers had made a great sensation of the robbery.

A good deal has been said of Mark Twain's drawling speech. This peculiarity is not natural, but acquired. When he was a small boy he spoke so rapidly that his family constantly remonstrated with him with the result that he went to the opposite extreme. When angry or excited, he can snap his words off as short as anyone.

The cabin in which Mark and Bob Howland lived in Aurora, in 1862, endured until a few years ago. It was a sort of dugout, to the roof of which the wandering billy goat of inquiring mind had access from the hillside above. A picture of this cabin—the old Nevada home—would form a striking contrast to Mark's present fine residence in Hartford. The Hartford dwelling is a structure of many gables and angles, and at the rear or east end projects a veranda, intended to represent the hurricane deck of a Mississippi steamboat. In summer, with the shade of the surrounding chestnut trees cooling the air, this open deck is a pleasant lounging-place. Seated in it, dressed in white linen, Mark imagines himself on board one of the floating palaces of the Father of Waters, while his thoughts often revert to the still earlier days of reportorial work in the mining regions of the wild Washoe.

—Dan De Quille (William Wright),
California Illustrated Magazine 4, July 1893,
reprinted in *Dan De Quille, The Washoe Giant:
A Biography and Anthology*, Richard A. Dwyer
and Richard E. Lingenfelter, eds., Reno:
University of Nevada Press, 1990

AMBROSE BIERCE (1905–06)

Letter to George Harvey, November 19, 1905
Dear Sir,

I regret that I am unable to accept your kind invitation to the Mark Twain dinner. New York is such a long way off and the walking so bad. I rejoice, however, in everything—even overeating—that tends to the greater glory of the only man in America who, always talking, writing and doing, has never to my knowledge said or done a foolish thing.

Letter to George Sterling, May 6, 1906

No, I never had any row (nor much acquaintance) with Mark Twain—met him but two or three times. Once with Stoddard in London. I think pretty well of him, but doubt if he cared for me and can't, at the moment, think of any reason why he *should* have cared for me.

—Ambrose Bierce, letters to George Harvey
and George Sterling, 2003, pp. 144, 151

WILLIAM JAMES (1907)

On my last night [in New York] I dined with Norman Hapgood, along with men who were successfully and happily in the vibration. H. and his most winning-faced young partner, Collier, Jerome, Peter Dunne, F.M. Colby, and Mark Twain. (The latter, poor man, is only good for monologue, in his old age, or for dialogue at best, but he's a dear little genius all the same.)

—William James, letter to Henry James,
February 1907, from *The Letters of*
William James, Boston, 1920, II: 264

GEORGE BERNARD SHAW
"SHAW MEETS TWAIN AND EXPLAINS HIM" (1907)

George Bernard Shaw (1856–1950) was the Irish playwright and critic, author of numerous well-known plays including *Arms and the Man, Saint Joan, Pygmalion*, and *Major Barbara*. His bibliography is a long one. Shaw was a controversial figure with strongly held views. He was a central figure in the English socialist Fabian Society.

This article describes a chance meeting between Shaw and Mark Twain. Shaw's biographer, Archibald Henderson, was on the same boat and train as Twain and befriended him. He would publish, in 1911, the first proper biography of Twain.

It is worth noting that the work Shaw asks Mark Twain about is "The Jumping Frog of Calaveras County." Even in 1907, Twain's best-known work was, to some, his first internationally published one. Shaw also questions, the degree of seriousness in his work, as many others would after Twain's death. Twain's own antics at the impromptu press conference seem to belie Shaw's own claims. Students interested in popular and critical perceptions and receptions of Mark Twain may find useful material here.

Of further interest is Twain's closing description of his life, which seems almost a spoof of his actual life. Is there even a joke here, or is Twain speaking in earnest? Differentiating between the two becomes increasingly complex as Twain's life and writing proceed.

English Reporters Learn That He Always
Writes with Serious Intent
THEY TAKE COPIOUS NOTES

And Twain Tells Them How He Goes Through His
Day and Other Things.

Special Cablegram.
Copyright 1907 by the NEW YORK TIMES CO.

LONDON, June 18.—"A number of these pests," said Bernard Shaw to Mark Twain, indicating by a gesture that he was referring to a great congregation of English newspaper reporters who stood about him and Twain in a great circle, "just asked me whether you were really serious when you wrote 'The Jumping Frog.'"

Thus was opened a brief conversation that followed the introduction of Mr. Shaw to Mr. Clemens by Prof. Victor H. Henderson. Mr. Clemens had come to receive a degree from Oxford University. Prof. Henderson had crossed with him on the Minneapolis and had come up to London with him on the boat express. Mr. Shaw had come to St. Pancras station to meet Prof. Henderson, who is an old friend of his.

"Yes," Shaw went on, "these pests asked me that, and I told them what I thought to be the truth."

"No doubt," broke in Twain, "I'm sure that you did me full justice. I have every confidence that I was quite safe in your hands."

"Certainly you were," asserted Mr. Shaw. "I told them that I had read everything good that you had written, and I was able to give them the fullest assurance that you always wrote seriously.

"Mr. Shaw," said Twain, "I assure you that I can return the compliment." With this Twain winked at the English journalists, who at once burst into laughter that somewhat disturbed Mr. Shaw's equanimity. He did not know that Twain was loaded.

Just as the merriment was subsiding, a nondescript individual with a basket under his arm broke through the journalistic circle and invited attention to a young bull pup.

"'Arf a guinea buys 'im, Guv'nor," he insinuatingly remarked to Mr. Shaw, "'Arf a guinea, only two dollars 'n 'arf for the best bull pup in England. Larst one I've got, Guv'nor."

"I'm not an American," protested Mr. Shaw. "Sell him to Twain. He has got American money."

But Twain, although he deeply longed for the bull pup, resisted the temptation to buy. Directly he had got rid of the pup peddler, he bade good-bye to Mr. Shaw and moved to a cab. By that time he had been more than three hours under the examination and cross-examination of the newspaper men, but he was not tired. He seemed to enjoy every minute of the time.

It was my fortune to meet him on the deck of the Minneapolis while he was taking his ante-breakfast promenade. I gave him the latest copies of THE NEW YORK TIMES and received his thanks.

"I always like to read THE NEW YORK TIMES," he said. "It prints only the news that's fit to print, and as I have been told I am in my second childhood, I like to read a paper which I know will not exert any contaminating influence on me. Old men cannot be too careful, you know."

Before he could say any more the London reporters got at him, every man with a notebook in his hand. Twain had a delightful time with them. They fired all sorts of questions at him, and he fired back all sorts of answers, every one of which was religiously recorded in the note books.

"Is the world growing better?" one youthful scribe inquired, and Twain solemnly answered.

"Yes, I think so. You know, I have been here almost seventy-two years, and—but, really you must not ask me to say more on this subject. I am a very modest man, and prefer not to speak of my achievements."

Some of the other questions reminded me of passages in "Innocents Abroad."

In the course of the morning Twain gave out a new scheme according to which he regulated his daily life. He asked the reporters to be very careful to take down his words accurately, as the publication of the scheme might be brought to be helpful to others.

"Every morning," said he, "as soon as I'm up, I smoke a cigar, and then have breakfast at 8 o'clock. After breakfast, I smoke another cigar, and then go back to bed. At half past 10 I smoke another cigar and start dictating to my stenographer. I finish at 12 o'clock, and doze off till 1. I smoke another cigar and eat lunch. Then I go back to bed and read what the newspapers have to say about me. I smoke more cigars until half past 6. Then three assistants dress me for dinner, evening parties, &c., after which I associate with elite society till 1 o'clock in the morning. I never go to bed till my daughter turns out the lights, and then I smoke in the dark.

"My constitution is improving all the time."

—George Bernard Shaw, "Shaw Meets Twain
and Explains Him," *New York Times*, June 19, 1907

FERRIS GREENSLET (1908)

In December, 1874, [Thomas Bailey] Aldrich, desirous of embellishing therewith his library at Ponkapog, asked Mark Twain for his picture. Mr. Clemens obligingly began sending him one a day. After two weeks Aldrich mildly protested against the photographic deluge, with the result that, on New Year's Day, 1875, he received twenty separate copies of the effigies of Mr. Clemens, in twenty separate covers.

—Ferris Greenslet, from *The Life of
Thomas Bailey Aldrich*, Boston:
Houghton Mifflin, 1908, p. 112

JEROME K. JEROME
"JEROME'S FIRST MEETING WITH HIM" (1910)

Very few knew that Mark Twain was living in London. Our little girls met at a gymnasium, and revealed to one another the secret of their parentage. So that I wrote to him, and he and his daughter—his wife, always a sufferer, was too ill to accompany him—came and dined with us in a little house that looked out upon Hyde Park. It was our first meeting. I had anticipated, to confess the truth, feeling slightly in awe of him, and, was, in consequence, somewhat shocked at the attitude of Hail-fellow-well-met that my little girl, after staring at him for a good half-minute, assumed towards him for the rest of the evening. We sat talking, looking out upon the silent park, till pretty late; and it struck me as curious, turning back into the house after having seen him and his daughter into their cab, that neither of us had made a single joke nor told a funny story. I met him, perhaps, some half a dozen times after that, but we were never alone again. In public he always carried—a little wearily, so it seemed to me—the burden of the professional humorist, and at such times I thought wistfully of the man of deep feeling and broad sympathies—of the grave, earnest, shrewdly whimsical thinker—I should like to have met and talked with again.

—Jerome K. Jerome, "Jerome's First Meeting with
Him," *The Bookman,* London, June 1910, p. 116

E.V. Lucas "E.V. Lucas and Twain at a 'Punch Dinner'" (1910)

To me "Huckleberry Finn" is Mark Twain's best book—and, indeed, one of the best books by any one—and next to that I put "Tom Sawyer" and then a volume that exists only in fancy made up of passages from all the others, down to the "Tramp Abroad" and "Life on the Mississippi," in which those early works, "Roughing It," "The Innocents at Home," and the "Jumping Frog" collection, are very strongly represented. But "Huckleberry Finn" and "Tom Sawyer" stand just as they were written: every word counts. In the next edition of "Huckleberry Finn," however, I hope that the long and wonderful extract from it that is now to be read in small type only in Chapter III. of "Life on the Mississippi" will be set in its true place.

I met Mark Twain only once. It was on his last visit to London, when he was present at the special *Punch* dinner given in his honour. . . .

[H]is informal speech . . . swung between recollections of London in the 'seventies, the wildest chaff of his old friend Sir Henry Lucy, and passages that were almost too emotional.

In meeting him at last face to face, I was surprised by his size. I had always thought of him as long and gaunt; but he was quite a small man, and his lines were soft. I was surprised also by the almost tremulous gentleness of his expression, but that I imagine was a late acquisition: it had come with age and bereavement. His voice a little disappointed me. One had heard so much of the famous drawl; but, possibly through careful cultivation of a similar mechanism by humorists of our own, I was not carried away by it. But everything that he said was good, and his choice of words seemed to me extremely felicitous.

Not long afterwards I had occasion to write to him about something, and recalled the evening to his mind. In reply, he asked me to go and stay with him at Stormfield, but as his letter began "My dear Lucy," I did not go.

—E.V. Lucas, "E.V. Lucas and Twain at a
'Punch Dinner,'" *The Bookman,* London,
June 1910, pp. 116–117

WILLIAM DEAN HOWELLS (1910)

"Probably no man was closer to Mark Twain, during his active writing career, than was Howells," wrote George Ade. He might have added: Probably no man has been more consistently blamed for leading Mark Twain into the realm of genteelism, of inferior thinking, and of poor decision making. "It seems incredible," wrote H.L. Mencken, "that two men so unlike should have found common denominators for a friendship lasting forty years. . . . The one wrote English as Michelangelo hacked marble, broadly, brutally, magnificently; the other was a maker of pretty waxen groups."

William Dean Howells was born in Ohio. His father was a newspaper editor, and so Howells began his writing career, like Twain (and Artemus Ward), as a printer. Howell's path soon differed from that of Twain or Artemus, however. While Twain's writing instantly tended toward humor, Howells notes that "Inwardly I was a poet." His calling was, then, always more respectable. In 1860 Howells wrote a campaign biography for Abraham Lincoln, for which he would be repaid with a consulship in Venice.

"If there was any one in the world who had his being more wholly in literature than I had in 1860, I am sure I would not have known where to find him," Howells wrote in *Literary Friends and Acquaintance* (1901), adding that if such a person did exist, "I doubt he could have been found nearer the centres of literary activity than I was." Accordingly, in 1860 Howells made his pilgrimage first to Boston to meet James Russell Lowell, then to Concord to meet Nathaniel Hawthorne, Ralph Waldo Emerson, Bronson Alcott, and Henry David Thoreau. These were not all singular successes, but, undaunted, Howells continued his pilgrimage to New York, in search of Whitman. He found him in Charles Pfaff's beer cellar.

So began his career in literature, tenaciously seeking out the "centres of literary activity." And so Howells became, by and by, "the dean of American letters." This might be viewed as glorified social climbing and has been faulted by some critics as indicative of a congenital shortcoming: Howells always wanted to belong and to conform. H.L. Mencken called him "an urbane and highly respectable gentleman, a sitter on committees . . . a placid conformist." From when they met, after Howells wrote a favorable review of *The Innocents Abroad*, such a philosophy was pressed on Twain, with (it is argued) dire consequences.

Be that as it may, Howells's eulogistic account of Twain, written quickly after Twain's death, is simultaneously touching, intimate, and shrewd. Howells had almost unmatched access to Twain, and—unlike many of

Twain's closer circle—Howells was an accomplished author. He was well equipped to understand and interpret Twain's life and works, however squeamish he may have been about certain Victorian niceties which seem fatuous to the present-day reader. Like Dan De Quille, Howells has the discernment to notice the telling details—those that may seem trivial but in fact reveal a deeper, though not obvious, facet of the author. In the following excerpts, Howells remarks on Twain's sealskin coat, for instance, which was conspicuous in proper Boston, but which of course signalled Twain's frontier aesthetic (one tending toward the exaggerated and the wild). Twain's early awkwardness among the literati is hereby presaged.

In Twain's stumbling overtures to the literary establishment Howells was often present, if not his sponsor. So we hear through Howells of the famous Whittier birthday dinner; of the exchange between Twain and Matthew Arnold; or of Twain's failure to impress James Russell Lowell, an anti-Semite who suspected that Twain was secretly Jewish.

Howells remembers conversations and collaborations, the table talk of the intellectual Twain, but also he remembers events and journeys made only in the name of friendship and affection, recollections that arguably reveal more about Twain, since they were not intended to promote heady, ostentatious discussion or lead to publication finally. For instance, there is the seemingly idle conversation in which Howells wonders to Twain "why we hate the past so," to which Twain responds ("from the depths of his own consciousness"), "It's so damned humiliating." Here alone is matter enough to justify a thesis equal to the one maintained by Van Wyck Brooks.

Elsewhere Howells tries generously to make sense of the misanthropy of the later Twain, rather than shying away from discussing it as a more superficial memoirist might. Howells's account is clearly marked by a desire to do his friendship proper justice, coupled with a desire—occasionally awkward—to tell a truth. "It is best to be honest in this matter," he writes at one stage; "he would have hated anything else."

Nevertheless, H.L. Mencken criticized Howells's account here, finding that Twain was presented as "a Mark whose Himalayan outlines are discerned but hazily through a pink fog of Howells." He continues:

> There is a moral note in the tale—an obvious effort to palliate, to touch up, to excuse. The poor fellow, of course, was charming, and there was talent in him, but what a weakness he had for thinking aloud—and such shocking thoughts! What oaths in his speech! What awful cigars he smoked! How barbarous his contempt for the strict sonata form!

Mencken is unfair to Howells, exaggerating his failings, but this provides a good example of the rumblings abroad in critical circles.

Students interested in the personal view of Twain, by one who was there and had the literary equipment to adequately record it will find rich material here. Howells admits to his own squeamishness at some of Twain's terminology, for instance, and tries valiantly to explain their social differences in such regards. Any student exploring the Twain-Howells relationship should, naturally, look here then.

———

Throughout my long acquaintance with him his graphic touch was always allowing itself a freedom which I cannot bring my fainter pencil to illustrate. He had the Southwestern, the Lincolnian, the Elizabethan breadth of parlance, which I suppose one ought not to call coarse without calling one's self prudish; and I was often hiding away in discreet holes and corners the letters in which he had loosed his bold fancy to stoop on rank suggestion; I could not bear to burn them, and I could not, after the first reading, quite bear to look at them. I shall best give my feeling on this point by saying that in it he was Shakespearian, or if his ghost will not suffer me the word, then he was Baconian.

At the time of our first meeting, which must have been well toward the winter, Clemens (as I must call him instead of Mark Twain, which seemed always somehow to mask him from my personal sense) was wearing a sealskin coat, with the fur out, in the satisfaction of a caprice, or the love of strong effect which he was apt to indulge through life. I do not know what droll comment was in Fields's mind with respect to this garment, but probably he felt that here was an original who was not to be brought to any Bostonian book in the judgment of his vivid qualities. . . .

We were natives of the same vast Mississippi Valley; and Missouri was not so far from Ohio but that we were akin in our first knowledges of woods and fields as we were in our early parlance. I had outgrown the use of mine through my greater bookishness, but I gladly recognized the phrases which he employed for their lasting juiciness and the long-remembered savor they had on his mental palate.

I have elsewhere sufficiently spoken of his unsophisticated use of words, of the diction which forms the backbone of his manly style. If I mention my own greater bookishness, by which I mean his less quantitative reading, it is to give myself better occasion to note that he was always reading some vital book. It might be some out-of-the-way book, but it had the root of the human matter in it: a volume of great trials; one of the supreme autobiographies; a signal passage of history, a narrative of travel, a story of captivity, which gave him life at first-hand. As I remember, he did not care much for fiction, and in that sort he had certain distinct loathings; there were certain authors whose names he seemed not so much to pronounce as to spew out of his mouth. Goldsmith was one of these, but his prime abhorrence was my dear and honored prime favorite, Jane Austen. He once said to me, I suppose after he had been reading some of my unsparing praises of her—I am always praising her, "*You* seem to think that woman could write," and he forbore withering me with his scorn, apparently because we had been friends so long, and he more pitied than hated me for my bad taste. He seemed not to have any preferences among novelists; or at least I never heard him express any. He used to read the modern novels I praised, in or out of print; but I do not think he much liked reading fiction. As for plays, he detested the theatre, and said he would as lief do a sum as follow a plot on the stage. He could not, or did not, give any reasons for his literary abhorrences, and perhaps he really had none. But he could have said very distinctly, if he had needed, why he liked the books he did. I was away at the time of his great Browning passion, and I know of it chiefly from hearsay; but at the time Tolstoy was doing what could be done to make me over Clemens wrote, "That man seems to have been to you what Browning was to me." I do not know that he had other favorites among the poets, but he had favorite poems which he liked to read to you, and he read, of course, splendidly. I have forgotten what piece of John Hay's it was that he liked so much, but I remembered how he fiercely revelled in the vengefulness of William Morris's *Sir Guy of the Dolorous Blast*, and how he especially exulted in the lines which tell of the supposed speaker's joy in slaying the murderer of his brother:

> "I am threescore years and ten,
>   And my hair is nigh turned gray,
> But I am glad to think of the moment when
>   I took his life away."

Generally, I fancy his pleasure in poetry was not great, and I do not believe he cared much for the conventionally accepted masterpieces of literature. He liked to find out good things and great things for himself; sometimes he would discover these in a masterpiece new to him alone, and then, if you brought his ignorance home to him, he enjoyed it, and enjoyed it the more you rubbed it in.

Of all the literary men I have known he was the most unliterary in his make and manner. I do not know whether he had any acquaintance with Latin, but I believe not the least; German he knew pretty well, and Italian enough late in life to have fun with it; but he used English in all its alien derivations as if it were native to his own air, as if it had come up out of American, out of Missourian ground. His style was what we know, for good and for bad, but his manner, if I may difference the two, was as entirely his own as if no one had ever written before. I have noted before this how he was not enslaved to the consecutiveness in writing which the rest of us try to keep chained to. That is, he wrote as he thought, and as all men think, without sequence, without an eye to what went before or should come after. If something beyond or beside what he was saying occurred to him, he invited it into his page, and made it as much at home there as the nature of it would suffer him. Then, when he was through with the welcoming of this casual and unexpected guest, he would go back to the company he was entertaining, and keep on with what he had been talking about. He observed this manner in the construction of his sentences, and the arrangement of his chapters, and the ordering or disordering of his compilations. I helped him with a Library of Humor, which he once edited, and when I had done my work according to tradition, with authors, times, and topics carefully studied in due sequence, he tore it all apart, and "chucked" the pieces in wherever the fancy for them took him at the moment. He was right: we were not making a text-book, but a book for the pleasure rather than the instruction of the reader, and he did not see why the principle on which he built his travels and reminiscences and tales and novels should not apply to it; and I do not now see, either, though at the time it confounded me. On minor points he was, beyond any author I have known, without favorite phrases or pet words. He utterly despised the avoidance of repetitions out of fear of tautology. If a word served his turn better than a substitute, he would use it as many times in a page as he chose. . . .

Now and then he would try a little stronger language than *The Atlantic* had stomach for, and once when I sent him a proof I made him observe that I had left out the profanity. He wrote back: "Mrs. Clemens opened that proof, and lit into the room with danger in her eye. What profanity? You see, when I read the manuscript to her I skipped that." It was part of his joke to pretend a violence in that gentlest creature which the more amusingly realized the situation to their friends.

I was always very glad of him and proud of him as a contributor, but I must not claim the whole merit, or the first merit of having him write for us.

It was the publisher, the late H. O. Houghton, who felt the incongruity of his absence from the leading periodical of the country, and was always urging me to get him to write. I will take the credit of being eager for him, but it is to the publisher's credit that he tried, so far as the modest traditions of *The Atlantic* would permit, to meet the expectations in pay which the colossal profits of Clemens's books might naturally have bred in him. Whether he was really able to do this he never knew from Clemens himself, but probably twenty dollars a page did not surfeit the author of books that "sold right along just like the Bible." . . .

There is an incident of this time so characteristic of both men that I will yield to the temptation of giving it here. After I had gone to Hartford in response to Clemens's telegram, Matthew Arnold arrived in Boston, and one of my family called on his, to explain why I was not at home to receive his introduction: I had gone to see Mark Twain. "Oh, but he doesn't like *that* sort of thing, does he?" "He likes Mr. Clemens very much," my representative answered, "and he thinks him one of the greatest men he ever knew." I was still Clemens's guest at Hartford when Arnold came there to lecture, and one night we went to meet him at a reception. While his hand laxly held mine in greeting, I saw his eyes fixed intensely on the other side of the room. "Who—who in the world is that?" I looked and said, "Oh, that is Mark Twain." I do not remember just how their instant encounter was contrived by Arnold's wish, but I have the impression that they were not parted for long during the evening, and the next night Arnold, as if still under the glamour of that potent presence, was at Clemens's house. I cannot say how they got on, or what they made of each other; if Clemens ever spoke of Arnold, I do not recall what he said, but Arnold had shown a sense of him from which the incredulous sniff of the polite world, now so universally exploded, had already perished. It might well have done so with his first dramatic vision of that prodigious head. Clemens was then hard upon fifty, and he had kept, as he did to the end, the slender figure of his youth, but the ashes of the burnt-out years were beginning to gray the fires of that splendid shock of red hair which he held to the height of a stature apparently greater than it was, and tilted from side to side in his undulating walk. He glimmered at you from the narrow slits of fine blue-greenish eyes, under branching brows, which with age grew more and more like a sort of plumage, and he was apt to smile into your face with a subtle but amiable perception, and yet with a sort of remote absence; you were all there for him, but he was not all there for you. . . .

Once when I came on from Cambridge he followed me to my room to see that the water was not frozen in my bath, or something of the kind, for it was very cold weather, and then hospitably lingered. Not to lose time in banalities I began at once from the thread of thought in my mind. "I wonder why we hate the past so," and he responded from the depths of his own consciousness, "It's so damned humiliating," which is what any man would say of his past if he were honest; but honest men are few when it comes to themselves. Clemens was one of the few, and the first of them among all the people I have known. I have known, I suppose, men as truthful, but not so promptly, so absolutely, so positively, so almost aggressively truthful. He could lie, of course, and did to save others from grief or harm; he was not stupidly truthful; but his first impulse was to say out the thing and everything that was in him. To those who can understand it will not be contradictory of his sense of humiliation from the past, that he was not ashamed for anything he ever did to the point of wishing to hide it. He could be, and he was, bitterly sorry for his errors, which he had enough of in his life, but he was not ashamed in that mean way. What he had done he owned to, good, bad, or indifferent, and if it was bad he was rather amused than troubled as to the effect in your mind. He would not obtrude the fact upon you, but if it were in the way of personal history he would not dream of withholding it, far less of hiding it.

He was the readiest of men to allow an error if he were found in it. In one of our walks about Hartford, when he was in the first fine flush of his agnosticism, he declared that Christianity had done nothing to improve morals and conditions, and that the world under the highest pagan civilization was as well off as it was under the highest Christian influences. I happened to be fresh from the reading of Charles Loring Brace's *Gesta Christi*; or, *History of Humane Progress*, and I could offer him abundant proofs that he was wrong. He did not like that evidently, but he instantly gave way, saying he had not known those things. Later he was more tolerant in his denials of Christianity, but just then he was feeling his freedom from it, and rejoicing in having broken what he felt to have been the shackles of belief worn so long. He greatly admired Robert Ingersoll, whom he called an angelic orator, and regarded as an evangel of a new gospel—the gospel of free thought. He took the warmest interest in the newspaper controversy raging at the time as to the existence of a hell; when the noes carried the day, I suppose that no enemy of perdition was more pleased. He still loved his old friend and pastor, Mr. Twichell, but he no longer went to hear him preach his sane and beautiful sermons, and was, I think, thereby the greater loser. Long before that I had asked him if he went regularly to church, and he groaned out: "Oh yes, I go. It 'most kills me, but I go," and I did not need his telling me to understand that he went because his wife wished it. He did tell me, after they both ceased to go, that it had finally come to her saying, "Well, if you are to be lost, I want to be lost with you." He could accept that willingness for supreme sacrifice and exult in it because of the supreme truth as he saw it. After they had both ceased to be formal Christians, she was still grieved by his denial of immortality, so grieved that he resolved upon one of those heroic lies, which for love's sake he held above even the truth, and he went to her, saying that he had been thinking the whole matter over, and now he was convinced that the soul did live after death. It was too late. Her keen vision pierced through his ruse, as it did when he brought the doctor who had diagnosticated her case as organic disease of the heart, and, after making him go over the facts of it again with her, made him declare it merely functional.

To make an end of these records as to Clemens's beliefs, so far as I knew them, I should say that he never went back to anything like faith in the Christian theology, or in the notion of life after death, or in a conscious divinity. It is best to be honest in this matter; he would have hated anything else, and I do not believe that the truth in it can hurt any one. . . .

The part of him that was Western in his Southwestern origin Clemens kept to the end, but he was the most desouthernized Southerner I ever knew. No man more perfectly sensed and more entirely abhorred slavery, and no one has ever poured such scorn upon the second-hand, Walter-Scotticized, pseudo-chivalry of the Southern ideal. He held himself responsible for the wrong which the white race had done the black race in slavery, and he explained, in paying the way of a negro student through Yale, that he was doing it as his part of the reparation due from every white to every black man. He said he had never seen this student, nor ever wished to see him or know his name; it was quite enough that he was a negro. About that time a colored cadet was expelled from West Point for some point of conduct "unbecoming an officer and gentleman," and there was the usual shabby philosophy in a portion of the press to the effect that a negro could never feel the claim of honor. The man was fifteen parts white, but, "Oh yes," Clemens said, with bitter irony, "it was that one part black that undid him." It made him a "nigger" and incapable of being a gentleman. It was to blame for the whole thing. The fifteen parts white were guiltless.

Clemens was entirely satisfied with the result of the Civil War, and he was eager to have its facts and meanings brought out at once in history. He ridiculed the notion, held by many, that "it was not yet time" to philosophize the events of the great struggle; that we must "wait till its passions had cooled," and "the clouds of strife had cleared away." He maintained that the time would never come when we should see its motives and men and deeds more clearly, and that now, now, was the hour to ascertain them in lasting verity. Picturesquely and dramatically he portrayed the imbecility of deferring the inquiry at any point to the distance of future years when inevitably the facts would begin to put on fable. . . .

He did not care much to meet people, as I fancied, and we were greedy of him for ourselves; he was precious to us; and I would not have exposed him to the critical edge of that Cambridge acquaintance which might not have appreciated him at, say, his transatlantic value. In America his popularity was as instant as it was vast. But it must be acknowledged that for a much longer time here than in England polite learning hesitated his praise. In England rank, fashion, and culture rejoiced in him. Lord mayors, lord chief justices, and magnates of many kinds were his hosts; he was desired in country houses, and his bold genius captivated the favor of periodicals which spurned the rest of our nation. But in his own country it was different. In proportion as people thought themselves refined they questioned that quality which all recognize in him now, but which was then the inspired knowledge of the simple-hearted multitude. I went with him to see Longfellow, but I do not think Longfellow made much of him, and Lowell made less. He stopped as if with the long Semitic curve of Clemens's nose, which in the indulgence of his passion for finding every one more or less a Jew he pronounced unmistakably racial. It was two of my most fastidious Cambridge friends who accepted him with the English, the European entirely—namely, Charles Eliot Norton and Professor Francis J. Child. Norton was then newly back from a long sojourn abroad, and his judgments were delocalized. He met Clemens as if they had both been in England, and rejoiced in his bold freedom from environment, and in the rich variety and boundless reach of his talk. Child was of a personal liberty as great in its fastidious way as that of Clemens himself, and though he knew him only at second hand, he exulted in the most audacious instance of his grotesquery, as I shall have to tell by-and-by, almost solely. I cannot say just why Clemens seemed not to hit the favor of our community of scribes and scholars, as Bret Harte had done, when he came on from California, and swept them before him, disrupting their dinners and delaying their lunches with impunity; but it is certain he did not, and I had better say so. . . .

At heart Clemens was romantic, and he would have had the world of fiction stately and handsome and whatever the real world was not; but he was not romanticistic, and he was too helplessly an artist not to wish his own work to show life as he had seen it. . . .

When Messrs. Houghton & Mifflin became owners of *The Atlantic Monthly*, Mr. Houghton fancied having some breakfasts and dinners, which should bring the publisher and the editor face to face with the contributors, who were bidden from far and near. Of course, the subtle fiend of advertising, who has now grown so unblushing bold, lurked under the covers at these banquets, and the junior partner and the young editor had their joint and separate fine anguishes of misgiving as to the taste and the principle of them; but they were really very simple-hearted and honestly meant hospitalities, and they prospered as they ought, and gave great pleasure and no pain. I forget some of the "emergent occasions," but I am sure of a birthday dinner most unexpectedly accepted by Whittier, and a birthday luncheon to Mrs. Stowe, and I think a birthday dinner to Longfellow; but the passing years have left me in the dark as to the pretext of that supper at which Clemens made his awful speech, and came so near being the death of us all. At the breakfasts and luncheons we had the pleasure of our lady contributors' company, but that night there were only men, and because of our great strength we survived.

I suppose the year was about 1879, but here the almanac is unimportant, and I can only say that it was after Clemens had become a very valued contributor of the magazine, where he found himself to his own great explicit satisfaction. He had jubilantly accepted our invitation, and had promised a speech, which it appeared afterward he had prepared with unusual care and confidence. It was his custom always to think out his speeches, mentally wording them, and then memorizing them by a peculiar system of mnemonics which he had invented. On the dinner-table a certain succession of knife, spoon, salt-cellar, and butter-plate symbolized a train of ideas, and on the billiard-table a ball, a cue, and a piece of chalk served the same purpose. With a diagram of these printed on the brain he had full command of the phrases which his excogitation had attached to them, and which embodied the ideas in perfect form. He believed he had been particularly fortunate in his notion for the speech of that evening, and he had worked it out in joyous self-reliance. It was the notion of three tramps, three dead-beats, visiting a California mining-camp, and imposing themselves upon the innocent miners as respectively Ralph Waldo Emerson, Henry Wadsworth Longfellow, and Oliver Wendell Holmes. The humor of the conception must prosper or must fail according to the mood of the hearer, but Clemens felt sure of compelling this to sympathy, and he looked forward to an unparalleled triumph.

But there were two things that he had not taken into account. One was the species of religious veneration in which these men were held by those nearest them, a thing that I should not be able to realize to people remote from them in time and place. They were men of extraordinary dignity, of the thing called *presence*, for want of some clearer word, so that no one could well approach them in a personally light or trifling spirit. I do not suppose that anybody more truly valued them or more piously loved them than Clemens himself, but the intoxication of his fancy carried him beyond the bounds of that regard, and emboldened him to the other thing which he had not taken into account—namely, the immense hazard of working his fancy out before their faces, and expecting them to enter into the delight of it. If neither Emerson, nor Longfellow, nor Holmes had been there, the scheme might possibly have carried, but even this is doubtful, for those who so devoutly honored them would have overcome their horror with difficulty, and perhaps would not have overcome it at all.

The publisher, with a modesty very ungrateful to me, had abdicated his office of host, and I was the hapless president, fulfilling the abhorred function of calling people to their feet and making them speak. When I came to Clemens I introduced him with the cordial admiring I had for him as one of my greatest contributors and dearest friends. Here, I said, in sum, was a humorist who never left you hanging your head for having enjoyed his joke; and then the amazing mistake, the bewildering blunder, the cruel catastrophe was upon us. I believe that after the scope of the burlesque made itself clear, there was no one there, including the burlesquer himself, who was not smitten with a desolating dismay. There fell a silence, weighing many tons to the square inch, which deepened from moment to moment, and was broken only by the hysterical and blood-curdling laughter of a single guest, whose name shall not be handed down to infamy. Nobody knew whether to look at the speaker or down at his plate. I chose my plate as the least affliction, and so I do not know how Clemens looked, except when I stole a glance at him, and saw him standing solitary amid his appalled and appalling listeners, with his joke dead on his hands. From a first glance at the great three whom his jest had made its theme, I was aware of Longfellow sitting upright, and regarding the humorist with an air of pensive puzzle, of Holmes busily writing on his menu, with a well-feigned effect of preoccupation, and of Emerson, holding his elbows, and listening with a sort of Jovian oblivion of this nether world in that lapse of memory which saved him in those later years from so much bother. Clemens must have dragged his joke to the climax and left it there, but I cannot say this from any sense of the fact. Of what happened afterward at the table where the immense, the wholly innocent, the truly unimagined affront was offered, I have no longer the least remembrance. I next remember being in a room of the hotel, where Clemens was not to sleep, but to toss in despair, and Charles Dudley Warner's saying, in the gloom, "Well, Mark, *you're* a funny fellow." It was as well as anything else he could have said, but Clemens seemed unable to accept the tribute.

I stayed the night with him, and the next morning, after a haggard breakfast, we drove about and he made some purchases of bric-à-brac for his house in Hartford, with a soul as far away from bric-à-brac as ever the soul of man was. He went home by an early train, and he lost no time in writing back to the three divine personalities which he had so involuntarily seemed to flout. They all wrote back to him, making it as light for him as they could. I have heard that Emerson was a good deal mystified, and in his sublime forgetfulness asked, Who was this gentleman who appeared to think he had offered him some sort of annoyance? But I am not sure that this is accurate. What I am sure of is that Longfellow, a few days after, in my study, stopped before a photograph of Clemens and said, "Ah, he is a *wag!*" and nothing more. Holmes told me, with deep emotion, such as a brother humorist might well feel, that he had not lost an instant in replying to Clemens's letter, and assuring him that there had not been the least offence, and entreating him never to think of the matter again. "He said that he was a fool, but he was God's fool," Holmes quoted from the letter, with a true sense of the pathos and the humor of the self-abasement.

To me Clemens wrote a week later, "It doesn't get any better; it burns like fire." But now I understand that it was not shame that burnt, but rage for a blunder which he had so incredibly committed. That to have conceived of those men, the most dignified in our literature, our civilization, as impersonable by three hoboes, and then to have imagined that he could ask them personally to enjoy the monstrous travesty, was a break, he saw too late, for which there was no repair. Yet the time came, and not so very long afterward, when some mention was made of the incident as a mistake, and he said, with all his fierceness, "But I don't admit that it *was* a mistake," and it was not so in the minds of all witnesses at second hand. The morning after the dreadful dinner there came a glowing note from Professor Child, who had read the newspaper report of it, praising Clemens's burlesque as the richest piece of humor in the world, and betraying no sense of incongruity in its perpetration in the presence of its victims. I think it must always have ground in Clemens's soul, that he was the prey of circumstances, and that if he had some more favoring occasion he could retrieve his loss in it by giving the thing the right setting. Not more than two or three years ago, he came to try me as to trying it again at a meeting of newspaper men in Washington. I had to own my fears, while I alleged Child's note on the other hand, but in the end he did not try it with the newspaper men. I do not know whether he has ever printed it or not, but since the thing happened I have often wondered how much offence there really was in it. I am not sure but the horror of the spectators read more indignation into the subjects of the hapless drolling than they felt. But it must have been difficult for them to bear it with equanimity. To be sure, they were not themselves mocked; the joke was, of course, beside them; nevertheless, their personality was trifled with, and I could only end by reflecting that if I had been in their place I should not have liked it myself. Clemens would have liked it himself, for he had the heart for that sort of wild play, and he so loved a joke that even if it took the form of a liberty, and was yet a good joke, he would have loved it. But perhaps this burlesque was not a good joke. . . .

He was apt to wear himself out in the vehemence of his resentments; or, he had so spent himself in uttering them that he had literally nothing more to say. You could offer Clemens offences that would anger other men and he did not mind; he would account for them from human nature; but if he thought you had in any way played him false you were anathema and maranatha forever. Yet not forever, perhaps, for by-and-by, after years, he would be silent. There were two men, half a generation apart in their succession, whom he thought equally atrocious in their treason to him, and of whom he used to talk terrifyingly, even after they were out of the world. He went farther than Heine, who said that he forgave his enemies, but not till they were dead. Clemens did not forgive his dead enemies; their death seemed to deepen their crimes, like a base evasion, or a cowardly attempt to escape; he pursued them to the grave; he would like to dig them up and take vengeance upon their clay. So he said, but no doubt he would not have hurt them if he had had them living before him. He was generous without stint; he trusted without measure, but where his generosity was abused, or his trust betrayed, he was a fire of vengeance, a consuming flame of suspicion that no sprinkling of cool patience from others could quench; it had to burn itself out. He was eagerly and lavishly hospitable, but if a man seemed willing to batten on him, or in any way to lie down upon him, Clemens despised him unutterably. In his frenzies of resentment or suspicion he would not, and doubtless could not, listen to reason. But if between the paroxysms he were confronted with the facts he would own them, no matter how much they told against him. . . .

He had begun before that to amass those evidences against mankind which eventuated with him in his theory of what he called "the damned human race." This was not an expression of piety, but of the kind contempt to which he was driven by our follies and iniquities as he had observed them in himself as well as in others. It was as mild a misanthropy, probably, as ever caressed the objects of its malediction. But I believe it was about the year 1900 that his sense of our perdition became insupportable and broke out in a mixed abhorrence and amusement which spared no occasion, so that I could quite understand why Mrs. Clemens should have found some compensation, when kept to her room by sickness, in the reflection that now she should not hear so much about "the damned human race." He told of that with the same wild joy that he told of overhearing her repetition of one of his most inclusive profanities, and her explanation that she meant him to hear it so that he might know how it sounded. The contrast of the lurid blasphemy with her heavenly whiteness should have been enough to cure any one less grounded than he in what must be owned was as fixed a habit as smoking with him. When I first knew him he rarely vented his fury in that sort, and I fancy he was under a promise to her which he kept sacred till the wear and tear of his nerves with advancing years disabled him. Then it would be like him to struggle with himself till he could struggle no longer and to ask his promise back, and it would be like her to give it back. His profanity was the heritage of his boyhood and young manhood in social conditions and under the duress of exigencies in which everybody swore about as impersonally as he smoked. It is best to recognize the fact of it, and I do so the more readily because I cannot suppose the Recording Angel really minded it much more than that Guardian Angel of his. It probably grieved them about equally, but they could equally forgive it. Nothing came of his pose regarding "the damned human race" except his invention of the Human Race Luncheon Club. This was confined to four persons who were never all got together, and it soon perished of their indifference.

In the earlier days that I have more specially in mind one of the questions that we used to debate a good deal was whether every human motive was not selfish. We inquired as to every impulse, the noblest, the holiest in effect, and he found them in the last analysis of selfish origin. Pretty nearly the whole time of a certain railroad run from New York to Hartford was taken up with the scrutiny of the self-sacrifice of a mother for her child, of the abandon of the lover who dies in saving his mistress from fire or flood, of the hero's courage in the field and the martyr's at the stake. Each he found springing from the unconscious love of self and the dread of the greater pain which the self-sacrificer would suffer in forbearing the sacrifice. If we had any time left from this inquiry that day, he must have devoted it to a high regret that Napoleon did not carry out his purpose of invading England, for then he would have destroyed the feudal aristocracy, or "reformed the lords," as it might be called now. He thought that would have been an incalculable blessing to the English people and the world. Clemens was always beautifully and unfalteringly a republican. None of his occasional misgivings for America implicated a return to monarchy. Yet he felt passionately the splendor of the English monarchy, and there was a time when he gloried in that figurative poetry by which the king was phrased as "the Majesty of England." He rolled the words deep-throatedly out, and exulted in their beauty as if it were beyond any other glory of the world. . . .

When Clemens returned to America with his family, after lecturing round the world, I again saw him in New York, where I so often saw him while he was shaping himself for that heroic enterprise. He would come to me, and talk sorrowfully over his financial ruin, and picture it to himself as the stuff of some unhappy dream, which, after long prosperity, had culminated the wrong way. It was very melancholy, very touching, but the sorrow to which he had come home from his long journey had not that forlorn bewilderment in it. He was looking wonderfully well, and when I wanted the name of his elixir, he said it was plasmon. He was apt, for a man who had put faith so decidedly away from him, to take it back and pin it to some superstition, usually of a hygienic sort. Once, when he was well on in years, he came to New York without glasses, and announced that he and all his family, so astigmatic and myopic and old-sighted, had, so to speak, burned their spectacles behind them upon the instruction of some sage who had found out that they were a delusion. The next time he came he wore spectacles freely, almost ostentatiously, and I heard from others that the whole Clemens family had been near losing their eyesight by the miracle worked in their behalf. Now, I was not surprised to learn that "the damned human race" was to be saved by plasmon, if anything, and that my first duty was to visit the plasmon agency with him, and procure enough plasmon to secure my family against the ills it was heir to for evermore. I did not immediately understand that plasmon was one of the investments which he had made from "the substance of things hoped for," and in the destiny of a disastrous disappointment. But after paying off the creditors of his late publishing firm, he had to do something with his money, and it was not his fault if he did not make a fortune out of plasmon. . . .

I cannot say whether or not he believed that his wife would recover; he fought the fear of her death to the end; for her life was far more largely his than the lives of most men's wives are theirs. For his own life I believe he would never have much cared, if I may trust a saying of one who was so absolutely without pose as he was. He said that he never saw a dead man whom he did not envy for having had it over and being done with it. Life had always amused him, and in the resurgence of its interests after his sorrow had ebbed away he was again deeply interested in the world and in the human race, which, though damned, abounded in subjects of curious inquiry. When the time came for his wife's removal from York Harbor I went with him to Boston, where he wished to look up the best means of her conveyance to New York. The inquiry absorbed him: the sort of invalid-car he could get; how she could be carried to the village station; how the car could be detached from the eastern train at Boston and carried round to the southern train on the other side of the city, and then how it could be attached to the Hudson River train at New York and left at Riverdale. There was no particular of the business which he did not scrutinize and master, not only with his poignant concern for her welfare, but with his strong curiosity as to how these unusual things were done with the usual means. With the inertness that grows upon an aging man he had been used to delegating more and more things, but of that thing I perceived that he would not delegate the least detail. . . .

Next I saw him dead, lying in his coffin amid those flowers with which we garland our despair in that pitiless hour. After the voice of his old friend Twichell had been lifted in the prayer which it wailed through in broken-hearted supplication, I looked a moment at the face I knew so well; and it was patient with the patience I had so often seen in it: something of puzzle, a great silent dignity, an assent to what must be from the depths of a nature whose tragical seriousness broke in the laughter which the unwise took for the whole of him. Emerson, Longfellow, Lowell, Holmes—I knew them all and all the rest of our sages, poets, seers, critics, humorists; they were like one another and like other literary men; but Clemens was sole, incomparable, the Lincoln of our literature.

—William Dean Howells, *My Mark Twain,* 1910

Joaquin Miller (1912)

He was shy as a girl, although time was already coyly flirting white flowers at his temples, and could hardly be coaxed to meet the learned and great who wanted to take him by the hand.

—Joaquin Miller, 1912,
quoted in Paine, I: 461

AMBROSE BIERCE (1913)

O yes, I suppose I look like the late Mark Twain—I've been mistaken for him all my life, sometimes most amusingly.

> —Ambrose Bierce, letter to Amy L. Wells,
> September 21, 1913, Bierce, 2003, p. 242

C.C. GOODWIN "SAMUEL L. CLEMENS— 'MARK TWAIN'" (1913)

Charles Carroll Goodwin was a reporter for the Virginia City *Enterprise* along with Mark Twain, Dan De Quille, and Rollin M. Daggett. He became a Judge. Bernard DeVoto, in his unquenchable vendetta against Van Wyck Brooks and his followers, claimed this text as a talisman and a knockout punch to their theories, since it evidences, he crowed, "the sheer worthlessness" of Brooks's chapter on Nevada. "It is most unwise of any one to develop notions about Nevada, or Mark Twain's years there, without taking Judge Goodwin's 'As I Remember Them' into account," he gravely chides. DeVoto, as a cub reporter in the West, knew the judge personally as "as a white-haired gentleman who smoked stogies." As DeVoto says, Goodwin's memoir is a valuable firsthand account of events that remain rather murky. Any student examining Twain's Nevada apprentice years on the *Enterprise* should consult Goodwin. Equally, any student explaining the "dialogue" between Brooks and DeVoto should read Goodwin and measure how well it tallies with either critic's view.

Most of the intelligent people of the world are familiar with the personal appearance of Mark Twain, as he was on earth. Of medium height and weight, dark complexion, eyes and hair like an Indian, a strong, expressive face, a beautiful head, as a man; and one, who, when a baby, must have been a mother's darling; and as she held him to her breast she fondly believed that he would grow up to be not only bright and respectable, but a wonder among his fellow-men. I have an idea that a mother's thought, if intense enough, makes its impression upon the child before or after birth, and that that impression lasts and in a measure controls the child through all its life. And I am ready to believe that what was best in Mark Twain came of that impression.

Abraham Lincoln was born in squalor; his childhood was so pitiable that men recoil when they read the story of it. Through one fierce winter the rude house in which he lived had but three sides to it, the fourth was open to the pitiless winds that swept across the Indiana prairies. But perhaps it was through that open side of the house that the great angel came, and noting the rude cradle within, bent and touched the lips of the sleeping child with the signet of immortality. But it is more acceptable to believe that the mother, destitute of all other treasures save that baby, so yearned with love about it and so impressed her life upon it that as the years went by, the fruition of those hopes was reached and that thus the man became immortal.

Mark Twain was born in Florida, Monroe county, Missouri. There is nothing to show that he was different from the other boys around him.

Missouri was crude in many ways when he was a boy, but it had great old forests which gave out nuts and wild bees in the autumn, and there were fields where "roasting ears," cantaloupes and watermelons grew, and forest and field supplied plenty of joys to boyhood. The chances, too, are that Mark fell in love very early, and possibly that event of his life was later the inspiration of "Tom Sawyer." Then he wandered off to the big river in Missouri and by a sort of natural gravity we hear of him first as an assistant pilot on a Mississippi steamboat. Later, I believe, he became a real pilot, though an old man has been reported recently as saying that he taught him what he knew as a pilot, but told him that he never would be a good one—that he was too funny.

The first I heard of him was when he began to write communications for the *Territorial Enterprise*, published in Virginia City, and his communications were signed "Mark Twain." There is a little interim between the time that he ceased to be a pilot and the time when he became a miner in Nevada that I cannot connect by any data that I can secure. It was whispered that early in 1861 he was for a time in the Rebel army. It is possible that he was one of the Missouri State guards. If he was, he grew tired of the work pretty soon. It is quite possible that he had an experience like another Missourian—a learned judge that I once knew. He told me that they organized a Confederate company or two in St. Joe, that they raised the Confederate flag over the courthouse, and when they met by day or by night they were wont to say to each other, "We would like to see a Yankee army try to lower that flag." Then he added:

"One morning a special train pulled into St. Joe, five companies of General Lyon's regular soldiers 'detrained,' and forming in column marched to the courthouse. The colonel in command detailed a lieutenant to go up and take down the flag and substitute the American flag. It was done, the lieutenant returned and took his place. Then, by order, the command saluted the old flag, and taking the Confederate flag with them, marched back to the train, boarded it and pulled out of town."

Then he said: "We looked in each other's faces. None of us felt like going up and taking down that flag, for we had seen, though on a small scale, the real flag, borne by real soldiers, under real discipline, and somehow the idea came into our minds that we were not very much warriors after all, and that there were several lessons which we would have to learn before we could call ourselves thorough veteran soldiers, irrepressible and invincible."

Maybe Mark Twain had a little experience like that, but that is mere speculation. I know nothing about it except that by his own confession he was once a Confederate soldier.

The first I ever heard of him in Nevada was after the territory was organized. James W. Nye of New York (the famous Nye) was appointed governor and Orion Clemens, a brother of Mark Twain, was appointed secretary of the territory. At that time Carson, the capitol, was a young town. The increase in houses did not keep up with the increase in people. Most of the houses were of the original California style—rude boards outside, and the partitions made, not out of studding and lath and plaster, but of canvas covered with paper, which houses had the disadvantage of taking all privacy away from the occupants. It was in one of these houses that Orion Clemens was installed on his arrival in Carson. His room was fitted up with mahogany or black walnut furniture—black walnut was the rage in those days—and there one day the occupants in the next room heard a man come into the secretary's office, heard him push a chair to one side, heard something very much like what is heard when a man puts his feet on the table, and then they heard a drawling voice say:

"You're playin' Hades out here, Brother Orion, are you not? Fine furniture, fine office, everything. But they'll drop on you after a while, Brother Orion. They will find out about you, about half as much as I know now, and you'd better go back to your oxen. Oxen are your strong suit, Brother Orion."

With Nye, when he came from New York, came a young man named Robert Howland. He was one of those "Don't-care-a-cent" young men, ready for any lark, afraid of nothing in the world; jolly, cordial, a man for men to like at first sight and for women to be charmed with. He and Mark Twain soon contracted a friendship for each other, and when the news came in from Aurora, one hundred miles south of Carson, of the great discoveries in that camp, these two young men formed a partnership and in some way got to Aurora. There they bought or built a rude cabin and passed the cold winter therein. Years later Bob used to tell that in that bleak winter it was the wont of Mark Twain and himself to go out at night, steal the empty fruit cans, oyster cans, empty champagne bottles and bottles that once held booze, from the rear of saloons and boarding houses, carry and pile them up in the rear of their own cabin to give it an opulent look, that passers-by in the daylight might say, "My, but those fellows must be flush with money!"

As the Fourth of July grew near, Mark wrote a Fourth of July oration, signed it "Mark Twain," and sent it to the local paper, in which it was copied. It began with the words, "I was sired by the great American Eagle and borne by a continental dam." This struck the fancy of Joseph T. Goodman, the owner and editor of the *Territorial Enterprise* in Virginia City, and he wrote to Mark that if he was not making more money mining than he would as local reporter on the *Enterprise*, he would hold a place for him. A few days later, when Mr. Goodman was entertaining some friends in the sanctum, a man walked in, shod in stogy shoes, wearing Kentucky jean pants, a hickory shirt and a straw hat, all very much travel worn, and in addition had a roll of ancient blankets on one shoulder. He shrugged that shoulder, dropped the blankets, and staring from one man to another, finally drawled out, "My name is Clemens." That was Mark's introduction to real journalism in Nevada.

But in a few days Mark was clothed and in his right mind—and just here a word about his *nom de plume*. The most authentic account that we have of it was Mark's explanation that a bright man used to write stories in New Orleans and sign them "Mark Twain," and when the man died Mark stole the *nom de plume*. He gave other reasons during his lifetime. One was that it was to shorten the work of the territorial legislature of Nevada so that members could refer to him, not as "that disreputable, lying, characterless, character-smashing, unscrupulous fiend who reports for the *Territorial Enterprise*, but as 'Mark Twain.'" Another story was that he got it from a roustabout on the steamboat, when they were near dangerous banks and the lead had to be thrown, and he would report "Mark one" or "Mark Twain." It is no matter whether he invented it or stole it, he wronged no one else and he made the title so famous that thousands know it who do not know his real name.

That coming to the *Enterprise* was the making of Mark Twain. I doubt very much whether he ever would have been famous at all except for his experience there. He found an atmosphere different from what he ever dreamed of being in. The office was filled with bright men, the town was filled with bright men. There he saw men that had made fortunes quickly, others who were trying to make fortunes quickly, and he saw other men who never had fortunes and never expected them. And he would hear them rail at the millionaires and say that the fact that they had money was a sure sign of how little God thought of money, judging by the men he gave it to. R. M. Daggett was on the *Enterprise*, and from his example he learned that when it was necessary to call a man names, there were no expletives too long or too expressive to be hurled in rapid succession to emphasize the utter want of character of the man assailed. Dan De Quille was working with him, too. He used to write famous stories on almost any subject, and he knew all about the gift of using adjectives. It was contagious in that office. It reached to the composing room. There were typesetters there who could hurl anathemas at bad copy which would have frightened a Bengal tiger. The news editor could damn a mutilated dispatch in twenty-four languages.

There was a compositor named Jim Connely. At that time the *Enterprise* was a six-day newspaper. Jim used to work faithfully through the week, but Saturday night he would "load up." Sometimes the load would last him over Sunday, and when he reached the office Monday morning he was a little trembly. One Monday morning he tried to distribute type for a few minutes, but laid down the stick, saying that his eyes were bad, wondering if he was going to be blind before he died, and thought he would go outside and take a spin around the block and see if he would not feel better. He did so. Probably he partook of three or four jolts while going around the block, for when he came back and picked up his composing stick, another printer asked him how his eyes were. He answered, "Fine." The rear windows of the *Enterprise* looked over the lower hills and out upon the twenty-six mile desert beyond. And as Jim said, "Fine!" he pointed out of a window and said: "Can you see that gray wolf on the twenty-six mile desert? I see him plain."

That was the character of society that Mark was introduced to, and outside there were the brightest lawyers, doctors and the shrewdest men of affairs in the world, and Mark got pointers from them all. If he wrote a good thing they would praise him and tell him to keep on, that there was something in him sure. If Homer nodded with him sometimes they would hold him up to scorn the next day; but he noticed through all that nothing was too extravagant for them in the way of description, and nothing too fine.

Mark Twain did not like a joke a bit if he was the victim. The boys of the *Enterprise* office made him a formal presentation of a meerschaum pipe. He was exceedingly pleased, but when he found next day that he could buy any number of such pipes at $1.50 each, it filled his soul with a desire to murder somebody, and he did not outgrow the feeling for a month.

Wells Fargo's coach was robbed of $25,000 at the Mound House, half way between Virginia City and Carson. A week later some of the wild chaps in Virginia City held up Mark Twain on the divide between Virginia City and Gold Hill and took his watch and money. He thought it was a genuine hold-up, and decided to go the next evening to San Francisco for a brief vacation.

As he was sitting in the coach in front of the International Hotel waiting for the hour of departure, the same gang, headed by George Birdsall, approached the stage and passed him a package done up in paper. He tore the paper open and saw inside his watch, and realized that his robbery was all a fake, and with his drawl said:

"It is all right, gentlemen, but you did it a damn sight too well for amateurs. Never mind this little dab of mine, but what did you do with the $25,000 that you took from Wells Fargo last week?"

He was in San Francisco when that city suffered a severe shock of earthquake. It happened one Sabbath morning about ten o'clock and Mark wrote a description of it to the *Enterprise*. The files of the *Enterprise* were burned and the letter, I believe, is lost to all the world: but some things about it seemed to me at the time about the jolliest writing that ever Mark Twain did. I believe I can recall a few paragraphs of it from memory almost word for word. He said:

"When that earthquake came on Sunday morning last there was but one man in San Francisco that showed any presence of mind, and he was over in Oakland. He did just what I thought of doing, what I would have done had I had any opportunity—he went down out of his pulpit and embraced a woman. The newspapers said it was his wife. Maybe it was, but if it was it was a pity. It would have shown so much more presence of mind to have embraced some other gentleman's wife.

"A young man came down from the fifth story of a house on Stockton street, with no clothing on except a knitted undershirt, which came about as near concealing his person as the tin foil does a champagne bottle. Men shouted to him, little boys yelled at him, and women besought him to take their sunbonnets, their aprons, their hoop skirts, anything in the world and cover himself up and not stand there distracting people's attention from the earthquake. He looked all around and then he looked down at himself, and then he went upstairs. I am told he went up lively.

"Pete Hopkins was shaken off of Telegraph Hill, and on his way down landed on a three-story brick house (Hopkins weighed four hundred and thirty pounds), and the papers, always misrepresenting things, ascribed the destruction of the house to the earthquake."

And so the letter ran on and on for a column and a half of the old, long, wide columns of the *Enterprise*, and every line was punctuated with fun.

He finally went to Honolulu for a vacation. There he completed a lecture which he had been preparing, and returning to San Francisco, delivered it. A great hit was in the advertising, which announced that the doors would be open at 7:30 o'clock and the trouble would begin at eight. A little later he joined an excursion party to the Mediterranean and its shores, from which he wrote the famous "Innocents Abroad." He took the manuscript to a portly publisher in New York, and, throwing it down on his desk with his card, said:

"I'd like to get that stuck into antimony." (Types are made of antimony.) The publisher looked at the manuscript, then glanced at the card, then looking up to Mark, said:

"Who are your references, Mr. Clemens?"

He replied: "I haven't any in the world. There are only two men I could apply to. One is Joe Goodman, the other is Jerry Driscoll, and they would not count, because they'd lie for me just as I'd lie for them."

Since then the world has known the history of Mark Twain. As I said above, it was the making of Mark Twain to go to work on the *Enterprise*. It opened a new world to him. All his life before he had been mostly with ordinary people, but there he found the majority of people were bright as dollars, as brave as lions, all alert, all generous, all ready to give credit where credit was due and none afraid to criticise anybody or anything else. And over all was the steadying influence of Mr. Joseph T. Goodman, the owner and editor of the paper. I think Mark Twain out of pure gratitude to him should have left him a part of his fortune. Goodman himself is as brave a man as ever lived, a thorough journalist, with magnificent journalistic judgment, and he steadied Mark through the years and was Mark's particular inspiration. Indeed, the affection of Twain for Goodman all his life was made clear in his own autobiography.

When he went east and his first book came out and he was hailed as a genius, he might have gone to the dogs had he not met the woman who became his wife and who was his salvation. That changed the whole course of his life, awakened new hopes, changed all his prospects; gave him to see how much there was in a refined life. Then when he made his home in Hartford and all his associates were refined and educated people, the change from his former life was an epoch to him; and still there are some things about him which are a mystery to those who knew him well. There is no evidence that in his boyhood he was fond of study or fond of literature; he wrote nothing that attracted especial attention until after he was thirty years of age.

It is not strange that he wrote so many humorous things, but the style of his writing is a perpetual mystery. Where did he get that? His English was always perfect, and it was of a high class which draws readers to his work every day.

We wish for the sake of his fame that he would oftener have done what Shakespeare did—all at once break out in a dozen lines of such majesty and beauty that it thrills people and always will. However, his fame is secure enough; his work was a distinct addition to the literature of the United States. But could some one have followed him about and taken down his remarks every day and compiled them in a book, it would outsell all his works, for he was funnier every hour in his conversation than anything he ever wrote.

I met "Josh Billings" as he came west a few days before he died. I said: "Of course, Mr. Shaw, you know Mark Twain?"

"Oh, yes," was the reply. "I went to his hotel in New York last week to see him and was told that he was over in Jersey lecturing, but would be back about midnight.

"Mark had a parlor and bed-room and out of the parlor another bed-room opened. They gave me this bed-room. I retired, leaving the door open. About 2 a.m. Mark came in. He turned up the gas, came to my bedside and said, 'Hello, Josh.' I asked him where he had been. 'Over in Jersey lecturing,' was his answer. I asked him if he had a good time.

"With a look of sorrow, he said: 'Had a devil of a time. Just before the lecture was to begin, a young man came to me and asked me to come with him. He led me to where there was a hole in the drop curtain, and with much emotion said, "Please look through this. The old gentleman with the white hair to the left of the center aisle, in an orchestra chair, is my father."' Then with a gulp he explained that the old gentleman had been afflicted with a settled melancholy for a long time, and that if I could say anything to rouse him it would be an immense favor to the whole family. I said, 'All right.' The curtain went up and my lecture began. After two or three minutes I shot a joke at the audience, but meant it for the old man. It didn't faze him. A little later I tried another joke at him; it didn't faze him. Still a little later I gathered myself up and hurled my masterpiece at him. The audience yelled, but the old man didn't even smile. Then I thought that I could not devote all my time to him, that something was due the audience, and so went on and finished my lecture.

"Then the young man came and in a soft voice inquired if I had succeeded in arousing the interest of the father. "'Not a blamed bit,' I replied. 'He sat there as though he did not hear a word.'

"'I guess he didn't,' said the Reuben. 'A powder mill explosion twenty years ago smashed the drums in his ears and since then he has been as deaf as a post.' Here Mark added, 'And I had no weapons.'"

When the *Lusitania* first came to New York, he was invited aboard the great ship and shown around. When the inspection was over, he casually remarked that he would tell Noah about that ship.

I hope he has found Noah now, and all the rest of the "old boys" that have gone over on the other side; and if he has, I predict that whether it is up above or down below, a ripple of laughter will follow his footsteps in either place through all eternity.

—C.C. Goodwin, "Samuel Clemens—'Mark Twain,'"
As I Remember Them, Salt Lake City, 1913, pp. 250–259

HENRY W. FISHER (1922)

These accounts were written—or dictated—at the prompting of Twain's cantankerous bibliographer, Merle Johnson. Johnson describes Henry Fisher as "one of the most widely known correspondents in foreign parts." Fisher first met Mark Twain in Chicago in 1879, at a dinner for President Ulysses Grant, and Fisher was a correspondent in Berlin when Twain and family were there (in winter 1891, what Fisher calls Twain's "troubled Berlin days"). Fisher also saw Twain later, when both men were living in London.

While they were never, as Fisher concedes, "hail-fellow-well-met," as Merle Johnson writes, "Fisher was in a unique position for contact" with Twain, and his stories, recalled with the use of old diaries and a journalist's fine memory, give a different view of a period otherwise familiar only through Twain's letters. Fisher gives us the garrulous off-the-cuff Twain.

Virginia City *Enterprise* reporter C.C. Goodwin had remarked how

> could some one have followed [Twain] about and taken down his remarks every day and compiled them in a book, it would outsell all his works, for he was funnier every hour in his conversation than anything he ever wrote.

Fisher's memoir (though hardly a bestseller) is such a book. Students investigating the unfurnished Mark Twain, portrayed in his "off the record" persona, caught in a natural setting, and recorded nearly verbatim by an expert journalist, should consult Fisher's accounts.

"Pa Used to Be a Terrible Man"

With Mark's daughter Susie, I was walking in the Berlin Thiergarten one afternoon when we encountered a very rough specimen of the genus tramp.

"Look at him," said Susie. "You know, Pa, too, was an awful man before Mamma took him in hand and married him." And with added seriousness, she continued: "He used to swear and swear, and then swear again, and the only thing that he didn't do that was bad was to let cards and liquor alone—some kinds of liquor."

It is too bad that I forgot Mark's comment on the above when I told him.

Mark, Bismarck, Lincoln, and Darwin

I had been to see Bismarck to help boom Bryan for the Presidency, when that gentleman happened to get defeated for the Senate.

"And is old Bismarck still reading those trashy French novels?" inquired Mark.

"Much worse," I said.

"Started Paul de Kock over again?"

"Worse still. He is reading Mark Twain now."

"You don't say. Since when the reform?"

"Since his daughter-in-law, Herbert's wife, the little Countess Hoyos, gave him a set for Christmas."

"Hoyos, Hoyos. I met some people of that name in Italy."

"Your fair patroness hails from Trieste, or neighborhood."

"How do you know that Bismarck not only owns, but reads, my books?" demanded Mark.

"Because he asked me whether there are still steamer loads of Yankees going picnicking in Palestine with Mark Twain for a bear-leader. The old Prince told me he read 'Innocents Abroad' twice, and memorized the best things in it to relate to his grandchildren."

"Quite a compliment—I do wish Bismarck hadn't been such a rascal—in politics, I mean—for in private life he was quite a gentleman, I understand.

Mark was genuinely proud of Bismarck's partiality for his books, even if it came late in the day.

"Do you know," he once said, "that I gave Charles Darwin the strength to write some of his most famous and epoch-making volumes? How? I am told that, when the great scientist was utterly fagged out with study, investigation, and with the manifold experiments he was carrying on, he would read my 'Innocents' or 'Tom Sawyer' or, maybe a Harper Magazine story, for a half hour or an hour. Then he would go to work again and later was ready for bed. Only when this here Mark Twain had lulled his nerves into proper condition, Darwin wooed sleep, I am told, but I can't vouch for the truth of this story."

On another occasion Mark said: "I was born too late to help ease Lincoln's hours of worry. Ward Hill Lamon, whom we met in Berlin, told me more than once that Lincoln would have been a constant reader of my 'literature' if he had lived long enough to enjoy my books, and none know Lincoln better than Lamon.

"And when my girls admonish me to behave in company, it always recalls the stories Lamon told me about old Abe's awkwardness.

"When Abe and he were riding circuit in Illinois, they carried their office in their hats, and Abe contracted the habit of pulling off his hat from the back so as not to spill any papers. That was all right on the circuit, but in the White House it looked undignified. So Mrs. Lincoln asked Lamon, a most courtly gentleman, to remonstrate with the President and teach him to take off his hat 'decently.' 'Decently' was the word she used, said Lamon. He continued:

"'I did my best during a night's smoker, Mr. Seward helping me, and the President proved a good enough scholar for any high school of courtesy. Eight or ten times he took off his hat properly, without a reminder of any sort. Then, at the good-night, I tried him again. "Let's do it in the right courtly fashion," I said, doffing my chapeau like the Count of Monte Cristo.

"'Here goes,' said the President, reached his right hand back, and pulled off his stovepipe in the old Illinois circuit style.'

"You see," concluded Mark, "it was no use trying to make a courtier of Lincoln. The same here."

An English Lover of Kings and a Hater

"Look at those fools going to pieces over old Doc Johnson—call themselves Americans and lick-spittle the toady who grabbed a pension from the German King of England that hated Americans, tried to flog us into obedience and called George Washington traitor and scoundrel."

Thus spoke Mark Twain in the Doctor Johnson room of the Cheshire Cheese, the Strand, where the old thoroughfare becomes "the Street of Ink" or Newspaper Row, and while we were enjoying the famous meat pie served there on certain days of the week.

"You are pleased to occupy Miss Evelyn's seat," whispered James the waiter, looking at Mark.

"Miss Evelyn—what?" demanded our friend.

James blushed. "Miss Evelyn, why—Miss Evelyn, the beautiful young American lady who came with the millionaire, Mr. People, coming to the Cheese, ninety-nine per cent. Do so because they don't know the man, and the others because they feel tickled to honor a writer a hundred and fifty years or so after he is good and rotten."

"Read Johnson plentifully, I suppose," mocked Bram Stoker, famous as author, critic, barrister and Henry Irving's associate.

"Not guilty—never a written word of his," answered honest Mark. "I gauge Johnson's character by his talks with that sot Bozzy, whom foolish old Carlyle called the greatest biographer ever because, I suppose, Bozzy interviewed Johnson on such momentous questions as: 'What would you do, sir, if you were locked up in the Tower with a baby?' "

"Well, what would *you* do," asked Bram.

"Throw it out of the window to a passing milkman, if it was weaned and if there was no cow around," said Mark.

Slang Not in Mark's Dictionary

Seldom or never did I hear Mark use slang—whether he thought himself above it in the matter of provoking laughter, or whether he disliked it, I can't tell. He used to keep the Berlin or Vienna embassy, or whatever the resort happened to be, in a roar by telling of billiard balls "the size of walnuts" and of a billiard table "as big as the State of Rhode Island," but such a word as "Biggity" never escaped him.

An American "slangy" person says: "I'll be jiggered" or something. Mark put that phrase differently: "*You* be damned if I didn't scream like a wet peacock with all his tail feathers mussed."

The ordinary run of humorists delight in fussing about hotel bills. Mark affected to "be mad clean through" at impositions practiced upon him by foreigners, and clenched both fists as he remarked: "We paid the heavy bill, about *six cents.*"

If Mark had used the slang loved by the vaudevillians he would be as widely unread in the Scandinavian countries, in modern Greece and in Russia as are the latter. "I never like riddles and jaw-breakers," he said to a member of the firm of Chatto and Windus in London one day, after the gentleman "had caught another foreign country for him," "but I guess cannibals and Pollacks alike love to be surprised, and the grotesque, always unexpected in arriving."

"During my stay in Stockholm some one read the following from one of my books (translated): 'The solemn steadfastness of the deep made the ship roll sideways.' Great laughter. 'And she kicked up behind!' At that the house shook and rocked and quivered with merriment and my fame was firmly established in Sweden. If I had told the audience that 'Her Majesty's dress crept along the floor for three minutes (count 'em) after the queen had gone,' they would have risen to a man and kissed me."

Mark "No Gentleman"

Mark didn't resort to profanity when he wanted to lambaste man or measure. I once heard him say to Mrs. Clemens: "I will write him that 'his mind is all caked up, that as an idiot he is simply immeasurable.'"

"And I will call him a snug person full of pedantic proclivities; and further, 'a long-eared animal' (and striking an attitude)—'a mule hostler with his pate full of axle grease.' "

"All right," said gentle Mrs. Livy, "do so by all means, but take care not to send the letter."

"Livy, dear, let me get it off my chest," pleaded Mark, "for 'Hotel Normandie, Paris,' would be just the place to date such an epistle from. Don't you remember the 'Madame's speech' to the effect that 'one must expect neither tact nor delicacy from Mark Twain?' "

The "Madame" referred to was Madam Blanc, the critic of one of the chief French reviews, already mentioned.

"The vagabond and adventurer, who from crown to sole remained a gentleman" (I forgot from which magazine that is quoted) fairly reveled "in the French Madame's abomination of his lowly self."

"You remind me of Charles II," I said to him once, referring to that confusing habit of his, and was going to "substantiate" when he interrupted.

"I can guess what you mean, but never mind, for all you know I may be Charlie's reincarnation. Charles, you wanted to say, had only three stories up his sleeve and these he told over and over again for new ones to Nell and the rest of the bunch. And varied them so cleverly and disguised them so well, that his audience never got on to the fact that His Majesty had been chestnutting. As for me, I can only hope that I will succeed as well as Charlie did."

In Berlin I once heard Susie Clemens—ill-fated, talented girl, who died so young—say to her father: "Grouch again! They *do* say that you can be funny when company is around—too bad that you don't consider Henry Fisher company."

"Out of the mouth of sucklings," quoth Clemens and gave Susie the twenty marks she was after, and he kissed her: "Goodby, little blackmailer, and don't tell your mamma how you worked that fool papa of yours."

Indeed, Mark was not always the humorist the public mind pictures him. Very often, for long hours at a time, in our intercourse extending over thirty years, he was decidedly serious, while at other times he grumbled at everything and everybody. His initial object in choosing me for his "bear-leader" was to add to his stock of knowledge on foreign affairs and to correct erroneous ideas he might have acquired from books. Since I had resided many years on the Continent, and had command of the languages he lacked, he asked me to pilot him around Berlin, Paris, and Vienna, and on such occasions his talk was more often deep and learned than laughter-provoking. In an afternoon or morning's work—getting atmosphere, *i.e.,* "the hang of things" German or Austrian, as Mark called it—he sometimes dropped two or three memorable witticisms, but familiar intercourse in the long run left no doubt of the fact that a very serious vein bordering on melancholy underlay his mask of bonhomie. On the other hand a closer or more intelligent student of life never lived. He was as conscientious, as true, and as simple as Washington Irving.

Those occasional lapses into dejection notwithstanding, it struck me that Mark extracted his humor out of the bounty and abundance of his own nature. Hench his tinkling grotesquerie, unconventionality, whimsicality, play of satire, and shrieking irony, between touches of deep seriousness. . . .

In later years I met Mark repeatedly during his several London seasons, for, liking his society, I called at Brown's or his apartment whenever he came to England, myself being engaged in literary work there. We were never on terms of particular intimacy—hail-fellows-well-met, yes! "Hello, Mark"— "Hello Henry W.—you here again?" We stuck verbally to the formula of the old Chicago days, and I was glad to be of use to him when it suited his fancy. Moreover, I was vastly interested in Mark's books, short stories, and essays, but found him rather inclined to talk shop unless it was the other fellow's.

Rudyard Kipling he used to designate "the militant spokesman of the Anglo-Saxon races," and he sometimes spoke with near-admiration of Bernard Shaw, "whose plays are popular from London to St. Petersburg, from Christiania to Madrid, from Havre to Frisco, and from Frisco to the Antipodes, while mine are nowhere."

After I visited Tolstoy at Yasnaya Polyana he said to me: "Lucky dog, you have broken bread with the man who commands, and almost monopolizes, the thought of the world."

—Henry W. Fisher, from *Abroad with*
Mark Twain and Eugene Field:
Tales They Told to a Fellow Correspondent,
New York: Nicholas L. Brown, 1922,
pp. 70, 103–104, 116–118, 150–151,
175–176, 177, xv–xvii, xvii–xix

GENERAL

What will quickly become apparent to the diligent reader of the reviews and essays collected here is how the questions that are now most routinely posed of Twain's writing—questions of race and attitudes about slavery, questions in regard to class, gender, and identity—are scarcely addressed in the early commentary on Twain's work. Literary criticism was not the rigorous institution it is today. It existed only in what may now seem a relatively primitive form. In addition, each era develops its own set of concerns and preoccupations. Attitudes about race and slavery were slowly evolving in Twain's lifetime, which included the Civil War. A writer such as Barrett Wendell, for instance, who was integral to the advancement of American literature as a subject worthy of study, also held proslavery, imperialistic prejudices. If he seemed to recoil from his own views at times, he still serves to illustrate the state of critical inquiry in the nineteenth century.

Comparisons, meanwhile, are often made to writers who are less known to current readers. Oliver Wendell Holmes, whose pithy New England books of table talk centered around the figure of the "Autocrat," is invoked several times, usually as a foil to Twain or a gauge of what Twain is not. Other names include John Phoenix (George Horatio Derby, one of the earliest California-based humorists and an important influence on American humor) and Petroleum Vesuvius Nasby (David Ross Locke, a Toledo-based satirist during the Civil War who was vigorously opposed to slavery and the Confederacy). The names of forgotten or overlooked humorists such as Doesticks or Orpheus C. Kerr are recalled. Undoubtedly most frequent of all, however, are those comparisons to Artemus Ward.

Artemus Ward was the pen name of Charles Farrar Browne, a Maine-born humorist whose biography closely resembled Twain's in many respects. Browne was born in 1834, the year before Samuel Clemens, and, as with Clemens, his father died while Charles was young, forcing the boy to find employment. He worked in a printing office run by his brother (again, mirroring Clemens). Learning the trade, he moved to Boston at eighteen where he worked as a printer's devil or apprentice, possible typesetting Clemens's first publication in the East, a generic piece of frontier humor titled "The Dandy Frightening the Squatter."

From Boston, Browne traveled south (Samuel Clemens headed north), an itinerant working variously as a schoolteacher and a printer. He wound up in Cleveland, where he became the local editor of the *Plain Dealer*. From there, he created the character of "Artemus Ward," a small-time showman modeled somewhat after P.T. Barnum, a persona that soon enough became confused with his own identity. Artemus's fame grew, so much that he was feted in England, where he traveled in 1866 and where he died of tuberculosis in Southampton the following year, at the height of his fame and at the age of only thirty-two.

Ward's premature death (and the void it left) serve as a backdrop to Twain's slowly budding career. Mark Twain was conceived popularly, for some time, as the protégé of Artemus Ward. It is true that Artemus got Twain published in the *New York Mercury* and then in the *Saturday Press*. It is also true that Twain capitalized on his connection with Artemus for a time, in sketches such as "My First Interview with Artemus Ward" and a lecture recalling Artemus. In time, perhaps, the debt became infuriating to Twain, who, with little exception, consistently expressed fondness for his dead friend, nevertheless. It bothers certain Twain supporters, as can be seen, from William Dean Howells to Bernard DeVoto, who claimed unequivocally (and rather awkwardly) that "of Ward's manner, his approach, and the content of his humor nothing of Mark's possesses anything at all."

Students should decide for themselves. Was there a campaign to represent Mark Twain in a certain light? There are two camps that begin to emerge in these reviews. One—which can be summarized as haughty and snobbish—seems to resent all suggestions that this uncouth pretender might possibly be considered a writer of authentic literature. The other camp confounds the first by trying to claim Mark Twain as an author of fine romances and serious ideas and often dismissing the humorous work as juvenilia. R.E. Phillips, then, argues that "by far the largest part of Mark Twain's work is serious." Others equivocate between the two—and William Dean Howells provides one example of this position. While he recognizes

Twain's more serious aspects and on occasion campaigned hard to have Twain taken seriously, he sees equally a trap in insisting too much:

> What we should all wish to do is to keep Mark Twain what he has always been: a comic force unique in the power of charming us out of our cares and troubles, united with as potent an ethic sense of the duties , public and private, which no man denies in himself without being false to other men. (Howells, 1901)

This is something of an admission in Howells, who is among the best-represented commentators in this section. "We" have a duty to control what "Mark Twain" is, and so Howells tries, redefining Twain for new audiences, reconfiguring the canon to reflect new tastes.

There is no similar debate on the "Americanism" of Mark Twain. Perhaps more than any writer before him, Twain can unhesitatingly be called "all-American." Never mind that Twain himself remarked that

> There isn't a single human characteristic that can be safely labelled "American." There isn't a single human ambition, or religious trend, or drift of thought, or peculiarity of education, or code of principles, or breed of folly, or style of conversation, or preference for a particular subject of discussion, or form of legs or trunk or head or face or expression or complexion, or gait, or dress or manners, or disposition, or any other human detail, inside or outside, that can rationally be generalized as "American."
>
> Whenever you have found what seems to be an "American" peculiarity, you have only to cross a frontier or two, or go down or up in the social scale, and you perceive that it has disappeared. And you can cross the Atlantic and find it again.
> ("What Paul Bourget Thinks of Us," 1895)

Again, in the London speech of 1899, Twain stressed (to an English audience, of course) that he had been reared on English authors: "They must not claim credit in America for what was given to them so long ago. They must only claim that they trimmed this, that and the other, and so changed their subject that they seemed to be original." Nevertheless, the emphasis on the Americanism of Mark Twain pervades numerous essays included here. It is present, of course, in Hemingway's oft-repeated remark in *The Green Hills of Africa* that "All modern literature comes from one book by Mark Twain called *Huckleberry Finn*." An unusual dissenting voice can be found in F.R. Leavis's essay on *Pudd'nhead Wilson*.

It may prove useful to students to follow the development of a consensus view of Twain. Gradually, over time, the "tardy voice of the professional critic assented" (Stuart P. Sherman). Twain became acceptable and was assimilated into an American canon. How was this achieved? Respectable champions had to campaign for Twain, and they did; Howells was at the forefront, of course, but also academics such as Barrett Wendell and Brander Matthews secured for Twain a higher reputation than he had previously enjoyed.

Those texts emphasized as Twain's "masterpieces" vary with time also. By 1901, Brander Matthews could pronounce *Huckleberry Finn* "the finest of his books," but, at least for a while, Howells was endeavoring to sell Twain as an author, like Hawthorne, of "romances." Many critics resolutely tried to distance Twain from his early humor, with Howells at their lead then as well, while others such as Harry Peck tenaciously (or obstinately) maintained that "The Jumping Frog" was the best work and that Twain's maturation was a decline: "It shows just how far a man who was once a great humourist can fall."

This plaint haunts Twain's reviews, particularly as his experiments to craft a successful fictional prose work became more urgent. While one half of the reviewers chafed at Twain's "buffoonery," his "broad," "coarse" and "vulgar" "grotesqueries," the other half was pining for the simple days of the "genial humorist." Division characterizes Twain; it is present even in his name ("twain" meaning "two") and in his having two names, therefore two identities. (Although too much has perhaps been made of this, since a *nom de plume* was used as a matter of course among nineteenth-century American humorists.) Twain famously used twins, impostors, and doubles throughout his fiction. He had, he remarked, numerous doubles (Ambrose Bierce was one of them). It should stand to reason, then, that he had two camps of critics.

"Literary opinions change as time progresses," William Phelps wrote in 1907, and as the twentieth century began, a struggle to define Twain emerged. The academy and the haughtier critics were trying to claim him as one of the masters of literature, comparable to Cervantes and Molière, Emerson and Hawthorne. They accordingly had to reconcile him to the "fastidious niceness of the professional critic" (the phrase is from T.M. Parrott), a project best achieved by marginalizing the early humorous writings. Other critics wanted to reclaim Twain as the earthy writer of vernacular, the bestseller of subscription books and train platform kiosks. As the academic acolytes take up Twain, certain commonplaces recur. Mark Twain is "purely American"; soon, everybody reiterates this.

He is ethical, not a "mere humorist." Consensus crystallizes. The reader might well wonder what Mark Twain, who so often challenged such conventional, uncritical repetition, thought of this.

Other readers, such as Harry Thurston Peck, were disgusted by what Twain had become and noted that had his *Extracts from Adam's Diary* been written by anybody "without a great name, no amount of 'pull' or adroit argument would have enabled him to palm them off on a first-class metropolitan daily as 'Sunday Special' matter." Critical readers might decide for themselves when critics are or are not engaged in such "adroit argument."

Another fight over the ownership of Twain was waged between Europe—chiefly England—and the United States. Many American critics no doubt felt rebuked when Mark Twain was embraced with greater critical fervor in England than in his native country. From the earliest pirated editions of Twain, his work was embraced hungrily by the English public, both popular and critical. It became a well-established fact that the Americans were behind the English in developing an appreciation for Twain. Consequently, when he returned to the United States from Europe in the 1890s, as William Dean Howells recalls, "his countrymen . . . kept it up in honor of him past all precedent." By 1909, Archibald Henderson could brag about Twain "preferring Connecticut to Camelot" and speak of "the average American's complacent and chuckling satisfaction in his country's possession of . . . Mark Twain."

Certain changes can be detected in the tone of the criticism over time. As H.L. Mencken describes it, "critical opinion of Mark has gradually evolved from scorn into indifference, and from indifference into toleration, and from toleration into apologetic praise, and from apologetic praise in to hearty praise" (1913). This change does not seem solely due to Twain's writing. As the posthumous summaries indicate, many critics felt that Twain's last fifteen years actually showed a conspicuous decline in his literary powers; yet his popularity blossomed in those years.

The rise in popularity, then, reflects events in Twain's own public life. Since so much of his writing was essentially autobiographical, it is not surprising that his life became a public narrative or myth. For instance, there is his triumphal return from Europe in 1900, having recovered from bankruptcy by embarking on a worldwide lecture tour (as described in *Following the Equator*). A tone of sycophancy enters certain essays about Twain at this time, orchestrated by those whom Mencken delicately terms the "drovers of rah-rah boys" (1917). "Yet these closing years were irradiated by a splendor of mature success almost unmatched in the history of literature," Howells wrote in 1913. "It seemed as if the world were newly roused to a sense of his pre-eminence." This global illumination unfortunately took the shape of routine and therefore somewhat empty compliments littering so-called reviews in lieu of discriminating criticism.

Conversely, after Twain's death in 1910, a backlash can be discerned, as if, with the author no longer living, it was safe to drub the work of his final years. Some critics go about this task with some savagery. Professor Harry Thurston Peck values little of Twain's work written after *Roughing It* (to his credit, he said as much while Twain was still alive). Twain's death also reinvented the author once more, through Paine's biography and his editions of the *Letters* and the *Notebooks* and then the steady stream of posthumous works, prompting H.L. Mencken to comment that "Mark Twain dead is beginning to show far different and more brilliant colors than those he seemed to wear during life" (November 1917).

To paraphrase Mark Twain, "Which was the dream?" Furthermore, "What is man?," Fred Lewis Pattee wrote in 1915, only five years after Twain's death, that "the man himself is becoming a mere legend, shadowy and more and more distorted." Not a small amount of the debates that fairly rage at times over Twain come down to opposing views of his sense of humor. One critic, failing to see the joke in *The Innocents Abroad*, dismisses it. Another critic finds it hilarious and vaunts it for all time. Once again, the man with two names prompts radically different interpretations.

Bret Harte "From California" (1866)

This early review of Mark Twain, for an eastern audience, recalls the time when Bret Harte and Mark Twain were still on good terms. This was not, of course, the earliest "puff" for Twain in the East. "Jim Smiley and His Jumping Frog" had appeared, through the kind offices of Artemus Ward, in Henry Clapp's New York Bohemian journal, the *Saturday Press*, in November 1865. Ward had endorsed Twain even earlier, facilitating the reprinting of two of his sketches in the New York *Sunday Mercury* as far back as January 1864.

In the East at this time there were many pseudonymous humorists writing squibs, hoaxes, and burlesques of the journalism of the day. Twain might well have been lost among this sheer glut of names if not for notices like Harte's. This critique is significant for being the first of many such pieces that seek to differentiate Twain from the mass of humorists, likewise beginning the long task of retrieving him from the enduring shadow of Artemus Ward.

This passage will be useful to students writing on the tempestuous Twain-Harte relationship and also to students concerned with Twain's early public maturation from a "mere humorist" into a canonical writer.

Samuel Clemens, better known as "Mark Twain," the Honolulu correspondent of the Sacramento Union, took advantage of the queen's visit to deliver a most entertaining lecture upon the Sandwich Islands. He had a crowded house and a brilliant success, and in this initial effort at once established his reputation as an eccentric lecturer whose humor surpassed Artemus Ward's with the advantage of being of a more legitimate quality. He had already acquired, here and abroad, considerable fame as an original and broadly humorous writer, but he took his audience by storm. He intends repeating the lecture through the state and is urged by his friends to extend his tour even to the East. His humor is peculiar to himself; if of any type, it is rather of the western character of ludicrous exaggeration and audacious statement, which perhaps is more thoroughly national and American than even the Yankee delineations of Lowell. His humor has more motive than that of Artemus Ward; he is something of a satirist, although his satire is not always subtle or refined. He has shrewdness and a certain hearty abhorence [*sic*] of shams which will make his faculty serviceable to mankind. His talent is so well based that he can write seriously and well when he chooses, which is perhaps the best test of true humor. His faults are crudeness, coarseness, and an occasional

Panurge-like plainness of statement. I am particular in these details, for I believe he deserves this space and criticism, and I think I recognize a new star rising in this western horizon.

—Bret Harte, "From California," Springfield
(Massachusetts) *Daily Republican*,
November 10, 1866

CHARLES HENRY WEBB (1867)

The "Advertisement" to Twain's first book, *The Celebrated Jumping Frog of Calaveras County and Other Sketches* (1867), was provided by "John Paul." This was the pen name of the book's publisher, Charles Henry Webb, the founder and publisher of the influential literary journal the *Californian* and a humorist in his own right.

Webb continues Bret Harte's project of distancing Twain from the run-of-the-mill humorists he was published with. Moral purpose is again emphasized. The Civil War had only recently ended, and the sometimes wild and vicious humor of the antebellum days seemed, by then, morally bankrupt. An air of reconstruction pervaded literature as well as politics. So Webb remarks on how Twain never sinks to the misspelling buffoonery of his peers (meaning, most prominently, Artemus Ward). "Humor is only a fragrance, a decoration. Often it is merely an odd trick of speech and of spelling," he dictated in his notes for an autobiography. Nonetheless, Twain was not above using misspelling in his humor (and Artemus Ward, conversely, exceeded the same).

By 1905, Twain's view of Webb, as with Harte, had changed dramatically: "I hate both the name and the memory of Charles Henry Webb, liar and thief." This "Advertisement" is, nevertheless, significant for students of Mark Twain's literary development, as an early form of a manifesto.

"Mark Twain" is too well known to the public to require a formal introduction at my hands. By his story of the Frog, he scaled the heights of popularity at a single jump, and won for himself the sobriquet of The Wild Humorist of the Pacific Slope. He is also known to fame as The Moralist of the Main; and it is not unlikely that as such he will go down to posterity. It is in his secondary character, as humorist, however, rather than in the primal one of moralist, that I aim to present him in the present volume. And here a ready explanation will be found for the somewhat fragmentary character of many of these sketches; for it was necessary to snatch threads of humor wherever they could be found—very often detaching them from serious articles and moral essays with which they were woven and entangled. Originally written for newspaper publication, many of the articles referred to events of the day, the interest of which has now passed away, and contained local allusions, which the general reader would fail to understand; in such cases excision became imperative. Further than this, remark or comment is unnecessary. Mark Twain never resorts to tricks of spelling nor rhetorical buffoonery for the purpose of provoking a laugh; the vein of his humor runs too rich and deep to make surface-gilding necessary. But there are few who can resist the quaint similes, keen satire, and hard good sense which form the staple of his writings.

—Charles Henry Webb, "Advertisement"
in *Jumping Frog*, 1867

Ellen Tucker Emerson (1873)

The daughter of Ralph Waldo Emerson would later prove an important go-between in negotiating Twain's redemption after he obliviously offended the Boston establishment with his "Whittier Birthday Speech." Ellen's remarks about her father's preferences bear out the similar claims in her later letter to Livy Clemens. This letter is useful to any student striving to find common ground between Mark Twain and Emerson.

Dear Mother,
    You have asked how Father felt about the newspaper slips. If it is a slip about the college, he is pleased. If it is about Mr Greely [sic] or Dickens he is displeased. Judge Hoar's letter and that about Mr. Tyndall's lecture, and both the Mark Twain letters have been his perfect delight.

—Ellen Tucker Emerson, letter to
Lydian Emerson, January 12, 1873

Henry James (1875)

Although they knew each other as Americans abroad and as littérateurs with common friends (Howells most obviously, but Twain would become friends in due time with Henry's brother, William), the novelist, short story writer, and critic Henry James wrote little concerning Mark Twain. Here, as an incidental remark in a review of a forgotten novel, Henry James flippantly dismisses Twain as a sort of social ill.

Twain's biographer Archibald Henderson has described Henry James again dismissing Twain, this time remarking that "one must be a very rudimentary person to enjoy Mark Twain." Students interested in finding similarities between these two very different major forces in late-nineteenth-century American letters should turn to this passage.

As Professor Masson indicates, the danger that the extreme "respectability" of each of these great men [Luther, Goethe and Milton] might operate as a blight upon their poetic faculty was not averted by the interposition of the sense of humor. We know how little of this faculty they possessed. What made them great was what we have called their consistency—the fact that their seriousness, their solemnity, their "respectability" was on so large and unbroken a scale. They were men of a proud imagination—even when Wordsworth condescended to the poetry of village idiots and little porringers. In the day of Mark Twain there is no harm in being reminded that the absence of drollery may, at a stretch, be compensated by the presence of sublimity.

—Henry James, *The Nation*, February 18, 1875,
review of David Masson, *Three Devils: Luther's,
Milton's, and Goethe's. With Other Essays*,
London: Macmillan, 1874

ROBERT UNDERWOOD JOHNSON
"A NEW BOOK BY MARK TWAIN" (1877)

Johnson is reviewing Mark Twain's Patent Self-Pasting Scrap Book, the only one of his many earnestly puzzled-out inventions to actually elicit a profit. Ironically, in the promotional material, Twain wrote that his purpose was not to make money but to "economize the profanity in the country." This was managed by cleverly sidestepping that endless application of glue that is usually associated with scrapbooks. Johnson amusingly treats the scrapbook as another of Twain's literary efforts. Of course, as Twain's bibliographer Merle Johnson tersely put it, "'Mark Twain's Scrap Book' is a patented pasting device, not a literary production."

It needs not skillful reading between the lines of this last volume by Mr. Clemens to see that it is essentially an autobiography. The experiences of the author, his trials, his failures, and his final success are patent on every page. Even in the illustrations, one may read the story of his eventful career. Though with rare modesty he has suppressed the most sacred facts of his life, it takes but an ordinary imagination to peer through the palings of his father's fence (see cut on page 25) and behold him in the sportive innocence of childhood, throwing his grandmother's gridiron (see cut on page 27) at the neighbor's cat. How easy to discern in this incident the budding of those distinguished editorial faculties of later years! Here, too (page 97), is a view of the brick-yard in which—though he says it not, we know from other sources—he worked for years. In fact, there is an air of brick-yard throughout the whole of this volume, which it is impossible to attribute to any other literary mood than reminiscence. The volatility of his youth is also plainly to be seen. If we are not at fault, the inference to be drawn from the book is, that for many years the author could stick to nothing; but that, in later years, his power of application has notably increased. Yet, we must frankly admit that we have found but few irregularities in the whole volume. Further on (pages 124–137) are given numerous sketches from the author's life on the Mississippi. The one of the pontoon bridges (page 126)—which, it may not be generally known, were used at the times of the overflow of Western rivers—seems to us hardly enough to the point. We think we can detect Mr. Clemens's hand in the sketch from which this view was made; it has, in common with the gridiron, already referred to, a certain individuality bordering on mannerism. (Can we be mistaken in supposing that the gridiron must have come from Mr. Clemens's hand?) Nor do we like so well the view of the Hannibal and St. Joe Railroad (page 140), on which Mr. Clemens went to California in '49; if we should be asked to name its principal fault, we should have to complain of the perspective. The views of the stratification of gold in the California mines (page 153), as it appeared to the imagination of Mr. Clemens, have a touch of that quaint humor so characteristic of him. We could wish the text were fuller in regard to this part of the author's romantic life, but we must do him the justice to remember that the title of this book only promises fragmentary sketches; though, as the title modestly suggests, they are not easily displaced from the memory.

But we did not mean to follow Mr. Clemens through the whole of the checkered career exhibited in this volume. It is a book to which readers could easily become attached. Many a lesson of patience and moderation may be learned from the parallels he has here drawn. Artists, even architects, will find much in the drawings to encourage them, while, among the quotations, many a scholar will gladly welcome the frequent lines of Arabic, the smoothness and flow of which are quite beyond praise. The style of the book, though occasionally labored, has none of the discursiveness heretofore so noticeable in Mr. Clemens's work, but is evenly sustained throughout. The compositor's work is almost without flaw. We have found a few instances of "wrong fonts," but, so far, not a single error in the leading. We must, however, protest against the insertion by the publishers, at the close, of the cut of the ladder by which Mr. Clemens rose to fame.

It is quite safe to say that no such work has ever been given to the public; the price per copy is from $1.25 to $3.50, according to style of binding, etc.

—Robert Underwood Johnson, "A New Book
by Mark Twain," *Scribner's Monthly* 13,
April 1877, pp. 874–875

JOEL CHANDLER HARRIS (1882)

Joel Chandler Harris was the author of the "Uncle Remus" stories—classic delineations of folk tales, centering around Brer Rabbit and narrated by the fictitious former slave Remus on a Georgia plantation. Mark Twain was an admirer of Harris's work—he considered his rendition of African-American vernacular unmatched. In 1881, the year before this review appeared, Twain contacted Harris to propose that they collaborate on a lecture tour with the author George Henry Cable. When they met, Twain discovered that Harris was far too shy to read his work aloud, and Harris was dropped from the plan.

In this review of Twain's collection *The Stolen White Elephant* (1882), Harris significantly draws attention to Twain's hostility toward conventional publishing. All of Twain's significant works through 1880 were sold through the subscription-only American Publishing Company. Students investigating Mark Twain's (extremely complex and checkered) publishing history should read Harris's words. What difference might it have made to Twain, as a writer, that he was published through a book subscription company? William Dean Howells also singles out this peculiarity in *My Mark Twain*. Osgood, Mark Twain's publisher here, was also publishing Emerson, Henry James, Howells, and Longfellow, among others. Does this acceptance into a more literary circle of publishing authors mark a change in Twain's fortunes (and writing)?

Howells remarks also on exaggeration and American humor, finding Twain distinct from the general "trash" that was readily available. Harris, like John Nichol, also addresses Twain's powers of description, although while Nichol sees this power in decline, Harris sees it as blooming.

———

The announcement of a new book by this genial humorist is rather in the nature of a surprise. Only the other day, accompanied by Mr. Osgood himself, who is a gentleman of marvelous social and business resources, Mr. Clemens was journeying up and down the Mississippi in search of material for a new volume. Nobody knows whether it is to be a comedy or an emotional drama, but it has been hinted that the reconstructed Missourian will endeavor to repay some of the venerable pilots who puff, and blow, and gas on the Father of Waters for remembering him so readily. Meantime, while all this was going on, the Osgoods in Boston were hurrying forward this volume, the advance sheets of which have reached us. Heretofore, Mr. Clemens, who is in the habit of looking keenly after his interests, has not displayed any fondness for publishers. He has been inclined to look upon them as the inventors of a new and profitable method of highway robbery, and he has had a theory that a man who writes a book ought to secure at least as large a share of the profits as the man who prints it. Doubtless he has not given up his theory. It is a very comfortable one, and has been the means of bringing him in a couple of hundred thousand dollars, more or less. But he seems to have met his fate, so far as publishers are concerned, in Mr. Osgood, for this volume, published in Boston yesterday, is the first book which Mr. Clemens has entrusted to the regular channels of the book trade, the only one which may be bought of any bookseller who may desire to keep it in stock. This is the beginning of a new policy on the part of the author, and, as he is one of the few literary men in the country who have an eye for business, it can hardly be said to be an experiment. In its general character, the book is similar to Mark Twain's well known "Sketches," of which more than one hundred thousand copies have been sold. It consists of eighteen sketches and short stories, the first of which, "The Stolen White Elephant," gives it its title. In other climes than ours, this story might seem to be a stupendous exaggeration, and yet it is merely a humorous development of facts. It is in fact a pungent satire upon the fraudulent concerns known as detective agencies, and, as a satire, it points its own pithy moral. This is the unctuous feature that separates Mr. Clemens's writings widely and permanently from the host of imitators that have sprung up, and from the bulk of the so-called humor of the day.

Exaggeration is ludicrous, but it is not genuine humor; and the difference between Mark Twain and those who give forth exaggerations only is the fundamental difference that exists between emptiness and pungency. It is the difference that makes trash of one and literature of the other. A little study of the most (apparently) reckless sketch in this volume will show that it has a purpose beyond that which lies upon the surface—the keen blade of the satire is sheathed in a most kindly humor which by no means interferes with the carving arrangements. Witness, for instance, the side-splitting essay "On the Decay of the Art of Lying, read at a Meeting of the Historical and Antiquarian Club of Hartford." After one is through laughing at the humor of this essay, then one has an opportunity to discover that it is really a satire upon the social environment which compels people to lie in spite of themselves. There is another quality of Mr. Clemens's writings, which has never been appreciated at its full value because it has grown up quietly under the shadow of his humor. We allude to his remarkable powers of description displayed not only in connection with the people he meets, but in connection with the scenery which happens to strike his fancy. We should select "Some Rambling Notes of an Idle Excursion" as by far the best sketch from a literary point of view to be found in the new volume. The humor is delightful, the character drawing is exceptionally fine, and the descriptions of natural scenery—little bits of color here and there—are genuine revelations. They are thoroughly sympathetic, showing that the man who gave the first impulse to what has come to be a wild riot of American humor, has a keen appreciation of the subtler manifestations of character as well as he [sic] faculty of interpreting the manifestations of nature. Nothing need be said of the humor; that is understood as a matter of course. When it doesn't drown out everything else, it subsides into a gentle undertone and then it is at its best. Here is a pretty little picture of Bermuda:

"The country roads curve and wind hither and thither in the delightfulest way, unfolding pretty surprises at every turn; billowy masses of oleander that seem to float out from behind distant projections like the pink-cloud banks of sunset; sudden plunges among cottages and gardens, life and activity, followed by as sudden plunges into the sombre twilight and stillness of the woods; flitting visions of white fortresses and beacon towers pictured against the sky on remote hill-tops; glimpses of shining green sea caught for a moment through opening headlands, then lost again; more woods and solitude; and by and by another turn lays bare, without warning, the full sweep of the inland ocean, enriched with its bars of soft color, and graced with its wandering sails."

This was Mr. Clemens speaking. Presently Mr. Twain has the floor. What is he saying?

"We have a tree that bears grapes, and just as calmly and unostentatiously as a vine would do it. We saw an India rubber tree, but out of season, possibly, as there were no shoes on it, nor suspenders, nor anything that a person could properly expect to find there. This gave it an impressively fraudulent look. There was exactly one mahogony [sic] tree on the island. I know this to be reliable, because I saw a man who said he had counted it many a time and could not be mistaken. He was a man with a hare-lip and a pure heart, and everybody said he was true as steel. Such men are all too few."

Mr. Clemens's humorous perceptions enable him to go to the very core of charater [sic], and his later work, notably "The Prince and the Pauper," shows a remarkable development of the sense of artistic purpose and proportion. Putting this and that and some other things together, we may remark that should he finally write the American novel that everybody is waiting for, some would probably be surprised, but there are a great many others who would receive the information as a matter of course. Meanwhile, those who are content to wait for that performance can pass away a portion of the time very pleasantly by securing this volume of sketches.

—Joel Chandler Harris, review of
*The Stolen White Elephant, Atlanta
Constitution*, June 11, 1882

WILLIAM DEAN HOWELLS "MARK TWAIN" (1882)

In reading the many reviews of Mark Twain's work by the American novelist and critic William Dean Howells, and specifically after his review of *The Innocents Abroad* in 1869, readers should exercise some critical caution. Bear in mind that Howells was reviewing the work of a close friend and occasional collaborator. Are Howells's opinions to be valued less because of this? At what point does criticism become promotion?

One of the most noteworthy aspects of this article is Howells's attempt to locate Twain's place in an American humorist tradition and, more importantly, to divorce or exempt him from it: "Mark Twain transcends all other American humorists in the universal qualities."

While John Nichol, writing in the same year as Howells, found Artemus Ward to be the redeeming figure in the American humor invasion, Howells places Twain far outside this tradition—a positioning he would uphold for the next thirty years. Howells offers a telling analysis of the humorists who came before Twain (and before Reconstruction). They were "on the side of slavery, of drunkenness and of irreligion; the friends of civilization were their prey; their spirit was thoroughly vulgar and base." After the Civil War, a note of squeamishness enters letters, and Howells was one of its chief proponents.

Students exploring the reinvention of Mark Twain, his rehabilitation from a Jacksonian to a proper Victorian, will find plenty of material here. Is Howells's campaign for Mark Twain comparable to the Widow Douglas's "sivilizing" of Huckleberry Finn? Does Howells speak for Twain, or for his would-be "sivilizers"? Why were Howells and Twain so embarrassed of their pasts? ("The average American is the man who has risen; . . . he has very often known squalor; and now, in his prosperity, he regards the past with a sort of large, pitying amusement.") This is an argument that remains active among scholars.

Howells also considers Twain's ethical speculations, his literary strengths, and his popularity and wonders how he translates so well abroad when he is as American as "boarding-house hash." Students might compare Howell's incredulous view with that held by Thomas Hardy, in the entry following this one, when Hardy remarks on how "Mark Twain did more than any other man to make plain people in England understand plain people in America." Conversely, Howells notes later how Twain avoids lifting tone and quip from Dickens or Thackeray, when many of his contemporaries shamelessly indulged in openly aping the two. Students researching either the American quality of Twain or seeking explanations for Twain's inordinate international success should look here.

Finally, of *Tom Sawyer*, Howells argues that the novel contains "an excess of reality," again casting Howells, in the view of many later critics, as a stiff and starchy prude, ill-equipped to criticize, much less edit, Mark Twain.

In one form or other, Mr. Samuel L. Clemens has told the story of his life in his books, and in sketching his career I shall have to recur to the leading facts rather than to offer fresh information. He was remotely of Virginian origin and more remotely of good English stock; the name was well known before his time in the South, where a senator, a congressman, and other dignitaries had worn it; but his branch of the family fled from the destitution of those vast landed possessions in Tennessee, celebrated in *The Gilded Age*, and went very poor to Missouri. Mr. Clemens was born on November 30, 1835, at Florida in the latter State, but his father removed shortly afterward to Hannibal, a small town on the Mississippi, where most of the humorist's boyhood was spent. Hannibal as a name is hopelessly confused and ineffective; but if we can know nothing of Mr. Clemens from Hannibal, we can know much of Hannibal from Mr. Clemens, who, in fact, has studied a loafing, out-at-elbows, down-at-the-heels, slaveholding Mississippi River town of thirty years ago, with such strong reality in his boy's romance of *Tom Sawyer*, that we need inquire nothing further concerning the type. The original perhaps no longer exists anywhere; certainly not in Hannibal, which has grown into a flourishing little city since Mr. Clemens sketched it. In his time the two embattled forces of civilization and barbarism were encamped at Hannibal, as they are at all times and everywhere; the morality of the place was the morality of a slaveholding community: fierce, arrogant, one-sided—this virtue for white, and that for black folks; and the religion was Calvinism in various phases, with its predestinate aristocracy of saints and its rabble of hopeless sinners. Doubtless, young Clemens escaped neither of the opposing influences wholly. His people like the rest were slaveholders; but his father, like so many other slaveholders, abhorred slavery—silently, as he must in such a time and place. If the boy's sense of justice suffered anything of that perversion which so curiously and pitiably maimed the reason of the whole South, it does not appear in his books, where there is not an ungenerous line, but always, on the contrary, a burning resentment of all manner of cruelty and wrong.

The father, an austere and singularly upright man, died bankrupt when Clemens was twelve years old, and the boy had thereafter to make what scramble he could for an education. He got very little learning in school, and like so many other Americans in whom the literary impulse is native, he turned to the local printing-office for some of the advantages from which he was otherwise cut off. Certain records of the three years spent in the Hannibal *Courier* office are to be found in Mark Twain's book of sketches; but I believe there is yet no history anywhere of the *wanderjahre*, in which he followed the life of a jour printer, from town to town, and from city to city, penetrating even so far into the vague and fabled East as Philadelphia and New York.

He returned to his own town—his *patria*—sated, if not satisfied, with travel, and at seventeen he resolved to "learn the river" from St. Louis to New Orleans as a steamboat pilot. Of this period of his life he has given a full account in the delightful series of papers, *Piloting on the Mississippi*, which he printed seven years ago in the *Atlantic Monthly*. The growth of the railroads and the outbreak of the Civil War put an end to profitable piloting, and at twenty-four he was again open to a vocation. He listened for a moment to the loudly calling drum of that time, and he was actually in camp for three weeks on the rebel side; but the unorganized force to which he belonged was disbanded, and he finally did not "go with his section" either in sentiment or in fact. His brother having been appointed Lieutenant-Governor of Nevada Territory, Mr. Clemens went out with him as his private secretary; but he soon resigned his office and withdrew to the mines. He failed as a miner, in the ordinary sense; but the life of the mining-camp yielded him the wealth that the pockets of the mountain denied; he had the Midas touch without knowing it, and all these grotesque experiences have since turned into gold under his hand. After his failure as a miner had become evident even to himself, he was glad to take the place of local editor on the Virginia City *Enterprise*, a newspaper for which he had amused himself in writing from time to time. He had written for the newspapers before this; few Americans escape that fate; and as an apprentice in the Hannibal *Courier* office his humor had embroiled some of the leading citizens, and impaired the fortunes of that journal by the alienation of several delinquent subscribers.

But it was in the *Enterprise* that he first used his pseudonym of "Mark Twain," which he borrowed from the vernacular of the river, where the man heaving the lead calls out "Mark *twain*!" instead of "Mark *two*!" In 1864, he accepted, on the San Francisco *Morning Call*, the same sort of place which he had held on the *Enterprise*, and he soon made his *nom de guerre* familiar "on that coast"; he not only wrote "local items" in the *Call*, but he printed humorous sketches in various periodicals, and, two years later, he was sent to the Sandwich Islands as correspondent of a Sacramento paper.

When he came back he "entered the lecture-field," as it used to be phrased. Of these facts there is, as all English-speaking readers know, full record in *Roughing It*, though I think Mr. Clemens has not mentioned there his association with that extraordinary group of wits and poets, of whom Mr. Bret Harte, Mr. Charles Warren Stoddard, Mr. Charles H. Webb, Mr. Prentice Mulford, were, with himself, the most conspicuous. These ingenious young men, with the fatuity of gifted people, had established a literary newspaper in San Francisco, and they brilliantly co-operated to its early extinction.

In 1867, Mr. Clemens made in the *Quaker City* the excursion to Europe and the East which he has commemorated in *The Innocents Abroad*. Shortly after his return he married, and placed himself at Buffalo, where he bought an interest in one of the city newspapers; later he came to Hartford, where he has since remained, except for the two years spent in a second visit to Europe. The incidents of this visit he has characteristically used in *A Tramp Abroad*; and, in fact, I believe the only book of Mr. Clemens's which is not largely autobiographical is *The Prince and the Pauper*: the scene being laid in

England, in the early part of the sixteenth century, the difficulties presented to a nineteenth-century autobiographer were insurmountable.

The habit of putting his own life, not merely in its results but in its processes, into his books, is only one phase of the frankness of Mr. Clemens's humorous attitude. The transparent disguise of the pseudonym once granted him, he asks the reader to grant him nothing else. In this he differs wholly from most other American humorists, who have all found some sort of dramatization of their personality desirable if not necessary. Charles F. Browne, "delicious" as he was when he dealt with us directly, preferred the disguise of "Artemus Ward" the showman; Mr. Locke likes to figure as "Petroleum V. Nasby," the cross-roads politician; Mr. Shaw chooses to masquerade as the saturnine philosopher "Josh Billings"; and each of these humorists appeals to the grotesqueness of misspelling to help out his fun. It was for Mr. Clemens to reconcile the public to humor which contented itself with the established absurdities of English orthography; and I am inclined to attribute to the example of his immense success, the humane spirit which characterizes our recent popular humor. There is still sufficient flippancy and brutality in it; but there is no longer the stupid and monkeyish cruelty of motive and intention which once disgraced and insulted us. Except the political humorists, like Mr. Lowell—if there were any like him—the American humorists formerly chose the wrong in public matters; they were on the side of slavery, of drunkenness, and of irreligion; the friends of civilization were their prey; their spirit was thoroughly vulgar and base. Before "John Phoenix," there was scarcely any American humorist—not of the distinctly literary sort—with whom one could smile and keep one's self-respect. The great Artemus himself was not guiltless; but the most popular humorist who ever lived has not to accuse himself, so far as I can remember, of having written anything to make one morally ashamed of liking him. One can readily make one's strictures; there is often more than a suggestion of forcing in his humor; sometimes it tends to horse-play; sometimes the extravagance overleaps itself, and falls flat on the other side; but I cannot remember that in Mr. Clemens's books I have ever been asked to join him in laughing at any good or really fine thing. But I do not mean to leave him with this negative praise; I mean to say of him that as Shakespeare, according to Mr. Lowell's saying, was the first to make poetry all poetical, Mark Twain was the first to make humor all humorous. He has not only added more in bulk to the sum of harmless pleasures than any other humorist; but more in the spirit that is easily and wholly enjoyable. There is nothing lost in literary attitude, in labored dictionary funning, in affected quaintness, in dreary dramatization, in artificial "dialect"; Mark Twain's humor is as simple in form and as direct as the statesmanship of Lincoln or the generalship of Grant.

When I think how purely and wholly American it is, I am a little puzzled at its universal acceptance. We are doubtless the most thoroughly homogeneous people that ever existed as a great nation. There is such a parity in the experiences of Americans that Mark Twain or Artemus Ward appeals as unerringly to the consciousness of our fifty millions as Goldoni appealed to that of his hundred thousand Venetians. In our phrase, we have somehow all "been there"; in fact, generally, and in sympathy almost certainly, we have been there. In another generation or two, perhaps, it will be wholly different; but as yet the average American is the man who has risen; he has known poverty, and privation, and low conditions; he has very often known squalor; and now, in his prosperity, he regards the past with a sort of large, pitying amusement; he is not the least ashamed of it; he does not feel that it characterizes him any more than the future does. Our humor springs from this multiform American experience of life, and securely addresses itself—in reminiscence, in phrase, in its whole material—to the intelligence bred of like experience. It is not of a class for a class; it does not employ itself with the absurdities of a tailor as a tailor; its conventions, if it has any, are all new, and of American make. When it mentions hash we smile because we have each somehow known the cheap boarding-house or restaurant; when it alludes to putting up stoves in the fall, each of us feels the grime and rust of the pipes on his hands; the introduction of the lightning-rod man, or the book-agent, establishes our brotherhood with the humorist at once. But how is it with the vast English-speaking world outside of these States, to which hash, and stovepipes, and lightning-rod men and book-agents are as strange as lords and ladies, dungeon-keeps and battlements are to us? Why in fine should an English chief justice keep Mark Twain's books always at hand? Why should Darwin have gone to them for rest and refreshment at midnight when spent with scientific research?

I suppose that Mark Twain transcends all other American humorists in the universal qualities. He deals very little with the pathetic, which he nevertheless knows very well how to manage, as he has shown, notably in the true story of the old slave-mother; but there is a poetic lift in his work, even when he permits you to recognize it only as something satirized. There is always the touch of nature, the presence of a sincere and frank manliness in what he says, the companionship of a spirit which is at once delightfully open and deliciously shrewd. Elsewhere I have tried to persuade the reader that his humor is at its best the foamy break of the strong tide of earnestness in him. But it would be limiting him unjustly to describe him as a satirist; and it is hardly practicable to establish him in people's minds as a moralist; he has made them laugh too long; they will not believe him serious; they think some joke is always intended. This is the penalty, as Doctor Holmes has pointed out, of making one's first success as a humorist. There was a paper of Mark Twain's printed in the *Atlantic Monthly* some years ago and called "The Facts Concerning the Late Carnival of Crime in Connecticut," which ought to have won popular recognition of the ethical intelligence underlying his humor. It was, of course, funny; but under the fun it was an impassioned study of the human conscience. Hawthorne or Bunyan might have been proud to imagine that powerful allegory, which had a grotesque force far beyond either of them. It had been read before a literary club in Hartford; a reverend gentleman had offered the author his pulpit for the next Sunday if he would give it as a homily there. Yet it quite failed of the response I had hoped for it, and I shall not insist here upon Mark Twain as a moralist; though I warn the reader that if he leaves out of the account an indignant sense of right and wrong, a scorn of all affectation and pretence, an ardent hate of meanness and injustice, he will come indefinitely short of knowing Mark Twain.

His powers as a story-teller were evident in hundreds of brief sketches before he proved them in *Tom Sawyer* and *The Prince and the Pauper*. Both of these books, aside from their strength of characterization, are fascinating as mere narratives, and I can think of no writer living who has in higher degree the art of interesting his reader from the first word. This is a far rarer gift than we imagine, and I shall not call it a subordinate charm in Mark Twain's books, rich as they otherwise are. I have already had my say about *Tom Sawyer*, whose only fault is an excess of reality in portraying the character and conditions of Southwestern boyhood as it was forty years ago, and which is full of that poetic sympathy with nature and human nature which I always find in Mark Twain. *The Prince and the Pauper* has particularly interested me for the same qualities which, in a study of the past, we call romantic, but which alone can realize the past for us. Occasionally the archaic diction gives way and lets us down hard upon the American parlance of the nineteenth century; but mainly the illusion is admirably sustained, and the tale is to be valued not only in itself, but as an earnest of what Mr. Clemens might do in fiction when he has fairly done with autobiography in its various forms. His invention is of the good old sort, like De Foe's more than that of any other English writer, and like that of the Spanish picaresque novelists, Mendoza and the rest; it flows easily from incident to incident, and does not deepen into situation. In the romance it operates as lightly and unfatiguingly as his memory in the realistic story.

His books abound in passages of dramatic characterization, and he is, as the reader knows, the author of the most successful American play. I believe Mr. Clemens has never claimed the reconstruction of Colonel Sellers for the stage; but he nevertheless made the play, for whatever is good in it came bodily from his share of the novel of *The Gilded Age*. It is a play which succeeds by virtue of the main personage, and this personage, from first to last, is quite outside of the dramatic action, which sometimes serves and sometimes does not serve the purpose of presenting Colonel Sellers. Where the drama fails, Sellers rises superior and takes the floor; and we forget the rest. Mr. Raymond conceived the character wonderfully well, and he plays it with an art that ranks him to that extent with the great actors; but he has in nowise "created" it. If any one "created" Colonel Sellers, it was Mark Twain, as the curious reader may see on turning again to the novel; but I suspect that Colonel Sellers was never created, except as other men are; that he was found somewhere and transferred, living, to the book.

I prefer to speak of Mr. Clemens's artistic qualities because it is to these that his humor will owe its perpetuity. All fashions change, and nothing more wholly and quickly than the fashion of fun; as any one may see by turning back to what amused people in the last generation; that stuff is terrible. As Europe becomes more and more the playground of Americans, and every scene and association becomes insipidly familiar, the jokes about the old masters and the legends will no longer be droll to us. Neither shall we care for the huge Californian mirth, when the surprise of the picturesquely mixed civilization and barbarism of the Pacific Coast has quite died away; and Mark Twain would pass with the conditions that have made him intelligible, if he were not an artist of uncommon power as well as a humorist. He portrays and interprets real types, not only with exquisite appreciation and sympathy, but with a force and truth of drawing that makes them permanent. Artemus Ward was very funny, that can never be denied; but it must be owned that the figure of the literary showman is as wholly factitious as his spelling; the conception is one that has to be constantly humored by the reader. But the innumerable characters sketched by Mark Twain are actualities, however caricatured—and, usually, they are not so very much caricatured. He has brought back the expression of Western humor to sympathy with the same orthography of John Phoenix; but Mark Twain is vastly more original in form. Derby was weighed upon by literary tradition; he was "academic" at times, but Mr. Clemens is never "academic." There is no drawing from casts; in his work evidently the life has everywhere been studied: and it is his apparent unconsciousness of any other way of saying a thing except the natural way that makes his books so restful and refreshing. Our little nervous literary sensibilities may suffer from his extravagance, or from other traits of his manner, but we have not to beat our breasts at the dread apparition of Dickens's or Thackeray's hand in his page. He is far too honest and sincere a soul for that; and where he is obliged to force a piece of humor to its climax—as sometimes happens—he does not call in his neighbors to help; he does it himself, and is probably sorry that he had to do it.

I suppose that even in so slight and informal a study as this, something like an "analysis" of our author's humor is expected. But I much prefer not to make it. I have observed that analyses of humor are apt to leave one rather serious, and to result in an entire volatilization of the humor. If the prevailing spirit of Mark Twain's humor is not a sort of good-natured self-satire, in which the reader may see his own absurdities reflected, I scarcely should be able to determine it.

—William Dean Howells, "Mark Twain,"
Century, September 1882

Thomas Hardy (1883)

Thomas Hardy was an acclaimed English novelist and poet. His novels include *Far From the Madding Crowd, Jude the Obscure,* and *Tess of the D'Urbervilles*, among many works set in the fictional county of Wessex (which corresponds closely with the southern and southwestern parts of England). Hardy's poetry and fiction can ring unremittingly bleak, so his affection for Mark Twain's work might seem surprising. Hardy once asked William Dean Howells: "Why don't people understand that Mark Twain is not merely a great humorist? He's a very remarkable fellow in a very different way."

The Early Life of Thomas Hardy, ostensibly written by his second wife, Florence, was actually the work of Hardy himself. Published in 1928, it includes this excerpt from Hardy's diary entry of June 23, 1883, in which Hardy recalls the legend of Twain at the Whittier birthday dinner, adding a final, apparently apocryphal, twist to the tale. Hardy's amusement at Twain's predicament is itself humorous.

Students comparing Twain to his British contemporaries, or those students interested in the wider repercussions of Twain's gaffe at the Whittier dinner, should consult Hardy's words.

"*June 25.* Dined at the Savile with Gosse. Met W. D. Howells of New York there. He told me a story of Emerson's loss of memory. At the funeral of Longfellow he had to make a speech. 'The brightness and beauty of soul', he began, 'of him we have lost, has been acknowledged wherever the English language is spoken. I've known him these forty years; and no American, whatever may be his opinions, will deny that in—in—in—I can't remember the gentleman's name—beat the heart of a true poet.'

"Howells said that Mark Twain usually makes a good speech. But once he heard him fail. In his speech he was telling a story of an occasion when he was in some western city, and found that some impostors personating Longfellow, Emerson, and others had been there. Mark began to describe these impostors, and while doing it found that Longfellow, Emerson, etc. were present, listening, and, from a titter or two, found also that his satirical description of the impostors was becoming regarded as an oblique satirical description of the originals. He was overspread by a sudden cold chill, and struggled to a lame ending. He was so convinced that he had given offence that he wrote to Emerson and Longfellow, apologizing. Emerson could not understand the letter, his memory of the incident having failed him, and wrote to Mark asking what it meant. Then Mark had to tell him what he wished he had never uttered; and altogether the fiasco was complete."

—Thomas Hardy, from *The Early Life of*
Thomas Hardy, Florence Hardy, New York:
Macmillan, 1928, pp. 208–209

WILLIAM DEAN HOWELLS
"THE EDITOR'S STUDY" (1887)

Howells wrote "The Editor's Study" column in *Harper's Monthly* for six years. His view shows an obvious alteration from the one held by the same author five years earlier, when he chided Twain's "excess of reality" in the delineation of Tom Sawyer. By 1887, realism had become Howells's watchword, and he now upholds Twain's fidelity to the real as an example to follow.

Of subordinate fiction, of the sort which neither informs nor nourishes, a correspondent writes us, in sad conviction of the fact that the great mass of those who can read and write seem to ask for nothing better: "Do you think our novel-reading public cares much for any masterpiece? It appears to me that the ordinary or uncultivated mind revolts from anything much higher than itself. Here is another lofty stair to climb; here is a new dialect of thought, and even of language, to struggle with; here is somebody insulting us by speaking a foreign tongue." There is suggestion in this, and truth enough for serious pause; and yet we think that it hardly does justice to the power of the ordinary mind to appreciate the best. Much of the best fails of due recognition, but enough of the best gets it to make us hopeful that when literature comes close to life, even ordinary minds will feel and know its charm. We think that there is proof of this in the vast popularity of our humorists, in the fame of the greatest, whose pseudonym is at this moment as well known, in America at least, as the name of Shakespeare. We need not blink any of his shortcomings in recognizing that his books are masterpieces of humor; they are so, and yet our public does care for them in prodigious degree, and it cares for them because incomparably more and better than any other American books they express a familiar and almost universal quality of the American mind, they faithfully portray a phase of American life, which they reflect in its vast kindliness and good-will, its shrewdness and its generosity, its informality, which is not formlessness; under every fantastic disguise they are honest and true. That is all we ask of fiction—sense and truth; we cannot prophesy that every novel which has them will have the success of *The Innocents Abroad*, or of *Roughing It*, but we believe recognition wide and full will await it. Let fiction cease to lie about life; let it portray men and women as they are, actuated by the motives and the passions in the measure we all know; let it leave off painting dolls and working them by springs and wires; let it show the different interests in their true proportions; let it forbear to preach pride and revenge, folly and insanity, egotism and prejudice, but frankly own these for what they are, in whatever figures and occasions they appear; let it not put on fine literary airs; let it speak the dialect, the language, that most Americans know—the language of unaffected people everywhere— and we believe that even its masterpieces will find a response in all readers.

—William Dean Howells, "The Editor's Study," *Harper's Monthly*, May 1887

OSCAR WILDE "THE CHILD-PHILOSOPHER" (1887)

The Irish dramatist, poet, critic, and wit Oscar Wilde here demonstrates his appreciation of Mark Twain's "amazing and amusing record" of American schoolchildren. When Wilde lived on Tite Street, in London's Chelsea district, he entertained many celebrities, including Mark Twain.

Though the Oracles are dumb, and the Prophets have taken to the turf, and the Sibyls are reduced to telling fortunes at bazaars, the ancient power of divination has not yet left the world. Mr. Mark Twain's fascinating article, in the current number of the Century Magazine, on "English as She is Taught" in his native country, throws an entirely new light on that *enfant terrible* of a commercial civilisation, the American child, and reminds us that we may all learn wisdom from the mouths of babes and sucklings. For the mistakes made by the interesting pupils of the American Board-Schools are not mistakes springing from ignorance of life or dulness of perception; they are, on the contrary, full of the richest suggestion, and pregnant with the very highest philosophy. No wonder that the American child educates its father and mother, when it can give us such luminous definitions as the following:—

> *Republican*, a sinner mentioned in the Bible.
> *Demagogue*, a vessel containing beer and other liquids.
> *The Constitution of the United States*, that part of the book at the end that nobody reads.
> *Plagiarist*, a writer of plays.
> *Equestrian*, one who ask questions.
> *Tenacious*, ten acres of land.
> *Quaternions*, a bird, with a flat beak and no bill, dwelling in New Zealand.
> *Franchise*, anything belonging to the French.

The last definition points very clearly to the fact that the fallacy of an extended Franchise is based on the French theory of equality, to which the child-philosopher seems also to allude when he says that—

> Things which are equal to each other are equal to anything else,

while the description of the Plagiarist is the most brilliant thing that has been said on modern literature for some time.

How true, also, in their directness and simplicity of phrase are such aphorisms as:—

> Some of the best fossils are found in theological cabinets.
> There are a good many donkeys in theological gardens.
> We should endeavour to avoid extremes—like those of wasps and bees.
> Congress is divided into civilised, half civilised, and savage.
> Climate lasts all the time, and weather only a few days.

The Constitution of the United States was established to ensure domestic hostility.

The body is mostly composed of water, and about one half is avaricious tissue.

How excellent are these views on History:—

The Puritans founded an insane asylum in the wilds of America.

The middle ages come in between antiquity and posterity.

Henry the Eight was famous for being a great widower having lost several wives.

Julius Caesar was really a very great man. He was a very great soldier and wrote a book for beginners in Latin.

The Stamp Act was to make everybody stamp all materials, so they should be null and void.

The only form of Government in Greece was a limited monkey.

How delightful these literary criticisms:—

Bulwell is considered a good writer.

Gibbon wrote a history of his travels in Italy. This was original.

Wm. Wordsworth wrote the Barefoot Boy and Immitations on Immortality.

A sort of sadness kind of shone in Bryant's poem.

Chaucer was the father of English pottery.

Holmes is a very profligate and amusing writer.

Sir Walter Scott, Charles Brontë, Alfred the Great, and Johnson were the first great novelists.

Chaucer was succeeded by H. Wads. Longfellow, an American writer. His writings were chiefly prose, and nearly one hundred years elapsed.

How valuable these results of a scientific education! How clearly they exemplify the importance of physiology as the basis of culture!

Physillogigy is to study about your bones, stummick, and vertebry.

The gastric juice keeps the bones from creaking.

The olfactory nerve enters the cavity of the orbit, and is developed into the special sense of hearing.

Nor should the influence of mathematics in developing a logical habit of mind be overlooked. How well it is shown in the following:—

A circle is a round straight line with a hole in the middle.
To find the number of square feet in a room, you multiply the room by
    the number of the feet. The product is the result.
The weight of the earth is found by comparing a mass of known lead
    with that of a mass of unknown lead.
Inertia is the negative quality of passiveness, either in recoverable latency
    or incipient latescence.

The metaphysical subtlety of the last statement shows that the child-philosopher is perfectly qualified to become a member of the psychical and the hermetic societies, and that with a little more study, he might develop into the most esoteric of all the Brompton Buddhists. Indeed, we sincerely hope that when the next bevy of beauties land on our shores from America, they will bring with them one specimen at least of the native school boy. For many of his utterances are obviously mystical, and possess that quality of absolute unintelligibility that is the peculiar privilege of the verbally inspired. In the case of such aphorisms, as—

The leopard is watching his sheep.
They had a strawberry vestibule.
The coercion of some things is remarkable; as bread and molasses.
The supercilious girl acted with vicissitude when the perennial time
    came.
You should take caution, and be precarious.

we must clearly, like Mr. Posket in "The Magistrate," read between the lines, and recognise that what to the uninitiated seems nonsense or platitude, to the humble transcendentalist is pure revelation. What a *trouvaille*, also, for Parliamentary speakers of the old school of Mr. Conybeare and Mr. Bradlaugh is the child-philosopher's list of word definitions! If mendacious only means "what can be mended," mercenary "one who feels for another," and parasite "a kind of umbrella," it is evident that latent, in the very lowest citizen of our community, lie capacities for platform oratory hitherto unsuspected. Even women, most complex of all modern problems, are analysed with a knowledge that in Europe is confined to poets and dandies. "They make fun of boys," says the child-philosopher, "and then turn round and love them."

Mr. Mark Twain deserves our warmest thanks for bringing to light the true American genius. American patriots are tedious, American millionaires go bankrupt, and American beauties don't last, but the schoolboy seems to be eternally delightful; and when the world has grown weary of Boston novelists, and tired of the civilisation of the telephone, the utterances of the child-philosopher will be treasured by the scientific historian as the best criticism upon modern education, the best epigram upon modern life.

—Oscar Wilde, "The Child-Philosopher,"
Court and Society Review, vol. IV,
no. 146, April 20, 1887

ANDREW LANG "ON THE ART OF MARK TWAIN" (1891)

Andrew Lang's review of Mark Twain, written regrettably at Twain's request (see Twain's letter to Lang regarding *A Connecticut Yankee*), begins by locating him in a larger context—in Lang's musings on the state of "Culture." In a refrain familiar to this day, Lang explains how alienated he feels from the doyens of culture and how at its heart it seems to him now superficial and inauthentic. Lang uses Mark Twain as an instrument to indict this culture.

Twain, he says, is dismissed by the supposed cultural elite as a "Barbarian." While Lang cannot defend *A Connecticut Yankee,* he does defend *Huckleberry Finn*, preferring it to Harriet Beecher Stowe's *Uncle Tom's Cabin*, since the former was written "without partisanship and without 'a purpose.'" Students comparing literary treatments of slavery may find Lang's work useful. Lang notes that, by speaking through Huck Finn, Twain was able to imbue his work with a seriousness lacking in his previous fiction. He compares Huck Finn to Odysseus and Twain to Homer—perhaps this is the first instance of such a comparison. It certainly is not the last. Students discussing the common ground between *Huckleberry Finn* and Homer's *Odyssey* should read Lang closely.

Lang praises Twain's descriptive powers (successive reviewers also note that Twain was becoming adept at description) but faults the "burlesque" ending, which would remain a subject of great debate well into the twentieth century. The fault is redeemed, though, according to Lang, by Tom Sawyer's "real unconscious heroism." Furthermore, Lang pronounces *Huckleberry Finn* "the great American novel," one which has gone unnoticed by culture's snobbish radar. This article is valuable because it anticipates views of Twain and of *Huckleberry Finn* that would fully develop in the next century.

The duty of self-examination is frequently urged upon us by moralists. No doubt we should self-examine our minds as well as our conduct now and then, especially when we have passed the age in which we are constantly examined by other people. When I attempt to conduct this delicate inquiry I am puzzled and alarmed at finding that I am losing Culture. I am backsliding. I have not final perseverance, unless indeed it is Culture that is backsliding and getting on to the wrong lines. For I ought to be cultured: it is my own fault if I have not got Culture.

I have been educated till I nearly dropped; I have lived with the earliest Apostles of Culture, in the days when Chippendale was first a name to conjure with, and Japanese art came in like a raging lion, and Ronsard was the favourite poet, and Mr. William Morris was a poet too, and blue and green were the only wear, and the name of Paradise was Camelot. To be sure, I cannot say that I took all this quite seriously, but 'we too have played' at it, and know all about it. Generally speaking, I have kept up with Culture. I can talk (if desired) about Sainte-Beuve, and Mérimée, and Félicien Rops: I could rhyme 'Ballades,' when they were 'in,' and knew what a *pantoom* was. I am acquainted with the scholia on the Venetus A. I have a pretty taste in Greek gems. I have got beyond the stage of thinking Mr. Cobden Sanderson a greater binder than Bauzonnet. With practice, I believe I could do an epigram of Meleager's into a bad imitation of a sonnet by Joachim du Bellay, or a sonnet of Bellay's into a bad imitation of a Greek epigram. I could pass an examination in the works of M. Paul Bourget. And yet I have not Culture. For Culture has got into new regions where I cannot enter, and, what is perhaps worse, I find myself delighting in a great many things which are under the ban of Culture.

This is a dreadful position, which makes a man feel like one of those Liberal politicians who are always 'sitting on the fence,' and who follow their party, if follow it they do, with the reluctant acquiescence of the prophet's donkey. Not that I do follow it. I cannot rave with pleasure over Tolstoi, especially as he admits that 'the Kreutzer Sonata' is not 'only his fun' but a kind of Manifesto. I have tried Hartmann, and I prefer Plato. I don't like poems by young ladies in which the verses neither scan nor rhyme, and the constructions are all linguistically impossible. I am shaky about Blake, though I am stalwart about Mr. Rudyard Kipling.

This is not the worst of it. Culture has hardly a new idol but I long to hurl things at it. Culture can scarcely burn anything, but I am impelled to sacrifice to that same. I am coming to suspect that the majority of Culture's modern disciples are a mere crowd of very slimly educated people, who have no natural taste or impulse; who do not really know the best things in literature; who have a feverish desire to admire the newest thing, to follow the latest artistic fashion; who prate about 'style' without the faintest acquaintance with the ancient examples of style, in Greek, French, or English; who talk about the classics and criticise the classical critics and poets, without being able to read a line of them in the original. Nothing of the natural man is left in these people; their intellectual equipment is made up of ignorant vanity, and eager desire of novelty, and a yearning to be in the fashion.

Take, for example—and we have been a long time in coming to him— Mark Twain. If you praise him among persons of Culture, they cannot believe that you are serious. They call him a Barbarian. They won't hear of him, they hurry from the subject; they pass by on the other side of the way. Now I do not mean to assert that Mark Twain is 'an impeccable artist', but he is just as far from being a mere coarse buffoon. Like other people, he has his limitations. Even Mr. Gladstone, for instance, does not shine as a Biblical critic, nor Mark Twain as a critic of Italian art nor as a guide to the Holy Land. I have abstained from reading his work on an American at the Court of King Arthur, because here Mark Twain is not, and cannot be, at the proper point of view. He has not the knowledge which would enable him to be a sound critic of the ideal of the Middle Ages. An Arthurian Knight in New York or in Washington would find as much to blame, and justly, as a Yankee at Camelot. Let it be admitted that Mark Twain often and often sins against good taste, that some of his waggeries are mechanical, that his books are full of passages which were only good enough for the corner of a newspaper. . . .

If the critics are right who think that art should so far imitate nature as to leave things at loose ends, as it were, not pursuing events to their conclusions, even here 'Huckleberry Finn' should satisfy them. It is the story of the flight down the Mississippi of a white boy and a runaway slave. The stream takes them through the fringes of life on the riverside; they pass feuds and murders of men, and towns full of homicidal loafers, and are intermingled with the affairs of families, and meet friends whom they would wish to be friends always. But the current carries them on: they leave the murders unavenged, the lovers in full flight; the friends they lose for ever; we do not know, any more than in reality we would know, 'what became of them all.' They do not return, as in novels, and narrate their later adventures.

As to the truth of the life described, the life in little innocent towns, the religion, the Southern lawlessness, the feuds, the lynchings, only persons who have known this changed world can say if it be truly painted, but it looks like the very truth, like an historical document. Already 'Huckleberry Finn' is an historical novel, and more valuable, perhaps, to the historian than 'Uncle Tom's Cabin,' for it is written without partisanship, and without 'a purpose.' The drawing of character seems to be admirable, unsurpassed in its kind. By putting the tale in the mouth of the chief actor, Huck, Mark Twain was enabled to give it a seriousness not common in his work, and to abstain from comment. Nothing can be more true and more humorous than the narrative of this outcast boy, with a heart naturally good, with a conscience torn between the teaching of his world about slavery and the promptings of his nature. In one point Mark Twain is Homeric, probably without knowing it. In the Odyssey, Odysseus frequently tells a false tale about himself, to account for his appearance and position when disguised on his own island. He shows extraordinary fertility and appropriateness of invention, wherein he is equalled by the feigned tales of Huckleberry Finn. The casual characters met on the way are masterly: the woman who detects Huck in a girl's dress; the fighting families of Shepherdson and Grangerford; the homicidal Colonel Sherborne, who cruelly shoots old Boggs, and superbly quells the mob of would-be lynchers; the various old aunts and uncles; the negro Jim; the two wandering impostors; the hateful father of Huck himself. Then Huck's compliment to Miss Mary Jane, whom he thought of afterwards 'a many and a many million times,' how excellent it is! 'In my opinion she had more sand in her than any girl I ever see; in my opinion she was just full of sand. It sounds like flattery, but it ain't no flattery. And when it comes to beauty—and goodness, too—she lays over them all.' No novel has better touches of natural description; the starlit nights on the great river, the storms, the whole landscape, the sketches of little rotting towns, of the woods, of the cotton-fields, are simple, natural, and visible to the mind's eye. The story, to be sure, ends by lapsing into burlesque, when Tom Sawyer insists on freeing the slave whom he knows to be free already, in a manner accordant with 'the best authorities.' But even the burlesque is redeemed by Tom's real unconscious heroism. There are defects of taste, or passages that to us seem deficient in taste, but the book remains a nearly flawless gem of romance and of humour. The world appreciates it, no doubt, but 'cultured critics' are probably unaware of its singular value. A two-shilling novel by Mark Twain, with an ugly picture on the cover, 'has no show,' as Huck might say, and the great American novel has escaped the eyes of those who watch to see this new planet swim into their ken. And will Mark Twain never write such another?

One is enough for him to live by, and for our gratitude, but not enough for our desire.

—Andrew Lang, "On the Art of Mark Twain,"
Illustrated News of the World (London),
reprinted in *The Critic* (New York),
July 25, 1891, pp. 45–46

WILLIAM MONTGOMERY CLEMENS (1894)

Unlike Cyril Clemens, Will Clemens could not even claim to be a cousin many times removed. Nevertheless, this is perhaps the first full biography of Twain, as can be seen in Mark Twain's letter to Will Clemens, included in this volume.

Nevertheless, the author's praise for his subject is slightly muted. He was "not even a good journalist," Clemens opines, and he does not hesitate to regard Charles Dickens as "the greater genius." Like others, Clemens remarks on the Americanism of Mark Twain, particularly as embodied in his social transformation. Again, the origin of the tale "Punch Brothers, Punch" is given, along with an interesting adaptation of that tale by the English poet Algernon Charles Swinburne, which indicates, if little else, how various Twain's audience was.

From the days of "Yankee Doodle" and the "Frogs of Windham," two gems of early American humor written in the Revolutionary period, until near the close of the war of the Rebellion, the recognized American humorist, the wit who could cause a laugh to go rippling, bubbling around the world, was a creation unknown to American literature. However, out of respect and admiration for their genius, their wit and humor, we must not fail in giving proper credit to Francis Hopkinson, Samuel Peters, John Trumbull, George F. Hopkins, William T. Thompson, Seba Smith, Joseph C. Neal, Orpheus C. Kerr, George H. Derby and a host of others, for bringing out in the American prints, those native characteristics, the drollness of the yankee and the wit of the early days, but not until after the Rebellion did America produce a humorist of world-wide reputation. When civil strife was ended, and the American began a new career, almost a new existence, there came to the surface a new school of native humor. The names of Mark Twain, Artemus Ward, Josh Billings and one or two others, became household words. Their funny sayings caused the Englishman to smile between his bites of beef. Their droll humor forced our German cousin to shake his sides with laughter. Their witty bon mots occasioned prolonged mirth from our friends in France. Not until then did we become known as a nation of humorists, and from that day the fame of our wits has extended throughout the entire world. To-day a ripple of mirth starting on the banks of Mud Flat Creek, will end in a hurricane of laughter on the Thames or the Seine.

There was something so purely American in the humor of Mark Twain, that his work soon made for him a place in native literature. As a representative of American life and character his name extended even beyond the confines of the continent of Europe, into all lands and among all peoples. In Paris one cannot purchase a Bible at the book stall, but one may find "Roughing It" at every corner. In Rome, "The Innocents Abroad" is one of the staples in the book marts. In Hongkong you will find Mark Twain. Everywhere they read him.

The career of Mark Twain is a romance. His life is a curious medley of pathos and poverty, with an occasional laugh to help along over the rough places. He was a wild, reckless boy, a poor printer, not even a good journalist, an adventurer, a wanderer. He was a sort of human kaleidoscope. He then became a wit, a scholar, a public speaker, a man of family and a millionaire. All this is but typical of America, of American life and American character.

Mark Twain is more than a mere Punch and Judy show. With his droll humor there comes information. He gives the reader a full dinner, not merely dessert. He tells you more about the Mississippi river than an old steamboatman. He gives you a world of information about Germany and Switzerland. He is better than a guide book for the Holy Land. What that greater genius Charles Dickens has done for fiction, Mark Twain does for humor. He is an ideal reporter. He minutely tells us all about a thing, tells us what he sees and hears, describes a man, a mule or a monarchy in excellent form, and makes one laugh at the same time.

Some years ago I was prompted to write the genial Mr. Clemens for an introduction or preface to a little volume of mine, long since buried by the sands of time. His reply was this:

Hartford, Conn., Nov. 18.
"WILL M. CLEMENS.

"My Dear Friend: Your letter received. God bless your heart. I would like ever so much to comply with your request, but I am thrashing away at my new book, and am afraid that I should not find time to write my own epitaph, in case I was suddenly called for.

"Wishing you and your book well, believe me,

"Yours truly,

SAMUEL L. CLEMENS."

Not long ago the gifted humorist sent me a printed slip of his career, taken from "Men of the Time." Upon the margin of this, he wrote the following:

"MY DEAR CLEMENS:

"I haven't any humorous biography—the facts don't admit of it. I had this sketch from "Men of the Time" printed on slips to enable me to study my history at my leisure.

S. L. CLEMENS."

By nature, a serious, thoughtful man, he is deeply in earnest at times, yet seldom has he ventured to deal with the pathetic in his writings. Occasionally he pens a careful, serious communication, like the following, for instance. which he addressed to a young friend of mine:

Hartford, Jan. 16, 1881.

"MY DEAR BOY:

How can I advise another man wisely, out of such a capital as a life filled with mistakes? Advise him how to avoid the like? No—for opportunities to make the same mistakes do not happen to any two men. Your own experiences may possibly teach you, but another man's can't. I do not know anything for a person to do but just peg along, doing the things that offer, and regretting them the next day. It is my way and everybody's.

"Truly yours,

S. L. CLEMENS."

In this modest volume I do not attempt to analyze the humor of Mark Twain. As Howells says: "Analyses of humor are apt to leave one rather serious, and to result in an entire volatilization of the humor." There is romance, and adventure, and thrilling interest surrounding the life of the prince of humorists, and I have endeavored to gather together some of these interesting facts. His satire and wit speak for themselves.

THE AUTHOR. . . .

HIS FIRST LITERARY SUCCESS.

During the following winter Mark Twain sojourned at the National capital, working at odd moments upon the initial chapter of his "Innocents Abroad." His Bohemian habits were retained in every particular, at least the statement is warranted by a friend who writes of Mark's life at this time:

"His room was a perfect chaos, his table a curiosity in its way. On it could be seen anything—from soiled manuscript to old boots. He never laid his paper on the table when writing, partly because there was no available space and partly because the position so necessitated was too much for his lazy bones. With both feet plunged in manuscript, chair tilted back and note-book and pencil in hand he did all the writing I ever saw him do. An ordinary atmosphere would not suffice to set in motion the stream of Mark's ideas. It must first be thoroughly saturated with the vilest tobacco smoke, which he puffed from a villainous pipe—said pipe having never received a cleaning—as many newspaper friends of those days can testify. He regarded this pipe as his salvation from bores, taking a ghastly delight in puffing away like a locomotive when an undesirable visitor dropped in, and eagerly watching the paleness which gradually crept over the face of the enemy as the poisonous stuff got in its work."

One day while Mark was busily engaged with his work, in his dingy little room, a tall, sallow-faced man, with a miserable expression of countenance, and a deep, consumptive cough, entered the room and without an invitation sat down. Turning to the visitor, Clemens said:

"Well."

The visitor said "Well."

"What can I do for you?" asked the humorist.

"Well, nothin' in particular. I heard 'em say that you are the man that writes funny things, and as I have several hours to loaf around before the train leaves, I thought I would come around and get you to make me laugh a little. I ain't had a good laugh in many a day, and I didn't know but what you mout accommodate me."

Clemens scowled at the man, who, thinking that the humorist was presenting him with a specimen of facial fun, began to titter.

"That'll do fust rate, cap'n, but I'd ruther hear you talk. I can make a mouth at a man about as easy as any fellow you ever saw, an' w'at I want is a few words from you that'll jolt me like a wagin had backed agin me."

"My friend, I am very busy to-day, and—"

"Yes, I know all that. I am very busy myself, except that I've got about two hours to loaf, an' as I said jest now, I'd like for you to get off something that I can take home. W'y, I can go around an' git the drinks on it for a week."

"Won't you have a cigar?" asked Clemens, desirous of learning whether the man was a smoker.

"No, I never could stand a seeggah."

The humorist smiled, and taking up his pipe, filled it up with strong tobacco, and began to puff. "I'll keep him in here, now," mused the smoker, "until he is as sick as a dog. I wouldn't consent to his departure, if he was to get down on his knees and pray for deliverance."

"Nothing does a man more good than a hearty laugh," the visitor said, coughing as a cloud of smoke surrounded his head. "Wah, hoo, wah, hoo! Don't you think it is a leetle close in here?"

"Oh, no," replied Mark, arising, and locking the door.

"I like a little fresh a'r, 'specially when thar's so much smoke in a room."

"Oh, there's air enough here. How did you leave all the folks?"

"Well, Gabe, my youngest—wah, hoo, wah, hoo—ain't as peart as he mout be, but all the others air stirrin'. You ain't got no chillun, I reckon?"

"No," the humorist replied, as he vigorously puffed his pipe.

"Well, I'm sorry for you. Thar ain't nothin' that adds to a man's nachul enjoyment like chillun. That boy Gabe, what I was talkin' about jest now, w'y, I wouldn't give him up fur the finest yoke of steers you ever seen."

"You wouldn't?"

"No sir, wouldn't tech 'em with a ten-foot pole would refuse 'em pine blank. Podner, don't you—wah, hoo, wah, hoo—think it's a gettin' a little too clost in here now?"

"No, not a bit, just right."

"Well, I don't know the style in this place, but I'll try an' put up with it."

After a moment's silence the visitor continued:

"When I left home, Mur—that's my wife—said to me, says she, 'Now, say, while you are thar, don't smoke that cob pipe.' I wanted to follow her advice, but I put my—wah, hoo, wah, hoo,—old fuzee in my jeans, an' now I b'l'eve I'll take a smoke."

He took out a cob pipe, and a twist of new tobacco, known in his neighborhood as "Tough Sam," whittled off a handful, filled his pipe, lighted it, placed his feet on the stove and went to work. Mark soon began to snuff the foul air, but he was determined to stand it. The visitor blew smoke like a tar kiln. Mark grew restless. Beads of cold perspiration began to gather on his brow. Throwing down his pipe, he hastily unlocked the door, and fled. On the sidewalk he met a friend.

"Hello, Clemens, what's the matter?"

Twain related what had occurred.

"Oh, you mean that fellow in brown jeans?"

"Yes."

"You ought to have had better sense than to light your pipe in his presence."

"Why?"

"Because he's a member of the Arkansas Legislature." . . .

In 1876, there appeared in the *Atlantic Monthly*, that famous fragment, "Punch Brothers, Punch with care." It had a curious origin. Early in April, 1875, the city line of the New York and Harlem railroad company having adopted the punch system, posted in the panels of their cars a card of information and instruction to conductors and passengers, both of whom were indirectly requested to watch the other. It read as follows:

> The CONDUCTOR, when be receives a Fare, must immediately PUNCH in
> the presence of the passenger,
> A BLUE Trip Slip for an 8 Cents Fare,
> A BUFF Trip Slip for a 6 Cents Fare,
> A PINK Trip Slip for a 3 Cents Fare,
> FOR COUPON AND TRANSFER TICKETS,
> PUNCH THE TICKETS.

The poesy of the thing was discovered almost as "immediately" as the conductor "immediately" punched and all sorts of jingles were accommodated to the measure. In September the first poem appeared in print and various versions appeared in the New York and Boston newspapers.

In the January, 1876, *Atlantic*, Mark Twain's "Literary Nightmare" appeared with the following version:

> "Conductor, when you receive a fare,
> Punch in the presence of the passenjare!
> A blue trip slip for an eight-cent fare,
> A buff trip slip for a six-cent fare,
> A pink trip slip for a three-cent fare;
> Punch in the presence of the passenjare!
>   CHORUS.
> Punch, brothers, punch with care!
> Punch in the presence of the passenjare!

Said Mark: "I came across these jingling rhymes in a newspaper, a little while ago, and read them a couple of times. They took instant and entire possession of me. All through breakfast they went waltzing through my brain, and when, at last, I rolled up my napkin, I could not tell whether I had eaten anything or not. I had carefully laid out my day's work the day before—a thrilling tragedy in the novel which I am writing. I went to my den to begin my deed of blood. I took up my pen, but all I could get it to say was, "Punch in the presence of the passenjare." I fought hard for an hour, but it was useless. My head kept humming, "A blue trip slip for an eight-cent fare, a buff trip slip for a six-cent fare," and so on and so on, without peace or respite. The day's work was ruined—I could see that plainly enough. I gave up and drifted down town, and presently discovered that my feet were keeping time to that relentless jingle. When I could stand it no longer I altered my step. But it did no good; those rhymes accommodated themselves to the new step and went on harassing me just as before. I returned home and suffered all the afternoon; suffered all through an unconscious and unrefreshing dinner; suffered, and cried, and jingled all through the evening; went to bed and rolled, tossed and jingled right along, the same as ever; got up at midnight frantic, and tried to read; but there was nothing visible upon the whirling page except "Punch! punch in the presence of the passenjare." By sunrise I was out of my mind, and everybody marvelled and was distressed at the idiotic burden of my ravings.—"

The Literary Nightmare awakened horse car-poets throughout the world. Algernon Charles Swinburne in *La Revue des Deux Mondes*, had a brief copy of French verses, written with all his well-known warmth and melody.

LE CHANT DU CONDUCTEUR.

Ayant ete paye le conducteur
Percera en pleine vue du voyageur,
    Quand il rocoit trois sous un coupon vert,
    Un coupon jaune pour six sous c'est l'affaire,
    Et pour huit sous c'est un coupon couleur,
De-rose, en pleine vue du voyageur.
    CHOEUR.
Donc, percez soigneusement, mes freres,
Tout en pleine vue des voyageurs, etc.

The *Western*, an enterprising St. Louis magazine, had a terrible attack, and addressing "Marco Twain" it came out in a Latin anthem, with the following chorus:

Pungite, fratres, pungite,
Pungite cum amore

Pungite pro vectore
Diligentissime pungite.

—William Montgomery Clemens, from *Mark
Twain: His Life and Work. A Biographical
Sketch*, Chicago: F. Tennyson Neely,
1894, pp. 7–12, 80–86, 119–123

H.H. BOYESEN
"THE PLAGUE OF JOCULARITY" (1895)

Hjalmar Hjorth Boyesen provides here a valuable account touching on
Mark Twain's acquaintance with the great Russian novelist Ivan Turgenev
(or "Tourgueneff"), as well as the negative, somewhat humorless views
on Twain held by French novelist Alphonse Daudet. Students interested
in Twain's reputation among his international peers will find much of
use in this memoir. Those who have read Andrew Lang's piece indicting
the slavish devotees of "Culture" might detect an echo of the dismis-
sive superiority often issuing from the cosmopolitan literary salons of
Paris. Furthermore, Turgenev enters into that vast and ongoing dialogue
on what constitutes an "American," which qualities are exclusively
"American," and the extent of Twain's "Americanism."

It is, to my mind, a highly significant fact that humor is the only literary
product which we export. Occasionally, to be sure, an American novel is
translated into French and German; but, generally speaking, our serious
literature is in no great demand in any European country. The only
contemporary American authors who have really an international fame are
Bret Harte and Mark Twain. Their books, in atrocious flamboyant covers, are
to be found on every railway news-stand in England and on the Continent.
The Queen of Italy was reported, some years ago, to have asked an American
if we had any other living authors than Bret Harte and Mark Twain. In 1879,
during a prolonged sojourn in Paris, I had the pleasure of introducing the
latter to Tourgueneff and receiving the Russian author's cordial thanks for
having brought the famous humorist to see him.

"Now, there," he exclaimed, "is a real American—the first American who
has had the kindness to conform to my idea of what an American ought to be.
He has the flavor of the soil. Your other friends, Mr. A. and Mr. G., might as well
be Europeans. They are excellent gentlemen, no doubt, but they are flavorless."

One evening, during the same year, when I went with Tourgueneff to a stag party at the house of a renowned *littéruteur*, the conversation turned upon American humor. Several French men present, among others Alphonse Daudet, declared that the excellence of American humor had been greatly exaggerated. It seemed to them grotesque rather than funny.

"There appeared some American stories, a short time ago, in the *Revue Des Deux Mondes*," said Daudet, "they were by Mark Twain; I could see nothing at all humorous in any of them."

"What were they?" I asked.

"There was one named 'The Jumping Frog,'" he replied, "a pitiful tale about two men who made a wager about a frog, one betting that he could jump to a certain height, the other betting that he could not; then, when the time comes to test the jumping ability of the frog, it is found that he has been stuffed full of shot, and of course, he cannot jump."

"Well," I queried, determined to uphold my friend, Clemens, "isn't that rather funny?"

"No," Daudet replied decidedly, "I feel too sorry for the poor frog."

All the rest, except Tourgueneff, joined in this verdict. He thought the story had been so badly translated, that its real flavor was lost in the French version. He thereupon told an incident from *Roughing It* (I think), in order to prove that American humor was not lacking in salt. It was the story of an inundation on the plains. A party of emigrants have encamped in their wagons on a little hillock, while the water keeps rising round about them. Days pass and starvation stares them in the face. Every one has to eat the most dreadful things. "I," says the author, ate my boots. *The holes tasted the best.*"

"Now," cried Tourgueneff, "isn't that delightfully funny?"

All agreed, though with some qualifications, that a point had been made in favor of Tourgueneff's contention.

"But," objected a well-known editor, "how is it possible for a civilized man to live among a people who are always joking? In Mark Train's *Innocents Abroad* there is a perpetual strain of forced jocularity, which at last grows to be deadly wearisome. The author tortures himself to find the jocular view of all things, sacred and profane. Now, what I want to know is this: Is this attitude typically American? To me it is essentially juvenile and barbaric.

I took up the cudgels, of course, for Mark Twain, and declared unblushingly that the jocular attitude toward life was not typically American. But since then I have changed my mind. I have come to the conclusion that nothing is more" typically American" than this more or less forced jocularity. In the Western States, and largely also in the East, the man who does not habitually joke is voted dull, and is held to be poor company. Entertainment, at all social gatherings, consists in telling funny stories, and every man who has a social ambition takes care to provide himself with as large a fund as possible of humorous sayings and doings, which he doles out as occasion may demand.

—H.H. Boyesen, "The Plague of Jocularity,"
North American Review, vol. 161, no. 468,
November 1895, pp. 531–533

Theodore Dreiser
"The Literary Shower" (1896)

Journalist and novelist Theodore Dreiser published his own journal, *Ev'ry Month*, in which this review of Twain's novel *Personal Recollections of Joan of Arc* appeared. *Joan of Arc* was first published anonymously, and when Twain revealed his authorship it did not improve sales particularly. It is just as well, then, that he wrote it, in his own words, "for love & not for lucre." Critics have not favored the work, while Twain thought it was his best. It is worth noting, however, that Twain had a strange, sentimental attraction to Joan of Arc. This was compounded by his associating Joan with Susy, his daughter who died only a year after the book's publication. This sentimental association perhaps heightened Twain's affection for the book, as well as softened any critic who might otherwise have slammed the novel.

―――

Mark Twain, plain, of great wisdom and thorough understanding, and humorist on principle, has come forward as an historical novelist with his *Personal Recollections of Joan of Arc*, which story has been running through Harper's since April, 1895, and has now appeared in book form. Although the critics are already dissecting the interesting work and exhibiting its weak points from historical and fictional standpoints, yet it is generally admitted that the effort is one of considerable importance and well worth ranging beside the other works of Mr. Clemens. This rugged old humorist, with his strong alloy of plain sense, has the faith and the interest of the mass of the American people to a greater degree, quite, than any other living writer. His sense and sympathy seems even to have come nearer to the level of the every day understanding of the people, who see many of their own characteristics mirrored in those of the children of his fancy. Twain has been a long time living and thinking, and is thoroughly in touch with the life of to-day. He is not primarily a man of letters. Fortunately for American literature and for the permanent fame of a man whom no one can know without loving and honoring, the creator of "Tom Sawyer" is far more than a mere man of letters, even a great one; he is something far more than a mere humorist, even a thoroughly genial and whole-souled one—he is a great writer. Like Balzac himself he can afford to let the critic smile and dissect at leisure, serene in the consciousness that he has in some measure understood and expressed the wondrous workings of the human heart.

—Theodore Dreiser, "The Literary Shower,"
Ev'ry Month 2, June 1896, pp. 2–6

WILLIAM DEAN HOWELLS (1897)

In this "review" to commemorate the first uniform edition of Twain's earlier works, Howells takes the opportunity to reenvisage and reinvent Mark Twain for a "new circle of his readers," blandly dismissing the "preoccupations of his older friends." For Howells, the new Twain, with the emphasis now on his "romances" rather than on the "studies or sketches," is the better one. This new Twain is "at heart a poet." With such formulations, Howells continues here to conduct what was to be a lifelong campaign against those readers who mistake Twain for a "mere humorist." He accordingly predicts that *The Innocents Abroad* and *Roughing It* will soon partake of "the relish of the grotesque merely."

Howells also hungrily anticipates "that great American novel which [Twain] could give us," explicitly discounting *Huckleberry Finn* as a candidate. He calls for "the real novel which he has given us the right to expect of him." Did Twain ever deliver the "novel of the average American life" that Howells is angling for here? No proper novel ever emanated from Mark Twain following this article. Does this, then, suggest that Howells was disappointed with his friend?

Because Howells chooses to emphasize the author of the "romances" here, he gives particular attention to *Huckleberry Finn, A Connecticut Yankee in King Arthur's Court,* and *Personal Recollections of Joan of Arc.* He has faltering praise for the latter book, hesitatingly and euphemistically calling it a noble failure.

Students researching the part Howells played in Twain's success and development—whether it is mostly as a cheerleader or as a bowdlerizing editor (here he chides Twain's "words . . . that I should like to blot") will find powerful ammunition here.

The welcome which the new edition of Mark Twain's works (there ought to be a word of greater cheerfulness for the sort of things he has done in literature) is proof not only of the willingness of people to have them in some uniform size and shape, but of a vitality in the books themselves which appeals to a new generation of readers, and will appeal to the lovers of imaginative humor after many more generations have grown old. I do not fix the number of these, partly because I doubt the use of that sort of thing; partly because I do not know it; and partly because I care more for the books than for their readers, past, present, or future. I care very much indeed for the books, for they embody, I think, the best of our national humor, considering it as to both quality and quantity, or as Mark Twain himself would prefer to say, taking it by and large. There is enough, and to spare, of American humor, but it has often been the vision of American things through the spectacles of more or less alien scholarship, or culture, or civilization, or whatever we like to call it; but in Mark Twain we have the national spirit as it is seen with our own eyes. In other humorists, it is our life appearing through literature; in him it is literature appearing through our life. Before him even the indigenous humorists had to help themselves out with preposterous caricature and impossible parlance and painful misspelling; but he gave voice to our humor in terms which needed none of these aids, but was the unmistakably recognizable speech of the American race, caught equally from the lips of the people and the columns of their newspapers.

I.

I am glad upon the whole to have his stories come first in the new edition, for I think that they represent him at his most imaginative and best; and if what I have been saying is at all true they more largely represent American character than any other American books. It is well also, I think, that the new circle of his readers should first realize his greatness as an artist in fiction, unswayed by the preoccupations of his older friends with the studies and sketches that came before his romances. He was always constructive and creative, but I believe with Mr. Brander Matthews that he has never been rated at his true worth as a story-teller; and I doubt whether Mr. Clemens himself knows that he is strongest in this sort, or that he will be remembered as the author of Huckleberry Finn, Tom Sawyer, The Prince and the Pauper, and The Connecticut Yankee at King Arthur's Court, after people have begun diffidently to wait for one another to say who wrote The Innocents Abroad and Roughing It. That will be a very long time yet, and I hope that before it arrives he will have done indefinitely more for my theory of his talent (I have confessed that it is not altogether mine) by writing that great American novel which he could give us. It would not be the novel which its anticipative critics have begun lately to make undesirable again; but it would be a novel of the average American life, such as no one else could write, or is at least so well fitted to write.

In the mean while I am very well content with the four romances we already have from him; and I am not at all sorry to have them accompanied by his later sketches which are of the same imaginative character. I do not mean here the studies of Life on the Mississippi, which are the direct and graphic records of his own experience as a steamboat pilot, but those other sketches, like that delicious satire, About Magnanimous Incident Literature, or that wonderful allegory, or parable, or apologue, so incomparably vivid, of Some Facts Concerning the Recent Carnival of Crime in Connecticut, which has to do with the ever-tormenting question of conscience. If I were to choose anything of the author's that would upon the whole most nearly represent the peculiar quality of his gift, I should choose this.

I think I should; but perhaps not. Nothing is more characteristic of a great talent (and I believe Mark Twain's one of the greatest) than its refusal to be illustrated by anything short of its whole range. In a certain sort, The Prince and the Pauper, and The Adventures of Huckleberry Finn, are about equally representative of a mind inalienably contemporaneous and of a fancy at home in all times and places. The author is too honest ever to palter with the truth, and in whatever romantic form he dealt with the past he must deal faithfully with it, for the behoof of those who love the truth, or ought to love it, anyway. The Prince and the Pauper is not less coldly real in its historic details than it is wildly fantastic in its inventions. It is a very charming story, it is very touching, it is deeply moving and significant. It was the first direct expression of that profound sympathy with the wronged, the helpless, the down-trodden, which has since often uttered itself in the work of our incomparable humorist and humanist.

I value it for this reason, which is one of the reasons why I value The Adventures of Huckleberry Finn. I was going to say that was a far greater book; but what would have been the use? Those who like The Prince and the Pauper best may do so without molestation from me in their preference. I will only insist upon my own, and try to hint my sense of the *breadth* of the story I prefer. It followed in order of time the history of Tom Sawyer, which approved itself one of the best boys' books ever written by the deep hold it took upon the boy's heart in old and young; and it surpassed that book in the variety if not freshness of its incidents, the novelty to literature of the life it portrayed, and the keenly felt and unerringly presented character. To be sure there is some caricature in it, and of course it does not always respect its convention of the town drunkard's son telling his own story. These are not minor faults; they break the illusion for the time, but in spite of them, the Southwest lives in that book, as it lives nowhere else, with its narrow and rude conditions, its half-savage heroisms, its vague and dim aspirations, its feuds and its fights, its violence, its squalor, its self-devotion, all in the shadow of that horrible cloud of slavery darkening both the souls and the minds of men. There are moments of almost intolerable pathos in the book, and also of a lofty joy, which is not less sublime because of the grotesque forms it takes. One of these is that of Huck Finn's resolution to violate the false conscience slavery has bred in him, and to be true to the slave rather than to his owner, though he goes to hell for it. Perhaps this is one of the places where the author comes too near speaking for his creation; but much might be said in favor of the risk he runs, and for what it achieves it was richly worth taking. After all the end reached in Huck Finn's mind is what an ignorant but generous spirit would have reasoned to, and the humorous implications were simply invaluable.

I like Huck Finn, as I like The Prince and the Pauper, for the reality in it. Both books have their machinery, and I have about the same pleasure in making believe with the author that the town drunkard's son could tell his story, as I have in supposing that the king's son could change places with the beggar's and see England from the beggar's point of view. Both lose in probability through their final possibility, and it is when the author puts his story quite beyond the range of possibility, that he wins for it a measure of probability equal to that which he loses when he demands less of the imagination. For some such reason as this, none of his romances seems to me so great as The Connecticut Yankee at King Arthur's Court.

There are two kinds of fiction that I like almost equally well: a real novel and a pure romance; and I joyfully accept the Connecticut Yankee as one of the greatest romances ever imagined. I believe I shall always like it best of Mark Twain's stories until he writes the real novel which he has given us the right to expect of him. It is a mighty stroke of poetry, an effect of the happiest daring in its conception, worked out with bold and unsparing fidelity. If you suppose that a Yankee of our day from East Hartford magically finds himself in the Britain of Arthur's time, you have the ground of inexhaustible contrasts and of almost invariable triumphs for our century and our civilization; but the author has the true historical sense, and he does not judge the past by the present, or rather he does not condemn it. He condemns the barbarism of the past only as it is continued into the present; and I suppose it is this which made the book such an offence to the English. Their droll anachronism of king, nobles, and commons was mirrored in all its grotesqueness in this fable of Arthur's land; but if it had not been for their fierce rejection of the picture one might have thought that the author had been dealing with a mere spectre, and bearing on altogether too hard in his ridicule of the divine right of monarchy and aristocracy. The outburst against him, however, was sufficient witness that there was still vitality in the superstition; and so much honor for it that a republican must not be suffered to laugh at it. In fact the story might seem to rebuke the inequality and iniquity of our own status, too; and if it is ever to become a manual of democracy in our schools, as some have hoped, the text must be carefully guarded with notes explaining that our system, with its privileges, its monopolies, and its injunctions, is of quite another nature from that of Britain in either the sixth or the nineteenth century. What it can safely do for young readers, whose hands it may fall into, is to teach them a just abhorrence of the ugliness and foulness of the past, which was beautiful and glorious only in the instincts of humanity, feeble and perverted and baffled as they mostly were, but still essentially the same in all ages.

He makes you sensible of this in the tender compassion which seems to me the key-note of The Prince and the Pauper, and in the pathetic mystery which he has even deepened upon the memory of Joan of Arc. Probably he did not do all that he hoped to do in that book for the ideal of self-devotion that was in his mind; and I could myself have preferred that he should have clothed his witness of her life in some such modern guise as that of his Connecticut Yankee instead of his Sieur le Conte, though I know that this would have been striking the same note twice. As it is, though Sieur le Conte is often lapsing out of mediaeval France and dropping down among us in latter-day America, the romance has that double charm of historic truth and inventive power which makes all the author's studies of the past so living. It presents us an image of the peasant girl of Domremy which many will rather venerate than the saint recognized in her tardy canonization.

II.

I must not give too serious a cast to the recognition of our great humorist on the side which I am sometimes vexed that people neither see nor care to see. That is something which will no doubt duly impress them in time and I may very well leave it. But when I came to look over this new edition of his books and to feel him so personally present in them, I could not help wishing others to value him for qualities besides his humor. I could not help hoping that they would note how there is no word of all his writing that flatters or even suffers wrong. There are many words of his that I should like to blot, because they grate upon my nerves, or offend my taste, but there is nothing that I could desire unsaid because it is untrue or ungenerous. In fine, what I am trying to make appear is that this humorist of ours is at heart a poet; and if such a notion of him taxes too heavily the generation that stands nearest him, I turn confidently to that which will in a way know him better. I like to think that there is already some proof of this in the acceptance of these works of his imagination by a new generation of readers. Not that I think less of his other books than they deserve; for I value them most profoundly. Above anything in our literature, they embody and express a national mood that I would not have forgotten: the high, hopeful, jubilant mood of our expansion after the great civil war, when we thought we had done it all and had only to rest forever, and take our ease, and our fill of laughter. Never again shall any people know such a mood, till the peoples do justice; but it was ours once, and it is recorded in Mark Twain's earlier books as nowhere else. They will always have an immense historical value, but they will become old much sooner than his stories, which indeed will not become old at all, any more than Don Quixote, or Robinson Crusoe, or the Pilgrim's Progress, or the Arabian Nights. It will not be such a great while before the parlance, the whole attitude in the Innocents Abroad, and in Roughing It, will begin to have the relish of the grotesque merely. We shall then wonder if the color which the author took from his time and imparted to it, was really the complexion of life; but with the stories it will not be so. Tom Sawyer and Huck Finn are enduring types of universal boyhood; their lifelikeness substantiates the truth of their local conditions already past. The historical group of romances, so fantastically conceived, are essentially real, and you trust their report of the past because you cannot question their truth to human nature. In these we see what the author calls the white Indians of Arthur's time, the barbarians of the later Plantagenets' reigns, and the bigots and blackguards of mediaeval France, with the modern light upon them. The powerful lens does not caricature or belie them because it reports their ugliness, and it will not bring them under condemnation with any reader who shares the author's historical sense. He makes you feel at all times that the past was what had then to be, and that it is abhorrent only in the survival to our own time of its ideals and errors. The spirit of his books is thoroughly scientific. He perceives that the first impulse of the man of the past was to believe, and then to act upon his belief; and that the first impulse of the modern man is to doubt, and then to reason upon his doubt. The difference is that which has mainly led humanity to wash up, and so largely to leave off rapine and murder; but the evolution is not yet complete, and the effect of these romances, their indirect and important effect, is to make the reader realize this fact.

—William Dean Howells,
Harper's Monthly, February 13, 1897

Brander Matthews (1899)

Brander Matthews had received a light drubbing from Twain in "Fenimore Cooper's Literary Offenses" (1895), when Twain quoted Matthews praising Cooper and remarked that "As a rule I am quite willing to accept Brander Matthews' literary judgments and applaud his lucid and graceful phrasing of them; but that particular statement needs to be taken with a few tons of salt." This irreverence came easily, because the two had been friends since the 1870s.

Matthews's essay appeared as the introductory comments to the complete edition of Mark Twain's *Works*. It is not likely, in other words, to include any great attack on Twain's reputation. Nevertheless, it has served as an important consideration of Twain's status as a writer. It also offered an opportunity to revise Twain's image for a new readership; to "unmake" the old opinion "and to remake it." With a new, uniform edition comes a certain respectability, after all. Nathaniel Hawthorne had been revamped with two new uniform collections (the Autograph and the Old Manse editions) in 1900, for instance, and the Centenary Edition of Ralph Waldo Emerson's *Complete Works*, overseen by his son Edward, would follow in the next few years (1903–04). Such a project being undertaken was, in itself, a token of literary worth.

Howells stated that such an edition enhances Twain's writing with the "dignified presence which most of us have thought their due." He dismisses the individual original editions as "matchlessly ugly subscription volumes." Evidently, then as now, the form that books assumed influenced a reader's estimate of the work independent of the content. This edition was pronounced by Howells as fit "to be set on the shelf of a gentleman's library." Brander Matthews's "singularly intelligent and agreeable essay" was the gate through which the reader entered, the lens through which the *Works* was to be perceived.

Brander Matthews was a professor at Columbia University and an influential critic. Like Barrett Wendell's valued support, Matthews's favorable view attests to an acceptance of Twain at a level beyond the magazine reviewers. No doubt he was chosen as the author of the *Works'* introduction for the clout that an esteemed critic could bring to Twain. (Howells, for instance, was influential and respectable enough, but he was not an academic and could not confer that level of acceptance.)

Matthews begins by redefining any uniform notion of a "reading public." There are many publics, ranging from a high, sophisticated one to a low one that laughs at broadest comedy. The project here, it seems, is to securely shift Twain's main audience from low to high. First his biography is offered, again. Students tracking evolving perceptions of Mark Twain might compare these different tellings of the Twain biography. Which episodes are emphasized by which writers, and what do these episodes signify? For instance, when Matthews singles out for praise Twain's marriage to Livy Langdon as "another of those happy unions of which there have been so many in the annals of American authorship," what sort of ideology is Matthews blithely reinforcing?

Ironically, Matthews claims a likeness (although only a biographical one) between Twain and the British novelist Sir Walter Scott, whom Twain blamed for the Civil War. Such a comparison carried implications, though. Scott's work was, of course, collected in uniform editions that to this day are viewed in some households as required bookshelf furnishings as much as they are considered literature. Matthews distances Twain from the "comic copy" of Artemus Ward and John Phoenix, drawing a comparison instead to Cervantes and the French comedic dramatist Molière. Again, by such redefinitions a new audience is courted. For Matthews, Twain is "to be compared with the masters of literature." Artemus and Squibob are ejected, then, and Geoffrey Chaucer, Jonathan Swift, Henry Fielding, Benjamin Franklin, Emerson, Hawthorne, and James Russell Lowell are duly rallied as the new peers of Mark Twain.

Matthews emphasises Twain's moral streak. "Mark Twain is always an advocate of the sterling ethical standard." He never laughed at the Italian Old Masters, though it might have seemed so. He was laughing at ignorant snobs. In Palestine, while unimpressed, Twain keeps his reverence. (Elsewhere, Matthews remarks that Twain is "no respecter of persons.") Students following the changing critical view of Twain should note Matthews's version of him. Here is a reverent, ethical stalwart. Is this consistent with previous estimates? Has Twain himself changed, or are his critics and supporters "unmaking" and "remaking" him according to their own agenda? Matthews finds the "romances" inferior to the three Mississippi novels (*Tom Sawyer*, *Huckleberry Finn*, and *Pudd'nhead Wilson*) which have a "flavor of the soil about them." It is by these novels that Twain is "likely to live the longest." The competing definitions of the Twain canon continue. *A Connecticut Yankee* is "iconoclastic" rather than irreverent, while *Joan of Arc* is coolly dismissed.

A certain detectable squeamishness suggests that Mark Twain is still not completely assimilated by the academics. He is "always accurate, however unacademic," his "instinct for the exact word is not always unerring" (Howells claimed the opposite earlier); he is "not free from slang," but his style is "modern." While Matthews stresses the American quality of Twain—by this time, a standard comment in any Twain criticism—he emphasizes repeatedly Twain's resemblance to Cervantes and Molière, as though Twain is best served by those comparisons (and not with comparisons to John Phoenix and Artemus Ward).

Students tracing the developing critical attitudes to Twain will find an important change, whether accurate or not, in Matthews's introduction. Students exploring Twain's debt to Cervantes, Molière, or the "masters of literature" should likewise consult this passage.

It is a common delusion of those who discuss contemporary literature that there is such an entity as the "reading public," possessed of a certain uniformity of taste. There is not one public; there are many publics—as many, in fact, as there are different kinds of taste; and the extent of an author's popularity is in proportion to the number of these separate publics he may chance to please. Scott, for example, appealed not only to those who relished romance and enjoyed excitement, but also to those who appreciated his honest portrayal of sturdy characters. Thackeray is preferred by ambitious youth who are insidiously flattered by his tacit compliments to their knowledge of the world, by the disenchanted who cannot help seeing the petty meannesses of society, and by the less sophisticated in whom sentiment has not gone to seed in sentimentality. Dickens in his own day bid for the approval of those who liked broad caricature (and were therefore pleased with Stiggins and Chadband), of those who fed greedily on plentiful pathos (and were therefore delighted with the deathbeds of Smike and Paul Dombey and Little Nell) and also of those who asked for unexpected adventure (and were therefore glad to disentangle the melodramatic intrigues of Ralph Nickleby).

In like manner the American author who has chosen to call himself Mark Twain has attained to an immense popularity because the qualities he possesses in a high degree appeal to so many and so widely varied publics—first of all, no doubt, to the public that revels in hearty and robust fun, but also to the public which is glad to be swept along by the full current of adventure, which is sincerely touched by manly pathos, which is satisfied by vigorous and exact portrayal of character, and which respects shrewdness and wisdom and sanity and a healthy hatred of pretense and affectation and sham. Perhaps no one book of Mark Twain's—with the possible exception of *Huckleberry Finn*—is equally a favorite with all his readers; and perhaps some of his best characteristics are absent from his earlier books or but doubtfully latent in them. Mark Twain is many sided; and he has ripened in knowledge and in power since he first attracted attention as a wild Western funny man. As he has grown older he has reflected more; he has both broadened and deepened. The writer of "comic copy" for a mining-camp newspaper has developed into a liberal humorist, handling life seriously and making his readers think as he makes them laugh, until to-day Mark Twain has perhaps the largest audience of any author now using the English language. To trace the stages of this evolution and to count the steps whereby the sagebrush reporter has risen to the rank of a writer of world-wide celebrity, is as interesting as it is instructive.

I

SAMUEL LANGHORNE CLEMENS was born November 30, 1835, at Florida, Missouri. His father was a merchant who had come from Tennessee and who removed soon after his son's birth to Hannibal, a little town on the Mississippi. What Hannibal was like and what were the circumstances of Mr. Clemens's boyhood we can see for ourselves in the convincing pages of *Tom Sawyer*. Mr. Howells has called Hannibal "a loafing, out-at-elbows, down-at-the-heels, slave-holding Mississippi town"; and Mr. Clemens, who silently abhorred slavery, was of a slave-owning family.

When the future author was but twelve his father died, and the son had to get his education as best he could. Of actual schooling he got little and of book learning still less, but life itself is not a bad teacher for a boy who wants to study, and young Clemens did not waste his chances. He spent six years in the printing office of the little local paper,—for, like not a few others on the list of American authors that stretches from Benjamin Franklin to William Dean Howells, he began his connection with literature by setting type. As a journeyman printer the lad wandered from town to town and rambled even as far east as New York.

When he was nineteen he went back to the home of his boyhood and presently resolved to become a pilot on the Mississippi. How he learned the river he has told us in *Life on the Mississippi*, wherein his adventures, his experiences, and his impressions while he was a cub pilot are recorded with a combination of precise veracity and abundant humor which makes the earlier chapters of that marvelous book a most masterly fragment of autobiography. The life of a pilot was full of interest and excitement and opportunity, and what young Clemens saw and heard and divined during the years when he was going up and down the mighty river we may read in the pages of *Huckleberry Finn* and *Pudd'nhead Wilson*. But toward the end of the fifties the railroads began to rob the river of its supremacy as a carrier; and in the beginning of the sixties the Civil War broke out and the Mississippi no longer went unvexed to the sea. The skill, slowly and laboriously acquired, was suddenly rendered useless, and at twenty-five the young man found himself bereft of his calling. As a border state, Missouri was sending her sons into the armies of the Union and into the armies of the Confederacy, while many a man stood doubting, not knowing which way to turn. The ex-pilot has given us the record of his very brief and inglorious service as a soldier of the South. When this escapade was swiftly ended, he went to the Northwest with his brother, who had been appointed Territorial Secretary of Nevada. Thus the man who had been born on the borderland of North and South, who had gone East as a jour printer, who had been again and again up and down the Mississippi, now went West while he was still plastic and impressionable; and he had thus another chance to increase that intimate knowledge of American life and American character which is one of the most precious of his possessions.

While still on the river he had written a satiric letter or two which found their way into print. In Nevada he went to the mines and lived the life he has described in *Roughing It*, but when he failed to "strike it rich," he naturally drifted into journalism and back into a newspaper office again. The *Virginia City Enterprise* was not overmanned, and the newcomer did all sorts of odd jobs, finding time now and then to write a sketch which seemed important enough to permit of his signature. He now began to sign himself Mark Twain, taking the name from a call of the man who heaves the lead on a Mississippi River steamboat, and who cries, "By the mark, three," "Mark twain," and so on. The name of Mark Twain soon began to be known to those who were curious in newspaper humor. After a while he was drawn across the mountains to San Francisco, where he found casual employment on the *Morning Call*, and where he joined himself to a little group of aspiring literators which included

Mr. Bret Harte, Mr. Noah Brooks, Mr. Charles Henry Webb, and Mr. Charles Warren Stoddard.

It was in 1867 that Mr. Webb published Mark Twain's first book, *The Celebrated Jumping Frog of Calaveras*; and it was in 1867 that the proprietors of the *Alta California* supplied him with the funds necessary to enable him to become one of the passengers on the steamer *Quaker City*, which had been chartered to take a select party on what is now known as the Mediterranean trip. The weekly letters, in which he set forth what befell him on this journey, were printed in the *Alta* Sunday after Sunday, and were copied freely by the other Californian papers. These letters served as the foundation of a book published in 1869 and called *The Innocents Abroad*, a book which instantly brought to the author celebrity and cash.

Both of these valuable aids to ambition were increased by his next step, his appearance on the lecture platform. Mr. Noah Brooks, who was present at his first attempt, has recorded that Mark Twain's "method as a lecturer was distinctly unique and novel. His slow, deliberate drawl, the anxious and perturbed expression of his visage, the apparently painful effort with which he framed his sentences, the surprise that spread over his face when the audience roared with delight or rapturously applauded the finer passages of his word-painting, were unlike anything of the kind they had ever known." In the thirty years since that first appearance the method has not changed, although it has probably matured. Mark Twain is one of the most effective of platform speakers and one of the most artistic, with an art of his own which is very individual and very elaborate in spite of its seeming simplicity.

Although he succeeded abundantly as a lecturer, and although he was the author of the most widely circulated book of the decade, Mark Twain still thought of himself only as a journalist; and when he gave up the West for the East he became an editor of the *Buffalo Express*, in which he had bought an interest. In 1870 he married; and it is perhaps not indiscreet to remark that his was another of those happy unions of which there have been so many in the annals of American authorship. In 1871 he removed to Hartford, where his home has been ever since; and at the same time he gave up newspaper work.

In 1872 he wrote *Roughing It*, and in the following year came his first sustained attempt at fiction, *The Gilded Age*, written in collaboration with Mr. Charles Dudley Warner. The character of "Colonel Mulberry Sellers" Mark Twain soon took out of this book to make it the central figure of a play which the late John T. Raymond acted hundreds of times throughout the United States, the playgoing public pardoning the inexpertness of the dramatist in favor of the delicious humor and the compelling veracity with which the chief character was presented. So universal was this type and so broadly recognizable its traits that there were few towns wherein the play was presented in which some one did not accost the actor who impersonated the ever-hopeful schemer to declare: "I'm the original of *Sellers*! Didn't Mark ever tell you? Well, he took the *Colonel* from me!"

Encouraged by the welcome accorded to this first attempt at fiction, Mark Twain turned to the days of his boyhood and wrote *Tom Sawyer*, published in 1875. He also collected his sketches, scattered here and there in newspapers and magazines. Toward the end of the seventies he went to Europe again with his family; and the result of this journey is recorded in *A Tramp Abroad*, published in 1880. Another volume of sketches, *The Stolen White Elephant*, was put forth in 1882; and in the same year Mark Twain first came forward as a historical novelist—if *The Prince and the Pauper* can fairly be called a historical novel. The year after, he sent forth the volume describing his *Life on the Mississippi*; and in 1884 he followed this with the story in which that life has been crystallized forever, *Huckleberry Finn*, the finest of his books, the deepest in its insight, and the widest in its appeal.

This Odyssey of the Mississippi was published by a new firm, in which the author was a chief partner, just as Sir Walter Scott had been an associate of Ballantyne and Constable. There was at first a period of prosperity in which the house issued the *Personal Memoirs* of Grant, giving his widow checks for $350,000 in 1886, and in which Mark Twain himself published *A Connecticut Yankee at King Arthur's Court*, a volume of *Merry Tales*, and a story called *The American Claimant*, wherein Colonel Sellers reappears. Then there came a succession of hard years; and at last the publishing house in which Mark Twain was a partner failed, as the publishing house in which Walter Scott was a partner had formerly failed. The author of *Huckleberry Finn* at sixty found himself suddenly saddled with a load of debt, just as the author of *Waverley* had been burdened full threescore years earlier; and Mark Twain stood up stoutly under it, as Scott had done before him. More fortunate than the Scotchman, the American has lived to pay the debt in full.

Since the disheartening crash came, he has given to the public a third Mississippi River tale, *Pudd'nhead Wilson*, issued in 1894; and a third historical novel *Joan of Arc*, a reverent and sympathetic study of the bravest figure in all French history, printed anonymously in *Harper's Magazine* and then in a volume acknowledged by the author in 1896. As one of the results of a lecturing tour around the world he prepared another volume of travels, *Following the Equator*, published toward the end of 1897. Mention must also be made of a fantastic tale called *Tom Sawyer Abroad*, sent forth in 1894, of a volume of sketches, *The Million Pound Bank-Note*, assembled in 1893, and also of a collection of literary essays, *How to Tell a Story*, published in 1897.

This is but the barest outline of Mark Twain's life—such a brief summary as we must have before us if we wish to consider the conditions under which the author has developed and the stages of his growth. It will serve, however, to show how various have been his forms of activity—printer, pilot, miner, journalist, traveler, lecturer, novelist, publisher—and to suggest the width of his experience of life.

II

A humorist is often without honor in his own country. Perhaps this is partly because humor is likely to be familiar, and familiarity breeds contempt. Perhaps it is partly because (for some strange reason) we tend to despise those who make us laugh, while we respect those who make us weep—forgetting that there are formulas for forcing tears quite as facile as the formulas for forcing smiles. Whatever the reason, the fact is indisputable that the humorist must pay the penalty of his humor; he must run the risk of being tolerated as a mere fun maker, not to be taken seriously, and unworthy of critical consideration. This penalty has been paid by Mark Twain. In many of the discussions of American literature he is dismissed as though he were only a competitor of his predecessors, Artemus Ward and John Phoenix, instead of being, what he is really, a writer who is to be classed—at whatever interval only time may decide—rather with Cervantes and Molière.

Like the heroines of the problem plays of the modern theater, Mark Twain has had to live down his past. His earlier writing gave but little promise of the enduring qualities obvious enough in his later works. Mr. Noah Brooks has told us how he was advised, if he wished to "see genuine specimens of American humor, frolicsome, extravagant, and audacious," to look up the sketches which the then almost unknown Mark Twain was printing in a Nevada newspaper. The humor of Mark Twain is still American, still frolicsome, extravagant, and audacious; but it is riper now and richer, and it has taken unto itself other qualities existing only in germ in these firstlings of his muse. The sketches in *The Jumping Frog* and the letters which made up *The Innocents Abroad* are "comic copy," as the phrase is in newspaper offices—comic copy not altogether unlike what John Phoenix had written and Artemus Ward, better indeed than the work of these newspaper humorists (for Mark Twain had it in him to develop as they did not), but not essentially dissimilar.

And in the eyes of many who do not think for themselves, Mark Twain is only the author of these genuine specimens of American humor. For when the public has once made up its mind about any man's work, it does not relish any attempt to force it to unmake this opinion and to remake it. Like other juries, it does not like to be ordered to reconsider its verdict as contrary to the facts of the case. It is always sluggish in beginning the necessary readjustment, and not only sluggish, but somewhat grudging. Naturally it cannot help seeing the later works of a popular writer from the point of view it had to take to enjoy his earlier writings. And thus the author of *Huckleberry Finn* and *Joan of Arc* is forced to pay a high price for the early and abundant popularity of *The Innocents Abroad*.

No doubt, a few of his earlier sketches were inexpensive in their elements; made of materials worn threadbare by generations of earlier funny men, they were sometimes cut in the pattern of his predecessors. No doubt, some of the earliest of all were crude and highly colored, and may even be called forced, not to say violent. No doubt, also, they did not suggest the seriousness and the melancholy which always must underlie the deepest humor, as we find it in Cervantes and Molière, in Swift and in Lowell. But even a careless reader, skipping through the book in idle amusement, ought to have been able to see in *The Innocents Abroad* that the writer of that liveliest of books of travel was no mere merry-andrew, grinning through a horse-collar to make sport for the groundlings; but a sincere observer of life, seeing through his own eyes and setting down what he saw with abundant humor, of course, but also with profound respect for the eternal verities.

George Eliot in one of her essays calls those who parody lofty themes "debasers of the moral currency." Mark Twain is always an advocate of the sterling ethical standard. He is ready to overwhelm an affectation with irresistible laughter, but he never lacks reverence for the things that really deserve reverence. It is not at the Old Masters that he scoffs in Italy, but rather at those who pay lip service to things which they neither enjoy nor understand. For a ruin or a painting or a legend that does not seem to him to deserve the appreciation in which it is held he refuses to affect an admiration he does not feel; he cannot help being honest—he was born so. For meanness of all kinds he has a burning contempt; and on Abelard he pours out the vials of his wrath. He has a quick eye for all humbugs and a scorching scorn for them; but there is no attempt at being funny in the manner of the cockney comedians when he stands in the awful presence of the Sphinx. He is not taken in by the glamour of Palestine; he does not lose his head there; he keeps his feet; but he knows that he is standing on holy ground; and there is never a hint of irreverence in his attitude.

A Tramp Abroad is a better book than *The Innocents Abroad*; it is quite as laughter-provoking, and its manner is far more restrained. Mark Twain was then master of his method, sure of himself, secure of his popularity; and he could do his best and spare no pains to be certain that it was his best. Perhaps there is a slight falling off in *Following the Equator*; a trace of fatigue, of weariness, of disenchantment. But the last book of travels has passages as broadly humorous as any of the first; and it proves the author's possession of a pithy shrewdness not to be suspected from a perusal of its earliest predecessor. The first book was the work of a young fellow rejoicing in his own fun and resolved to make his readers laugh with him or at him; the latest book is the work of an older man, who has found that life is not all laughter, but whose eye is as clear as ever and whose tongue is as plain-spoken.

These three books of travel are like all other books of travel in that they relate in the first person what the author went forth to see. Autobiographic also are *Roughing It* and *Life on the Mississippi*, and they have always seemed to me better books than the more widely circulated travels. They are better because they are the result of a more intimate knowledge of the material dealt with. Every traveler is of necessity but a bird of passage; he is a mere carpetbagger; his acquaintance with the countries he visits is external only; and this acquaintanceship is made only when he is a full-grown man. But Mark Twain's knowledge of the Mississippi was acquired in his youth; it was not purchased with a price; it was his birthright; and it was internal and complete. And his knowledge of the mining camp was achieved in early manhood when the mind is open and sensitive to every new impression. There is in both these books a fidelity to the inner truth, a certainty of touch, a sweep of vision, not to be found in the three books of travels. For my own part I have long thought that Mark Twain could securely rest his right to survive as an author on those opening chapters in *Life on the Mississippi* in which he makes clear the difficulties, the seeming impossibilities, that fronted those who wished to learn the river. These chapters are bold and brilliant, and they picture for us forever a period and a set of conditions, singularly interesting and splendidly varied, that otherwise would have had to forego all adequate record.

III

It is highly probable that when an author reveals the power of evoking views of places and of calling up portraits of people such as Mark Twain showed in *Life on the Mississippi*, and when he has the masculine grasp of reality Mark Twain made evident in *Roughing It*, he must needs sooner or later turn from mere fact to avowed fiction and become a story-teller. The long stories which Mark Twain has written fall into two divisions—first, those of which the scene is laid in the present, in reality, and mostly in the Mississippi Valley, and second, those of which the scene is laid in the past, in fantasy mostly, and in Europe.

As my own liking is a little less for the latter group, there is no need for me now to linger over them. In writing these tales of the past Mark Twain was making up stories in his head; personally I prefer the tales of his in which he has his foot firm on reality. *The Prince and the Pauper* has the essence of boyhood in it; it has variety and vigor; it has abundant humor and plentiful pathos; and yet I for one would give the whole of it for the single chapter in which Tom Sawyer lets the contract for whitewashing his aunt's fence.

Mr. Howells has declared that there are two kinds of fiction he likes almost equally well—"a real novel and a pure romance"; and he joyfully accepts *A Connecticut Yankee at King Arthur's Court* as "one of the greatest romances ever imagined." It is a humorous romance overflowing with stalwart fun; and it is not irreverent, but iconoclastic, in that it breaks not a few disestablished idols. It is intensely American and intensely nineteenth century and intensely democratic—in the best sense of that abused adjective. The British critics were greatly displeased with the book;—and we are reminded of the fact that the Spanish still somewhat resent *Don Quixote* because it brings out too truthfully the fatal gap in the Spanish character between the ideal and the real. So much of the feudal still survives in British society that Mark Twain's merry and elucidating assault on the past seemed to some almost an insult to the present. But no critic, British or American, has ventured to discover any irreverence in *Joan of Arc*, wherein, indeed, the tone is almost devout and the humor almost too much subdued. Perhaps it is my own distrust of the so-called historical novel, my own disbelief that it can ever be anything but an inferior form of art, which makes me care less for this worthy effort to honor a noble figure. And elevated and dignified as is the *Joan of Arc*, I do not think that it shows us Mark Twain at his best; although it has many a passage that only he could have written, it is perhaps the least characteristic of his works. Yet it may well be that the certain measure of success he has achieved in handling a subject so lofty and so serious, will help to open the eyes of the public to see the solid merits of his other stories, in which his humor has fuller play and in which his natural gifts are more abundantly displayed.

Of these other stories three are "real novels," to use Mr. Howells's phrase; they are novels as real as any in any literature. *Tom Sawyer* and *Huckleberry Finn* and *Pudd'nhead Wilson* are invaluable contributions to American literature—for American literature is nothing if it is not a true picture of American life and if it does not help us to understand ourselves. *Huckleberry Finn* is a very amusing volume, and a generation has read its pages and laughed over it immoderately; but it is very much more than a funny book; it is a marvelously accurate portrayal of a whole civilization. Mr. Ormsby, in an essay which accompanies his translation of *Don Quixote*, has pointed out that for a full century after its publication that greatest of novels was enjoyed chiefly as a tale of humorous misadventure, and that three generations had laughed over it before anybody suspected that it was more than a mere funny book. It is perhaps rather with the picaresque romances of Spain that *Huckleberry Finn* is to be compared than with the masterpiece of Cervantes; but I do not think it will be a century or take three generations before we Americans generally discover how great a book *Huckleberry Finn* really is, how keen its vision of character, how close its observation of life, how sound its philosophy, and how it records for us once and for all certain phases of Southwestern society which it is most important for us to perceive and to understand. The influence of slavery, the prevalence of feuds, the conditions and the circumstances that make lynching possible—all these things are set before us clearly and without comment. It is for us to draw our own moral, each for himself, as we do when we see Shakespeare acted.

Huckleberry Finn, in its art, for one thing, and also in its broader range, is superior to *Tom Sawyer* and to *Pudd'nhead Wilson*, fine as both these are in their several ways. In no book in our language, to my mind, has the boy, simply as a boy, been better realized than in *Tom Sawyer*. In some respects *Pudd'nhead Wilson* is the most dramatic of Mark Twain's longer stories, and also the most ingenious; like *Tom Sawyer* and *Huckleberry Finn*, it has the full flavor of the Mississippi River, on which its author spent his own boyhood, and from contact with the soil of which he always rises reinvigorated.

It is by these three stories, and especially by *Huckleberry Finn*, that Mark Twain is likely to live longest. Nowhere else is the life of the Mississippi Valley so truthfully recorded. Nowhere else can we find a gallery of Southwestern characters as varied and as veracious as those Huck Finn met in his wanderings. The histories of literature all praise the *Gil Blas* of Le Sage for its amusing adventures, its natural characters, its pleasant humor, and its insight into human frailty; and the praise is deserved. But in every one of these qualities *Huckleberry Finn* is superior to *Gil Blas*. Le Sage set the model of the picaresque novel, and Mark Twain followed his example; but the American book is richer than the French—deeper, finer, stronger. It would be hard to find in any language better specimens of pure narrative, better examples of the power of telling a story and of calling up action so that the reader cannot help but see it, than Mark Twain's account of the Shepherdson–Grangerford feud, and his description of the shooting of Boggs by Sherbourn and of the foiled attempt to lynch Sherbourn afterward.

These scenes, fine as they are, vivid, powerful, and most artistic in their restraint, can be matched in the two other books. In *Tom Sawyer* they can be paralleled by the chapter in which the boy and the girl are lost in the cave, and Tom, seeing a gleam of light in the distance, discovers that it is a candle carried by Indian Joe, the one enemy he has in the world. In *Pudd'nhead Wilson* the great passages of *Huckleberry Finn* are rivaled by that most pathetic account of the weak son willing to sell his own mother as a slave "down the river." Although no one of the books is sustained throughout on this high level, and although, in truth, there are in each of them passages here and there that we could wish away (because they are not worthy of the association in which we find them), I have no hesitation in expressing here my own conviction that the man who has given us four scenes like these is to be compared with the masters of literature; and that he can abide the comparison with equanimity.

IV

Perhaps I myself prefer these three Mississippi Valley books above all Mark Twain's other writings (although with no lack of affection for those also) partly because these have the most of the flavor of the soil about them. After veracity and the sense of the universal, what I best relish in literature is this native aroma, pungent, homely, and abiding. Yet I feel sure that I should not rate him so high if he were the author of these three books only. They are the best of him, but the others are good also, and good in a different way. Other writers have given us this local color more or less artistically, more or less convincingly: one New England and another New York, a third Virginia, and a fourth Georgia, and a fifth Wisconsin; but who so well as Mark Twain has given us the full spectrum of the Union? With all his exactness in reproducing the Mississippi Valley, Mark Twain is not sectional in his outlook; he is national always. He is not narrow; he is not Western or Eastern; he is American with a certain largeness and boldness and freedom and certainty that we like to think of as befitting a country so vast as ours and a people so independent.

In Mark Twain we have "the national spirit as seen with our own eyes," declared Mr. Howells; and, from more points of view than one, Mark Twain seems to me to be the very embodiment of Americanism. Self-educated in the hard school of life, he has gone on broadening his outlook as he has grown older. Spending many years abroad, he has come to understand other nationalities, without enfeebling his own native faith. Combining a mastery of the commonplace with an imaginative faculty, he is a practical idealist. No respecter of persons, he has a tender regard for his fellow man. Irreverent toward all outworn superstitions, he has ever revealed the deepest respect for all things truly worthy of reverence. Unwilling to take pay in words, he is impatient always to get at the root of the matter, to pierce to the center, to see the thing as it is. He has a habit of standing upright, of thinking for himself, and of hitting hard at whatsoever seems to him hateful and mean; but at the core of him there is genuine gentleness and honest sympathy, brave humanity and sweet kindliness. Perhaps it is boastful for us to think that these characteristics which we see in Mark Twain are characteristics also of the American people as a whole; but it is pleasant to think so. Mark Twain has the very marrow of Americanism. He is as intensely and as typically American as Franklin or Emerson or Hawthorne. He has not a little of the shrewd common sense and the homely and unliterary directness of Franklin. He is not without a share of the aspiration and the elevation of Emerson; and he has a philosophy of his own as optimistic as Emerson's. He possesses also somewhat of Hawthorne's interest in ethical problems, with something of the same power of getting at the heart of them; he, too, has written his parables and apologs wherein the moral is obvious and unobtruded. He is uncompromisingly honest; and his conscience is as rugged as his style sometimes is.

No American author has to-day at his command a style more nervous, more varied, more flexible, or more various than Mark Twain's. His colloquial ease should not hide from us his mastery of all the devices of rhetoric. He may seem to disobey the letter of the law sometimes, but he is always obedient to the spirit. He never speaks unless he has something to say; and then he says it tersely, sharply, with a freshness of epithet and an individuality of phrase, always accurate, however unacademic. His vocabulary is enormous, and it is deficient only in the dead words; his language is alive always, and actually tingling with vitality. He rejoices in the daring noun and in the audacious adjective. His instinct for the exact word is not always unerring, and now and again he has failed to exercise it; but there is in his prose none of the flatting and sharping he censured in Fenimore Cooper's. His style has none of the cold perfection of an antique statue; it is too modern and too American for that, and too completely the expression of the man himself, sincere and straightforward. It is not free from slang, although this is far less frequent than one might expect; but it does its work swiftly and cleanly. And it is capable of immense variety. Consider the tale of the Blue Jay in *A Tramp Abroad*, wherein the humor is sustained by unstated pathos; what could be better told than this, with every word the right word and in the right place? And take Huck Finn's description of the storm when he was alone on the island, which is in dialect, which will not parse, which bristles with double negatives, but which none the less is one of the finest passages of descriptive prose in all American literature.

V

After all, it is as a humorist pure and simple that Mark Twain is best known and best beloved. In the preceding pages I have tried to point out the several ways in which he transcends humor, as the word is commonly restricted, and to show that he is no mere fun maker. But he is a fun maker beyond all question, and he has made millions laugh as no other man of our century has done. The laughter he has aroused is wholesome and self-respecting; it clears the atmosphere. For this we cannot but be grateful. As Lowell said, "let us not be ashamed to confess that, if we find the tragedy a bore, we take the profoundest satisfaction in the farce. It is a mark of sanity." There is no laughter in Don Quixote, the noble enthusiast whose wits are unsettled; and there is little on the lips of Alceste the misanthrope of Molière; but for both of them life would have been easier had they known how to laugh. Cervantes himself, and Molière also, found relief in laughter for their melancholy; and it was the sense of humor which kept them tolerantly interested in the spectacle of humanity, although life had pressed hardly on them both. On Mark Twain also life has left its scars; but he has bound up his wounds and battled forward with a stout heart, as Cervantes did, and Molière. It was Molière who declared that it was a strange business to undertake to make people laugh; but even now, after two centuries, when the best of Molière's plays are acted, mirth breaks out again and laughter overflows.

It would be doing Mark Twain a disservice to liken him to Molière, the greatest comic dramatist of all time; and yet there is more than one point of similarity. Just as Mark Twain began by writing comic copy which contained no prophecy of a masterpiece like *Huckleberry Finn*, so Molière was at first the author only of semiacrobatic farces on the Italian model in no wise presaging *Tartuffe* and *The Misanthrope*. Just as Molière succeeded first of all in pleasing the broad public that likes robust fun, and then slowly and step by step developed into a dramatist who set on the stage enduring figures plucked out of the abounding life about him, so also has Mark Twain grown, ascending from *The Jumping Frog* to *Huckleberry Finn*, as comic as its elder brother and as laughter-provoking, but charged also with meaning and with philosophy. And like Molière again, Mark Twain has kept solid hold of the material world; his doctrine is not of the earth earthy, but it is never sublimated into sentimentality. He sympathizes with the spiritual side of humanity, while never ignoring the sensual. Like Molière, Mark Twain takes his stand on common sense and thinks scorn of affectation of every sort. He understands sinners and strugglers and weaklings; and he is not harsh with them, reserving his scorching hatred for hypocrites and pretenders and frauds.

At how long an interval Mark Twain shall be rated after Molière and Cervantes it is for the future to declare. All that we can see clearly now is that it is with them that he is to be classed—with Molière and Cervantes, with Chaucer and Fielding, humorists all of them, and all of them manly men.

—Brander Matthews, 1899

BARRETT WENDELL (1900)

In a time when university courses scarcely acknowledged American literature, even within the United States, Harvard University English professor Barrett Wendell pioneered its study and, for better or worse, introduced English composition and creative writing into the standard curriculum. He was a biographer of Cotton Mather, whose life sometimes resembled his subject's. Like Mather, Wendell was the heir (on his father's side) to a venerable New England tradition. Like Mather, he was both influential and controversial. Also like Mather, he ended his days increasingly isolated due to anachronistic views—in Wendell's case, his views on class and race. He was a snob in a time of social reform.

Any particular disposition toward his native land's literature might not be immediately easy to discern, then, in the chapter titled "The West." It appears as almost an afterthought to Wendell's long *Literary History of America*. Fred Lewis Pattee sardonically renamed Wendell's book "A Literary History of Harvard University, with Incidental Glimpses of the Minor Writers of America." Wendell himself described this study to William James thus: "In sentiment it is Tory, pro-slavery, and imperialistic; all of which I fear I am myself."

Wendell interestingly locates Twain's writing alongside the works of two English writers: Frances Trollope's study *Domestic Manners of the Americans* (1832) and Charles Dickens's novel *Martin Chuzzlewit* (1844). These two works were viewed by many Americans as attacks by ingrates on their own culture, made by writers who had partaken of the country's hospitality and generosity and who, in Dickens's case, they had formerly admired. What might it signify for Wendell to list Twain's Mississippi writings alongside those of Dickens and Trollope? What tradition does Wendell place Twain in?

Wendell considers also the connection between newspapers and the advancement of a native American humor. By doing so, he looks back at the development of American humor, finding a precedent for Mark Twain in Benjamin Franklin. (Mark Twain might disagree with this, if one credits the view held in the 1870 squib "The Late Benjamin Franklin.") Yet Wendell also displays a squeamish ambivalence to works of Western journalism, which he compares to the minstrel shows of the 1840s. Is the word he is awkwardly skirting "democracy"? Finally, having briskly dismissed Artemus Ward as "far from reputable," Wendell finds a lineage connecting the savage pro-Union Civil War satirist David Ross Locke ("Petroleum V. Nasby") and Twain, who retains Nasby's "contagious vitality."

Wendell provides an unusual view, that of a self-professed snob from Harvard who recoiled from the common herd, who nevertheless finds great value in Mark Twain's work in a time when most conservative critics remained aloof. Does this concession mark a change in the critical consensus regarding Mark Twain? Students tracing patterns in critical attitudes toward Twain should certainly take note.

Our chief concern, however, is not with politics or even with society; it is rather with those aspects of feeling and temper which tend toward something which the West has not yet achieved,—namely, literary expression. Glimpses of these, as they appeared to foreign eyes, are to be found in the familiar old books of travel which formerly so incensed Americans against Mrs. Trollope; and a little later in those caricatures of "Martin Chuzzlewit" which so displeased American sensibilities that American readers are prone to forget how the same book caricatures the English too, in such figures as Mr. Pecksniff and Mrs. Sarah Gamp. A very different picture of the Middle West, a little later, is to be found in a book which in certain moods ones is disposed for all its eccentricity to call the most admirable work of literary art as yet produced on this continent. This is that Odyssean story of the Mississippi to which Mark Twain gave the grotesque name of "Huckleberry Finn." The material from which he made this book he carelessly flung together a year or two before in a rambling series of reminiscences called "Life on the Mississippi." Mrs. Trollope, "Martin Chuzzlewit," "Life on the Mississippi," and "Huckleberry Finn" will combine to give a fair notion of Western life and character before the Civil War. . . .

As you grow familiar with American newspapers, it appears that besides their chief function of purveying news in a manner welcome to uneducated readers they undertake to provide such readers with fragmentary matter of which the substance comes nearer to literature. In recognised "departments," you will find many items of general information; many scraps of verse, too, some of which approaches poetry; and, above all, in most papers of much pretension you are apt to find regular contributions intended simply to make you laugh.

Mainly from this source,—the comic columns of American newspapers,— there has tended to develop a kind of native expression hardly recognised forty years ago and now popularly supposed to be our most characteristic. This is what is commonly called American humour.

Some vein of humour, of coarse, has existed in America almost from the beginning. In the admirable analytic index of Stedman and Hutchinson's "Library of American Literature," American humor is held to have existed as early as 1647, when Nathaniel Ward, minister of Ipswich, published his "Simple Cobbler of Agawam," a work which contains satirical sketches of character in the regular seventeenth-century manner. There was plenty of conventional humour, too, in the literature of the American Revolution. Hopkinson's "Battle of the Kegs," however, the most familiar example of this, needs only comparison with Cowper's neatly contemporary "John Gilpin" to reveal that its chief American trait is a somewhat unskillful touch. Franklin's humour was somewhat more national; that letter of his to a London newspaper, about 1760, proved the most hard-headed and versatile of eighteenth-century Americans to have been capable of a grave confusion of fact and nonsense which reminds one of Mark Twain's. Among our acknowledged men of letters, in later days, several have won recognition largely by means of their humorous passages. Irving's "Knickerbockers," for example, founded his reputation by just such confusion of literal statement with extravagance as made Franklin's letter amusing fifty years before and Mark Twain's "Innocents Abroad" fifty years later; in all three, you are constantly perplexed as to what is so and what not. . . .

Whatever the strength or the weakness of the writers whom we have considered, their fun, like their seriousness and their commonplace, is of the sort which characterises gentlemen. Democratic though our country be, those actually recognised as our men of letters, even if, like Franklin or Whittier, of simple origin, have generally possessed in their ripeness a personal dignity, at once conscious and willingly acknowledged. In momentarily distinguished form, then, American humour first declared itself. The form which has been developing in Western newspapers has other traits.

The chief of these, which is inherent in the popularity of Western journalism, is hard to define, but palpable and vital. It amounts to a general assumption that everybody whom you address will entirely understand whatever you say. Such an assumption implies broad human feeling. We all know that men differ not only in temperament, but also in accordance with the conditions of their lives; and most of us are over-conscious of such differences. Now and again, however, you come across somebody who contagiously assumes that for all our differences every human being is really human, and so that everybody's emotions, sublime or ridiculous, may generally be excited in the same way. A familiar example of the temper now in mind pervaded a kind of entertainment frequent in America thirty or forty years ago,—the negro minstrel shows, now tending to vanish in performances, like those of London music halls. In these shows a number of men would daub their faces with burnt cork, would dress themselves in preposterous burlesque of the florid taste still characteristic of negroes, and sitting in a row would sing songs and tell stories. The songs were sometimes sentimental, the stories almost always extravagantly comic; but underlying one and all was an assumption that everybody who heard what the performers said was familiar with everything they knew,—not only with local allusions and human nature, but also with the very names and personal oddities of the individuals they mentioned. To phrase the thing colloquially, the whole performance assumed that we were all in the crowd. You will find a touch of this temper in Falstaff, plenty of it in Sancho Panza; you will find it, too, in the conventional personages of the old European stage,—Policinello or Sganarelle; you will find it in the mountebanks who have plied their trade throughout human history. This temper is obviously akin to that broadly human feeling which underlies all great works of lasting art. The more we can assume that everybody is human, the more human our literary work will be.

Some such trait as this pervades the "funny" columns of American newspapers, particularly in the West; and it is mostly from these columns that American humour has emerged into what approach it has made to literary form. . . .

Though, in general, American newspaper humour is not so significant, it has retained from Nasby's day the sort of contagious vitality found throughout his writings; and in one or two cases of men still living it has emerged into something more notable. In one case, indeed, it has resulted in literary work so characteristically American, and so wildly varied, that while happily the author in question is not yet a posthumous subject for such study as ours, it is impossible not to mention his name. If there be any contemporary work at once thoroughly American, and, for all its errors of taste, full of indications that the writer's power would have been exceptional anywhere, it is that of Mr. Clemens, more widely known as Mark Twain.

—Barrett Wendell, from *A Literary History of America*, New York: Charles Scribner's Sons, 1900, pp. 502–503, 507–508, 509–510, 513

HARRY THURSTON PECK
"AS TO MARK TWAIN" (1901)

Peck was a Latin professor at Columbia University, as well as the editor of the *Bookman*, in which this article appeared. It is worth noting that Twain had apparently become a fierce subject of debate among academics. Peck's comments may duly be compared to those of Barrett Wendell contained elsewhere in this volume. Peck was clearly stung by Twain's humorous dismissal of Sir Walter Scott, and here he seeks to redress the balance.

Peck draws attention to a change in the public perception of Twain since his "return to the country of his birth." Twain has become favored, Peck writes, and all reports concerning him are "indiscriminate eulogy." It has reached the stage where Twain himself requests a change of note. This, Professor Peck attempts to do.

Peck's view, though unfashionable at its time, rings rather truer to the present reader. He predicts that Mark Twain shall be remembered as a humorist and that his enduring characters are Huckleberry Finn and Tom Sawyer (and Colonel Sellers). He is correct that *Joan of Arc* is an oddity. This essay is diametrically opposed to the one written by William Dean Howells four years earlier. Howells tries to induce the reader to forget Twain the humorist and embrace Twain of the romances; Peck predicts that the humorist will prevail and the romances are an aberration. "A hundred years from now it is very likely that *The Jumping Frog* alone will be remembered." Students comparing competing critical views of Mark

Twain might profitably compare these two articles. Peck, at any rate, provides a valuable dissenting voice at a time when unchecked praise of Twain is proliferating.

———

At a recent meeting of the Nineteenth Century Club Mark Twain delivered himself of some observations upon the subject of Sir Walter Scott as a novelist. He said that Scott can be read with interest by a boy of sixteen and can be re-read with interest by the same person after he has reached the age of ninety, but that between one's first and second childhood Scott is hardly to be reckoned with. It would have been well had Mr. Clemens extended his observations a little further in order to inform his audience at precisely what age his own historical novels may be regarded as interesting any human being. It is a subject on which we have ourselves endeavoured to secure some first-hand information and have ingloriously failed. We know of one gentleman who succeeded in reading *Joan of Arc* to the end; but he was a book reviewer and had to do it because he was a conscientious man. We tried it several times, and then gave it up because of its egregious dulness. We should like to know whether Mr. Clemens supposes that the various beautiful editions of Scott's works that have lately been issued in England and in this country have been issued solely for the benefit of boys and dotards. Then there is the sumptuous reprint of Lockhart's *Life of Scott*, published in five large volumes by the Macmillan Company. This appears to show that not only do very many persons thoroughly enjoy the reading of what Scott wrote down himself, but that they also like to read about him—a liking that has been further gratified by the publication of a smaller life of the great romancer composed by Mr. James Hay. There does not, therefore, seem to be any reason for serious disquietude with regard to Scott; but we fear that we cannot say as much for Mr. Clemens.

Mr. Clemens has of late and since his return to the country of his birth been very conspicuously in what one of our magazines delights to call 'the public eye.' He has succeeded in beating down a cabman's charges to the extent of a quarter of a dollar—which, of course, was a public-spirited thing for him to do. He has attended innumerable dinners and other functions, and has made innumerable speeches at them. He has said some things about the responsibility of our leading citizens for the present condition of our municipal government, and thus has pleased the city newspapers. The speakers who have introduced him to his audiences have invariably beslavered him with praise, and life has been to him of late what Mr.

Grover Cleveland many years ago described as just 'one grand sweet song.' Mr. Clemens himself, with certain compunctions which we believe to have been sincere, has from time to time requested these perfervid gentlemen to change their note and to say something that should be an antidote to indiscriminate eulogy. None of them complied; and, therefore, Mr. Clemens will no doubt be doubly grateful that we are not possessed of a mind of such obliquity as not to take him at his word. Putting aside all prejudice and looking at his work in a purely achromatic way, a critical and truthful judgment upon Mark Twain can be summed up in a very exiguous space. Mark Twain is first and last and all the time, so far as he is anything, a humourist and nothing more. He wrote *The Jumping Frog* and *Innocents Abroad* and *Roughing It*, and these are all the real books that he ever wrote. He set forth the typically American characters of Colonel Sellers and Tom Sawyer and Huckleberry Finn, and these are all the real characters that he ever drew. His later publications that are humorous in intention contain many gleams of the old Mark Twain; but, taken as entities, you cannot read them from beginning to end. Some unduly optimistic persons who are fond of literary cults grown under glass have tried very hard to make the world believe that Mr. Clemens has great gifts as a serious novelist and romancer. By dint of iteration the world, perhaps, has temporarily come to think that this is true; but all the same, it will not read these novels and romances, and it thereby shows that common sense and real discrimination may exist in practice even while they hold no place in theory. A hundred years from now it is very likely that *The Jumping Frog* alone will be remembered, just as out of all that Robert Louis Stevenson composed, the world will ultimately keep in memory the single tale of *Dr. Jekyll and Mr. Hyde*.

This spasmodic and ephemeral outburst of enthusiasm over Mr. Clemens emphasises for the thousandth time a melancholy truth about contemporary criticism. When a writer is doing good and forceful work and winning readers and laying the foundation and erecting the superstructure of an enviable reputation, our critics, even though they may admire him, have not the 'sand' to say so. They are poor dumb sheep that never dare to take the lead in anything; but they stand around with unintelligent and foolish bleatings until some one whom they are not afraid to follow shall tell them what they ought to say. When Kipling was doing his finest work, such as he has never equalled in these later years, the critics did not dare to take him seriously. He was so unconventional and rough and strong that he frightened them; and so they slunk timidly behind their ink-stands and said little feeble nothings and joked a little and called him a mere journalist, and then looked around to see if any one was going to hit them. After they found out that his work was instinct with true genius, and that he was in reality the one real literary phenomenon of the last quarter of our century, they all rushed in at once and spattered him with praise and daubed him over with their flattery, and did their very best to make him seem absurd. By this time, as it happened, Kipling's best had all been done, and he was entering upon a period of a decline which may or may not turn out to be temporary. But the critics were as blind to his decadence as they had been previously blind to his great power; and, therefore, all the things they should have said about his early work they said about his later, so that he has been going on for the last two years receiving praise and admiration that are clearly a misfit. The same thing is quite true concerning Mr. Clemens. In the speeches that he has lately made he has said some things that recalled his earlier humour, but in the majority of his utterances the humour has been forced and the laughter which it has evoked has been extremely hollow. Yet just because it was Mark Twain, and because Mark Twain was once a true, spontaneous and original humourist, the poor creatures who write about him believe that everything he says must be amusing and delightful. If they do not feel the fun of it themselves they think they ought to, and they write about it just as though they did.

—Harry Thurston Peck,
"As to Mark Twain," January 1901

Ambrose Bierce "Wit and Humor" (1903)

While the critics were arguing their cases for Mark Twain as humorist or romancer (or, simply, author of literature), his old associate Ambrose Bierce had no doubt. Twain was a humorist. For Bierce, whose concerns are not the same as those of Howells (whom he despised), the opposition is not between humor and literature at all but between wit and humor. Even in 1903, the old names of Josh Billings and Artemus Ward are resurrected and Mark Twain's placed alongside them.

In a matter of this kind it is easier to illustrate than to define. Humor (which is not inconsistent with pathos, so nearly allied are laughter and tears) is Charles Dickens, wit is Alexander Pope. Humor is Dogberry, wit is Mercutio. Humor is Artemus Ward, John Phoenix, Josh Billings, Bill Nye, Mark Twain —their name is legion; for wit we must brave the perils of the deep; it is "made in France" and hardly bears transportation. All Americans are humorous; if any are born witty Heaven help them to emigrate! You shall not meet an American and talk with him two minutes but he will say something humorous; in ten days he will say nothing witty.... Humor is tolerant, tender; its ridicule caresses; wit stabs, begs pardon—and turns the weapon in the wound. Humor is a sweet wine, wit a dry; we know which is preferred by the connoisseur.

—Ambrose Bierce, "Wit and Humor,"
San Francisco *Examiner*, March 23, 1903

BARRETT WENDELL WITH
CHESTER NOYES GREENOUGH (1904)

Four years after his *Literary History,* Wendell collaborated with Chester Noyes Greenough on an edition for use in schools. In this new, longer reckoning, Wendell is less hesitant with his praise and more effusive. He is perhaps the first to call *Huckleberry Finn* a "masterpiece"—even "the masterpiece of literature in America."

A self-confessed imperialist, Wendell also praises the mature, political Twain, "whether you agree with him or not." Wendell arguably recasts Twain more effectively than Howells, since his praise comes more reluctantly, lauding his "honourable maturity" and "manly honesty." Students exploring public perceptions of Twain should note this recognition and acceptance, not only by a Harvard conservative but also by the editor of an influential textbook. Is this a turning point in the wider perception of Mark Twain?

Equally, it should be asked, in exonerating Twain from all charges of "spiritual vulgarity," "errors of taste," or coarseness, is Barrett Wendell also whitewashing Mark Twain and denying his, as Wendell phrased it elsewhere, "contagious vitality"?

SAMUEL LANGHORNE CLEMENS, "Mark Twain," (1835–), after an apprenticeship to a printer, became a pilot on the Mississippi River in 1851. Later he tried mining, and still later journalism, in California. Thence he removed to Hawaii, and finally to Hartford, Connecticut, where he lived till lately. In 1884 he founded the publishing firm of C. L. Webster & Company; he lost heavily by its failure. His subsequent labor to pay its debts suggests the similarly heroic efforts of Sir Walter Scott. His first book, *The Jumping Frog and Other Sketches*, came out in 1867, *Innocents Abroad* in 1869, *Adventures of Tom Sawyer* in 1876, *Life on the Mississippi* in 1883, *Adventures of Huckleberry*

Finn in 1885, *Pudd'nhead Wilson* in 1894, and *Personal Recollections of Joan of Arc* in 1895–1896.

The earlier work of Mark Twain seemed broadly comic—only another manifestation of that rollicking sort of journalistic fun which is generally ephemeral. As the years have passed, however, he has slowly distinguished himself more and more from anyone else. No other living writer, for one thing, so completely exemplifies the kind of humor which is most characteristically American—a shrewd sense of fact expressing itself in an inextricable confusion of literal statement and wild extravagance, uttered with no lapse from what seems unmoved gravity of manner.

But this is by no means the sum of him, nor yet his deepest merit. His more careful books show a grasp of his subject, a power of composition on the grand scale, unapproached by any other popular American. For all its faults of superficial taste, and for all its extravagance of dialect, *Huckleberry Finn* proves, as one compares it with its rough material, carelessly collected in *Life on the Mississippi*, nothing short of a masterpiece. And it proves as well, when one has read it over and over again, to be among the few books in any literature which preserve something like a comprehensive picture of an entire state of society. In this aspect it is Odyssean, just as *Don Quixote* is. There are moods when one is tempted to call it, despite its shortcomings, the masterpiece of literature in America.

It was this power of construction on a large scale, combined with profound human sympathy, which made more than one competent critic recognize Mark Twain's hand in the originally anonymous *Personal Recollections of Joan of Arc*. In this he showed himself an historical novelist of positive importance. His more recent work has been apt to have the increasing seriousness of his honorable maturity. He has fearlessly written of public matters, and of various social and philosophic follies, and, whether you agree with him or not, you cannot fail to recognize his manly honesty, his unbroken vigor of thought and phrase, and his ripe individuality. His persistent humor proves less and less a matter of wildness or extravagance. It is his peculiar method of courageously commenting on life.

And throughout his work one finds innumerable turns of thought and of phrase which could proceed only from one whose whole being was born and developed not in one part of America or another, but surely and only in America. No one was ever, in the better sense of the word, a more instinctive and whole-souled man of the people. No one was ever more free from the spiritual vulgarity, as distinguished from mere errors of taste, which sometimes makes men of the people seem coarse. No one was ever more broadly human—sometimes with a broadness which the fastidious may lament, oftener with a breadth of sympathy which should shame whoever fails to share it. Mark Twain is often odd, but never eccentric. There is nowhere a sounder heart or a more balanced head than reveal themselves throughout the work of this man with whom none but Americans can quite feel complete fellowship, and with whom no true American can fail to feel it.

Walt Whitman has sometimes been called the most characteristic of Americans. But there can be little doubt that, long after the whims of Whitman have obscured what power was in him, the sanity and vigor of Mark Twain will persistently show what the American spirit of his time really and truly was. This spirit has been broadly popular, odd in its expression, none too reverent in phrase or manner, often deceptive, consequently, to those whom phrase and manner may readily mislead, but full of good sense, full of kindly humor, and, above all, eager, while recognizing all the perversities of fact, to persevere towards righteousness.

> — Barrett Wendell with Chester Noyes Greenough,
> *A History of Literature in America*, New York:
> Charles Scribner's Sons, 1904, pp. 421–424

Harry Thurston Peck
"Mark Twain at Ebb Tide" (1904)

There is something unutterably pathetic about a book like Mark Twain's *Extracts from Adam's Diary*. It shows just how far a man who was once a great humourist can fall. We thought when we read 'A Double-Barrelled Detective Story' that Mark Twain could do no worse. But we were wrong. The other book may have been more ridiculous; but this one is more pitiable. We glance at the paper wrapper; we see the advertisement of the 'Complete Works of Mark Twain'; we read the titles: *The Adventures of Huckleberry Finn, The Jumping Frog of Calaveras, Life on the Mississippi, The Gilded Age, The Innocents Abroad, The Adventures of Tom Sawyer*, and we remember a man who through the sheer strength and originality of his genius won the world's laughter. Then we read *Extracts from Adam's Diary*. Had these Extracts been written by a man without a great name, no amount of 'pull' or adroit argument would have enabled him to palm them off on a first-class metropolitan daily as 'Sunday Special' matter.

> —Harry Thurston Peck, "Mark Twain
> at Ebb Tide," May 1904

HAMMOND LAMONT
"MARK TWAIN AT SEVENTY" (1905)

Hammond Lamont begins by recalling the seventieth birthday celebrations held for Mark Twain in 1905. Among the speakers at the celebration were William Dean Howells, Brander Matthews (representing the academy, presumably), and Andrew Carnegie (representing big business). A transcript was published as a supplement to *Harper's Weekly*. Odes were read and toasts proposed. As Lamont discerns, this event was a further step in cementing Twain's place within the literary establishment, his promotion to the high table and toward canonization. "Bret Harte . . . is dead," Lamont pronounces bluntly; and the literary West once exemplified by Harte and Twain is a distant memory.

There is a dissenting tone to this account. Anti-Harvard, antiacademic, and anti–Boston Brahmin in tone, it can be read as a counterblast to Brander Matthews's essay. Lamont revives and celebrates Twain as a "literary pariah," author of "words of the people as the people understand them," reclaiming Twain from the high table. Students seeking a view of Twain alternative to that of the establishment should consult Lamont's contentions.

≈≈≈ ≈≈≈ ≈≈≈

The most significant thing about the dinner to Mark Twain on December 5 was the greeting from forty of the leading men of letters of England. No other American author, we are confident, could receive such a tribute. In the opinion of foreigners, Mark Twain is the greatest of living American writers. An interesting side-light is thrown on his fame by an incident in Kipling's first visit to America, some fifteen years ago. Mark Twain was the man of whom Kipling had heard, and whom, above others, he wished to see. In the interval since then his reputation has grown, both at home and abroad. Bret Harte, whose name was often coupled with his, is dead. No one is left to dispute his preeminence, or even to compare with him.

He did not, however, come into his own at once. People were suspicious of him because he was not born and bred to the literary traditions of Boston, New York, or Philadelphia. Nor did he, when at last he had fairly started on his career, accept the conventions of his generation and conform to the standards of either of these three centres of culture. He was not reared with Hawthorne, Lowell, Longfellow, and Holmes; and consequently New England pitied him. He never attended the so-called 'Knickerbocker School'; and New York saw at once that he suffered much from lack of early advantages. True, his essays and sketches used to appear in the staid pages of the *Atlantic*, but they were a horrible shock to the dowager duchesses of Boston. The *Atlantic*, however, was erratic. It not only tolerated Mark Twain, but for a time it was edited by a man named Thomas Bailey Aldrich, who had not graduated from Harvard, indeed had never attended college, and who was therefore not a member of the Brahmin caste. These literary pariahs, however, occasionally get on in spite of deficiencies in taste and education. Mr. Aldrich, for example, managed to write some things that people have condescended to read. Indeed, one of his stories, 'Marjorie Daw,' so took the fancy of a budding author that, changing the name of the personages of the tale, he kindly offered to sell it to the *Evening Post*. What is worth stealing must have some merit. Mark Twain's success has been more dazzling than Mr. Aldrich's—and with good reason.

He knows America and knows it whole. Born in Missouri seventy years ago, he saw every type of man, woman, and child, white and black, that lived in the vast Mississippi Valley. As pilot on a Mississippi steamboat he made the acquaintance of the pioneers from New England, New York, Pennsylvania, and the Western Reserve, who pushed across the prairies and filled the vacant lands of Illinois, Iowa, Wisconsin, Minnesota, Nebraska, and Kansas. He was scarcely less at home in the Gulf States, for which the Mississippi was the great highway. As Territorial secretary of Nevada and editor of the Virginia City *Enterprise*, he knew at first hand the mining camps of the Pacific Coast, the gamblers, the railway builders, and the politicians. He has dwelt for many years in the East. He has travelled extensively. He has read widely. With some native talent to start with, he has in the slow course of time picked up almost as good an equipment for literary work as a man will get in four years at Harvard or Columbia.

He has not devoted himself to carving cherry-stones according to academic rules, but to the best of his ability he has written books to read. Delicate questions of usage have not troubled him any more than they troubled Shakspere or Defoe; he has had larger problems on his mind. We do not, we trust, undervalue choice, exact, and even academic English. A careless, sloppy style is not virtue. Misusing words and taking the edge off their meaning is the favorite amusement of fools. But Mark Twain has had stories to tell—big ones and good ones. His swift, racy style—words of the people as the people understand them—smelling of the soil, is as excellent in its kind as the classic sentences of Hawthorne. In *Huckleberry Finn* and *Tom Sawyer* he had matter enough to last an ordinary novelist a lifetime. That, after all, is the essential. The manner, we admit, is not that of the late Walter Pater in *Marius the Epicurean*. It is—if the two writers be at all commensurable—far better.

Yet it is the bulk of Mark Twain's work, rather than the admirable handling of details, that gives it power. To say nothing of his ventures into historical romance—he has shown us on an extensive scale surpassingly vivid pictures of many phases of our life. 'Here,' cry his European eulogists, 'is America as it is or was.' They are right. *Huckleberry Finn* is a cross-section of Missouri and lower Illinois. You may rise from the perusal, feeling that you have actually lived there, that you know intimately a whole social stratum of ante-bellum days, and that you have enjoyed one of the most entertaining and moving tales in our language. The episode of that feud between the Grangerfords and the Shepherdsons, with the men running along the river-bank, shooting at the swimming boys, and shouting 'Kill them! kill them!' grips the memory like those stirring scenes where Crusoe came upon the footprints of the savages and the outlaws stormed the castle of Front de Boeuf.

In saying this we mean that Mark Twain is a much greater man than the humorist of *The Jumping Frog*. That he is a humorist of the first rank no discriminating person has dreamed of denying for the last thirty years. But he is a humanist as well, if we accept the term in its broader sense—one versed in human affairs. His humor has served to keep clear and steady his vision of human relations, has helped him to pierce the sophistries of politicians, and to test the fleeting fashions of a day by eternal principles, has closed his ears to the passing cries of party, and enabled him to stand with courage, and to lift a voice that carries far, for justice and mercy to all men, of all colors, in all lands.

—Hammond Lamont, "Mark Twain at Seventy,"
The Nation, December 14, 1905

WILLIAM LYON PHELPS "MARK TWAIN" (1907)

If one can detect a note of dissension in Hammond Lamont's account of Twain's seventieth birthday, Yale professor William Phelps provides a conservative view of Mark Twain. His bias is unambiguous; at one juncture he gushes that "I wish that Mr. Howells might live forever." Elsewhere: "In these earnest pages, our national humorist [that is, Twain] appears as the true knight." For whatever reason, this essay was singled out for praise by Mark Twain.

The Yale professor Phelps had come to Hartford in February 1907 to give a lecture on Twain. When word of its content reached Twain, he responded that "when a man like Phelps speaks, the world gives attention." Twain was at this time under fire from a library that had banned his latest work, *Eve's Diary*, from its shelves. A harried Twain felt redeemed by Phelps's praise. "Some day I hope to meet him and thank him for his courage for saying those things out in public," he wrote to a friend. "Custom is, to think a handsome thing in private but tame it down in the utterance." One wonders if Twain was aware of the blizzard of hurrahs being published about him at this time.

For this reason, if none other, the essay is worthy of attention. This was a portrait that Twain endorsed. Does Twain likewise endorse the opinions spouted in the essay? Mark Twain "shows us the wretched condition of the common people," Phelps writes, "their utter ignorance and degradation." Is this a fair reading of Twain's work? Phelps is even more controversial on questions of race. Twain gives the reader both points of view, Phelps says. Here is the "living dread of the negro that he will be sold down the river," while here is "the beautiful side of slavery," that is, the "wonderfully beautiful, patriarchal side." Students investigating Mark Twain's sometimes ambivalent feelings on race and slavery should read very closely here. Again, with no great subtlety, Phelps writes of Jim in *Huckleberry Finn*: "The peculiar harmlessness of Jim is beautiful to contemplate." Was this how Twain preferred to be interpreted? Did he endorse such values (that African Americans were beautiful when harmless, that slavery as a patriarchal institution was likewise "beautiful")?

Elsewhere, again, Phelps remarks flippantly that "the Irish and the Negro" are "light-hearted and careless," but "the Americans" are serious and nervous at heart. "We like Mark Twain's humor, not because we are frivolous, but because we are just the reverse. I have never known a frivolous person who really enjoyed or appreciated Mark Twain."

Students interested in the variety of critical views of Mark Twain will find a fertile, if unpleasant, source here. Phelps closes with an unnecessary jab at Walt Whitman (the poet was detested by conservative critics). "Mark Twain is our great Democrat," Phelps trumpets, before qualifying this by asserting that Nathaniel Hawthorne is the greatest of all American novelists.

———

During the last twenty years, a profound change has taken place in the attitude of the reading public toward Mark Twain. I can remember very well when he was regarded merely as a humorist, and one opened his books with an anticipatory grin. Very few supposed that he belonged to literature;

and a complete, uniform edition of his *Works* would perhaps have been received with something of the mockery that greeted Ben Jonson's folio in 1616. Professor Richardson's *American Literature*, which is still a standard work, appeared originally in 1886. My copy, which bears the date 1892, contains only two references in the index to Mark Twain, while Mr. Cable, for example, receives ten; and the whole volume fills exactly 990 pages. Looking up one of the two references, we find the following opinion:

> But there is a class of writers, authors ranking below Irving or Lowell, and lacking the higher artistic or moral purpose of the greater humorists, who amuse a generation and then pass from sight. Every period demands a new manner of jest, after the current fashion. . . . The reigning favorites of the day are Frank R. Stockton, Joel Chandler Harris, the various newspaper jokers, and "Mark Twain." But the creators of *Pomona* and *Rudder Grange*, of *Uncle Remus and His Folk-lore Stories* and *Innocents Abroad*, clever as they are, must make hay while the sun shines. Twenty years hence, unless they chance to enshrine their wit in some higher literary achievement, their unknown successors will be the privileged comedians of the republic. Humor alone never gives its masters a place in literature; it must co-exist with literary qualities, and must usually be joined with such pathos as one finds in Lamb, Hood, Irving or Holmes.

It is interesting to remember that before this pronouncement was published, *Tom Sawyer* and *Huckleberry Finn* had been read by thousands. Professor Richardson continued: "Two or three divisions of American humor deserve somewhat more respectful treatment," and he proceeds to give a full page to Petroleum V. Nasby, another page to Artemus Ward and two and one-half pages to Josh Billings, while Mark Twain had received less than four lines. After stating that, in the case of authors like Mark Twain, "temporary amusement, not literary product, is the thing sought and given," Professor Richardson announces that the department of fiction will be considered later. In this "department," Mark Twain is not mentioned at all, although Julian Hawthorne receives over three pages!

I have quoted Professor Richardson at length, because he represents an attitude toward Mark Twain that was common all during the eighties. Another college professor, who is today one of the best living American critics, says in his *Initial Studies in American Letters* (1895), "Though it would be ridiculous to maintain that either of these writers [Artemus Ward and Mark Twain] takes rank with Lowell and Holmes, . . . still it will not do to ignore them as mere buffoons, or even predict that their humors will soon be forgotten." There is no allusion in his book to *Tom Sawyer* or *Huckleberry Finn*, nor does the critic seem to regard their creator as in any sense a novelist. Still another writer, in a passing allusion to Mark Twain, says, "Only a very small portion of his writing has any place as literature."

Literary opinions change as time progresses; and no one could have observed the remarkable demonstration at the seventieth birthday of our great national humorist without feeling that most of his contemporaries regarded him, not as their peer, but as their Chief. Without wishing to make any invidious comparisons, I cannot refrain from commenting on the statement that it would be "ridiculous" to maintain that Mark Twain takes rank with Oliver Wendell Holmes. It is, of course, absolutely impossible to predict the future; the only real test of the value of a book is Time. Who now reads Cowley? Time has laughed at so many contemporary judgments that it would be foolhardy to make positive assertions about literary stock quotations one hundred years from now. Still, guesses are not prohibited: and I think it not unlikely that the name of Mark Twain will outlast the name of Holmes. American Literature would surely be the poorer if the great Boston Brahmin had not enlivened it with his rich humor, his lambent wit and his sincere pathos; but the whole content of his work seems slighter than the big American prose epics of the man of our day.

Indeed, it seems to me that Mark Twain is our foremost living American writer. He has not the subtlety of Henry James or the wonderful charm of Mr. Howells; he could not have written *Daisy Miller*, or *A Modern Instance*, or *Indian Summer*, or *The Kentons*—books of which every American should be proud, for they exhibit literary quality of an exceedingly high order. I have read these books over and over again, with constantly increasing profit and delight. I wish that Mr. Howells might live forever, and give to every generation the pure intellectual joy that he has given to ours. But the natural endowment of Mark Twain is still greater. Mr. Howells has made the most of himself; God has done it all for Mark Twain. If there be a living American writer touched with true genius, whose books glow with the divine fire, it is he. He has always been a conscientious artist; but no amount of industry could ever have produced a *Huckleberry Finn*.

When I was a child at the West Middle Grammar School of Hartford, on one memorable April day, Mark Twain addressed the graduating class. I was thirteen years old, but I have found it impossible to forget what he said. The subject of his "remarks" was Methuselah. He informed us that Methuselah lived to the ripe old age of nine hundred and sixty-nine. But he might as well have lived to be several thousand—nothing happened. The speaker told us that we should all live longer than Methuselah. Fifty years of Europe are better than a cycle of Cathay, and twenty years of modern American life are longer and richer in content than the old patriarch's thousand. Ours will be the true age in which to live, when more will happen in a day than in a year of the flat existence of our ancestors. I cannot remember his words; but what a fine thing it is to hear a speech, and carry away an idea!

I have since observed that this idea runs through much of his literary work. His philosophy of life underlies his broadest burlesque—for *A Connecticut Yankee in King Arthur's Court* is simply an exposure of the "good old times." Mark Twain believes in the Present, in human progress. Too often do we apprehend the Middle Ages through the glowing pages of Spenser and Walter Scott; we see only glittering processions of "ladies dead and lovely knights." Mark Twain shows us the wretched condition of the common people, their utter ignorance and degradation, the coarseness and immorality of technical chivalry, the cruel and unscrupulous ecclesiastical tyranny and the capricious insolence of the barons. One may regret that he has reversed the dynamics in so glorious a book as Malory's *Morte d'Arthur*, but, through all the buffoonery and roaring mirth with which the knights in armor are buried, the artistic and moral purpose of the satirist is clear. If I understand him rightly, he would have us believe that *our* age, not theirs, is the "good time;" nay, ours is the age of magic and wonder. We need not regret in melancholy sentimentality the picturesqueness of bygone days, for we ourselves live, not in a material and commonplace generation, but in the very midst of miracles and romance. Merlin and the Fay Morgana would have given all their petty skill to have been able to use a telephone or a phonograph, or to see a moving picture. The sleeping princess and her castle were awakened by a kiss; but in the twentieth century a man in Washington touches a button, and hundreds of miles away tons of machinery begin to move, fountains begin to play and the air resounds with the whir of wheels. In comparison with today, the age of chivalry seems dull and poor. Even in chivalry itself our author is more knightly than Lancelot; for was there ever a more truly chivalrous performance than Mark Twain's essay on Harriet Shelley, or his literary monument to Joan of Arc? In these earnest pages, our national humorist appears as the true knight.

Mark Twain's humor is purely American. It is not the humor of Washington Irving, which resembles that of Addison and Thackeray; it is not delicate and indirect. It is genial, sometimes outrageous, mirth—laughter holding both his sides. I have found it difficult to read him in a library or on a street-car, for explosions of pent-up mirth or a distorted face are apt to attract unpleasant attention in such public places. Mark Twain's humor is boisterous, uproarious, colossal, overwhelming. As has often been remarked, the Americans are not naturally a gay people, like the French; nor are we light-hearted and careless, like the Irish and the Negro. At heart, we are intensely serious, nervous, melancholy. For humor, therefore, we naturally turn to buffoonery and burlesque, as a reaction against the strain and tension of life. Our attitude is something like that of the lonely author of the *Anatomy of Melancholy*, who used to lean over the parapet of Magdalen Bridge, and shake with mirth at the horrible jokes of the bargemen. We like Mark Twain's humor, not because we are frivolous, but because we are just the reverse. I have never known a frivolous person who really enjoyed or appreciated Mark Twain.

The essence of Mark Twain's humor is Incongruity. The jumping frog is named Daniel Webster; and, indeed, the intense gravity of a frog's face, with the droop at the corners of the mouth, might well be envied by many an American Senator. When the shotted frog vainly attempted to leave the earth, he shrugged his shoulders "like a Frenchman." Bilgewater and the Dolphin on the raft are grotesquely incongruous figures. The rescuing of Jim from his prison cell is full of the most incongruous ideas, his common-sense attitude toward the whole transaction contrasting strangely with that of the romantic Tom. Along with the constant incongruity goes the element of surprise—which Professor Beers has well pointed out. When one begins a sentence, in an apparently serious discussion, one never knows how it will end. In discussing the peace that accompanies religious faith, Mark Twain says that he has often been impressed with the calm confidence of a Christian with four aces. Exaggeration—deliberate, enormous hyperbole—is another feature. Rudyard Kipling, who has been profoundly influenced by Mark Twain, and has learned much from him, often employs the same device, as in "Brugglesmith." Irreverence is also a noteworthy quality. In his travel-books, we are given the attitude of the typical American Philistine toward the wonders and sacred relics of the Old World, the whole thing being a gigantic burlesque on the sentimental guide-books which were so much in vogue before the era of Baedeker. With so much continuous fun and mirth, satire and burlesque, it is no wonder that Mark Twain should not always be at his best. He is doubtless sometimes flat, sometimes coarse, as all humorists since Rabelais have been. The wonder is that his level has been so high. I remember, just before the appearance of *Following the Equator*, I had been told that Mark Twain's inspiration was finally gone, and that he could not be funny if he tried. To test this, I opened the new book, and this is what I found on the first page:

> We sailed for America, and there made certain preparations. This took but little time. Two members of my family elected to go with me. Also a carbuncle. The dictionary says a carbuncle is a kind of jewel. Humor is out of place in a dictionary.

Although Mark Twain has the great qualities of the true humorist—common sense, human sympathy and an accurate eye for proportion—he is much more than a humorist. His work shows very high literary quality, the quality that appears in first-rate novels. He has shown himself to be a genuine artist. He has done something which many popular novelists have signally failed to accomplish—he has created real characters. His two wonderful boys, Tom Sawyer and Huckleberry Finn, are wonderful in quite different ways. The creator of Tom exhibited remarkable observation; the creator of Huck showed the divine touch of imagination. Tom is the American boy—he is "smart." In having his fence whitewashed, in controlling a pool of Sabbath-school tickets at the precise psychological moment, he displays abundant promise of future success in business. Huck, on the other hand, is the child of nature, harmless, sincere and crudely imaginative. His reasonings with Jim about nature and God belong to the same department of natural theology as that illustrated in Browning's *Caliban*. The night on the raft with Jim, when these two creatures look aloft at the stars, and Jim reckons the moon laid them, is a case in point.

> We had the sky up there, all speckled with stars, and we used to lay on our backs and look up at them, and discuss about whether they was made or only just happened. Jim he allowed they was made, but I allowed they happened; I judged it would have took too long to *make* so many. Jim said the moon could 'a' *laid* them; well, that looked kind of reasonable, so I didn't say nothing against it, because I've seen a frog lay most as many, so of course it could be done. We used to watch the stars that fell, too, and see them streak down. Jim allowed they'd got spoiled and was hove out of the nest.

Again, Mark Twain has so much dramatic power that, were his literary career beginning instead of closing, he might write for us the great American play that we are still awaiting. The story of the feud between the Grangerfords and the Shepherdsons is thrillingly dramatic, and the tragic climax grips one by the heart. The shooting of the drunken Boggs, the gathering of the mob and its control by one masterful personality, belong essentially to true drama, and are written with power and insight. The pathos of these scenes is never false, never mawkish or overdone; it is the pathos of life itself. Mark Twain's extraordinary skill in descriptive passages shows, not merely keen observation, but the instinct for the specific word—the one word that is always better than any of its synonyms, for it makes the picture real—it creates the illusion, which is the essence of all literary art. The storm, for example:

> It was my watch below till twelve, but I wouldn't 'a' turned in anyway if I'd had a bed, because a body don't see such a storm as that every day in the week, not by a long sight. My souls, how the wind did scream along! And every second or two there'd come a glare that lit up the white-caps for a half a mile around, and you'd see the islands looking dusty through the rain, and the trees thrashing around in the wind; then comes a *h-whack!*—bum! bum! bumble-umble-um-bum-bum-bum-bum—and the thunder would go rumbling and grumbling away, and quit—and then *rip* comes another flash and another sockdolager. The waves most washed me off the raft sometimes, but I hadn't any clothes on, and didn't mind. We didn't have no trouble about snags; the lightning was glaring and flittering around so constant that we could see them plenty soon enough to throw her head this way or that and miss them.

Tom Sawyer and *Huckleberry Finn* are prose epics of American life. The former is one of those books—of which *The Pilgrim's Progress*, *Gulliver's Travels* and *Robinson Crusoe* are supreme examples—that are read at different periods of one's life from very different points of view; so that it is not easy to say when one enjoys them the most—before one understands their real significance or after. Nearly all healthy boys enjoy reading *Tom Sawyer*, because the intrinsic interest of the story is so great, and the various adventures of the hero are portrayed with such gusto. Yet it is impossible to outgrow the book. The eternal Boy is there, and one cannot appreciate the nature of boyhood properly until one has ceased to be a boy. The other masterpiece, *Huckleberry Finn*, is really not a child's book at all. Children devour it, but they do not digest it. It is a permanent picture of a certain period of American history, and this picture is made complete, not so much by the striking portraits of individuals placed on the huge canvas, as by the vital unity of the whole composition. If one wishes to know what life on the Mississippi really was, to know and understand the peculiar social conditions of that highly exciting time, one has merely to read through this powerful narrative, and a definite, coherent, vivid impression remains.

By those who have lived there, and whose minds are comparatively free from prejudice, Mark Twain's pictures of life in the South before the war are regarded as, on the whole, nearer the truth than those supplied by any other artist. One reason for this is the aim of the author; he was not trying to support or defend any particular theory—no, his aim was purely and wholly artistic. In *Uncle Tom's Cabin*, a book by no means devoid of literary art, the red-hot indignation of the author largely nullified her evident desire to tell the truth. If one succeeds in telling the truth about anything whatever, one must have something more than the *desire* to tell the truth; one must know how to do it. False impressions do not always, probably do not commonly, come from deliberate liars. Mrs. Stowe's astonishing work is not really the history of slavery; it is the history of abolition sentiment. On the other hand, writers so graceful, talented and clever as Mr. Page and Mr. Hopkinson Smith do not always give us pictures that correctly represent, except locally, the actual situation before the war; for these gentlemen seem to have *Uncle Tom's Cabin* in mind.

Mark Twain gives us both points of view; he shows us the beautiful side of slavery—for it had a wonderfully beautiful, patriarchal side—and he also shows us the horror of it. The living dread of the negro that he would be sold down the river, has never been more vividly represented than when the poor woman in *Pudd'nhead Wilson* sees the water swirling against the snag, and realizes that she is bound the wrong way. That one scene makes an indelible impression on the reader's mind, and counteracts tons of polemics. The peculiar harmlessness of Jim is beautiful to contemplate. Although he and Huck really own the raft, and have taken all the risk, they obey implicitly the orders of the two tramps who call themselves Duke and King. Had that been a raft on the Connecticut River, and had Huck and Jim been Yankees, they would have said to the intruders, "Whose raft is this, anyway?"

Mark Twain may be trusted to tell the truth; for the eye of the born caricature artist always sees the salient point. Caricatures often give us a better idea of their object than a photograph; for the things that are exaggerated, be it a large nose, or a long neck, are, after all, the things that differentiate this particular individual from the mass. Everybody remembers how Tweed was caught by one of Nast's cartoons.

Mark Twain is through and through American. If foreigners really wish to know the American spirit, let them read Mark Twain. He is far more American than their favorite specimen, Walt Whitman. The essentially

American qualities of common sense, energy, enterprise, good humor and Philistinism fairly shriek from his pages. He reveals us in our limitations, in our lack of appreciation of certain beautiful things, fully as well as he pictures us in coarser but more triumphant aspects. It is, of course, preposterous to say that Americans are totally different from other humans; we have no monopoly of common sense and good humor, nor are we all hide-bound Philistines. But there is something pronounced in the American character, and the books of Mark Twain reveal it. He has also more than once been a valuable and efficient champion. Without being an offensive and blatant Jingo, I think he is well satisfied to be an American.

Mark Twain is our great Democrat. Democracy is his political, social and moral creed. His hatred of snobbery, affectation and assumed superiority is total. His democracy has no limits; it is bottomless and far-reaching. Nothing seems really sacred to him except the sacred right of every individual to do exactly as he pleases; which means, of course, that no one can interfere with another's right, for then democracy would be the privilege of a few, and would stultify itself. Not only does the spirit of democracy breathe out from all his greater books, but it is shown in specific instances, such as "Travelling with a Reformer;" and Mark Twain has more than once given testimony for his creed, without recourse to the pen.

At the head of all American novelists, living and dead, stands Nathaniel Hawthorne, unapproached, possibly unapproachable. His fine and subtle art is an altogether different thing from the art of our mighty, democratic, national humorist. But Literature is wonderfully diverse in its content; and the historian of American Letters, in the far future, will probably find it impossible to omit the name of Mark Twain, whose books have warmed human hearts all over the world.

—William Lyon Phelps, "Mark Twain,"
North American Review, CLXXXV,
July 5, 1907, pp. 540–548

SIGMUND FREUD "CONTRIBUTION TO A QUESTIONNAIRE ON READING" (1907)

In this, the earliest indication of Freud's fondness for the work of Mark Twain, the German father of psychoanalysis includes a book of Twain's sketches in his "top ten" favorite books. Freud's inclusion of the work (perhaps *Sketches New and Old* [1875], or possibly a German collection) is notable, since it runs counter to the trend of the criticism that precedes it. The majority of Twain's critics minimize the importance of the early sketches; Freud, although he does not explain how he arrived at his choice, apparently finds greater matter in them than the novels or travelogues.

Any students performing a Freudian analysis of Twain's work should undoubtedly be aware of this top ten, however little it explains. Are Twain's sketches, for instance, more open to psychoanalysis? Are they closer to the literature Freud analyzes elsewhere, such as E.T.A. Hoffman's short story "The Sandman"?

⸺

You ask me to name 'ten good books' for you, and refrain from adding to this any word of explanation. Thus you leave to me not only the choice of the books but also the interpretation of your request. Accustomed to paying attention to small signs, I must then trust the wording in which you couch your enigmatical demand. You did not say: 'the ten most magnificent works (of world literature)', in which case I should have been obliged to reply, with so many others: Homer, the tragedies of Sophocles, Goethe's *Faust*, Shakespeare's *Hamlet, Macbeth*, etc. Nor did you say the 'ten most significant books', among which scientific achievements like those of Copernicus, of the old physician Johann Weier on the belief in witches, Darwin's *Descent of Man*, and others, would then have found a place. You did not even ask for 'favourite books', among which I should not have forgotten Milton's *Paradise Lost* and Heine's *Lazarus*. I think, therefore, that a particular stress falls on the 'good' in your phrase, and that with this predicate you intend to designate books to which one stands in rather the same relationship as to 'good' friends, to whom one owes a part of one's knowledge of life and view of the world—books which one has enjoyed oneself and gladly commends to others, but in connection with which the element of timid reverence, the feeling of one's own smallness in the face of their greatness, is not particularly prominent.

I will therefore name ten such 'good' books for you which have come to my mind without a great deal of reflection.

Multatuli, Letters and Works. [Cf. p. 133 *n*.]
Kipling, *Jungle Book.*
Anatole France, *Sur la pierre blanche.*
Zola, *Fécondité.*
Merezhkovsky, *Leonardo da Vinci.*
G. Keller, *Leute von Seldwyla.*

C. F. Meyer, *Huttens letzte Tage*.
Macaulay, *Essays*.
Gomperz, *Griechische Denker*.
Mark Twain, *Sketches*.

—Sigmund Freud, "Contribution to a
Questionnaire on Reading," first published in
*Vom Lesen und von guten Büchern, eine Rundfrage
veranstaltet von der Redaktion der 'Neuen Blätter
für Literatur und Kunst'*, Vienna, 1907, ix.,
English translation by K.R. Eissler

ARCHIBALD HENDERSON "MARK TWAIN" (1909)

In an increasingly cosmopolitan world, certain writers had risen to international fame. Among these were Rudyard Kipling, George Bernard Shaw, and Leo Tolstoy. Foremost and unparalleled in this regard, however, was Mark Twain. This was because humor is universal and favors no class above another. In this company, Twain has transcended the nineteenth century. Henderson presents Twain's contemporaries as the German philosopher Friedrich Nietzsche and the Norwegian playwright Henrik Ibsen, each, in his way, a prophet of modernism.

As well as revisiting (in Brander Matthews's words "unmaking and remaking") Twain as a modernist, Henderson remakes him as a cosmopolite. Yet, unlike Henry James, Twain is "at home even in his own country." Henderson also addresses the darker aspects of Twain's work. This contemporary of Nietzsche was "too heretical for the Hartford Club of orthodox religionists," with his doubts of the existence of free will (doubts that echo Emerson at his most bleak, in "Fate"). This resignation to the grim aspect of Twain's thought marks a more sophisticated, less genteel tone than many of the preceding surveys (Howells, Matthews, and Phelps, for example). Henderson's portrait of Twain the "sociologist" might even be viewed as the first modern account of Twain.

Henderson reports firsthand from conversations with Twain—he was an early biographer of Twain—and these exchanges are plundered for this essay. Students delving into Twain's theories, particularly those concerning humor and nationality, will find relevant material in Henderson's words. Any students interested in Twain as a protomodernist should consult this essay too.

I've a theory that every author while living has a projection of himself, a sort of eidolon, that goes about in near and distant places and makes friends and enemies for him out of folk who never knew him in the flesh. When the author dies this phantom fades away, not caring to continue business at the old stand. Then the dead writer lives only in the impression made by his literature; this impression may grow sharper or fainter, according to the fashions and new conditions of the time.—*Letter of Thomas Bailey Aldrich to William Dean Howells, December 23, 1901.*

Despite the average American's complacent and chuckling satisfaction in his country's possession of that superman of humor, Mark Twain, there is room for serious doubt whether a realization of the unique and incomparable position of Mark Twain in the republic of letters has fully dawned upon the American consciousness. On reflection, the number of living writers to whom can justly be attributed what a Frenchman would call *mondial éclat* is startlingly few. It was not so many years ago that Rudyard Kipling, with vigorous, imperialistic note, won for himself the unquestioned title as militant spokesman for the Anglo-Saxon race. Today, Bernard Shaw has a fame more world-wide than that of any other literary figure in the British Isles, and his dramas are played from Madrid to Helsingfors, from Budapest to Stockholm, from Vienna to St. Petersburg, from Paris to Berlin. Since Ibsen's death, Tolstoi exerts unchallenged the profoundest influence upon the thought and consciousness of the world—not so much by his intellect as by the passionate integrity of his moral aspiration. But, in a sense not easily misunderstood, Mark Twain has a place in the minds and hearts of the great mass of humanity throughout the civilized world which, if measured in terms of affection, sympathy, and spontaneous enjoyment, is without a parallel.

The robust nationalism of Kipling challenges the defiant opposition of foreigners; while his reportorial realism offends many an inviolable canon of European taste. With all his incandescent wit and radiant comic irony, Bernard Shaw makes his most vivid impression upon the upper strata of society; while his legendary character is perpetually standing in the light of the serious reformer. Tolstoi's works are Russia's greatest literary contribution to posterity; yet his extravagant ideals, his unrealizable hopes, in their almost maniacal mysticism, continue to detract from his fame. If Mark Twain makes a more generally popular appeal, it is because the instrument of his appeal is the universal solvent of humor. That *eidolon* of which Aldrich speaks—a compact of good humor, robust sanity, and large-minded humanity—has diligently "gone about in near and distant places," everywhere making warm and lifelong friends of folk of all nationalities who have never known Mark Twain in the flesh. The stevedore on the dock, the motorman on the street-car, the newsboy on the street, the riverman on the Mississippi—all speak with exuberant affection of this quaint figure in his white suit, ever wreathed in clouds of tobacco smoke. In one day an emperor and a *concierge* vie with each other in tributes of admiration and esteem for the man and his works. It is Mark Twain's imperishable glory, not simply that his name is more widely known than that of any other living man, but that it is remembered with infinite and irrepressible zest.

Not without wide significance in its bearing upon the general outlines of contemporary literature is the circumstance that Mark Twain served his apprenticeship to letters in the high school of journalism. Rudyard Kipling awoke the world with a start by the crude, almost barbaric cry of his journalese; and Bernard Shaw acquired that trenchant and forthright style, which imparts such an air of heightened verisimilitude to his plays, in the ranks of the new journalism. "The writer who aims at producing the platitudes which are 'not for an age, but for all time,'" says Bernard Shaw, "has his reward in being unreadable in all ages; while Plato and Aristophanes trying to knock some sense into the Athens of their day, Shakespeare peopling that same Athens with Elizabethan mechanics and Warwickshire hunts, Ibsen photographing the local doctors and vestrymen of a Norwegian parish, Carpaccio painting the life of St. Ursula exactly as if she were a lady living in the next street to him, are still alive and at home everywhere among the dust and ashes of many thousands of academic, punctilious, most archaeologically correct men of letters and art who spent their lives haughtily avoiding the journalist's vulgar obsession with the ephemeral." Mark Twain began by studying the people and period he knew, in relation to his own life; and in writing of his time *à propos* of himself, succeeded in telling the truth about humanity in general and for any time. If it be true that the intellectual life of America for the most part takes its cue from the day, while Europe derives hers from history, then Mark Twain is a typical product of American literature as defined by Johannes V. Jensen: "journalism under exceptionally favorable conditions." Whatever modicum of truth may lurk in this definition, certain it is that Mark Twain is the greatest genius evolved by natural selection out of the ranks of American journalism. Crude, rudimentary, and often coarse as much of his writing was, it bore upon it the fresh stamp of contemporary actuality.

While Mark Twain has solemnly averred that humor is a "subject which has never had much interest" for him, it is nothing more than a commonplace to say that it is as a humorist and as a humorist only that the world persists in regarding him. The philosophy of his early life was what George Meredith has aptly termed the "philosophy of the Broad Grin"; and Mark Twain has had a great struggle to "live down his past." Mr. Gilbert Chesterton once said that "American humor, neither unfathomably absurd like the Irish, nor transfiguringly lucid and appropriate like the French, nor sharp and sensible and full of the realities of life like the Scotch, is simply the humor of imagination. It consists in piling towers on towers and mountains on mountains; of heaping a joke up to the stars and extending it to the end of the world." This partial and somewhat conventional foreign conception of American humor is admirably descriptive of the cumulative and sky-breaking humor of the early Mark Twain. Then no exaggeration was too absurd for him, no phantasm too unreal, no climax too extreme. After a while he learned on the platform that the unpardonable sin is to "sell" an audience, and in the study that "comic copy" will never win real fame.

In spite of these wholesome lessons learned through actual experience, Mark Twain has had to pay in full the penalty of comic greatness. The world is loath to accept a popular character at any rating other than its own. Whosoever sets to himself the task of amusing the world must realize the almost insuperable difficulty of inducing the world to regard him as a serious thinker. *"C'est une étrange entreprise que celle de faire rire les honnêtes gens,"* says Molière; and the strangeness of the undertaking is no less pronounced than the rigor of its obligations. Mark Twain began his career as a professional humorist and fun-maker; and the man in the street is not easily persuaded that the basis of the comic is not uncommon nonsense, but glorified common sense. The French have a fine-flavored distinction in *ce qui remue* from *ce qui émeut*, and if *remuage* was the defining characteristic of *A Tramp Abroad*, *Roughing It*, and *Innocents Abroad*, there was much of deep and genuine emotion in *Life on the Mississippi*, *Tom Sawyer*, *Huckleberry Finn*, and *Pudd'nhead Wilson*. Think of that admirable passage in which he portrays the marvellous spell laid upon him by that mistress of his youth, the great river:

> The face of the water in time became a wonderful book—a book which was a dead language to the uneducated passenger, but which told its mind to me without reserve, delivering its most cherished secrets as if it uttered them with a voice. And it was not a book to be read over and thrown aside, for it had a new story to tell every day.... There was never so wonderful a book written by man.... When I had mastered the language of this water, and

had come to know every trifling feature that bordered the great river as familiarly as I knew the letters of the alphabet, I had made a valuable acquisition. But I had lost something, too. I had lost something which could never be restored to me while I lived. All the grace, the beauty, the poetry, had gone out of the majestic river. . . . A day came when I began to cease from noting the glories and the charms which the moon and the sun and the twilight wrought upon the river's face: another day came when I ceased altogether to note them.

Even today, though long since dissociated in fact from the category of Artemus Ward, John Phoenix, Josh Billings, and Petroleum V. Nasby, Mark Twain can never be sure that his most solemn utterance may not be drowned in roars of thoughtless laughter. "It has been a very serious and a very difficult matter," Mr. Clemens lately remarked to me, "to doff the mask of humor with which the public has always seen me adorned. It is the incorrigible practice of the public, in this or in any country to see only humor in a humorist, however serious his vein. Not long ago I wrote a poem, which I never dreamed of giving to the public, on account of its seriousness; but on being invited to address the women students of a certain great university, I was persuaded by a near friend to read this poem. At the close of my lecture I said: 'Now, ladies, I am going to read you a poem of mine'—which was greeted with bursts of uproarious laughter. 'But this is a truly serious poem,' I asseverated—only to be greeted with renewed and, this time, more uproarious laughter. Nettled by this misunderstanding, I put the poem in my pocket, saying, 'Well, young ladies, since you do not believe me *serious*, I shall not read the poem,' at which the audience almost went into convulsions of merriment."

Humor, it must be remembered, is a function of nationality. The same joke, as related by an American, a Scotsman, an Irishman, a Frenchman, carries with it a distinctive racial flavor and individuality of approach. Indeed, it is open to question whether most humor is not essentially local in its nature, requiring some specialized knowledge of some particular locality. After reading George Ade's *Fables in Slang*, Mr. Andrew Lang was driven to the desperate conclusion that humor varies with the parallels of latitude, a joke in Chicago being a riddle in London! If one would lay his finger upon the secret of Mark Twain's world-wide popularity as a humorist, he must find that secret primarily in the universality and humanity of his humor. Mark Twain is a master in the art of broad contrast; incongruity lurks on the surface of his humor; and there is about it a staggering and cyclopean surprise. But these are mere surface qualities, more or less common, though at lower power, to all forms of humor. Nor is Mark Twain's international reputation as a humorist to be attributed to any tricks of style, to any breadth of knowledge, or even to any depth of intellectuality. His hold upon the world is due to qualities not of the head, but of the heart. I once heard Mr. Clemens say that humor is the key to the hearts of men, for it springs from the heart; and worthy of record is his dictum that there is far more of feeling than of thought in genuine humor.

Mark Twain has a remarkable feeling for words and their uses; and the merit of his style is its admirable adaptation to the theme. And though Mr. Henry James may have said that one must be a very rudimentary person to enjoy Mark Twain, there is unimpeachable virtue in a rudimentary style in treatment of rudimentary—or, as I should prefer to phrase it, fundamental—things. Mark Twain has always written with utter individuality, untrammelled by the limitations of any particular sect of art. Style bears translation ill; in fact, translation is not infrequently impossible. But as Mr. Clemens once pointed out to me, *humor has nothing to do with style*. Mark Twain's humor has international range, since, constructed out of a deep comprehension of human nature and a profound sympathy for human relationships and human failings, it successfully surmounts the difficulties of translation into alien tongues.

Mark Twain is a great figure, not because he is an American, paradoxical and even unpatriotic as this may sound, but because he is America's greatest cosmopolitan. He is a true cosmopolitan in the Higginsonian sense in that, unlike Mr. Henry James, he is "at home even in his own country." Above all, he has sympathized with and admired the citizens of every nation, seeking beneath the surface veneer the universal traits of that nation's humanity. It is a matter, not of argument, but of fact, that he has made far more damaging admissions concerning America than concerning any other nation. He disclaims any "attitude" toward the world, for the very simple reason that his relation toward all peoples has been one of effort at comprehension and identification with them in feeling. Lafcadio Hearn best succeeded in interpreting poetry to his Japanese students by freeing it from all artificial and local restraints, and using as examples the simplest lyrics which go straight to the heart and soul of man. And his remarkable lecture on *Naked Poetry* is the most signal illustration of his profoundly suggestive mode of interpretation. In the same way Mark Twain as humorist has sought the highest common factor of all nations. "My secret, if there is any secret," Mr. Clemens said to me, "is to create humor independent of local conditions.

Though studying humanity as exhibited in the people and localities I best knew and understood, I have sought to winnow out the encumbrance of the local. *Humor, like morality, has its eternal verities.* Most American humorists have not been widely famous because they have failed to create humor independent of local conditions not found or realized elsewhere."

It must be conceded that the history of literature furnishes forth no great international figures whose fame rests solely upon the basis of humor, however human, however sympathetic, however universal that humor may be. Behind that humor must lurk some deeper and more serious implication which gives breadth and solidity to the art-product. Genuine humor, as Landor has pointed out, requires a "sound and capacious mind, which is always a grave one." There is always a breadth of philosophy, a depth of sadness, or a profundity of pathos in the very greatest humorists. Both Rabelais and La Fontaine were reflective dreamers; Cervantes fought for the progressive and the real in pricking the bubble of Spanish chivalry; and Molière declared that, for a man in his position he could do no better than attack the vices of his time with ridiculous likenesses. Though exhibiting little of the melancholy of Lincoln, Mark Twain has much of the Yankee shrewdness and bed-rock common sense of Franklin; and commingled with all his boyish and exuberant fun is a note of pathos subdued but unmistakable. That "disposition for hard hitting with a moral purpose to sanction it," which George Meredith pronounces the national disposition of British humor, is Mark Twain's racial hereditament; and it is, perhaps, because he relates us to our origins, as Mr. Brander Matthews has suggested, that Mark Twain is the foremost of American humorists. It is impossible to think of him in his maturer development as other than a moralist. His impassioned and chivalric defence of Harriet Shelley, his eloquent tribute to the Maid of Orleans, his philippic against King Leopold and the atrocities in the Congo, are all, in essence, vindications of the moral principle. "Was it Heaven or Hell?" in its simple pathos, and "The Man that Corrupted Hadleyburg," in its shrieking irony, present that same transvaluation of current moral values which marks the age of Nietzsche, of Ibsen, of Tolstoi, of Zola, and of Shaw. In her unfinished biography of him, Mark Twain's little daughter Susy credited him with being "as much of a pholosopher [sic] as anything"; and insists that "he is more interested in earnest books and earnest subjects to talk upon than in humorous ones." Mr. Clemens' first essay on a philosophical subject—doubting the existence of free will and declaring that every man was under the immitigable compulsion of his temperament, his training, and his environment—was too heretical for the Hartford Club of orthodox religionists to which he belonged; and so was never read. But in the last thirty years he has amplified his original conception into a philosophical and ethical system; and to-day his injunction for right living is best concretized in these words: "Diligently train your ideals upward and still upward toward a summit where you will find your chiefest pleasure in conduct which, while contenting you, will be sure to confer benefits upon your neighbors and the community." As Lassalle once said, "History forgives mistakes and failures, but not want of conviction." In Mark Twain posterity will never be called upon to forgive any want of conviction.

Mark Twain is a great humorist—more genial than grim, more good-humored than ironic, more given to imaginative exaggeration than to intellectual sophistication, more inclined to pathos than to melancholy. He is a great story-teller; and he has enriched the literature of the world with a gallery of portraits so human in their veracious likeness as to rank them with the great figures of classic comedy. He is a remarkable observer and faithful reporter, never allowing himself, in Ibsen's phrase, to be "frightened by the venerableness of the institution;" and his sublimated journalism reveals a mastery of the naively comic thoroughly human and democratic. He is the most eminent product of our American democracy; and, in profoundly shocking Great Britain by preferring Connecticut to Camelot, he exhibited that robustness of outlook, that buoyancy of spirit, and that faith in the contemporary which stamps America in perennial and inexhaustible youth. Throughout his long life he has been a factor of high ethical influence in our civilization; and the philosopher and the humanitarian look out from the twinkling eyes of the humorist.

But, after all, Mark Twain's supremest title to distinction as a great writer inheres in his mastery in that highest sphere of thought, embracing religion, philosophy, morality, and even humor, which we call sociology. Mr. Bernard Shaw once remarked to me that he regarded Poe and Mark Twain as America's greatest achievements in literature; and that he thought of Mark Twain primarily, not as humorist, but as sociologist. "Of course," he added, "Mark Twain is in much the same position as myself: he has to put matters in such a way as to make people who would otherwise hang him believe he is joking!" And Mark Twain once said that whenever he had diverged from custom and principle to utter a truth, the rule has been that the hearer hadn't strength of mind enough to believe it. There is a "sort of contemporaneous posterity" which has registered its verdict that Mark Twain is the world's greatest living humorist; but there is yet to come that greater posterity of the future which will, I dare say, class Mark Twain as

America's greatest sociologist in letters. He is the historian in art of a varied and unique phase of civilization on this continent that has passed forever. And it is inconceivable that any future investigator into the sociological phase of that civilization can fail to find priceless and unparalleled documents in the wild yet genial, rudimentary yet sane, boisterous yet universally human writings of Mark Twain.

It is a far cry from the steamboat on the Mississippi to the Italianate villa, from the overalls of the river pilot to the gray and scarlet of the Oxford gown. And in recalling the various vicissitudes of his varied life the mind irresistibly reverts to that day when Mark Twain, at the age of sixty, accompanied by his wife, set forth to retrieve his fallen fortunes. When the publishing-house in which he was interested, against his advice and through no fault of his own, continued a policy which led to ruin, Mr. and Mrs. Clemens discovered that even if they sacrificed all their effects they could pay the creditors only about forty cents on the dollar. But Mrs. Clemens' passion for morals manifested itself, and they agreed together that at any cost they must pay nothing less than dollar for dollar. With her courageous company, Mr. Clemens began his career a second time, setting off on a tramp abroad which has ended in "Stormfield" and autumn peace. With obligations satisfied, business integrity magnificently maintained, and fortune made, Mr. Clemens has earned that dignified and honorable leisure for congenial work and humanitarian service it was the tragic fate of Sir Walter Scott never to realize. Nothing can disturb the even tenor of his care-free existence—not even that direst of all terrors to the man of letters, the expiration of copyright. For he has incorporated the very name of *Mark Twain*!

—Archibald Henderson, "Mark Twain,"
Harper's Monthly 118, May 1909, pp. 948–955

H.L. MENCKEN "NOVELS AND OTHER BOOKS–MOSTLY BAD" (1909)

Henry Louis Mencken, the journalist, essayist, and critic renowned for his withering but brilliant attacks on pomp and deception, in literature and politics alike, has been called "a true child of Mark Twain, as fearless as his greater ancestor and feared in exactly the same way by the dry as dust and the conventional" (Henry Seidel Canby, "The Status of American Criticism"). Mencken would become, over the years, the most incisive, acerbic, and influential critic in the United States. Prescient and shrewd, he would identify and vaunt the great works of modernism.

Mencken returned to considerations of Mark Twain regularly in his career. This is his first such estimate, a review of Mark Twain's last book published in his lifetime. *Is Shakespeare Dead?* was an inquiry into the true identity of the author of Shakespeare's plays, a late foray into a sort of literary conspiracy theory, interspersed with autobiographical musings.

Mark Twain tends toward the "Baconian" theory, while Mencken is a firm "Stratfordian." More significantly, Mencken rates *Huckleberry Finn* alone as equal to all the works of Poe, Hawthorne, Cooper, Holmes, Howells, and James. He regrets, though, that there has been nothing of any matter published over Twain's signature since before *Following the Equator*. Students interested in how Twain was perceived by the new generation of critics and thinkers should look here.

Mark Twain's argument that Shakespeare did not write the Shakespearean plays is based upon the fact that little authentic information about the Bard has come down to us. If Shakespeare had really done the work himself, says Mark, instead of merely lending his name to some other man, his contemporaries would have recognized him as a great man, and would have been at pains to seek him out, talk to him and leave records of his acts and opinions. As it is, we have only a few facts about his parentage and a few obscure entries in the court papers of Stratford and London.

Assuming that this statement of the historical material at hand is correct—which it is not—the fallacy of the author's reasoning must yet be plain. All that he proves, indeed, is that the majority of Shakespeare's contemporaries were densely blind to his enormous genius. They regarded him, perhaps, as a successful theatrical manager and an ingenious maker of stage plays, but that he was a world figure and one with Aeschylus and Solomon never occurred to them. If it had, they would have sought him out; and if it had appeared that he was not the real author of the plays he claimed, they would have sought out that real author. In a word, the absence of contemporary news of Shakespeare proves only the absence of contemporary appreciation.

Those friends of the poet who were capable of formulating some notion of his true stature—such men as Jonson, Heminge and Condell—were in no doubt as to his reality and honesty. Their testimony is direct and specific; they say that he wrote the plays credited to him. And it is certainly safe to suppose that they knew, for they met him almost daily. They saw the prompt books of his theater, with his autograph corrections; they were his intimates; they paid tribute to him when he died. That the testimony of these men is to be rebutted by the fact that the tradesmen of Stratford did not recognize the Immortal in their midst is an absurdity.

Mr. Clemens's book, indeed, makes sorry reading for those who hold him in reverence. He is, by great odds, the most noble figure America has ever given to English literature. Having him, we may hold up our heads when Spaniards boast of Cervantes and Frenchmen of Molière. His one book, *Huckleberry Finn*, is worth, I believe, the complete works of Poe, Hawthorne, Cooper, Holmes, Howells and James, with the entire literary output to date of Indiana, Pennsylvania and all the States south of the Potomac thrown in as makeweight. But since *Following the Equator*, his decline has been almost pathetic. Once a great artist, he is now merely a public character. He has gone the road of Wycherley; the old humanity and insight have given place to the smartness of the town wit. Let us try to forget this latter-day Mark Twain, with his pot boilers and his wheezes, and remember only the incomparable Mark Twain that was— and will be through the ages—just as we try to forget that the Thackeray who wrote *Barry Lyndon* also wrote *Lovell the Widower*, and that the Shakespeare who wrote *Much Ado About Nothing* wrote also *Cymbeline*.

—H.L. Mencken, "Novels and Other Books–
Mostly Bad," *Smart Set* 28, August 1909,
pp. 156–157

Unsigned (1910)

The word to fit Mark Twain is not easily found. To say of him that he was a humourist is to pervert language. Comic—at times irresistibly so—perhaps; but not humorous. The comic mood is nowhere near to humour. His best work is a mere overflow of mental good spirits; and, unless the reader be equally full-bodied, he may find himself depressed from sheer reaction. He was first among the funny men of America—a country which can never become seriously minded or reflective enough to produce a humourist. His spirit and tone were very near to those of our own comic press. This is not the time for humour. People want to be amused boisterously, and pay their funny men to that end, just as the mediaeval baron paid his fool.

Mark Twain was the best of them all. The secret of his success was this: to please his fellows he had simply to be himself—to give himself the rein. His vein was the vein of Elizabethan farce. However crude the absurdity it went down with his readers, because it was forced down. Literally he made his readers laugh. That is why he bored so many of them. With his faults he had the supreme excuse that condones many of the artistic blemishes in Shakespeare's early farces—he was vital.

—Unsigned, *Saturday Review* 109,
April 23, 1910, p. 516

ARNOLD BENNETT "ARNOLD BENNETT CONSIDERS TWAIN WAS A DIVINE AMATEUR" (1910)

This curt, unsentimental "tribute" is by the prolific English author of short stories, plays, essays, self-help books, and novels such as *The Old Wives Tale* and the *Clayhanger* trilogy. Bennett recalls earlier criticisms that asserted that Twain could not sustain a narrative but was best represented in constituent episodes. The values of "construction" so lauded by Bennett were soon to be trampled in turn, whereupon *Huckleberry Finn* would be celebrated as a "modern" novel for its very looseness of construction. Any student comparing Twain to his British peers might find Bennett's comments useful.

I never saw Mark Twain. Personally I am convinced that his best work is to be found in the first half of "Life on the Mississippi." The second half is not on the same plane. Episodically, both "Huckleberry Finn" and "Tom Sawyer" are magnificent, but as complete works of art they are of quite inferior quality. Mark Twain was always a divine amateur, and he never would or never could appreciate the fact (to which nearly all Anglo-Saxon writers are half or totally blind), that the most important thing in any work of art is its construction. He had no notion of construction, and very little power of self-criticism. He was great in the subordinate business of decoration, as distinguished from construction; but he would mingle together the very best and the very worst decorations. The praise poured out on his novels seems to me exceedingly exaggerated. I like his travel-sketches; by their direct, disdainful naîveté they remind me of Stendhal's. I should be disposed to argue that he has left stuff which will live for a long time among us Anglo-Saxons, but not that he was complete enough to capture Europe.

—Arnold Bennett, "Arnold Bennett Considers
Twain Was a Divine Amateur," *Bookman* 38,
London, June 1910, p. 118

Various Authors
"Tributes to Mark Twain" (1910)

In these tributes assembled for the *North American Review*, more sentiment is evident than in Arnold Bennett's dry critique. Nevertheless,
some strong matter is to be found. Even amid his eulogy, the business-
man Andrew Carnegie wonders why Mark Twain, who came from a
background as humble as his own, could then doubt that Shakespeare
was the author of those works attributed to him. Like "Ploughman
Burns" (that is, the Scottish poet Robert Burns) and like Mark Twain, why
couldn't Shakespeare have come from little? Is this not the essence of
the achievements of a democracy? The question is significant for any
students researching Twain's thoughts on class and authorship.

Booker T. Washington, the former slave, educator, and spokesman for
African-American rights, provides a tribute to Twain that is of importance to
any students writing on Twain and race. He discourses on Jim in *Huckleberry
Finn* (unfortunately misremembering him as "the colored boy"—while Jim's
age is not stated, he has a wife and two children). Washington views Twain
as characteristically southern. Students investigating potential southern
qualities in Twain's work might turn to this selection.

Meanwhile, Hamlin Garland, predominantly a short story writer (*Main
Travelled Roads* being his best-known collection) views Twain as "the mid-
Western American." Readers discern their own region in the pan-American
Twain. The novelist Booth Tarkington, author of *The Magnificent Ambersons*
and *Penrod,* among other works, views Twain as representative of the
entire United States: "he *was* the American spirit." Also like Sherman, he
compares Twain to Walt Whitman, who was, almost twenty years after his
death, becoming another synonym for American democracy. The humorist
George Ade warns against the practice of comparing Twain's works. Twain
wrote "what he wanted to write when he felt that it should be written." Any
student comparing one Twain text to another should heed his words.

Finally, Brander Matthews sums up Twain's oeuvre as "unequal." Critics
must not be sentimental; it is to their credit that they will even speak ill of
the well-loved dead. Matthews predicts a further "remaking" of Twain's
reputation: "the next generation will drop out the half of his writings and
the generation after may winnow what is left."

"Mark Twain gone!"—such the refrain that comes to my lips at intervals.
The gayety of nations eclipsed, the most original genius of our age and one of
the sweetest, noblest men that ever lived.

Fortunate was I that we met many years ago upon the ocean and became friends. He told me, much to my surprise, that the idea of "A Yankee at the Court of King Arthur" came from reading my first literary outburst written at high noon when the sun casts no shadow, "Triumphant Democracy"; also he called my attention to the heading of a chapter in "Pudd'nhead Wilson," of which I was the author. I was young then and naturally greatly flattered that the business man should be hailed as fellow author. The intimacy continued to grow until I could safely consider myself one of his circle. My admiration for him increased as I knew him better, until great as the author was, the man, the friend, took first place.

When the business trial of his life came and he decided that the question was not what he owed others, but what was due to himself that should govern, be chose the latter and travelled the world over and conquered. He undertook Sir Walter Scott's task and triumphed, paying every creditor not the forty cents on the dollar they offered to take, but every cent of his debt. There comes to men in life critical moments which test whether they be of clay or the pure gold. Mark Twain proved himself the latter.

No man knew Mark Twain who had not seen him aroused by some mean, detestable action which violated his sense of justice. In his wrath he was indeed terrible. One has only to read his condemnation of the capture of Aguinaldo, the Filipino General, to realize this. It exceeds the strongest philippics of Junius. In reading his support of the Baconian theory *in re* Shakespeare, one wonders how he could reject the miracle of an uneducated wool-carder producing the unapproachable gems when his own career gives us something of the very same nature, as does that of that other original genius, Ploughman Burns. Truly surprising, almost exceeding belief, are these miracles had we not such proofs that they really were performed. No one has ventured to rob the Scottish poet of his gems. Mark Twain is one of the brotherhood.

"If there's another life, he lives in bliss. If there be none, he made the best of this." Let us follow his example.

"Nothing is here for tears, nothing to wail
Or knock the breast. No weakness, no contempt,
Dispraise or blame, nothing but well and fair
And what may quiet us in a death so noble."

And yet—and yet—I find the tears drop as I write.
ANDREW CARNEGIE.

* * *

Once he said to me:

"I came in with Halley's comet. I should like to stay until its return and go out with it."

That was a year ago. The night he died Halley's comet was visible in the sky. What a star to be born under, and how like he was to that radiant visitor! Where others were great, he was supreme; where others shone and sparkled, he blazed out transcendent; we had but to see him rise among his fellows to realize how his stately splendor bedimmed them all.

ALBERT BIGELOW PAINE.

* * *

It was my privilege to know the late Samuel L. Clemens for a number of years. The first time I met him was at his home in Hartford. Later I met him several times at his home in New York City and at the Lotus Club. It may be I became attached to Mr. Clemens all the more strongly because both of us were born in the South. He had the Southern temperament, and most that he has written has the flavor of the South in it. His interest in the negro race is perhaps expressed best in one of his most delightful stories, "Huckleberry Finn." In this story, which contains many pictures of Southern life as it was fifty or sixty years ago, there is a poor, ignorant negro boy who accompanies the heroes of the story, Huckleberry Finn and Tom Sawyer, on a long journey down the Mississippi on a raft.

It is possible the ordinary reader of this story has been so absorbed in the adventures of the two white boys that he did not think much about the part that "Jim"—which was, as I remember, the name of the colored boy—played in all these adventures. I do not believe any one can read this story closely, however, without becoming aware of the deep sympathy of the author in "Jim." In fact, before one gets through with the book, one cannot fail to observe that in some way or other the author, without making any comment and without going out of his way, has somehow succeeded in making his readers feel a genuine respect for "Jim," in spite of the ignorance he displays. I cannot help feeling that in this character Mark Twain has, perhaps unconsciously, exhibited his sympathy and interest in the masses of the negro people.

My contact with him showed that Mr. Clemens had a kind and generous heart. I think I have never known him to be so stirred up on any one question as he was on that of the cruel treatment of the natives in the Congo Free State. In his letter to Leopold, the late King of the Belgians, in his own inimitable way he did a service in calling to the attention of the world the cruelties practised upon the black natives of the Congo that had far-reaching results. I saw him several times in connection with his efforts to bring about reforms in the Congo Free State, and he never seemed to tire of talking on the subject and planning for better conditions.

As a literary man he was rare and unique, and I believe that his success in literature rests largely upon the fact that he came from among the common people. Practically all that he wrote had an interest for the commonest man and woman. In a word, he succeeded in literature as few men in any age have succeeded, because he stuck close to nature and to the common people, and in doing so he disregarded in a large degree many of the ordinary rules of rhetoric which often serve merely to cramp and make writers unnatural and uninteresting.

Few, if any, persons born in the South have shown in their achievements what it is possible for one individual to accomplish to the extent that Mr. Clemens has. Surrounded in his early childhood by few opportunities for culture or conditions that tended to give him high ideals, he continued to grow in popular estimation and to exert a wholesome influence upon the public to the day of his death.

The late Mr. H. H. Rogers, who was, perhaps, closer to Mr. Clemens than any one else, said to me at one time that Mr. Clemens often seemed irritated because people were not disposed to take him seriously; because people generally take most that he said and wrote as a mere jest. It was this fact to which he referred, I have no doubt, when at a public meeting in the interest of Tuskegee at Carnegie Hall a few years ago, he referred to himself in a humorous vein as a moralist, saying that all his life he had been going about trying to correct the morals of the people about him. As an illustration of the deep earnestness of his nature, I may mention the fact that Mr. Rogers told me that at one time Mr. Clemens was seriously planning to write a life of Christ, and that his friends had hard work to persuade him not to do it for fear that such a life might prove a failure or would be misunderstood.

As to Mark Twain's successor, he can have none. No more can such a man as Mark Twain have a successor than could Phillips Brooks or Henry Ward Beecher. Other men may do equally interesting work in a different manner, but Mark Twain, in my opinion, will always stand out as a unique personality, the results of whose work and influence will be more and more manifest as the years pass by.

BOOKER T. WASHINGTON.

* * *

The steadiest American home-body, distressed by what he sees in his newspapers, weeklies and monthlies, must know moments nowadays when, despite his patriotism, our country suggests nothing more than a gigantic loot and a voluminous but despairing cry of "Stop Thief!" The gloomy moment passes quickly before the second thought that all this is only surface and is nothing vital to the real America that flies a banner starry indeed. For my part, always when I think of that true United States, part of the thought is Mark Twain. For, complete citizen of the world as he was, he was the American Spirit. And oh! how that spirit spoke in him—and *from* him, from that great pen, now quiet.

... He was not only a master builder; he was a master critic, too. But it was never men he condemned or fought—only their cruelties and stupidities. What he hated most, I think, were the stupidities that are cruel.

His presence here made the world a more "reassuring" place to live in than it had been before. Everything seemed safer because he was with us. For the multitude who read all he wrote, it was like a child having a grown person's hand in the dark.

He came of the West and of the South, and at first belonged to them. Then he belonged to the whole country; then to all the world. After that all the world belonged to him.

It is incredible that he is dead. He couldn't be. So he must be—"just away."

BOOTH TARKINGTON.

* * *

MARK TWAIN was a sore disappointment to iconoclasts who love to hold funeral services over living celebrities. He had the rare story-teller's sense of knowing just how often to summon his audience and when to leave it waiting for more. He was about the only popular humorist who never endured the chagrin of hearing applause die away. He used a combination of artistic sense and every-day common horse sense in never crowding his output simply because there was eager demand for it. Every writer is measured by his own high-water mark, and the lay critic often seems disposed to draw unfavorable comparisons. Every book by Mark Twain was so different from the one preceding that comparisons were impossible. He had the courage and the divine inspiration to write what he wanted to write when he felt that it should be written. He never was in danger of becoming that pathetic reminder of the year before, the exploded humorist.

GEORGE ADE.

* * *

Mark Twain is not all of Samuel Clemens. He was much more than humorous. He was a great fictionist and a rough-hewn stylist uttering himself in his own way, which was a large, direct and forceful way. No amount of Old World contact could destroy his quaint drawl, and not all his reading nor his acquired personal knowledge of other writers could conventionalize his method. He remained the mid-Western American and literary democrat to the last.

I shall never forget the impression he made upon me when I called upon him in London some twelve years ago. The hotel in which he was staying was one of those highly refined, almost completely femininized, institutions with which the west end of London is furnished, but when the shock-haired, keen-eyed man from Missouri took my hand and said "Howdy" I felt at home. I thought him then as I think him now: one of the greatest of American authors. Not of the cultured type, but of the creative type. A figure to put beside Walt Whitman as a representative of our literary democracy.

Let me also say that to me he was a most distinctive and powerful orator. I was fortunate enough to hear his speech at the Lotus Club on the occasion of his return from "Following the Equator," at which time he feelingly announced to us that he had paid off the debt with which for so long a time he had been burdened. It was humorous, of course, but it was more than that; it was a brave and manly and exultant speech.

I heard him also at the dinner given on his sixty-seventh birthday, and there again he made all other speakers seem tame. No other orator save Ingersoll ever seemed to me so vital and so spontaneous. I have heard him on other occasions and always there was that marvellous power of creating phrases, of making old words seem new. As Howells says, "He wrote like a primitive," so I say he spoke like one who used words fresh from the mint with the sheen of their minting still upon them. Every letter of his speech was vital with the breath of his personality. This was the secret of his amazing hold upon his audiences all over the world.

Hamlin Garland.

* * *

He was a pretty big man—I sometimes wonder if he were not quite the most commanding literary personality of this period. Certainly no other man has succeeded in gripping so many people in so many parts of the world as he, and it does not seem natural to have a world without Mark Twain in it. One's

sorrow is mitigated somewhat by the thought of his loneliness of late years, as
well as of the feeling that he probably wanted to go.

JOHN KENDRICK BANGS.

* * *

Contemporaries are prone to judge an artist by the bulk of his work or by the
average of it; but, luckily, posterity gauges him only by his best. It measures
him by the summits of his accomplishment and not by the foot-hills or
the valleys. Few authors will profit more by this wiser choice of the years
to come than Mark Twain, since his writing was curiously unequal, with
a wide chasm yawning between his loftiest work and his lowest; his touch
was often uncertain and his taste was on occasion perverse. But his best is
very high in quality; the peaks of his achievement tower aloft unchallenged
and indisputable. No one of the men of letters of his time bids fair to loom
larger in the perspective of time. It may be that the next generation will drop
out the half of his writings and the generation after may winnow what is
left. Yet enough will withstand the drastic process; our grandchildren will
gladly make friends with Tom Sawyer and Huck Finn; and they will grow up
to delight in the most veracious passages of "Roughing It" and "Life on the
Mississippi" and "A Tramp Abroad."

Mark Twain was great in many ways and especially in four—as a humorist,
as a story-teller, as a stylist and as a moralist. Now and again his humor was
fantastic and arbitrary, perhaps even mechanical; but at its richest it was
irresistible, rooted in truth, sustained by sincerity and supported by a manly
melancholy—which became more plainly visible as he broadened his outlook
on life. His native gift of story-telling, the compelling power of his narrative,
was cultivated by conscious art, until one could not choose but hear,
submitting ourselves wholly to the spell he cast upon us; of their kind there
is nothing more vivid in fiction than the Shepherdson–Grangerford feud and
the shooting of Boggs by Sherburn, with the subsequent attempt to lynch
the latter. As a master of English prose he has not received the appreciation
he deserved, for he could call up an unforgettable picture with the utmost
economy of stroke; Huck Finn's description of the storm at night when he
is alone on the island may be set by the side of the vision of the Jungfrau
by moonlight in "A Tramp Abroad." And his sturdy morality, inspired by a
detestation of sham and of affectation as ingrained as Molière's, ought to be
evident to all who have pondered his analysis of Cecil Rhodes in "Following
the Equator," and especially to all who have meditated upon "The Man that

Corrupted Hadleyburg," a masterpiece of stern irony which Swift would not have disowned and which is free from the corroding misanthropy that Swift might have bestowed upon it.

A great artist in humor and in narrative and in style, a great moralist—and a great man in himself.

Brander Matthews.

—Various Authors, "Tributes to Mark Twain,"
North American Review, June 1910

George Ade "Mark Twain and the Old Time Subscription Book" (1910)

The Chicago humorist George Ade's memoir of Twain recalls, as William Dean Howells does elsewhere, with only a grimace, the age of "subscription books" (or as Howells calls them, the "matchlessly ugly subscription volumes . . . the hideous blocks and bricks of which the visible temple of the humorist's fame was first builded"). Twain's earliest books (excepting his very first, *The Jumping Frog*) were made available to the public in the manner described by Ade. Such an account is valuable to any students researching the publishing methods of the nineteenth century, including how books were marketed and how they were consumed. Students interested in the social details and politics of reading will find this useful also. Most of the books bought on a subscription plan fulfilled a role more as furniture than as literature. As Ade remembers, "Nobody really wanted these books." What purpose did they serve then? And how did the arrival of Twain in this market subvert the tradition? To what degree was Twain's final popularity based on his strange publishing history?

In *My Mark Twain* (1910), Howells remembers one of his earliest meetings with Twain, when Twain made him and Thomas Bailey Aldrich envious of the facts and figures regarding subscription publishing:

> An army of agents was overrunning the country with the prospectuses of his books, and delivering them by the scores of thousands in completed sale. Of *The Innocents Abroad* he said, "It sells right along just like the Bible." . . . [H]e lectured Aldrich and me on the folly of that mode of publication in the trade which we had thought it the highest success to achieve a chance in. "Anything but subscription publication is printing for private circulation," he maintained, and he so won upon our greed and hope that on the

way back to Boston we planned the joint authorship of a volume
adapted to subscription publication.

———— ·/// ————— ·/// ———— ·///————

Mark Twain should be doubly blessed for saving the center table from utter
dullness. Do you remember that center table of the seventies? The marble top
showed glossy in the subdued light that filtered through the lace curtains,
and it was clammy cold even on hot days. The heavy mahogany legs were
chiseled into writhing curves from which depended stern geometrical
designs or possibly bunches of grapes. The Bible had the place of honor and
was flanked by subscription books. In those days the house never became
cluttered with the ephemeral six best sellers. The new books came a year
apart, and each was meant for the center table, and it had to be so thick and
heavy and emblazoned with gold that it could keep company with the bulky
and high-priced Bible.

Books were bought by the pound. Sometimes the agent was a ministerial
person in black clothes and stove-pipe hat. Maiden ladies and widows, who
supplemented their specious arguments with private tales of woe, moved from
one small town to another feeding upon prominent citizens. Occasionally the
prospectus was unfurled by an undergraduate of a freshwater college working
for the money to carry him another year.

The book-agents varied, but the book was always the same,—many pages,
numerous steel engravings, curly-cue tail-pieces, platitudes, patriotism,
poetry, sentimental mush. One of the most popular, still resting in many a
dim sanctuary, was known as "Mother, Home, and Heaven." A ponderous
collection of "Poetical Gems" did not involve the publishers in any royalty
entanglements. Even the "Lives of the Presidents" and "Noble Deeds of the
Great and Brave" gave every evidence of having been turned out as piecework by needy persons temporarily lacking employment on newspapers. Let
us not forget the "Manual of Deportment and Social Usages," from which the
wife of any agriculturist could learn the meaning of R.S.V.P. and the form to
be employed in acknowledging an invitation to a levee.

Nobody really wanted these books. They were purchased because
the agents knew how to sell them, and they seemed large for the price,
and besides, every well-furnished home had to keep something on the
center table.

Subscription books were dry picking for boys. Also they were accessible
only on the Sabbath after the weekly scouring. On week-days the boys
favored an underground circulating library, named after Mr. Beadle, and

the hay-mow was the chosen reading room. Let one glorious exception be made in the case of "Dr. Livingstone's Travels in Africa," a subscription book of forbidding size, but containing many pictures of darkies with rings in their noses.

Just when front-room literature seemed at its lowest ebb, so far as the American boy was concerned, along came Mark Twain. His books looked, at a distance, just like the other distended, diluted, and altogether tasteless volumes that had been used for several decades to balance the ends of the center table. The publisher knew his public, so he gave a pound of book for every fifty cents, and crowded in plenty of wood-cuts and stamped the outside with golden bouquets and put in a steel engraving of the author, with a tissue paper veil over it, and "sicked" his multitude of broken-down clergymen, maiden ladies, grass widows, and college students on to the great American public.

Can you see the boy a Sunday morning prisoner, approach the new book with a dull sense of foreboding, expecting a dose of Tupper's "Proverbial Philosophy"? Can you see him a few minutes later when he finds himself linked arm-in-arm with Mulberry Sellers or Buck Fanshaw or the convulsing idiot who wanted to know if Christopher Columbus was sure-enough dead? No wonder he curled up on the hair-cloth sofa and hugged the thing to his bosom and lost all interest in Sunday-school. "Innocents Abroad" was the most enthralling book ever printed until "Roughing It" appeared. Then along came "The Gilded Age," "Life on the Mississippi," and "Tom Sawyer," one cap sheaf after another. While waiting for a new one we read the old ones all over again.

The new uniform edition with the polite little pages, high-art bindings, and all the boisterous wood-cuts carefully expurgated can never take the place of those lumbering subscription books. They were our early friends and helped us to get acquainted with the most amazing story-teller that ever captivated the country boys and small-town boys all over America.

While we are honoring Mark Twain as a great literary artist, a philosopher, and a teacher, let the boys of the seventies add their tribute. They knew him for his miracle of making the subscription book something to be read and not merely looked at. He converted the Front Room from a Mausoleum into a Temple of Mirth.

—George Ade, "Mark Twain and the Old Time
Subscription Book," *Review of Reviews* 41,
June 1910, pp. 703–704

Simeon Strunsky (1910)

This shrewd article is less about Mark Twain than it is about how critics
and journalists write about Mark Twain. As such, it is highly useful to any
student assembling a sophisticated study of how Mark Twain was perceived, presented, and manipulated by critics.

    Strunsky's complaint—that to deny that Twain was "primarily a fun-
maker" is to deny the plain facts, stated clearly in his writing—anticipates
Bernard DeVoto's response to Van Wyck Brooks, the final selection in this
section. It is worth noting, however, that Twain himself was foremost in
trying to distance himself from the title "mere humorist."

⇒◆⇐ ⇒◆⇐ ⇒◆⇐

Mark Twain's memory may suffer from a certain paradoxical habit we
have fallen into when passing judgment on the illustrious dead. The habit
consists in picking out for particular commendation in the man what one
least expects. If the world thinks of him as a great humorist, the point to
make is that at bottom he was really a philosopher. If his shafts struck at
everybody and everything, the thing to say is that he liked best what he hit
hardest. If one of his books sold five thousand copies, the attempt is made
to base his future fame on the comparatively unknown book. The motive
behind such reasoning is commendable enough. It is the desire not to judge
superficially, the desire to get at the 'real' man behind the mask which all
of us, according to tradition, wear in life. It is a praiseworthy purpose, but,
in the hands of the unskilled or the careless, a perilous one. And worse
than either in the intellectual snob whose business it is constitutionally
to disagree with the obvious. We make no attempt to classify the writer
who has declared that Mark Twain, when he wrote *Innocents Abroad*, was
terribly in earnest; that he set out to satirize and was funny only because
he could not help it. This represents the extreme of a tendency that is made
manifest on every side, to turn Mark Twain into everything but what he
was—a great compeller of laughter.

    One gets dreadfully weary of such topsy-turvy criticism. There are times
when one would like to believe that Napoleon will be remembered because
he won Austerlitz and Marengo, and not because he divided up France into a
vast number of small peasant holdings; that Lincoln was a great man because
he signed the Proclamation of Emancipation and wrote the Gettysburg
address, and not because he kept his temper under criticism and in adversity.
It is well to try to pierce behind the veil of Maya, but no amount of analysis
can do away with the popularly accepted beliefs that mothers are primarily

maternal, that actresses' talents lie in the direction of the stage, that joyful people laugh, and that people who make wry faces are either pessimists or dyspeptics. What use is there in trying to make a serious book out of the *Innocents Abroad*, when we know well that the Mark Twain who wrote it was primarily a fun-maker? For ourselves, we confess that we have been unable to find any grave purpose in the 'Jumping Frog of Calaveras.' We recall the Hawaiian stranger whom Mark Twain kissed for his mother's sake before robbing him of his small change. We recall the horse he rode in Honolulu; it had many fine points, and our traveller hung his hat upon one of them. We recall that other horse behind which he went driving one Sunday with the lady of his choice; it was a milk-dealer's horse on week-days, and it persisted in travelling diagonally across the street and stopping before every gate. These adventures are easy to recall, but the hidden serious purpose within them remains hidden from us.

The serious element in Mark Twain the man and the writer, it would, of course, be futile to deny. His hatred of sham, his hatred of cruelty, his hatred of oppression, appear in the *Innocents Abroad*, as they do in his *Connecticut Yankee* and in his bitter assaults on the Christian Scientists and the American missionaries in China of the Boxer days. But to say that Mark Twain was a great humorist because he was an intensely serious man is not true, whatever truth there may be in the formula that humorists are humorists because they are men of sorrow. We would reverse the formula. We would say that humorists are often sad because they are humorists, and that from much laughing the rebound must necessarily be towards much grief. If it is commonly asserted that the humorist laughs because of the incongruities of life, it is, nevertheless, just as safe to maintain that the man born to laughter will be driven by his instincts to search out incongruities. There was no fundamental pessimism in Mark Twain. As Mr. Howells brings out in his chapter of reminiscences in the last *Harper's*, Mr. Clemens had the soul of untamed boyishness. He was boyish in his exuberance of manner, in his taste for extraordinary clothes, and in his glee at earning a great deal of money:

> The postals [announcing his share of the daily profits from the *Gilded Age*] used to come about dinner-time, and Clemens would read them aloud to us in wild triumph. $150–$200–$300 were the gay figures which they bore, and which he flaunted in the air before he sat down at table, or rose from it to brandish, and then, flinging his napkin into his chair, walked up and down to exult in.

One thing there was in Mark Twain that was not apparently boyish or simple. Mr. Howells asserts positively that in his later years Twain believed neither in the Christian theology, in God, nor in immortality:

> All his expressions to me were of a courageous renunciation of any hope of living again, or elsewhere seeing those he had lost. He suffered terribly in their loss, and he was not fool enough to try ignoring his grief. He knew that for that there were but two medicines; that it would wear itself out with the years, and that meanwhile there was nothing for it but those respites in which the mourner forgets himself in slumber. I remember that in a black hour of my own when I was called down to see him, as he thought from sleep, he said, with an infinite, an exquisite compassion, 'Oh, did I wake you, did I *wake* you?' Nothing more, but the look, the voice, were everything; and while I live they cannot pass from my sense.

Here at last we have the disillusion that is said to dwell in the innermost soul of the great humorist. But here, too, we seem to feel that the gray vision of the future was with him not a cause, but a result. When the buoyant soul sinks back upon itself it is apt to feel the riddle of life very keenly indeed.

—Simeon Strunsky, *The Nation*, June 30, 1910

G.K. Chesterton "Mark Twain" (1910)

Gilbert Keith Chesterton was an English essayist, novelist, and short story writer, author of among other works *The Man Who Was Thursday* and the "Father Brown" stories. As an essayist, he enjoyed considerable influence in his day, alongside his friend Hilaire Belloc. As literary mandarins, they plug the breach between the Victorian era and the modern one.

Mark Twain's writing has "mad logic carried further and further into the void." His tall tales recall the construction of a New York apartment building (or a Peking pagoda). Such terminology reinvents Twain for the twentieth century, hinting at the "absurdism" or even nihilism that lurks at the back of some humor ("black humor"), a comic nihilism that would be exhibited later in the century by authors such as John Barth, Donald Barthelme, and William Gass.

The urban comparison to New York architecture (later to Chicago and Philadelphia) particularly takes Twain far from the southern or midwestern impressions offered by Booker T. Washington and Hamlin

Garland previously in this section. Students examining Twain's modernity, or his relation to the city, should consult Chesterton. Students interested in Twain as an influence on postwar American fiction should also consult Chesterton.

The dichotomy between whether Twain is a wit or a humorist is alive in this article. Chesterton disagrees with Professor Peck, also previously included here, finding Twain to be a wit. Wit, Chesterton insists, "is a more manly exercise than fiddling or fooling; wit requires an intellectual athleticism, because it is akin to logic." Chesterton returns to his impression of "arithmetical progression" in Twain's humor (or rather, his wit), a resort to "more and more frantic lengths of deduction." This progression is tied to the "mad lucidity" and the "wild wit" and also to New York architecture.

In forming this thesis, Chesterton, like Peck, returns to Twain's early stories for his sources: "How I Edited an Agricultural Paper" and the Horace Greeley stories from *Roughing It*. Unlike Arnold Bennett, Chesterton discerns a structure to Twain's writing (that is, to the shorter works). It is ascending, exaggerative, "almost apocalyptic" even. Students endeavoring to write on the use of structure (or its absence) in Mark Twain's writing should consider Chesterton's theory.

Mark Twain's laughter was like the falls at Niagara ("almost one of the vulgarities of Nature"). Samuel Clemens, however, was lonely and severe. This psychobiographical conceit of separating Twain and Clemens, exemplified by Justin Kaplan's biography *Mr. Clemens and Mark Twain* (1966), has an early exponent here. Such a separation leads to the psychological speculation best exemplified by Van Wyck Brooks's *The Ordeal of Mark Twain* (1920).

We are always told that there is something specially sinister in the death of a great jester. I am not so sure about the point myself, seeing that so many thousand human beings, diplomatists, financiers, kings, bankers, and founders of philosophies, are engaged in functions far more ultimately fruitless and frivolous than really making the smallest schoolboy laugh. If the death of a clown makes pantomimes for a moment tragic, it is also true that the death of a statesman makes statesmanship for a moment highly comic; the irony cuts both ways. But in the case of Mark Twain there is a particular cause which at once emphasises and complicates this contrast between the comic and the serious. The point I mean is this: that while Mark Twain's literary merits were very much of the uproarious and topsy-turvy kind, his personal merits were very much of the stoical or even puritanical kind. While irresponsibility was the energy in his writings, an almost excessive responsibility was the energy in his character. The artistic European might feel that he was, perhaps, too comic when he was comic; but such a European would also feel that he was too serious when he was serious.

The wit of Mark Twain was avowedly and utterly of the extravagant order. It had that quality of mad logic carried further and further into the void, a quality in which many strange civilizations are at one. It is a system of extremes, and all extremes meet in it; thus houses piled one on top of the other is the ideal of a flat in New York and of a pagoda in Pekin. Mark Twain was a master of this mad lucidity. He was a wit rather than a humorist; but I do not mean by this (as so many modern people will certainly fancy) that he was something less than a humorist. Possibly, I think, he was something more than a humorist. Humour, a subtle relish for the small incongruities of society, is a thing that exists in many somewhat low society types, in many snobs and in some sneaks. Like the sense of music, it is exquisite and ethereal; but, like the sense of music, it can exist (somehow or other) in utter blackguards or even in utter blockheads; just as one often meets a fool who can really play the fiddle, so one often meets a fool who can really play the fool. But wit is a more manly exercise than fiddling or fooling; wit requires an intellectual athleticism, because it is akin to logic. A wit must have something of the same running, working, and staying power as a mathematician or a metaphysician. Moreover, wit is a fighting thing and a working thing. A man may enjoy humour all by himself; he may see a joke when no one else sees it; he may see the point and avoid it. But wit is a sword; it is meant to make people feel the point as well as see it. All honest people saw the point of Mark Twain's wit. Not a few dishonest people felt it.

But though it was wit it was wild wit, as wild as the pagoda in China or the other pagodas in New York. It was progressive, and the joke went forward by arithmetical progression. In all those excruciating tales of his, which in our youth made us ill with laughing, the idea always consisted in carrying some small fact or notion to more and more frantic lengths of deduction. If a man's hat was as high as a house Mark Twain would think of some way of calling it twenty times higher than a house. If his hat was smashed as flat as a pancake, Mark Twain would invent some startling and happy metaphor to prove that it was smashed twenty times flatter than a pancake. His splendid explosive little stories, such as that which describes how he edited an agricultural paper, or that which explains how he tried to decipher a letter from Horace Greeley, have one tremendous essential of great art. I mean that the excitement mounts up perpetually; the stories grow more and more comic, as a tragedy should grow more and more tragic. The rack, tragic or comic, stretches a man until something breaks inside him. In tragedy it is his heart, or, perhaps, his stiff neck. In farce I do not quite know what it is—perhaps his funny-bone is dislocated; perhaps his skull is slightly cracked.

Anyhow, the humour or wit of Mark Twain was of this ascending and exaggerative order. As such it was truly mountainous, and almost apocalyptic. No writer of modern English, perhaps, has had such a genius for making the cow jump over the moon; that is, for lifting the heaviest and most solemn absurdity high up into the most starry adventures. He was never at a loss for a simile or a parable, and they were never, strictly speaking, nonsense. They were rather a kind of incredible sense. They were not suddenly inconsequent, like Lewis Carroll; rather they were unbearably consequent, and seemed capable of producing new consequences for ever. Even that fantastic irreverence and fantastic ignorance which sometimes marked his dealings with elements he insufficiently understood, were never abrupt departures, but only elaborate deductions from his idea. It was quite logical that when told that a saint's heart had burst his ribs he should ask what the saint had had for dinner. It was quite logical that his delightful musician, when asked to play music appropriate to the Prodigal Son, should play, "We all get blind drunk when Johnny comes marching home." These are things of real wit, like that of Voltaire; though they are not uttered with the old French restraint, but with a new American extravagance. Voltaire is to them as the Rhone is to Niagara; not inferior in quality, but merely in quantity, for Niagara is not only one of the violences, but almost one of the vulgarities of Nature. The laughter of Mark Twain was like Niagara.

Such was Mark Twain; such was not Samuel Clemens. His lonely figure stands up in strange solitude and severity against the confusion and extravagance of the background of his works. The virtues which we have all now to regret in their return to God were specially virtues rather of the restrained than of the riotous or sympathetic order. We know, indeed, that he rose from the ranks, in the sense that he was poor and pugnacious in a rich and pugnacious society; that he came of Southern folk, served with the heroic Southern armies, but that the greater part of his life was such a scramble of incalculable successes and unavoidable failures as Stevenson has well described in the one convincing picture of a good American, Jim Pinkerton, in *The Wrecker*. The words Stevenson used of Pinkerton might quite truly be used of Clemens. "He was stuffed full of manly virtues. Thrift and courage glowed in him." When his hair was white and his soul heavy with years an accident led him into liabilities which the law would have discharged by the ordinary arrangements of bankruptcy. The old man refused to accept the ordinary arrangements which the law allowed him. He set to work strenuously, writing and lecturing as if he were at the beginning of his life rather than at the end of it. He repaid his unrecognised and unlegal debt, and a little later he died. Thus the primary paradox is emphasised almost in the article of death; the man whom ten million people had adored as a tom-fool was too serious even for the expectation of his own creditors.

The credit of such glowing thrift and courage (to quote an admirable phrase again) must be ascribed to something or somebody; I will no longer disguise the dreadful fact that I ascribe it exactly where Mark Twain would have ascribed it. I ascribe it to the Republican virtue of America. Of course, if Mark Twain had said that in so many words, everybody in England would have thought he was making one of his best jokes; whereas, in truth, he would have been indulging in one of his worst pieces of seriousness. Somebody in an advanced Socialist paper that I saw the other day said that Mark Twain was a cynic. I suppose there never was a person so far removed from cynicism as Mark Twain. A cynic must at least mean a man who is flippant about serious things; about things that he thinks serious. Mark Twain was always serious to the verge of madness. He was not serious about St. Francis; he did not think St. Francis serious. He honestly supposed the marvels of St. Francis to be some ecclesiastical trick of Popes and Cardinals. He did not happen to know that the Franciscan movement was something much more certainly popular than the revolution that rent America from England. He derided King Arthur's Court as something barbaric. He did not happen to know that the only reason why that dim and highly dubious Court has made a half-entry into history is that it stood, if it ever stood at all, for the remnant of high civilization against the base advance of barbarism. He did not happen to know that, in his time, St. Francis stood for the ballot-box. He did not happen to know that, in his time, King Arthur stood for the telephone. He could never quite get rid of the American idea that good sense and good government had begun quite a little while ago; and that the heavier a monumental stone was to lift the more lightly it might be thrown away. But all these limitations of his only re-emphasise the ultimate fact he never laughed at a thing unless he thought it laughable. He was an American; that is, an unfathomably solemn man. Now all this is due to a definite thing, an historical thing, called Republican virtue. It was worth while to issue the Declaration of Independence if only that Mark Twain might declare his independence also.

In this the great humorist not only represents his country, but a big mistake about his country. The apparent clamour and complexity of America is very superficial; America is not really advanced or aggressively civilized. New York, Philadelphia, Chicago are jokes; just such tall jokes as Mark Twain would have made. American commerce is all one tall story; American commerce is a vast American lie. But the American lie is a very serious, separate, and authoritative institution, which could only exist among a singularly truthful people. Behind these extravagances, whether in words or wealth, whether in books or bricks, there remains a grave simplicity which is truly American. The genuine value of the Yankee is not his forwardness. Rather it is his backwardness that is the real beauty of the Yankee. There is in the depths of him the rural stillness of an intellectual backwater: he is a great rustic. The log-hut, and not the sky-scraper, is the American home. Therefore, despite the revolting vices of wealth and all the vulgarities of unhistorical individualism, there does remain in the Americans a certain average of virile virtues, equality, hard work, patriotism, and a plain ideality. Corrupt fatigue is uncommon; unclean despair is almost unknown. You could not have made Mark Twain even understand either of these things. He was radiant with a rectitude none the less noble for being slightly naive; he carried everywhere those powerful platitudes that are like clubs of stone. With these he hammered Calvinism in his youth and Christian Science in his old age. But he was not an "advanced" thinker, not a mind in revolt; rather he was a conservative and rustic grandfather older than all such follies. But this strength in him and his country truly came from a great spirit which England resisted and has forgotten; the spirit which, when all is said, made it no nonsense to compare Washington to Cincinnatus; the austere love of liberty and of the ploughshare and the sword.

—G.K. Chesterton, "Mark Twain,"
T.P.'s Weekly, April/May 1910

MERLE JOHNSON (1910)

Merle Johnson provided the first proper bibliography of the works of Mark Twain. He was a "commercial artist" and book dealer, legendary among Twain scholars and collectors for his cantankerousness. "In case you didn't know it, all of Merle's correspondence isn't printable," chuckled *The Twainian*, "those of you who knew the fellow can vouch for that." While the good bibliographer must be exacting in his main work, there is an impressionistic, humorous, and sometimes strongly opinionated tenor to Johnson's observations. For this reason, some of his ostensibly bibliographical remarks have interest to the scholar of Mark Twain.

Bibliographical information is itself interesting in Twain's instance. Johnson's bibliography describes in a way otherwise not apparent the struggle between English and American audiences for Twain. "Europe, Canada, and the United States vied for the first publication of his work," Johnson reports. It might surprise the American reader to learn then that "nearly all the books were first issued in England." Why did this happen? Was the market superior, the audience larger or more responsive in some other manner? Furthermore, Johnson's remarks about attitudes to the "fine differences between editions" will be revealing for students concerned with the state of publishing and authorship in the late nineteenth century, particularly with reference to Twain.

Finally, in a section subtitled "Notes," Johnson provides information regarding Mark Twain's attitude toward interviewers (interesting when read alongside Theodore Dreiser's "Mark Twain: Three Contacts") and to book illustrators. Students writing about the uses of illustration in Mark Twain's work, especially the extent of Twain's collaboration with his artists, will be fascinated by this excerpt.

—⌇⌇⌇— —⌇⌇⌇— —⌇⌇⌇—

Samuel Langhorne Clemens, who lived and wrote under the pseudonym "Mark Twain," was born in Florida, Missouri, November 30, 1835, and died in Redding, Connecticut, April 21, 1910.

This bibliography of his printed work is not the place for an extended résumé of the literary value of his output; it is rather a catalogue to facilitate the researches of the many, present and future, interested in his writings. Little attempt will be made to distinguish between the individual characteristics of the various books or articles with regard to the quality of humor, moral teaching, interest, or probable value. Mark Twain has been variously regarded as merely an entertaining humorist, and as a great and profound philosopher; his own point of view probably changed with the years as his mental horizon changed and widened. A preface to one of his early works states: "I am not offering this work to the reader as either law or gospel, upon any point, principle, or subject; but only as a trifle to occupy himself with when he has nothing to do and does not wish to whistle." Yet most of his very latest work was controversial and philosophical, and just before his death he wrote: "I like myself best when I am serious."

Personally, I regard most of his better-known works as Americana of the greatest value, as impossible to duplicate as the paintings of Remington depicting an age that has vanished; those books portray the making of the nineteenth-century American, his whimsical humor and exaggeration, his roughness, his fineness, his ready sympathy, his strength, his weakness, from boyhood to old age: they are history, as Dickens books are history, in the best sense of all.

Mark Twain's literary production covered a period of practically five decades. His range of activities included newspaper, magazine, book, and speech. He lived in a dozen places, from Honolulu to Vienna. Europe, Canada, and the United States vied for the first publications of his work. . . .

It must be taken into account that the bulk of Mark Twain's work was published before the date of international copyright, and his popularity made him the victim of "pirates" of every degree. Whatever the author's feelings on the subject may have been, these "pirated" works are of as much importance to the collector as those regularly copyrighted. Naturally, the printing dates of these pirated works can be found in no such regular channels as government records. Even the government records of the copyright editions have been incomplete. Many books filed in government offices at time of printing have been lost. Of some of the early books, publishers, printers, binders, illustrators, all lie in their graves, and Mr. Clemens himself never had the collector's interest in remarking the fine differences between editions so necessary to state exactly in a bibliography. Neither author nor publishers felt the importance of preserving the first copies from the press. . . .

The largest point at issue for the collector who does not wish to be omnivorous in his purchases, lies between the English and American editions. (In most cases the Canadian publications can be eliminated as "Firsts" because the English editions preceded them.)

Many bibliophiles claim with authority that the collector should choose for a preferential set of those books published in the author's own country, even if some of the items have been previously issued in another country. In the Twain case nearly all the books were first issued in England, some pirated, but most by arrangement for purposes of copyright protection before the passage of the present act. . . .

Mr. Clemens has been interviewed countless times by newspapers and magazine writers. His refreshing and original views always made good reading for the public. He could be grave or gay as suited the topic. It became so the custom in New York for the editors to send reporters to him on any and all occasions, that he was forced to draw the line, limiting them to the day of his departure for some distant point, and the day of his return. The same questions arise in regard to interviews as with speeches, chiefly as to accuracy of reporting. I once saw a scrap-book containing newspaper interviews which had been submitted to Mr. Clemens by some ardent admirer, and the author had margined it with his comments. Some had merely a confirmatory "O.K.," others had more extended comments, and but one was denied in toto; surely Mr. Clemens found a far less percentage of "Mendacious Journalism" than other of our public men. On the one interview which he did not choose to remember giving to the press, which purported to be a reply to a society leader's previous article, he margined, in effect, "I would be as apt to discuss this with Mrs. A— as with the cat."

Here is Mark Twain's own idea of the interview as he has met it:

> "I have, in my time, succeeded in writing some very poor stuff, which I have put in pigeon-holes until I realized how bad it was, and then destroyed it. But I think the very poorest article I ever wrote and destroyed was better worth reading than any interview with me that was ever published. I would like just once to interview myself in order to show the possibilities of interview." . . .

Mr. Clemens' attitude toward illustrators and college-men was typical of newspaper editors of his time; since then employers have learned to recognize and even stimulate merit in those unfortunate classes. Dan Beard contributed the following to the New York *American* concerning his first meeting with Mark Twain to discuss the illustration of a book. Mr. Beard endeavors to give in type a representation of Mark's peculiar drawl:

> "'Mr. Beard, I—do—not—want—to—inflict—any—mental— agony—upon—you nor subject you—to—any—undue suffering, but—I—do wish—you'd read—the—book before—you make the— pictures.'

"I assured him that I had already read the manuscripts thoroughly three times, and he replied by opening a prominent magazine at his elbow, to a very beautiful picture of an old gentleman with a smooth face, which the text described as having a flowing white beard, remarking, as he did so:

> "'From—a—casual—reference—to—the   current— m a g a z i n e s—I—d i d   n o t—s u p p o s e—t h a t—w a s— the   usual—custom—with—illustrators. Now, Mr. Beard, you—know—my—character—of—the—Yankee He—is—a—common, uneducated—man. He's   a   good— telegraph—operator;   he—can—make—a—Colt's—revolver—

or—a—Remington—gun, but—he's—a—perfect—ignor-amus. He's—a—good—foreman—for—a—manufacturer, can survey—land—and—run—a—locomotive; in other—words, he—had—neither—the—refinement—nor—the—weakness— of—a—college—education. In—conclusion—I—want— to—say, that—I—have—endeavored—to—put—in—all—t he coarseness—and—vulgarity—into—the—Yankee— in—King—Arthur's—Court—that is—necessary, and— rely—upon—you—for—all—that—refinement—and delicacy—of—humor—which—your—facile—pen—can— depict. Glad to have met you, Mr. Beard.' " . . .

To show Mark Twain's relation to the physical appearance of his books, letters from his illustrators are of interest. Says Lucius Wolcott Hitchcock:

"I went to Mr. Clemens' house to see about the *Horse's Tale*. He had a little, old photograph of one of his children, who had died when a child, and he wanted me to work 'that little face' into the picture of the little girl in the story. I asked him if there was any further suggestion he wanted to make about what scenes of the story to take, etc., but he said: 'No, it's just this way about that. I find the artist knows more about what will make a good picture than I do. What I thought a good subject for a picture isn't worth a hang, and something I should not have thought of at all makes a very good one, so I will leave all that with you.' At the same time he gave me a photo of the cats he wanted me to use in the drawing of the old general.

"When the *Horse's Tale* drawings were finished, I took them down for him to see. He came into his study in a bathgown and pipe. These was no place to put the drawings where they could be seen but on the floor. So the old man dropped down on the floor like a child to look them over. He was pleased with them all far beyond their merits. He thought the drawing of the child looked like the original, and of the 'moonlight' he said, 'A very eloquent horse!' "

Dan Beard writes:

"I would rather work for Mark Twain than any man I ever met. First, because his writings are so full of imagination, so full of ideas, that each paragraph would make a good subject for a picture, a cartoon, or an illustration; second, because Mark Twain himself has a quicker perception and a keener appreciation of thoughtful, earnest work than any author for whom I have worked or *met*; third, because he was never niggardly with his praise, never waited for one to ask him how he liked the illustration, but of his own volition, and without suggestion from the artist, he would take time to sit down and write a personal letter of commendation for the work which pleased him; fourth, because he did not try to draw the pictures for the illustrator himself, as do most authors and publishers. Said he: 'Dan—if-a-man-comes-to-me-an'-says-Mr.-Clemens-I-want-you-to-write-me-a-book, I'll write it for him, but-if-he-comes-to-me and says-he-wants-me-to-write-a-book-'n'-then-tells-me-what-to-write, I'll-say-Dang-you, go-hire-a-type-writer.'

"When I had finished the illustrations for the now rare Webster Edition of *The Yankee in King Arthur's Court,* Mark set me a dignified, courtly letter of encouragement and commendation. When I finished the book, he wrote: 'There are hundred of artists who could illustrate this one. What a lucky day I went netting for lightning-bugs and caught a meteor. Live for ever. Mark.' "

Mr. Clemens had ideas of his own on the proper illustration of certain books, and insisted on their being carried out. The contract for pictures to accompany the separate edition of *Eve's Diary* had actually been led to a certain artist whose work had hitherto given great satisfaction, when Mark interposed with a demand for a different style of work for that particular book. It was with considerable effort that the exact style of decoration and allegorical pictures he desired was obtained.

Then again, for *Joan of Arc* he wished nothing humorous, but suggested that the pictures convey the sense of mysticism and allegory which he claimed was lacking, or only partially indicated in his text.

—Merle Johnson, from *A Bibliography
of the Work of Mark Twain,* New York:
Harper and Brothers, 1910, pp. v–vi, vii,
viii–xiii, 152–153, 159–160, 160–162

H.L. MENCKEN "TWAIN AND HOWELLS" (1911)

Whenever a new generation of critics comes to redefine Twain, one of the mysteries and frustrating obstacles to their comprehension is Twain's intimate friendship with William Dean Howells, expressed well if bluntly here by H.L. Mencken. This essay also marks an important challenge to Howells's "version" of Mark Twain. Howells was Twain's friend but also his mentor, adviser, and editor. Mencken's short piece here might be viewed as the first salvo of the battle to redefine a Twain independent of Howells's "simpering, coquettish, overcorseted" bowdlerization. Mencken's piece marks a formal challenge; Howells could not dominate the literary perceptions of Twain anymore.

The name of *My Mark Twain*, by William Dean Howells, is well chosen, for the book is less a record of events than an attempt at a personal interpretation. The Mark Twain that we see in it is a Mark Twain whose gaunt Himalayan outlines are discerned but hazily through a pink fog of Howells. There is an evident effort to palliate, to tone down, to apologize. The poor fellow, of course, was charming, and there was a lot of merit in some of the things he wrote—but what a weakness he had for thinking aloud! What oaths in his speech! What awful cigars he smoked! How barbarous his contempt for the strict sonata form! It seems incredible, indeed, that two men so unlike as Clemens and Howells should have found common material for a friendship lasting forty-four years. The one derived from Rabelais, Chaucer, the Elizabethans and Benvenuto Cellini—buccaneers of the literary high seas, loud laughers, law breakers, giants of an elder day; the other came down from Jane Austen, Washington Irving and Hannah More. The one wrote English as Michelangelo hacked marble, broadly, brutally, magnificently; the other was a maker of pretty waxen groups. The one was utterly unconscious of the means whereby he achieved his staggering effects; the other was the most toilsome, fastidious and self-conscious of craftsmen. Read the book. It will amuse you; better still, it will instruct you. If you get nothing else out of it, you will at least get some notion of the abysmal difference between the straightforward, clangorous English of Clemens and the simpering, coquettish, overcorseted English of the later Howells.

—H.L. Mencken, "Twain and Howells,"
Smart Set, January 1911

WILLIAM DEAN HOWELLS (1913)

The publication of Albert Bigelow Paine's epic three-volume *Mark Twain: A Biography* (1912) provides occasion enough for another re-evaluation

by William Dean Howells, further to *My Mark Twain* (1910). Some anxiety appears evident in Howells's prediction for the longevity of Twain's
reputation. His "primary question" here is, "how long Mark Twain will
last as a humorist." Even in 1913, Howells feels compelled to criticize
Artemus Ward and Petroleum V. Nasby. This is particularly strange given
that Howells had written an enthusiastic introduction to a new edition of
Artemus Ward's Best Stories for Harper and Brothers the previous year.

Howells struggles with the undeniable darkness of Twain's final
philosophy, his misanthropy and his atheism. Twain was "at times furiously
intolerant of others' belief in a divine Fatherhood and a life after death."
He dismisses Twain's last work, *Is Shakespeare Dead?*, as "preposterous"
and sums up his friend as "essentially an actor—that is, a child—that is,
a poet." H.L. Mencken would vigorously contest this last characterization
in the entry that follows.

Howells importantly also registers his approval for Paine's depiction of
Twain. While Paine was the official biographer and knew Twain intimately,
to later Twain scholars he has come to represent something of a problem.
Paine willingly whitewashed aspects of Twain's life and his opinions that
were deemed unpleasant by the Twain estate (that is, Twain's surviving
daughter, Clara) and was prone to extend this Victorian squeamishness to
editions of Twain's works; for instance, *The Mysterious Stranger*, published
posthumously in 1916, was interpolated with numerous fussy intrusions
written by Paine.

Additionally, Paine was the first editor of the "Mark Twain Papers,"
that vast mass of unedited manuscripts, that remained unpublished. As
well as writing the biography, he edited the *Letters* (1917), an edition of
the *Autobiography* (1924), and the *Notebooks* (1935). Students assessing
Paine's depiction of Twain will find no dissenting opinion in Howells.
Students regarding the Howells-Twain friendship might find some
interesting new developments in Howells's perception of Twain.

The question of how long he will last as a humorist, or how long he will
dominate all other humorists in the affection of his fellow-men, is something
that must have concerned Mark Twain in his life on earth. If he still lives
in some other state, the question does not concern him so much, except as
he would be loath to see good work forgotten; but, as he once lived here, it
must have concerned him intensely because he loved beyond almost any
other man to make the world sit up and look and listen. The question of his
lasting primacy is something that now remains for us survivors of him to

answer, each according to his thinking; and it renews itself in our case with unexpected force from the reading of Mr. Albert Bigelow Paine's story of his personal and literary life.

Of course, if we are moderately honest and candid, we must all try to shirk the question, for it would be a kind of arrogant hypocrisy to pretend that we had any of us a firm conviction on the point. For our own part, the Easy Chair's part, we prefer only to say that if the world ever ceased to love and to value his humor it would do so to its peculiar loss, for, as we have always held, the humor of no other is so mixed with good-will to humanity, and especially to that part of humanity which most needs kindness. Beyond this we should not care to go in prophecy, and in trying to guess Mark Twain's future from the past of other humorists we should not care to be comparative. There are only three or four whom he may be likened with, and, not to begin with the ancients, we may speak in the same breath of Cervantes, of Molière, of Swift, of Dickens, among the moderns. None of these may be compared with him in humanity except Dickens alone, whose humanity slopped into sentimentality, and scarcely counts more than the others'.

But Dickens even surpassed Mark Twain in characterizing and coloring the speech of his time. We who read Dickens in his heyday not only read him, we talked him, and slavishly reverberated his phrase when we wished to be funny. No one does that to-day, and no one ever did that with Mark Twain. Such a far inferior humorist as Artemus Ward stamped the utterance of his contemporaries measurably as much as Dickens and much more than Mark Twain, but this did not establish him in the popular consciousness of posterity; it was of no more lasting effect than the grotesqueries of Petroleum V. Nasby, or than the felicities of baseball parlance which Mr. George Ade has so satisfyingly reported. The remembrance of Mark Twain does not depend upon the presence of a like property in his humor, and its absence has little to do with the question which we have been inviting the reader to evade with us. . . .

It would not be easy for Mark Twain's surviving friends to find the drama of his closing years misrepresented in any important scene or motive. He was, like every one else, a complex nature but a very simple soul, and something responsive to him in his biographer is what has most justified Clemens in his choice of him for the work. The greatest of our humorists, perhaps the greatest humorist who ever lived, is here wonderfully imagined by a writer who is certainly not a great humorist. From first to last it seems to us that Mr. Paine has read Mark Twain aright. He has understood him as a boy in the primitive Southwestern circumstance of his romantic childhood; he has brought a clairvoyant sympathy to the events of the wild youth adventuring in every path inviting or forbidding him; he has truly seen him as he found himself at the beginning of his long climb to an eminence unequaled in the records of literary popularity; and he has followed him filially, affectionately, through the sorrows that darkened round him in his last years. Another biographer more gifted, or less gifted, than this very single-hearted historian might have been tempted to interpret a personality so always adventurous, so always romantic, so always heroic, according to his own limitations; but Mr. Paine has not done this folly. Whether knowingly or not, he has put himself aside, and devotedly adhered to what we should like to call his job. But he has not done this slavishly; he has ventured to have his own quiet opinion of Mark Twain's preposterous advocacy of the Baconian myth, and if he calls his fierce refusal of all the accepted theologies a philosophy, it is apparently without his entire acceptance of the refusal as final and convincing.

Mark Twain, indeed, arrived at the first stage of the scientific denial of the religious hope of mankind; he did not reach that last stage where Science whimsically declares that she denies nothing. He was at times furiously intolerant of others' belief in a divine Fatherhood and a life after death; he believed that he saw and heard all nature and human nature denying it; but when once he had wreaked himself in his bigotry of unbelief, he was ready to listen to such poor reasons as believers could give for the faith that was in them. In his primary mood he might have relaxed them to the secular arm for a death by fire, but in his secondary mood he would have spared them quite unconditionally, and grieved ever after for any harm he meant them. We think the chapters of Mr. Paine's book dealing with this phase are of very marked interest, both as records and as interpretations. He has known how to take it seriously, but not too seriously, to respect it as the cast of a man who thought deeply and felt intensely concerning the contradictions of the mortal scene, yet through his individual conditioning might any moment burst into self-mockery. This witness of his daily thinking, while reverently dissenting from the conclusions which he could not escape, is able the more closely to portray that strange being in whose most tempestuous excess there was the potentiality of the tenderest, the humblest, the sweetest patience.

Every part of his eventful life, every phase of his unique character is fascinating, and as a contribution to the human document which the book embodies is of high importance; but the most important chapters of the book, the most affecting, the most significant, are those which relate to Clemens's life from the death of his eldest daughter and the break of his wonderful prosperity to that ultimate moment in his earthly home when he ceased from the earth with a dignity apparently always at his command. It was as if he had chosen his way of dying, and it is justly to the praise of his historian that he shows an unfailing sense of the greatness which was not unfailing. It was part of Mark Twain's noble humanity that it was perfect only at moments. It was a thing of climaxes, as his literature was, with the faults and crudities marking it almost to the last, but often with a final effect, an ultimate complexion which could not be overpraised in the word sublime. He was essentially an actor—that is, a child—that is, a poet—with no taint of mere histrionism, but always suffering the emotions he expressed. He suffered them rather than expressed them in his later years, when his literature grew less and less and his life more and more. This formed the supreme opportunity of his biographer, and it was not wasted upon him. His record of the long close, with its fitful arrests and its fierce bursts of rebellion against tragic fate is portrayed with constant restraint as well as courageous veracity to an effect of beauty which the critical reader must recognize at the cost of any and every reservation. The death of his eldest daughter left this aging child pitifully bewildered; the loss of his wife and the close of one of the loveliest love-stories that was ever lived realized for him the solitude which such a stroke makes the world for the survivor; and then the sudden passing of his youngest daughter, whom he alone knew in the singular force of her mind, were the events which left him only the hope of dying.

Yet these closing years were irradiated by a splendor of mature success almost unmatched in the history of literature. It seemed as if the world were newly roused to a sense of his pre-eminence. Wealth flowed in upon him, and adversity was a dream of evil days utterly past; honors crowded upon him; his country and his city thronged him; the path which his old feet trod with yet something of their young vigor was strewn with roses; the last desire of his fame-loving soul was satisfied when the greatest university in the world did his claim to her supreme recognition justice. It was for his biographer to show the gloom of these later years broken and illumined by these glories, and, when their light could not pierce it, to show him, a gray shadow amid the shadows, but walking their dark undauntedly, and sending from it his laugh oftener than his moan. It is his biographer's praise that he has done this so as to make us feel the qualities of the fact; as in the earlier records he makes us feel the enchantment, the joy, the rapture of the man's experience. If we have not yet answered our primary question, how long Mark Twain will last as a humorist, we must content ourselves with the belief that while the stories of men's lives delight, this book will keep him from being forgotten as a man.

—William Dean Howells, review of
Paine's *Life of Mark Twain*, *Harper's Monthly*,
January 1913

H.L. MENCKEN "THE BURDEN OF HUMOR" (1913)

In a review of Paine's biography, of which he approves, Mencken asks: "What is the origin of the prejudice against humor?" He provides his own answer: because "the average man is far too stupid to make a joke." This thesis is well applied to the public and critical attitude toward Twain, who was "the noblest literary artist, who ever set pen to paper on American soil." Twain was unmatched for debunking flimflam and pretension, for uttering the penetrating truths, but he was neglected because he also wrote humorously.

Inevitably, Mencken locates the worst source of this prejudice in William Dean Howells. With his campaign to minimize the comic aspect of Twain, Howells evidenced "a subtle fear of allowing [Twain] too much merit, of an ineradicable disinclination to take him quite seriously." Mencken challenges both Howells and William Lyon Phelps for their characterization of Twain as a "child" (see previous section).

Noting the fluctuating fortunes of Twain at the hands of the critics, Mencken sets himself up as the prophet of a "stage of unqualified enthusiasm" soon to come. He then provides his "statement of faith": *Huckleberry Finn* is a classic, exceeding Dickens's *Nicholas Nickleby*, Laurence Sterne's *Tristram Shandy* or Henry Fielding's *Tom Jones*; it will outlast any other American book of the period 1800–1860 (with "perhaps three exceptions"); Twain had the clearest perception of life of any American, "not excepting Emerson"; that he wrote "better English" than Washington Irving or Nathaniel Hawthorne; and that in four books (*Huckleberry Finn*, *Life on the Mississippi*, *Captain Stormfield's Visit to Heaven*—an unusual choice—and *A Connecticut Yankee*) Twain exceeds the worth of all the works of Cooper, Irving, Holmes, and Whittier, among others, combined. Mencken dignifies Twain over Whitman and not below Poe. "I believe that he was the true father of our national literature, the first genuinely American artist of the blood royal," he writes. "Such is my feeling at the moment, and such has been my feeling for many a moon."

This statement is important for its seriousness and its lack of Howellsian equivocations. Mencken's "statement of faith" precedes Ernest Hemingway's better-known statement in *The Green Hills of Africa* that followed twenty-two years later that "all modern American literature comes from one book by Mark Twain called *Huckleberry Finn.* . . . It's the best book we've had. All American writing comes from that." Mencken's statement says the same and more (and Hemingway, of course, read Mencken).

What is the origin of the prejudice against humor? Why is it so dangerous, if you would keep the public confidence, to make the public laugh?

Is it because humor and sound sense are essentially antagonistic? Has humanity found by experience that the man who sees the fun of life is unfitted to deal sanely with its problems? I think not. No man had more of the comic spirit in him than William Shakespeare, and yet his serious reflections, by the sheer force of their sublime obviousness, have pushed their way into the race's arsenal of immortal platitudes. So, too, with Æsop, and with Lincoln and Johnson, to come down the scale. All of these men were humorists, and yet all of them performed prodigies of indubitable wisdom. And contrariwise, many an undeniable pundit has had his guffaw. Huxley, if he had not been the greatest intellectual duellist of his age, might have been its greatest wit. And Beethoven, after soaring to the heights of tragedy in the first movement of the Fifth Symphony, turned to the divine fooling, the irresistible bull-fiddling of the *scherzo.*

No, there is not the slightest disharmony between sense and nonsense, humor and respectability, despite the almost universal tendency to assume that there is. But, why, then, that widespread error? What actual fact of life lies behind it, giving it a specious appearance of reasonableness? None other, I am convinced, than the fact that the average man is far too stupid to make a joke.

He may *see* a joke and love a *joke*, particularly when it floors and flabbergasts some person he dislikes, but the only way he can himself take part in the priming and pointing of a new one is by acting as its target. In brief, his personal contact with humor tends to fill him with an accumulated sense of disadvantage, of pricked complacency, of sudden and crushing defeat; and so, by an easy psychological process, he is led into the idea that the thing itself is incompatible with true dignity of character and intellect. Hence his deep suspicion of jokers, however their thrusts. 'What a damphool!'—this same half-pitying tribute he pays to wit and butt alike. He cannot separate the virtuoso of comedy from his general concept of comedy itself, and that concept is inextricably mixed with memories of foul ambuscades and mortifying hurts. And so it is not often that he is willing to admit any wisdom in a humorist, or to condone frivolity in a sage.

In all this, I believe, there is a plausible explanation of the popular, and even of the critical attitude toward the late Samuel Langhorne Clemens (Mark Twain). Unless I am so wholly mistaken that my only expiation lies in suicide, Mark was the noblest literary artist, who ever set pen to paper on American soil, and not only the noblest artist, but also one of the most profound and sagacious philosophers. From the beginning of his maturity down to his old age he dealt constantly and earnestly with the deepest problems of life and living, and to his consideration of them he brought a truly amazing instinct for the truth, an almost uncanny talent for ridding the essential thing of its deceptive husks of tradition, prejudice, flubdub and balderdash. No man, not even Nietzsche, ever did greater execution against those puerilities of fancy which so many men mistake for religion, and over which they are so eager to dispute and break heads. No man had a keener eye for that element of pretense which is bound to intrude itself into all human thinking, however serious, however painstaking, however honest in intent. And yet, because the man had humor as well as acumen, because he laughed at human weakness instead of weeping over it, because he turned now and then from the riddle of life to the joy of life—because of this habit of mind it is the custom to regard him lightly and somewhat apologetically, as one debarred from greatness by unfortunate infirmities.

William Dean Howells probably knew him better than any other human being, but in all that Howells has written about him one is conscious of a conditioned admiration, of a subtle fear of allowing him too much merit, of an ineradicable disinclination to take him quite seriously. The Mark that Howells draws is not so much a great artist as a glorious *enfant terrible*. And even William Lyon Phelps, a hospitable and penetrating critic, wholly loose of orthodox shackles—even Phelps hems and haws a bit before putting Mark above Oliver Wendell Holmes, and is still convinced that *The Scarlet Letter* is an incomparably finer work of art than *Huckleberry Finn*.

Well, such notions will die hard, but soon or late, I am sure, they will inevitably die. So certain am I, indeed, of their dying that I now formally announce their death in advance, and prepare to wait in patience for the delayed applause. In one of his essays Dr. Phelps shows how critical opinion of Mark has gradually evolved from scorn into indifference, and from indifference into toleration, and from toleration into apologetic praise, and from apologetic praise into hearty praise. The stage of unqualified enthusiasm is coming—it has already cast its lights before England—and I am very glad to join the lodge as a charter member. Let me now set down my faith, for the literary archaeologists of day after tomorrow:

I believe that *Huckleberry Finn* is one of the great masterpieces of the world, that it is the full equal of *Don Quixote* and *Robinson Crusoe*, that it is vastly better than *Gil Blas*, *Tristram Shandy*, *Nicholas Nickleby* or *Tom Jones*. I believe that it will be read by human beings of all ages, not as a solemn duty but for the honest love of it, and over and over again, long after every book written in America between the years 1800 and 1860, with perhaps three exceptions, has disappeared entirely save as a classroom fossil. I believe that Mark Twain had a clearer vision of life, that he came nearer to its elementals and was less deceived by its false appearances, than any other American who has ever presumed to manufacture generalizations, not excepting Emerson. I believe that, admitting all his defects, he wrote better English, in the sense of cleaner, straighter, vivider, saner English, than either Irving or Hawthorne. I believe that four of his books—*Huck*, *Life on the Mississippi*, *Captain Stormfield's Visit to Heaven*, and *A Connecticut Yankee*—are alone worth more, as works of art and as criticisms of life, than the whole output of Cooper, Irving, Holmes, Mitchell, Stedman, Whittier and Bryant. I believe that he ranks well above Whitman and certainly not below Poe. I believe that he was the true father of our national literature, the first genuinely American artist of the blood royal.

Such is my feeling at the moment, and such has been my feeling for many a moon. If any gentleman in the audience shares it, either wholly or with qualifications, then I advise him to buy and read the biography of Mark lately published by Albert Bigelow Paine (*Harper*), for therein he will find an elaborate, painstaking and immensely interesting portrait of the man, and sundry shrewd observations upon the writer.

Not that I agree with Paine in all his judgments. Far from it, indeed. It seems to me that he gets bogged hopelessly when he tries to prove that *The Innocents Abroad* is a better book than *A Tramp Abroad*, that he commits a crime when he puts *Joan of Arc* above *Huck Finn*, and that he is too willing to join Howells and other such literary sacristans in frowning down upon Mark's clowning, his weakness for vulgarity, his irrepressible maleness. In brief, Paine is disposed, at times, to yield to current critical opinion against what must be his own good sense. But when you have allowed for all this— and it is not obtrusive—the thing that remains is a vivid and sympathetic biography, a book with sound merit in every chapter of it, a mountain of difficulties triumphantly surmounted, a fluent and excellent piece of writing.

Paine tells everything that is worth hearing, whether favorable to Mark or the reverse, and leaves out all that is not worth hearing. One closes the third volume with unbounded admiration for the industry of the biographer, and with no less admiration for his frankness and sagacity. He has given us a rich and colorful book, presenting coherently a wise selection from a perfect chaos of materials. The Mark Twain that emerges from it is almost as real as Huckleberry Finn.

And what a man that Mark Twain was! How he stood above and apart from the world, like Rabelais come to life again, observing the human comedy, chuckling over the eternal fraudulence of man! What a sharp eye he had for the bogus, in religion, politics, art, literature, patriotism, virtue! What contempt he emptied upon shams of all sorts—and what pity! Mr. Paine reveals for us very clearly, by quotation and exposition, his habitual attitude of mind. He regarded all men as humbugs, but as humbugs to be dealt with gently, as humbugs too often taken in and swindled by their own humbuggery. He saw how false reasoning, false assumptions, false gods had entered into the very warp and woof of their thinking; how impossible it was for them to attack honestly the problems of being; how helpless they were in the face of life's emergencies. And seeing all this, he laughed at them, but not often with malice. What genuine indignation he was capable of was leveled at life itself and not at its victims. Through all his later years the riddle of existence was ever before him. He thought about it constantly; he discussed it with everyone he knew; he made copious notes of his speculations. But he never came to any soothing custom made conclusion. The more he examined life, the more it appeared to him to be without meaning, and even without direction; the more he pondered upon the idea of God, the more a definite idea of God eluded him. In the end, as Mr. Paine tells us, he verged toward a hopeless pessimism. Death seemed to him a glad release, an inestimable boon. When his daughter Jean died, suddenly, tragically, he wrote to her sister: 'I am so glad she is out of it and safe—safe!'

It is this reflective, philosophizing Clemens who stands out most clearly in Mr. Paine's book. In his own works, our glimpses of him are all too brief. His wife and his friends opposed his speculations, perhaps wisely, for the artist might have been swallowed up in the sage. But he wrote much to please himself and left a vast mass of unpublished manuscript behind him. Certainly it is to be hoped that these writings will see the light, and before long. One book described by Mr. Paine, *Three Thousand Years Among the Microbes*, would appear to be a satire so mordant and so large in scale that his admirers have a plain right to demand its publication. And there should be a new edition, too, of his confession of doubt, *What is Man?* of which a few copies were printed for private distribution in 1905. Yet again we have a right to ask for most if not all of his unpublished stories and sketches, many of which were suppressed at the behest of Mrs. Clemens, for reasons no longer worth considering. There is good ground for believing that his reputation will gain rather than suffer by the publication of these things, and in any case it can withstand the experiment, for *Huck Finn* and *Life on the Mississippi* and the *Connecticut Yankee* will remain, and so long as they remain there can be no question of the man's literary stature. He was one of the great artists of all time. He was the full equal of Cervantes and Molière, Swift and Defoe. He was and is the one authentic giant of our national literature.

—H.L. Mencken, "The Burden of Humor,"
Smart Set 38, February 1913, pp. 151–154

SIGMUND FREUD (1914)

The Viennese neurologist and father of psychoanalysis here tells the history of the psychoanalytic movement and the various divergent branches that formed as erstwhile colleagues (Adler and Jung) "seceded" from Freud's authority. Freud crowns this recollection with a quotation from Mark Twain's story "My Watch—An Instructive Little Tale" (1870). Students applying Freudian analysis to Mark Twain's work will be especially curious to see how Freud used Twain, in turn, to explain his work. In the same study, Freud remarks

> In the course of these years I have read, perhaps a dozen times . . . that psychoanalysis was now dead, that it was finally overcome and settled. The answer to all this would have to read like the telegram from Mark Twain to the newspaper that falsely announced his death: "The report of my death is grossly exaggerated." After each of these death-notices, psychoanalysis has gained new followers and co-workers and has created for itself new organs. Surely to be reported dead is an advance over being treated with dead silence!

Just as Adler's researches brought something new to psychoanalysis, a piece of the ego–psychology, and paid only too dearly for this gift by repudiating all the fundamental analytic principles, in the same way Jung and his adherents have based their fight against psychoanalysis upon a new contribution to the same. They have traced in detail ... how the material of the sexual ideas originating in the family complex and in the incestuous object selection can be used to represent the highest ethical and religious interests of mankind, that is, they have explained a remarkable case of sublimation of the erotic impelling forces and the transformation of the same into strivings that can no longer be called erotic. . . . But the world would have exclaimed that ethics and religion had been sexualized. I cannot help assuming "finally" that the investigators found themselves quite unequal to the storm they had to face. Perhaps the storm began to rage in their own bosoms. The previous theological history of so many of the Swiss workers [i.e., psychoanalyst followers of the Swiss Carl Jung] is as important in their attitude to psychoanalysis as is the socialistic record of Adler for the development of his "psychology." One is reminded of Mark Twain's famous story about the fate of his watch and to the speculative remark with which he closed it: "And he used to wonder what became of all those unsuccessful tinkers, and gunsmiths, and shoemakers, and blacksmiths; but nobody could ever tell him."

—Sigmund Freud, from *On the History of the Psychoanalytic Movement*, translated by A.A. Brill, New York: The Nervous and Mental Disease Publishing Company, 1917, pp. 52–53

FRED LEWIS PATTEE (1915)

Next to Stuart P. Sherman, Fred Lewis Pattee was H.L. Mencken's preferred whipping boy and representative of collegiate obliviousness. This was unfair, however—Mencken's tastes were his own, and whimsical as anybody's, but he postulated them as though they were objective fact. Pattee was another pioneer of American literary studies when the subject was not universally seen as entirely fit for study. Pattee also—like Van Wyck Brooks and Bernard DeVoto—had an encyclopedic knowledge of American literature, both high and low, which he puts to good use here. While this chapter comes from a survey of American literature, and

Pattee necessarily repeats a familiar chronology, he makes original connections and independent emphases.

For example, he describes the four year "college course" as a riverboat pilot "cub," a period in Twain's career often passed over blithely. In this apprenticeship Samuel Clemens acquired his lifelong sensitivity to sham and pretension, Pattee argues; on those decks he acquired his ear for the vernacular of the American West. Students investigating the influence of Twain's piloting years on his later writing career will find Pattee's analysis helpful.

Pattee re-establishes Clemens in the milieus that forged his literary persona, those certain sites of cultural transmission where significant parts of the apprenticeship were served. Pattee pays close attention to places and their denizens, such as the crowd at Virginia City, Nevada, or the Bohemians in San Francisco. Mark Twain did not emerge fully developed from a void, although his supporters and sometimes Twain himself may have tried to revise history so that it seemed he did. Furthermore, he had mentors before William Dean Howells, like Bret Harte, however much he may have later come to hate him. Pattee reclaims these earlier sites and figures. Students interested in questions of early influence on Mark Twain will be greatly rewarded by Professor Pattee's account.

When Pattee assays *The Innocents Abroad*, he again locates the oddity of the project, how incongruous it was as a piece of travel writing, emerging from the "unique" California of the 1860s. Twain's predecessors in this department were authors such as the pretentious poet Bayard Taylor, who wrote empty prose poems to the sublime, travel guides by the handful with humorless and sentimental descriptions of the "holy shrines" of the Old World. This was the sort of work, now happily forgotten but in its time bestselling, that Twain purposely burlesqued. Such skewering did not differentiate between high subjects and low: "The new American democracy was speaking. To the man who . . . had learned in the school of Horace Bixby there was no high and no low save as measured, not by appearances or by tradition, but by intrinsic worth."

As Pattee returns Twain to his earliest scenes of creativity and inspiration, he recalls unlikely key figures (like Bixby) and lesser-known but (Pattee argues) key sentences, including that which prefaces *The Innocents Abroad*: "I am sure I have written at least honestly, whether wisely or not."

⚊⚊⚊   ⚊⚊⚊   ⚊⚊⚊

With Mark Twain, American literature became for the first time really national. He was the first man of letters of any distinction to be born west of the Mississippi. He spent his boyhood and young manhood near the heart of the continent, along the great river during the vital era when it was the boundary line between known and unknown America, and when it resounded from end to end with the shouts and the confusion of the first great migration from the East; he lived for six thrilling years in the camps and the boom towns and the excited cities of Nevada and California; and then, at thirty-one, a raw product of the raw West, he turned his face to the Atlantic Coast, married a rare soul from one of the refined families of New York State, and settled down to a literary career in New England, with books and culture and trips abroad, until in his old age Oxford University could confer upon him—"Tom Sawyer," whose schooling in the ragged river town had ended before he was twelve—the degree that had come to America only as borne by two or three of the Brahmins of New England. Only America, and America at a certain period, could produce a paradox like that.

Mark Twain interpreted the West from the standpoint of a native. The group of humorists who had first brought to the East the Western spirit and the new laughter had all of them been reared in the older sections. John Phoenix and Artemus Ward and Josh Billings were born in New England, and Nasby and many of the others were natives of New York State. All of them in late boyhood had gone West as to a wonderland and had breathed the new atmosphere as something strange and exhilarating, but Mark Twain was native born. He was himself a part of the West; he removed from it so as to see it in true perspective, and so became its best interpreter. Hawthorne had once expressed a wish to see some part of America "where the damned shadow of Europe has never fallen." Mark Twain spent his life until he was thirty in such unshadowed places. When he wrote he wrote without a thought of other writings; it was as if the West itself was dictating its autobiography. . . .

The first crisis in the boy's life came in his twelfth year, when the death of his father sent him as an apprentice to a country newspaper office, that most practical and most exacting of all training schools for youth. Two years on the Missouri *Courier*, four years on the Hannibal *Journal*, then the restlessness of his clan sent him wandering into the East even as it had sent Artemus Ward and Nasby into the West. For fifteen months he served as compositor in New York City and Philadelphia, then a great homesickness for the river came upon him. From boyhood it had been his dream to be the pilot of a Mississippi steamboat; all other professions seemed flat and lifeless compared with that satisfying and boundless field of action; and it is not strange that in

April, 1857, we find him installed as Horace Bixby's "cub" at the beginning of a new career.

During the next four years he gave himself heart and soul to the almost superhuman task of committing to memory every sandbar and point and landmark in twelve hundred miles of a shifting, treacherous river. The difficulties he has explained fully in his book. It was a college course of four years, and no man ever had a better one. To quote his own words:

> In that brief, sharp schooling I got personally and familiarly acquainted with all the different types of human nature that are to be found in fiction, biography, or history. When I find a well-drawn character in fiction or biography, I generally take a warm personal interest in him, for the reason that I have known him before—met him on the river.

It taught him far more than this. The pilot of a great Mississippi boat was a man with peculiar responsibilities. The lives of the passengers and the safety of the cargo were absolutely in his hands. His authority was above even the captain's. Only picked men of courage and judgment with a self-reliance that never wavered in any crisis were fit material for pilots. To quote Horace Bixby, the most noted of them all:

> There were no signal lights along the shore in those days, and no searchlights on the vessels; everything was blind, and on a dark, misty night in a river full of snags and shifting sand-bars and changing shores, a pilot's judgment had to be founded on *absolute certainty*.

Under such conditions men were valued only for what they actually could do. There was no entrance into the inner circle of masters of the river save through genuineness and real efficiency. Sentimentalizing and boasting and sham died instantly in that stern atmosphere. To live for four years in daily contact with such men taught one coarseness of speech and an appalling fluency in the use of profanity, but it taught one at the same time to look with supreme contempt upon inefficiency and pretense.

The "cub" became at length a pilot, to be entrusted after a time with some of the finest boats on the river. He became very efficient in his hard-learned profession so conspicuously so that he won the commendation even of Bixby, who could say in later years, "Sam Clemens never had an accident either as a steersman or as a pilot, except once when he got aground for a few hours in the *bagasse* (cane) smoke, with no damage to any one." But the war put a sudden end to the piloting. The river was closed, and in April, 1861, he went reluctantly back to Hannibal. "I loved the profession far better than any I have ever followed since," he declared in his later years, "and I took a measureless pride in it." It is very possible that but for the war and the change which it wrought upon the river, Mark Twain might have passed his whole life as a Mississippi pilot.

II

After a few weeks in a self-recruited troop that fell to pieces before it could join the Confederate army, the late pilot, now twenty-six years old, started by stage coach across the Plains with his brother Orion, who had just been appointed secretary to the new Governor of Nevada. It was Mark Twain's entry upon what, in college terms, may be called his graduate course. It was six years long and it covered one of the most picturesque eras in the history of Western America. For a few restive months he remained at Carson City as his brother's assistant, then in characteristic fashion he broke away to join the excited tide of gold seekers that was surging through all the mountains of Nevada. During the next year he lived in mining camps with prospectors and eager claim-holders. Luck, however, seemed against him; at least it promised him little as a miner, and when the Virginia City *Enterprise*, to which he had contributed letters, offered him a position on its staff of reporters, he jumped at the opportunity.

Now for two years he lived at the very heart of the mining regions of the West, in Virginia City, the home of the Comstock lode, then at its highest boom. Everything about him—the newness and rawness of things, the peculiar social conditions, the atmosphere of recklessness and excitement, the money that flowed everywhere in fabulous quantities—everything was unique. Even the situation of the city was remarkable. Hingston, who visited it with Artemus Ward while Mark Twain was still a member of the *Enterprise* staff, speaks of it as "perched up on the side of Mt. Davidson some five or six thousand feet above sea level, with a magnificent view before us of the desert.... Nothing but arid rocks and sandy plains sprinkled with sage brush. No village for full two hundred miles, and any number of the worst type of Indians—the Goshoots—agreeably besprinkling the path." Artemus Ward estimated its population at twelve thousand. He was impressed by its wildness, "its splendid streets paved with silver ore," "its unadulterated cussedness," its vigilance committee "which hangs the more vicious of the pestiferous crowd," and its fabulous output of silver which is "melted down into bricks the size of common house bricks, then loaded into huge wagons, each drawn by eight and twelve mules, and sent off to San Francisco."

It was indeed a strange area of life that passed before the young Mississippi pilot. For two winters he was sent down to report the new legislature of the just-organized territory, and it was while engaged in this picturesque gala task that he sent back his letters signed for the first time Mark Twain. That was the winter of 1863. It was time now for him to seek a wider field. Accordingly, the following May he went down to San Francisco, where at length he found employment on the *Morning Call*.

Now for the first time the young reporter found himself in a literary atmosphere. Poets and sketch-writers and humorists were everywhere. There was at least one flourishing literary journal, the *Golden Era*, and its luxuriously appointed office was the literary center of the Pacific Coast. "Joaquin Miller recalls from an old diary, kept by him then, having seen Adah Isaacs Menken, Prentice Mulford, Bret Harte, Charles Warren Stoddard, Fitzhugh Ludlow, Mark Twain, Orpheus C. Kerr, Artemus Ward, Gilbert Densmore, W.S. Kendall, and Mrs. Hitchcock assembled there at one time." Charles Henry Webb was just starting a literary weekly, the *Californian*, and when, a year later, Bret Harte was made its editor, Mark Twain was added to the contributing staff. It was the real beginning of his literary career. He received now helpful criticism. In a letter written in after years to Thomas Bailey Aldrich he says:

> Bret Harte trimmed and trained and schooled me patiently until he changed me from an awkward utterer of coarse grotesqueness to a writer of paragraphs and chapters that have found a certain favor in the eyes of even some of the very decentest people in the land.

To the *Californian* and the *Era* he now contributed that series of sketches which later was drawn upon for material for his first published book. But the old restlessness was upon him again. He struck out into the Tuolumne Hills with Jim Gillis as a pocket miner and for months lived as he could in shacks and camps, panning between drenching showers worthless gravel, expecting every moment to find gold. He found no gold, but he found what was infinitely richer. In later years in a letter to Gillis he wrote:

> It makes my heart ache yet to call to mind some of those days. Still it shouldn't, for right in the depths of their poverty and their pocket-hunting vagabondage lay the germ of my coming good fortune. You remember the one gleam of jollity that shot across our dismal

sojourn in the rain and mud of Angel's Camp—I mean that day we sat around the tavern and heard that chap tell about the frog and how they filled him with shot. And you remember how we quoted from the yarn and laughed over it out there on the hillside while you and dear old Stoker panned and washed. I jotted the story down in my note-book that day, and would have been glad to get ten or fifteen dollars for it—I was just that blind. But then we were so hard up. I published that story, and it became widely known in America, India, China, England, and the reputation it made for me has paid me thousands and thousands of dollars since.

The publication in New York, May 1, 1867, of *The Celebrated Jumping Frog of Calaveras County and Other Sketches* and the delivery a week later by the author of *The Jumping Frog* of a lecture on the Sandwich Islands marks the end of the period of preparation in Mark Twain's life. A new American author had arrived.

III

Send this Mississippi pilot, printer, adventurer, miner in rough camps of the Sierras, to Paris, Italy, Constantinople, and the Holy Land, and what will be his impressions? For an answer we must read *The Innocents Abroad*. It will be no *Outre Mer*, we are certain of that, and no *Pencillings by the Way*. Before a line of it was written an atmosphere had been created unique in American literature, for where, save in the California of 1867, was there ever optimism, nay, romanticism, that could reply instantly to the young reporter who asked to be sent on a Don Quixote pilgrimage to Europe and the Orient, "Go. Twelve hundred and fifty dollars will be paid for you before the vessel sails, and your only instructions are that you will continue to write at such times and from such places as you deem proper, and in the same style that heretofore secured you the favor of the readers of the *Alta California*"?

It was not to be a tour of Europe, as Longfellow and Willis and Taylor had made it, the pilgrimage of a devotee to holy shrines; it was to be a great picnic with sixty-seven in the picnic party. Moreover, the recorder of it was bound by his instructions to report it in the style that had won him California fame. It was to be a Western book, written by a Westerner from the Western standpoint, but this does not imply that his Western readers expected an illiterate production full of coarseness and rude wit. California had produced a school of poets and romancers; she had serious literary journals, and she was proud of them. The letters, if California was to set her stamp of approval upon them, must have literary charm; they must have, moreover, freshness and originality; and they must sparkle with that spirit of humor which already had begun to be recognized as a native product.

We open the book and linger a moment over the preface:

> Notwithstanding it is only the record of a picnic, it has a purpose, which is, to suggest to the reader how *he* would be likely to see Europe and the East if he looked at them with his own eyes instead of the eyes of those who traveled in those countries before him. I make small pretence of showing any one how he *ought* to look at objects of interest beyond the sea—other books do that, and therefore, even if I were competent to do it, there is no need.
>
> I offer no apologies for any departures from the usual style of travel-writing that may be charged against me—for I think I have seen with impartial eyes, and I am sure I have written at least honestly, whether wisely or not.

Let us read the book straight through. We are impressed with the fact that, despite the supposition of its first readers, it is not primarily a humorous work. It is a genuine book of travels. It is first of all an honest record, even as its author averred. In the second place it is the book of a young man, a young man on a lark and full of the highest spirits. The world is good—it is a good show, though it is full of absurdities and of humbugs that should be exposed. The old stock jokes of the grand tour—the lack of soap, the charge for candles, the meeting of supposed foreigners who break unexpectedly into the best of English, and all the well-known others—were new to the public then and they came with freshness. Then it is the book of one who saw, even as he claimed, with his own eyes. This genuine American, with his training on the river and the wild frontier where men and things are what they *are*, no more and no less, will be impressed only with genuineness. He will describe things precisely as he sees them. Gibraltar "is pushed out into the sea on the end of a flat, narrow strip of land, and is suggestive of a 'gob' of mud on the end of a shingle"; of the Coliseum: "everybody recognizes at once that 'looped and windowed' bandbox with a side bitten out"; and of a famous river: "It is popular to admire the Arno. It is a great historical creek with four feet in the channel and some scows floating around. It would be a very passable river if they would pump some water into it." That was not written for a joke: it was the way the Arno honestly impressed the former Mississippi pilot.

He is not always critical. Genuineness and real worth never fail to impress him. Often he stands before a landscape, a city, a cathedral, as enthusiastic as any of the older school of travelers. The book is full of vivid descriptions, some of them almost poetic in their spirit and diction. But things must be what they pretend to be, or they will disgust him. Everywhere there is scorn for the mere echoer of the enthusiasm of others. He will not gush over an unworthy thing even if he knows the whole world has gushed over it. Da Vinci's "Last Supper," painted on a dilapidated wall and stained and scarred and dimmed, may once have been beautiful, he admits, but it is not so now. The pilgrims who stand before it "able to speak only in catchy ejaculations of rapture" fill him with wrath. "How can they see what is not visible?" The work of the old masters fills him always with indignation. They painted not Hebrews in their scriptural pieces, but Italians. "Their nauseous adulation of princely patrons was more prominent to me and claimed my attention more than the charms of color." "Raphael pictured such infernal villains as Catherine and Marie de Medicis seated in heaven conversing familiarly with the Virgin Mary and the angels (to say nothing of higher personages), and yet my friends abuse me because I am a little prejudiced against the old masters."

Here we have a note that was to become more and more emphatic in Mark Twain's work with every year he lived: his indignation at oppression and insincerity. The cathedrals of Italy lost their beauty for him when he saw the misery of the population. He stood before the Grand Duomo of Florence. "Like all other men I fell down and worshiped it, but when the filthy beggars swarmed around me the contrast was too striking, too suggestive, and I said 'O sons of classic Italy, *is* the spirit of enterprise, of self-reliance, of noble endeavor, utterly dead within yet? Curse your indolent worthlessness, why don't you rob your church?' Three hundred happy, comfortable priests are employed in that cathedral."

Everywhere he strikes out at sentimentality. When he learns how Abelard deliberately sacrificed Héloïse to his own selfish ideals, he bursts out: "The tons of sentiment I have wasted on that unprincipled humbug in my ignorance! I shall throttle down my emotions hereafter, about this sort of people, until I have read them up and know whether they are entitled to any tearful attentions or not." He is eager to see a French "grissette," but having seen one, bursts out in true Artemus Ward fashion: "Aroint thee, wench! I sorrow for the vagabond student of the Latin Quarter now, even more than formerly I envied him. Thus topples to the earth another idol of my infancy." The story of Petrarch's love for Laura only fills him with pity for the outrageously treated "Mr. Laura," the unknown husband of the heroine, who bore the burden but got none of the glory, and when they tell the thrilling legend of the old medieval castle, he makes only the comment, "Splendid legend—splendid lie—drive on!"

It was a blow at the whole school of American travel writers; it marked the passing of an era. Bret Harte in the first volume of the *Overland Monthly* (1868), was the first to outline the Western standpoint:

> The days of sentimental journeyings are over. The dear old book of travel . . . is a thing of the past. Sentimental musings on foreign scenes are just now restricted to the private diaries of young and impressible ladies and clergymen with affections of the bronchial tubes. . . . A race of good humored, engaging iconoclasts seem to have precipitated themselves upon the old altars of mankind, and like their predecessors of the eighth century, have paid particular attention to the holy church. Mr. Howells has slashed one or two sacred pictorial canvasses with his polished rapier; Mr. Swift has made one or two neat long shots with a rifled Parrott, and Mr. Mark Twain has used brickbats on stained glass windows with damaging effect. And those gentlemen have certainly brought down a heap of rubbish.

It was the voice of the new West and of the new era. With *The Innocents Abroad* begins the new period in American literature. The book is full of the new after-the-war Americanism that did its own thinking, that saw with its own eyes, that put a halo upon nothing save genuineness and substantial worth. It must not be forgotten that America even in the new seventies was still mawkish with sentimentality. The very year *The Innocents Abroad* appeared, *Gates Ajar* sold twenty editions. Mark Twain came into the age like the Goths into Rome. Stand on the solid earth, he cried. Look with your own eyes. Worship nothing but truth and genuineness. Europe is no better than America. Como is beautiful, but it is not so beautiful as Tahoe. Why this eternal glorification of things simply and solely because it is the conventional thing to glorify them? "The critic," he wrote in later years to Andrew Lang, "has actually imposed upon the world the superstition that a painting by Raphael is more valuable to the civilizations of the earth than is a chromo; and the august opera more than the hurdy-gurdy and the villagers' singing society; and the Latin classics than Kipling's far-reaching bugle note; and Jonathan Edwards than the Salvation Army." The new American democracy was speaking. To the man who for four years had learned in the school of Horace Bixby there was no high and no low save as measured, not by appearances or by tradition, but by intrinsic worth.

IV

It has been customary in libraries to place the earlier works of Mark Twain on the same shelf as those of Artemus Ward and Josh Billings. To the thousands who laughed at him as he lectured from year to year he was a mere maker of fun. The public that bought such enormous editions of *The Innocents Abroad* and *Roughing It* bought them as books to laugh over. What shall we say to-day of Mark Twain's humor? A generation has arisen to whom he is but a tradition and a set of books; what is the verdict of this generation?

First of all, it is necessary that we examine the man himself. Nature seems to have forced him into the ranks of the comedians. From his mother he inherited a drawl that was inexpressibly funny; he had a laughable personality, and a laughable angle from which he looked at life. He could no more help provoking mirth than he could help being himself. Moreover, he had been thrown during his formative years into a veritable training school for humorists. On the river and in the mines and the raw towns and cities of the West, he had lived in a gale of high spirits, of loud laughter, of practical jokes, and droll stories that had gone the rough round of the boats or the camps. His humor, therefore, was an echo of the laughter of elemental men who have been flung into conditions full of incongruities and strange contrasts. It is the humor of exaggeration run wild, of youthful high spirits, of rough practical jokes, of understatement, of irreverence, and gross absurdity.

But the personality of Mark Twain no longer can give life to his humor; the atmosphere in which it first appeared has gone forever; the man himself is becoming a mere legend, shadowy and more and more distorted; his humor must be judged now like that of Cervantes and Shakespeare, apart from author and times. How does it stand the test? Not at all well. There are the high spirits of the new West in it—that element has not evaporated—and there is in it a personal touch, a drollery that was his individual contribution to humor. There was a certain drawl in his pen as well as in his tongue. It is this alone that saves much of his humorous work from flatness. Concerning *The Jumping Frog*, for instance, Haweis asks in true British way, "What, I should like to know, is the fun of saying that a frog who has been caused to swallow a quantity of shot cannot jump so high as he could before?" The answer is that there is no fun save in the way the story is told; in other words, save in the incomparable drawl of Mark Twain's pen. One can only illustrate:

> The feller . . . give it back to Smiley, and says, very deliberate, "Well, I don't see no pints about that frog that's any better'n any other frog."

"May be you don't," Smiley says. "May be you understand frogs, and may be you don't understand 'em; may be you've had experience, and may be you ain't, only a amature, as it were. Any ways I've got my opinion, and I'll risk forty dollars that he can out-jump any frog in Calaveras county."

And the feller studied a minute, and then says, kinder sad like, "Well, I'm only a stranger here, and I ain't got no frog; but if I had a frog, I'd bet you!"

Or take this episode from *The Innocents Abroad* where he tells of his sensations one night as a boy upon awakening and finding the body of a murdered man on the floor of his room:

I went away from there. I do not say that I went away in any sort of a hurry, but I simply went—that is sufficient. I went out at the window, and I carried the sash along with me. I did not need the sash, but it was handier to take it than it was to leave it, and so I took it. I was not scared, but I was considerably agitated.

All this and the hundreds of pages like it in *The Innocents Abroad* and *Roughing It* and the later books is excellent drollery, but had Mark Twain written nothing else than this he would be as dead now as an author as even "Doesticks." His drollery is best in the work that lies nearest to the source of his first inspiration. As the Western days faded from his memory, his comedy became more and more forced, until it could reach at last the inane flatness of *Adam's Diary* and flatter still, *Eve's Diary*.

The humor that lives, however, is not drollery; it must be embodied in a humorous character like Falstaff, for instance, or Don Quixote. The most of Mark Twain's fun comes from exaggerated situations with no attempt at characterization, and therein lies his weakness as a humorist. Huckleberry Finn and Colonel Sellers come the nearest to being humorous creations, but Huckleberry Finn is but a bit of *genre*, the eternal bad boy in a Pike County costume, and Colonel Sellers is but a preliminary study toward a character, a shadowy figure that we feel constantly to be on the point of jumping into greatness without ever actually arriving. Narrowly as he may have missed the mark in these two characters, Mark Twain cannot be classed with the great humorists.

V

There are three Mark Twains: there is Mark Twain, the droll comedian, who wrote for the masses and made them laugh; there is Mark Twain, the indignant protester, who arose ever and anon to true eloquence in his denunciation of tyranny and pretense; and there is Mark Twain, the romancer, who in his boyhood had dreamed by the great river and who later caught the romance of a period in American life. The masterpiece of the first is *The Jumping Frog*, of the second *The Man that Corrupted Hadleyburg*, and of the third *Life on the Mississippi* and *Roughing It*.

It is this third Mark Twain that still lives and that will continue to live in American literature. He saw with distinctness a unique area of American life. As the brief and picturesque era faded away he caught the sunset glory of it and embodied it in romance—the steamboat days on the river in the slavery era, the old régime in the South, the barbarism of the Plains, the great buffalo herds, the wild camps in the gold fields of Nevada and California. In half a dozen books: *Roughing It, Life on the Mississippi, The Gilded Age* (a few chapters of it), *Tom Sawyer, Huckleberry Finn, Pudd'nhead Wilson*, he has done work that can never be done again. The world that these books depict has vanished as completely as the Bagdad of Haroun al Raschid. Not only has he told the story of this vanished world, illustrating it with descriptions and characterizations that are like Flemish portraits, but he has caught and held the spirit of it, and he has thrown over it all the nameless glow of romance. It is as golden a land that he leads us through as any we may find in Scott, and yet it was drawn from the life with painstaking care. Scott and Bulwer and Cooper angered Mark Twain. They were careless of facts, they were sentimental, they misinterpreted the spirit of the times they depicted and the men and women who lived in them, but these six books of Mark Twain may be placed among the source books of American history. Nowhere else can one catch so truly certain phases of the spirit of the mid-nineteenth century West. Over every page of them may be written those words from the preface of *The Innocents Abroad*, "I am sure I have written at least honestly, whether wisely or not."

The books are six chapters of autobiography. *Tom Sawyer* and *Huckleberry Finn* are recollections of that boyhood by the river after so long a time had elapsed that the day-dreams and boyish imaginings were recorded as real happenings; *Life on the Mississippi* records that romantic adventure of his young manhood as he recalled it in later days when the old piloting era had vanished like a dream of boyhood; *The Gilded Age*, a book of glorious fragments, has in it his uncle James Lampton drawn from life and renamed Colonel Sellers; *Roughing It* bubbles over with the joy and the high spirits and the excitement of those marvelous days when the author and the West were young together; and *Pudd'nhead Wilson* gives the tragedy of slavery as it passed before his boyish eyes. These books and *The Innocents Abroad* are Mark Twain's contribution to the library of American classics. The rest of his enormously large output, despite brilliant passages here and there, does not greatly matter.

They are not artistic books. The author had little skill in construction. He excelled in brilliant dashes, not in long-continued effort. He was his own Colonel Sellers, restless, idealistic, Quixotic. What he did he did with his whole soul without restraint or sense of proportion. There is in all he wrote a lack of refinement, kept at a minimum, to be sure, by his wife, who for years was his editor and severest critic, but likely at any moment to crop out. His books, all of them, are monotones, a running series of episodes and descriptions all of the same value, never reaching dramatic climax. The episodes themselves, however, are told with graphic intensity; some of them are gems well-nigh perfect [such as the] picture of the famous pony express of the Plains. . . .

The steamboat race and the explosion in chapter four of *The Gilded Age* have few equals in any language for mere picturing power. He deals largely with the out-of-doors. His canvases are bounded only by the horizon: the Mississippi, the great Plains, the Rocky Mountains, Mono Lake, the Alkali Deserts, and the Sierras—he has handled a continent. Only Joaquin Miller and John Muir have used canvases as vast. Huckleberry Finn's floating journey down the river on his raft has in it something of the spirit of *The Odyssey* and *Pilgrim's Progress* and *Don Quixote*. Had Mark Twain's constructive skill and his ability to trace the growth of a human soul been equal to his picturing power, his Defoe-like command of detail and situation, and his mastery of phrase and of narrative, he might have said the last word in American fiction. He was a product of his section and of his education. College and university would have made of him an artist like Holmes, brilliant, refined, and messageless. It would have robbed him of the very fountain-head of his power. It was his to work not from books but from life itself, to teach truth and genuineness of life, to turn the eyes of America from the romance of Europe to her own romantic past.

VI

If Artemus Ward is Touchstone, Mark Twain is Lear's Fool. He was a knightly soul, sensitive and serious, a nineteenth-century knight errant who would protect the weak of the whole world and right their wrongs. The genuineness and honesty that had been ground into his soul on the river and in the mines where a man was a man only when he could show true manliness, were a part of his knightly equipment. When financial disaster came to him, as it had come to Scott, through no fault of his own, he refused to repudiate the debt as he might have done with no discredit to himself, and, though old age was upon him, he set out to earn by his own efforts the whole enormous amount. And he discharged the debt to the full. He had, moreover, the true knight's soul of romance. The *Morte d'Arthur* and the chronicles of Joan of Arc, his favorite reading, contained the atmosphere that he loved. He fain would have given his generation "pure literature," but they bade him back to his cap and bells. Richardson, as late as 1886, classed him with the purveyors of "rude and clownish merriment" and advised him to "make hay while the sun shines."

So he jested and capered while his heart was heavy with personal sorrows that came thick upon him as the years went by, and with the baseness and weakness and misery of humanity as the spectacle passed under his keen observation. Yet in it all he was true to himself. That sentence in the preface tells the whole story: "I have written at least honestly." His own generation bought his books for the fun in them; their children are finding now that their fathers bought not, as they supposed, clownish ephemerae, but true literature, the classics of the period.

And yet—strange paradox!—it was the cap and bells that made Mark Twain and that hastened the coming of the new period in American literature. The cap and bells it was that made him known in every hamlet and in every household of America, north and south and east and west, and in all lands across all oceans. Only Cooper and Mrs. Stowe of all our American authors are known so widely. This popularity it was that gave wings to the first all-American literature and that inspired a new school of American writers. After Mark Twain American literature was no longer confined to Boston and its environs; it was as wide as the continent itself.

—Fred Lewis Pattee, from *A History of
American Literature Since 1870*, 1915

H.L. Mencken (1917)

In three different essays in his *Book of Prefaces*, Mencken returns to the figure of Twain. In an essay on Theodore Dreiser, he cites William Lyon Phelps on the subject of Twain's neglect by "the favourite national critics of that era," before assailing Phelps for neglecting Theodore Dreiser in the same way. His conclusion: "College professors, alas, never learn anything." Students interested either in the evolution of the critical reception of Twain, or in comparing the careers of Twain and Dreiser, should pay close attention to Mencken here.

Meanwhile, in one of his best-known essays, "Puritanism as a Literary Force," Mencken finds Twain guilty of "Philistinism" and "Puritanism." While several critics have commented vaguely on Twain's "Calvinist" upbringing (see, for instance, Howells, 1918), Mencken explores how Puritanism is expressed in Twain's writing, even (or indeed especially) in a work as early and seemingly jovial as *The Innocents Abroad*. Sounding suspiciously similar to his sworn foe Stuart P. Sherman, Mencken grouses sourly at "such coarse and ignorant clowning," faulting Twain's refusal to appreciate the beauty of the old masters and the Catholic Church.

Students tracing the strain of Calvinism or Puritanism alleged to exist in Mark Twain's writing will find an excellent source in Mencken's essay.

⸺◦⁄◦⁄◦⸺ ⸺◦⁄◦⁄◦⸺ ⸺◦⁄◦⁄◦⸺

This conviction that human life is a seeking without a finding, that its purpose is impenetrable, that joy and sorrow are alike meaningless, you will see written largely in the work of most great creative artists. It is obviously the final message, if any message is genuinely to be found there, of the nine symphonies of Ludwig van Beethoven, or, at any rate, of the three which show any intellectual content at all. Mark Twain, superficially a humourist and hence an optimist, was haunted by it in secret, as Nietzsche was by the idea of eternal recurrence: it forced itself through his guard in "The Mysterious Stranger" and "What is Man?" . . .

Dr. William Lyon Phelps, the Lampson professor of English language and literature at Yale, opens his chapter on Mark Twain in his "Essays on Modern Novelists" with a humorous account of the critical imbecility which pursued Mark in his own country down to his last years. The favourite national critics of that era (and it extended to 1895, at the least) were wholly blind to the fact that he was a great artist. They admitted him, somewhat grudgingly, a certain low dexterity as a clown, but that he was an imaginative writer of the first rank, or even of the fifth rank, was something that, in their insanest moments, never so much as occurred to them. Phelps cites, in particular, an ass named Professor Richardson, whose "American Literature," it appears, "is still a standard work" and "a deservedly high authority"—apparently in colleges. In the 1892 edition of this *magnum opus*, Mark is dismissed with less than four lines, and ranked below Irving, Holmes and Lowell—nay, actually below Artemus Ward, Josh Billings and Petroleum V. Nasby! The thing is fabulous, fantastic, *unglaublich*—but nevertheless true. Lacking the "higher artistic or moral purpose of the greater humourists" (*exempli gratia*, Rabelais,

Molière, Aristophanes!!), Mark is dismissed by this Professor Balderdash as a hollow buffoon. . . . But stay! Do not laugh yet! Phelps himself, indignant at the stupidity, now proceeds to credit Mark with a moral purpose! . . . Turn to "The Mysterious Stranger," or "What is Man?" . . .

College professors, alas, never learn anything. The identical gentleman who achieved this discovery about old Mark in 1910, now seeks to dispose of Dreiser in the exact manner of Richardson. That is to say, he essays to finish him by putting him into Coventry, by loftily passing over him. "Do not speak of him," said Kingsley of Heine; "he was a wicked man!" Search the latest volume of the Phelps revelation, "The Advance of the English Novel," and you will find that Dreiser is not once mentioned in it. The late O. Henry is hailed as a genius who will have "abiding fame"; Henry Sydnor Harrison is hymned as "more than a clever novelist," nay, "a valuable ally of the angels" (the right-thinker complex! art as a form of snuffling!), and an obscure Pagliaccio named Charles D. Stewart is brought forward as "the American novelist most worthy to fill the particular vacancy caused by the death of Mark Twain"—but Dreiser is not even listed in the index. And where Phelps leads with his baton of birch most of the other drovers of rah-rah boys follow. . . .

On the one hand, the writer who would deal seriously and honestly with the larger problems of life, particularly in the rigidly-partitioned ethical field, is restrained by laws that would have kept a Balzac or a Zola in prison from year's end to year's end; and on the other hand the writer who would proceed against the reigning superstitions by mockery has been silenced by taboos that are quite as stringent, and by an indifference that is even worse. For all our professed delight in and capacity for jocosity, we have produced so far but one genuine wit—Ambrose Bierce—and, save to a small circle, he remains unknown today. Our great humourists, including even Mark Twain, have had to take protective colouration, whether willingly or unwillingly, from the prevailing ethical foliage, and so one finds them levelling their darts, not at the stupidities of the Puritan majority, but at the evidences of lessening stupidity in the anti-Puritan minority. In other words, they have done battle, not against, but *for* Philistinism—and Philistinism is no more than another name for Puritanism. Both wage a ceaseless warfare upon beauty in its every form, from painting to religious ritual, and from the drama to the dance—the first because it holds beauty to be a mean and stupid thing, and the second because it holds beauty to be distracting and corrupting.

Mark Twain, without question, was a great artist; there was in him something of that prodigality of imagination, that aloof engrossment in the human comedy, that penetrating cynicism, which one associates with the great artists of the Renaissance. But his nationality hung around his neck like a millstone; he could never throw off his native Philistinism. One ploughs through "The Innocents Abroad" and through parts of "A Tramp Abroad" with incredulous amazement. Is such coarse and ignorant clowning to be accepted as humour, as great humour, as the best humour that the most humorous of peoples has produced? Is it really the mark of a smart fellow to lift a peasant's cackle over "Lohengrin"? Is Titian's chromo of Moses in the bullrushes seriously to be regarded as the noblest picture in Europe? Is there nothing in Latin Christianity, after all, save petty grafting, monastic scandals and the worship of the knuckles and shin-bones of dubious saints? May not a civilized man, disbelieving in it, still find himself profoundly moved by its dazzling history, the lingering remnants of its old magnificence, the charm of its gorgeous and melancholy loveliness? In the presence of all beauty of man's creation—in brief, of what we roughly call art, whatever its form—the voice of Mark Twain was the voice of the Philistine. A literary artist of very high rank himself, with instinctive gifts that lifted him, in "Huckleberry Finn" to kinship with Cervantes and Aristophanes, he was yet so far the victim of his nationality that he seems to have had no capacity for distinguishing between the good and the bad in the work of other men of his own craft. The literary criticism that one occasionally finds in his writings is chiefly trivial and ignorant; his private inclination appears to have been toward such romantic sentimentality as entrances school-boys; the thing that interested him in Shakespeare was not the man's colossal genius, but the absurd theory that Bacon wrote his plays. Had he been born in France (the country of his chief abomination!) instead of in a Puritan village of the American hinterland, I venture that he would have conquered the world. But try as he would, being what he was, he could not get rid of the Puritan smugness and cocksureness, the Puritan distrust of new ideas, the Puritan incapacity for seeing beauty as a thing in itself, and the full peer of the true and the good.

It is, indeed, precisely in the works of such men as Mark Twain that one finds the best proofs of the Puritan influence in American letters, for it is there that it is least expected and hence most significant. Our native critics, unanimously Puritans themselves, are anaesthetic to the flavour, but to Dr. Kellner, with his half-European, half-Oriental culture, it is always distinctly perceptible. He senses it, not only in the harsh Calvinistic fables of Hawthorne and the pious gurglings of Longfellow, but also in the poetry of Bryant, the tea-party niceness of Howells, the "maiden-like reserve" of James Lane Allen, and even in the work of Joel Chandler Harris. What! A Southern

Puritan? Well, why not? What could be more erroneous than the common assumption that Puritanism is exclusively a Northern, a New England, madness? The truth is that it is as thoroughly national as the kindred belief in the devil, and runs almost unobstructed from Portland to Portland and from the Lakes to the Gulf. It is in the South, indeed, and not in the North, that it takes on its most bellicose and extravagant forms. Between the upper tier of New England and the Potomac river there was not a single prohibition state—but thereafter, alas, they came in huge blocks! . . .

In the seventies and eighties, with the appearance of such men as Henry James, William Dean Howells, Mark Twain and Bret Harte, a better day seemed to be dawning. Here, after a full century of infantile romanticizing, were four writers who at least deserved respectful consideration as literary artists, and what is more, three of them turned from the conventionalized themes of the past to the teeming and colourful life that lay under their noses. But this promise of better things was soon found to be no more than a promise. Mark Twain, after "The Gilded Age," slipped back into romanticism tempered by Philistinism, and was presently in the era before the Civil War, and finally in the Middle Ages, and even beyond. . . .

The tale might be lengthened. Mark Twain, in his day, felt the stirrings of revolt, and not all his Philistinism was sufficient to hold him altogether in check. If you want to find out about the struggle that went on within him, read the biography by Albert Bigelow Paine, or, better still, "The Mysterious Stranger" and "What is Man?" Alive, he had his position to consider; dead, he now speaks out. In the preface to "What is Man?" dated 1905, there is a curious confession of his incapacity for defying the taboos which surrounded him. The studies for the book, he says, were begun "twenty-five or twenty-seven years ago"—the period of "A Tramp Abroad" and "The Prince and the Pauper." It was actually written "seven years ago"—that is, just after "Following the Equator" and "Personal Recollections of Joan of Arc." And why did it lie so long in manuscript, and finally go out stealthily, under a private imprint?[1] Simply because, as Mark frankly confesses, he "dreaded (*and could not bear*) the disapproval of the people around" him. He knew how hard his fight for recognition had been; he knew what direful penalties outraged orthodoxy could inflict; he had in him the somewhat pathetic discretion of a respectable family man. But, dead, he is safely beyond reprisal, and so, after a prudent interval, the faithful Paine begins printing books in which, writing knowingly behind six feet of earth, he could set down his true ideas without fear. Some day, perhaps, we shall have his microbe story, and maybe even his picture of the court of Elizabeth.

Note

1. The first edition for public sale did not appear until June, 1917, and in it the preface was suppressed.

—H.L. Mencken, *A Book of Prefaces,*
New York: Knopf, 1917, p. 15 ("Joseph Conrad"),
pp. 131–132 ("Theodore Dreiser"), pp. 202–206,
217, 222–224 ("Puritanism as a Literary Force")

RING LARDNER "THREE STORIES A YEAR ARE ENOUGH FOR A WRITER" (1917)

Ring Lardner was a popular humorist, sports columnist, and author of essays, dramas, and short stories. He is probably remembered best for his series of mock letters from a baseball player, *You Know Me Al* (1916). Lardner wrote in a vernacular style, whose lineage—followed back far enough—might be traced to Mark Twain's Huck. Or so the reader might suppose. Ring Lardner refutes any influence. His testimony suggests, perhaps more strongly than many of those gathered here, the opinion of the disinterested reader. He prefers George Ade.

Mr. Lardner is not one of those who pay unstinted homage to the memory of Mark Twain. To a question as to the name of the greatest humorist that America had produced, he said:

"Well, I wouldn't consider Mark Twain our greatest humorist. I guess that George Ade is. Certainly he appeals to us more than Mark Twain does because he belongs to our own time. He writes of the life we are living, and Mark Twain's books deal with the life which we know only by hearsay. I suppose my forebears would say that Mark Twain was a much greater humorist than George Ade.

"But I never saw one of Mark Twain's characters, while I feel that I know every one about whom George Ade writes. You see, I didn't travel along the Mississippi River in Mark Twain's youth, so I don't know his people. Harry Leon Wilson is a great humorist, and Finley Peter Dunne. But I'll bet Finley Peter Dunne is sick of writing Irish dialect!"

"But as to Mark Twain," said the reporter, "you admire his 'Huckleberry Finn,' don't you?"

"Yes," said Mr. Lardner, "but I like Booth Tarkington's 'Penrod' stories better. I've known Booth Tarkington's boys and I've not known those of Mark

Twain. Mark Twain's boys are tough and poverty-stricken and they belong to a period very different from that of our own boys. But we all know Penrod and his friends.

"No, I certainly don't believe that Mark Twain is our greatest American humorist. Some of his fun is spontaneous, but a great deal of it is not."

—Ring Lardner, "Three Stories a Year Are
Enough for a Writer," *New York Times Magazine*,
March 25, 1917, section six, p.14

H.L. Mencken "Si Mutare Potest Aethiops Pellum Suam" (1917)

The Mysterious Stranger having escaped the public hangman, Albert Bigelow Paine now ventures upon the open publication of Mark Twain's *What Is Man?* Of this book I have often discoursed at length; Mark wrote it back in the '80's, but did not print it until 1906, and then only in an edition limited to 250 copies, and not for sale. It contains, in brief, two ideas, neither of them very startling, the first being that man, in Dr. Crile's phase, is an adaptive mechanism, and the second being that altruism, when analyzed, always turns out to be self-interest in a long-tailed coat. These ideas, as I say, are not startling—most men of any intelligence subscribe to them today—but when they first occurred to Mark they were less prevalent, and so they shook him up a bit, and he set them down with the air of a boy pulling the cat's tail, and was afraid to circulate them. Even now they meet with horrified opposition from such pillars of forgotten nonsense as the *New York Times Review of Books*. In the issue for June 3 there is a long editorial denouncing them as naughty, and stating that "one refuses to believe that the book voices the settled, mature convictions held by Mr. Clemens—at least one does not wish to believe it." Refuses? On what ground? No more than a glance at Paine's life of Mark is sufficient to prove that he not only held to them to the last, but that he was fond of extending them and reinforcing them. If he was anything at all in this world, he was an absolute skeptic and determinist; nothing offended and enraged him more than the sloppy idealism and optimism which the *Times* now seeks to ram down his aesophagus. That such bosh should be seriously printed as criticism is surely a sorry indication of the depths to which criticism is sunk in These States.

But let us not be impatient. The fact that Mark was an intelligent man is one that will penetrate the caputs of the national grandmas of letters only slowly. They began by greeting him as a childish buffoon; they proceeded to hail him a purveyor of refined entertainment; they are now in the stage of praising him as a chaser of the blues—in the *Times* phrase, one "who has done so much, through his joyous humor, to lighten the burdens of his generation." Such judgments are worse than errors; they are indecencies. It is as if Italian organ-grinders should essay to estimate Beethoven. The truth about Mark is that he was a colossus, that he stood head and shoulders above his country and his time, that even the combined pull of Puritanism without and Philistinism within could not bring him down to the national level. The result is that he remains mysterious—a baffling puzzle to the critics of the country. Read Howells' *My Mark Twain* if you would see how even the utmost personal intimacy can leave a second-rate man with only a vague and inaccurate picture of a first-rate man.

> —H.L. Mencken, from "Si Mutare Potest
> Aethiops Pellum Suam," *Smart Set* 53,
> September 1917, pp. 142–143

H.L. Mencken "Mark Twain's Americanism" (1917)

H.L. Mencken's campaign to redefine perceptions of Twain was widely waged in 1917, with these two further estimates. In the first salvo Mencken tries to identify anew the three stages of Twain's career (as he was perceived): "They began by greeting him as a childish buffoon; they proceeded to hail him a purveyor of refined entertainment; they are now in the stage of praising him as a chaser of the blues."

In the second salvo, Mencken refines his characterizations further: First, Twain was as a "hollow buffoon, a brother to Josh Billings and Petroleum V. Nasby." This failing, "they made him a comic moralist," followed by a promotion to "the rank of Thomas Bailey Aldrich and William Dean Howells." Now, Mencken predicts, they "must overrehaul him again." Twain is no longer to be perceived as "the amiable old grampa of letters." In Mencken's incarnation he is a vengeful radical. Students researching Mark Twain's later material, particularly those works that were published posthumously, will find a strong exponent of them in H.L. Mencken.

Critics today writing about the authors of the nineteenth century can routinely find, revealed in cold print, many of their most privately held views simply by consulting the published journals or correspondence. Mencken is of the first generation to have access to such materials, so here we find him surprised by Horace Traubel's revelation that Walt Whitman believed Twain "misses fire" or by Paine's detail of how Twain and Howells visited Emerson only a few weeks before Emerson died, and how they "went again in the evening, not to see him, but to stand reverently outside and look at his house" (Paine 1912, II:735). Such reverence, at least for Emerson, has little place in Mencken's version of Twain. "The simple fact is that *Huckleberry Finn* is worth the whole work of Emerson," he argues mathematically, "with two-thirds of the work of Whitman thrown in for make-weight." Emerson was indebted to German transcendentalism, while Edgar Allan Poe "was a foreigner in every line he wrote," and *Leaves of Grass* "might have been written in London quite as well as in Brooklyn." That is a matter of opinion sure to be contested by many. Mencken's claim, however, is that of all the vaunted American Renaissance writers, Mark Twain alone was an authentic American in his writing. Students interested in Twain's Americanism, or in questions of Americanism in literature generally, will find this heady essay difficult to ignore.

―――― ―――― ――――

When Mark Twain died, in 1910, one of the magnificos who paid public tribute to him was William H. Taft, then President of the United States. "Mark Twain," said Dr. Taft, "gave real intellectual enjoyment to millions, and his works will continue to give such pleasure to millions yet to come. He never wrote a line that a father could not read to a daughter."

The usual polite flubdub and not to be exposed, perhaps, to critical analysis. But it was, in a sense, typical of the general view at that time, and so it deserves to be remembered for the fatuous inaccuracy of the judgment in it. For Mark Twain dead is beginning to show far different and more brilliant colors than those he seemed to wear during life, and the one thing no sane critic would say of him to-day is that he was the harmless fireside jester, the mellow chautauquan, the amiable old grampa of letters that he was once so widely thought to be.

The truth is that Mark was almost exactly the reverse. Instead of being a mere entertainer of the mob, he was in fact a literary artist of the very highest skill and sophistication, and, in all save his superficial aspect, quite unintelligible to Dr. Taft's millions. And instead of being a sort of Dr. Frank Crane in cap and bells, laboriously devoted to the obvious and the uplifting, he was a destructive satirist of the utmost pungency and relentlessness, and the most bitter critic of American platitude and delusion, whether social, political or religious, that ever lived.

Bit by bit, as his posthumous books appear, the true man emerges, and it needs but half an eye to see how little he resembles the Mark of national legend. Those books were written carefully and deliberately; Mark wrote them at the height of his fame; he put into them, without concealment, the fundamental ideas of his personal philosophy—the ideas which colored his whole view of the world. Then he laid the manuscripts away, safe in the knowledge that they would not see the light until he was under six feet of earth. We know, by his own confession, why he hesitated to print them while he lived; he knew that fame was sweet and he feared that they might blast it. But beneath that timorousness there was an intellectual honesty that forced him to set down the truth. It was really comfort he wanted, not fame. He hesitated, a lazy man, to disturb his remaining days with combat and acrimony. But in the long run he wanted to set himself straight.

Two of these books, *The Mysterious Stranger* and *What Is Man?* are now published, and more may be expected to follow at intervals. The latter, in fact, was put into type during Mark's lifetime and privately printed in a very limited edition. But it was never given to the public, and copies of the limited edition bring $40 or $50 at book auctions to-day. Even a pirated English edition brings a high premium. Now, however, the book is issued publicly by the Harpers, though without the preface in which Mark explained his reasons for so long withholding it.

The ideas in it are very simple, and reduced to elementals, two in number. The first is that man, save for a trace of volition that grows smaller and smaller the more it is analyzed, is a living machine—that nine-tenths of his acts are purely reflex, and that moral responsibility, and with it religion, are thus mere delusions. The second is that the only genuine human motive, like the only genuine dog motive or fish motive or protoplasm motive is self interest—that altruism, for all its seeming potency in human concerns, is no more than a specious appearance—that the one unbroken effort of the organism is to promote its own comfort, welfare and survival.

Starting from this double basis, Mark undertakes an elaborate and extraordinarily penetrating examination of all the fine ideals and virtues that man boasts of, and reduces them, one after the other, to untenability and absurdity. There is no mere smartness in the thing. It is done, to be sure, with a sly and disarming humor, but at bottom it is done quite seriously and with the highest sort of argumentative skill. The parlor entertainer of Dr. Taft's eulogy completely disappears; in his place there arises a satirist with something of Rabelais's vast resourcefulness and dexterity in him, and all of Dean Swift's devastating ferocity. It is not only the most honest book that

Mark ever did; it is, in some respects, the most artful and persuasive as a work of art. No wonder the pious critic of *The New York Times*, horrified by its doctrine, was forced to take refuge behind the theory that Mark intended it as a joke.

In *The Mysterious Stranger* there is a step further. *What Is Man?* analyzes the concept of man; *The Mysterious Stranger* boldly analyzes the concept of God. What, after all, is the actual character of this Being we are asked to reverence and obey? How is His mind revealed by His admitted acts? How does His observed conduct toward man square with those ideals of human conduct that He is said to prescribe, and whose violation He is said to punish with such appalling penalties?

These are the questions that Mark sets for himself. His answers are, in brief, a complete rejection of the whole Christian theory—a rejection based upon a wholesale *reductio ad absurdum*. The thing is not mere mocking; it is not even irreverent; but the force of it is stupendous. I know of no agnostic document that shows a keener sense of essentials or a more deft hand for making use of the indubitable. A gigantic irony is in it. It glows with a profound conviction, almost a kind of passion. And the grotesque form of it—a child's story—only adds to the sardonic implacability of it.

As I say, there are more to come. Mark in his idle moments was forever at work upon some such riddling of the conventional philosophy, as he was forever railing at the conventional ethic in his private conversation. One of these pieces, highly characteristic, is described in Albert Bigelow Paine's biography. It is an elaborate history of the microbes inhabiting a man's veins. They divine a religion with the man as God; they perfect a dogma setting forth his desires as to their conduct; they engaged in a worship based upon the notion that he is immediately aware of their every act and jealous of their regard and enormously concerned about their welfare. In brief, a staggering satire upon the anthropocentric religion of man—a typical return to the favorite theme of man's egoism and imbecility.

All this sort of thing, to be sure, has its dangers for Mark's fame. Let his executors print a few more of his unpublished works—say, the microbe story and his sketch of life at the court of Elizabeth—and Dr. Taft, I dare say, will withdraw his *pronunciamento* that "he never wrote a line that a father could not read to his daughter." Already, indeed, the lady reviewers of the newspapers sound an alarm against him, and the old lavish praise of him begins to die down to whispers. In the end, perhaps, the Carnegie libraries will put him to the torture, and *The Innocents Abroad* will be sacrificed with *What Is Man?*

But that effort to dispose of him is nothing now. Nor will it succeed. While he lived he was several times labeled and relabeled, and always inaccurately and vainly. At the start the national guardians of letters sought to dismiss him loftily as a hollow buffoon, a brother to Josh Billings and Petroleum V. Nasby. This enterprise failing, they made him a comic moralist, a sort of chautauquan in motley, a William Jennings Bryan armed with a slapstick. Foiled again, they promoted him to the rank of Thomas Bailey Aldrich and William Dean Howells, and issued an impertinent amnesty for the sins of his youth. Thus he passed from these scenes—ratified at last, but somewhat heavily patronized.

Now the professors must overhaul him again, and this time, I suppose, they will undertake to pull him down a peg. They will succeed as little as they succeeded when they tried to read him out of meeting in the early '80s. The more they tackle him, in fact, the more it will become evident that he was a literary artist of the very first rank, and incomparably the greatest ever hatched in these states.

One reads with something akin to astonishment of his superstitious reverence for Emerson—of how he stood silent and bareheaded before the great transcendentalist's house at Concord. One hears of him, with amazement, courting Whittier, Longfellow and Holmes. One is staggered by the news, reported by Traubel, that Walt Whitman thought "he mainly misses fire." The simple fact is that *Huckleberry Finn* is worth the whole work of Emerson with two-thirds of the work of Whitman thrown in for make-weight, and that one chapter of it is worth the whole work of Whittier, Longfellow and Holmes.

Mark was not only a great artist; he was pre-eminently a great American artist. No other writer that we have produced has ever been more extravagantly national. Whitman dreamed of an America that never was and never will be; Poe was a foreigner in every line he wrote; even Emerson was no more than an American spigot for European, and especially German, ideas. But Mark was wholly of the soil. His humor was American. His incurable Philistinism was American. His very English was American. Above all, he was an American in his curious mixture of sentimentality and cynicism, his mingling of romanticist and iconoclast.

English Traits might have been written by any one of half a dozen Germans. The tales of Poe, printed as translations from the French, would have deceived even Frenchmen. And *Leaves of Grass* might have been written in London quite as well as in Brooklyn. But in *Huckleberry Finn*, in *A Connecticut Yankee* and in most of the short sketches there is a quality that is unmistakably and overwhelmingly national. They belong to our country and our time quite as obviously as the skyscraper or the quick lunch counter. They are as magnificently American as the Brooklyn Bridge or Tammany Hall.

Mark goes down the professorial gullet painfully. He has stuck more than once. He now seems fated to stick again. But these gaggings will not hurt him, nor even appreciably delay him. Soon or late the national mind will awake to the fact that a great man was among us—that in the midst of all our puerile rages for dubious foreigners we produced an artist who was head and shoulders above all of them.

—H.L. Mencken, "Mark Twain's Americanism,"
New York Evening Mail, November 1, 1917, p. 9

Ezra Pound "Three Views of H.L. Mencken" (1918)

It is a great blessing that at last some one with fibre tough enough to read Mark Twain, and intelligence enough to perceive the part which is not simple "Hee-Haw", has at last diagnosed Mark Twain's trouble.... Mr Mencken ... has given a correct diagnosis. He has put his finger on the plague spot. My own detestation of Twain has stayed vague for a number of years; there were too many more important things to attend to; I could not be bothered to clarify this patch of vagueness. A detestation of a man's tonality does not necessitate a blindness to his abilities. And when a man's rightnesses have been so lied against as Twain's were in America, one could be well content to conceal a private and unimportant detestation. One could not express a dislike of any man, for instance, whose posthumous publications have been so lied about and distorted as Twain's final pessimistic expressions.

—Ezra Pound, "Three Views of H.L. Mencken,"
Little Review 4:9, January 1918, pp. 10–12

William Dean Howells (1918)

Aged eighty-one and only two years from his death, William Dean Howells casts his eye once more back at his friend. The occasion was the publication of Twain's letters. Howells reviews Twain's bibliography again, noting now the autobiographical aspect in his works. Twain insert-ed "his immortal part" in *The Gilded Age*, in the character of Mulberry Sellers; in *A Connecticut Yankee* he was the Boss. Students investigating autobiographical aspects of Twain's writing will be intrigued by these late musings from Howells.

Howells's thoughts on Twain at the end mirror, in ironic ways, Mencken's. Both remark on Twain as the "average American." The fierce emphasis on Americanism and patriotism may reflect their period as much as it reflects Twain in himself. America had been involved in a war with Germany for nearly a year, a war mentioned explicitly by Howells when he suggests that Twain "forecast" World War I. (The war is surely in the background also when Mencken derides "dubious foreigners" in his review of November 1917.) Since Twain had already been equated with the American flag by Stuart P. Sherman in 1910, some of these comments may count as much abstract flag-waving as incisive literary criticism.

Both Twain and Howells also identify the Puritan, or here "Calvinistic," aspect of Twain. Mencken's use of the word "Puritan" is more nebulous than Howells's sense of Calvinism here, but students interested in those aspects of Puritanism in Twain's writing will find Howells's view compelling when read alongside Mencken's.

—·— —·— —·—

Mr. Albert Bigelow Paine has ended his very faithful and intelligent labors on the biography of a man nearer and dearer to his generation than any other author, in two volumes of *Mark Twain's Letters*. Unless more material should unexpectedly offer itself, these letters will tell us the last we shall be told of one who can never be told enough of, and who tells himself in them more explicitly and directly than in all his other work. Every author tells himself in his work, if his work is inventive; and no writer can imagine traits or characteristics or qualities which do not already exist in human nature as it is actually or potentially known to him from himself. With Mark Twain this is verified first and last in his books, whether they are the crude effect of newspaper reporting, or the play of controlless fancy, or ostensibly the record of travel. The book which first made him universally known, *Innocents Abroad*, is almost entirely autobiography, although it is a story of travel in the strangest guise that travel ever took on under unprecedented conditions. Still closer to personal experience is *Roughing It*, which is the Wild West variously speaking from the Wildest Westerner ever inspired by the things happening either to him or to others. *The Gilded Age*, or Mark Twain's half of it, embodies a part of his immortal part in Mulberry Sellers, and in *A Connecticut Yankee at the Court of King Arthur*—one of the most poetic inventions in all fiction—the Boss is the reflex of Mark Twain's bold and lovable soul. Tom Sawyer is the boy who was Mark Twain and Huck Finn is the boy whom no one but such a boy as Tom Sawyer could have realized. In *The Personal Recollections of Joan of Arc* it is the Arthurian Yankee and Missourian boy who heroically befriend the immortal Maid; and the same spirit in *Following the Equator* reduces the facts of travel, to their proper level below the emotions of the traveler. In his slightest and crudest sketch we feel the cordial hand-clasp of the author, and hear his kind, brave American voice speaking from himself and of himself to his American, his human counterpart in the reader. The letters addressed to his friends are scarcely less intimately addressed to the general reader. Each of them holds as much of himself as he could put into it, pressed down and running over, no matter how little or large the measure of it. They are each written from some vital occasion, and never from an impulse invited or pretended. If ever he starts involuntarily from some unreal motive he is presently in full earnest, throbbing and hammering away like one of the high pressure steamboats of his own Mississippi. Any of the famous epistles of the past, like Pope's or Walpole's, or Lady Mary Montagu's, or Byron's, or Carlyle's, show fictitious and factitious in their pose of intentional literature beside these letters of Mark Twain which are the more of universal import because of their intensely individual appeal.

The reader of this magazine already knows the quality of the letters gathered here, but not their variety and scope. None of them could be spared from a study of the nature and character of the man, and no one who wishes to know him truly will find himself shut from the intimacy of a soul which had no reserves, no pretences, no manner of falsehood, not even false shame. He is sometimes ashamed, and then he is ashamed with reason, or with the belief that he has reason. The reader who is of the same make, the good average American make, will be, first of all, glad of the letters which Mark Twain wrote to his mother in his boyhood when he left home and until he had grown a gray-haired man. At times the letters joke her, at times cheer her, but always tenderly caress her with his boyish affection. It is known to those who know Mr. Paine's biography how simple often to rudeness the early circumstances of Mark Twain's life were, but if anything were needed to testify to the inner beauty of his life these letters of the young boy and the old boy to his mother will convince the witness least acquainted with the average American life.

To this end the letters of this wonderful collection are tense with what Mark Twain felt and thought at the time he wrote them, and in their complex they constitute the history of that philosophy of the world which became honestly his in its denial of a conscious Creator and its affirmation of the failure of whatever force wrought the creation of man. By birth and by marriage he was of the Calvinistic faith which bowed the neck of most Americans in the early eighteen seventies, and then began to break of its own impossibility and to substitute the prevailing scientific agnosticism. His personal unreligion went far back in his early life. The faith he had been taught in his childhood passed with his childhood; but it held against his reason and remained in his affection long after it had ceased in his conviction, and until his churchgoing became a meaningless form. Then when he turned from the form the heroic woman who had no life apart from his could only say, "Well, if he must be lost, I do not wish to be saved," and their Christianity ceased to be a creed and remained a life. Probably the change was not so profound when it became open as even she had imagined; the sorrows which time accumulated upon them were those which life brings. They were of the common lot, and no special tragedy. The least part of their trouble was that loss of fortune which he so heroically bore and she so heroically inspired him to bear, but the death of his children would seem to have struck him with a sort of dismay, as if no one else had known the like, and it finds naive utterance in the letters. The gayety goes out of them, not lastingly, but again and again after it has come back. The gloom deepens around him to the end; he fights it away, he downs it again and again; but the doubt that has always haunted him, hardens into denial and effects itself at last in such an allegory as *The Mysterious Stranger* who bedevils a world without reason and without pity.

Of course the thing will not do, and there are times when the cry of pain becomes a burst of laughter turning upon the unreason of the reasoning; but any one who leaves out the tragedy of the great humorist's suffering leaves the part of Hamlet out of life's play of Hamlet. No humorist knew better than he that there is a time to laugh and a time to weep, and that absence from felicity cannot be lifelong. Almost to the very last, he steadfastly denied himself the hope of life hereafter, though before the very last, but then only at the entreaty of those dearest who stood nearest him, he is said to have permitted this hope, with a murmur, a look.

It does not greatly matter. The fact does not impeach the veracity of what had gone before in the books, or in the letters which went before the books. None of the letters, idly begun, failed of final significance; and the perception of the lasting verity of the actualities touched upon sometimes took on the character of forecast. Such a strain breaks out in a letter written eighteen years ago to the friend who had hated equally with him the war of England upon the Boer Republics. "Privately speaking, this is a sordid and criminal war, and in every way shameful and excuseless. Every day I write (in my head) bitter magazine articles about it, but I have to stop at that, *for England must not fail. It would mean an inundation of Russian and German political degradation, which would envelop the globe and steep it in a sort of Middle Age night and slavery, which would last until Christ comes again. Even if wrong—and she is wrong—England must be upheld. He is an enemy of the human race who shall speak against her now."* Is there any one presently treating or talking of the actual situation who could more clearly and strongly divine our duty toward our Motherland, often our Step-Motherland, or more strongly urge it? If this is wisdom concerning that little wicked war of England's *against* Liberty eighteen years ago, how profoundly wise it is concerning her war *for* Liberty now—her war, *our* war, humanity's war! Has the truth about Germany been said more clearly, potently, finally?

—William Dean Howells,
Harper's Monthly, March 1918

WALDO FRANK (1919)

Our America was written as part of a sort of cultural exchange with the French during World War I. Waldo Frank, a novelist and the editor of a "little magazine," *The New Republic*, was commissioned by two French intellectuals to write what was effectively a Greenwich Village guide to America. The result is bohemian, flippant, impressionistic, and pretentious.

Waldo Frank's text has been credited with providing the first Freudian analysis of Mark Twain's work. "The leaders of a tomorrow forced to spiritual discovery are men of letters," he writes. "These men needed to break with the restricted reality of their fathers." This provides an index to the tone of the book. Students interested in the Freudian analysis of Twain's writing will find at least a historical curiosity here.

To Waldo Frank, Twain's sole work of consequence was *Huckleberry Finn*: After its publication, "Mark Twain lived twenty-six years longer. That voice never spoke again." Frank recalls seeing Mark Twain give a lecture to a room full of blind people, at first trying to speak seriously and eventually, amid laughter, giving up. Similar versions of this story with slight variations seem to have circulated. Frank hated Twain at the time. Now he does not. Nevertheless, rancor remains for William Dean Howells, who was, to a rising generation of writers, absolutely representative of the old, staid, stuffy past: the "restricted reality" of the fathers.

If nothing else, Frank's impressions of Huck and Mark serve as an indicator of the way Twain was viewed by the younger generation, members of the New York avant-garde (to whom "the sentiment of the majority"—what Van Wyck Brooks calls "gospel to the old-fashioned Westerner"—was anathema). Students interested in the different perceptions of Mark Twain across society will find this entry diverting.

⎯⎯ ⎯⎯ ⎯⎯

But the land of the pioneer has had a more heroic victim. Jack London was a man of talent: Mark Twain was a man of genius. The mind of Jack London was brilliant: the soul of Mark Twain was great. . . .

Out of the bitter wreckage of his long life, one great work emerges by whose contrasting fire we can observe the darkness. This work is *Huckleberry Finn*. It must go down in history, not as the expression of a rich national culture like the books of Chaucer, Rabelais, Cervantes, but as the voice of American chaos, the voice of a precultural epoch. Mark Twain kept this book long at his side. Ostensibly, it was the sequel to *The Adventures of Tom Sawyer* which appeared in 1875. "Huck" came nine years later. In it for once, the soul of Mark Twain burst its bonds of false instruction and false ideal, and found voice. Mark Twain lived twenty-six years longer. That voice never spoke again.

Huckleberry Finn is the simple story of a young white lad, born on the banks of the Mississippi who, with an escaped slave named Jim, builds a raft and floats down the mighty current. Mark Twain originally had meant it to be nothing else: had meant it for the mere sequel of another tale. But his theme was too apt a symbol. Into it he poured his soul.

Huck is a candid ignorant courageous child. He is full of the cunning and virtue of the resilient savage. He wears the habiliments of the civilization from which he comes, loosely, like trinkets about his neck. He and his companion build a raft and float. At night they veer their craft into the shallows or sleep on land. They have many adventures. The adventures that Huck has are the material of pioneering life. He always *happens* upon them. At times, he is a mere spectator: at time enforced accessory. Always, he is passive before a vaster fact. Huck is America. And Huck *floats* down the current of a mighty Stream.

Huckleberry Finn is the American epic hero. Greece had Ulysses. America must be content with an illiterate lad. He expresses our germinal past. He expresses the movement of the American soul through all the sultry climaxes of the Nineteenth Century.

The Mississippi with its countless squalid towns and its palatial steamboats was a ferment of commingled and insoluble life. All the elements of the American East and all the elements of Europe seethed here, in the hunt of wealth. A delirium of dreams and schemes and passions, out of which shaped our genius for invention and exploitation. The whole gamut of American beginnings ran with the river. And Huck along. One rises from the book, lost in the beat of a great rhythmic flow: the unceasing elemental march of a vast life, cutting a continent, feeding its soil. And upon the heaving surface of this Flood, a human child: ignorant, joyous and courageous. The American soul like a midge upon the tide of a world.

Mark Twain was fifty when this work appeared. The balance of his literary life, before and after, went mostly to the wastage of half-baked, half-believed, half-clownish labor. And underneath the gibes and antics of the professional jester, brooded the hatred and resentment of a tortured child. Mark Twain, in his conscious mind, shared his people's attitude of contempt for "art and spiritual matters"—shared their standards of success. Mark Twain strove to make money and to please! This great soul came to New York and felt ashamed before the little dancing-masters of the magazines; felt humble before Richard Watson Gilder and William Dean Howells! Shared their conviction that he was only a crude, funny writer from Missouri; changed the texts of his books to suit their fancy. Mark Twain did not believe in his soul, and his soul suffered. Mark Twain believed, with his fellows, that the great sin was to be unpopular and poor, and his soul died. His one great work was the result of a burst of spirit over the dikes of social inhibition and intellectual fear. *Leaves of Grass* came in consequence of a similar bursting of the floodgates. American expression has ever had to break through the bars of pioneer conviction. But in the case of Whitman, the spirit remained free.

I recall vividly the one time I ever saw Mark Twain. There was a Benefit Performance for some Association for the Blind, in the ball-room of a New York hotel. My father took me. The platform was filled with blind men and women; silent faces that had somehow won serenity from their deprivation above the turmoil of those who saw. Joseph H. Choate was the chairman. My father told me that he was our Ambassador to England, and that he was the leader of the American Bar. I remember my vague and unresolved discomfort, looking at Mr. Choate. He had a bland and empty face. The face of a gigantic child. His well-groomed body curved with gracious gestures. It also was child-like, sweet, untrammeled. No passion seemed to have ruffled this great man: no harsh experience stamped him. He seemed to me the symbol of respectable vapidity. I did not realize that he was rather more the symbol of a world which barred experience—the true Ambassador of the pioneer.

Mr. Choate arose and spoke solemn, touching words. Speaking, his face wrinkled with complacence. A blind man was led to the piano: he played. A blind woman sang. And then, a tall spare person, natively graceful, naively timid, swung forward from his place among the blind. A vast shock of white hair fell from the clear forehead. Mark Twain! He opened his mouth. He hesitated. The long, nasal twang of the lower Middle-West came with his words. Mark Twain—the humorist—America's funny man! His words were diffident and sad. But everybody laughed. Mark Twain drew back. Turning half about, he seemed to take some heartening he needed from the unseeing eyes, from the wan smiles behind him. He began again. Mark Twain's Western twang. The ball-room laughed once more. . . . For five minutes, the sad soul struggled with this reality about him—this reality that would laugh. His face was strained: his body seemed loose and nervous: his transparent voice withdrew gradually from the obtuse glee of his hearers. And then, Mark Twain gave up. He relaxed. He launched into an anecdote. The audience settled back, wreathed in smiles that somehow suggested to me the folds of an obese body. And Mark Twain rambled on. His jokes came slow and listless. He stood there almost still, with his back to the rows of them who could not see, and dropped the ungainly humor from his mouth. And the audience before him spouted it, guzzled it, roared with delight. At last, Mark Twain stopped. He fell back from the high applause to his seat and was out of sight among the sightless.

I remember how at that time I hated this noble-looking fool. It seemed to me that all the shallowpates I knew called Mark Twain their favorite author, bored me with quotations from his books. I hated Mark Twain because of them who seemed to love him. Now, I love him, because I faintly understand what a cross such love must have bound upon his back.

Mark Twain went through life, lost in a bitter blindness that is far more terrible than the hate of men like Schopenhauer or Jonathan Swift. The mighty pessimists were fertile: they plowed great fields with their wrath and sowed them with their love. Mark Twain's was the misery of a love too feeble to create. In his later days, he wrote a book entitled *What is Man?* It is the confession of his despondency, and its elucidation. It is the profane utterance of a defeated soul bent upon degrading the world to the low level where it was forced to live, whence came its ruin. An Old Man, in wooden dialogue, proves to a Young Man the folly of all human aspiration: proves to him that man is a machine:

YOUNG MAN: Do you believe in the doctrine that man is equipped with an intuitive perception of good and evil?

OLD MAN: Adam hadn't it.

YOUNG MAN: But has man acquired it since?

OLD MAN: No: I think he has no intuition of any kind. He gets all his ideas, all his impressions from the outside.

—The *reductio ad absurdum* of extraversion. And in the mouth of a man who by every inner circumstance and gift was an intuitive giant, belonged to the number of great artists! But Mark Twain knew that this was not the sort of book that his American readers wanted. So out of deference to their taste, or lack of confidence in his own, he hid it among his papers, where it was discovered at his death. Until the end, he held forward to the public gaze the painted and powdered visage of a clown.

The clown tragedy of Mark Twain is prelude to the American drama. The generic Clemens was a tender and dreaming and avid spirit, in love with beauty, in love with love. But he was born in the ranks of a hurling and sweating army. He forced himself to move with it at its own pace. He forced himself to take on its measures of success: to take on that distrust of life and love which so well defended the principal business of its march. For this betrayal of his soul, his soul brought him bitterness, and the mass of his works are failures.

Mark Twain was a giant. Or a giant he would have grown to be, had he been nurtured at his nation's breast. But the centrifugal force was overwhelming. Mark Twain was flung away in outer darkness: where he did not belong, and where only lesser men adapt themselves to live. If we look for Miracle upon these Western plains, we must seek elsewhere.

—Waldo Frank, *Our America*,
pp. 38–44, 1919

Van Wyck Brooks (1920)

Surely the greatest "unmaking" and "remaking" of the way readers viewed Twain, Van Wyck Brooks's thesis (called a "defeatist thesis" by the *Twainian* magazine) would be best engaged and most famously challenged by Bernard DeVoto in *Mark Twain's America*, published twelve years later. Their competing interpretations of Mark Twain's life and work have divided Twain studies ever since. The influence of Brooks can clearly be seen, for instance, in the caustic (and inferior) account by Edgar Lee

Masters (*Mark Twain: A Portrait*, 1938), or the derivative and floundering "analysis" by Theodore Dreiser ("Mark the Double Twain," *The English Journal*, 24:8, October 1935), which are both at times flagrantly lifted from Brooks.

> It is an established fact, if I am not mistaken, that these morbid feelings of sin, which have no evident cause, are the result of having transgressed some inalienable life-demand peculiar to one's nature. It is as old as Milton that there are talents which are "death to hide," and I suggest that Mark Twain's "talent" was just so hidden. That bitterness of his was the effect of a certain miscarriage in his creative life . . . of which he was himself almost wholly unaware, but which for him destroyed the meaning of life. . . .
>
> Does this seem too rash a hypothesis?

So begins Brooks's analysis; and many have since answered him in the affirmative.

Certainly, Brooks is unrelenting. Countless details of Twain's life are pored over and shown to prove the Brooks "hypothesis." Alternatively, it might be said that his study is simply remarkably fertile. All earlier criticism seems light and conservative compared to this one. Brooks's text marks a change in critical attitudes. *The Ordeal of Mark Twain* was published in the period of James Joyce and T.S. Eliot; it was published two years before *Ulysses* and *The Wasteland*, and it shares with those works a simultaneous familiarity with, and irreverence for, the past. Furthermore, in an age when sexual matters were slowly becoming fair subjects of critical discourse, Brooks is the first to bring Twain's private life into discussion. Paine's biography, of course, aids him in this venture, however unwittingly.

Going back over Paine's biography, Brooks finds that Twain's father was a "mere pathetic shadow" while his mother was (in Freudian terms) a "castrating" Calvinist, inculcating her son with an urgent but somewhat directionless capitalism. Her influence blighted Twain's development, according to Brooks: "All his life he had to be mothered by somebody." With this start—best characterized by a harrowing deathbed scene with his father—Twain was unsurprisingly insecure, in turn a "megalomaniac," while warped and distilled by prissy overseers and surrogate "parents" into what was, in Brooks's eyes, an artistic failure. Twain's redemption lies in *Huckleberry Finn*, in which the author somehow smuggled out his more radical visions from the mouths of babes, while his censors (Livy and Howells) were preoccupied with *The Prince and the Pauper*.

It is Brooks who best establishes a tradition that sees William Dean Howells and Olivia Clemens as the two censors of Twain's genius. Like Ambrose Bierce before him, Brooks sees Twain's marriage to Livy as an application as a "candidate for gentility"—a central stage in that "pursuit of prestige" which sprang from his miserable vow to his mother. This vow meant that Twain divided himself between the dutiful son or husband or friend and the wayward spirit that recoiled from convention. This division explains his recurring attraction to themes of twins and doubles, "dual personalities." Students interested in the use of doubling in Twain's work should consult Brooks.

Brooks extends his criticism to whole scenes and traditions, and it is for this too that he was later criticized, particularly by Bernard DeVoto. Taking his lead from Paine's biography, Brooks views the frontier—here, Nevada—as an environment "inflexibly opposed . . . to the development of individuality," where the sole motivation is avarice and "a life of chronic nervous exasperation" is inevitable. This avarice and exasperation led Twain unwittingly into the authorship of humor, a form that Twain actually hated. (At least, so says Brooks.)

Any student wishing to acquire a good sense of the history of Twain criticism cannot afford to ignore Brooks's account. It represents a major change in how critics view the author. Any student attempting a Freudian analysis of Twain or his work should likewise look to Brooks as a foundation for such research. Students interested in how Twain's biography—his marriage, his family, his friendships—affected his literature should read Brooks.

Can we, then, accept any of the usual explanations of Mark Twain's pessimism? Can we attribute it, with Mr. Paine, to the burdens of debt under which he labored now and again, to the recurring illnesses, the death of those he loved? No, for these things would have modified his temperament, not his point of view; they would have saddened him, checked his vitality, given birth perhaps to a certain habit of brooding, and this they did not do. We have, in addition to his own testimony, the word of Mr. Paine: "More than any one I ever knew, he lived in the present." Of the misfortunes of life he had neither more nor less than other men, and they affected him neither more nor less. To say anything else would be to contradict the whole record of his personality.

No, it was some deep malady of the soul that afflicted Mark Twain, a malady common to many Americans, perhaps, if we are to judge from that excessive interest in therapeutics which he shared with so many millions of his fellow-countrymen. . . .

In fact, the more one scans the later pages of Mark Twain's history the more one is forced to the conclusion that there was something gravely amiss with his inner life. There was that frequently noted fear of solitude, that dread of being alone with himself which made him, for example, beg for just one more game of billiards at 4 o'clock in the morning. There were those "daily self-chidings" that led him to slay his own conscience in one of the most ferocious of his humorous tales. That conscience of his—what was it? Why do so many of his jokes turn upon an affectation, let us say, of moral cowardice in himself? How does it happen that when he reads "Romola" the only thing that "hits" him "with force" is Tito's compromise with his conscience? Why those continual fits of remorse, those fantastic self-accusations in which he charged himself, we are told, with having filled Mrs. Clemens's life with privations, in which he made himself responsible first for the death of his younger brother and later for that of his daughter Susy, writing to his wife, according to Mr. Paine, that he was "wholly and solely responsible for the tragedy, detailing step by step with fearful reality his mistakes and weaknesses which had led to their downfall, the separation from Susy, and this final, incredible disaster"? Was there any reason why, humorously or otherwise, he should have spoken of himself as a liar, why he should have said, in reply to his own idea of writing a book about Tom Sawyer's after-life: "If I went on now and took him into manhood, he would just lie, like all the one-horse men in literature, and the reader would conceive a hearty contempt for him"? That morbid feeling of having lived in sin, which made him come to think of literature as primarily, perhaps, the confession of sins—was there anything in the moral point of view of his generation to justify it, in this greatly-loved writer, this honorable man of business, this zealous reformer, this loyal friend? . . .

No, there was a reason for Mark Twain's pessimism, a reason for that chagrin, that fear of solitude, that tortured conscience, those fantastic self-accusations, that indubitable self-contempt. It is an established fact, if I am not mistaken, that these morbid feelings of sin, which have no evident cause, are the result of having transgressed some inalienable life-demand peculiar to one's nature. It is as old as Milton that there are talents which are "death to hide," and I suggest that Mark Twain's "talent" was just so hidden. That bitterness of his was the effect of a certain miscarriage in his creative life, a balked personality, an arrested development of which he was himself almost wholly unaware, but which for him destroyed the meaning of life. The spirit of the artist in him, like the genie at last released from the bottle, overspread in a gloomy vapor the mind it had never quite been able to possess.

Does this seem too rash a hypothesis? It is, I know, the general impression that Mark Twain quite fully effectuated himself as a writer. Mr. Howells called him the "Lincoln of our literature," Professor William Lyon Phelps describes him as one of the supreme novelists of the world, Professor Brander Matthews compares him with Cervantes, and Bernard Shaw said to him once: "I am persuaded that the future historian of America will find your works as indispensable to him as a French historian finds the political tracts of Voltaire." These were views current in Mark Twain's lifetime, and similar views are common enough to-day. "Mark Twain," says Professor Archibald Henderson, "enjoys the unique distinction of exhibiting a progressive development, a deepening and broadening of forces, a ripening of intellectual and spiritual powers from the beginning to the end." To Mr. John Macy, author of what is, on the whole, the most discerning book that has been written on our literature, he is "a powerful, original thinker." And finally, Mr. H. L. Mencken says: "Mark Twain, without question, was a great artist. There was in him something of that prodigality of imagination, that aloof engrossment in the human comedy, that penetrating cynicism, which one associates with the great artists of the Renaissance." An imposing array of affirmations, surely! And yet, unless I am mistaken, these last few years, during which he has become in a way so much more interesting, have witnessed a singular change in Mark Twain's reputation. Vividly present he is in the public mind as a great historic figure, as a sort of archtype of the national character during a long epoch. Will he not continue so to be for many generations to come? Undoubtedly. By whom, however, with the exception of two or three of his books, is he read? Mr. Paine, I know, says that "The Innocents Abroad" sells to this day in America in larger quantity than any other book of travel. But a number of explanations might be given for this, as for any other mob phenomenon, none of which has anything to do with literary fame in the proper sense. A great writer of the past is known by the delight and stimulus which he gives to mature spirits in the present, and time, it seems to me, tends to bear out the assertion of Henry James that Mark Twain's appeal is an appeal to rudimentary minds. "Huckleberry Finn," "Tom Sawyer," a story or two like "The Man That Corrupted Hadleyburg," a sketch or two like "Traveling with a Reformer" and a few chapters of "Life on the Mississippi,"—these, in any case, can already be said to have "survived" all his other work. And are these writings, however beautiful and important, the final expressions of a supreme artistic genius, one of the great novelists of the world, a second Cervantes? Arnold Bennett, I think, forecast the view that prevails to-day when he called their author the "divine amateur" and said of "Huckleberry Finn" and "Tom Sawyer" that while they are "episodically magnificent, as complete works of art they are of quite inferior quality."

So much for what Mark Twain actually accomplished. But if he had not been potentially a great man could he have so impressed, so dazzled almost every one who came into direct, personal contact with him? . . .

Wherever he walked among men he trailed with him the psychic atmosphere of a planet as it were all his own. Gigantic, titanic were the words that came to people's lips when they tried to convey their impression of him, and when he died it seemed for the moment as if one of the fixed stars had fallen in space.

This was the force, this the energy which, through Mark Twain's pen, found such inadequate expression. He was, as Arnold Bennett says, a "divine amateur"; his appeal is, on the whole, what Henry James called it, an appeal to rudimentary minds. But is not that simply another way of saying, in the latter case, that his was a mind that had not developed, and in the former, that his was a splendid genius which had never found itself?

It is the conclusion borne out by Mark Twain's own self-estimate. His judgments were, as Mr. Paine says, "always unsafe": strictly speaking, he never knew what to think of himself, he was in two minds all the time. This, in itself a sign of immaturity, serves to warn us against his formal opinions. When, therefore, one appeals for evidence to Mark Twain's estimate of himself it is no conscious judgment of his career one has in mind but a far more trustworthy judgment, the judgment of his unconscious self. This he revealed unawares in all sorts of ways. . . .

Mark Twain was a megalomaniac; only a megalomaniac could have advertised, as he did, for post-mortem obituaries of himself. But does that sort of megalomania express a genuine self-confidence? Does it not suggest rather a profound, uneasy desire for corroboration? Of this the famous episode of his Oxford degree is the most striking symbol. "Although I wouldn't cross an ocean again for the price of the ship that carried me, I am glad to do it," he wrote, "for an Oxford degree." Many American writers have won that honor; it is, in fact, almost a routine incident in a distinguished career. In the case of Mark Twain it became a historic event: it was for him, plainly, of an exceptional significance, and all his love for gorgeous trappings could never account for the delight he had in that doctor's gown—"I would dress that way all the time, if I dared," he told Mr. Paine—which became for him a permanent robe of ceremony. And Mark Twain at seventy-two, one of the most celebrated men in the world, could not have cared so much for it if it had been a vindication merely in the eyes of others. It must have served in some way also to vindicate him in his own eyes; he seized upon it as a sort of talisman, as a reassurance from what he considered the highest court of culture, that he really was one of the elect.

Yes, that naïve passion for the limelight, for "walking with kings" and hobnobbing with job lots of celebrities, that "revelling," as Mr. Paine calls it, "in the universal tribute"—what was its root if not a deep sense of insecurity, a desire for approval both in his own eyes and in the eyes of all the world? During those later years in New York, when he had become so much the professional celebrity, he always timed his Sunday morning walks on Fifth Avenue for about the hour when the churches were out. Mr. Paine tells how, on the first Sunday morning, he thoughtlessly suggested that they should turn away at Fifty-ninth Street in order to avoid the throng and that Clemens quietly remarked, "I like the throng." "So," says Mr. Paine, "we rested in the Plaza Hotel until the appointed hour. . . . We left the Plaza Hotel and presently were amid the throng of outpouring congregations. Of course he was the object on which every passing eye turned, the presence to which every hat was lifted. I realized that this open and eagerly paid homage of the multitude was still dear to him, not in any small and petty way, but as the tribute of a nation." And must not the desire for approval and corroboration, the sense of insecurity, have been very deep in a quick-tempered, satirical democrat like Mark Twain, when he permitted his associates to call him, as Mr. Paine says they did, "the King"? Actual kings were with him nothing less than an obsession: kings, empresses, princes, archduchesses—what a part they play in his biography! He is always dragging them in, into his stories, into his letters, writing about his dinners with them, and his calls upon them, and how friendly they are, and what gorgeous funerals they have. And as with kings, so also with great men, or men who were considered great, or men who were merely notorious. He makes lists of those he has known, those he has spent evenings with—Mark Twain, to whom celebrity was the cheapest thing going! Is there not in all this the suggestion of an almost conscious weakness clutching at strength, the suggestion of some kind of failure that sets a premium upon almost any kind of success?

Turn from the man to the writer; we see again this same desire for approval, for corroboration. Mark Twain was supported by the sentiment of the majority, which was gospel to the old-fashioned Westerner; he had the golden opinion of Mr. Howells, in his eyes the arbiter of all the elegances; he had virtually the freedom of *The Atlantic Monthly*, and not only its freedom but a higher rate of payment than any other *Atlantic* contributor. Could any

American man of letters have had more reason to think well of himself? Observe what he thought. "I haven't as good an opinion of my work as you hold of it," he writes to Mr. Howells in 1887, "but I've always done what I could to secure and enlarge my good opinion of it. I've always said to myself, 'Everybody reads it and that's something—it surely isn't pernicious, or the most acceptable people would get pretty tired of it.' And when a critic said by implication that it wasn't high and fine, through the remark, 'High and fine literature is wine,' I retorted (confidentially to myself), 'Yes, high and fine literature is wine, and mine is only water; but everybody likes water.'" That is frank enough; he is not always so. There is a note of unconscious guile, the guile of the peasant, of the sophisticated small boy, in the letter he wrote to Andrew Lang, beseeching a fair hearing in England for the "Connecticut Yankee." He rails against "the cultivated-class standard"; he half poses as an uplifter of the masses; then, with a touch of mock-noble indignation, he confesses to being a popular entertainer, fully convinced at least that there are two kinds of literature and that an author ought to be allowed to put upon his book an explanatory line: "This is written for the Head," or "This is written for the Belly or the Members." No plea more grotesque or more pathetic was ever written by a man with a great reputation to support. It shows that Mark Twain was completely ignorant of literary values: had he not wished upon literature, as it were, a separation between the "Head" and the "Belly" which, as we shall see, had simply taken place in himself? Out of his own darkness he begs for the word of salvation from one who he thinks can bestow it.

Mark Twain, in short, knew very well—for I think these illustrations prove it—that there was something decidedly different between himself and a great writer. In that undifferentiated mob of celebrities, great, and less great, and far from great, amid which he moved for a generation, he was a favored equal. But in the intimate presence of some isolated greatness he reverted to the primitive reverence of the candidate for the mystagogue. Was it Emerson? He ceased to be a fellow writer, he became one of the devout Yankee multitude. Was it Browning? He forgot the man he had so cordially known in the poet whom he studied for a time with the naïve self-abasement of a neophyte. . . .

I think we are in a position now to understand that boundless comic impudence of Mark Twain's, that comic impudence which led him to propose to Edwin Booth in 1873 a new character for "Hamlet," which led him to telegraph to W. T. Stead: "The Czar is ready to disarm. I am ready to disarm. Collect the others; it should not be much of a task now"; which led him, at the outset of his career, to propose the conundrum, "Why am I like the

Pacific Ocean?" and to answer it thus: "I don't know. I was just asking for information." Tempting Providence, was he not, this child of good fortune? Literally, yes; he was trying out the fates. If he had not had a certain sense of colossal force, it would never have occurred to him, however humorously, to place himself on an equality with Shakespeare, to compare his power with that of the Czar and his magnitude with that of the Pacific Ocean. But, on the other hand, it would never have occurred to him to make these comparisons if he had felt himself in possession, in control, of that force. Men who are not only great in energy but masters of themselves let their work speak for them; men who are not masters of themselves, whose energy, however great, is not, so to speak, at the disposal of their own spirits, are driven, as we see Mark Twain perpetually driven, to seek corroboration from without; for his inner self, at these moments, wished to be assured that he really was great and powerful like the Pacific and Shakespeare and the Czar. He resembled those young boys who have inherited great fortunes which they own but cannot command; the power is theirs and yet they are not in control of it; consequently, in order to reassure themselves, they are always "showing off." We are not mistaken, therefore, in feeling that in this comic impudence Mark Twain actually was interrogating destiny, feeling out his public, in other words, which had in its hands the disposal of that ebullient energy of his, an energy that he could not measure, could not estimate, that seemed to him simply of an indeterminable, untestable, and above all uncontrollable abundance. . . .

We are in possession now, it seems to me, of the secret of Mark Twain's mechanistic philosophy, the philosophy of that little book which he called his "Bible," "What Is Man?" He was extremely proud of the structure of logic he had built up on the thesis that man is a machine, "moved, directed, commanded by *exterior* influences, *solely*," that he is "a chameleon, who takes the color of his place of resort," that he is "a mere coffee-mill," which is permitted neither "to supply the coffee nor turn the crank." He confesses to a sort of proprietary interest and pleasure in the validity of that notion. "Having found the Truth," he says, "preceiving that beyond question man has but one moving impulse—the contenting of his own spirit—and is merely a machine and entitled to no personal merit for what he does, it is not humanly possible for me to seek further. The rest of my days will be spent in patching and painting and puttying and calking my priceless possession and in looking the other way when an imploring argument or a damaging fact approaches." You see how it pleases him, how much it means to him, that final "Truth," how he clings to it with a sort of defiant insolence against the "imploring argument," the "damaging fact"? "Man originates nothing," he says, "not even a thought.... Shakespeare could not create. He was a machine, and machines do not create." Faith never gave the believer more comfort than this philosophy gave Mark Twain.

But is it possible for a creative mind to find "contentment" in denying the possibility of creation? And why should any one find pride and satisfaction in the belief that man is wholly irresponsible, in the denial of "free will"? One remembers the fable of the fox and the sour grapes, one remembers all those forlorn and tragic souls who find comfort in saying that love exists nowhere in the world because they themselves have missed it. Certainly it could not have afforded Mark Twain any pleasure to feel that he was "entitled to no personal merit" for what he had done, for what he had achieved in life; the pleasure he felt sprang from the relief his theory afforded him, the relief of feeling that he was not responsible for what he had failed to achieve—namely, his proper development as an artist. He says aloud, "Shakespeare could not create," and his inner self adds, "How in the world, then, could I have done so?" He denies "free will" because the creative life is the very embodiment of it—the emergence, that is to say, the activity in a man of one central, dominant, integrating principle that turns the world he confronts into a mere instrument for the registration of his own preferences. There is but one interpretation, consequently, which we can put upon Mark Twain's delight in the conception of man as an irresponsible machine: it brought him comfort to feel that if he was, as he said, a "sewing-machine," it was the doing of destiny, and that nothing he could have done himself would have enabled him to "turn out Gobelins."

From his philosophy alone, therefore, we can see that Mark Twain was a frustrated spirit, a victim of arrested development, and beyond this fact, as we know from innumerable instances the psychologists have placed before us, we need not look for an explanation of the chagrin of his old age. He had been balked, he had been divided, he had even been turned, as we shall see, against himself; the poet, the artist in him, consequently, had withered into the cynic and the whole man had become a spiritual valetudinarian.

But this is a long story: to trace it we shall have to glance not only at Mark Twain's life and work, but also at the epoch and the society in which he lived. . . .

One, and one only, an influence tragic in its ultimate consequences, the influence of Mark Twain's mother. That poor, taciturn, sunstruck failure, John Clemens, was a mere pathetic shadow beside the woman whose portrait Mark Twain has drawn for us in the Aunt Polly of "Tom Sawyer." She who was regarded as a "character" by all the town, who was said to have been "the handsomest girl and the wittiest, as well as the best dancer, in all Kentucky," who was still able to dance at 80, and lived to be 87, who belonged, in short, to "the long-lived, energetic side of the house," directed her children, we are told—and we can believe it—"with considerable firmness." And what was the inevitable relationship between her and this little boy? "She had a weakness," says Mr. Paine, "for the child that demanded most of her mother's care. . . . All were tractable and growing in grace but little Sam . . . a delicate little lad to be worried over, mothered, or spanked and put to bed." In later life, "you gave me more uneasiness than any child I had," she told him. In fact, she was always scolding him, comforting him, forgiving him, punishing and pleading with him, fixing her attention upon him, exercising her emotions about him, impressing it upon his mind for all time, as we shall come to see that woman is the inevitable seat of authority and the fount of wisdom.

We know that such excessive influences are apt to deflect the growth of any spirit. Men are like planets in this, that for them to sail clear in their own orbits the forces of gravity have to be disposed with a certain balance on all sides: how often, when the father counts for nothing, a child becomes the satellite of its mother, especially when that mother's love has not found its normal expression in her own youth! We have seen that Mark Twain's mother did not love her husband; that her capacity for love, however, was very great is proved by the singular story revealed in one of Mark Twain's letters: more than sixty years after she had quarreled with that young Lexington doctor, and when her husband had long been dead, she, a woman of eighty or more, took a railway journey to a distant city where there was an Old Settlers' convention because among the names of those who were to attend it she had noticed the name of the lover of her youth. "Who could have imagined such a heart-break as that?" said Mr. Howells, when he heard the story. "Yet it went along with the fulfillment of every-day duty and made no more noise than a grave under foot." It made no noise, but it undoubtedly had a prodigious effect upon Mark Twain's life. When an affection as intense as that is balked in its direct path and repressed it usually, as we know, finds an indirect outlet; and it is plain that the woman as well as the mother expressed itself in the passionate attachment of Jane Clemens to her son. We shall note many consequences of this fact as we go on with our story. We can say at least at this point that Mark Twain was, quite definitely, in his mother's leading-strings.

What was the inevitable result? I have said, not, I hope, with too much presumption, that Mark Twain had already shown himself the born, predestined artist, that his whole nature manifested what is called a tendency toward the creative life. For that tendency to become conscious, to become purposive, two things were necessary: it must be able, in the first place, to assert itself and in the second place to embody itself in a vocation; to realize itself and then to educate itself, to realize itself in educating itself. And, as we know, the influences of early childhood are, in these matters, vitally important. If Jane Clemens had been a woman of wide experience and independent mind, in proportion to the strength of her character, Mark Twain's career might have been wholly different. Had she been catholic in her sympathies, in her understanding of life, then, no matter how more than maternal her attachment to her son was, she might have placed before him and encouraged him to pursue interests and activities amid which he could eventually have recovered his balance, reduced the filial bond to its normal measure and stood on his own feet. But that is to wish for a type of woman our old pioneer society could never have produced. We are told that the Aunt Polly of "Tom Sawyer" is a speaking portrait of Jane Clemens, and Aunt Polly, as we know, was the symbol of all the taboos. The stronger her will was, the more comprehensive were her repressions, the more certainly she became the inflexible guardian of tradition in a social régime where tradition was inalterably opposed to every sort of personal deviation from the accepted type. "In their remoteness from the political centers of the young Republic," says Mr. Howells, in "The Leatherwood God," of these old Middle Western settlements, "they seldom spoke of the civic questions stirring the towns of the East; the commercial and industrial problems which vex modern society were unknown to them. Religion was their chief interest." And in the slave States it was not the abolitionist alone whose name was held, as Mr. Paine says, "in horror," but every one who had the audacity to think differently from his neighbors. Jane Clemens, in short, was the embodiment of that old-fashioned, cast-iron Calvinism which had proved so favorable to the life of enterprising action but which perceived the scent of the devil in any least expression of what is now known as the creative impulse. She had a kind heart, she was always repenting and softening and forgiving; it is said that whenever she had to drown kittens, she warmed the water first. But this, without opening any channel in a contrary direction, only sealed her authority! She won her points as much by kindness as by law. Besides, tradition spoke first in her mind; her hand was quicker than her heart; in action she was the madonna of the hairbrush. And what, specifically, was it that she punished? Those furtive dealings of Huck and Tom with whitewash and piracy were nothing in the world—and that is why all the world loves them—but the first stirrings of the normal aesthetic sense, the first stirrings of individuality.

Already I think we divine what was bound to happen in the soul of Mark Twain. The story of "Huckleberry Finn" turns, as we remember, upon a conflict: "the author," says Mr. Paine, "makes Huck's struggle a psychological one between conscience and the law, on one side, and sympathy on the other." In the famous episode of Nigger Jim, "sympathy," the cause of individual freedom, wins. Years later, in "The Mysterious Stranger," Mark Twain presented the parallel situation we noted in the last chapter: "we found," says the boy who tells that story, "that we were not manly enough nor brave enough to do a generous action when there was a chance that it could get us into trouble." Conscience and the law, we see, had long since prevailed in the spirit of Mark Twain, but what is the conscience of a boy who checks a humane impulse but "boy terror," as Mr. Paine calls it, an instinctive fear of custom, of tribal authority? The conflict in "Huckleberry Finn" is simply the conflict of Mark Twain's own childhood. He solved it successfully, he fulfilled his desire, in the book, as an author can. In actual life he did not solve it at all; he surrendered. . . .

But the circumstances that surrounded Mark Twain were not merely passively unfavorable to his own self-discovery; they were actively, overwhelmingly unfavorable. He was in his mother's leading-strings, and in his mother's eyes any sort of personal self-assertion in choices, preferences, impulses was, literally, sinful. Thus the whole weight of the Calvinistic tradition was concentrated against him at his most vulnerable point. His mother, whom he could not gainsay, was unconsciously but inflexibly set against his genius; and destiny, which always fights on the side of the heaviest artillery, delivered, in his twelfth year, a stroke that sealed her victory.

Mark Twain's father died. Let Mr. Paine picture the scene:

"The boy Sam was fairly broken down. Remorse, which always dealt with him unsparingly, laid a heavy hand on him now. Wildness, disobedience, indifference to his father's wishes, all were remembered; a hundred things, in themselves trifling, became ghastly and heartwringing in the knowledge that they could never be undone. Seeing his grief, his mother took him by the hand and led him into the room where his father lay. 'It is all right, Sammy,' she said. 'What's done is done, and it does not matter to him any more; but here by the side of him now I want you to promise me——.' He turned, his eyes streaming with tears, and flung himself into her arms. 'I will promise anything,' he sobbed, 'if you won't make me go to school! Anything!' His mother held him for a moment, thinking, then she said: 'No, Sammy, you need not go to school any more. Only promise me to be a better boy. Promise not to break my heart.' So he promised her to be a faithful and industrious man, and upright, like his father. His mother was satisfied with that. The sense of honor and justice was already strong within him. To him a promise was a serious matter at any time; made under conditions like these it would be held sacred. That night—it was after the funeral—his tendency to somnambulism manifested itself. His mother and sister, who were sleeping together, saw the door open and a form in white enter. Naturally nervous at such a time, and living in a day of almost universal superstition, they were terrified and covered their heads. Presently a hand was laid on the coverlet, first at the foot, then at the head of the bed. A thought struck Mrs. Clemens: 'Sam!' she said. He answered, but he was sound asleep and fell to the floor. He had risen and thrown a sheet around him in his dreams. He walked in his sleep several nights in succession after that. Then he slept more soundly."

Who is sufficiently the master of signs and portents to read this terrible episode aright? One thing, however, we feel with irresistible certitude, that Mark Twain's fate was once for all decided there. That hour by his father's corpse, that solemn oath, that walking in his sleep—we must hazard some interpretation of it all, and I think we are justified in hazarding as most likely that which explains the most numerous and the most significant phenomena of his later life.

To a hypersensitive child such as Mark Twain was at eleven that ceremonious confrontation with his father's corpse must, in the first place, have brought a profound nervous shock. Already, we are told, he was "broken down" by his father's death; remorse had "laid a heavy hand on him." But what was this remorse; what had he done for grief or shame? "A hundred things in themselves trifling," which had offended, in reality, not his father's heart but his father's will as a conventional citizen with a natural desire to raise up a family in his own likeness. Feeble, frantic, furtive little feelings out of this moody child, the first wavering steps of the soul, that is what they have really been, these peccadillos, the dawn of the artist. And the formidable promptings of love tell him that they are sin! He is broken down indeed; all those crystalline fragments of individuality, still so tiny and so fragile, are suddenly shattered; his nature, wrought upon by the tense heat of that hour, has become again like soft wax. And his mother stamps there, with awful ceremony, the composite image of her own meager traditions. He is to go forth the Good Boy by *force majeure*, he is to become such a man as his father would have approved of, he is to retrieve his father's failure, to recover the lost gentility of a family that had once been proud, to realize that "mirage of wealth" that had ever hung before his father's eyes. And to do so he is not to quarrel heedlessly with his bread and butter, he is to keep strictly within the code, to remember the maxims of Ben Franklin, to respect all the prejudices and all the conventions; above all, he is not to be drawn aside into any fanciful orbit of his own! . . . Hide your faces, Huck and Tom! Put away childish things, Sam Clemens; go forth into the world, but remain always a child, your mother's child! In a day to come you will write to one of your friends, "We have no *real* morals, but only artificial ones—morals created and preserved by the forced suppression of natural and healthy instincts." Never mind that now; your mother imagines her heart is in the balance—will you break it? . . . Will you promise? . . . And the little boy, in the terror of that presence, sobs: "Anything!"

"There is in every man," said Sainte-Beuve, "a poet who dies young." In truth, the poet does not die; he falls into a fitful trance. It is perfectly evident what happened to Mark Twain at this moment: he became, and his immediate manifestation of somnambulism is the proof of it, a dual personality. If I were sufficiently hardy, as I am not, I should say that that little sleepwalker who appeared at Jane Clemens's bedside on the night of her husband's funeral was the spirit of Tom Sawyer, come to demand again the possession of his own soul, to revoke that ruthless promise he had given. He came for several nights, and then, we are told, the little boy slept more soundly, a sign, one might say, if one were a fortune-teller, that he had grown accustomed to the new and difficult rôle of being two people at once! The subject of dual personality was always, as we shall see, an obsession with Mark Twain; he who seemed to his friends such a natural-born actor, who was, in childhood, susceptible not only to somnambulism but to mesmeric control, had shown from the outset a distinct tendency toward what is called dissociation of consciousness. His "wish" to be an artist, which has been so frowned upon and has encountered such an insurmountable obstacle in the disapproval of his mother, is now repressed, more or less definitely, and another wish, that of winning approval, which inclines him to conform with public opinion, has supplanted it. The individual, in short, has given way to the type. The struggle between these two selves, these two tendencies, these two wishes or groups of wishes, will continue throughout Mark Twain's life, and the poet, the artist, the individual, will make a brave effort to survive. From the death of his father onward, however, his will is definitely enlisted on the side opposed to his essential instinct. . . .

Now, whatever was true of America during the Gilded Age was doubly true of Nevada, where, as Mr. Paine says, "all human beings, regardless of previous affiliations and convictions, were flung into the common fusing-pot and recast into the general mold of pioneer." Life in the gold-fields was, in fact, an infinite intensification of pioneering, it was a sort of furnace in which all the elements of human nature were transmuted into a single white flame, an incandescence of the passion of avarice. If we are to accept Mark Twain's description in "Roughing It" of the "flush times" in Virginia City, we can see that the spirit of the artist had about as good a chance of survival and development there as a butterfly in a blazing chimney: "Virginia had grown to be the 'livest' town, for its age and population, that America had ever produced. The side-walks swarmed with people. The streets themselves were just as crowded with quartz-wagons, freight-teams, and other vehicles. . . . Joy sat on every countenance, and there was a glad, almost fierce, intensity in every eye that told of the money-getting schemes that were seething in every brain and the high hope that held sway in every heart. Money was as plenty as dust. . . . There were military companies, fire companies, brass bands, banks, hotels, theaters, 'hurdy-gurdy houses,' wide-open gambling palaces, political pow-wows, civic processions, street-fights, murders, inquests, riots, a whiskey mill every fifteen steps, a dozen breweries, and half a dozen jails and station-houses in full operation, and some talk of building a church. The 'flush times' were in magnificent flower! . . . The great 'Comstock lode' stretched its opulent length straight through the town from North to South, and every mine on it was in diligent process of development."

This was the spirit of Mark Twain's new environment, a spirit inflexibly opposed, as we can see, to the development of individuality. Had Mark Twain been free, it might have been a matter of indifference to him; he might have gone his own way and amused himself with the astonishing spectacle of the gold-fields and then taken himself off again. But Mark Twain was not free; he was, on the contrary, bound in such a way that, far from being able to stand aloof from his environment, he had to make terms with it. For what obligations had he not incurred! To become such a conventional citizen as his father would have approved of, to make money and restore the fallen fortunes of his family—that old pledge was fixed in the back of his mind, where it had been confirmed by his failure to discover and assert any independent principle of his own. Furthermore, he now had his own financial record to live up to. It was the lucrativeness and prestige of the pilot's career that had originally enabled him to adopt it, and we know what pride he had had in his "great triumph," in being a somebody at last: his brother Orion had considered it a "disgrace" to descend to the trade of printing: they were gentleman's sons, these Clemenses! He had had, in short, a chance to exercise and educate his creative instinct while at the same time doing what was expected of him. And now, when he had lost his guiding-line, more was expected of him than ever! His salary, at twenty-three, on the river, had been $250 a month, a vastly greater income certainly than his father had ever earned: at once and of course, we are told, he had become, owing to this fact, the head of the Clemens family. "His brother Orion was ten years older," says Mr. Paine, "but he had not the gift of success. By common consent, the young brother assumed permanently the position of family counselor and financier." These circumstances, I say, compelled Mark Twain to make terms with public opinion. He could not fall too far behind the financial pace his piloting life had set for him, he was bound to recover the prestige that had been his and to shine once more as a conspicuous and important personage, he had to "make good" again, quickly and spectacularly: that was a duty which had also become a craving. How strongly he felt it we can see from one of his Nevada letters in which he declares earnestly that he will never look upon his mother's face again, or his sister's, or get married, or revisit the "Banner State," until he is a rich man. . . .

It is a significant fact, under these circumstances, that Mark Twain failed as a miner. He had good luck, now and then, enough to make wealth a tantalizing possibility. He describes, though we are told with exaggeration, how he was once "a millionaire for ten days." But he failed as a miner precisely because he was unable to bring to his new work any of those qualities that had made him so successful as a pilot. Concentration, perseverance, above all, judgment—these were the qualities that former career had given birth to. The craftsman's life had instantly matured him; the life of sheer exploitation, in spite of his sense of duty, in spite of the incentives of his environment, in spite of the prospects of wealth and prestige it offered him, could not fuse his spirit at all. It only made him frantic and lax by turns. He went off prospecting, and with what result? "One week of this satisfied me," he said. "I resigned." Then he flung himself into quartz-mining. "The letters which went from the Aurora miner to Orion," we are told, "are humanly documentary. They are likely to be staccato in their movement; they show nervous haste in their composition, eagerness, and suppressed excitement; they are not always coherent; they are seldom humorous, except in a savage way; they are often profane; they are likely to be violent. Even the handwriting has a terse look; the flourish of youth has gone out of it. Altogether they reveal the tense anxiety of the gambling mania." Then the pendulum swings to the other extreme: he is utterly disgusted and has but one wish, to give up everything and go away. "If Sam had got that pocket," said one of his comrades, of his last exploit, "he would have remained a pocket-miner to the end of his days"; but he would have got it if he had been able to bring to the situation any of the qualities he would have brought to a critical situation on the Mississippi. It is quite plain that he failed simply because he did not care enough about money, merely as money, to succeed. His real self, the artist, in short, could not develop, and yet, repressed as it was, it prevented him from becoming whole-heartedly anything else. We shall see this exhibited throughout the whole of Mark Twain's business life.

So here was Mark Twain face to face with a dilemma. His unconscious desire was to be an artist, but this implied an assertion of individuality that was a sin in the eyes of his mother and a shame in the eyes of society. On the other hand, society and his mother wanted him to be a business man, and for this he could not summon up the necessary powers in himself. The eternal dilemma of every American writer! It was the dilemma which, as we shall see in the end, Mark Twain solved by becoming a humorist. . . .

[I]n becoming a humorist he felt that in some way he was selling rather than fulfilling his own soul.

Why this was so we cannot consider at present: the time has not yet come to discuss the psychogenesis and the significance of Mark Twain's humor. But that it was so we have ample evidence. Mr. Cable tells how, to his amazement, once, when he and Clemens were giving a public reading together, the latter, whom he had supposed happy and satisfied with his triumphant success, turned to him on their way back to the hotel and said with a groan, "Oh, Cable, I am demeaning myself—I am allowing myself to be a mere buffoon. It's ghastly. I can't endure it any longer." And all the next day, Mr. Cable says, he sedulously applied himself, in spite of the immense applause that had greeted him, to choosing selections for his next reading which would be justified not only as humor but as literature and art. This is only one of many instances of Mark Twain's lifelong revolt against a rôle which he apparently felt had been thrust upon him. It is enough to corroborate all our intuitions regarding the reluctance with which he accepted it. . . .

One further, final proof. In 1865 "The Jumping Frog" was published in New York, where, according to one of the California correspondents, it was "voted the best thing of the day." How did Clemens, who was still in the West, receive the news of his success? "The telegraph," says Mr. Paine, "did not carry such news in those days, and it took a good while for the echo of his victory to travel to the Coast. When at last a lagging word of it did arrive, it would seem to have brought disappointment, rather than exaltation, to the author. Even Artemus Ward's opinion of the story had not increased Mark Twain's regard for it as literature. That it had struck the popular note meant, as he believed, failure for his more highly regarded work. In a letter written January 20, 1866, he says these things for himself: 'I do not know what to write; my life is so uneventful. I wish I was back there piloting up and down the river again. Verily, all is vanity and little worth—save piloting. To think that, after writing many an article a man might be excused for thinking tolerably good, those New York people should single out a villainous backwoods sketch to compliment me on!—"Jim Smiley and His Jumping Frog"—a squib which would never have been written but to please Artemus Ward.'" He had thought so little of that story indeed that he had not even offered it to *The Californian*, the magazine to which he was a staff contributor: "he did not," says Mr. Paine, "regard it highly as literary material." We can see in that letter the bitter prompting of his creative instinct, in rebellion against the course he has drifted into; we can see how his acquisitive instinct, on the other hand, forbids him to gainsay the success he has achieved. "I am in for it," he writes to his brother. "I must go on chasing [phantoms] until I marry, *then* I am done with literature and all other bosh—that is, literature wherewith to please the general public. I shall write to please myself then." Marriage, he says to himself, is going to liberate him, this poor, ingenuous being!—this divided soul who has never been able to find any other criterion than that of an environment which knows no criterion but success. His destiny, meanwhile, has passed out of his own hands: that is the significance of the "victory" of "The Jumping Frog." As Mr. Paine says, with terrible, unconscious irony: "The stone rejected by the builder was made the cornerstone of his literary edifice."

So much for Mark Twain's motives in becoming a humorist. He had adopted this rôle unwillingly, as a compromise, at the expense of his artistic self-respect, because it afforded the only available means of satisfying that other instinct which, in the unconsciousness of his creative instinct, had become dominant in him, the gregarious, acquisitive instinct of the success-loving pioneer. . . .

When he adopted humor as a profession, therefore, he was falling back upon a line he had previously rejected, and this implied that he had ceased to be the master of his own destiny. In short, the artist in him having failed to take the helm, he had become a journalist, and his career was now at the mercy of circumstance. . . .

To win fame and fortune, meanwhile, as his parents had wished him to do, had now become his dominant desire, and almost every one he met knew more about the art of success than he did. He had to "make good," but in order to do so he had to subject himself to those who knew the ropes. Consequently, whoever excelled him in skill, in manners, in prestige, stood to him *in loco parentis*; and, to complete the ironic circle, he was endlessly grateful to those who led him about, like a Savoyard bear, because he felt, as was indeed true, that it was to them he owed the success he had attained. This is the real meaning of Mr. Paine's remark: "It was always Mark Twain's habit to rely on somebody."

The list of those to whom he deferred is a long and varied one. In later years, "he did not always consult his financial adviser, Mr. Rogers," we are told, "any more than he always consulted his spiritual adviser Twichell, or his literary adviser Howells, when he intended to commit heresies in their respective provinces." But these were the exceptions that proved the rule: in general, Mark Twain abandoned himself to the will and word of those who had won his allegiance. There was Artemus Ward, there was Anson Burlingame, there was Henry Ward Beecher: what they told him, and how he obeyed, we have just seen. There was Bret Harte, who, he said, "trimmed and trained and schooled me patiently until he changed me from an awkward utterer of coarse grotesquenesses to a writer of paragraphs and chapters that have found a certain favor in the eyes of even some of the very decentest people in the land." Above all, and among many others, there was Mr. Howells, who, from the first moment, "won his absolute and unvarying confidence in all literary affairs": indeed, adds Mr. Paine, "in matters pertaining to literature and to literary people in general he laid his burden on William Dean Howells from that day." It was to Howells that he said, apropos of "The Innocents Abroad": "When I read that review of yours I felt like the woman who was so glad her baby had come white." It has become the custom with a certain school of critics to assert that Mark Twain's spiritual rights were in some way infringed by his associates and especially by his wife, the evident fact being that he craved authority with all the self-protective instinct of the child who has not learned safely to go his own way and feels himself surrounded by pitfalls. "There has always been somebody in authority over my manuscript and privileged to improve it," he wrote in 1900, with a touch of angry chagrin, to Mr. S. S. McClure. But the privilege had always emanated from Mark Twain himself.

In short, having lost the thread of his life and committed himself to the pursuit of prestige, Mark Twain had to adapt himself to the prevailing point of view of American society. "The middle class," says a contemporary English writer, Mr. R. H. Gretton, "is that portion of the community to which money is the primary condition and the primary instrument of life"; if that is true, we can understand why Matthew Arnold observed that the whole American population of his time belonged to the middle class. When, accordingly, Mark Twain accepted the spiritual rule of the majority, he found himself leading, to use an expression of bridge-players, from his weakest suit. It was not as a young writer capable of great artistic achievements that he was valued now, but as a promising money-maker capable of becoming a plutocrat. And meanwhile, instead of being an interesting individual, he was a social inferior. His uncouth habits, his lack of education, his outlandish manners and appearance, his very picturesqueness—everything that made foreigners delight in him, all these raw materials of personality that would have fallen into their natural place if he had been able to consummate his freedom as an artist, were mill-stones about the neck of a young man whose salvation depended upon his winning the approval of bourgeois society. His "outrageousness," as Mr. Howells calls it, had ceased to be the sign of some priceless, unformulated force; it had become a disadvantage, a disability, a mere outrageousness! That gift of humor was a goldmine—so much every one saw: Mark Twain was evidently cut out for success. But he had a lot of things to live down first! He was, in a word, a "roughneck" from the West, on probation; and if he wanted to get on, it was understood that he had to qualify. We cannot properly grasp the significance of Mark Twain's marriage unless we realize that he had been manoeuvered into the rôle of a candidate for gentility.

But, here, in order to go forward, we shall have to go back. What had been Mark Twain's original, unconscious motive in surrendering his creative life? To fulfill the oath he had taken so solemnly at his dead father's side; he had sworn to "make good" in order to please his mother. In short, when the artist in him had abdicated, the family man, in whom personal and domestic interests and relations and loyalties take precedence of all others, had come to the front. His home had ever been the hub of Mark Twain's universe: "deep down," says Mr. Paine, of the days of his first triumphs in Nevada, "he was lonely and homesick; he was always so away from his own kindred." And at thirty-two, able to go back to his mother "without shame," having at last retrieved his failure as a miner, he had renewed the peculiar filial bond which had remained precisely that of his infancy. Jane Clemens was sixty-four at this time, we are told, "but as keen and vigorous as ever—proud (even if somewhat critical) of this handsome, brilliant man of new name and fame who had been her mischievous, wayward boy. She petted him, joked with him, scolded him, and inquired searchingly into his morals and habits. In turn, he petted, comforted and teased her. She decided that he was the same Sam, and always would be—a true prophecy." It was indeed so true that Mark Twain, who required authority as much as he required affection, could not fail now to seek in the other sex some one who would take his mother's place. All his life, as we know, he had to be mothered by somebody, and he transferred this filial relation to at least one other person before it found its bourn first in his wife and afterward in his daughters. This was "Mother" Fairbanks of the *Quaker City* party, who had, we are told, so large an influence on the tone and character of those travel letters which established his fame. "She sewed my buttons on," he wrote—he was thirty-two at the time—"kept my clothing in presentable form, fed me on Egyptian jam (when I behaved), lectured me awfully ... and cured me of several bad habits." It was only natural, therefore, that he should have accepted the rule of his wife "implicitly," that he should have "gloried," as Mr. Howells says, in his subjection to her. "After my marriage," he told Professor Henderson, "she edited everything I wrote. And what is more—she not only edited my works—she edited me!" What, indeed, were Mark Twain's works in the totality of that relationship? What, for that matter, was Olivia Clemens? She was more than a person, she was a symbol. ...

"Eve's Diary," written by Mark Twain shortly after his wife's death, is said to figure their relationship: Adam there is the hewer of wood and the drawer of water, a sort of Caliban, and Eve the arbiter in all matters of civilization. "It has low tastes," says Beauty of this Beast. "Some instinct tells me that eternal vigilance is the price of supremacy." And how Mrs. Clemens exercised it! There is something for the gods to bewail in the sight of that shorn Samson led about by a little child who, in the profound somnolence of her spirit, was merely going through the motions of an inherited domestic piety. "Her life had been circumscribed," says Mr. Paine, "her experiences of a simple sort"; but she did not hesitate to undertake "the work of polishing and purifying her life companion. She had no wish to destroy his personality, to make him over, but only to preserve his best, and she set about it in the right way—gently, and with a tender gratitude in each achievement." To preserve his best! "She sensed his heresy toward the conventions and forms which had been her gospel; his bantering, indifferent attitude toward life—to her always so serious and sacred; she suspected that he even might have unorthodox views on matters of religion." That was before they were married: afterward, "concerning his religious observances her task in the beginning was easy enough. Clemens had not at that time formulated any particular doctrines of his own. ... It took very little persuasion on his wife's part to establish family prayers in their home, grace before meals, and the morning reading of a Bible chapter." Thus was reëstablished over him that old Calvinistic spell of his mother's, against which he had so vainly revolted as a child: preserving his "best," as we can see, meant preserving what fitted into the scheme of a good husband, a kind father and a sagacious man of business after the order of the Jervis Langdons of this world, for Olivia Clemens had never known any other sort of hero. "In time," says Mr. Paine, with a terrible unconscious irony, "she saw more clearly with his vision, but this was long after, when she had lived more with the world, had become more familiar with its larger needs, and the proportions of created things." It was too late then; the mischief had long been done. Mark Twain frightened his wife and shocked her, and she prevailed over him by an almost deliberate reliance upon that weakness to which he, the chivalrous Southerner—the born cavalier, in reality—could not fail to respond. Why did she habitually call him "Youth"? Was it not from an instinctive sense that her power lay in keeping him a child, in asserting the maternal attitude which he could never resist? He had indeed found a second mother now, and he "not only accepted her rule implicitly," as Mr. Howells says, "but he rejoiced, he gloried in it." He teased her, he occasionally enjoyed "shivering" her "exquisite sense of decorum"; but he, who could not trust his own judgment and to whom, consequently, one taboo was as reasonable as another, submitted to all her taboos as a matter of course. "I would quit wearing socks," he said, "if she thought them immoral." . . .

For what sort of taste was it that Mark Twain had to satisfy? Hardly a taste for the frank, the free, the animated, the expressive! The criticism he received was purely negative. We are told that Mrs. Clemens and her friends read Meredith "with reverential appreciation," that they formed a circle of "devout listeners" when Mark Twain himself used to read Browning aloud in Hartford. Profane art, the mature expression of life, in short, was outside Mrs. Clemens's circle of ideas; she could not breathe in that atmosphere with any comfort; her instinctive notion of literature was of something that is read at the fireside, out loud, under the lamp, a family institution, vaguely associated with the Bible and a father tempering the wind of King James's English to the sensitive ears and blushing cheek of the youngest daughter. Her taste, in a word, was quite infantile. "Mrs. Clemens says my version of the blindfold novelette, 'A Murder and a Marriage,' is 'good.' Pretty strong language for her," writes Mark Twain in 1876; and we know that when he was at work on "Huckleberry Finn" and "The Prince and the Pauper," she so greatly preferred the latter that Mark Twain really felt it was rather discreditable of him to pay any attention to "Huckleberry Finn" at all. "Imagine this fact," he wrote to Howells; "I have even fascinated Mrs. Clemens with this yarn for youth. My stuff generally gets considerable damning with faint praise out of her, but this time it is all the other way. She is become the horse-leech's daughter, and my mill doesn't grind fast enough to suit her. This is no mean triumph, my dear sir." And shortly afterward he wrote to his mother: "I have two stories, and by the verbal agreement they are both going into the same book; but Livy says they're not, and by George I she ought to know. She says they're going into separate books, and that one of them is going to be elegantly gotten up, even if the elegance of it eats up the publisher's profits and mine, too." It was "The Prince and the Pauper," a book that anybody might have written but whose romantic medievalism was equally respectable in its tendency and infantile in its appeal, that Mrs. Clemens felt so proud of: "nobody," adds Mr. Paine, "appears to have been especially concerned about Huck, except, possibly the publisher." Plainly it was very little encouragement that Mark Twain's natural genius received from these relentless critics to whom he stood in such subjection, to whom he offered such devotion; for Mr. Howells, too, if we are to accept Mr. Paine's record, seconded him as often as not in these innocuous, infantile ventures, abetting him in the production of "blindfold novelettes" and plays of an abysmal foolishness. As for Mark Twain's unique masterpiece, "Huckleberry Finn," "I like it only tolerably well, as far as I have got," he writes, "and may possibly pigeonhole or burn the MS. when it is done"; to which Mr. Paine adds: "It did not fascinate him as did the story of the wandering prince. He persevered only as the story moved him. Apparently, he had not yet acquired confidence or pride enough in poor Huck to exhibit him, even to friends." And quite naturally! His artistic self-respect had been so little developed, had been, in fact, so baffled and abashed by all this mauling and fumbling that he could take no pride in a book which was, precisely, the mirror of the unregenerate past he was doing his best to live down.

Behold Mrs. Clemens, then, in the rôle of critic and censor. A memorandum Mark Twain made at the time when he and she were going over the proofs of "Following the Equator" shows us how she conceived of her task. It is in the form of a dialogue between them:

> Page 1,020, 9th line from the top. I think some other word would be better than "stench." You have used that pretty often.
> But can't I get it in anywhere? You've knocked it out every time.
> Out it goes again. And yet "stench" is a noble, good word.
> Page 1,038. I hate to have your father pictured as lashing a slave boy.
> It's out, and my father is whitewashed.

Page 1,050, 2nd line from the bottom. Change "breech-clout."
It's a word that you love and I abominate. I would take that and
"offal" out of the language.

You are steadily weakening the English tongue, Livy.

We can see from this that to Mrs. Clemens virility was just as offensive
as profanity, that she had no sense of the difference between virility
and profanity and vulgarity, that she had, in short, no positive taste, no
independence of judgment at all. We can see also that she had no artistic ideal
for her husband, that she regarded his natural liking for bold and masculine
language, which was one of the outward signs of his latent greatness, merely
as a literary equivalent of bad manners, as something that endangered their
common prestige in the eyes of conventional public opinion. She condemned
his writings, says Mr. Paine, specifically, "for the offense they might give
in one way or another"; and that her sole object, however unconscious, in
doing this was to further him, not as an artist but as a popular success, and
especially as a candidate for gentility, is proved by the fact that she made him,
as we observe in the incident of his father and the slave boy, whitewash not
only himself but his family history also. And in all this Mr. Howells seconded
her. "It skirts a certain kind of fun which you can't afford to indulge in," he
reminds our shorn Samson in one of his letters; and again, "I'd have that
swearing out in an instant," the "swearing" in this case being what he himself
admits is "so exactly the thing Huck would say"—namely, "they comb me all
to hell." As for Mark Twain himself, he took it as meekly as a lamb. Mr. Paine
tells of a certain story he had written that was disrespectful to the Archbishop
of Canterbury. Forbidden to print it, he had "laboriously translated it into
German, with some idea of publishing it surreptitiously; but his conscience
had been too much for him. He had confessed, and even the German version
had been suppressed." And how does he accept Mr. Howells's injunction
about the "swearing" in "Huckleberry Finn"? "Mrs. Clemens received the
mail this morning," he writes, "and the next minute she lit into the study with
danger in her eye and this demand on her tongue, 'Where is the profanity
Mr. Howells speaks of?' Then I had to miserably confess that I had left it out
when reading the MS. to her. Nothing but almost inspired lying got me out
of this scrape with my scalp. Does your wife give you rats, like that, when you
go a little one-sided?"

They are very humiliating, these glimpses of great American writers
behind the scenes, given "rats" by their wives whenever they stray for an
instant from the strait and narrow path that leads to success. "Once," writes

Mr. Paine, "when Sarah Orne Jewett was with the party—in Rome—he remarked that if the old masters had labeled their fruit one wouldn't be so likely to mistake pears for turnips. 'Youth,' said Mrs. Clemens, gravely, 'if you do not care for these masterpieces yourself, you might at least consider the feelings of others'; and Miss Jewett, regarding him severely, added, in her quaint Yankee fashion: 'Now you've been spoke to!'" Very humiliating, very ignominious, I say, are these tableaux of "the Lincoln of our literature" in the posture of an ignorant little boy browbeaten by the dry sisters of Culture-Philistia. Very humiliating, and also very tragic! . . .

And is there any other explanation of his "Elizabethan breadth of parlance"? Mr. Howells confesses that he sometimes blushed over Mark Twain's letters, that there were some which, to the very day when he wrote his eulogy on his dead friend, he could not bear to reread. Perhaps if he had not so insisted, in former years, while going over Mark Twain's proofs, upon "having that swearing out in an instant," he would never have had cause to suffer from his having "loosed his bold fancy to stoop) on rank suggestion." Mark Twain's verbal Rabelaisianism was obviously the expression of that vital sap which, not having been permitted to inform his work, had been driven inward and left there to ferment. No wonder he was always indulging in orgies of forbidden words. Consider the famous book, "1601," that "fireside conversation in the time of Queen Elizabeth": is there any obsolete verbal indecency in the English language that Mark Twain has not painstakingly resurrected and assembled there? He, whose blood was in constant ferment and who could not contain within the narrow bonds that had been set for him the riotous exuberance of his nature, had to have an escape-valve, and he poured through it a fetid stream of meaningless obscenity—the waste of a priceless psychic material! Mr. Paine speaks of an address he made at a certain "Stomach Club" in Paris which has "obtained a wide celebrity among the clubs of the world, though no line of it, or even its title, has ever found its way into published literature." And who has not heard one or two of the innumerable Mark Twain anecdotes in the same vein that are current in every New York publishing house?

In all these ways, I say, these blind, indirect, extravagant, wasteful ways, the creative self in Mark Twain constantly strove to break through the censorship his own will had accepted, to cross the threshold of the unconscious. "A literary imp," says Mr. Paine, "was always lying in wait for Mark Twain, the imp of the burlesque, tempting him to do the *outré*, the outlandish, the shocking thing. It was this that Olivia Clemens had to labor hardest against." Well she labored, and well Mark Twain labored with her! It was the spirit of the artist, bent upon upsetting the whole apple-cart of bourgeois conventions. They could, and they did, keep it in check; they arrested it and manhandled it and thrust it back; they shamed it and heaped scorn upon it and prevented it from interfering too much with the respectable tenor of their daily search for prestige and success. They could baffle it and distort it and oblige it to assume ever more complicated and grotesque disguises in order to elude them, but they could not kill it. In ways of which they were unaware it escaped their vigilance and registered itself in a sort of cipher, for us of another generation who have eyes to read, upon the texture of Mark Twain's writings.

For is it not perfectly plain that Mark Twain's books are shot through with all sorts of unconscious revelations of this internal conflict? In the Freudian psychology the dream is an expression of a suppressed wish. In dreams we do what our inner selves desire to do but have been prevented from doing either by the exigencies of our daily routine, or by the obstacles of convention, or by some other form of censorship which has been imposed upon us, or which we ourselves, actuated by some contrary desire, have willingly accepted. Many other dreams, however, are not so simple: they are often incoherent, nonsensical, absurd. In such cases it is because two opposed wishes, neither of which is fully satisfied, have met one another and resulted in a "compromise"—a compromise that is often as apparently chaotic as the collision of two railway trains running at full speed. These mechanisms, the mechanisms of the "wish-fulfillment" and the "wish-conflict," are evident, as Freud has shown, in many of the phenomena of everyday life. Whenever, for any reason, the censorship is relaxed, the censor is off guard, whenever we are day-dreaming and give way to our idle thoughts, then the unconscious bestirs itself and rises to the surface, gives utterance to those embarrassing slips of the tongue, those "tender playfulnesses," that express our covert intentions, slays our adversaries, sets our fancies wandering in pursuit of all the ideals and all the satisfactions upon which our customary life has stamped its veto. In Mark Twain books, or rather in a certain group of them, his "fantasies" we can see this process at work. . . .

Just before Mark Twain's death, he recalled, says Mr. Paine, "one of his old subjects, Dual Personality, and discussed various instances that flitted through his mind—Jekyll and Hyde phases in literature and fact." One of his old subjects, Dual Personality! Could he ever have been aware of the extent to which his writings revealed that conflict in himself? Why was he so obsessed by journalistic facts like the Siamese Twins and the Tichborne case, with its theme of the lost heir and the usurper? Why is it that the idea of changelings in the cradle perpetually haunted his mind, as we can see from "Pudd'nhead Wilson" and "The Gilded Age" and the variation of it that constitutes "The Prince and the Pauper"? The prince who has submerged himself in the rôle of the beggar-boy—Mark Twain has drawn himself there, just as he has drawn himself in the "William Wilson" theme of "The Facts Concerning the Recent Carnival of Crime in Connecticut," where he ends by dramatically slaying the conscience that torments him. And as for that pair of incompatibles bound together in one flesh—the Extraordinary Twins, the "good" boy who has followed the injunctions of his mother and the "bad" boy of whom society disapproves—how many of Mark Twain's stories and anecdotes turn upon that same theme, that same juxtaposition!—does he not reveal there, in all its nakedness, as I have said, the true history of his life?

We have observed that in Pudd'nhead's aphorisms Mark Twain was expressing his true opinions, the opinions of the cynic he had become owing to the suppression and the constant curdling as it were of the poet in him. While his pioneer self was singing the praises of American progress and writing "A Connecticut Yankee at the Court of King Arthur," the disappointed poet kept up a refrain like this: "October 12, the discovery. It was wonderful to find America, but it would have been more wonderful to lose it." In all this group of writings we have been discussing, however, we can see that while the censorship had been sufficiently relaxed in the general confusion of his life to permit his unconscious to rise to the surface, it was still vigilant enough to cloak its real intentions. It is in secret that Pudd'nhead jots down his saturnine philosophy; it is only in secret, in a private diary like Pudd'nhead's, that young Lord Berkeley, in "The American Claimant," thinks of recording his views of this fraudulent democracy where "prosperity and position constitute rank." Here, as in the malevolent, Mephistophelian "passing stranger" of "The Man That Corrupted Hadleyburg," Mark Twain frankly images himself. But he does so, we perceive, only by taking cover behind a device that enables him to save his face and make good his retreat. Pudd'nhead is only a crack-brained fool about things in general, even if he is pretty clever with his finger-print invention—otherwise he would find something better to do than to spend his time writing nonsense; and as for Lord Berkeley, how could you expect a young English snob to know anything about democracy? That was the reaction upon which Mark Twain could safely count in his readers; they would only be fooling themselves, of course, they would know that they were fooling themselves: but in order to keep up the great American game of bluff they would have to forgive *him*! As long as he never hit below the belt by speaking in his own person, in short, he was perfectly secure. And Mark Twain, the humorist, who held the public in the hollow of his hand, knew it.

It is only after some such explanation as this that we can understand the supremacy among all Mark Twain's writings of "Huckleberry Finn." Through the character of Huck, that disreputable, illiterate little boy, as Mrs. Clemens no doubt thought him, he was licensed to let himself go. We have seen how indifferent his sponsors were to the writing and the fate of this book: "nobody," says Mr. Paine, "appears to have been especially concerned about Huck, except, possibly, the publisher." The more indifferent they were, the freer was Mark Twain! Anything that little vagabond said might be safely trusted to pass the censor, just because he was a little vagabond, just because, as an irresponsible boy, he could not, in the eyes of the mighty ones of this world, know anything in any case about life, morals and civilization. That Mark Twain was almost, if not quite, conscious of his opportunity we can see from his introductory note to the book: "Persons attempting to find a motive in this narrative will be prosecuted; persons attempting to find a moral in it will be banished; persons attempting to find a plot in it will be shot." He feels so secure of himself that he can actually challenge the censor to accuse him of having a motive! Huck's illiteracy, Huck's disreputableness and general outrageousness are so many shields behind which Mark Twain can let all the cats out of the bag with impunity. He must, I say, have had a certain sense of his unusual security when he wrote some of the more cynically satirical passages of the book, when he permitted Colonel Sherburn to taunt the mob, when he drew that picture of the audience who had been taken in by the Duke proceeding to sell the rest of their townspeople, when he has the King put up the notice, "Ladies and Children not Admitted," and add: "There, if that line don't fetch them, I don't know Arkansaw!" The withering contempt for humankind expressed in these episodes was of the sort that Mark Twain expressed more and more openly, as time went on, in his own person; but he was not indulging in that costly kind of cynicism in the days when he wrote "Huckleberry Finn." He must, therefore, have appreciated the license that little vagabond, like the puppet on the lap of a ventriloquist, afforded him. This, however, was only a trivial detail in his general sense of happy expansion, of ecstatic liberation. "Other places do seem so cramped up and smothery, but a raft don't," says Huck, on the river; "you feel mighty free and easy and comfortable on a raft." Mark Twain himself was free at last!—that raft and that river to him were something more than mere material facts. His whole unconscious life, the pent-up river of his own soul, had burst its bonds and rushed forth, a joyous torrent! Do we need any other explanation of the abandon, the beauty, the eternal freshness of "Huckleberry Finn"? Perhaps we can say that a lifetime of moral slavery and repression was not too much to pay for it. Certainly, if it flies like a gay, bright, shining arrow through the tepid atmosphere of American literature, it is because of the straining of the bow, the tautness of the string, that gave it its momentum.

Yes, if we did not know, if we did not feel, that Mark Twain was intended for a vastly greater destiny, for the rôle of a demiurge, in fact, we might have been glad of all those petty restrictions and misprisions he had undergone, restrictions that had prepared the way for this joyous release. No smoking on Sundays! No "swearing" allowed! Neckties having to be bothered over! That everlasting diet of Ps and Qs, petty Ps and pettier Qs, to which Mark Twain had had to submit, the domestic diet of Mrs. Clemens, the literary diet of Mr. Howells, those second parents who had taken the place of his first—we have to thank it, after all, for the vengeful solace we find in the promiscuous and general revolt of Huckleberry Finn. . . .

Perhaps we can best surprise the secret of this humor by noting Mark Twain's instinctive reaction to the life in Nevada. It is evident that in many ways, and in spite of his high spirits and high hopes, he found that life profoundly repugnant to him: he constantly confesses in his diary and letters, indeed, to the misery it involves. "I do hate to go back to the Washoe," he writes, after a few weeks of respite from mining. "We fag ourselves completely out every day." He describes Nevada as a place where the devil would feel homesick: "I heard a gentleman say, the other day, that it was the 'd——dest country under the sun'—and that comprehensive conception I fully subscribe to. It never rains here, and the dew never falls. No flowers grow here, and no green thing gladdens the eye. . . . Our city lies in the midst of a desert of the purest—most unadulterated and uncompromising—*sand*." And as with the setting—so with the life. "High-strung and neurotic," says Mr. Paine, "the strain of newspaper work and the tumult of the Comstock had told on him": more than once he found it necessary—this young man of twenty-eight—"to drop all work and rest for a time at Steamboat Springs, a place near Virginia City, where there were boiling springs and steaming fissures in the mountain-side, and a comfortable hotel." That he found the pace in California just as difficult we have his own testimony; with what fervor he speaks of the "d——n San Francisco style of wearing out life," the "careworn or eager, anxious faces" that made his brief escape to the Sandwich Islands—"God, what a contrast with California and the Washoe"!—ever sweet and blessed in his memory. Never, in short, was a man more rasped by any social situation than was this young "barbarian," as people have called him, by what people also call the free life of the West. We can see this in his profanity, which also, like his humor, came to the front in Nevada and remained one of his prominent characteristics through life. We remember how "mad" he was, "clear through," over the famous highway robbery episode: he was always half-seriously threatening to kill people; he threatened to kill his best friend, Jim Gillis. "To hear him denounce a thing," says Mr. Paine, "was to give one the fierce, searching delight of galvanic waves"; naturally, therefore, no one in Virginia, according to one of the Gillis brothers, could "resist the temptation of making Sam swear." Naturally; but from all this we observe that Mark Twain was living in a state of chronic nervous exasperation.

Was this not due to the extraordinary number of repressions the life of pioneering involved? It is true that it was, in one sense, a free life. It was an irresponsible life, it implied a break with civilization, with domestic, religious and political ties. Nothing could be freer in that sense than the society of the gold-seekers in Nevada and California as we find it pictured in "Roughing It." Free as that society was, nevertheless, scarcely any normal instinct could have been expressed or satisfied in it. The pioneers were not primitive men, they were civilized men, often of gentle birth and education, men for whom civilization had implied many restraints, of course, but innumerable avenues also of social and personal expression and activity to which their natures were accustomed. In escaping responsibility, therefore, they had only placed themselves in a position where their instincts were blocked on every side. There were so few women among them, for instance, that their sexual lives were either starved or debased; and children were as rare as the "Luck" of Roaring Camp, a story that shows how hysterical, in consequence of these and similar conditions, the mining population was. Those who were accustomed to the exercise of complex tastes and preferences found themselves obliged to conform to a single monotonous routine. There were criminal elements among them, too, which kept them continually on their guard, and at best they were so diverse in origin that any real community of feeling among them was virtually impossible. In becoming pioneers they had, as Mr. Paine says, to accept a common mold; they were obliged to abdicate their individuality, to conceal their differences and their personal pretensions under the mask of a rough good-fellowship that found expression mainly in the nervously and emotionally devastating terms of the saloon, the brothel and the gambling-hall. Mark Twain has described for us the "gallant host" which peopled this hectic scene, that army of "erect, bright-eyed, quick-moving, strong-handed young giants—the very pick and choice of the world's glorious ones." Where are they now? he asks in "Roughing It." "Scattered to the ends of the earth, or prematurely aged or decrepit—or shot or stabbed in street affrays—or dead of disappointed hopes and broken hearts—all gone, or nearly all, victims devoted upon the altar of the golden calf." We could not have a more conclusive proof of the total atrophy of human nature this old Nevada life entailed.

Innumerable repressions, I say, produced the fierce intensity of that life, which burnt itself out so quickly. We can see this, indeed, in the fact that it was marked by an incessant series of eruptions. The gold-seekers had come of their own volition, they had to maintain an outward equilibrium, they were sworn, as it were, to a conspiracy of masculine silence regarding these repressions, of which, in fact, in the intensity of their mania, they were scarcely aware. Nevertheless, the human organism will not submit to such conditions without registering one protest after another; accordingly, we find that in the mining-camps the practical joke was, as Mr. Paine says, "legal tender," profanity was almost the normal language, and murder was committed at all hours of the day and night. Mark Twain tells how, in Virginia City, murders were so common that they were scarcely worth more than a line or two in the newspaper, and "almost every man" in the town, according to one of his old friends, "had fought with pistols either impromptu or premeditated duels." We have just noted that for Mark Twain this life was a life of chronic nervous exasperation. Can we not say now that, in a lesser degree, it was a life of chronic nervous exasperation for all the pioneers? . . .

We are now in a position to understand why all the writers who were subjected to these conditions became humorists. The creative mind is the most sensitive mind, the most highly individualized, the most complicated in its range of desires: consequently, in circumstances where individuality cannot register itself, it undergoes the most general and the most painful repression. The more imaginative a man was the more he would naturally feel himself restrained and chafed by such a life as that of the gold-seekers. He, like his comrades, was under the necessity of making money, of succeeding— the same impulse had brought him there that had brought every one else; we know how deeply Mark Twain was under this obligation, an obligation that prevented him from attempting to pursue the artistic life directly because it was despised and because to have done so would have required just those expressions of individuality that pioneer life rendered impossible. On the other hand, sensitive as he was, he instinctively recoiled from violence of all kinds and was thus inhibited by his own nature from obtaining those outlets in "practical jokes," impromptu duels and murder to which his companions constantly resorted. Mr. Paine tells us that Mark Twain never "cared for" duels and "discouraged" them, and that he "seldom indulged physically" in practical jokes. In point of fact, he abhorred them. "When grown-up people indulge in practical jokes," he wrote, forty years later, in his Autobiography, "the fact gauges them. They have lived narrow, obscure and ignorant lives, and at full manhood they still retain and cherish a job-lot of left-over standards and ideals that would have been discarded with their boyhood if they had then moved out into the world and a broader life. There were many practical jokers in the new Territory." After all those years he had not outgrown his instinctive resentment against the assaults to which his dignity had had to submit! To Mark Twain, in short, the life of the gold-fields was a life of almost infinite repression: the fact, as we have seen, that he became a universal butt sufficiently proves how large an area of individuality as it were had to submit to the censorship of public opinion if he was to fulfill his pledge and "make good" in Nevada.

Here we have the psychogenesis of Mark Twain's humor. An outlet of some kind that prodigious energy of his was bound to have, and this outlet, since he had been unable to throw himself whole-heartedly into mining, had to be one which, in some way, however obliquely, expressed the artist in him. That expression, nevertheless, had also to be one which, far from outraging public opinion, would win its emphatic approval. Mark Twain was obliged to remain a "good fellow" in order to succeed, in order to satisfy his inordinate will-to-power; and we have seen how he acquiesced in the suppression of all those manifestations of his individuality—his natural freedom of sentiment, his love of reading, his constant desire for privacy—that struck his comrades as "different" or "superior." His choice of a pen-name, as we have noticed, proves how urgently he felt the need of a "protective coloration" in this society where the writer was a despised type. Too sensitive to relieve himself by horseplay, he had what one might call a preliminary recourse in his profanity, those "scorching, singeing blasts" he was always directing at his companions, and that this in a measure appeased him we can see from Mr. Paine's remark that his profanity seemed "the safety-valve of his high-pressure intellectual engine. . . . When he had blown off he was always calm, gentle, forgiving and even tender." We can best see his humor, then, precisely as Mr. Paine seems to see it in the phrase, "Men laughed when they could no longer swear"—as the expression, in short, of a psychic stage one step beyond the stage where he could find relief in swearing, as a harmless "moral equivalent," in other words, of those acts of violence which his own sensitiveness and his fear of consequences alike prevented him from committing. By means of ferocious jokes—and most of Mark Twain's early jokes are of a ferocity that will hardly be believed by any one who has not examined them critically—he could vent his hatred of pioneer life and all its conditions, those conditions that were thwarting his creative life; he could, in this vicarious manner, appease the artist in him, while at the same time keeping on the safe side of public opinion, the very act of transforming his aggressions into jokes rendering them innocuous.

—Van Wyck Brooks, *The Ordeal of Mark Twain,*
New York: E.P. Dutton and Co., 1920, pp. 9–10,
12, 14–16, 16–17, 17–21, 21–22, 24–25, 32–36,
39–42, 74–76, 79–80, 84, 87–89, 95, 101–105,
114–116, 120–124, 185–187, 193–196,
199–202, 203–205

WORKS

THE JUMPING FROG
OF CALAVERAS COUNTY

In reading the earliest reviews of Mark Twain, in which his name is spelled incorrectly ("Mr. Clements"), students can develop an idea of the early reception and perceptions of Mark Twain. A sense of his lack of a public profile, on the East Coast at least, is evident in the overwhelming attention paid not to the book's author but to Charles Henry Webb, who published the book and, as John Paul, wrote the preface. The reviewer for the *Brooklyn Eagle*, for instance, speaks only of Webb. Mark Twain's virtues, if there are any, enter the review solely by association with Webb.

When Twain is afforded attention for his own merits, foremost among them is praise of what he does not do: the absence of any misspelling in his humor. This merit was emphasized by Webb in his foreword, which many reviewers have subsequently paraphrased. The American public was evidently sick of such playful distortion of the language. Ironically, Artemus Ward—its best-known proponent—had all but abandoned the practice several years earlier, although he was obliged to revive it when he was in London to please *Punch* magazine (to which he was contributing) and an English audience still hungry for such whimsy. David Ross Locke, who wrote as Petroleum V. Nasby, was meanwhile turning to conventional novels. The American public's hunger for a humor based on cacography (that is, misspelling), a trend that had been in evidence for three decades, seemed to all but evaporate, mysteriously, after the Civil War. In this regard, Mark Twain's book had struck the right note.

Ward died, at the height of his fame and powers, on March 6, 1867, only two months before the publication of *The Jumping Frog*. Reviewers, and presumably readers, were looking for a replacement to fill this sudden gap. The reviewer for the *Round Table* asserts, then, that Mark Twain has "succeeded to the vacant chair of the lamented Artemus Ward." How fortuitous the death of Ward was to Twain's popularity cannot now be established with certainty. Nevertheless, Ward's misfortune served Twain well.

Another virtue of Twain's collection, noticed by the *Round Table* reviewer, is that it is "well calculated to unbend the thoughts which may be too much stretched by care." The Civil War had ended two years earlier, with Reconstruction continuing apace. While many of Twain's contemporaries among the humorists wrote virulent, partisan pieces during the Civil War (particularly Petroleum V. Nasby) or featured the Civil War as a recurring backdrop, with Abraham Lincoln and Jefferson Davis as characters (an approach adopted by Artemus Ward), Twain's book assiduously avoided such divisive, upsetting subject matter. As the reviewer for the *San Francisco Evening Bulletin* writes, in praise, he "don't propose to attempt reforming the world." This would, of course, change with time.

Still, the book was not universally admired. Most critical attention is paid to the title story, which was syndicated in innumerable newspapers and came to define Twain early in his career. The tale thereby became a millstone around Twain's neck. To his mother and sister Pamela he called the title work a "villainous backwoods sketch"—a phrase recalled by Van Wyck Brooks in *The Ordeal of Mark Twain* as evidence that Twain never even wanted to write humor.

To compound his chagrin, the rest of his work was seen by one critic as "dreary, and often worse." Twain could easily have been remembered for the one piece only, like his contemporary Robert Burdette, the now forgotten author of a well-loved piece titled "The Rise and Fall of the Mustache."

—◦◦◦— —◦◦◦— —◦◦◦—

Mark Twain (1866)

My Dear Mother and Sister,—

I do not know what to write; my life is so uneventful. I wish I was back there piloting up and down the river again. Verily, all is vanity and little worth—save piloting.

To think that, after writing many an article a man might be excused for thinking tolerably good, those New York people should single out a villainous backwoods sketch to compliment me on!—"Jim Smiley and His Jumping Frog"—a squib which would never have been written but to please Artemus Ward, and then it reached New York too late to appear in his book.

But no matter. His book was a wretchedly poor one, generally speaking, and it could be no credit to either one of us to appear between its covers.

—Mark Twain, letter to Mrs. Jane Clemens
and Mrs. Pamela Moffett, January 20, 1866

Unsigned "New Publications/ Miscellaneous" (1867)

In a handsomely printed and tastefully bound little volume, called the *Jumping Frog*, which is the initial venture of Mr. C. H. Webb as a publisher, "Mark Twain" presents himself as a candidate for the honors of a humorist. "Mark Twain" is, we believe, the *nom de plume* of Mr. Samuel Clements, who, although a Missourian by birth, has for the last year had his residence in California. There his contributions to the weekly journals secured him a wide popularity, and this volume serves to introduce him to the lovers of humor in the Atlantic States. The sketch from which the book takes its name was first published several years ago, and at that time was widely circulated through the newspapers. It is a fair specimen of the whimsical fancies in which the book abounds, and, although there are other sketches nearly equal to it in merit, it is appropriately assigned the leading place because it has done more than any other single paper to secure for the writer whatever reputation he may have. "Mark Twain" differs from the other recent writers of his class in not resorting to the adventitious aid of bad spelling to make his jokes seem more absurd, and this is, of course, decidedly in his favor. There is a great deal of quaint humor and much pithy wisdom in his writings, and their own merit, as well as the attractive style in which they are produced, must secure them a popularity which will bring its own profit. . . .

—Unsigned, "New Publications/Miscellaneous,"
New York Times, May 1, 1867, p. 2

Unsigned "The Citizen's Book Table" (1867)

Let no one hereafter speak of the inhumanity and grasping selfishness of publishers—except, of course, the owners of rejected manuscripts. For the publishing fraternity is henceforth to be honored by the presence of C. H. Webb—he of the *Californian*, of "Liffith Lank," of "St. Twel'mo," and of a thousand and one jokes that have sparkled in the pages of newspaper and magazine from Boston to San Francisco. Happy is the man whose book Webb shall publish. Having been himself one of us, unquestionably a fellow-feeling toward the impecunious author will produce those results in the bosom of C. H. Webb, publisher to which the poet so neatly refers. Particularly happy is Mark Twain, brother Californian and brother humorist of the publisher, in securing so genial a sponsor for his new born book. We welcome both publisher and author to the Atlantic metropolis, and sympathize tenderly with deserted San Francisco, which must be terribly dull, now that the twain have left its halls of dazzling light, it may be for years, and then again it may not.

(Any one who is stupid enough to suppose that a pun is intended by the words "the twain," must have a very low opinion of the moral tone which pervades *The Citizen* office. Being merely human we have our faults and weaknesses, but we do not pun in bad grammar.)

The story of the "Jumping Frog" has been frequently published in various Atlantic papers, and is almost as well-known here as it is on the Pacific slope. It is altogether the jolliest story that we have ever been fortunate enough to laugh over. "Humorous," or "comic," does not begin to express its peculiar character. It is thoroughly, perfectly, inexpressibly jolly, and is entirely unrivaled in its peculiar style of excellence.

Mark Twain is a genuine humorist. He does not depend on misspelling, or on punning, for the comic effect of his sketches, but on legitimate wit and humor. Perhaps his chief characteristic is his habit of bringing two utterly incongruous things in close juxtaposition. He imitates no one, but his humor is thoroughly and entirely his own.

We don't propose to spoil these sketches by making unsatisfactory and aggravating extracts from them, but strongly urge every one to get the book without delay. Read it, and you will find yourself the owner of a good substantial laugh that will last you till Webb publishes his "St. Twel'mo." And then be ready for another.

—Unsigned, New York Citizen, "The
Citizen's Book Table," May 4, 1867, p. 4

Unsigned (1867)

C. H. Webb has been known on the Pacific coast for a number of years by humorous, philosophical, and satirical contributions to the California press. His introduction to the reading public of the Atlantic States occurred in the columns of the New York *Times*, through "Liffith Lank," one of the cleverest travesties that has appeared in a long time. Charles Reade's peculiarities of style as betrayed in *Griffith Gaunt* were well apprehended and most effectively presented. The success of "Liffith" has prepared the way for this neatly gotten-up volume of sketches. Mr. Paul says in a brief preface that Mark Twain is known as "The Moralist of the Main," no less than "The Wild Humorist of the Pacific Slope." It is as a humorist he appears in this volume. The sketches were originally written for the newspapers.

—Unsigned, Brooklyn Eagle,
May 7, 1867, p. 4

UNSIGNED (1867)

As Mark Twain's lecture was successful, we may say of his book, what is the fact, that it is a mistake. The story of the "Jumping Frog" is one of the best of its kind that we remember; but the remainder of the little book, with one or two exceptions, is dreary, and often worse. It is not suited to this longitude.

—Unsigned, *New York Evening Post*,
May 8, 1867, p. 2

UNSIGNED (1867)

Mr. Clements ("Mark Twain"), the Wild Humorist of the Pacific Slope, Lecturer on the Sandwich Islands, Citizen of Nevada and Pilgrim to the Holy Land has introduced himself most favorably to all "Eastern people," as the rest of mankind are called in California, by a little book full of good hard sense, wit pure, sparkling and sharp as a diamond of first water, and humor genial and inexhaustible. Without resorting to tricks of spelling or any other buffoonery "Mark Twain" will surprise his readers most unexpectedly into inextinguishable laughter by many a touch that smacks of what seems to be the distinctive characteristic of American wit and humor—a proclivity to exaggeration. But even his exaggerations are not exaggerated beyond all bounds—they leave you with the impression that he could have stretched them twice as far if he had chosen "to be as funny as he can." . . . His famous lecture on the Sandwich Islands drew a full house last Monday night.

—Unsigned, *New York Herald*,
May 12, 1867, p. 5

UNSIGNED (1867)

In the double capacity of lecturer and humorist, Mark Twain has succeeded to the vacant chair of the lamented Artemus Ward. In both there is a strongly marked nationality, a keen appreciation of the ridiculous, and a love of fun untinged with cynicism. The advantages arising from this two-fold exercise of an author's talents are obvious: his reputation as a speaker increases the demand for his works, and his popularity as a writer awakens the reader's curiosity to see and hear him. Besides—what is worthy of mention—it saves the critic the trouble of introducing to the world the aspirant to literary distinction; the world has an opportunity to see and judge for itself.

The book before us consists of a collection of amusing sketches, airily and jauntily put together, well calculated to unbend the thoughts which may be too much stretched by care, and are apparently suggested by the exhilarating atmosphere of California. In "The Jumping Frog" the fun principally consists in the quaint manner of telling the story; the phraseology in this and the "Spirit" chapters is decidedly droll. "Answers to Correspondents" are very amusing, and although stern disciplinarians and distributors of tracts might object to the moral iconoclasm of "The Story of the Bad Little Boy Who Didn't Come to Grief," the rising generation, whose terrors have been awakened by narrations of the punishments which inevitably follow small derelictions from duty, will acknowledge to our author a large debt of gratitude. We commend this little volume to all who seek a few moments' relaxation from the serious cares of life, and who concur in believing that

"Care to our coffin adds a nail, no doubt;
And ev'ry grin so merry draws one out."

—Unsigned, *Round Table*,
May 25, 1867, p. 332

UNSIGNED (1867)

Mark Twain's long-promised book is out. It is entitled *The Celebrated Jumping Frog of Calaveras County, and Other Sketches*, consisting mainly of papers contributed to various California journals. It appears under the patronage of C. H. Webb, by whom it purports to be edited and published, though the type, paper and binding would seem to indicate that it came from the house of George W. Carleton & Co. As a specimen of bookcraft it is not creditable. It has a cheap look and bears evidence of having been hurried through the press without proper supervision. Mark Twain deserves better treatment at the hands of his printer and publisher. He is eminently worthy of being heralded in the best style of the best publishing house in the country. We regard him as by far the best of our second-rate humorists. He is superior to Artemus Ward, for his fun has a purpose to it, and is worth a hundred Petroleum V. Nasbys and Josh Billingses. He is something more than a mere writer of funny sayings. Beneath the surface of his pleasantry lies a rich vein of serious thought. He instructs as well as amuses and even his broadest jokes have a moral more or less obvious. He is at times a little more coarse than one could wish, but he is never wicked. We feel, in reading him, that he is a good honest fellow at bottom, who wishes everybody well, but don't propose to attempt reforming the world on his own hook, and don't expect the Millennium to come during his life-time. Most of the sketches are too long for our crowded columns, but the following, entitled "The Story of the Bad Little Boy Who Didn't Come to Grief," is a fair specimen of the quality of the author as a humorist.

—Unsigned, *San Francisco Evening Bulletin*, June 1, 1867, p. 1

UNSIGNED (1867)

The Pacific humorist, who has already made his mark in the East, enters upon the dignity of book life with an old friend and literary comrade as a publisher. The relations between publishers and authors being proverbially precarious, an early difference between Mark Twain and John Paul is to be feared. A large sale is insured by the dedication, which is a tribute to a multitudinous individual: "To John Smith. . . ." The volume, which is edited by John Paul, contains a selection from the mass of the contributions of the humorist to the Pacific press. "The Celebrated Jumping Frog of Calaveras County," like Robb's story of "Swallowing Oysters Alive," or Sut Lovegood's story of the Exploded Dog, is sufficient warrant for the flourish of fame. It is at once a revelation of character—for Jim Smiley is a type of a class—the seizure of a ludicrous situation, and a narration full of the local flavor of a mining camp. Other sketches that accompany the wonderful frog story are suggestive of Phoenix, as for instance, "The Killing of Julius Caesar 'Localized,'" and the "Brief Biographical Sketch of George Washington." The "Story of the Bad Little Boy who Didn't Come to Grief" is a sharp satire on the stories which are supposed to be particularly edifying in the Sunday schools, but which fail to teach that virtue is its own reward. The satirist is right, for, as a matter of fact, the bad boy does not always or inevitably come to grief. The sketch entitled "Lucretia Smith's Soldier" risibly hits off the sentimental yarns of which the late war was prolific. This we quote: (Quoted in full.)

Although some of the sketches from the pen of Mark Twain are in the vein of other humorists, he deserves to be regarded as an "original," for he combines qualities which are to be found united in no rival writer. The strong sense, keen observation, unctuous, hearty manner, lively conception of character, quick perception of oddity in everyday life and satirical power, which are the property of Mark, could not, as an aggregate of merit, be claimed for Artemus Ward or Orpheus C. Kerr, and it can hardly be regarded as an ebullition of provincial preference if we predict for our Pacific humorist a more enduring fame than either has achieved.

—Unsigned, *Sacramento Union*,
June 6, 1867, p. 1

UNSIGNED (1867)

We hereby present our thanks to Messrs. Routledge for giving to the British public one of the funniest books that we have met with for a long time—*The Celebrated Jumping Frog*, by Mark Twain. The author is an American, and was, we believe, the editor of a paper called *The Californian*, in which many of the stories in the present volume appeared. "Mark Twain" is, of course, a *nom de plume*, like Artemus Ward or Orpheus C. Kerr, for these American humourists seem shy of coming before the public with their real names, and prefer to assume fanciful *sobriquets*. The first story in this little book is "The Celebrated Jumping Frog of Calaveras County," which belonged to a certain Jim Smiley, a gentleman remarkable for his propensity to bet upon anything and everything. The frog's name was "Dan'l Webster," and, though a wonderful jumper, we read, "You never see a frog more modest and straightfor'ard as he was, for all he was so gifted." How Smiley bet on him and how poor Dan'l was the victim of the most shameful foul play the reader must find out for himself, the story is too long to tell here, and too good to spoil by curtailment. "Aurelia's Unfortunate Young Man" is equally good, and the item which the editor himself couldn't understand is a most delicious piece of mystification. In several of the sketches we get a charming insight into American usages. We are told, for instance, that young "bucks and heifers" always come it strong on panoramas because it "gives them a chance of tasting one another's mugs in the dark." Our readers will hardly recognise the seductive process of osculation in this expression. We learn also some facts about the dress of our fair cousins across the Atlantic, with which we are ashamed to say we were previously unacquainted. A young lady's attire at a ball is thus described:

> Miss R. P., with that repugnance to ostentation in dress which is so peculiar to her, was attired in a simple white lace collar, fastened with a neat pearl button *solitaire*. The fine contrast between the sparkling vivacity of her natural optic and the steadfast attentiveness of her placid glass eye, was the subject of general and enthusiastic remark.

There are no misspellings, no contortions of words in Mark Twain; his fun is entirely dependent upon the inherent humour in his writings. And although many jokers have sent us *brochures* like the present from the other side of the Atlantic, we have had no book fuller of more genuine or more genial fun than the *Celebrated Jumping Frog*. Our advice to our readers, therefore, is immediately to invest a shilling in it, and over a pipe and what Mr. Swiveller called a "modest quencher," to sit down and have the hearty laugh that we can promise them from its perusal.

—Unsigned, *Fun*, N.S., 6,
October 19, 1867, p. 65

DAN DE QUILLE (1874)

Mark Twain has been republishing some of his sketches in pamphlet form; 32 pages, price two-bits—"Jumping Frog," etc. He keeps grinding these things over and over as long as he thinks there is a cent in them. I have his last batch and will send you the pamphlet as soon as I have glanced it over. I never could see much in the "Jumping Frog," yet that yarn was the one which first brought Mark into notice. The story was told him by an old chap who still lives in his cabin in Amador County, California. Gillis, our news editor, knows the old fellow well and was with Mark when he told him the yarn. The only funny thing about it is the idea of loading a frog with shot.

—Dan De Quille, letter to his sister Lou,
June 14, 1874, from Richard A. Dwyer and
Richard E. Lingenfelter, eds., *Dan De Quille,
the Washoe Giant: A Biography and Anthology*,
Reno: University of Nevada Press, 1990, p. 32

THE INNOCENTS ABROAD

The Innocents Abroad was compared to the multitude of travel books of its day. A trove of books was written by "unnumbered sentimental and pious pilgrims," featuring rote descriptions of the "Grand Tour" of Europe, largely notable for their often excessive reverence for the select sites visited. The "famous localities," as Bret Harte has it, "of which a great many six hundred and fifty pages have been, at various times, written by various tourists." William Dean Howells describes the prevailing tone and subject of these works, when he writes of "the blissfulness of bliss."

By 1837, this type of travel memoir had become notorious. "Authors we have, in numbers," Ralph Waldo Emerson remarks in *The American Scholar*, "who have written out their vein, and who, moved by a commendable prudence, sail for Greece or Palestine ... to replenish their merchantable stock."

This convention of traveler's awe perhaps made Twain's irreverence even more pronounced. Nevertheless, his lack of the requisite awe charmed many readers. As the Virginia City *Enterprise* reviewer notes, Twain "presents foreign scenes to the eye of every individual so nearly in the light in which he would have viewed them himself." Or, as "Tom Folio" phrases it, he "saw things as they were, not as they have been described by poets and romancers." The differentiation is an important one. Twain was not highfalutin; he did not demand genteel appreciation but spoke to the innocent, the philistine, and the vandal in his readers. He was appreciated by more than just the philistines, however. Ellen Emerson recalled how her father, Ralph Waldo, "often asked us to repeat certain passages of *The Innocents Abroad*." The learned Bostonian "Tom Folio," meanwhile, compares Twain's account of Palestine to a work by the seventeenth-century minister and author Thomas Fuller called *A Pisgah Sight of Palestine* (1650).

The Innocents Abroad introduced William Dean Howells to Mark Twain ("Mr. Clements"), and his review in turn led to the first meeting of these two writers, who established a friendship that endured for forty years. Surprisingly, Howells began by refusing to analyze "the character of American humor"—which was something of a journalistic chestnut by this time. Howells notes the singular lack of instruction to the book ("the didactic ... is not Mr. Clements's prevailing mood") but finds that "pure human nature," the sort that "rarely gets into literature," is Twain's best subject. The book is not about traveling abroad but rather about travelers abroad. The journey is often merely a swiftly abandoned premise for a more general and willful meandering: "Almost any topic, and any event of the author's past life, he finds pertinent to the story of European and Oriental travel." Howells notes approvingly a "continuous incoherence" to Twain's narrative. Bret Harte, meanwhile, praises its "lawlessness and audacity."

Much is made of the book's physical aspect as a consumer product: its size ("about the size of *The Family Physician*"), its illustrations, and the fact that it is published through a subscription company. Bret Harte notes with canny amusement the incongruity of Twain's work among the usual fare of the subscription publisher ("an Indian spring in an alkaline literary desert"). Twain is an "image-breaker," writes Harte, and the "whole affair was a huge practical joke." Twain would probably balk at such a description in later years, and he and Harte had a falling out in due course. Harte, unlike Howells, finds tracts of sentiment ("he is *really* sentimental") and lecturing in *The Innocents Abroad*. He also notes that Twain, for all his irreverence, meekly followed the dictates of the Grand Tour and his Baedeker travel guide, not extending his subversion to his itinerary or his route. In noting this, Harte anticipates those later critics who bemoaned Twain's lack of discernment in matters of culture. Again presaging later critics, he shrewdly points out Twain's hatred of all cant "except, of course, the cant of materialism."

The Old World, unsurprisingly, evidenced a more mixed reaction to *The Innocents Abroad*, best represented at its negative extreme by the London *Saturday Review*'s anonymous reviewer. Here is an early case made against the "ugly American," the American abroad, a favorite subject of Henry James. To the *Saturday Review*'s writer, he is "as offensive as the worst kind of Cockney tourist," harsh words indeed. Accepting that "Mr. Mark Twain is of course not as simple as he affects to be," the reviewer seemingly misses the satire of the book; though he could actually ultimately be in on the joke, since he locates many of the funniest portions of the book, however apparently straight faced and aggrieved.

Mark Twain responded to this review (apparently without having actually read it) in the December 1870 issue of the *Galaxy*. Despite the London reviewer's caveat that he recognizes the dry jokes present in the text, Twain composed an exaggerated satire of the review exploding the criticisms to the point of absurdity. Ambrose Bierce, like many other American journalists reading it, believed it to be a real review. The matter became further complicated when certain journalists claimed that Twain was himself "sold," or fooled, by the London reviewer, who was himself expressing a bit of dry humor of his own. In Twain's final description of the furor, there seems a clear confusion among all parties as to which article is being referred to, the genuine London review or Twain's burlesque of it. By the end of the fiasco (recounted by Arthur Bigelow Paine), Twain's own sense of humor has tapered off dramatically. Students of Twain's relation to the reviewers, and particularly to his reception in England, will find this tortuous, backfired prank fascinating, if it can be untangled in the first place.

The complex reception of the book in England is further evidenced by Twain's later account of the Englishman reading *The Innocents Abroad* on a train without smiling once or the genuinely humorless review by

Henry Harland, who is mystified as to why Twain's work "is still a book one likes" (he puts it down to "the downright barbarism of the book"). Arthur Bigelow Paine, with hindsight, remarks (unlike Ambrose Bierce) that "English readers of culture, critical readers, rose to an understanding of Mark Twain's literary value with a greater promptness than did the same class of readers at home."

UNSIGNED REVIEW IN THE *VIRGINIA CITY TERRITORIAL ENTERPRISE* (1869)

The thousand friends and admirers of our old co-worker, Sam Clemens, will doubtless be pleased to know that an opportunity has come to procure his book of travels in Europe and the Holy Land. A lady arrived in town yesterday who will canvass the State for the sale of the work, and as it is only sold by subscription, parties will bear in mind that this will be their only chance of procuring it without considerable trouble. The book is admirably gotten up and contains 651 pages, illustrated by 234 cuts. No other such entertaining account of travel, we venture to say, was ever written, and none—as the author declares his purpose to have been—that presents foreign scenes to the eye of every individual so nearly in the light in which he would have viewed them himself. But it is unnecessary for us to speak of its merits or demerits, as everybody will buy it and all that could be said would pass unheeded in the enjoyment of the work itself.

—Unsigned, *Virginia City Territorial Enterprise*, October 7, 1869, p. 3

WILLIAM DEAN HOWELLS (1869)

The character of American humor, and its want of resemblance to the humor of Kamtschatka and Patagonia,—will the reader forgive us if we fail to set down here the thoughts suggested by these fresh and apposite topics? Will he credit us with a self-denial proportioned to the vastness of Mr. Clements's very amusing book, if we spare to state why he is so droll, or—which is as much to the purpose—why we do not know? This reticence will leave us very little to say by way of analysis; and, indeed, there is very little to say of *The Innocents Abroad* which is not of the most obvious and easy description. The idea of a steamer-load of Americans going on a prolonged picnic to

Europe and the Holy Land is itself almost sufficiently delightful, and it is perhaps praise enough for the author to add that it suffers nothing from his handling. If one considers the fun of making a volume of six hundred octavo pages upon this subject, in compliance with one of the main conditions of a subscription book's success, bigness namely, one has a tolerably fair piece of humor, without troubling Mr. Clements further. It is out of the bounty and abundance of his own nature that he is as amusing in the execution as in the conception of his work. And it is always good-humored humor, too, that he lavishes on his reader, and even in its impudence it is charming; we do not remember where it is indulged at the cost of the weak or helpless side, or where it is insolent, with all its sauciness and irreverence. The standard shams of travel which everybody sees through suffer possibly more than they ought, but not so much as they might; and one readily forgives the harsh treatment of them in consideration of the novel piece of justice done on such a traveller as suffers under the pseudonym of Grimes. It is impossible also that the quality of humor should not sometimes be strained in the course of so long a narrative; but the wonder is rather in the fact that it is strained so seldom.

Mr. Clements gets a good deal of his fun out of his fellow-passengers, whom he makes us know pretty well, whether he presents them somewhat caricatured, as in the case of the "Oracle" of the ship, or carefully and exactly done, as in the case of such a shrewd, droll, business-like, sensible, kindly type of the American young man as "Dan." We must say also that the artist who has so copiously illustrated the volume has nearly always helped the author in the portraiture of his fellow-passengers, instead of hurting him, which is saying a good deal for an artist; in fact, we may go further and apply the commendation to all the illustrations; and this in spite of the variety of figures in which the same persons are represented, and the artist's tendency to show the characters on mules where the author says they rode horseback.

Of course the instructive portions of Mr. Clements's book are of a general rather than particular character, and the reader gets as travel very little besides series of personal adventures and impressions; he is taught next to nothing about the population of the cities and the character of the rocks in the different localities. Yet the man who can be honest enough to let himself see the realities of human life everywhere, or who has only seen Americans as they are abroad, has not travelled in vain and is far from a useless guide. The very young American who told the English officers that a couple of our gunboats could come and knock Gibraltar into the Mediterranean Sea; the American who at a French restaurant "talked very loudly and coarsely, and laughed boisterously, where all others were so quiet and well behaved," and who ordered "wine, sir!" adding, to raise admiration in a country where wine is as much a matter of course as soup, "I never dine without wine, sir"; the American who had to be addressed several times as Gordon, being so accustomed to hear the name pronounced Gorrdong, and who had forgotten most English words during a three months' sojourn in Paris; the Americans who pitilessly made a three days' journey in Palestine within two days, cruelly overworking the poor beasts they rode, and overtaxing the strength of their comrades, in order not to break the Sabbath; the American Pilgrims who travelled half round the world to be able to take a sail on the Sea of Galilee, and then missed their sole opportunity because they required the boatman to take them for one napoleon when he wanted two;—these are all Americans who are painted to peculiar advantage by Mr. Clements, and who will be easily recognized by such as have had the good fortune to meet them abroad.

The didactic, however, is not Mr. Clements's prevailing mood, nor his best, by any means. The greater part of his book is in the vein of irony, which, with a delicious impudence, he attributes to Saint Luke, declaring that Luke, in speaking of the winding "street, called Straight" in Damascus, "is careful not to commit himself; he does not say it is the street which *is* straight, but the 'street which is *called* Straight.' It is a fine piece of irony; it is the only facetious remark in the Bible, I believe." At Tiberias our author saw the women who wear their dowry in their head-dresses of coins. "Most of these maidens were not wealthy, but some few have been kindly dealt with by fortune. I saw heiresses there, worth, in their own right,—worth, well, I suppose I might venture to say as much as nine dollars and a half. But such cases are rare. When you come across one of these, she naturally puts on airs." He thinks the owner of the horse "Jericho," on which he travelled towards Jerusalem, "had a wrong opinion about him. He had an idea that he was one of those fiery, untamed, steeds, but he is not of that character. I know the Arab had this idea, because when he brought the horse out for inspection in Beirout, he kept jerking at the bridle and shouting in Arabic, 'Ho! will you? Do you want to run away, you ferocious beast, and break your neck?' when all the time the horse was not doing anything in the world, and only looked like he wanted to lean up against something and think. Whenever he is not shying at things or reaching after a fly, he wants to do that yet. How it would surprise his owner to know this!" In this vein of ironical drollery is that now celebrated passage in which Mr. Clements states that he was affected to tears on coming, a stranger in a strange land, upon the grave of a blood-relation,—the tomb of Adam; but that passage is somewhat more studied in tone than most parts of the book, which are written with a very successful approach in style to colloquial drolling. As Mr. Clements writes of his experiences, we imagine he would talk of them; and very amusing talk it would be: often not at all fine in matter or manner, but full of touches of humor,—which if not delicate are nearly always easy,—and having a base of excellent sense and good feeling. There is an amount of pure human nature in the book, that rarely gets into literature; the depths of our poor unregeneracy—dubious even of the blissfulness of bliss—are sounded by such a simple confession as Mr. Clements makes in telling of his visit to the Emperor of Russia: "I would as soon have thought of being cheerful in Abraham's bosom as in the palace of an Emperor." Almost any topic, and any event of the author's past life, he finds pertinent to the story of European and Oriental travel, and if the reader finds it impertinent, he does not find it the less amusing. The effect is dependent in so great degree upon this continuous incoherence, that no chosen passage can illustrate the spirit of the whole, while the passage itself loses half in separation from the context. Nevertheless, here is part of the account given by Mr. Clements of the Pilgrims' excursion to the river Jordan, over roads supposed to be infested by Bedouins; and the reader who does not think it droll as it stands can go to our author for the rest.

> I think we must all have determined upon the same line of tactics, for it did seem as if we never would get to Jericho. I had a notoriously slow horse, but somehow I could not keep him in the rear, to save my neck. He was forever turning up in the lead. In such cases I trembled a little, and got down to fix my saddle. But it was not of any use. The others all got down to fix their saddles, too. I never saw such a time with saddles. It was the first time any of them had got out of order in three weeks, and now they had all broken down at once. I tried walking, for exercise—I had not had enough in Jerusalem searching for holy places. But it was a failure. The whole mob were suffering for exercise, and it was not fifteen minutes till they were all on foot and I had the lead again. . . .
>
> . . . We were moping along down through this dreadful place, every man in the rear. Our guards—two gorgeous young Arab sheiks, with cargoes of swords, guns, pistols, and daggers on board—were loafing ahead.
>
> "Bedouins!"
>
> Every man shrunk up and disappeared in his clothes like a mud-turtle. My first impulse was to dash forward and destroy the Bedouins. My second was to dash to the rear to see if there were any

coming in that direction. I acted on the latter impulse. So did all the others. If any Bedouins had approached us, then, from that point of the compass, they would have paid dearly for their rashness.

Under his *nom de plume* of Mark Twain, Mr. Clements is well known to the very large world of newspaper-readers; and this book ought to secure him something better than the uncertain standing of a popular favorite. It is no business of ours to fix his rank among the humorists California has given us, but we think he is, in an entirely different way from all the others, quite worthy of the company of the best.

—William Dean Howells, *Atlantic Monthly* 24,
December 1869, pp. 764–766

REVIEWER WRITING AS "TOM FOLIO" (1869)

MARK TWAIN'S NEW BOOK. What would the great old romantic voyagers and travellers, the heroes of Hackluyt and Purchas, say of the monster Yankee picnic to Europe and the Holy Land? I think that if those worthies were to get hold of a copy of Mark Twain's account of the excursion, there would be laughter in Elysium. At any rate, I can hardly believe it possible for an earthly reader—unless, indeed, like Charles Lamb's Scotchman, he is joke-proof—to peruse Twain's new book, *The Innocents Abroad*, without "laughing consumedly." The work, however, though rich in joke and jest is not, like Gilbert à Becket's dreary comic histories, a merely funny book. On the contrary, it is a very full and matter-of-fact record of travel in Europe and the East, delightfully flavored with humor and plentifully spiced with wit. Addison's sober citizen complained that there were too many plums and no suet in his pudding, but no one can say that Twain's literary pudding is wanting in suet or too full of plums.

Our author is not one of the "one-eyed travellers," mentioned by Whateley, who see "a great deal of some particular class of objects, and are blind to all others," but a shrewd, quick-witted person, who travelled with his eyes very wide open, and saw things as they were, not as they have been described by poets and romancers. It is not, however, so much for its new, truthful and pleasant pictures of Old World places and people, as for the delicious wit and humor scattered so freely up and down the book, that one praises and prizes *The Innocents Abroad*. And it is such good humor, too, most of it, and with all its freedom and riot, touching gently and lovingly all serious things. I have been reading Fuller's *Pisgah Sight of Palestine*, and derived no little amusement by comparing his descriptions of the Holy Land with Mark Twain's. Fuller, though as pious and reverent as a saint, was a rare wit and humorist, and his book on Palestine is brimming over with merry quibbles and jocular humor. Although some of Mark Twain's levities might have displeased the witty old divine, I think that he would have laughed loud and long at the passage concerning the tomb of Adam.

—Reviewer Writing as "Tom Folio,"
Boston *Daily Evening Transcript*,
December 15, 1869, p. 1

BRET HARTE (1870)

Six hundred and fifty pages of open and declared fun—very strongly accented with wood-cuts at that—might go far toward frightening the fastidious reader. But the Hartford publishers, we imagine, do not print for the fastidious reader, nor do traveling book agents sell much to that rarely occurring man, who prefers to find books rather than let them find *him*. So that, unless he has already made "Mark Twain's" acquaintance through the press, he will not probably meet him until, belated in the rural districts, he takes from the parlor table of a country farm-house an illustrated Bible, Greeley's *American Conflict*, Mr. Parton's apocryphal *Biographies*, successively and listlessly, and so comes at last upon "Mark Twain's" *Innocents* like a joyous revelation—an Indian spring in an alkaline literary desert. For the book has that intrinsic worth of bigness and durability which commends itself to the rural economist, who likes to get a material return for his money. It is about the size of *The Family Physician*, for which it will doubtless be often mistaken—with great advantage to the patient.

The entire six hundred and fifty pages are devoted to an account of the "steamship *Quaker City*'s excursion to Europe and the Holy Land," with a description of certain famous localities of which a great many six hundred and fifty pages have been, at various times, written by various tourists. Yet there is hardly a line of Mr. Clemens' account that is not readable; and none the less, certainly, from the fact that he pokes fun at other tourists, and that the reader becomes dimly conscious that Mr. Clemens' fellow-passengers would have probably stopped this gentle satirist from going with them could they have forecast his book. The very title—*The Innocents Abroad*—is a suggestive hint of the lawlessness and audacity in which the trip is treated. We shall not stop to question the propriety of this feature: it is only just to

Mr. Clemens to say, that the best satirists have generally found their quarry in the circle in which they moved, and among their best friends; but we contend that if he has, by this act, choked off and prevented the enthusiastic chronicling of the voyage by any of his fellow-passengers, who may have been sentimentally inclined, he is entitled to the consideration of a suffering world; and it shall stand in extenuation of some mannerism that is only slang, some skepticism that lacks the cultivation which only makes skepticism tolerable, and some sentiment that is only rhetoric.

And so, with an irreverence for his fellow-pilgrims which was equaled only by his scorn for what they admired, this hilarious image-breaker started upon his mission. The situation was felicitous, the conditions perfect for the indulgence of an humor that seems to have had very little moral or esthetic limitation. The whole affair was a huge practical joke, of which not the least amusing feature was the fact that "Mark Twain" had embarked in it. Before the *Quaker City* reached Fayal, the first stopping-place, he had worked himself into a grotesque rage at every thing and every body. In this mock assumption of a righteous indignation, lies, we think, the real power of the book, and the decided originality of Mr. Clemens' humor. It enables him to say his most deliberately funny things with all the haste and exaggeration of rage; it gives him an opportunity to invent such epithets as "animated outrage," and "spider-legged gorilla," and apply them, with no sense of personal responsibility on the part of reader or writer. And the rage is always ludicrously disproportionate to the cause. It is "Mr. Boythorn," without his politeness, or his cheerful intervals. For, when "Mark Twain" is not simulating indignation, he is *really* sentimental. He shows it in fine writing—in really admirable rhetoric, vigorous and picturesque—but too apt, at times, to suggest the lecturing attitude, or the reporter's flourish. Yet it is so much better than what one had any right to expect, and is such an agreeable relief to long passages of extravagant humor, that the reader is very apt to overlook the real fact, that it is often quite as extravagant.

Yet, with all his independence, "Mark Twain" seems to have followed his guide and guidebooks with a simple, unconscious fidelity. He was quite content to see only that which every body else sees, even if he was not content to see it with the same eyes. His record contains no new facts or features of the countries visited. He has always his own criticism, his own comments, his own protests, but always concerning the same old facts. Either from lack of time or desire, he never stepped out of the treadmill round of "sights." His remarks might have been penciled on the margins of Murray. This is undoubtedly a good way to correct the enthusiasm or misstatements of other tourists; but is, perhaps, hardly the best method of getting at the truth for one's self. As a conscientious, painstaking traveler, "Mark Twain," we fear, is not to be commended. But that his book would have been as amusing, if he had been, is a matter of doubt.

Most of the criticism is just in spirit, although extravagant, and often too positive in style. But it should be remembered that the style itself is a professional exaggeration, and that the irascible pilgrim, "Mark Twain," is a very eccentric creation of Mr. Clemens'. We can, perhaps, no more fairly hold Mr. Clemens responsible for "Mark Twain's" irreverence than we could have held the late Mr. Charles F. Browne to account for "Artemus Ward's" meanness and humbuggery. There may be a question of taste in Mr. Clemens permitting such a man as "Mark Twain" to go to the Holy Land at all; but we contend that such a traveler would be more likely to report its external aspect truthfully than a man of larger reverence. And are there not Lamartines, Primes, and unnumbered sentimental and pious pilgrims to offset these skeptics—or, as our author would say, such "animated outrages"—as Ross Browne, Swift, "Mark Twain," *et al.*

To subject Mr. Clemens to any of those delicate tests by which we are supposed to detect the true humorist, might not be either fair or convincing. He has caught, with great appreciation and skill, that ungathered humor and extravagance which belong to pioneer communities—which have been current in bar-rooms, on railways, and in stages—and which sometimes get crudely into literature, as "a fellow out West says." A good deal of this is that picturesque Western talk which we call "slang," in default of a better term for inchoate epigram. His characters speak naturally, and in their own tongue. If he has not that balance of pathos which we deem essential to complete humor, he has something very like it in that serious eloquence to which we have before alluded. Like all materialists, he is an honest hater of all cant—except, of course, the cant of materialism—which, it is presumed, is perfectly right and proper. To conclude: after a perusal of this volume, we see no reason for withholding the opinion we entertained before taking it up, that Mr. Clemens deserves to rank foremost among Western humorists; and, in California, above his only rival, "John Phoenix," whose fun, though more cultivated and spontaneous, lacked the sincere purpose and larger intent of "Mark Twain's."

—Bret Harte, review of *The Innocents Abroad*,
Overland Monthly, January 1870, pp. 100–101

Ambrose Bierce "A Joke on the Saturday Review" (1870)

Probably the most delicious joke of the season is the *Saturday Review*'s article upon Mark Twain's *Innocents Abroad*. The *Saturday* gravely analyzes this piece of screaming fun, and severely condemns it in detail. It seems never to have entered the reviewer's opaque pate, that the book is not a perfectly serious composition, and he has been informed, upon what be esteems good authority, that it "has been adopted by the schools and colleges of the several States as a textbook!" Naturally be is disgusted at the "brutal ignorance that pervades the American nation." Now we have never told a lie in our life, and the universe has a touching faith in our entire veracity, but in this case we have not the faintest hope that we shall be believed. That the *Saturday Review*, the very brain of English periodical literature, should have committed so dense a piece of stupidity, is simply incredible. In affirming that it *did*, we feel the pangs of martyrdom—feel that we have sacrificed a reputation dearer to us than wife or children, in the cause of naked truth. We expect hereafter to be avoided by every one who has not actually read the article in question. We can only repeat that what we relate is strictly true, and add that the average English critic is a dumb beast of dense cuticular rhinocerosity.

—Ambrose Bierce, "A Joke on the *Saturday Review*," *News Letter*, November 2, 1870

Mark Twain "An Entertaining Article" (1870)

Perhaps the most successful flights of the humor of Mark Twain have been descriptions of the persons who did not appreciate his humor at all. We have become familiar with the Californians who were thrilled with terror by his burlesque of a newspaper reporter's way of telling a story, and we have heard of the Pennsylvania clergyman who sadly returned his "Innocents Abroad" to the book-agent with the remark that "the man who could shed tears over the tomb of Adam must be an idiot." But Mark Twain may now add a much more glorious instance to his string of trophies. The "Saturday Review," in its number of October 8, reviews his book of travels, which has been republished in England, and reviews it seriously. We can imagine the delight of the humorist in reading this tribute to his power; and indeed it is so amusing in itself that he can hardly do better than reproduce the article in full in his next monthly Memoranda.

(Publishing the above paragraph thus gives me a sort of authority for reproducing the *Saturday Review*'s article in full in these pages. I dearly wanted to do it, for I cannot write anything half so delicious myself. If I had a cast-iron dog that could read this English criticism and preserve his austerity, I would drive him off the doorstep.—EDITOR MEMORANDA.)

(From the London *Saturday Review*.)

REVIEWS OF NEW BOOKS

THE INNOCENTS ABROAD. A Book of Travels. By Mark Twain. London: Hotten, publisher. 1870.

Lord Macaulay died too soon. We never felt this so deeply as when we finished the last chapter of the above-named extravagant work. Macaulay died too soon—for none but he could mete out complete and comprehensive justice to the insolence, the impertinence, the presumption, the mendacity, and, above all, the majestic ignorance of this author.

To say that the *Innocents Abroad* is a curious book, would be to use the faintest language—would be to speak of the Matterhorn as a neat elevation, or of Niagara as being "nice" or "pretty." "Curious" is too tame a word wherewith to describe the imposing insanity of this work. There is no word that is large enough or long enough. Let us, therefore, photograph a passing glimpse of book and author, and trust the rest to the reader. Let the cultivated English student of human nature picture to himself this Mark Twain as a person capable of doing the following-described things—and not only doing them, but with incredible innocence *printing them* calmly and tranquilly in a book. For instance:

He states that he entered a hair-dresser's in Paris to get shaved, and the first "rake" the barber gave with his razor it *loosened his "hide"* and *lifted him out of his chair.*

This is unquestionably exaggerated. In Florence he was so annoyed by beggars that he pretends to have seized and eaten one in a frantic spirit of revenge. There is of course no truth in this. He gives at full length a theatrical programme seventeen or eighteen hundred years old, which he professes to have found in the ruins of the Coliseum, among the dirt and mold and rubbish. It is a sufficient comment upon this statement to remark that even a cast-iron programme would not have lasted so long under such circumstances. In Greece he plainly betrays both fright and flight upon one occasion, but with frozen effrontery puts the latter in this falsely tame form: "We *sidled* toward the Piraeus." "Sidled," indeed! He does not hesitate to intimate that at Ephesus, when his mule strayed from the proper course, he got down, took him under his arm, carried him to the road again, pointed him right, remounted, and went to sleep contentedly till it was time to restore the beast to the path once more. He states that a growing youth among his ship's passengers was in the constant habit of appeasing his hunger with soap and oakum between meals. In Palestine he tells of ants that came eleven miles to spend the summer in the desert and brought their provisions with them; yet he shows by his description of the country that the feat was an impossibility. He mentions, as if it were the most commonplace of matters, that he cut a Moslem in two in broad daylight in Jerusalem, with Godfrey de Bouillon's sword, and would have shed more blood *if he had had a graveyard of his own*. These statements are unworthy a moment's attention. Mr. Twain or any other foreigner who did such a thing in Jerusalem would be mobbed, and would infallibly lose his life. But why go on? Why repeat more of his audacious and exasperating falsehoods? Let us close fittingly with this one: he affirms that "in the mosque of St. Sophia at Constantinople I got my feet so stuck up with a complication of gums, slime, and general impurity, that I *wore out more than two thousand pair of bootjacks* getting my books off that night, and even then some Christian hide peeled off with them." It is monstrous. Such statements are simply lies—there is no other name for them. Will the reader longer marvel at the brutal ignorance that pervades the American nation when we tell him that we are informed upon perfectly good authority that this extravagant compilation of falsehoods, this exhaustless mine of stupendous lies, this *Innocents Abroad*, has actually been adopted by the schools and colleges of several of the States as a text-book!

But if his falsehoods are distressing, his innocence and his ignorance are enough to make one burn the book and despise the author. In one place he was so appalled at the sudden spectacle of a murdered man, unveiled by the moonlight, that he jumped out of the window, going through sash and all, and then remarks with the most childlike simplicity that he "was not scared, but was considerably agitated." It puts us out of patience to note that the simpleton is densely unconscious that Lucrezia Borgia ever existed off the stage. He is vulgarly ignorant of all foreign languages, but is frank enough to criticize the Italians' use of their own tongue. He says they spell the name of their great painter "Vinci, but pronounce it Vinchy"—and then adds with a naivete possible only to helpless ignorance, "foreigners always spell better than they pronounce." In another place he commits the bald absurdity of putting the phrase "tare an ouns" into an Italian's mouth. In Rome he unhesitatingly believes the legend that St. Philip Neri's heart was so inflamed with divine love that it burst his ribs—believes it wholly because an author with a learned list of university degrees strung after his name endorses it—"otherwise," says this gentle idiot, "I should have felt a curiosity to know what Philip had for dinner." Our author makes a long, fatiguing journey to the Grotto del Cane on purpose to test its poisoning powers on a dog—got elaborately ready for the experiment, and then discovered that he had no dog. A wiser person would have kept such a thing discreetly to himself, but with this harmless creature everything comes out. He hurts his foot in a rut two thousand years old in exhumed Pompeii, and presently, when staring at one of the cinder-like corpses unearthed in the next square, conceives the idea that maybe it is the remains of the ancient Street Commissioner, and straightway his horror softens down to a sort of chirpy contentment with the condition of things. In Damascus he visits the well of Ananias, three thousand years old, and is as surprised and delighted as a child to find that the water is "as pure and fresh as if the well had been dug yesterday." In the Holy Land he gags desperately at the hard Arabic and Hebrew Biblical names, and finally concludes to call them Baldwinsville, Williamsburgh, and so on, "for convenience of spelling!"

We have spoken thus freely of this man's stupefying simplicity and innocence, but we cannot deal similarly with his colossal ignorance. We do not know where to begin. And if we knew where to begin, we certainly would not know where to leave off. We will give one more specimen, and one only. He did not know, until he got to Rome, that Michael Angelo was dead! And then, instead of crawling away and hiding his shameful ignorance somewhere, he proceeds to express a pious, grateful sort of satisfaction that he is gone and out of his troubles!

No, the reader may seek out the author's exhibitions of his uncultivation for himself. The book is absolutely dangerous, considering the multitude and variety of its misstatements, and the convincing confidence with which they are made. And yet it is a text-book in the schools of America.

The poor blunderer mouses among the sublime creations of the Old Masters, trying to acquire the elegant proficiency in art-knowledge, which he has a groping sort of comprehension is a proper thing for the travelled man to be able to display. But what is the manner of his study? And what is the progress he achieves? To what extent does he familiarize himself with the great pictures of Italy, and what degree of appreciation does he arrive at? Read:

"When we see a monk going about with a lion and looking up into heaven, we know that that is St. Mark. When we see a monk with a book and a pen, looking tranquilly up to heaven, trying to think of a word, we know that that is St. Matthew. When we see a monk sitting on a rock, looking tranquilly up to heaven, with a human skull beside him, and without other baggage, we know that that is St. Jerome. Because we know that he is always flying light in the matter of baggage. When we see other monks looking tranquilly up to heaven, but having no trade-mark, we always ask who those parties are. We do this because we humbly wish to learn."

He then enumerates the thousands and thousands of copies of these several pictures which he has seen, and adds with accustomed simplicity that he feels encouraged to believe that when he has seen "Some More" of each, and had a larger experience, he will eventually "begin to take an absorbing interest in them"—the vulgar boor.

That we have shown this to be a remarkable book, we think no one will deny. That it is a pernicious book to place in the hands of the confiding and uninformed, we think we have also shown. That the book is a deliberate and wicked creation of a diseased mind, is apparent upon every page. Having placed our judgment thus upon record, let us close with what charity we can, by remarking that even in this volume there is some good to be found; for whenever the author talks of his own country and lets Europe alone, he never fails to make himself interesting; and not only interesting, but instructive. No one can read without benefit his occasional chapters and paragraphs, about life in the gold and silver mines of California and Nevada; about the Indians of the plains and deserts of the West, and their cannibalism; about the raising of vegetables in kegs of gunpowder by the aid of two or three teaspoonfuls of guano; about the moving of small farms from place to place at night in wheelbarrows to avoid taxes; and about a sort of cows and mules in the Humboldt mines, that climb down chimneys and disturb the people at night. These matters are not only new, but are well worth knowing. It is a pity the author did not put in more of the same kind. His book is well-written and is exceedingly entertaining, and so it just barely escaped being quite valuable also.

(One month later)

Latterly I have received several letters, and see a number of newspaper paragraphs, all upon a certain subject, and all of about the same tenor. I here give honest specimens. One is from a New York paper, one is from a letter from an old friend, and one is from a letter from a New York publisher who is a stranger to me. I humbly endeavor to make these bits toothsome with the remark that the article they are praising (which appeared in the December *Galaxy*, and *pretended* to be a criticism from the London *Saturday Review* on my *Innocents Abroad*) *was written by myself, every line of it*:

> The *Herald* says the richest thing out is the "serious critique" in the London *Saturday Review*, on Mark Twain's *Innocents Abroad*. We thought before we read it that it must be "serious," as everybody said so, and were even ready to shed a few tears; but since perusing it, we are bound to confess that next to Mark Twain's "Jumping Frog" it's the finest bit of humor and sarcasm that we've come across in many a day.

(I do not get a compliment like that every day.)

> I used to think that your writings were pretty good, but after reading the criticism in *The Galaxy* from the *London Review*, have discovered what an ass I must have been. If suggestions are in order, mine is, that you put that article in your next edition of the *Innocents*, as an extra chapter, if you are not afraid to put your own humor in competition with it. It is as rich a thing as I ever read.

(Which is strong commendation from a book publisher.)

> The London Reviewer, my friend, is not the stupid, "serious" creature he pretends to be, *I* think; but, on the contrary, has a keen appreciation and enjoyment of your book. As I read his article in *The Galaxy*, I could imagine him giving vent to many a hearty laugh. But he is writing for Catholics and Established Church people, and high-toned, antiquated, conservative gentility, whom it is a delight to him to help you shock, while he pretends to shake his head with owlish density. He is a magnificent humorist himself.

(Now that is graceful and handsome. I take off my hat to my lifelong friend and comrade, and with my feet together and my fingers spread over my heart, I say, in the language of Alabama, "You do me proud.")

I stand guilty of the authorship of the article, but I did not mean any harm. I saw by an item in the Boston *Advertiser* that a solemn, serious critique on the English edition of my book had appeared in the London *Saturday Review*, and the idea of *such* a literary breakfast by a stolid, ponderous British ogre of the quill was too much for a naturally weak virtue, and I went home and burlesqued it—reveled in it, I may say. I never saw a copy of the real *Saturday Review* criticism until after my burlesque was written and mailed to the printer. But when I did get hold of a copy, I found it to be vulgar, awkwardly written, ill-natured, and entirely serious and in earnest. The gentleman who wrote the newspaper paragraph above quoted had not been misled as to its character.

If any man doubts my word now, I will kill him. No, I will not kill him; I will win his money. I will bet him twenty to one, and let any New York publisher hold the stakes, that the statements I have above made as to the authorship of the article in question are entirely true. Perhaps I may get wealthy at this, for I am willing to take all the bets that offer; and if a man wants larger odds, I will give him all he requires. But he ought to find out whether I am betting on what is termed "a sure thing" or not before he ventures his money, and he can do that by going to a public library and examining the London *Saturday Review* of October 8th, which contains the real critique.

Bless me, some people thought that *I* was the "sold" person!

P.S.—I cannot resist the temptation to toss in this most savory thing of all—this easy, graceful, philosophical disquisition, with its happy, chirping confidence. It is from the Cincinnati *Enquirer*:

> Nothing is more uncertain than the value of a fine cigar. Nine smokers out of ten would prefer an ordinary domestic article, three for a quarter, to fifty-cent Partaga, if kept in ignorance of the cost of the latter. The flavor of the Partaga is too delicate for palates that have been accustomed to Connecticut seed leaf. So it is with humor. The finer it is in quality, the more danger of its not being recognized at all. Even Mark Twain has been taken in by an English review of his *Innocents Abroad*. Mark Twain is by no means a coarse humorist, but the Englishman's humor is so much finer than his, that he mistakes it for solid earnest, and "larfs most consumedly."

A man who cannot learn stands in his own light. Hereafter, when I write an article which I know to be good, but which I may have reason to fear will not, in some quarters, be considered to amount to much, coming from an American, I will aver that an Englishman wrote it and that it is copied from a London journal. And then I will occupy a back seat and enjoy the cordial applause.

(Still later)

Mark Twain at last sees that the *Saturday Review*'s criticism of his *Innocents Abroad* was not serious, and he is intensely mortified at the thought of having been so badly sold. He takes the only course left him, and in the last *Galaxy* claims that *he* wrote the criticism himself, and published it in *The Galaxy* to sell the public. This is ingenious, but unfortunately it is not true. If any of our readers will take the trouble to call at this office we will show them the original article in the *Saturday Review* of October 8th, which, on comparison, will be found to be identical with the one published in *The Galaxy*. The best thing for Mark to do will be to admit that he was sold, and say no more about it.

The above is from the Cincinnati *Enquirer*, and is a falsehood. Come to the proof. If the *Enquirer* people, through any agent, will produce at *The Galaxy* office a London *Saturday Review* of October 8th, containing an article which, on comparison, will be found to be identical with the one published in *The Galaxy*, I will pay to that agent five hundred dollars cash. Moreover, if at any specified time I fail to produce at the same place a copy of the London *Saturday Review* of October 8th, containing a lengthy criticism upon the *Innocents Abroad*, entirely different, in every paragraph and sentence, from the one I published in *The Galaxy*, I will pay to the *Enquirer* agent another five hundred dollars cash. I offer Sheldon & Co., publishers, 500 Broadway, New York, as my "backers." Any one in New York, authorized by the *Enquirer*, will receive prompt attention. It is an easy and profitable way for the *Enquirer* people to prove that they have not uttered a pitiful, deliberate falsehood in the above paragraphs. Will they swallow that falsehood ignominiously, or will they send an agent to *The Galaxy* office. I think the Cincinnati *Enquirer* must be edited by children.

Note
1. Yes, I calculated they were pretty new. I invented them Myself.

—Mark Twain, "An Entertaining Article,"
Galaxy, December 1870

HENRY HARLAND "MARK TWAIN" (1899)

What is the explanation of Mark Twain's great, continued, and very peculiar popularity? I say peculiar, because Mark Twain is not merely, like Mr. Hall Caine and Miss Marie Corelli, popular with the masses; he is popular also with the remnant; his works are enjoyed and esteemed by people of taste and cultivation—and that, in spite of faults, of vices, which, one would imagine antecedently, must render any work, to people of taste and cultivation, utterly abhorrent.

Let us be cruel (that we may be kind in due season), and give to a few of Mark Twain's more conspicuous and constant vices their common names. In re-reading *The Innocents Abroad*, for instance, I think one cannot help being struck by the vulgarity that mars the book, and by the illiteracy, by the ignorance and the inaccuracy, by the narrowness, the provincialism, above all by the perpetual, the colossal irreverence. And yet, one reads *The Innocents Abroad* with pleasure, even perhaps with some degree of profit; it is still, for all its vices, and much as they offend one, it is still a book one likes. Why? What is the explanation?

I'm afraid we shall never discover the explanation, unless we begin by considering the vices somewhat closely. It will only be by recognising and eliminating them, that we shall obtain, in the end, the residue of saving virtues. And we may eliminate at the outset, if you will, we may condone as venial, Mark Twain's illiteracy, ignorance, and inaccuracy. When he alludes to the grave-digger's discourse over the skull of Yorick, when he mentions that the signal for the fighting on St. Bartholomew's Day was rung from the towers of Notre Dame, when he translates 'Genova la Superba' 'Genoa the Superb'—it is easy to lift an eyebrow, shrug a shoulder, smile, and pass on. Even when he tells us that the 'pax hominibus bonae voluntatis,' which he saw blazoned in gold on the walls of St. John Lateran, 'is not good scripture,' we can commend him, in charity, to the intercession of St. Jerome. But Mark Twain's vulgarity, his narrowness, his provincialism, his irreverence, are made of sterner stuff. They are in the very texture of his work, not merely on its surface—they are of its spirit, they inform it, they determine its savor; and they are all bound and mixed up together, they are inseparable; it is impossible to discuss one without connoting the others. They are different manifestations, as it were, of the same constitutional defect: a total inability, namely, to respect what he cannot understand; an instant conviction that what he cannot see does not exist, and that those who profess to see it are hypocrites—that what he does not believe is inevitably false, and that those who profess to believe it are either hypocrites or fools. As if a color-blind man were to condemn as fools or hypocrites those who profess to see blue in the Union Jack, or to admire the splendors of a sunset.

It is this constitutional defect, I fancy, which accounts for Mark Twain's most egregious solecisms, for his most unlovely blasphemies. It is this which leads him to the perpetration of his numberless cheap and dreary jests about the 'Old Masters.' It is this which so deprives him of any sense of proportion as to enable him to write seriously of Raphael, Michael Angelo, and Canova in the same breath; to explain that the exterior of St. Peter's is 'not one-twentieth part as beautiful as the Capitol at Washington'; to suggest that it is the supreme mission of art to 'copy nature with faultless accuracy'; to prefer the marble millinery which has occasioned most of us a shudder in the Campo Santo at Genoa to the 'damaged and dingy statuary' of the Louvre; to declare that 'wherever you find a Raphael, a Rubens, a Michael Angelo, or a Da Vinci, you find artists copying them, and the copies are always the handsomer. Maybe the originals were handsome when they were new, but they are not now.'

It is this terrible inability to respect what he cannot understand, this fatal readiness to despise those whose opinions he does not share, which makes it possible for Mark Twain to crack his ghastly jokes about death, his dreadful jokes at the expense of things that to the majority of civilised mankind are sacrosanct, his jokes at the expense of the saints, and the pictures and relics of the saints—nay, at the expense of more sacred relics still, at the expense of the Crown of Thorns and the True Cross. 'They say St. Mark had a tame lion, and used to travel with him—and everywhere that St. Mark went the lion was sure to go.' 'When we see a party looking tranquilly up to heaven, unconscious that his body is shot through with arrows, we know that that is St. Sebastian.' 'I think we have seen as much as a keg of these nails.' What nails? Nails from the True Cross, if you can believe me. It is always, I suppose, the same inability to respect what he cannot understand which makes it possible for Mark Twain to write facetiously of his travels in Palestine, and to crack a final joke about the True Cross in the presence of the Holy Sepulchre.

All this is surely very shocking; to some of us it must be very repulsive. Why is it, then, that in spite of all this we can still read Mark Twain with pleasure, perhaps with profit, still esteem him, and acknowledge his good right to the popularity, even with the remnant, which he has won? Why must we still reckon *The Innocents Abroad* among the books we like?

Well, certainly not, at any rate, certainly not because of its humor. The humor of the book, one is surprised to find on re-reading it after a lapse of years, is by no means its most salient feature nor its brightest merit—is indeed, for the most part, extremely thin, flat, and inexpensive. Sometimes, in our weaker moments, it may excite a pale flicker of a smile; never a laugh; never, never—*au grand jamais*—that deep internal glow which is our response to humor in its finer flower. But if it is not the humor of the book, what is it?

I wonder whether it isn't in some measure—no, in great measure—the downright barbarism of the book? The big, bluff, rough, honest barbarism of the book and of its writer? What Mark Twain cannot see, he cannot see at all; he cannot believe in it, he cannot allow for it; you and I are hypocrites (or fools) for professing to see it. But what he can see, he sees with the unwearied eyes of the barbarian, of one to whom the old world is new—of a shrewd, clear-headed barbarian, outspoken, fearless, sincere, who knows how to present his impressions lucidly, vividly. And it is necessarily interesting to get a clear-headed barbarian's impression of our old world, interesting and fascinating. He will gibe at our gods, mock at our sacred mysteries, profane our shrines, march booted and bare-headed upon our holy ground, he will outrage our sensibilities, trample upon our conventions, assault our prejudices and our fond illusions; but never mind. He cannot see what we can see, and we cannot hope to make him see it; but he will see much that we have not seen, and we (because the larger contains the less) shall be able, when he points it out, to see it with him. Fancy travelling through Europe with a keen-witted English-speaking pilgrim from the moon—visiting Paris and the Louvre with him, Rome and the Vatican, Naples, Constantinople, Athens, Como, and the Hellespont, and listening to his commentaries upon these familiar sights. Would it be instructive, suggestive, amusing, exhilarating? Well, Mark Twain, this pilgrim from the Mississippi valley, brings to Europe eyes very nearly as fresh as the moonman's. It is instructive, suggestive, amusing, exhilarating to travel with him. He speaks his own quaint manner of English with fluency and energy and picturesque eloquence; and he is good-humored and wholesome; and his heart is in the right place.

Of course, *The Innocents Abroad* is not the best of Mark Twain's books. *Roughing It*, I think, is a better book; I am sure *Tom Sawyer* and *Huckleberry Finn* are better books. But the qualities and the defects of *The Innocents Abroad* are the qualities and the defects of Mark Twain's temperament, and they are present in varying proportions in all his books: vulgarity, narrowness, irreverence, freshness of vision, honesty, good-humor, wholesomeness. Mr. Brander Matthews, in a 'Biographical Criticism' accompanying these volumes, says that Mark Twain 'must be classed with Molière and Cervantes.' But then Mr. Brander Matthews, in the same article, brackets the late Mr. J. R. Lowell also with Molière and Cervantes, and that somehow shakes one's faith in Mr. Matthews's judgment. Time will show.

The present 'edition de luxe' of Mark Twain's works is handsomely printed upon good imitation hand-made paper, and ornamented by some of the worst wash-drawings (by a Mr. Peter Newell) that it has ever been my lot to see. 'Theatre' is spelled 'theater,' 'centre' 'center,' and 'traveller' is allowed but a single 'l.'

—Henry Harland, "Mark Twain," London
Daily Chronicle, December 11, 1899

Mark Twain "Mark Twain's Own Account" (1907)

Through MacAlister, Mark Twain has been good enough to supply me with an account of a much earlier visit to the Club than any of those just named. He says:—

"About thirty-five years ago (1872) I took a sudden notion to go to England and get materials for a book about that not-sufficiently known country. It was my purpose to spy out the land in a very private way, and complete my visit without making any acquaintances. I had never been in England. I was eager to see it, and I promised myself an interesting time. The interesting time began at once, in the London train from Liverpool. It lasted an hour—an hour of delight, rapture, ecstasy. These are the best words I can find, but they are not adequate, they are not strong enough to convey the feeling which this first vision of rural England brought to me. Then the interest changed and took another form: I began to wonder why the Englishman in the other end of the compartment never looked up from his book. It seemed to me that I had not before seen a man who could read a whole hour in a train and never once take his eyes off his book. I wondered what kind of a book it might be that could so absorb a person. Little by little my curiosity grew, until at last it divided my interest in the scenery; and then went on growing until it abolished it. I felt that I must satisfy this curiosity before I could get back to my scenery, so I loitered over to that man's end of the carriage and stole a furtive glance at the book; it was the English edition of my 'Innocents Abroad!' Then I loitered back to my end of the compartment, nervous, uncomfortable, and sorry I had found out: for I remembered that up to this time I had never seen that absorbed reader smile. I could not look out at the scenery any more. I could not take my eyes from the reader and his book. I tried to get a sort of comfort out of the fact that he was evidently deeply interested in the book and manifestly never skipped a line, but the comfort was only moderate and was quite unsatisfying. I hoped he would smile once—only just once—and I kept on hoping and hoping, but it never happened. By and by I perceived that he was getting close to the end;

then I was glad, for my misery would soon be over. The train made only one stop in its journey of five hours and twenty minutes; the stop was at Crewe. The gentleman finished the book just as we were slowing down for the stop. When the train came to a standstill he put the book in the rack and jumped out. I shall always remember what a wave of gratitude and happiness swept through me when he turned the last page of that book. I felt as a condemned man must feel who is pardoned upon the scaffold with the noose hanging over him. I said to myself that I would now resume the scenery and be twice as happy in it as I had been before. But this was premature, for as soon as the gentleman returned, he reached into his hand-bag and got out the second volume! He and that volume constituted the only scenery that fell under my eyes during the rest of the journey. From Crewe to London he read in that same old absorbed way, but he never smiled. Neither did I."

> —Mark Twain, "Mark Twain's Own Account,"
> from *The Savage Club: A Medley of Historical
> Anecdote and Reminiscence*, Aaron Watson,
> London: T. Fisher Unwin, 1907, pp. 131–133

WILLIAM DEAN HOWELLS (1910)

The vividest impression which Clemens gave us two ravenous young Boston authors was of the satisfying, the surfeiting nature of subscription publication. An army of agents was overrunning the country with the prospectuses of his books, and delivering them by the scores of thousands in completed sale. Of the *Innocents Abroad* he said, "It sells right along just like the Bible," and *Roughing It* was swiftly following, without perhaps ever quite overtaking it in popularity. But he lectured Aldrich and me on the folly of that mode of publication in the trade which we had thought it the highest success to achieve a chance in. "Anything but subscription publication is printing for private circulation," he maintained, and he so won upon our greed and hope that on the way back to Boston we planned the joint authorship of a volume adapted to subscription publication. We got a very good name for it, as we believed, in *Memorable Murders*, and we never got farther with it, but by the time we reached Boston we were rolling in wealth so deep that we could hardly walk home in the frugal fashion by which we still thought it best to spare car fare; carriage fare we did not dream of even in that opulence.

> —William Dean Howells,
> *My Mark Twain*, 1910, pp. 7–8

ARTHUR BIGELOW PAINE (1912)

Meantime *The Innocents Abroad* had continued to prosper. Its author ranked mainly as a humorist, but of such colossal proportions that his contemporaries had seemed to dwindle; the mighty note of the "Frog of Calaveras" had dwarfed a score of smaller peepers. At the end of a year from its publication the *Innocents* had sold up to 67,000, and was continuing at the rate of several thousand monthly.

"You are running it in staving, tiptop, first-class style," Clemens wrote to Bliss. "On the average ten people a day come and hunt me up to tell me I am a benefactor! I guess that is a part of the program we didn't expect, in the first place."

Apparently the book appealed to readers of every grade. One hundred and fifteen copies were in constant circulation at the Mercantile Library, in New York, while in the most remote cabins of America it was read and quoted. Jack Van Nostrand, making a long horseback tour of Colorado, wrote:

> I stopped a week ago in a ranch but a hundred miles from nowhere. The occupant had just two books: the Bible and *The Innocents Abroad*—the former in good repair.

Across the ocean the book had found no less favor, and was being translated into many and strange tongues. By what seems now some veritable magic its author's fame had become literally universal. The consul at Hongkong, discussing English literature with a Chinese acquaintance, a mandarin, mentioned *The Pilgrim's Progress*.

"Yes, indeed, I have read it!" the mandarin said, eagerly. "We are enjoying it in China, and shall have it soon in our own language. It is by Mark Twain."

In England the book had an amazing vogue from the beginning, and English readers were endeavoring to outdo the Americans in appreciation. Indeed, as a rule, English readers of culture, critical readers, rose to an understanding of Mark Twain's literary value with greater promptness than did the same class of readers at home. There were exceptions, of course. There were English critics who did not take Mark Twain seriously, there were American critics who did. Among the latter was a certain William Ward, editor of a paper in Macon, Mississippi—*The Beacon*. Ward did not hold a place with the great magazine arbiters of literary rank. He was only an obscure country editor, but he wrote like a prophet. His article—too long to quote in full—concerned American humorists in general, from Washington Irving, through John Phoenix, Philander Doesticks, Sut Lovingwood,

Artemus Ward, Josh Billings and Petroleum V. Nasby, down to Mark Twain. With the exception of the first and last named he says of them:

> They have all had, or will have, their day. Some of them are resting beneath the sod, and others still live whose work will scarcely survive them. Since Irving no humorist in prose has held the foundation of a permanent fame except it be Mark Twain, and this, as in the case of Irving, is because he is a pure writer. Aside from any subtle mirth that lurks through his composition, the grace and finish of his more didactic and descriptive sentences indicate more than mediocrity.

The writer then refers to Mark Twain's description of the Sphinx, comparing it with Bulwer's, which he thinks may have influenced it. He was mistaken in this, for Clemens had not read Bulwer—never *could* read him at any length.

Of the English opinions, that of *The Saturday Review* was perhaps most doubtful. It came along late in 1870, and would hardly be worth recalling if it were not for a resulting, or collateral, interest. Clemens saw notice of this review before he saw the review itself. A paragraph in the Boston *Advertiser* spoke of *The Saturday Review as* treating the absurdities of the *Innocents* from a serious standpoint. The paragraph closed:

> We can imagine the delight of the humorist in reading this tribute to his power; and indeed it is so amusing in itself that he can hardly do better than reproduce the article in full in his next monthly "Memoranda."

The old temptation to hoax his readers prompted Mark Twain to "reproduce" in *The Galaxy*, not the *Review* article, which he had not yet seen, but an *imaginary Review* article, an article in which the imaginary reviewer would be utterly devoid of any sense of humor and treat the most absurd incidents of *The New Pilgrim's Progress* as if set down by the author in solemn and serious earnest. The pretended review began:

> Lord Macaulay died too soon. We never felt this so deeply as when we finished the last chapter of the above-named extravagant work. Macaulay died too soon; for none but he could mete out complete and comprehensive justice to the insolence, the impudence, the presumption, the mendacity, and, above all, the majestic ignorance of this author.

The review goes on to cite cases of the author's gross deception. It says:

> Let the cultivated English student of human nature picture to himself this Mark Twain as a person capable of doing the following described things; and not only doing them, but, with incredible innocence, printing them tranquilly and calmly in a book. For instance:
>
> He states that he entered a hair-dresser's in Paris to get a shave, and the first "rake" the barber gave him with his razor it loosened his "hide," and lifted him out of the chair.
>
> This is unquestionably extravagant. In Florence he was so annoyed by beggars that he pretends to have seized and eaten one in a frantic spirit of revenge. There is, of course, no truth in this. He gives at full length the theatrical program, seventeen or eighteen hundred years old, which he professes to have found in the ruins of the Colosseum, among the dirt and mold and rubbish. It is a sufficient comment upon this subject to remark that even a cast-iron program would not have lasted so long under the circumstances.

There were two and one-half pages of this really delightful burlesque which the author had written with huge enjoyment, partly as a joke on the *Review*, partly to trick American editors, who he believed would accept it as a fresh and startling proof of the traditional English lack of humor.

But, as in the early sage-brush hoaxes, he rather overdid the thing. Readers and editors readily enough accepted it as genuine, so far as having come from *The Saturday Review*; but most of them regarded it as a delicious bit of humor which Mark Twain himself had taken seriously, and was therefore the one sold. This was certainly startling, and by no means gratifying. In the next issue he undertook that saddest of all performances with tongue or pen: he explained his joke, and insisted on the truth of the explanation. Then he said:

> If any man doubts my word now I will kill him. No, I will not kill him; I will win his money. I will bet him twenty to one, and let any New York publisher hold the stakes, that the statements I have above made as to the authorship of the article in question are entirely true.

But the Cincinnati *Enquirer* persisted in continuing the joke—in "rubbing it in," as we say now. The *Enquirer* declared that Mark Twain had been intensely mortified at having been so badly taken in; that his explanation in the *Galaxy* was "ingenious, but unfortunately not true." The *Enquirer* maintained that *The Saturday Review* of October 8, 1870, did contain the article exactly as printed in the "Memoranda," and advised Mark Twain to admit that he was sold, and say no more about it.

This was enraging. Mark Twain had his own ideas as to how far a joke might be carried without violence, and this was a good way beyond the limits. He denounced the *Enquirer*'s statement as a "pitiful, deliberate falsehood," in his anger falling into the old-time phrasing of newspaper editorial abuse. He offered to bet them a thousand dollars in cash that they could not prove their assertions, and asked pointedly, in conclusion: "Will they swallow that falsehood ignominiously, or will they send an agent to the *Galaxy* office? I think the Cincinnati *Enquirer* must be edited by children." He promised that if they did not accept his financial proposition he would expose them in the next issue.

The incident closed there. He was prevented, by illness in his household, from contributing to the next issue, and the second issue following was his final "Memoranda" instalment. So the matter perished and was forgotten. It was his last editorial hoax. Perhaps he concluded that hoaxes in any form were dangerous playthings; they were too likely to go off at the wrong end.

—Arthur Bigelow Paine, from *Mark Twain: A Biography,* New York: Harper and Brothers, 1912, 1: pp. 426–430

THE ADVENTURES OF TOM SAWYER

The regional tensions evident in reviews of an earlier Twain work *Roughing It* are reinvigorated in Howells's review of *Tom Sawyer*. Howells compares Twain's book to a predecessor, Thomas Bailey Aldrich's *The Story of a Bad Boy* (1870), a comparison that will recur in several of the reviews included in this section. Howells sees Aldrich's *Bad Boy* as a "pleasant reprobate," "hemmed in" by established New England tradition, while Tom Sawyer is "the boy of the Southwest." Howells's opinion of the frontier remains unchanged from his earlier review of Twain's work; the novel's "St. Petersburg" setting is an "idle, shabby little Mississippi River town." It is fortunate, then, that Tom Sawyer "belongs to the better sort of people in it." Howells sees Tom as a product of frontier Calvinism, fearing God and struggling with "manifold sins. . . . In a word," Howells writes, "he is a boy."

Howells purposely tries to distinguish *Tom Sawyer* from the sort of humor customarily associated with the Southwest. Twain, he writes, provides "a sober and serious and orderly contrast to the sort of life that has come to represent the Southwest in literature." Fifty years later, Bernard DeVoto would hinge his study *Mark Twain's America* on an opposite assertion: that Twain was influenced by precisely that Southwest school of humor.

Howells's mystification of Mississippi is shared by Moncure Daniel Conway, an American minister and writer residing at the time in England, who wonders in similar awe about the "far frontiers of American civilisation" and elsewhere "the confines of civilisation," a "pioneer point."

Conway raises an important question, prompted by Twain's own preface to the book: Who is its intended audience? Is it intended first for adults or for boys? Aside from the boys, "it might be most prized by philosophers and poets." Students investigating the audience for Twain's novel will find a useful inquiry initiated by Conway. A different view of Twain's audience is provided by the reviewer for the London *Athenaeum*, who, prior to reading *Tom Sawyer*, could not disassociate Twain "from the railway-station" where his books were sold, apparently alongside Artemus Ward's works and copies of *The Diseases of Dogs*.

The same reviewer notes a change in direction; the new work is "consecutive," not fragmented. Carl Van Doren, writing more than forty years later, finds the novel structured rather like a play, "with exits and entrances not always motivated" and laments its "defects of structure." The characterization is paramount, while the "poetry and satire" of the novel entirely outweigh the narrative. Van Doren concedes, though, that this same loose structure allows for the "flexibility of the narrative, its easy, casual gait." Students of Twain's use (or not) of a narrative structure should take note.

Other English reviewers, such as Richard Littledale, hail the novel for "showing what kind of animal the American schoolboy is," an achievement not to be underrated. Thomas Hardy would one day remark similarly that, "Mark Twain did more than any other man to make plain people in England understand plain people in America." Carl Van Doren, detecting the same purpose in the text, is less approving, finding *Tom Sawyer* tending toward "the documentary side of the line which divides documents from works of art."

The reviewer for the *New York Times* concentrates on Twain's dual audience for this book, holding it up alongside Lewis Carroll's *Alice in Wonderland*, an exemplary tome that provided that rare "double appreciation," wherein "both parent and child agree in their conclusions." He seems to be in a state of some conflict over *Tom Sawyer*. On one hand, he recognizes that children's books of the past were "mostly constructed in one monotonous key" with facts and morals included "like bitter draughts or acrid pills." This duly noted, the reviewer frowns on a strain of "ugly realism" that has invaded children's literature recently, and he maintains that "courage, frankness, truthfulness, and self-reliance are to be inculcated in our lads."

Students exploring the status of children's literature in the United States at this time, and how *Tom Sawyer* differed from or affirmed the prevailing generic tendencies, will find this review valuable. The reviewer credits the realism of the book ("Matters are not told as they are fancied to be, but as they actually are"), and he particularly praises the character of Huckleberry Finn: "There is a reality about this boy which is striking." Nevertheless, the book would have benefited from less Injun Joe, less slitting of women's ears, and less of "the shadow of the gallows."

This conflict between the shadow of the gallows, between Southwest grotesquery on one side and the need to be wholesome and demonstrate "natural piety" on the other, excited doubts in Twain's mind as well. These doubts are attested to in William Dean Howells's later reminiscence of the book and its editing, particularly the part played by Olivia Clemens in shaping her husband's book. Those students interested in the degree of editorial influence enjoyed by Howells (and Livy Clemens), and the nature of that influence, will find these remarks significant.

Reflecting the changing tides of literary taste, the poet Edgar Lee Masters reviews the novel with a pedant's eye and criticizes it for lacking the proper realism. In discussing the novel's errors of vernacular, he sounds rather like the fabricated author in Twain's own hoax review of *The Innocents Abroad*, previously included in this section. Nevertheless, his view may serve students looking at questions of realism and local color in Twain's work.

WILLIAM DEAN HOWELLS (1876)

Mr. Aldrich has studied the life of A Bad Boy as the pleasant reprobate led it in a quiet old New England town twenty-five or thirty years ago, where in spite of the natural outlawry of boyhood he was more or less part of a settled order of things, and was hemmed in, to some measure, by the traditions of an established civilization. Mr. Clemens, on the contrary, has taken the boy of the Southwest for the hero of his new book, and has presented him with a fidelity to circumstance which loses no charm by being realistic in the highest degree, and which gives incomparably the best picture of life in that region as yet known to fiction. The town where Tom Sawyer was born and brought up is some such idle, shabby little Mississippi River town as Mr. Clemens has so well described in his piloting reminiscences, but Tom belongs to the better sort of people in it, and has been bred to fear God and dread the Sunday-school according to the strictest rite of the faiths that have characterized all the respectability of the West. His subjection in these respects does not so deeply affect his inherent tendencies but that he makes himself a beloved burden to the poor, tender-hearted old aunt who brings him up with his orphan brother and sister, and struggles vainly with his manifold sins, actual and imaginary. The limitations of his transgressions are nicely and artistically traced. He is mischievous, but not vicious; he is ready for almost any depredation that involves the danger and honor of adventure, but profanity he knows may provoke a thunderbolt upon the heart of the blasphemer, and he almost never swears; he resorts to any stratagem to keep out of school, but he is not a downright liar, except upon terms of after shame and remorse that make his falsehood bitter to him. He is cruel, as all children are, but chiefly because he is ignorant; he is not mean, but there are very definite bounds to his generosity; and his courage is the Indian sort, full of prudence and mindful of retreat as one of the conditions of prolonged hostilities. In a word, he is a boy, and merely and exactly an ordinary boy on the moral side. What makes him delightful to the reader is that on the imaginative side he is very much more, and though every boy has wild and fantastic dreams, this boy cannot rest till he has somehow realized them. Till he has actually run off with two other boys in the character of buccaneer, and lived for a week on an island in the Mississippi, he has lived in vain; and this passage is but the prelude to more thrilling adventures, in which he finds hidden treasures, traces the bandits to their cave, and is himself lost in its recesses. The local material and the incidents with which his career is worked up are excellent, and throughout there is scrupulous regard for the boy's point of view in reference to his surroundings and himself, which shows how rapidly Mr. Clemens has grown as an artist. We do not remember anything in which this propriety is violated, and its preservation adds immensely to the grown-up reader's satisfaction in the amusing and exciting story. There is a boy's love-affair, but it is never treated otherwise than as a boy's love-affair. When the half-breed has murdered the young doctor, Tom and his friend, Huckleberry

Finn, are really, in their boyish terror and superstition, going to let the poor old town-drunkard be hanged for the crime, till the terror of that becomes unendurable. The story is a wonderful study of the boy-mind, which inhabits a world quite distinct from that in which he is bodily present with his elders, and in this lies its great charm and its universality, for boy-nature, however human nature varies, is the same everywhere.

The tale is very dramatically wrought, and the subordinate characters are treated with the same graphic force that sets Tom alive before us. The worthless vagabond, Huck Finn, is entirely delightful throughout, and in his promised reform his identity is respected: he will lead a decent life in order that he may one day be thought worthy to become a member of that gang of robbers which Tom is to organize. Tom's aunt is excellent, with her kind heart's sorrow and secret pride in Tom; and so is his sister Mary, one of those good girls who are born to usefulness and charity and forbearance and unvarying rectitude. Many village people and local notables are introduced in well-conceived character; the whole little town lives in the reader's sense, with its religiousness, its lawlessness, its droll social distinctions, its civilization qualified by its slave-holding, and its traditions of the wilder West which has passed away. The picture will be instructive to those who have fancied the whole Southwest a sort of vast Pike County, and have not conceived of a sober and serious and orderly contrast to the sort of life that has come to represent the Southwest in literature. Mr. William M. Baker gives a notion of this in his stories, and Mr. Clemens has again enforced the fact here, in a book full of entertaining character, and of the greatest artistic sincerity.

Tom Brown and Tom Bailey are, among boys in books, alone deserving to be named with Tom Sawyer.

—William Dean Howells, *Atlantic*
Monthly 37, May 1876, pp. 621–622

MONCURE DANIEL CONWAY (1876)

This newest work of Mark Twain increases the difficulty of assigning that author a literary *habitat*. "American humorist" has for some time been recognised as too vague a label to attach to a writer whose "Jumping Frog" and other early sketches have been reduced to mere fragments and ventures by such productions as *The Innocents Abroad* and *The New Pilgrim's Progress*, in which, while the humour is still fresh, there is present an equal art in graphic description of natural scenery, and a fine sense of what is genuinely impressive in the grandeurs of the past. Those who have travelled with Mark Twain with some curiosity to observe the effect of the ancient world interpreted by a very shrewd eye, fresh from the newest outcome of civilisation, may have expected to find antiquity turned into a solemn joke, but they can hardly have failed to discover a fine discrimination present at each step in the path of the "new pilgrim"; while he sheds tears of a kind hardly relished by the superstitious or sentimental over the supposed grave of his deceased parent Adam, he can "listen deep" when any true theme from the buried world reaches his ear. Without being pathetic he is sympathetic, and there is also an innate refinement in his genius felt in every subject it selects and in its treatment of it. *Tom Sawyer* carries us to an altogether novel region, and along with these characteristics displays a somewhat puzzling variety of abilities. There is something almost stately in the simplicity with which he invites us to turn our attention to the affairs of some boys and girls growing up on the far frontiers of American civilisation. With the Eastern Question upon us, and crowned heads arrayed on the political stage, it may be with some surprise that we find our interest demanded in sundry Western questions that are solving themselves through a *dramatis personae* of humble folk whose complications occur in a St. Petersburg situated on the Missouri river. Our manager, we feel quite sure, would not for a moment allow us to consider that any other St. Petersburg is of equal importance to that for which he claims our attention. What is the deposition, death, or enthronement of a Sultan compared with the tragical death of "Injun Joe," the murderer, accidentally buried and entombed in the cavern where his stolen treasures are hid? There he was found.

> The poor unfortunate had starved to death. In one place, near at hand, a stalagmite had been slowly growing up from the ground for ages, builded by the water-drip from a stalactite overhead. The captive had broken off the stalagmite, and upon the stump had placed a stone, wherein he had scooped a shallow hollow to catch the precious drop that fell once in every three minutes with the dreary regularity of a clock-tick—a dessert-spoonful once in four and twenty hours. That drop was falling when the Pyramids were new; when Troy fell; when the foundations of Rome were laid when Christ was crucified; when the Conqueror created the British empire; when Columbus sailed; when the massacre at Lexington was "news." It is falling now; it will still be falling when all these things shall have sunk down the afternoon of history, and the twilight of tradition,

and been swallowed up in the thick night of oblivion. Has everything a purpose and a mission? Did this drop fall patiently during five thousand years to be ready for this flitting human insect's need? and has it another important object to accomplish ten thousand years to come? No matter. It is many and many a year since the hapless half-breed scooped out the stone to catch the priceless drops, but to this day the tourist stares longest at that pathetic stone and that slow-dropping water when he comes to see the wonders of McDougal's cave. Injun Joe's cup stands first in the list of the cavern's marvels; even "Aladdin's Palace" cannot rival it.

In such writing as this we seem to be reading some classic fable, such as the Persian Sâdi might point with his moral, "Set not your heart on things that are transitory; the Tigris will run through Bagdat after the race of Caliphs is extinct." Nor is this feeling of the dignity of his subject absent when the author is describing the most amusing incidents. Indeed, a great deal of Mark Twain's humour consists in the serious—or even at times severe—style in which he narrates his stories and portrays his scenes, as one who feels that the universal laws are playing through the very slightest of them. The following is a scene in which the principal actors are a dog, a boy, and a beetle, the place being the chapel:—

The minister gave out the hymn, and read it through with a relish, in a peculiar style which was much admired in that part of the country. His voice began on a medium key and climbed steadily up till it reached a certain point, where it bore with strong emphasis upon the topmost word and then plunged down as if from a spring-board:

Shall I be carried to the skies, on flow'ry beds of ease,

Whilst others fight to win the prize, and sail thro' bloody seas?

He was regarded as a wonderful reader. At church "sociables" he was always called upon to read poetry; and when he was through, the ladies would lift up their hands and let them fall helplessly in their laps, and "wall" their eyes, and shake their heads, as much as to say, "Words cannot express it; it is too beautiful, too beautiful for this mortal earth." After the hymn had been sung, the Rev. Mr. Sprague turned himself into a bulletin-board, and read off "notices" of meetings and societies and things till it seemed that the list would stretch out to the crack of doom—a queer custom which is still kept up in America, even in cities, away here in this age of abundant newspapers. Often, the less there is to justify a traditional custom, the harder it is to get rid of it.

And now the minister prayed. A good, generous prayer it was, and went into details: it pleaded for the church, and the little children of the church; for the other churches of the village; for the village itself; for the county; for the State; for the State officers; for the United States; for the churches of the United States; for Congress; for the President; for the officers of the Government; for poor sailors, tossed by stormy seas; for the oppressed millions groaning under the heel of European monarchies and Oriental despotisms; for such as have the light and the good tidings, and yet have not eyes to see nor ears to hear withal; for the heathen in the far islands of the sea; and closed with a supplication that the words he was about to speak might find grace and favor, and be as seed sown in fertile ground, yielding in time a grateful harvest of good. Amen.

There was a rustling of dresses, and the standing congregation sat down. The boy whose history this book relates did not enjoy the prayer, he only endured it—if he even did that much. He was restive all through it; he kept tally of the details of the prayer, unconsciously—for he was not listening, but he knew the ground of old, and the clergyman's regular route over it—and when a little trifle of new matter was interlarded, his ear detected it and his whole nature resented it; he considered additions unfair, and scoundrelly. In the midst of the prayer a fly had lit on the back of the pew in front of him and tortured his spirit by calmly rubbing its hands together, embracing its head with its arms, and polishing it so vigorously that it seemed to almost part company with the body, and the slender thread of a neck was exposed to view; scraping its wings with its hind legs and smoothing them to its body as if they had been coat-tails; going through its whole toilet as tranquilly as if it knew it was perfectly safe. As indeed it was; for as sorely as Tom's hands itched to grab for it they did not dare—he believed his soul would be instantly destroyed if he did such a thing while the prayer was going on. But with the closing sentence his hand began to curve and steal forward; and the instant the "Amen" was out the fly was a prisoner of war. His aunt detected the act and made him let it go.

The minister gave out his text and droned along monotonously through an argument that was so prosy that many a head by and by began to nod—and yet it was an argument that dealt in limitless fire and brimstone and thinned the predestined elect down to a company so small as to be hardly worth the saving. Tom counted the pages of the sermon; after church he always knew how many pages there had been, but he seldom knew anything else about the discourse. However, this time he was really interested for a little while. The minister made a grand and moving picture of the assembling together of the world's hosts at the millennium when the lion and the lamb should lie down together and a little child should lead them. But the pathos, the lesson, the moral of the great spectacle were lost upon the boy; he only thought of the conspicuousness of the principal character before the on-looking nations; his face lit with the thought, and he said to himself that he wished he could be that child, if it was a tame lion.

The scene we have selected is not so laughable, perhaps, as some others in the volume, but it indicates very well the kind of art in which Mark Twain is pre-eminent in our time. Every movement of boy, beetle, and poodle, is described not merely with precision, but with a subtle sense of meaning in every movement. Everything is alive, and every face physiognomical. From a novel so replete with good things, and one so full of significance, as it brings before us what we can feel is the real spirit of home life in the far West, there is no possibility of obtaining extracts which will convey to the reader any idea of the purport of the book. The scenes and characters cannot be really seen apart from their grouping and environment. The book will no doubt be a great favourite with boys, for whom it must in good part have been intended; but next to boys we should say that it might be most prized by philosophers and poets. The interior life, the everyday experiences, of a small village on the confines of civilisation and in the direction of its advance, may appear, antecedently, to supply but thin material for a romance; but still it is at just that same little pioneer point that humanity is growing with the greatest freedom, and unfolding some of its unprescribed tendencies. We can, indeed, hardly imagine a more felicitous task for a man of genius to have accomplished than to have seized the salient, picturesque, droll, and at the same time most significant features of human life, as he has himself lived it and witnessed it, in a region where it is continually modified in relation to new circumstances. The chief fault of the story is its brevity, and it will, we doubt not, be widely and thoroughly enjoyed by young and old for its fun and its philosophy.

—Moncure Daniel Conway, London
Examiner, June 17, 1876, pp. 687–688

Unsigned Review in the *Edinburgh Scotsman* (1876)

Mark Twain's appearance as a writer of a book for boys is justified by the result. His book, *The Adventures of Tom Sawyer*, though it has throughout strong American flavour, will delight all the lads who may get hold of it. We have made the experiment upon a youngster, and found that the reading of the book brought on constant peals of laughter. That is perhaps the best testimony that can be produced as to its amusing character. There is nothing in it of an unwholesome kind, so that parents need have no fear of trusting it into the hands of their boys. It is a book in which full knowledge of the habits of thought of lads is shown; and a full appreciation of the mischief which constitutes to a large extent their chief amusement.

—Unsigned Review in the *Edinburgh
Scotsman*, June 23, 1876, p. 2

Unsigned Review in the *Athenaeum* (1876)

The name of Mark Twain is known throughout the length and breadth of England. Wherever there is a railway-station with a bookstall his jokes are household words. Those whose usual range in literature does not extend beyond the sporting newspapers, the *Racing Calendar*, and the "Diseases of Dogs," have allowed him a place with Artemus Ward alongside of the handful of books which forms their library. For ourselves, we cannot dissociate him from the railway-station, and his jokes always rise in our mind with a background of Brown & Polson's Corn Flour and Taylor's system of removing furniture. We have read *The Adventures of Tom Sawyer* with different surroundings, and still have been made to laugh; and that ought to be taken as high praise. Indeed, the earlier part of the book is, to our thinking, the most amusing thing Mark Twain has written. The humour is not always uproarious, but it is always genuine and sometimes almost pathetic, and it is only now and then that the heartiness of a laugh is spoilt by one of those pieces of self-consciousness which are such common blots on Mark Twain's other books. *The Adventures of Tom Sawyer* is an attempt in a new direction. It is consecutive, and much longer than the former books, and as it is not put forward as a mere collection of *Screamers*, we laugh more easily, and find some relief in being able to relax the conventional grin expected from the reader of the little volumes of railway humour. The present book is not, and does not pretend to be a novel, in the ordinary sense of the word; it is not even a story, for that presupposes a climax and a finish; nor is it a mere boys' book of adventures. In the Preface the author says, "Although my book is intended mainly for the entertainment of boys and girls, I hope it will not be shunned by men and women on that account, for part of my plan has been to try pleasantly to remind adults of what they once were themselves, and of how they felt and thought and talked, and what queer enterprises they sometimes engaged in." Questions of intention are always difficult to decide. The book will amuse grown-up people in the way that humorous books written for children have amused before, but (perhaps fortunately) it does not seem to us calculated to carry out the intention here expressed. With regard to the style, of course there are plenty of slang words and racy expressions, which are quite in place in the conversations, but it is just a question whether it would not have been as well if the remainder of the book had not been written more uniformly in English.

—Unsigned Review in the *Athenaeum*,
2539, June 24, 1876, p. 851

Richard F. Littledale (1876)

In the sketches by which Mr. Clemens, who is pleased to call himself Mark Twain, first became known to the English public, there is one of a bad little boy who didn't come to grief, which is obviously capable of being indefinitely developed. Some such idea seems to have prompted the composition of *Tom Sawyer*, who is own brother, or at least cousin-german, to the bad Jim of the *Sketches*. He goes through a variety of adventures, for whose authenticity Mark Twain pledges himself, although they did not all happen to the same person, and the book, which is a very amusing one in parts, has a certain value as showing what kind of animal the American schoolboy is, and what odd fancies and superstitions he indulges and practises, or at least did some thirty or forty years ago. Traditions of the sort have such vitality, and are so readily handed down by one generation of schoolboys to another, that there is little reason to believe them extinct now; and those who are curious in such studies will note that some at least are survivals of old English usages themselves the detritus of a vanished Paganism; while the common-school discipline as depicted in *Tom Sawyer* will recall to a few at least Mr. George Macdonald's vigorous sketches of the Scottish parish-school in *Alec Forbes of Howglen*. In each case, the whole is differentiated by the conditions of American life; but the parentage cannot be mistaken, and no one could take *Tom Sawyer* for either French Canadian or Pennsylvania Dutch in descent and instincts. The book is designed primarily for boys, but older people also will find it worth looking through.

—Richard F. Littledale, *Academy* 9,
June 24, 1876, pp. 204–205

Unsigned Review in the London *Times* (1876)

Mark Twain belongs to a somewhat different school of writers from Miss Yonge, and *Tom Sawyer* is a characteristic production of his genius. We recognize the germ of it in the stories of the good and bad little boys, which went some way towards making their author's popularity. *Tom Sawyer*, as we are told in the Preface, is intended primarily for the amusement of children, but it is hoped that "it will not be shunned by men and women on that account, for part of my plan has been to try pleasantly to remind adults of what they once were themselves." How far Master Sawyer's eccentric experiences may come home in that way to American citizens we cannot pretend to say. To our English notions, Tom appears to have been a portentous phenomenon, and his eventful career exhibits an unprecedented precocity. His conceptions were as romantic as their execution was audacious. Holding all sedentary occupations in aversion, his cast of thought was as original as his quaint felicity of picturesque expression. We are very sure there are no such boys in this country, and even in the States it may be supposed that the breed has been dying out, for fully more than a generation has gone by since Tom was the glory and plague of his native village on the Mississippi. His remarkable talent for mischief would have made him an intolerable thorn in the flesh of the aunt who acted as a mother to him had it not been that his pranks and misconduct endeared him to that much-enduring woman. "Cuteness" is scarcely the word for Tom's ingrained artfulness. Take, by way of example, one of his earliest achievements. He is caught by his aunt in some flagrant delict, and condemned to whitewash the fence that runs in front of her cottage. Tom had planned to make one of a swimming party, and, what is more, he knows that he will be jeered by his playmates, and contempt is intolerable to his soaring spirit. So, when he sees Ben Rogers, whose satire he stands most in dread of, come puffing along the road, personating a high-pressure steamer, Tom buckles himself to his task with a will. He is so absorbed, in fact, in artistic enthusiasm that Ben's ribald mockery falls on unheeding ears, and Tom has actually to be twitched by the jacket before he turns to recognize his friend. Ere long Ben, who was bound for the river, is begging and praying to be permitted to have a turn with the brush. Tom is slow to be persuaded; had it been the back fence it might have been different, but his aunt is awful particular about this front one—

> Ben, I'd like to, honest injun; but Aunt Polly—well, Jim wanted to do it, but she wouldn't let him. Sid wanted to do it, but she wouldn't let Sid. Now, don't you see how I'm fixed? If you was to tackle this fence and anything was to happen to it.

The result is that Tom, as an immense favour, trades the privilege of a few minutes' painting for an apple. Each of the other boys, as he comes up in Ben's wake, makes a similar deal on his own account. Tom amasses a wealth of miscellaneous treasure, which he subsequently barters for a sufficiency of tickets of merit at the Sunday school to entitle him to walk off with the honours for which meritorious children have been toiling; while his aunt, to her intense surprise, finds her fence covered with several coatings of whitewash, and goes into raptures over Tom's capacity for work on the rare occasions when he chooses to apply himself. But, though anything but a bookish boy, Tom had paid considerable attention to literature of an eccentric kind, and, indeed, his knowledge of men and things was very much taken from his favourite authors. He runs away with a couple of comrades to follow the calling of pirates on an island of the Mississippi, the grand inducement being "that you don't have to get up mornings, and you don't have to go to school and wash and all that blame foolishness." After some days, when the trio are bored and half-starved and rather frightened, Tom plans a melodramatic return, and the missing ones emerge from the disused gallery of the church and present themselves to the congregation of weeping mourners, just as the clergyman's moving eloquence is dwelling on the virtues of the dear departed. Afterwards Tom, who "all along has been wanting to be a robber," but has never been able to find the indispensable cave, stumbles on the very thing to suit him. So he carries off a devoted follower who has been hardened for an outlaw's life by the habit of living on scraps and sleeping in empty hogsheads—Republican freedom from class prejudices seems to have been a marked feature among the boys of the Transatlantic St. Petersburg. He teaches Huck his duties as they are flying from the society of their kind out of the accumulated stores of his own erudition. "Who'll we rob?" asks Huck. "Oh, most anybody—waylay people; that's mostly the way." "And kill them?" "No, not always. Hide them in the cave till they can raise a ransom. You make them raise all they can off o' their friends, and after you've kept them a year, if it ain't raised, then you kill them. That's the general way. Only you don't kill the women; you shut up the women, but you don't kill them. They're always beautiful and rich and awfully scared. You take their watches and things, but you always take off your hat and talk polite. There ain't everybody as polite as robbers; you'll see that in any book. Well, the women get to loving you; and after they've been in the cave a week or two weeks they stop crying, and after that you couldn't get them to leave. If you drove them out they'd turn right round and come back. It's so in all the books.' In the course of their researches in the cavern they come on what Tom pronounces "an awful snug place for orgies." "What's orgies?" inquires Huck. "I dunno," says Tom very frankly; "but robbers always have orgies, and of course we've got to have them too."

We fear these elegant extracts give but a faint idea of the drollery in which the book abounds; for the fact is that the best part of the fun lies in the ludicrous individuality of Tom himself, with whom we have been gradually growing familiar. But we should say that a perusal of *Tom Sawyer* is as fair a test as one could suggest of anybody's appreciation of the humorous. The drollery is often grotesque and extravagant, and there is at least as much in the queer Americanizing of the language as in the ideas it expresses. Practical people who pride themselves on strong common sense will have no patience with such vulgar trifling. But those who are alive to the pleasure of relaxing from serious thought and grave occupation will catch themselves smiling over every page and exploding outright over some of the choicer passages.

—Unsigned Review in the London
Times, August 28, 1876, p. 4

Unsigned Review in the New York Times (1877)

Shades of the venerable Mr. Day, of the instructive Mrs. Barbauld, of the persuasive Miss Edgeworth! Had you the power of sitting today beside the reviewer's desk, and were called upon to pass judgment on the books written and printed for the boys and girls of today, would you not have groaned and moaned over their perusal? If such superlatively good children as Harry and Lucy could have existed, or even such nondescript prigs as Sandford and Merton had abnormal being, this other question presents itself to our mind: 'How would these precious children have enjoyed Mark Twain's *Tom Sawyer?*' In all books written for the amusement of children there are two distinct phases of appreciation. What the parent thinks of the book is one thing; what the child thinks of it is another. It is fortunate when both parent and child agree in their conclusions. Such double appreciation may, in most instances, simply be one in regard to the fitness of the book on the part of the parent. A course of reading entirely devoted to juvenile works must be to an adult a tax on time and patience. It is only once in many years that such a charming book as *Little Alice in Wonderland* is produced, which old and young could read with thorough enjoyment. If, thirty years ago, *Tom Sawyer* had been placed in a careful father's hands to read, the probabilities would have been that he would have hesitated before giving the book to his boy—not that Mr. Clemens' book is exceptional in character, or differs in the least, save in its cleverness, from a host of similar books on like topics which are universally read by children today. It is the judgment of the book-givers which has undoubtedly undergone a change, while youthful minds, being free from warp, twist, or dogma, have remained ever the same.

Returning then to these purely intellectual monstrosities, mostly the pen-and-ink offspring of authors and authoresses who never had any real flesh and blood creations of their own, there can be no doubt that had Sandford or Merton ever for a single moment dipped inside of *Tom Sawyer*'s pages, astronomy and physics, with all the musty old farrago of Greek and Latin history, would have been thrown to the dogs. Despite tasseled caps, starched collars, and all the proprieties, these children would have laughed uproariously over Tom Sawyer's 'cat and the pain-killer,' and certain new ideas might have had birth in their brains. Perhaps had these children actually lived in our times, Sandford might have been a Western steam-boat captain, or Merton a filibuster. *Tom Sawyer* is likely to inculcate the idea that there are certain lofty aspirations which Plutarch never ascribed to his more prosaic heroes. Books for children in former bygone periods were mostly constructed in one monotonous key. A child was supposed to be a vessel which was to be constantly filled up. Facts and morals had to be taken like bitter draughts or acrid pills. In order that they should be absorbed like medicines it was perhaps a kindly thinker who disguised these facts and morals. The real education swallowed in those doses by the children we are inclined to think was in small proportion to the quantity administered. Was it not good old Peter Parley who in this country first broke loose from conventional trammels, and made American children truly happy? We have certainly gone far beyond Mr. Goodrich's manner. There has come an amount of ugly realism into children's story-books, the advantages of which we are very much in doubt about.

Now, it is perfectly true that many boys do not adopt drawing-room manners. Perhaps it is better that little paragons—pocket Crichtons—are so rare. Still, courage, frankness, truthfulness, and self-reliance are to be inculcated in our lads. Since association is everything, it is not desirable that in real life we should familiarize our children with those of their age who are lawless or daredevils. Granting that the natural is the true, and the true is the best, and that we may describe things as they are for adult readers, it is proper that we should discriminate a great deal more as to the choice of subjects in books intended for children. Today a majority of the heroes in such books have longings to be pirates, want to run away with vessels, and millions of our American boys read and delight in such stories. In olden times the *Pirate's Own Book* with its death's-head and crossbones on the back, had no concealment about it. It is true, edition after edition was sold. There it was. You saw it palpably. There was no disguise about it. If a father or mother objected to their child's reading the *Pirate's Own Book*, a pair of tongs and a convenient fireplace ended the whole matter. Today the trouble is: that there is a decidedly sanguinary tendency in juvenile books. No matter how innocent, quiet, or tame may be the title of a child's book, there is no guarantee that the volume your curly-headed little boy may be devouring may not contain a series of adventures recalling Capt. Kidd's horrors. In the short preface of *Tom Sawyer*, Mr. Clemens writes, 'Although my book is intended mainly for the entertainment of boys and girls, I hope it will not be shunned by men and women on that account.' We have before expressed the idea that a truly clever child's book is one in which both the man and the boy can find pleasure. No child's book can be perfectly acceptable otherwise. Is *Tom Sawyer* amusing? It is incomparably so. It is the story of a Western boy, born and bred on the banks of one of the big rivers, and there is exactly that wild village life which has schooled many a man to self-reliance and energy. Mr. Clemens has a remarkable memory for those peculiarities of American boy-talk which the grown man may have forgotten, but which return to him not unpleasantly when once the proper key is sounded. There is one scene of a quarrel, with a dialogue, between Tom and a city boy which is perfect of its kind. Certain chapters in Tom's life, where his love for the schoolgirls is told, make us believe that for an urchin who had just lost his milk-teeth the affections out West have an awakening even earlier than in Oriental climes. In fact, Tom is a preternaturally precocious urchin. One admirable character in the book, and touched with the hand of a master, is that of Huckleberry Finn. There is a reality about this boy which is striking. An honest old aunt, who adores her scapegrace nephew, is a homely picture worked with exceeding grace. Mr. Clemens must have had just such a lovable old aunt. An ugly murder in the book, over-minutely described and too fully illustrated, which Tom and Huck see, of course, in a graveyard, leads, somehow or other, to the discovery of a cave, in which treasures are concealed, and to which Tom and Huck fall heirs. There is no cant about Mr. Clemens. A description of a Sunday-school in *Tom Sawyer* is true to the letter. Matters are not told as they are fancied to be, but as they actually are.

If Mr. Clemens has been wanting in continuity in his longer sketches, and that sustained inventive power necessary in dovetailing incidents, Tom, as a story, though slightly disjointed, has this defect less apparent. As a humorist, Mr. Clemens has a great deal of fun in him, of the true American kind, which crops out all over the book. Mr. Clemens has an audience both here and in England, and doubtless his friends across the water will re-echo 'the hearty laughs which the reading of *Tom Sawyer* will cause on this side of the world'. We are rather inclined to treat books intended for boys and girls, written by men of accredited talent and reputation, in a serious manner. Early impressions are the lasting ones. It is exactly such a clever book as *Tom Sawyer* which is sure to leave its stamp on younger minds. We like, then, the true boyish fun of Tom and Huck, and have a foible for the mischief these children engage in. We have not the least objection that rough boys be the heroes of a story-book. Restless spirits of energy only require judicious training in order to bring them into proper use. In the books to be placed into children's hands for purposes of recreation, we have a preference for those of a milder type than *Tom Sawyer*. Excitements derived from reading should be administered with a certain degree of circumspection. A sprinkling of salt in mental food is both natural and wholesome; any cravings for the contents of the castors, the cayenne and the mustard, by children, should not be gratified. With less, then, of Injun Joe and 'revenge', and 'slitting women's ears', and the shadow of the gallows, which throws an unnecessarily sinister tinge over the story, (if the book really is intended for boys and girls) we should have liked *Tom Sawyer* better.

—Unsigned Review, *New York Times*, January 13, 1877, p. 3

WILL CLEMENS (1894)

When "The Adventures of Tom Sawyer" appeared in 1876, the fame of Mark Twain was universal. In this volume he revealed the story of his boyhood days on the Mississippi, and his pranks and adventures in the town of Hannibal. It was published as a book for boys, and commanded an enormous sale, edition after edition being exhausted. In fact, "Tom Sawyer" sold better than any of his books, excepting "Innocents Abroad." In the meanwhile, "The Gilded Age" had been dramatized and the production of the comedy on the American stage netted the author large sums of money.

"Injin Jo" one of the principal characters in "Tom Sawyer" still lives at Hannibal, Mo., and is one of the noted individuals of the town. He drives an old white horse and a red express wagon, borne down on one side from long and hard service. Jo hauls trunks from the depot and chores around with his horse and wagon. He loves a dollar more than anybody else in the town, and out of his meagre earnings he has accumulated quite a fortune. He owns twelve tenement houses in Hannibal, ranging in value from $500 to $1,000 each yet from the clothes that he wears one would naturally think that he would be constantly in dread of the ragman coming along and casting him into a sack of old iron and rags.

—Will Clemens, *Mark Twain*,
1894, pp. 124–125

WILLIAM DEAN HOWELLS (1910)

I am surprised to find from the bibliographical authorities that it was so late as 1875 when he came with the manuscript of *Tom Sawyer*, and asked me to read it, as a friend and critic, and not as an editor. I have an impression that this was at Mrs. Clemens's instance in his own uncertainty about printing it. She trusted me, I can say with a satisfaction few things now give me, to be her husband's true and cordial adviser, and I was so. I believe I never failed him in this part, though in so many of our enterprises and projects I was false as water through my temperamental love of backing out of any undertaking. I believe this never ceased to astonish him, and it has always astonished me; it appears to me quite out of character; though it is certain that an undertaking, when I have entered upon it, holds me rather than I it. But however this immaterial matter may be, I am glad to remember that I thoroughly liked *Tom Sawyer*, and said so with every possible amplification. Very likely, I also made my suggestions for its improvement; I could not have been a real critic without that; and I have no doubt they were gratefully accepted and, I hope, never acted upon. I went with him to the horse-car station in Harvard Square, as my frequent wont was, and put him aboard a car with his MS. in his hand, stayed and reassured, so far as I counted, concerning it. I do not know what his misgivings were; perhaps they were his wife's misgivings, for she wished him to be known not only for the wild and boundless humor that was in him, but for the beauty and tenderness and "natural piety"; and she would not have had him judged by a too close fidelity to the rude conditions of Tom Sawyer's life. This is the meaning that I read into the fact of his coming to me with those doubts.

—William Dean Howells,
My Mark Twain, 1910, pp. 47–48

CARL VAN DOREN (1921)

The Adventures of Tom Sawyer took Mark Twain from epic to comedy. He first planned it as a play and when he decided upon another form for it he had in mind to write a story of boyhood which, like Aldrich's *Story of a Bad Boy*, should emphatically depart from the customary type of Sunday school fiction. But its departure from a type is one of the least memorable aspects of *Tom Sawyer*. Tom and Huck are, indeed, "bad" boys; they have done more than overhear profanity and smell the smoke of pipes; they play outrageous pranks in the fashion of the disapproved youngsters of all small American towns; their exploits have even led both *Tom Sawyer* and *Huckleberry Finn* to be at times barred by librarians in whom zeal exceeds imagination. These qualities in the heroes, however, only conform to the general quality of realism which characterizes *Tom Sawyer* throughout. To a delicate taste, indeed, the book seems occasionally overloaded with matters brought in at moments when no necessity in the narrative calls for them. The boyish superstitions, delectable as they are in themselves, tend to lug *Tom Sawyer* to the documentary side of the line which divides documents from works of art. Nor can the murder about which the story is built up be said to dominate it very thoroughly. The story moves forward in something the same manner as did the plays of the seventies, with exits and entrances not always motivated. And yet a taste so delicate as to resent these defects of structure would probably not appreciate the flexibility of the narrative, its easy, casual gait, its broad sweep, its variety of substance. Mark Twain drives with careless, sagging reins, but he holds the general direction. Most of his readers remember certain episodes, particularly the white-washing of the fence and the appearance of the boys at their own funeral, rather than the story as a whole. To inquire into the causes of this is to find that the plot of *Tom Sawyer* means considerably less than the characters. A hundred incidents beside those here chosen would have served as well; the characters are each of them unique. Certain of them come directly from the life, notably the vagabond Huckleberry Finn and Aunt Polly and Becky Thatcher, the Gang, and Tom Sawyer himself, who, though compounded of numerous elements, essentially reproduces the youthful figure of his creator. Such a mixture of rich humor and serious observation had never before been devoted to the study of a boy in fiction. Mark Twain smiles constantly at the absurd in Tom's character, but he portrays him in the dignity of full length; he does not laugh him into insignificance or lecture him into the semblance of a puppet. Boys of Tom's age can follow his fortunes without discomfort or boredom. At the same time, there are overtones which most juvenile fiction entirely lacks and which continue to delight those adults who Mark Twain said, upon finishing his story, alone would ever read it. At the moment he must have felt that the poetry and satire of *Tom Sawyer* outranked the narrative, and he was right. They have proved the permanent, at least the preservative, elements of a classic.

—Carl Van Doren, *The American Novel*,
New York: Macmillan, 1921, pp. 168–170

THE PRINCE AND THE PAUPER

Critics of Mark Twain's earlier work note the author's propensity for slipping in and out of different genres, moving among broad humor, autobiography, and serious reportage. The same tendency can be found by perusing a chronological bibliography of his works. Twain flitted eccentrically between a semiautobiographical novel of the old Southwest (*The Adventures of Tom Sawyer*) to a comic account of European travel (*A Tramp Abroad*) to a historical novel of sixteenth-century England (*The Prince and the Pauper*). If one formula or scheme failed, there was another one being lined up. To H.H. Boyesen, a friend of Twain's, this profit-led restlessness indicated only the mind of a true artist, ready to "forsake the field of assured success, and seek distinction in untried paths."

The same attitude is evident in Twain's frequent forays into business, which often ended in disaster. This failure to stick to any one given mode is central to the psychoanalysis of Twain presented by Van Wyck Brooks in *The Ordeal of Mark Twain* (1920). After the ambivalent critical response to *A Tramp Abroad,* Twain turned for a third time to the novel form. *The Prince and the Pauper* was the first of Twain's European historical novels. True to formless form, his next published book would be *Life on the Mississippi.*

Howells, in his prepublication promotional puff for the novel, pronounced it a "satire on monarchy" and a "manual of republicanism which might fitly be introduced in the schools." Twain is repackaged by his friend as "a man who has hitherto been known only as a humorist—a mere *farceur*—to most people." Were those previous criticisms of *A Tramp Abroad* portraying Twain as a hollow buffoon, "perpetually keyed up to the full bent of his comic powers" (the *San Francisco Evening Bulletin*), the basis for this conspicuous rehabilitation?

H.H. Boyesen was a crony of Howells's, one entirely friendly to Twain (they had met and socialized in Paris two years earlier). He was enlisted to review *The Prince and the Pauper,* this time for the *Atlantic Monthly.* Howells had only recently relinquished the editorship of the *Atlantic Monthly* in March 1881, and he had passed the editorship on to Thomas Bailey Aldrich, another friend of Twain's. So as he made this uncertain shift into historical romance, Twain was intimately connected to a friendly critical network. Likewise Joel Chandler Harris reviewed the novel using rapturous language. Harris, the author of the Uncle Remus stories and books, was in a friendly correspondence and negotiation with Twain at this time.

Boyesen believes that "no reader, not even a critical expert, would think of attributing to him, if his name were withheld from the title-page." This experiment actually was later essayed by Twain, when *Joan of Arc* was serialized in *Harper's Magazine* with no indication of its author. Students of Twain's style may be intrigued by this assertion. Is there anything recognizably Twainian about the novel, or is it without any resemblance to the works that precede it? Boyesen regards the book as such a departure that it would be "inappropriate to reckon it among that writer's works." If it is indeed so unlike his previous style, what recommends it exactly? Is it an improvement or a disappointment? Critics have been divided on this question since the book's publication.

Boyesen makes a significant distinction: that "it is indisputably by Clemens; it does not seem to be by Twain." Here is an early instance of what would become a critical cliché, separating "Mark Twain" from Samuel Clemens. In Boyesen's criticism of "Clemens," certain Twainian devices seem to crop up: For one, there is a notably "life-like verisimilitude" to the narrative. For another, there is "no pretense of a formal plot" to it. The sharply contrasting adventures of the pauper and the prince "constitute the whole tale." That is, Twain's narrative remains episodic. Boyesen blithely rates *The Prince and the Pauper* "far above any of the author's previous productions," finding "barely a flaw" in it. To accentuate the extent of this improvement, he drubs the previous works as "the most heterogeneous accumulations of ill-assorted material that ever defied the laws of literature." He concludes by remarking that "it will be interesting to watch for the popular estimate of this fascinating book."

To those parties not disposed to Twain forsaking humor, this new direction merely replaced incessant joking with "some four-hundred pages of careful tediousness, mitigated by occasional flashes of unintentional and unconscious fun." The trade is not a good one. The *Athenaeum* reviewer, who concludes that Twain has been earnestly researching history, remarks that "if to convert a brilliant and engaging humourist into a dull and painful romancer be necessarily a function of the study of history, it cannot be too steadily discouraged." Critics remained unsure about how to read the novel—the complaint that had haunted the reception of *A Tramp Abroad*. One critic only sees inadvertent humor in the narrative; others were equally perplexed. "Whether we were expected to laugh or cry we could not quite make out," writes the *Academy* critic, "but at all events we did neither." In this incarnation, he continues, Twain will only be laughed at, not with, by his young readers.

Joel Chandler Harris, on the other hand, derives only pleasure from the same confusion of tone, citing episodes "where tears and laughter go hand in hand—where the tragic and comic parade in grim relationship." He applauds the transformation of Twain from the "wild western burlesquer" to the "true literary artist."

The reviewer for the *Century* finds, like Howells, a satire on "kingcraft," albeit one "spun-out almost to tediousness." Students examining Twain's use of satire might peruse these reviews and decide whether they agree. The reviewer believes that the novel's purpose is "to prove that the humorous story-teller ... can be a literary purist, a scholar, and an antiquary." Viewed in this way, the novel becomes an exercise or an experiment. Indeed, it is significant that each of the reviewers is compelled to discourse at some length on perceptions of the author and his conspicuous *volte face*, or about-face, in some cases as much as they discourse on the work itself. The *Century* reviewer perhaps best articulates what aggravates the naysayers among the critics. "His recent humorous writings abound in passages of great excellence as serious compositions," he writes. Why, then, was it necessary for Twain to pointedly abandon his humorous work? The model suggested by Van Wyck Brooks, that Twain felt that his role as a humorist was humiliating, gains credibility in light of this particular round of reviews. "His unconscious desire was to be an artist, but this implied an assertion of individuality that was a sin in the eyes of his mother and a shame in the eyes of society," Brooks writes. "It was the dilemma which, as we shall see in the end, Mark Twain solved by becoming a humorist." If *The Prince and the Pauper* was his attempt to reclaim his true, higher destiny, it was not viewed universally as such. The critics, at least, preferred Twain as a humorist.

Hjalmar Hjorth Boyesen (1881)

Inclination to forsake the field of assured success, and seek distinction in untried paths, has shown itself a controlling impulse in many an artistic mind. Examples are most frequent, probably, amongst actors, whose eagerness to shine in unexpected situations, and to demonstrate merits apart from those by which they have achieved prominence, is a common characteristic. For reasons sufficiently obvious, these efforts of theatrical aspiration are seldom satisfactory; nor would they be likely to win applause, even if based upon sound judgment and sustained by positive ability. The actor, as a rule, must be content with fame in a single branch of his vocation, unless he is prepared to undertake a fresh career in regions where his person and his precedents are unknown. In other arts ambition is subject to no such restraints. If the power of versatility exists, it is fairly sure of recognition. A Doré may desert the narrower channel of his early fortune, and enlarge his fame in proportion to the breadth of his spreading canvas. Rossini, with a reputation founded upon dozens of dazzling comic operas, could not rest, in his old age, until he had produced a solemn mass which might stand beside the grave works of more majestic composers. Scott, after securing eminence enough to content his modest nature through the exercise of one gift, built himself secretly a higher renown by means of another. Bulwer's less brilliant light shone with a still greater variety of rays. The 'deed' may not in all cases be equal to the 'attempt,' but the evidences of determined endeavor to establish this sort of manifold claim upon public attention and regard have always been abundant, and will be as long as the imagination of men can be turned to creative account.

The publication of Mark Twain's new story, *The Prince and the Pauper*, supplies a rather striking instance in point,—or, at least, supplies material for illustration of the tendency of writers whose position is fixed and prosperous to give their faculties a new and unexpected range, and strive for a totally different order of production from any previously accomplished. It would be impertinent to pronounce too confidently upon the author's motive, but what he has done is, in one particular, plain to every comprehension. He has written a book which no reader, not even a critical expert, would think of attributing to him, if his name were withheld from the title-page. There is nothing in its purpose, its method, or its style of treatment that corresponds with any of the numerous works by the same hand. It is no doubt possible to find certain terms of phraseology, here and there, which belong to Mark Twain, and characteristically convey his peculiar ideas; but these are few, and would pass unnoticed as means of identification, although we recognize their familiarity readily enough, when we are already aware from whom they come. It is also possible to recall episodical passages in his earlier volumes—quaint legends and antique fantasies—which seem to be animated by a spirit similar to that of the present tale; but these, again, would have suggested nothing as to the origin of *The Prince and the Pauper*, if it had appeared anonymously. So far as Mark Twain is concerned, the story is an entirely new departure; so much so as to make it appear inappropriate to reckon it among that writer's works. It is indisputably by Clemens; it does not seem to be by Twain,—certainly not by the Twain we have known for a dozen or more years as the boisterous and rollicking humorist, whose chief function has been to diffuse hilarity throughout English-reading communities and make himself synonymous with mirth in its most demonstrative forms. Humor, in quite sufficient proportion, this tale does assuredly contain; but it is a humor growing freely and spontaneously out of the situations represented,—a sympathetic element, which appeals sometimes shrewdly, sometimes sweetly, to the senses, and is never intrusive or unduly prominent; sometimes, indeed, a humor so tender and subdued as to surprise those who are under its spell with doubts whether smiles or tears shall be summoned to express the passing emotion.

The book is not only a novelty of Mark Twain's handiwork; it is in some respects a novelty in romance. It is not easy to place it in any distinct classification. It lacks the essential features of a novel, and while principally about children, is by no means a tale exclusively for children, although the young may have their full share in the enjoyment of it. The subject is so absolutely simple that to know it beforehand deprives the reader of none of the pleasure he has a right to expect. There is no pretense of a formal plot, and all the charm is owing to the sincerity, the delicacy, and the true feeling with which the story is told. Two little boys (one a bright figure in history, the other a gem of fiction; the former King Edward the Sixth of England, the latter a pauper vagrant) accidentally exchange stations at the age of about twelve years, and each remains for several days in his strangely altered condition. A strong resemblance between the two, cooperating with accidents of time and place, makes it possible for the substitution to remain undetected. The sharply contrasting adventures of the pair constitute the whole tale. The incident of the exchange is the sole point that would seem to be hazardous for the narrator; but whether the skill is conscious or not, whether that particular passage gets its truthfulness from the author's own sense of its validity, or is carefully elaborated with a view to the reader's beguilement, it certainly presents no difficulty as it stands. The rest follows naturally and ingenuously. There is no strain upon credulity, for the characters come and go, live and breathe, suffer and rejoice, in an atmosphere of perfect reality, and with a vivid identity rarely to be found in fictions set in mediaeval days. The same life-like verisimilitude that is manifest in many pages of Scott, and throughout Reade's *Cloister and the Hearth*, glows in every chapter of this briefer chronicle of a real prince's fancied griefs and perils. To preserve an illusion so consistently, it would seem that the author's own faith in the beings of his creation must have been firm, from beginning to end of their recorded career. Unless the teller of a story believes it all himself, for the time, he can hardly impress such conviction as he does in this case upon the mind of the reader.

However skillful in invention a writer may be, it is certain that his work loses nothing of effect from a studious harmonization with the period in which it is placed. In *The Prince and the Pauper* this requirement has been scrupulously observed. The details are not made obtrusive, and the 'local color' is never laid on with excess; but the spirit of the age preceding that of Elizabeth is maintained with just the proper degree of art to avoid the appearance of artfulness. Critical examination shows that no inconsiderable labor has been given to the preservation of this air of authenticity; but the idea that the results of research are inflicted with malice aforethought is the last that would occur to any reader. On the other hand, if irrelevant phrases may be once or twice detected, their employment is obviously intentional,— the indulgence of some passing whim, the incongruity of which, it is taken for granted, will be excused for the sake of its fun. Such might easily be spared, no doubt, though they do no serious harm. It is in every way satisfactory to observe that the material accessories are brought into view with an accuracy which coherently supports the veracity of the narrative. Dresses, scenery, architecture, manners and customs, suffer no deviation from historical propriety. It would be a pity if our trust in the existence of the little pair of heroes, or of the well-proportioned figures that accompany them, were to be shaken by shortcomings in these respects. But there is no danger. The big-hearted protector of guileless childhood is as palpable to our senses as to the grateful touch of the prince's accolade. The one soft spot in the hard old monarch's nature reveals itself to our apprehension as clearly as to the privileged eyes of the courtiers at Westminster. The burly ruffian of the gutters, the patient, sore-afflicted mother, the gracious damsels of pure estate and breeding, the motley vagabonds of the highway, the crafty and disciplined councilors of the realm, the mad ascetic, and the varied throng of participants in the busy scenes portrayed,—all these take to themselves the shape and substance of genuine humanity, and stamp themselves on our perceptions as creatures too vital and real to be credited to fable land. We go beyond the author's cautious proposition in the prefatory lines, that the story 'could have happened:' we are sure that it ought to have happened, and we willingly believe it did happen.

It will be interesting to watch for the popular estimate of this fascinating book. Of the judgment of qualified criticism there can be little question. That it will be accorded a rank far above any of the author's previous productions is a matter of course. It has qualities of excellence which he has so long held in reserve that their revelation now will naturally cause surprise. Undoubtedly, the plan upon which most of his works have been framed called for neither symmetry, nor synthetic development, nor any of the finer devices of composition. Generally speaking, they served their purpose, without the least reference to the manner in which they were thrown together. They stood, and stand, at the head of all the genuine successes of modern comic writing; but, notwithstanding the frequent flashes of power that give them vigor, the felicities of characterization that brighten them, the pathos that chastens them, and no one can say how many other manifestations of cleverness, they remain the most heterogeneous accumulations of ill-assorted material that ever defied the laws of literature, and kept the public contentedly captive for half a score of years. Now the same public is called upon to welcome its old favorite in a new guise,—as the author of a tale ingenious in conception, pure and humane in purpose, artistic in method, and, with barely a flaw, refined in execution.

—Hjalmar Hjorth Boyesen, *Atlantic Monthly* 48,
December 1881, pp. 843–845

UNSIGNED REVIEW (1881)

To the innumerable admirers of *Roughing It* and *A Tramp Abroad*, *The Prince and the Pauper* is likely to prove a heavy disappointment. The author, a noted representative of American humour, has essayed to achieve a serious book. The consequences are at once disastrous and amazing. The volume, which deals with England in the days of Edward VI., and is announced as 'A Tale for Young People of all Ages', is only to be described as some four hundred pages of careful tediousness, mitigated by occasional flashes of unintentional and unconscious fun. Thus Mr. Clements, who has evidently been reading history, and is anxious about local colour, not only makes a point of quoting documents, and parading authorities, and being fearfully in earnest, but does so with a look of gravity and an evident sense of responsibility that are really delicious. On the whole, however, of Mr. Clements's many jokes, *The Prince and the Pauper* is incomparably the flattest and worst. To this, as a general reflection, it may be added that if to convert a brilliant and engaging humourist into a dull and painful romancer be necessarily a function of the study of history, it cannot be too steadily discouraged. Messrs. Chatto & Windus are the publishers.

—Unsigned Review in the *Athenaeum* 282,
December 24, 1881, p. 849

REVIEW ATTRIBUTED TO EDWARD PURCELL (1881)

This review is unsigned, but it was possibly written by the critic and editor Edward Sheridan Purcell.

Those who have discovered wit, wisdom, and good taste in Mark Twain's previous works will laugh beforehand at even an historical romance from his pen. But whether we were expected to laugh or cry we could not quite make out—on the whole, the volume seemed to be written *au grand sérieux*—but, at all events, we did neither. Against the happy thought which forms the backbone of the tale, we must really protest. A street Arab, one Tom, is supposed to have changed clothes with Edward VI. during Henry's last illness, to have played the part of a royal Christopher Sly, and reigned with much distinction till the real Edward, after dreadfully low adventures, steps forward at the coronation and claims his own. And this is intended for 'young people of all ages.' Mr. Clemens will permit us to point out that, if the young Britisher has once passed the age when such historical heresies must either be prohibited or extirpated by the rod, he will infallibly fall to criticising, and probably even to making fun at, instead of with, Mark Twain. Victor Hugo's veiled Wapentake, or Court of Arches, that synod of the English Church, is not more astounding than this picture of Reformation times—a misty atmosphere of Scott's chivalry in which floats all the flunkeyism, aristocratic oppression, and so forth, of all or any later period, as revealed to Columbia's stern eye. It is not worth while to multiply instances; let the absurd description of the young King's *levée* in chap. xviii. suffice, where the author exaggerates something he must have read somewhere about the ceremonies of the bedchamber introduced by Louis XIV. There is no excuse for this libel on the English Court. The list of thirteen officials, ending with the Primate, through whose hands the royal hose pass is concocted with peculiar clumsiness. Not even Cranmer would have stooped to hand the King's breeches, no matter how heavy the pockets felt. Foxe's classical work has apparently been consulted; burnings and boilings are done full justice to, and the general Protestant tone would be highly satisfactory were it not that the author is always fidgeting about certain 'Blue Laws of Connecticut.' From the Appendix (which, in its quotations from Hume, Mr. Timbs, and the erudite Dr. Trumbull, author of a Defence of the said Blue Laws, is quite a curiosity) we gather that this ponderous fantasia on English history is intended to show up British barbarism, and so, by contrast, to whitewash this embarrassing Blue business, which, in a solemn last general note in italics and capitals, he calls '*the first* SWEEPING DEPARTURE FROM JUDICIAL ATROCITY *which the "civilised" world had seen,*' and '*this humane and kindly Blue-Law Code.*' And why? Because our laws had 123 capital crimes, and the Blue Laws only fourteen. What those fourteen were he does not say. We think we can guess. The book is full of pictures in the spirited, florid old style. These will amuse the children. Naturally, the plot has suggested several comical situations, some of which are amusingly dwelt on; while a few smart sayings relieve the monotony of a prolix work singularly deficient in literary merit.

—Review Attributed to Edward Purcell,
Academy 20, December 24, 1881, p. 469

Joel Chandler Harris (1881)

The book comes upon the reading public in the shape of a revelation. Mr. Clemens is known wherever the English language is spoken as the foremost exponent of that species of humor which is peculiar enough to be called American, but which, in reality, is the humor of the broadest, and wildest, and most boisterous burlesque. Of this humor, "The Jumping Frog" is a fair specimen. In this field and in this vein, Mr. Clemens is without rival, albeit a host of writers have sprung up to pay him the tribute of imitation. In *The Prince and Pauper*, however, he has made a wide departure from his old methods—so much so that the contrast presents a phase of literary development unique in its proportions and suggestions. The wild western burlesquer, the builder of elephantine exaggerations and comicalities has disappeared, and in his stead we have the true literary artist. All that is really vital in the wild humor of Mark Twain is here, but it is strengthened and refined. The incongruities are nature's own, and they are handled with marvelous skill and deftness.

"I will set down a tale," says Mr. Clemens, by way of preface, "as it was told to me by one who had it of his father, which latter had it of his father, this last having in like manner had it of his father, and so on, back and still back, three hundred years and more the fathers transmitting it to the sons and so preserving it. It may be history, it may be only a legend, a tradition. It may have happened, it may not have happened; but it could have happened. It may be that the wise and the learned believed it in the old days; it may be that only the unlearned and the simple loved it and credited it." Through some whim the young prince, who afterward becomes Edward VI, exchanges garments with a beggar named Tom Canty, and goes into the streets of London. This whimsical masquerade costs both dear, for each is thereafter engaged in a conflict to regain his own position again, and each is accounted mad—Tom Canty when he declares that he is not the true prince, and Edward, when he announces to his companions in the streets that he is the heir-apparent to the throne of England. Dealing with the incongruities and contrasts that are possible to such a situation, the comic beads and bubbles of boisterous humor and exaggeration that have heretofore been the chief characteristic of the writings of Mark Twain are blown away by some happy wind; but the true wine of humor remains to give strength and flavor to a most delightful book. It is humor of the highest and most perfect kind—the kind that embodies, the best and purest emotions of the human heart, and that is as full of tenderness and tears as of laughter. There are episodes in Mr. Clemens's story where tears and laughter go hand in hand—where the tragic and comic parade in grim relationship—and all in response to and under the control of the most artistic treatment. But the book is something more than this. It is a powerful and an impressive study of character, wherein the complex relations that bind the highest human being to the lowest are treated with an insight as keen and a touch as faithful and as vivid as any modern writer has employed—and with a charming simplicity to which few writers ever attain. There is great temptation just here to analyze the artistic and moral purpose concealed beneath these delightful methods, and to say something of the art which has here caught and retained the manners and speech of the period of which the story treats; but our space will not admit of a formal review of this enjoyable volume—enjoyable in a larger sense than a mere narrative, no matter how picturesque such a narrative might be. It is sold only by subscription, and we know of no more appropriate gift for the holidays for old or young.

—Joel Chandler Harris, *Atlanta Constitution*,
December 25, 1881, p.11

UNSIGNED REVIEW IN *CENTURY MAGAZINE* (1882)

In his new book, Mark Twain has so far divested himself of his usual literary habit, that the reader is inclined now and then, as he follows the quaint story, to turn back to the title page in the expectation of finding that the famous humorist and satirist has been writing, incognito, as Mr. Clemens. *The Prince and the Pauper* is a curious mixture of fact and fancy. . . .

In many respects, *The Prince and the Pauper* is a remarkable book; it is certainly effective as a story, though it is spun-out almost to tediousness. It appears also to be overweighted with purpose. The least interesting part of the story, and that which as a whole is not essential to the main narrative, proceeds from the author's purpose to vindicate the 'humane and kindly' character of the Blue-Laws of Connecticut. Another purpose or effect of the story is to satirize kingcraft. This is cleverly done. The quiet satire, the ingenuity of the plot, and the clever development of the thoughts and motives of the Prince and the Pauper, in their changed circumstances, form the main interest of the story.

So far as it was the author's purpose to produce a work of art after the old models, and to prove that the humorous story-teller and ingenious homely philosopher, Mark Twain, can be a literary purist, a scholar, and an antiquary, we do not think his 'new departure' is a conspicuous success. It was not necessary for the author to prop his literary reputation with archaic English and a somewhat conventional manner. His recent humorous writings abound in passages of great excellence as serious compositions, and his serious, nervous style is the natural expression of an acute mind, that in its most fanciful moods is seldom superficial in its view. Indeed, it is because Mark Twain is a satirist, and in a measure a true philosopher, that his broadly humorous books and speeches have met with wide and permanent popular favor.

Considered as a work of art, *The Prince and the Pauper* is open to criticism. The author has taken great pains to be 'early English,' as they say in *Patience*, and his mild attempt to be aesthetic is almost necessarily artificial. In the conversation of the story, he attempts to reproduce the idiom of the time of Henry VIII., and the effort is well sustained. But the descriptive parts in which (if we may take the style of the preface as the key-note of his purpose) he also intended to keep the flavor of 'early English,' are a mixture of old and modern idiom, and the artistic unity of the work is frequently disturbed by quotations from old writers, and by the use of an occasional Americanism. Some of the fun sprinkled through the story grates on the ear. In speaking of the king's 'taster,' whose duty it was to make sure that poison had not been put into the royal food, the author wonders 'why they did not use a dog or a plumber.' At his first royal meal, the Pauper drinks out of the finger-bowl. There is an air of antiquity about this bit of fun, but is it 'early English'? A strangely obscure allusion appears on page 45. Here the reader is informed that the Prince 'snatched up and put away *an article of national importance.*' Five chapters farther on, it transpires that the great seal cannot be found, and at the end of the story the Prince proves his identity by remembering where he hid it. It will probably occur to few readers that the phrase 'an article of national importance' is a synonym for 'great seal'.

—Unsigned Review in *Century Magazine*,
March 23, 1882, pp. 783–784

HARRIET BEECHER STOWE (1887)

I am reading your Prince and Pauper for the fourth time, and I know it is the best book for young folks that was ever written.

—Harriet Beecher Stowe, quoted by Mark Twain
in a letter to Charles L. Webster, April 2, 1887,
from *Mr. Clemens and Mark Twain,* Justin Kaplan,
New York: Simon and Schuster, 1967, p. 240.

LIFE ON THE MISSISSIPPI

Life on the Mississippi, while it returned to the North American continent and Twain's own era, in addition to a subject that Twain knew intimately, failed to solve his enduring problems of maintaining a structure and of sticking to a clear genre. For this book, Twain collated a series of essays that he had written on "Old Times on the Mississippi," which were published in the *Atlantic Monthly* over the course of 1875. To this collection were appended further reminiscences of Twain's steamboat piloting past and then an account of his recent return to the Mississippi. On that journey, Twain traveled incognito on the steamboats until his identity was revealed, at which point he was invited to pilot the steamboat.

"Mr. Clemens as a Mississippi tourist is not to be compared with Mr. Clemens as a Mississippi pilot," complains the reviewer for the London *Athenaeum,* who pronounces the book a "disappointment." The old chapters are excellent, of course—"Mark Twain at his best"—but they are "already ancient history." Unfortunately, such an anthology begs the comparison of old and new, a "contrast . . . discomforting in the extreme." While in the old letters he was abundant, in the newer work, he is glib, "forced and ambitious" when formerly he was "easy and successful." Most tellingly, the reviewer finds Twain now to be "talking of things from the point of view of the professional American humorist." Self-consciousness has entered Twain's work. He writes as a paid humorist now, while before he wrote as a person. In short, for many readers and reviewers, the tourist has replaced the riverboat pilot.

The genteel recoil from "mere humor" that critics found frustrating in *The Prince and the Pauper* penetrates the new work also: "It is as though he were ashamed of having jested, and were determined to show that on occasion he can be as serious as any one else." When he jokes, he is "anxiously funny." The *Athenaeum* reviewer seems to compare obliquely Twain's talents to the Mississippi as Twain finds it on his return: "things had suffered a change that is almost indescribable."

The reviewer for the *Graphic* predicts a drop in popularity for this latest Twain book. Similarly, growing fatigue with Twain's writing forms the basis of a wager in the *Arkansaw Traveler,* a humor journal. "He has ceased to interest the public," says Twain's critic, and "the people have had enough of him. Now, nothing that he can write or ever has written would be received with any degree of favor." Artemus Ward's name rises up again when he is heralded as Twain's superior, at least in the opinion of the press. The bet is made and an experiment tried, whereby it is proved (albeit fraudulently) that Mark Twain still commands the interest of the newspapers. Strangely, neither article cites a failure in Twain's writing. There is simply a diminishing popularity. Students researching audience reception of Twain will find these brief notices puzzling and extremely provocative conjectures.

Not all notices were negative though. Lafcadio Hearn, then a denizen of New Orleans, praised the book. "Others have described the frontier life sketched in *Roughing It*, and the days of '49," he says, "but no other has ever touched the subject of Mississippi life except in ballads or brief stories." While much had been written by frontier humorists for magazines such as *The Spirit of the Times* and the *New Orleans Picayune*, it is true that no great work of similar length existed at the time. William Dean Howells recounts how a hotel porter and the German emperor both claimed *Life on the Mississippi* as their favorite book, making the same observation to explain their preference. Helen Keller also told Twain it was her favorite of his books. Twain was astonished that a woman could enjoy "such rough reading," although he conceded that "I don't know much about women. It would be impossible for a person to know less about women than I do." Students evaluating gender in Twain's work and life will be fascinated by this claim.

Unsigned Review in the
Chicago Tribune (1883)

James R. Osgood & Co. . . . have brought out the latest of the works of America's genial humorist, Mark Twain. As in its predecessors, much of the material contained in this volume has been in print before; but the body of the work consists of new matter, and the book itself is one of the best, if not *the* best, this writer has given to the public. It deals with a region and with phases of life with which Mr. Clemens is especially familiar. Born on the banks of the Mississippi, his career upon its waters familiarized him with all its vagaries, and he grew to manhood under such peculiar influences that he mingled with the people in the freest possible manner, and thus became especially well qualified to write of them and to talk about them. So this book now before us contains a rich and varied collection of pictures of the characteristic features of *Life on the Mississippi*. And, when viewed through Mr. Clemens' spectacles, when he acts as our guide, and makes his humorous running comments on the scenes successively unfolded before us, the journey cannot fail to interest, and the means of travel is a sure rest to the wearied mind. The author imparts a great deal of useful information, and his book is much more than a mere "funny" book. First, we have an account of the physical and historical aspects of the great Father of Waters; of the changes in its course, and its alterations in the formation of the land on either side; and then we are led to glance at "its slumberous first epoch in a couple of short chapters, at its second and wider-awake epoch in a couple more, at its flushest and widest-awake epoch in a good many succeeding chapters, and then at its comparatively tranquil present epoch in what is left of the book." Here is an amusing paragraph from the work, showing what may be expected in the future from the erratic conduct of this mighty river: (Quoted, chap. 17, from "(Therefore,) the Mississippi, between . . ." and ". . . investment of fact.")

After this preliminary discussion, Mr. Clemens includes some chapters previously issued both in magazine and in book form, in which he tells of his apprenticeship to a pilot; of the difficulties he had to master; of the association of pilots twenty-five years ago; of the famous riverboats and of their races; and gives vivid pictures of his life at this time, before he dreamed of filling a vacant niche as an American humorist. The War suspended his occupation as a pilot. He says:

> I had to seek another livelihood. So I became a silver-miner in Nevada; next, a newspaper-reporter; next, a gold-miner in California; next, a reporter in San Francisco; next, a special correspondent in the Sandwich Islands; next, a roving correspondent in Europe and the East; next, an instructional torchbearer on the lecture-platform; and finally I became a scribbler of books and an immovable fixture among the other rocks of New England.

The rest of the book gives a graphic account of the visit made last spring to his old haunts, and the reminiscences brought to mind by this trip. Of course, a good deal of exaggeration and of fiction is mingled with the author's narrative; but that only gives additional spice to the reading, and Mark Twain's volumes are not exactly intended to serve as guide-books. On the whole, the reader will find this an entertaining and interesting work, lavishly illustrated, and published in the handsome style characteristic of the house from which it emanates. . . .

—Unsigned Review in the *Chicago Tribune*, May 19, 1883, p. 9

LAFCADIO HEARN (1883)

Life on the Mississippi,—Mark Twain's new production, is a large volume of more than six hundred pages—much resembling in form the famous *Innocents Abroad* and *Roughing It*. Like those highly successful books, *Life on the Mississippi* has been illustrated with humorous engravings, the spirit of which will be appreciated by all familiar with the picturesque features of American river-life. A number of the early chapters are already familiar to readers of the *Atlantic*,—having been contributed to that periodical several years ago; but their interest has been greatly augmented, and their verisimilitude emphasized, by the drawings which now accompany them. The past and present types of steamboatmen are portrayed with a certain rough and lively humor in thorough keeping with the text.

Notwithstanding its lively spirit of fun, the volume is a more serious creation by far than *The Innocents Abroad*; and in some respects seems to us the most solid book that Mark Twain has written. Certainly the first two hundred and fifty pages possess a large historical value; and will be referred to in future years as trustworthy paintings of manners, customs, and social phases which have already been much changed, and will doubtless, before another generation, belong altogether to the past. But in addition to reminiscences of the old-time river-life, and the curious multitude of incidents and amusing experiences, one finds that the author has taken pains to collect and set forth almost every important fact connected with the Mississippi River—historical or geographical. These positive data rather gain than lose in weight by their humorous presentation; and it may safely be said that many persons who may read the opening chapters will obtain from them a better knowledge of what the Mississippi is, than they could gain by laborious study of physical geographies. When one finds upon page 25 the statement that "*nearly the whole of that one thousand three hundred miles of old Mississippi River which La Salle floated down in his canoe, two hundred years ago, is good solid dry land now*"—one gains a juster idea of the river's eccentricities than the perusal of many volumes of solid and statistical reports could give. Within less than five pages an astonishing variety of information is given in similarly compressed shape;—the whole natural history of the river, (its importance, its fickleness, its capacities of construction) is presented in a brief series of ingeniously epitomized paragraphs which, once read, will not easily be forgotten.

The most delightful part of the book is included in the autobiographical chapters—in the history of the author's early experience as a pilot's apprentice. These pages are full of laughing vividness, and paint the brighter side of old-fashioned river-life with such a delicate exaggeration of saliencies as that by which the peculiarities of English habits fifty years ago are perpetuated for us by the early artists of *Punch*. But there is a kernel of curious fact in every rich-flavored incident of humor. Here the book is absolutely unique;—it contains the only realistic history of piloting on the Mississippi in existence, and written by perhaps the only author of the century whose genius is thoroughly adapted to the subject treated. Indeed, one must have followed for years some peculiar river-calling in order to comprehend what steamboat life is, and appreciate its various presentations of tragedy, comedy, and poetry—to all of which we find ample justice done in the book before us. It is the sum of the experience of years; and no little art has been shown in selecting specimens from such a range of memoirs. The old-time flatboatmen and raftsmen—so famous in Mississippi River history—are capitally drawn; and we have a rare sketch of the lordly pilots of ante-bellum days, who drew their $250 or more per month, and were idolized by the fair of numberless little river-towns. Not less interesting is the brief history of the Pilots' Association in those days—an imperious monopoly which sustained many furious campaigns against steamboat owners, and almost invariably won the fight at last by dint of certain ingenious devices pleasantly recounted in Chapter XV.

Mark Twain's humor being of the most typically American sort, and rich in that imaginative quality which an ingenious foreign critic has compared to "sheet lightning, flashing over half a world at once," has won him that literary reputation in Europe formerly held by Artemus Ward. Ward is now old-fashioned; Twain occupies a far larger transatlantic position. His stories have been widely translated; and within the past six months we have seen as many of his sketches "done into French," for the Paris *Figaro*. Much of the dialectic fun was necessarily lost in the transmutation; but otherwise the comic element survived admirably in the French—a language especially well suited to the exaggerations of American humor. We fancy that the present work will have a larger success in Europe than its illustrated predecessors; for it is more novel in its character, and even more thoroughly American in its fun, and withal, more historically valuable. Others have described the frontier life sketched in *Roughing It*, and the days of '49; but no other has ever touched the subject of Mississippi life except in ballads or brief stories.

The last three hundred pages are devoted to the Mississippi Life of to-day as compared with that of before the war;—they represent the result of the author's Southern trip during the last inundation. This part of his history opens with the recital of a pleasant personal adventure, in which the author attempted to play *incognito* with an old pilot too sharp to be caught, who tells a wonderful yarn about a dredge-boat, which he calls by another name: (Quoted, chap. 24, from "'An alligator boat . . .'" through "'. . . around on alligators.'")

Finally, after a most interesting history of "alligator pilots," Mark Twain's mask is torn off, and he is put to the wheel in expiation of his attempt at mystification. He finds that even after twenty-years he has not forgotten how to manage a steamboat; but the river has so changed in the long interval that portions of its ante-bellum geography are no longer recognizable. He wants to go ashore subsequently, and so informs the captain: (Quoted, chap. 32, from "'Go ashore where?'" through "'. . . into the Mississippi'")

This spirit of fun never flags, even to the end of the book; but every page of humor is underlaid by some solid truth, often more or less grim, and bearing important witness for one side of that now vastly agitated subject—The Mississippi River Question. Here the reader will find a startling account of the changes of the Mississippi since the era of our civil war.

We have already published extracts from the chapter on New Orleans; but the author has given a great deal more space to our city and its features than the aforesaid extracts would suggest. Here and there he pokes some sharp fun at New Orleans' peculiarities,—especially regarding funerals and undertakers; but there is no malice in the satire and nobody is badly hurt. Some pleasant reminiscences of his visit appear,—his acquaintance with George W. Cable and others; and *The Times-Democrat* must acknowledge the handsome compliments paid to it throughout the volume, besides the republication in the appendix of Mr. Whitney's correspondence during the relief trip of the *Susie B.* in March 1882.

—Lafcadio Hearn, *New Orleans
Times-Democrat*, May 20, 1883, p. 4

Unsigned Review in the *Athenaeum* (1883)

Mr. Clemens's new book is a disappointment. To begin with, it has a vulgar red cover, it is cumbered with a quantity of illustrations of the cheapest and least suggestive American type, its lines are ungraceful; so that, coming as it does in an age of *Parchment Libraries* and *Petites Bibliothèques Elzéviriennes*, and *Éditions Jouaust*, it appears at once anomalous and offensive, and prejudices its readers against it as a book even before they get seriously to work upon it as literature. Nor is this the only thing that may be said against it. On examination its best part turns out to be years old—to be, in fact, a reprint of the vigorous and pleasant set of sketches published as 'Old Days on the Mississippi.' They are excellent, as we all know; they are in some ways the author's best work; but they are already ancient history. What is even more to the point, perhaps, they are vastly superior to their present environment. There is plenty of drollery, of American humour, in the new chapters; there is some good writing; not a little of the matter is interesting and novel; but they have none of the freshness and force of their predecessors. In his trials and triumphs as a Mississippi pilot Mr. Clemens had an admirable subject, and handled it with the greatest gusto imaginable. You feel as you read that what is written is the outcome of years of experience, is a record of memories mellow with age and instinct with the cheerful vitality that comes of retrospection; that the writer has thoroughly enjoyed his work; and that the production of his book has made him sincerely happy. From the new chapters the impression received is very different. Mr. Clemens as a Mississippi tourist is not to be compared with Mr. Clemens as a Mississippi pilot. His experiences seem all brand-new; his impressions are not remarkably profound; he is rather glib than abundant, rather restless than vivacious, rather forced and ambitious than easy and successful; his humour is too often strained, his narrative has too often the flavour of mere 'copy,' his cleverness has too often a likeness to that of the brilliant bagman. As he appears in 'Old Days on the Mississippi' he is the Mark Twain of *Roughing It* and the *Innocents at Home*; as he appears in the record of his cruise he is more or less the Mark Twain of the *New Pilgrim's Progress*, and certain chapters in the *Tramp Abroad*, and that dreadful book in which he tells the story of his impressions of the continent of Europe. In the one set of works, that is to say, he is fresh, vigorous, irresistibly amusing; in the other, he is merely parading his own vulgarity, and talking of things from the point of view of the professional American humourist. The contrast, as they know who are learned in Mark Twain, is discomforting in the extreme.

His opening chapter is a good example of the vices of his new method. Part of it he has got from books, and part of it—a very little part—is touched with his own experience. He begins it with geographical statistics, and tells us how the Mississippi is 4,300 miles long; how it discharges three times as much water as the St. Lawrence, and 338 times as much as the Thames; how it drains an area of forty-five degrees of longitude; how it discharges 406,000,000 tons of mud per annum into the Gulf of Mexico, and all the rest of it. The information is valuable no doubt; but in a book of this sort it is, on the whole, superfluous, and it certainly suggests the matter of an American lecture. In the next few pages Mr. Clemens picks himself up a little, and talks of the Mississippi's eccentricities: how it is given to the practice of 'cut offs,' how it is always changing its locality by 'moving bodily *side* ways,' how in thirty years it has increased the size of Prophet's island from 1,500 to 2,000 acres, and how in more instances than one 'it has shortened itself thirty miles at a single jump.' After this he becomes a mere compiler. It is as though he were ashamed of having jested, and were determined to show that on occasion he can be as serious as any one else. In this respect his second chapter is even more disappointing than his first.

But afterwards, for a dozen or fifteen chapters, we have to deal with 'Old Days on the Mississippi,' and we come in contact with Mark Twain at his best. They treat of a time when steamboating was a great industry, and along some thousands of miles of water-way the pilot was a creature of a superior race—a privileged and impeccable being. . . .

. . . He goes on to tell how the steamboat men and boys were heroes to the long-shore boys and men; how 'now and then we had a hope that if we lived and were good, God would permit us to be pirates . . . but the ambition to be a steamboatman always remained'; how, in course of time, disgusted and exasperated by the airs of boys upon steamboats, he ran away, and presently became apprentice to a pilot; how for a time he rejoiced and was glad, and how for a time he despaired and was wretched; how he had to learn the great river bit by bit, mark by mark, feature by feature, accident by accident, backwards and forwards, by day and night, in all its innumerable details; how in due course he became a pilot, and what manner of men the pilots, his contemporaries, were; how they talked, and how they worked, and how they earned tremendous wages, and how they towered above created things; of the feats they did, and the oaths they swore, and the airs they gave themselves; and how, at last, the war came and stopped their work, and broke up their corporation, and gave the river over to tugs and the shores to locomotives, and put an end to the Golden Age of steamboating, and took the heroic quality from piloting as completely as though it had never existed. He is on a level with his argument throughout. As we have said, he writes as one who enjoys his work. His fun is natural and spontaneous, his dialogue is everywhere admirable, and in certain places—in telling, for instance, how his master, Mr. Bixby, carried his boat past Hat Island in the teeth of darkness and a falling tide and the opinion of all the pilots aboard—he shows such a mastery of narrative, such a power of story-telling pure and simple, as is within the reach of few contemporaries or none.

When, years afterwards, Mr. Clemens returned to the river and revisited the scene of his former triumphs, he found that things had suffered a change that is almost indescribable. This change it is which is the matter of his new chapters. In itself it is of uncommon interest; but it has reacted on the writer's spirits, and though his account of it is easily read, it is not easily remembered. It is not that Mr. Clemens is found wanting either in sincerity or in ingenuity. On the contrary, he describes what he sees with point and propriety, he is anxiously funny, and he makes original remarks with immense application; he is responsible for certain pages on the mournful influence of Walter Scott and his share in the production of the peculiar 'chivalry' of the Southern States, which are monuments of misplaced and unhappy ambition. But his heart is not in his work. What is good in it deals with the past—is for the most part as though omitted from 'Old Days on the Mississippi.' The rest is mere reporting, and we cannot but regret that it was not published separately, and that the older and better matter was not left to take care of itself.

—Unsigned Review in the *Athenaeum*
2901, June 2, 1883, pp. 94–95

ROBERT BROWN (1883)

This pleasantly written and profusely illustrated volume is an English reprint of an American book the first portion of which appeared several years ago. It describes, with all the dry humour and often graphic power of Mr. Clemens, his experiences as an apprentice-pilot on board the great steamers plying between New Orleans and St. Louis in the far-away days to which the Southerner refers so sadly as 'befo' the wah.' The second section, which forms a sequel to the first, narrates a visit to the old scenes twenty-one years after the author had left 'the river.' The result is a singularly interesting work, though probably the earlier chapters will prove of most lasting value, for the later ones are more personal, and often needlessly padded with anecdotes and reminiscences which, however diverting, have a very remote, if any, connexion with the narrative.

The fun in Mr. Clemens' *Tramps Abroad* is frequently forced, and sometimes quite unsuited to the subject in hand. His American experiences have rarely this fault; the writer seems to feel the ground he is treading more secure, and his broad pleasantry is in better keeping with raftsmen, backwoods settlers, and gold-diggers than with monks, mountains, kings, cathedrals, and other sanctities of old-fashioned Europe. The description of the Mississippi, its steamboat captains, mates, and pilots, the broad-horns and their rough crews, the ague-shaken settlers roosting on fences while the 'river was out,' and the ways of the great valley of the vast American river as they existed before the war are in his best style. Half-a-century ago, the Mississippi Valley was the favourite field for English tourists; for in times where Concord coaches over corduroy roads were the only means of penetrating the continent, the river and its tributaries, covered with palatial steamers, were among the easiest highways through the centre of the United States, or its then farthest civilised boundaries. Marryat, Mrs. Trollope, Basil Hall—all the little army of literary visitors—have much to say about the Mississippi. Later travellers scarcely ever mention it, for they are so eager to rush West that, except where they catch a glimpse of it and the Missouri on their rapid run for the Rocky Mountains, the Father of Waters is strange to their note-books. The railways, in like manner, ruined the old steam-boating times, and humbled the pride of pilots—whose pride was the pride of kings—and even made the captains and mates regard ordinary passengers as of the same flesh and blood with themselves. The rise, decline, and fall of these potentates is told with admirable effect; and, leaving out of account a little characteristic exaggeration here and there, with minute fidelity. Now and then, an expert in American *facetiae* will detect a very old friend, disguised for the occasion; but these familiar faces in no way detract from the freshness of a volume which does not contain a dull page.

The book is indeed the best account of social life on the Mississippi with which we are acquainted. But it possesses an additional merit which possibly the author may disclaim—it embodies a clear and, take it all in all, very accurate account of the physical features of the river, its shiftings, and general vagaries. Specialists will, of course, turn to Humphrey and Abbot's stern tomes, or to the Reports of the Commission which is fast making piloting on the Mississippi as prosaic and easy as it is on the Elbe or the Thames; but less exigent people, whose thirst for knowledge is quenched with something less than quartos, may safely take 'Mark Twain' for their guide. The illustrations are rough, but graphic; and the book is altogether so good that we regret to see that the ardour which is lavished in scarlet and gold is unequal to the production of an index.

—Robert Brown, *Academy* 24,
July 28, 1883, p. 58

Unsigned Review in the
Arkansaw Traveler (1883)

Several weeks ago a well-known gentleman, while on a visit to the *Traveler*, took occasion to severely criticize Mark Twain's new book *[Life on the Mississippi]*. "He has ceased to interest the public;" the critic went on, "not that he has materially weakened in style, but because the people have had enough of him. Now, nothing that he can write or ever has written would be received with any degree of favor. I warrant you that if he had kept some of his letters until now, they would fall flat. It was different with Artemus Ward. Every scrap that Ward ever wrote is, upon discovery, taken up by the press."

"A hitherto unpublished letter from Mark Twain would be taken up by the newspapers," we suggested, and hereupon began such a speculative argument that at last we wagered a box of cigars, agreeing to settle the matter by producing a Twain letter. Of course there was no hitherto unpublished letter attainable, so a very rough imitation was "ground out," purporting to have been written in Memphis in 1859. The letter was published and was immediately reproduced by many of the leading newspapers in the country. The gentleman has left a box of cigars at the office, and we feel that it is our duty to share them with Mr. Clemens.

—Unsigned Review in the *Arkansaw Traveler,* August 4, 1883, p. 4

UNSIGNED REVIEW IN *GRAPHIC* (1883)

'Mark Twain,' in the earlier chapters of his new book, *Life on the Mississippi* (Chatto and Windus), gives such an admirable specimen of his powers as a serious writer of history, that one is almost tempted to wish that, for this occasion only, he would lay aside altogether his funny style, or at least subordinate it to purposes of serious literary work. But the old Adam cannot long be subdued. Mr. Clemens soon slips into his accustomed style; and almost before the reader is aware that he has changed from the graphic to the grotesque, he is deep in sketches of life and character in all of which the great river forms the background. Pilot's exploits, and the misfortunes of pilot's 'cubs,' river superstitions and river romances, tales of hard drinking, hard fighting, and hard swearing—these are the materials of which the book is made up. Sometimes the quaint humour is varied by some grisly tale of murder and revenge, such as 'A Thumb-Print, and What Came of It,' a peculiarly horrible story of a night watchman in a German morgue. That *Life on the Mississippi* will be as popular as the books by which 'Mark Twain's' name was made is not likely. Nevertheless it is well worth reading.

—Unsigned Review in *Graphic* 28, September 1, 1883, p. 231

WILLIAM DEAN HOWELLS (1910)

At that time I had become editor of *The Atlantic Monthly*, and I had allegiances belonging to the conduct of what was and still remains the most scrupulously cultivated of our periodicals. When Clemens began to write for it he came willingly under its rules, for with all his wilfulness there never was a more biddable man in things you could show him a reason for. He never made the least of that trouble which so abounds for the hapless editor from narrower-minded contributors. If you wanted a thing changed, very good, he changed it; if you suggested that a word or a sentence or a paragraph had better be struck out, very good, he struck it out. His proof-sheets came back each a veritable "mush of concession," as Emerson says. Now and then he would try a little stronger language than *The Atlantic* had stomach for, and once when I sent him a proof I made him observe that I had left out the profanity. He wrote back: "Mrs. Clemens opened that proof, and lit into the room with danger in her eye. What profanity? You see, when I read the manuscript to her I skipped that." It was part of his joke to pretend a violence in that gentlest creature which the more amusingly realized the situation to their friends.

I was always very glad of him and proud of him as a contributor, but I must not claim the whole merit, or the first merit of having him write for us. It was the publisher, the late H. O. Houghton, who felt the incongruity of his absence from the leading periodical of the country, and was always urging me to get him to write. I will take the credit of being eager for him, but it is to the publisher's credit that he tried, so far as the modest traditions of *The Atlantic* would permit, to meet the expectations in pay which the colossal profits of Clemens's books might naturally have bred in him. Whether he was really able to do this he never knew from Clemens himself, but probably twenty dollars a page did not surfeit the author of books that "sold right along just like the Bible."

We had several short contributions from Clemens first, all of capital quality, and then we had the series of papers which went mainly to the making of his great book, *Life on the Mississippi*. Upon the whole I have the notion that Clemens thought this his greatest book, and he was supported in his opinion by that of the *portier* in his hotel at Vienna, and that of the German Emperor, who, as he told me with equal respect for the preference of each, united in thinking it his best; with such far-sundered social poles approaching in its favor, he apparently found himself without standing for opposition. At any rate, the papers won instant appreciation from his editor and publisher, and from the readers of their periodical, which they expected to prosper beyond precedent in its circulation. But those were days of simpler acceptance of the popular rights of newspapers than these are, when magazines strictly guard their vested interests against them. The New York *Times* and the St. Louis *Democrat* profited by the advance copies of the magazine sent them to reprint the papers month by month. Together they covered nearly the whole reading territory of the Union, and the terms of their daily publication enabled them to anticipate the magazine in its own restricted field. Its subscription list was not enlarged in the slightest measure, and *The Atlantic Monthly* languished on the news-stands as undesired as ever.

—William Dean Howells, *My Mark Twain*,
New York: Harper and Brothers,
1910, pp. 19–21

THE ADVENTURES OF HUCKLEBERRY FINN

Although it is now revered as a definitive American classic, Twain's novel was not held in the highest esteem by its first wave of readers. One letter to Twain recalled the wager proffered by *Arkansaw Traveler*'s review of *Life on the Mississippi*:

> For God's sake give the suffering public a rest on your labored wit. Shoot your trash and quit it. You are only an imitator of Artemus Ward and a sickening one at that and we are all sick of you. For God's sake take a tumble and give us a rest.

Twain's own opinion was ambivalent. He had written *Huckleberry Finn* at the same time he produced *The Prince and the Pauper,* and he valued the latter novel much more highly. He did not expect the former title to sell well: "I am not able to see that anything can save Huck Finn from being another defeat," he wrote gloomily to his publisher, "unless you are looking to do it by tumbling books into the trade." Even later, when he looked back over his oeuvre, it was not *Huckleberry Finn* that he preferred but *Joan of Arc*. Howells and Livy Clemens agreed with him that *The Prince and the Pauper* was the superior novel; it was genteel and improving and wholesome. Post-Victorian readers tend to disagree.

Huckleberry Finn had an awkward start, even before it was published. Three thousand advance "prospectuses" were sent out containing "obscene" additions to the illustrations, which are now probably more amusing than they were at the time. The *New York World* writer tried to describe this mutilation without naming it outright. "A mere stroke of the awl would suffice to give to the cut an indecent character never intended by the author or engraver."

The misgivings of the book's author notwithstanding, *Huckleberry Finn* attracted plenty of advance interest, due in no small part to the fiasco prompted by the obscene plate and the subsequent lawsuit. Sensitive to Twain's late string of flops, his publishers promoted the book as "written in Mark Twain's old style." Indeed, the company promoted the book so aggressively that it attracted adverse notice. "No book has been put on the market with more advertising," the San Francisco *Bulletin* groused. "*Huckleberry Finn* has been introduced to the world as it were with a blare of trumpets." Twain's former employer, the San Francisco *Alta California*, weighed in by remarking that "[a]s a self-advertiser, Mark Twain has become more of a success than as a humorist, as is shown by the *Adventures of Huckleberry Finn.*"

In a friendly advance review, Brander Matthews views the novel as a "sequel" to *Tom Sawyer*. Unlike the majority of modern readers, Matthews sees Tom's intervention in the narrative as happening "in the very nick of time," casting Tom as "a young god from the machine." The *deus ex machina*, or "god out of the machine," was a convention used in certain classical Greek dramas. It was employed to neatly resolve difficult situations in the plot by the use of an omnipotent deity lowered onto the stage by a machine. Casting Tom in this role is perhaps an exaggeration. T.S. Perry, like many later writers (Ernest Hemingway is one), argue that Tom's intervention is an unnecessary and even irritating interruption. Carl Van Doren tolerantly concedes that the book's "hilarious comic force" prevents the narrative from collapsing into anticlimax. Students following the debate surrounding this ending will find Matthews's estimate a useful start.

Matthews notes with approval the novel's narrative shift after *Tom Sawyer*. While in the first novel readers saw Huck "from the outside," now he is seen "from the inside." These qualities that Matthews rates, qualities that mark a subjective, internally looking narrative, anticipate the modernist texts of the following century. The "great charm" of Twain's characters, he writes, is that

> they are not written about and about; they are not described and dissected and analysed; they appear and play their parts and disappear; and yet they leave a sharp impression of indubitable vitality and individuality.

There is no omniscient narrator, able to discern and explain conclusively everything that is happening. "We see everything through [Huck's] eyes," Matthews writes, and "they are his eyes and not a pair of Mark Twain's spectacles." Nor are Huck's comments "speeches put into his mouth by the author." T.S. Perry notices this same innovation:

> That is the way that a story is best told, by telling it, and letting it go to the reader unaccompanied by sign-posts or directions how he shall understand it and profit by it. Life teaches its lessons by implication, not by didactic preaching; and literature is at its best when it is an imitation of life and not an excuse for instruction.

This methodology would lead, in due time, to James Joyce's *Ulysses* and William Faulkner's *The Sound and the Fury*.

Twain was blessed with Matthews as an early reviewer, a critic who has the sophistication to see the book for its merits without the instinctive Victorian recoil from the new or the unusual. The reviewer is equal to the matter under examination, able to appreciate it for what it is and to anticipate what it will become. Matthews praises the "sober self-restraint" exhibited by the author for relaying without authorial comment scenes "which would have afforded the ordinary writer matter for endless moral and political and sociological disquisition." Perhaps for this reason, Matthews prophetically remarks of Huck that "Old maids of either sex will wholly fail to understand him or to like him, or to see his significance and his value." He would very soon be proved correct.

Matthews is especially good in noticing the differences between Huck and Tom. While Tom is bookish and "the child of respectable parents," Huck is "a walking repository of the juvenile folklore of the Mississippi Valley—a folklore . . . largely influenced by intimate association with the negroes." Matthews is already recognizing what Shelley Fisher Fishkin would explore at length more than a hundred years later in *Was Huck Black?* Students exploring racial characterization and also racial blurring in *Huckleberry Finn* will find this a strong starting point.

Finally, Matthews pronounces that this time Twain has turned away from his incessant clowning. While *Tom Sawyer* had the funnier isolated episodes, "the general level of the later story is perhaps higher than that of the earlier." While this may sound like faint praise to contemporary readers, Matthews's essay stands as a vital evaluation of *Huckleberry Finn* ahead of the conservative-led frenzy to follow.

Robert Bridges's review, filed less than a month after Brander Matthews's, demonstrates the conservative case against *Huckleberry*

Finn. Bridges sarcastically cites scenes of drunkenness, the death and mutilation of a pig, the southern feud that leads to "six to eight choice corpses," a tempered version of an obscene folktale ("a chapter for … church festivals"), a funeral, and "a rat episode in the cellar." To contemporary readers, this litany shows most clearly the unusual level of squeamishness exhibited by an earlier society. Students exploring the social context in which the novel was first published should, however, take note of these taboos. Only by knowing the dominant customs of the time can the full achievement of Twain's novel be appreciated. Bridges's piece is followed by a number of documents, some of which were not published in the literary columns of the papers, about the controversy between Mark Twain and the town of Concord, Massachusetts.

Concord is the town best known as the home of the freethinking Ralph Waldo Emerson, as well as the radical Henry David Thoreau (both men, by this time, were dead) and the educational reformer and writer Amos Bronson Alcott. The community's public library had a committee that decided which books should be available there and which should not. It became publicly known that *Huckleberry Finn* was an unsuitable book for children, and the committee had it duly banned from its library's shelves. That Concord, of all places, should take this position clearly communicates the social division that existed within the United States at the time. The committee first pronounced the book "coarse," "the veriest trash," and, tellingly, "more suited to the slums than to intelligent, respectable people."

Unfortunately, Concord equally had a poor reputation within the conservative press for an earlier radicalism (Emerson's "Divinity School Address" of 1838 and the subsequent transcendentalist movement that was centered there), so the library committee became the butt of jokes as well. Poking fun at the impenetrable philosophy of Ralph Waldo Emerson and Bronson Alcott, the *Boston Daily Globe* chided: "When Mark writes another book he should think of the Concord School of Philosophy and put a little more whenceness of the hereafter among his nowness of the here." Twain rejoiced in the publicity (if he did not actually laugh "in his sleeves"), and other conservatives condemned the Concord chapter for providing Twain with free publicity.

A more reasoned reviewer, from the San Francisco *Chronicle*, noted that the supposition that *Huckleberry Finn* was a "boy's book" was perhaps the first misreading, since "upon nine boys out of ten much of the humor, as well as the pathos, would be lost. The more general knowledge one has the better he is fitted to appreciate this book." The novel calls for a sophisticated reader. The boy who looks eagerly for a story in *Huckleberry Finn* will find frustration amid the rich "embroidery of jokes, sketches and sarcasm" in which "the story really forms the least part." The *Chronicle* reviewer reads the last part of the book, Jim's "rescue" by Huck and Tom, as a savvy burlesque of crime fiction. T.S. Perry recognizes this too but remains irritated by the intrusion ("the caricature of books of adventure leaves us cold"). Even more perceptively, the reviewer sees the tale as "the sharpest satire on the ante-bellum estimate of the slave." Any student examining representations of slavery in Twain should read the *Chronicle* review.

The reviewer closes his piece by noting the simple truth behind the grand squabble, that "[t]here is a large class of people who are impervious to a joke." As if in illustration of this fact, the *Boston Daily Advertiser* solemnly announces that "in matters of humor the tide has turned at last, and ... the old school of coarse, flippant and irreverent joke makers is going out, to return no more." This was, regrettably, to prove a correct assessment.

Eventually, the transcendentalist element of Concord society distinguished itself at least slightly in the wake of the library's ban. Franklin B. Sanborn was asked to write a review of *Huckleberry Finn* for the anti-Twain *Springfield Republican*, for which he was a regular columnist. The piece he submitted insisted defiantly that the novel "has a vein of deep morality beneath its exterior of falsehood and vice."

While Sanborn retains some squeamishness about subjects presumably deemed "grotesque" and "coarse" only at Harvard, he recognizes the historical worth of the novel and its moral import. "It is in effect an argument against negro-slavery, lynching, whisky-drinking, family feuds, promiscuous shooting, and nearly all the vices of Missouri in the olden time." He hails Twain's documentation of "the political history of the United States from 1854 to 1860," seeing in the character of Pap Finn "the drunken poor white of Missouri, upon whom Atchison and his betters relied to fight slavery into Kansas." Sanborn was well informed on this subject, having been a friend of and collaborator with the radical abolitionist John Brown. Sanborn locates Twain's novel within the bloody history of slavery. Students interested in the historical background and verity of Twain's novel will find Sanborn's account compelling.

Students analyzing Twain's complex war of words with the officials in Concord, Massachusetts, will find Sanborn's involvement provides a fascinating and independent view. Sanborn is also perhaps the first reviewer to read *Huckleberry Finn* as an allegory for a deeper, older myth.

In the twentieth century it became a matter of course to identify Huck with Odysseus, for instance (Carl Van Doren does so in 1921), but in 1885 Sanborn is already suggesting that "it is indeed a legend of prehistoric times, and for aught I know, may be a sun-myth or a freshet-myth, or the story of a geological period." This willingness to see a "sun-myth" in *Huckleberry Finn* distinguishes Sanborn from the general crowd at Concord, as well as most nineteenth-century readers of the novel. Any student exploring mythology in this novel will find a good foundation in Sanborn's reading.

Additional defenses of *Huckleberry Finn* come from Thomas Sergeant Perry, the friend of Henry James and William Dean Howells, who relishes the documentation of "the hideous fringe of civilization that then adorned that valley," and Joel Chandler Harris, who launches into a sociological analysis of "the American leisure class" in order to show that the fault lies with the newspaper critics. Twain responded with gratitude to Harris, "for the good word about Huck, that abused child of mine who has had so much unfair mud slung at him." Twain especially appreciated that this defense came from a southerner ("a man ... who has been where such boys live"). Students curious about how much of the Concord storm was a revival of hostility between the Confederate states and the Union will find Twain's letter revealing.

Later studies of *Huckleberry Finn* reflect the slow evolution of an idea: that the novel might be, should be, then is a key canonical text. Twain was delighted when Sir Walter Besant, the British novelist, critic, historian, and philanthropist, nominated Twain his "favorite novelist" and *Huckleberry Finn* Twain's best book. When Besant wrote the piece, in 1898, he reckoned his choice might be "perhaps unexpected," since it was not (at least not then) "one of the acknowledged masterpieces; ... a book which has already been reviewed over and over again." Besant praises the book for being pleasing—in different ways—at all stages of life. He praises the deadpan narrative in which Huck Finn never once cracks a smile: "[I]t is humorous because the narrator sees no humor in anything." Besant marvels at how long ago the events seem. "There are still, perhaps, country villages and places in the Central States ... where the people are simple and unsuspicious, and enjoy a red hot religion; but the world has moved, even for them." The world has moved also, it is obvious, for the gentlemen and ladies of the Concord Public Library, whose views now seem outmoded. In due course, as can be seen in such later reviews, the world catches up with Twain's novel.

Twelve years later, thus, H.L. Mencken could still ask, "How long does it take a new idea to gain lodgment in the professorial mind?" He ponders, specifically, the plodding resistance of the canon (as defined by academics) to *Huckleberry Finn*, lamenting the hiatus between the novel's publication and "its acceptance by any reputable professor of literature, tutor, lecturer or high school pundit as a work of art of the first rank." In another eleven years, the novel is (in Carl Van Doren's words) Twain's "masterpiece." Indeed, by 1921 the two contenders for the crown are *Huckleberry Finn* and *The Scarlet Letter*—two novels so sufficiently unalike that the decision is postponed indefinitely (although Van Doren gamely essays a comparison). Students reading these later reevaluations of *Huckleberry Finn* can trace the development of the interpretation of the novel as a "classic."

UNSIGNED REVIEW "MARK TWAIN IN A DILEMMA" (1884)

Huckleberry Finn, Mark Twain's new book, was complete last March, but owing to complications and differences with his publishers, it has not yet appeared, although it has been extensively announced—a prospectus of the story sent out and the opening chapters recently published in the *Century*. When the book was finished last month Mark Twain made a proposition in regard to its publication to the American Publishing Company of this city, which published his "Innocents Abroad" and his later works. From them the company, which heretofore had been but a small concern, achieved a reputation and standing equal to any of the older established publishing houses of the country. Mark Twain on his side obtained royalties amounting in all to over $400,000. When "Huckleberry Finn," the sequel to "Tom Sawyer," was completed, Twain again made a proposition to his publishers to produce this new work. Negotiations were commenced, but never completed. The parties could not agree to terms. Evidently Mark Twain considered that he had built up the American Publishing Company, while they seemed to think themselves the founders of his fame and fortune. Liberal royalties were offered Twain by the publishing company, but he refused to accept them. The final offer was that the profits should be divided, each of the parties to receive 50 per cent, of the proceeds from the sale of the new work. This proposition was not satisfactory to the author, who wanted 60 per cent of the profits. This offer the company refused to accept, and he determined on entering a new business—combining that of the publisher with that of author.

Mark Twain had a nephew residing in New York in whose business ability he had great confidence. This man, whose name is Charles L. Webster, is engaged in the book-publishing business at No. 658 Broadway. He entered into a partnership with his nephew to produce his new work and to supervise all the mechanical details of its production. The copy was all sent to him and by him given to the printers. In order to properly embellish the book the services of a leading metropolitan engraver were secured, and from this comes all the trouble into which Hartford's popular author is now plunged. The engravings, after having been cut on the plates, were sent to the electrotyper. One of the plates represented a man with a downcast head, standing in the foreground of a particularly striking illustration. In front of him was a ragged urchin with a look of dismay overspreading his countenance. In the background, and standing behind the boy, was an attractive-looking young girl, whose face was enlivened by a broad grin. Something which the boy or man had said or done evidently amused her highly. The title of the cut was "In a Dilemma; What Shall I do?"

When the plate was sent to the electrotyper a wicked spirit must have possessed him. The title was suggestive. A mere stroke of the awl would suffice to give to the cut an indecent character never intended by the author or engraver. It would make no difference in the surface of the plate that would be visible to the naked eye, but when printed would add to the engraving a characteristic which would be repudiated not only by the author, but by all the respectable people of the country into whose hands the volume should fall. The work of the engraver was successful. It passed the eye of the inspector and was approved. A proof was taken and submitted. If the alteration of the plate was manifested in the proof it was evidently attributed to a defect in the press and paper, which would be remedied when the volume was sent to the press. Now the work was ready for printing.

In issuing books to be sold by "subscription only" the publishers first strike off a large number of prospectuses, which are to be used by the agents when soliciting subscribers to the work. Some 3,000 of these prospectuses, with the defective cut, were presented and distributed to the different agents throughout the country. The entire work had passed the eyes of the various readers and inspectors and the glaring indecency of the cut had not been discovered. Throughout the country were hundreds of agents displaying the merits of the work and elaborating on the artistic work of the engravings. It was remarkable that while the defect was so palpable, none of the agents noticed it, or if he did, he failed to report it to the publishers. Possibly they might have considered the alteration intentional, as the title to the illustration was now doubly suggestive.

At last came a letter from the Chicago agent calling attention to the cut. Then there was consternation in the office of the publishers. Copies of the prospectus were hauled from the shelf and critically examined. Then for the first time it dawned on the publishers that such an illustration would condemn the work. Immediately all the agents were telegraphed to and the prospectuses were called in. The page containing the cut was torn from the book, a new and perfect illustration being substituted. Agents were supplied with the improved volumes and are now happy in canvassing for a work to which there can be no objection, while they smile at the prospects of heavy commissions. But the story leaked out. Several opposition publishers got hold of the cut, however, and these now adorn their respective offices.

—Unsigned Review, "Mark Twain in a Dilemma,"
New York World, November 27, 1884, p. 4

Brander Matthews "Huckleberry Finn" (1885)

The boy of to-day is fortunate indeed, and, of a truth, he is to be congratulated. While the boy of yesterday had to stay his stomach with the unconscious humour of *Sandford and Merton*, the boy of to-day may get his fill of fun and of romance and of adventure in *Treasure Island* and in *Tom Brown* and in *Tom Sawyer*, and now in a sequel to *Tom Sawyer*, wherein Tom himself appears in the very nick of time, like a young god from the machine. Sequels of stories which have been widely popular are not a little risky. *Huckleberry Finn* is a sharp exception to this general rule. Although it is a sequel, it is quite as worthy of wide popularity as *Tom Sawyer*. An American critic once neatly declared that the late G. P. R. James hit the bull's-eye of success with his first shot, and that for ever thereafter he went on firing through the same hole. Now this is just what Mark Twain has not done. *Huckleberry Finn* is not an attempt to do *Tom Sawyer* over again. It is a story quite as unlike its predecessor as it is like. Although Huck Finn appeared first in the earlier book, and although Tom Sawyer reappears in the later, the scenes and the characters are otherwise wholly different. Above all, the atmosphere of the story is different. *Tom Sawyer* was a tale of boyish adventure in a village in Missouri, on the Mississippi river, and it was told by the author. *Huckleberry Finn* is autobiographic; it is a tale of boyish adventure along the Mississippi river told as it appeared to Huck Finn. There is not in *Huckleberry Finn* any one scene quite as funny as those in which Tom Sawyer gets his friends to whitewash the fence for him, and then uses the spoils thereby acquired to attain the highest situation of the Sunday school the next morning. Nor is there any description quite as thrilling as that awful moment in the cave when the boy and the girl are lost in the darkness, and when Tom Sawyer suddenly sees a human hand bearing a light, and then finds that the hand is the hand of Indian Joe, his one mortal enemy; we have always thought that the vision of the hand in the cave in *Tom Sawyer* is one of the very finest things in the literature of adventure since Robinson Crusoe first saw a single footprint in the sand of the seashore. But though *Huckleberry Finn* may not quite reach these two highest points of *Tom Sawyer*, we incline to the opinion that the general level of the later story is perhaps higher than that of the earlier. For one thing, the skill with which the character of Huck Finn is maintained is marvellous. We see everything through his eyes—they are his eyes and not a pair of Mark Twain's spectacles. And the comments on what he sees are his comments—the comments of an ignorant, superstitious, sharp, healthy boy, brought up as Huck Finn had been brought up; they are not speeches put into his mouth by the author. One of the most artistic things in the book—and that Mark Twain is a literary artist of a very high order all who have considered his later writings critically cannot but confess—one of the most artistic things in *Huckleberry Finn* is the sober self-restraint with which Mr. Clemens lets Huck Finn set down, without any comment at all, scenes which would have afforded the ordinary writer matter for endless moral and political and sociological disquisition. We refer particularly to the account of the Grangerford–Shepherdson feud, and of the shooting of Boggs by Colonel Sherburn. Here are two incidents of the rough old life of the South-Western States, and of the Mississippi Valley forty or fifty years ago, of the old life which is now rapidly passing away under the influence of advancing civilization and increasing commercial prosperity, but which has not wholly disappeared even yet, although a slow revolution in public sentiment is taking place. The Grangerford–Shepherdson feud is a vendetta as deadly as any Corsican could wish, yet the parties to it were honest, brave, sincere, good Christian people, probably people of deep religious sentiment. Not the less we see them taking their guns to church, and, when occasion serves, joining in what is little better than a general massacre. The killing of Boggs by Colonel Sherburn is told with equal sobriety and truth; and the later scene in which Colonel Sherburn cows and lashes the mob which has set out to lynch him is one of the most vigorous bits of writing Mark Twain has done.

In *Tom Sawyer* we saw Huckleberry Finn from the outside; in the present volume we see him from the inside. He is almost as much a delight to any one who has been a boy as was Tom Sawyer. But only he or she who has been a boy can truly enjoy this record of his adventures, and of his sentiments and of his sayings. Old maids of either sex will wholly fail to understand him or to like him, or to see his significance and his value. Like Tom Sawyer, Huck Finn is a genuine boy; he is neither a girl in boy's clothes like many of the modern heroes of juvenile fiction, nor is he a 'little man,' a full-grown man cut down; he is a boy, just a boy, only a boy. And his ways and modes of thought are boyish. As Mr. F. Anstey understands the English boy, and especially the English boy of the middle classes, so Mark Twain understands the American boy, and especially the American boy of the Mississippi Valley of forty or fifty years ago. The contrast between Tom Sawyer, who is the child of respectable parents, decently brought up, and Huckleberry Finn, who is the child of the town drunkard, not brought up at all, is made distinct by a hundred artistic touches, not the least natural of which is Huck's constant reference to Tom as his ideal of what a boy should be. When Huck escapes from the cabin where his drunken and worthless father had confined him, carefully manufacturing a mass of very circumstantial evidence to prove his own murder by robbers, he cannot help saying, 'I did wish Tom Sawyer was there. I knowed he would take an interest in this kind of business, and throw in the fancy touches. Nobody could spread himself like Tom Sawyer in such a thing as that.' Both boys have their full share of boyish imagination; and Tom Sawyer, being given to books, lets his imagination run on robbers and pirates and genies, with a perfect understanding with himself that, if you want to get fun out of this life, you must never hesitate to make believe very hard; and, with Tom's youth and health, he never finds it hard to make believe and to be a pirate at will, or to summon an attendant spirit, or to rescue a prisoner from the deepest dungeon 'neath the castle moat. But in Huck this imagination has turned to superstition; he is a walking repository of the juvenile folklore of the Mississippi Valley—a folklore partly traditional among the white settlers, but largely influenced by intimate association with the negroes. When Huck was in his room at night all by himself waiting for the signal Tom Sawyer was to give him at midnight, he felt so lonesome he wished he was dead:

> The stars were shining, and the leaves rustled in the woods ever
> so mournful; and I heard an owl, away off, who-whooing about
> somebody that was dead, and a whippoorwill and a dog crying
> about somebody that was going to die; and the wind was trying

to whisper something to me, and I couldn't make out what it was, and so it made the cold shivers run over me. Then away out in the woods I heard that kind of a sound that a ghost makes when it wants to tell about something that's on its mind and can't make itself understood, and so can't rest easy in its grave, and has to go about that way every night grieving. I got so down-hearted and scared I did wish I had some company. Pretty soon a spider went crawling up my shoulder, and I flipped it off and it lit in the candle; and before I could budge it was all shriveled up. I didn't need anybody to tell me that that was an awful bad sign and would fetch me some bad luck, so I was scared and most shook the clothes off of me. I got up and turned around in my tracks three times and crossed my breast every time; and then I tied up a little lock of my hair with a thread to keep witches away. But I hadn't no confidence. You do that when you've lost a horseshoe that you've found, instead of nailing it up over the door, but I hadn't ever heard anybody say it was any way to keep off bad luck when you'd killed a spider.

And, again, later in the story, not at night this time, but in broad daylight, Huck walks along a road:

When I got there it was all still and Sunday-like, and hot and sunshiny—the hands was gone to the fields; and there was them kind of faint dronings of bugs and flies in the air that makes it seem so lonesome and like everybody's dead and gone; and if a breeze fans along and quivers the leaves, it makes you feel mournful, because you feel like it's spirits whispering—spirits that's been dead ever so many years—and you always think they're talking about you. As a general thing it makes a body wish *he* was dead, too, and done with it all.

Now, none of these sentiments are appropriate to Tom Sawyer, who had none of the feeling for nature which Huck Finn had caught during his numberless days and nights in the open air. Nor could Tom Sawyer either have seen or set down this instantaneous photograph of a summer storm:

It would get so dark that it looked all blue-black outside, and lovely; and the rain would thrash along by so thick that the trees off a little ways looked dim and spider-webby; and here would come a blast of wind that would bend the trees down and turn up the pale underside of the leaves; and then a perfect ripper of a gust would follow along and set the branches to tossing their arms as if they was just wild; and next, when it was just about the bluest and blackest—fst! it was as bright as glory, and you'd have a little glimpse of tree-tops a-plunging about away off yonder in the storm, hundreds of yards further than you could see before; dark as sin again in a second, and now you'd hear the thunder let go with an awful crash, and then go rumbling, grumbling, tumbling, down the sky towards the under side of the world, like rolling empty barrels down stairs—where it's long stairs and they bounce a good deal, you know.

The romantic side of Tom Sawyer is shown in most delightfully humorous fashion in the account of his difficult devices to aid in the easy escape of Jim, a runaway negro. Jim is an admirably drawn character. There have been not a few fine and firm portraits of negroes in recent American fiction, of which Mr. Cable's Bras-Coupé in the *Grandissimes* is perhaps the most vigorous, and Mr. Harris's Mingo and Uncle Remus and Blue Dave are the most gentle. Jim is worthy to rank with these; and the essential simplicity and kindliness and generosity of the Southern negro have never been better shown than here by Mark Twain. Nor are Tom Sawyer and Huck Finn and Jim the only fresh and original figures in Mr. Clemens's new book; on the contrary, there is scarcely a character of the many introduced who does not impress the reader at once as true to life—and therefore as new, for life is so varied that a portrait from life is sure to be as good as new. That Mr. Clemens draws from life, and yet lifts his work from the domain of the photograph to the region of art, is evident to any one who will give his work the honest attention which it deserves. Mr. John T. Raymond, the American comedian, who performs the character of Colonel Sellers to perfection, is wont to say that there is scarcely a town in the West and South-West where some man did not claim to be the original of the character. And as Mark Twain made Colonel Sellers, so has he made the chief players in the present drama of boyish adventure; they are taken from life, no doubt, but they are so aptly chosen and so broadly drawn that they are quite as typical as they are actual. They have one great charm, all of them—they are not written about and about; they are not described and dissected and analysed; they appear and play their parts and disappear; and yet they leave a sharp impression of indubitable vitality and individuality. No one, we venture to say, who reads this book will readily forget the Duke and the King, a pair of as pleasant 'confidence operators' as one may meet in a day's journey, who leave the story in the most appropriate fashion, being clothed in tar and feathers and ridden on a rail. Of the more broadly humorous passages—and they abound—we have not left ourselves space to speak; they are to the full as funny as in any of Mark Twain's other books; and, perhaps, in no other book has the humourist shown so much artistic restraint, for there is in *Huckleberry Finn* no mere 'comic copy,' no straining after effect; one might almost say that there is no waste word in it. Nor have we left ourselves room to do more than say a good word for the illustrations, which, although slight and unpretending, are far better than those to be found in most of Mark Twain's books. For one thing, they actually illustrate—and this is a rare quality in illustrations nowadays. They give the reader a distinct idea of the Duke and the King, of Jim and of Colonel Sherburn, of the Shepherdsons and the Grangerfords. They are all by one artist, Mr. E. W. Kemble, hitherto known to us only as the illustrator of the *Thompson Street Poker Club*, an amusing romance of highly-coloured life in New York.

—Brander Matthews, "Huckleberry Finn,"
Saturday Review 59, January 31, 1885,
pp. 153–154

ROBERT BRIDGES (1885)

Mark Twain is a humorist or nothing. He is well aware of the fact himself, for he prefaces the "Adventures of Huckleberry Finn" with a brief notice, warning persons in search of a moral, motive or plot that they are liable to be prosecuted, banished or shot. This is a nice little artifice to scare off the critics—a kind of "trespassers on these grounds will be dealt with according to law."

However, as there is no penalty attached, we organized a search expedition for the humorous qualities of this book with the following hilarious results:

A very refined and delicate piece of narration by Huck Finn, describing his venerable and dilapidated "pap" as afflicted with delirium tremens, rolling over and over, "kicking things every which way," and "saying there are devils ahold of him." This chapter is especially suited to amuse the children on long, rainy afternoons.

An elevating and laughable description of how Huck killed a pig, smeared its blood on an axe and mixed in a little of his own hair, and then ran off, setting up a job on the old man and the community, and leading them to believe him murdered. This little joke can be repeated by any smart boy for the amusement of his fond parents.

A graphic and romantic tale of a Southern family feud, which resulted in an elopement and from six to eight choice corpses.

A polite version of the "Giascutus" story, in which a nude man, striped with the colors of the rainbow, is exhibited as "The King's Camelopard; or, The Royal Nonesuch." This is a chapter for lenten parlor entertainments and church festivals. A side-splitting account of a funeral, enlivened by a "sick melodeum," a "long-legged undertaker," and a rat episode in the cellar.

—Robert Bridges, *Life* 5, February 26, 1885, p. 119

FRANKLIN B. SANBORN "MARK TWAIN AND LORD LYTTON" (1885)

Franklin B. Sanborn is a controversial figure among Thoreau scholars. He was a Harvard student who had made the well-trod pilgrimage to Concord to meet Emerson in 1854. Emerson had convinced Sanborn to open a private school there, where he taught Emerson's children, among others. Sanborn stayed and became the "indefatigable chronicler" and editor of Thoreau, Emerson, Bronson Alcott, and Ellery Channing. Sanborn's reputation is distinctly murky, however. He is remembered for his mean-spiritedness to other scholars and for having deliberately skewed facts about the Thoreau family, particularly Thoreau's parents. He also courted Emerson's daughter Edith, or thought he did. When she proved cool to him, Sanborn penned an angry letter that prompted a furious response from Emerson himself.

Sanborn was an abolitionist and was the New England contact for the antislavery agitator and martyr John Brown. Sanborn knew in advance of Brown's plans for the raid at Harpers Ferry and was later arrested in Concord for withholding this knowledge. He was soon freed. This intimacy with the facts about the violent disputes over slavery in Missouri and "Bleeding Kansas" makes him, for all his sins, an interesting reader and defender of *Huckleberry Finn*.

It would be difficult to make Englishmen believe that the adventures of Huckleberry Finn and Tom Sawyer are as important to the loose-girt muse of fiction as the high-bred sentiments of Lord Glenaveril and his German parson-Pylades,—yet such is the fact; and even as a work of dramatic art, the new book of Mark Twain has more merit than Lord Lytton's. I cannot subscribe to the extreme censure passed upon this volume, which is no coarser than Mark Twain's books usually are, while it has a vein of deep morality beneath its exterior of falsehood and vice, that will redeem it in the eyes of mature persons. It is not adapted to Sunday-school libraries, and should perhaps be left unread by growing boys; but the mature in mind may read it, without distinction of age or sex, and without material harm. It is in effect an argument against negro-slavery, lynching, whisky-drinking, family feuds, promiscuous shooting, and nearly all the vices of Missouri in the olden time, when Benton represented that state in the Senate; and before the people of western Missouri undertook to colonize Kansas in the interest of slavery, and then to force that institution upon the freemen who went there from the North. As a picture of Missouri life and manners it is simply invaluable, and goes farther to explain the political history of the United States from 1854 to 1860 than any other work I have seen,—and I have been reading in that direction of late. Huck Finn's father is the drunken poor white of Missouri, upon whom Atchison and his betters relied to fight slavery into Kansas; and the Grangerfords, Shepherdsons and Col. Sherburn are the gentlemen of courage and wealth who sometimes led on and sometimes thwarted the diabolism of the poor whites. I hardly know where one could find a more lively sketch of the fire-eating, affectionate, proud and courteous southern homicide than that given by poor Huck Finn in his account of the Grangerford family: (Quoted, chap. 17, from "Three big men . . ." through ". . . I tell you.")

This is a curious reproduction of the manners that prevailed in the time of Benton and Clay, and farther back, in the days of Andrew Jackson, who used to drink his morning draught as described, and then hand the tumbler to one of his suite, who would pour in water and drink the heeltap, as Huck Finn and Buck Grangerford do in this sketch. In other parts of the book there is exaggeration, and too much that is merely grotesque and coarse,—but in its best portions it is true to the life and very effective. There are needless complications in the plot, and there is more joking than is best for the story,—but on the whole the plot is not a bad one, and the joking is unavoidable and generally harmless, considering what the author's conception of his characters seems to be. Like all professed humorists, he carries the joke too far, and "runs it into the ground," but in its best estate his fun is irresistible, though it is very little helped by the so-called illustrations of his book. These throw some light on the housing, dress and external circumstances of the personages, but seldom reproduce, as the author does, their internal struggles and entanglements. There is hardly anything so true to human nature in the whole realm of casuistry as the young hero's meditations with himself over his duty regarding the runaway slave, Jim, when it first dawns upon the boy that he is an accomplice in the escape from slavery. (Quoted, chap. 16, from "I begun to . . ." through ". . . what she done."; from "Here was this . . ." through ". . . me no harm."; from "My conscience got . . . through ". . . troubles was gone.")

So he deceives the fugitive and sets out for the shore in the canoe, while his grateful companion says: "Jim won't ever forgit you, Huck; you's de bes' fren' Jim's ever had; en you's de *only* fren' ole Jim's got now." Huck then goes on: "I was paddling off, all in a sweat, to tell on him; but when he says this, it seemed to kind of take the tuck all out of me. I went along slow then, and I wasn't right down certain whether I was glad I started or whether I wasn't. When I was 50 yards off Jim says: 'Dah you goes, de ole true Huck; de only white genl-man dat ever kep' his promise to ole Jim.' Well, I just felt sick. But I says, I *got* to do it—I can't get *out* of it." However, he deceives two white men who are looking for runaways, gets $40 in gold out of them in compassion for his assumed father's sickness with the small-pox, and goes back to Jim without betraying him, "feeling bad and low, because I knowed very well I had done wrong." "Then I thought a minute, and says to myself, hold on—s'pose you'd a done right and give Jim up; would you felt better than what you do now? No, says I, I'd feel bad—I'd feel just the same way I do now. Well, then, says I, what's the use you learning to do right, when it's troublesome to do right, and ain't no trouble to do wrong, and the wages is just the same? I was stuck. I couldn't answer that. So I reckoned I wouldn't bother no more about it, but after this always do whichever come handiest at the time."

Good people must make no mistake about the teachings of this book; for although the author declares that "persons attempting to find a moral in it will be banished," and though the Concord library committee have banished the book itself as immoral, I can see nothing worse in it than in the story of Samson, which contains a great deal of deliberate lying, or the story of Noah, which has a good deal about drinking, rafting, and high water. It is indeed a legend of prehistoric times, and for aught I know, may be a sun-myth or a freshet-myth, or the story of a geological period. As a work of art it is an improvement on *Tom Sawyer* and has the air of reality which *The Prince and the Pauper* lacks. Lord Lytton should read it before finishing *Glenaveril*.

—Franklin B. Sanborn, "Mark Twain and
Lord Lytton," *Springfield Republican*,
April 27, 1885, pp. 2–3

THOMAS SERGEANT PERRY "OPEN LETTERS" (1885)

Mark Twain's *Tom Sawyer* is an interesting record of boyish adventure; but, amusing as it is, it may yet be fair to ask whether its most marked fault is not too strong adherence to conventional literary models? A glance at the book certainly does not confirm this opinion, but those who recall the precocious affection of Tom Sawyer, at the age when he is losing his first teeth, for a little girl whom he has seen once or twice, will confess that the modern novel exercises a very great influence. What is best in the book, what one remembers, is the light we get into the boy's heart. The romantic devotion to the little girl, the terrible adventures with murderers and in huge caves, have the air of concessions to jaded readers. But when Tom gives the cat Pain-Killer, is restless in church, and is recklessly and eternally deceiving his aunt, we are on firm ground—the author is doing sincere work.

This later book, *Huckleberry Finn*, has the great advantage of being written in autobiographical form. This secures a unity in the narration that is most valuable; every scene is given, not described; and the result is a vivid picture of Western life forty or fifty years ago. While *Tom Sawyer* is scarcely more than an apparently fortuitous collection of incidents, and its thread is one that has to do with murders, this story has a more intelligible plot. Huckleberry, its immortal hero, runs away from his worthless father, and floats down the Mississippi on a raft, in company with Jim, a runaway negro. This plot gives great opportunity for varying incidents. The travelers spend some time on an island; they outwit every one they meet; they acquire full knowledge of the hideous fringe of civilization that then adorned that valley; and the book is a most valuable record of an important part of our motley American civilization.

What makes it valuable is the evident truthfulness of the narrative, and where this is lacking and its place is taken by ingenious invention, the book suffers. What is inimitable, however, is the reflection of the whole varied series of adventures in the mind of the young scapegrace of a hero. His undying fertility of invention, his courage, his manliness in every trial, are an incarnation of the better side of the ruffianism that is one result of the independence of Americans, just as hypocrisy is one result of the English respect for civilization. The total absence of morbidness in the book—for the *mal du siècle* has not yet reached Arkansas—gives it a genuine charm; and it is interesting to notice the art with which this is brought out. The best instance is perhaps to be found in the account of the feud between the Shepherdsons and the Grangerfords, which is described only as it would appear to a semi-civilized boy of fourteen, without the slightest condemnation or surprise,—either of which would be bad art,—and yet nothing more vivid can be imagined. That is the way that a story is best told, by telling it, and letting it go to the reader unaccompanied by sign-posts or directions how he shall understand it and profit by it. Life teaches its lessons by implication, not by didactic preaching; and literature is at its best when it is an imitation of life and not an excuse for instruction.

As to the humor of Mark Twain, it is scarcely necessary to speak. It lends vividness to every page. The little touch in "Tom Sawyer," page 105, where, after the murder of which Tom was an eye-witness, it seemed "that his school-mates would never get done holding inquests on dead cats and thus keeping the trouble present to his mind," and that in the account of the spidery six-armed girl of Emmeline's picture in *Huckleberry Finn*, are in the author's happiest vein. Another admirable instance is to be seen in Huckleberry Finn's mixed feelings about rescuing Jim, the negro, from slavery. His perverted views regarding the unholiness of his actions are most instructive and amusing. It is possible to feel, however, that the fun in the long account of Tom Sawyer's artificial imitation of escapes from prison is somewhat forced; everywhere simplicity is a good rule, and while the account of the Southern *vendetta* is a masterpiece, the caricature of books of adventure leaves us cold. In one we have a bit of life; in the other Mark Twain is demolishing something that has no place in the book. Yet the story is capital reading, and the reason of its great superiority to "Tom Sawyer" is that is it, for the most part, a consistent whole. If Mark Twain would follow his hero through manhood, he would condense a side of American life that, in a few years, will have to be delved out of newspapers, government reports, county histories, and misleading traditions by unsympathetic sociologists.

—Thomas Sergeant Perry, "Open Letters,"
Century Magazine, May 30, 1885, pp. 171–172

JOEL CHANDLER HARRIS
"HUCKLEBERRY FINN AND HIS CRITICS" (1885)

A very deplorable fact is that the great body of literary criticism is mainly perfunctory. This is not due to a lack of ability or to a lack of knowledge. It is due to the fact that most of it is from the pens of newspaper writers who have no time to elaborate their ideas. They are in a hurry, and what they write is hurried. Under these circumstances it is not unnatural that they should take their cues from inadequate sources and give to the public opinions that are either conventional or that have no reasonable basis.

All this is the outcome of the conditions and circumstances of American life. There is no demand for sound criticism any more than there is a demand for great poetry. We have a leisure class, but its tastes run toward horses, yachting and athletic sports, in imitation of the English young men who occasionally honor these shores with their presence. The imitation, after all, is a limping one. The young Englishman of leisure is not only fond of outdoor sports, but of books. He has culture and taste, and patronizes literature with as much enthusiasm as he does physical amusements. If our leisure class is to imitate the English, it would be better if the imitation extended somewhat in the direction of culture.

The American leisure class—the class that might be expected to patronize good literature and to create a demand for sound, conservative criticism—is not only fond of horses, but is decidedly horsey. It is coarse and uncultivated. It has no taste in either literature or art. It reads few books and buys its pictures in Europe by the yard.

We are led to these remarks by the wholly inadequate verdict that has recently been given in some of the most prominent newspapers as to the merits of Mark Twain's new book, *The Adventures of Huckleberry Finn*. The critics seem to have gotten their cue in this instance from the action of the Concord library, the directors of which refused the book a place on their shelves. This action, as was afterwards explained, was based on the fact that the book was a work of fiction, and not because of the humorous characteristics that are popularly supposed to attach to the writings of Mr. Clemens. But the critics had got their cue before the explanation was made, and they straightway proceeded to inform the reading public that the book was gratuitously coarse, its humor unneccessarily broad, and its purpose crude and inartistic.

Now, nothing could be more misleading than such a criticism as this. It is difficult to believe that the critics who have condemned the book as coarse, vulgar and inartistic can have read it. Taken in connection with *The Prince and the Pauper*, it marks a clear and distinct advance in Mr. Clemens's literary methods. It presents an almost artistically perfect picture of the life and character in the southwest, and it will be equally valuable to the historian and to the student of sociology. Its humor, which is genuine and never-failing, is relieved by little pathetic touches here and there that vouch for its literary value.

It is the story of a half illiterate, high-spirited boy whose adventures are related by himself. The art with which this conception is dealt with is perfect in all its details. The boy's point of view is never for a moment lost sight of, and the moral of the whole is that this half illiterate boy can be made to present, with perfect consistency, not only the characters of the people whom he meets, but an accurate picture of their social life. From the artistic point of view, there is not a coarse nor vulgar suggestion from the beginning to the end of the book. Whatever is coarse and crude is in the life that is pictured, and the picture is perfect. It may be said that the humor is sometimes excessive, but it is genuine humor—and the moral of the book, though it is not scrawled across every page, teaches the necessity of manliness and self-sacrifice.

> —Joel Chandler Harris, "Huckleberry Finn
> and His Critics," *Atlanta Constitution*,
> May 26, 1885, p. 4

JOEL CHANDLER HARRIS "SYMPOSIUM ON THE HISTORICAL NOVEL" (1885)

But you were speaking of the historical novel. Well, it seems to me that every successful novel is, in a sense, historical. It must deal with a certain period of time and must give us veracious reports of the character and habits of people who lived in that period. Looking at the matter from this side, it may be said that Mr. Howells's "Silas Lapham" is as historical as "Janice Meredith." War is not the only material that goes to the making of history. In this sense, "The Scarlet Letter" is our greatest historical novel, and next to it we must place "Huckleberry Finn," though one is a romance and the other a report of character and manners. To-day is as much a part of history as yesterday, and the writer who embodies its atmosphere and action in a story of character will produce a historical novel.

> —Joel Chandler Harris, "Symposium on the
> Historical Novel," *Atlanta Journal,* n.d., reprinted
> in *Life and Letters of Joel Chandler Harris,*
> Julia Collier Harris, Boston: Houghton Mifflin,
> 1918, p. 566

MARK TWAIN (1885)

DEAR UNCLE REMUS:—

I thank you cordially for the good word about Huck, that abused child of mine who has had so much unfair mud flung at him. Somehow I can't help believing in him, and it's a great refreshment to my faith to have a man back me up who has been where such boys live, and knows what he is talking about.

> Sincerely yours
> S. L. CLEMENS

> —Mark Twain, letter to Joel Chandler Harris,
> 1885, from *Life and Letters of Joel Chandler
> Harris*, Julia Collier Harris, Boston:
> Houghton Mifflin, 1918, p. 566

SIR WALTER BESANT "MY FAVORITE NOVELIST AND HIS BEST BOOK" (1898)

I have been invited to write upon my "Favorite Novel." Alas, I have so many favorite novels! How can I incur the jealousy of all the others by selecting one as the favorite? Novels are live things; they love admiration; they resent neglect; they hate the preference of others. Like Charles Lamb, who loved every book because it was a book—except the Law List—I love every novel because it is a novel—except those which are not novels, but only shams. I love the novel of adventure; I find the "Three Musketeers" as delightful now as when I sat in a corner, breathless, panting, and followed, all a lifelong holiday, the fortunes of the Immortal Three who were Four. And I love the novel which portrays human life and society; whether it is *Tom Jones*, or *Humphrey Clinker*, or *Nicholas Nickleby*. And I love Charlotte Yonge's gentle girls; and Marryat's anything but gentle sailor; and Lever's swaggering soldier; and Jane Austen, and Maria Edgeworth, and Wilkie Collins, and Charles Reade, and Edgar Allan Poe, and Hawthorne, and Oliver Wendell Holmes—not to speak of living men and women by the score whose works I read with joy.

Of a novel I ask but one thing. "Seize me," I say—"seize me and hold me with a grip of steel. Make me deaf and blind to all the world so long as I read in thine enchanted pages. Carry me whither thou wilt. Play on me; do with me what thou wilt, at thine own sweet will. Make me shriek with pain; fill my eyes with tears and my heart with sorrow; let me laugh aloud, let me bubble over with the joy of silent mirth; let me forget that the earth is full of oppression and wickedness. Only seize me and hold me tight—immovable, rapt, hypnotized; deaf and blind to all the world."

I confess that unless this condition is fulfilled I cannot read a novel. Many novels I try to read, only to lay them down. A few such I have had to read on occasions—they were rare—when an editor has asked me to review a novel. To me it is more painful than words can tell to read such a book; it is more irksome than any convict's task to write a review of such a book. The only excuse that I will admit from a reviewer who dishonestly pronounces judgment on a book which he has not read is that the novel was one of the kind which cannot be read. If he pleads that excuse, I pity him and pass on. For this reason, also, I am in no hurry to take up any new novel. I like to have it "tasted" for me first. The tasting enables me to escape the attempt to read a great many new novels. As a rule I buy only those of which other people have already spoken. As a wise man and a philosopher, I take my recommendations not from the critics, but from the other people. Then, if a story possesses the gift of grip, I am ready to forgive all other sins. A novel cannot be really bad, though it may have many faults, if it seizes the reader and holds him spellbound till the last page.

These remarks prepare the way for a selection which is perhaps unexpected. I do not respond to the invitation by taking one of the acknowledged masterpieces; nor shall I worry myself to find something fresh to say about a book which has already been reviewed over and over again. Cervantes, Fielding, Dickens, Thackeray—all these I leave to the professors of literature, and to the critic of the big and serious "appreciation"—to him who estimates influence, finds out blemishes, and explores the sources. I am only a critic in so far as I really do know the points of a good novelist and something about the art of construction of a novel; and I prefer to apply this knowledge on the present occasion to a work of perhaps humbler pretensions, albeit a work of genius, and work which will live and will belong to the literature of the language. I speak of one of my favorites; not my single favorite. I love the book for a variety of excellent reasons, but not to the exclusion of other books. It is expected of a well regulated mind that it cannot love more than one woman at a time. This galling restriction applies not to the lover of novels, which, with poetry, are the fair women of literature. One can love them all—yes, all. So catholic is love in literature, so wide is his embrace, so universal; so free from jealousy are his mistresses.

The book which I have selected is Mark Twain's "Huckleberry Finn." At the outset I observe, and intend to respect, a warning after the title page to the effect that any person who may try to find a motive in the narrative will be prosecuted; that any person who may try to find a moral in it will be banished, and that persons attempting to find a plot will be shot.

Let us repeat this warning. Let us not try to find in "Huckleberry Finn" either motive, moral, or plot.

I lay it down as one of the distinctive characteristics of a good story that it pleases—or rather, seizes—every period of life; that the child, and his elder brother, and his father, and his grandfather, may read it with like enjoyment—not equal enjoyment, because as a man gets older and understands more and more what the world of men and women means, he reads between the lines and sees things which the child cannot see and cannot understand. Very likely, if the painting is true to nature, he sees things which the artist himself could not see or understand. The note of genius is that it suggests so much more than it meant to suggest, and goes so much deeper than the poet himself intended. To discover and to read the superadded letterpress, the invisible part of the printed page, is one of the compensations of age.

The first quality that I claim for this book, then, is that it does appeal to all ages and every age. The boy of twelve reads it with delight beyond his power of words to express; the young man reads it; the old man reads it. The book is a joy to all alike. For my own part, I have read it over and over again, yet always with delight and always finding something new in its pages.

There is no motive in the book; there is no moral; there is no plot. The book is like a panorama in which the characters pass across the stage and do not return. They follow each other with the unexpectedness belonging to a voyage down a river. All happens by chance; the finger of providence—which means the finger of Mark Twain—is nowhere visible. There is no motive; there is no moral; there is no plot. This directing, intervening, meddlesome finger you will find very often in the novel which does not permit itself to be read; it sticks out in the carpenter's novel. You see the thumb—it wants washing—in the novel made by rule. It is nowhere visible in *Huckleberry Finn*.

The book commends itself, to begin with, by the humorous treatment of perfectly serious situations. It is unconsciously humorous, it is humorous because the narrator sees no humor in anything. In some places, when an English boy would have rolled on the floor with laughing, the American boy relates the scene without a smile. Indeed, from beginning to end, there is hardly a smile. Yet, while all the situations lie open for sentiment, for moralizing, or for laughing, the actors are perfectly serious—and perfectly comic.

The reason of the serious nature of the performance is that the narrator is a boy whose experiences of life have not, so far, inclined him to look at things from a humorous point of view. He is the son of a drunken scoundrel, the disgrace and terror of the town.

He said he'd cowhide me till I was black and blue if I didn't raise some money for him. I borrowed three dollars from Judge Thatcher, and pap took it and got drunk and went a-blowing around and cussing and whooping and carrying on; and he kept it up all over town, with a tin pan, till 'most midnight. Then they jailed him; next day they had him before court and jailed him again for a week.

Even the boys in the town spoke of him as 'a man who used to lay drunk with the hogs in the tan yard.' It is with the gravest face that the boy speaks of his father; relates how he took the pledge in presence of the judge—who 'said it was the holiest time on record'—and broke it the next day; and how he had delirium tremens and tried to murder his son. With such a father; with no education; with no religion; living about in the woods; without respect of persons; untruthful whenever it seemed easier to conceal the truth; yielding when necessary; watchful of opportunities; not immoral, but unmoral—the boy starts off to tell his tale of adventure. Writers of fiction, of whom there are now so many, will understand the difficulty of getting inside the brain of that boy, seeing things as he saw them, writing as he would have written, and acting as he would have acted; and presenting to the world a true, faithful, and living *effigies* of that boy. The feat has been accomplished: there is no character in fiction more fully, more faithfully presented than the character of *Huckleberry Finn*. What that character finally appears, when the book is finished, when the glamour dies away, when the figure stands out plainly before us, I will endeavor to portray after touching on some of the points of *Huckleberry*'s pilgrimage.

The earlier chapters, with *Tom Sawyer* and the other boys, are hardly worthy to be taken as an introduction to the book. But they are soon got over. The adventures really begin with the boy's life in the cabin where his father has taken him. The man was always drunk, always abusing and threatening the boy, always falling about in his half drunk moments, and cursing.

Down he went in the dirt and rolled there and held his toes; and the cussing he done there laid over anything he had ever done previous. He said so, his own self, afterwards.

Observe the boy's standard as to cursing considered as fine art.

He escapes; he finds a canoe drifting down the river; he gets on board, takes certain steps which will make his father believe that he has been murdered, and paddles down the river to an island. The river is the mighty Mississippi; and now we are on or beside its waters and hear the swirl and the swish as the current rolls past the reeds and sedges of the island and washes the planks of the craft. We see the huge lumber rafts making their slow way with the stream; we hear, with the boy, the voice of the man on board—'Stern oars! Heave her head to stabboard!'

On his desert island the boy, perfectly happy, caught fish and broiled them; found wild strawberries—the *fraises à quatre saisons* which flourish all over the world; and went about exploring his kingdom. It was a glorious time, only it was difficult to get through the day. Presently he found another resident on the island, the runaway 'nigger' *Jim*, whom he knew very well. The white boy was so wild, so uncivilized, that even in a slave holding State he had imbibed no proper feeling as regards runaway slaves. He chummed with *Jim* immediately. The river rises; the island is under water; they live in a cave on a rock which is above the flood; they paddle about in the canoe, either on the river or among the woods; they pick up things that come floating down—among other things part of a lumber raft.

It was lucky they found the raft, because smoke had been seen on the island, and suspicion had arisen about the runaway 'nigger.' They decided to run away from their island and to make for the first point where a fugitive slave would be free. They loaded the raft with all they had; they carried their canoe on board; and in the dead of night they slipped off the island and so down stream. Where they were going to, whither the river would carry them, they never inquired. The book, you see, has no plot, no motive, no moral.

They ran about seven or eight hours every night, the current making four miles an hour. They fished as they slid down the stream. Sometimes they took a swim to keep off sleepiness.

It was a kind of solemn, drifting down the big still river, laying on our backs looking up at the stars, and we didn't feel like talking loud and it wasn't often that we laughed, only a little of a low chuckle.

Every night about ten o'clock, the boy went ashore to some village and bought ten or fifteen cents' worth of meal or bacon.

> Sometimes I lifted a chicken that wasn't roosting comfortable. Pap always said, 'Take a chicken when you get a chance, because if you don't want him yourself you can easy find somebody that does, and a good deed ain't never forgot.' I never see pap when he didn't want the chicken himself, but that is what he used to say, any way.

In the same way, the boy went into the fields and borrowed a watermelon or a 'mush melon' or a 'punkin' or some new corn. The book, you observe, has no moral.

They then take on board the immortal pair of rogues and vagabonds—the *King* and the *Duke*. Writes the young philosopher:

> It didn't take me long to make up my mind that these liars wasn't no kings and dukes at all, but just low down humbugs and frauds. But I never said nothing, never let on; kept it to myself. It's the best way; then you don't have no quarrels and don't get into no trouble.

The chapters with the *King* and the *Duke* are amazing for the sheer impudence of the two rogues and the remarks of the boy. He makes no remonstrance, he affects no indignation; he falls in with every pretense on which his assistance is required, and he watches all the time—watches for the chance to upset their little plans. And such plans! One sells quack medicines; plays and recites; lectures on mesmerism and phrenology; teaches singing and geography at schools for a change; does anything that comes handy. The other preaches temperance, also religion; gets up camp meetings; is a missionary; lays on hands for curing paralysis and the like. Together they agree to get up scenes from Shakspere [sic] especially the balcony scene in *Romeo and Juliet*; to discover water and treasure by means of the divining rod; to dissipate witch spells; to get subscriptions and advertisements for a bogus paper; to continue the preaching, and so on. The great *coup* was the personation of a man in England, brother of a man just deceased. This, in fact, very nearly came off; it would have come off, with a bag of six thousand dollars, but for the boy, who defeats their villainies: How he does this, how the older of the two rogues sells *Jim* for a runaway, how the two rascals, the *King* and the *Duke*, have to ride on a rail, how *Jim* is recovered, is well known by those who have read the book, and can be easily learned by those who have not. It is a book which, to repeat, has no moral. One does not expect the punishment of villainy; yet it is pleasant to catch this last glimpse of the *King* and the *Duke* thus honored by their grateful fellow citizens. This American custom of riding a rogue on a rail is not, as is generally supposed, an invention or a growth of the American people, though they are eminently inventive. It crossed the Atlantic from the old country, where, under the name of 'Riding the Stang'—a rail for the men, a basket for the women—it flourished in certain parts almost down to the present time.

Also, though the book has no moral, one is pleased to find the 'nigger' receiving his freedom at the end. And, although it has no plot, one is delighted to find that *Huckleberry* remains the same at the end as he began at the beginning. That blessed boy, who has told as many lies as there are pages in the book, is left impenitent.

> I reckon I got to light out for the Territory ahead of the rest, because
> Aunt Sally she's going to adopt me and civilize me, and I can't stand
> it. I been there before.

These are his parting words.

It was fifty years ago. Do you know what happened afterwards? I will
tell you. *Huckleberry*, of course, remained not civilized; he went to live with
Jim on Jackson Island. They had a raft and a canoe; they fished and shot
and trapped; they built a log hut. *Tom Sawyer* used to visit them till he was
taken away and sent to college and became a lawyer. He is now, as everybody
knows, the governor of his State, and may possibly become President.
Presently *Jim* died. Then *Huckleberry* was left alone. He still lives on Jackson
Island in his log hut. He is now an old man; his beard is as white as that of
the veteran fraud, the *King*; he is full of wisdom and wise thoughts; long and
lonely nights beneath the stars, watching the endless roll of the Mississippi,
have made him wise. Of the world he still knows nothing; of his ancient fibs
and tricks he is impenitent.

There is another side of the book. It belongs to the fifties, the old time
before the civil war, when the 'institution' was flourishing against all the
efforts of the Abolitionists. Without intending it—the book has no motive—
the boy restores for us that life in the Southern States. It is now so far off that
even those who are old enough to remember it think of it as a kind of dream.
Consider how far off it is. There is the elderly maiden lady, full of religion,
who tries to teach the boy the way to heaven. She herself is living, she says, so
as to go there. She has one old 'nigger' who has been with her all her life—a
faithful servant, an affectionate creature. This pious woman deliberately
proposes to sell the man—to *sell* him—for the sum of eight hundred dollars,
or one hundred and sixty pounds sterling. Only forty years ago! Yet how
far off! How far off! Is there, anywhere in the Southern States of today, any
living lady who could in cold blood sell an old servant into slavery among
strangers? Then there is the feud between the families of the *Grangerfords* and
the *Shepherdsons*. They have a feud—do families in the South have feuds and
go shooting each other now? It seems so far off; so long ago. The *Shepherdsons*
and the *Grangerfords* alike are all filled out with family pride; no descendant
of all the kingly houses of Europe could be prouder of family than these
obscure planters. They have no education; they shoot at each other whenever
they meet; they murder even the boys of either family. It is only a glimpse we
catch of them as we float down the Mississippi, but it belongs to a time so
long ago—so long ago.

There is another glimpse—of a riverside town. It consists of one street, of stores with awnings in front; loafers in wide straw hats and neither coat nor waistcoat lie and sit about. They do nothing; they borrow 'chaws' of tobacco of each other; the street is quite quiet and empty. Presently some wagons come in from the country, and the town is animated. It is a kind of market day. Then a drunken man rides amuck though the town, roaring and threatening. He threatens one prominent citizen so long that, after a while, the man says he has lost patience, and shoots the drunkened dead. It is all so long ago, you see. Or we are at a camp meeting—perhaps those meetings go on still, somewhere. There are a thousand people present. The meeting is provided with sheds for preaching and sheds for selling watermelons and lemonade. The young men go barefooted; the girls have sun-bonnets and linsey woolsey frocks. Some of them listen to the preaching; some sit out and carry on flirtations of the more elementary. People are invited to the mourners' bench; they crowd in, on the invitation, moved by the contagious emotion, weeping, crying, throwing themselves down in the straw. Among them, weeping more bitterly than the rest, is the wicked old *King*; he has got conviction of sin; he is broken down; he is on the mourners' bench. He is so contrite that you may hear his groans above all the rest. He begs permission to speak to the people; he confesses that he has been a pirate all his life; he is now repentant; he will be a pirate no more; he will go among his old friends and convert them. It will be difficult without money, but he will try—he will try. So they take up a collection for him, and he goes back to the raft, after kissing all the girls, with eighty seven dollars and twenty five cents in his purse. He had also found a three gallon keg of whisky, too, under a wagon. The good old man said, 'Take it all around, it laid over any day he'd ever put in, in the missionary line. Heathens,' he said, 'don't amount to shucks, alongside of pirates, to work a camp meeting with.' There are still, perhaps, country villages and places in the Central States, of which we of England know so little, where the people are simple and unsuspicious, and enjoy a red hot religion; but the world has moved, even for them. There are surely no country places left where such a ridiculous old fraud as the *King* could be believed. It may be objected that the characters are extravagant. Not so. They are all exactly and literally true; they are quite possible in a country so remote and so primitive. Every figure in the book is a type; *Huckleberry* has exaggerated none. We see the life—the dull and vacuous life—of a small township upon the Mississippi forty years ago; so far as I know, it is the only place where we can find that phase of life portrayed.

If the scenes and characters of the book are all life-like and true to nature, still more life-like is the figure of the boy as he stands out, at the end, when we close the volume, self revealed.

He is, to begin with, shrewd. It is a word which may have a good or a bad meaning; in the former sense, I think that shrewdness is a more common characteristic of the American than of the Englishman. I mean that he is more ready to question, to doubt, to examine, to understand. He is far more ready to exercise freedom of thought; far less ready to accept authority. His individuality is more intense; he is one against the world; he is more readily on the defensive. *Huckleberry*, therefore, however it may be with his countrymen at large, is shrewd. He questions everything. For instance, he is told to pray for everything. He tries it; he prays for fish hooks. None come; he worries over the matter a while, and then he concludes to let it go. If he has no religion, however, he has plenty of superstition; he believes all the wonderful things the 'nigger' *Jim* tells him: the ghosts and the signs of bad luck and good luck.

He has an immense natural love for the woods and forests; for the open air; for the great river laden with the rafts forever going down the stream; for the night as much as the day; for the dawn as much as the splendour of the noonday. . . .

If he loves the still and solemn night and the woods, he loves also the creatures in the woods—squirrels, turtles, snakes. He is a boy who belongs to the river, which he will never desert. His lies and his thievings and his acquiescence in frauds—to be sure, he was forced—do not affect his nature; he passes through these things and will shake them off and forget them. All his life he will live in the present, which is a part of the nomadic spirit. He will look on without indignation at the things men do around him; but his home will be on Jackson's Island in a log hut, alone, and far from the haunts of men. And he will never grow weary of watching the lumber rafts go by; or of sitting beside the mighty flood; or of watching the day break, and the sun set; or of lying in the shade so long as he can look at the snakes and the turtles or listen while a couple of squirrels 'set on a limb and jabber at him friendly.' Because, you see, there is no moral in this book; and no motive; and no plot.

—Sir Walter Besant, "My Favorite Novelist
and His Best Book," *Munsey's Magazine,*
February 18, 1898, pp. 659–664

H.L. Mencken "Popularity Index" (1910)

How long does it take a new idea to gain lodgment in the professorial mind? The irreverent ignoramus may be tempted to answer six days and six nights, or just as long as it took to manufacture and people the world; but any such answer would be a gross and obvious underestimate. Some day a painstaking statistician, putting aside his beloved death rates and export tables, will take the trouble to give us more satisfactory figures. He will determine, for example, with mathematical accuracy, just how many years, months, weeks and days elapsed between the publication of *The Origin of Species* and the abandonment of Genesis by the professor of "natural history" in, say, Amherst College. He will find out for us, again, exactly how long was required to make the first scholastic convert to Sidney Lanier's sound but revolutionary theory of English verse. And finally, he will measure for us, with a dependable tape, the hiatus between the appearance of *Huckleberry Finn* and its acceptance by any reputable professor of literature, tutor, lecturer or high school pundit as a work of art of the first rank.

This last hiatus, I suspect, was of exactly twenty-five years' length, to a day. And my suspicion is grounded upon three facts, to wit:

(A) On March 15, 1885, the first American edition of *Huckleberry Finn* was published in New York.

(B) On March 15, 1910, or just a quarter of a century later, the Adams Express Company dropped on my doorstep a copy of *Essays on Modern Novelists*, by William Lyon Phelps, a Harvard master of arts, a Yale doctor of philosophy, a former instructor in English at Harvard, and now the Lampson professor of English literature at Yale.

(C) I found in that book the first honest and hearty praise of *Huckleberry Finn*, by a college professor in good standing, that these eyes had ever encountered, and the first faint, trembling admission, by the same sort of professor, that Mark Twain was a greater artist than Oliver Wendell Holmes.

After all, the sun *do* move! After all, there is yet hope! If it is possible, in the year 1910, for a college professor to admit that Clemens was a greater artist than Holmes, without thereby imperiling his salary and the honor of his craft, then it may be possible by 1950 for him to admit that Clemens was a greater artist than Irving, than Lowell, than Fenimore Cooper, than all and sundry of the unbearable bores whose "works" are rammed into the heads of schoolboys by hunkerous pedagogues, and avoided as pestilences by everyone else.

Fortunately for Dr. Clemens, he didn't have to wait for the college professors. Long before the first of them began to harbor thoughts of treachery to the *Tales of a Traveler* and *The Last of the Mohicans*, a large number of less orthodox persons began to sense the colossal merits of *Huckleberry Finn*. One of the first of them, unless memory errs, was the late Sir Walter Besant, himself a writer of experience and very much alive to the difficulties of the trade. Back in the early '90's his remarkable analysis of the story was printed, and soon afterwards a number of distinguished English critics adopted his view of it. Then came the gradual disappearance of Mark Twain, the glorified buffoon, and the rise of Samuel Langhorne Clemens, the master of letters. He lived just long enough to see the metamorphosis of his fame accomplished. Twenty-five years ago the world roared over his extravagances and swore that they were fully as funny as the quips of Tom Hood and Petroleum V. Nasby, Bill Nye and Josiah Allen's Wife. Fifteen years ago there arose folk who were rash enough to compare him, with some hesitation, to Holmes and Sam. Foote, Farquhar and Wycherley. And finally, just before he died, it began to be bruited about that a literary artist of world rank was among us, the greatest that the United States had yet produced—a greater than all our Hawthornes and Lowellses—a peer to Swift, Fielding, and Defoe—perhaps even a peer to Cervantes, Molière and Rabelais.

There is no space here to discuss the grounds for that last theory. You will find them in parts of *A Connecticut Yankee*, in parts of *A Tramp Abroad* and other books, in every line of *Huckleberry Finn*. The pictures of the mighty Mississippi, as the immortal Huck presents them, do not belong to buffoonery or to pretty writing, but to universal and almost flawless art. Where, in all fiction, will you find another boy as real as Huck himself? In sober truth, his equals, young or old, are distressingly few in the world. Rabelais created two, Fielding one, Thackeray three or four and Shakespeare a roomful; but you will find none of them in the pages of Hawthorne or Poe or Cooper or Holmes. In Kipling's phrase, Huck stands upon his feet. Not a freckle is missing, not a scar, not a trick of boyish fancy, not a habit of boyish mind. He is, in brief, Everyboy—the archetype of all other boys—the most delightful boy that ever stole a ginger cake or tortured a cat.

—H.L. Mencken, "Popularity Index,"
Smart Set 31, June 1910, pp. 153–154

CARL VAN DOREN (1921)

Tom Sawyer cannot be discussed except in connection with its glorious sequel *The Adventures of Huckleberry Finn* (1885). "By and by," Mark Twain had written to Howells when he announced the completion of *Tom Sawyer*, "I shall take a boy of twelve and run him through life (in the first person)"; and he had begun the new book almost at once; but with characteristic uncertainty of taste he had lost interest in it and turned to struggle over a preposterous detective comedy which he wanted to name *Balaam's Ass*. Again in 1880 and finally in 1883 he came back to his masterpiece, published two years later. In spite of this hesitation and procrastination *Huckleberry Finn* has remarkable unity. To tell a story in the first person was second nature to Mark Twain. His travel books had so been told, no matter what non-autobiographical episodes he might elect to bring in. But he was more than a humorous liar; he was an instinctive actor; Sir Henry Irving regretted that Mark Twain had never gone upon the stage. Once he had decided to tell the story through Huck Finn's mouth he could proceed at his most effortless pace. And his sense of identity with the boy restricted him to a realistic substance as no principles of art, in Mark Twain's case, could have done. With the first sentence he fell into an idiom and a rhythm flawlessly adapted to the naïve, nasal, drawling little vagabond. "You don't know me without you have read a book by the name of *The Adventures of Tom Sawyer*; but that ain't no matter. That book was made by Mr. Mark Twain, and he told the truth, mainly. There was things which he stretched, but mainly he told the truth." It has been remarked that Huck appears rather more conscious of the charms of external nature than his Hannibal prototype, Tom Blankenship, doubtless was; and of course, strictly speaking, he rises above lifelikeness altogether by his gift for telling a long yarn which has artistic economy and satiric point. But something like this may be said of all heroes presented in the first person. Mark Twain, though for the time being he had relapsed to the shiftless lingo of his boyhood companion, was after all acting Huck for the sake of interpreting him; and interpretation enlarges the thing interpreted. Tom Sawyer acquires a new solidity by being shown here through the eyes of another boy, who, far from laughing at Tom's fanciful ways of doing plain tasks, admires them as the symptoms of a superior intelligence. After this fashion all the material of the narrative comes through Huck's perceptions. Mouthpiece for others, Huck is also mouthpiece for himself so competently that the whole of his tough, ignorant, generous, loyal, pyrotechnically mendacious nature lies revealed.

And yet virtues still larger than the structural unity thus imparted make *Huckleberry Finn* Mark Twain's masterpiece. In richness of life *Tom Sawyer* cannot compare with it. The earlier of the two books keeps close home in one sleepy, dusty village, illuminated only, at inconvenient moments, by Tom Sawyer's whimsies. But in *Huckleberry Finn* the plot, like Mark Twain's imagination, goes voyaging. Five short chapters and Huck leaves his native village for the ampler world of the picaresque. An interval of captivity with his father—that unpleasant admonitory picture of what Huck may some day become if he outgrows his engaging youthful fineness—and then the boy slips out upon the river which is the home of his soul. There he realizes every dream he has ever had. He has a raft of his own. He has a friend, the negro Jim, with the strength of a man, the companionableness of a boy, and the fidelity of a dog. He can have food for the fun of taking it out of the water or stealing it from along the shore. He sleeps and wakes when he pleases. The weather of the lower Mississippi in summer bites no one. At the same time, this life is not too safe. Jim may be caught and taken from his benefactor. With all his craft, Huck is actually, as a boy, very much at the mercy of the rough men who infest the river. Adventure complicates and enhances his freedom. And what adventure! It never ceases, but flows on as naturally as the river which furthers the plot of the story by conveying the characters from point to point. Both banks are as crowded with excitement, if not with danger, as the surrounding forest of the older romances. Huck can slip ashore at any moment and try his luck with the universe in which he moves without belonging to it. Now he is the terrified and involuntary witness of a cruel murder plot, and again of an actual murder. Now he strays, with his boy's astonished simplicity, into the Grangerford–Shepherdson vendetta and sees another *Romeo and Juliet* enacted in Kentucky. In the undesired company of the "king" and the "duke," certainly two as sorry and as immortal rogues as fiction ever exhibited, Huck is initiated into degrees of scalawaggery which he could not have experienced, at his age, alone; into amateur theatricals as extraordinary as the Royal Nonesuch and frauds as barefaced as the impostures practised upon the camp-meeting and upon the heirs of Peter Wilks. After sights and undertakings so Odyssean, the last quarter of the book, given over to Tom Sawyer's romantic expedients for getting Jim, who is actually free already, out of a prison from which he could have been released in ten minutes, is preserved from the descent into anticlimax only by its hilarious comic force. As if to make up for the absence of more sizable adventures, this mimic conspiracy is presented with enough art and enough reality in its genre studies to furnish an entire novel. That, in a way, is the effect of *Huckleberry Finn* as a whole: though the hero, by reason of his youth, cannot entirely take part in the action, and the action is therefore not entirely at first hand, the picture lacks little that could make it more vivid or veracious.

In the futile critical exercise of contending which is the greatest American novel, choice ordinarily narrows down at last to *The Scarlet Letter* and *Huckleberry Finn*—a sufficiently antipodean pair and as hard to bring into comparison as tragedy and comedy themselves. Each in its department, however, these two books do seem to be supreme. *The Scarlet Letter* offers, by contrast, practically no picture; *Huckleberry Finn*, no problem. Huck undergoes, it is true, certain naggings from the set of unripe prejudices he calls his conscience; and once he rises to an appealing unselfishness when, in defiance of all the principles he has been taught to value, he makes up his mind that he will assist the runaway slave to freedom. But in the sense that *The Scarlet Letter* poses problems, *Huckleberry Finn* poses none at all. Its criticism of life is of another sort. It does not work at the instigation of any doctrine, moral or artistic, whatever. As Hawthorne, after long gazing into the somber dusk over ancient Salem, had seen the universal drama of Hester and Dimmesdale and Chillingworth being transacted there, and had felt it rising within him to expression, so Mark Twain, in the midst of many vicissitudes remembering the river of his youthful happiness, had seen the panorama of it unrolling before him and also had been moved to record it out of sheer joy in its old wildness and beauty, assured that merely to have such a story to tell was reason enough for telling it. Having written *Life on the Mississippi* he had already reduced the river to his own language; having written *Tom Sawyer*, he had got his characters in hand. There wanted only the moment when his imagination should take fire at recollection and rush away on its undogmatic task of reproducing the great days of the valley. Had Mark Twain undertaken to make another and a greater *Gilded Age* out of his matter, to portray the life of the river satirically on the largest scale, instead of in such dimensions as fit Huck's boyish limitations of knowledge, he might possibly have made a better book, but he would have had to be another man. Being the man he was, he touched his peak of imaginative creation not by taking thought how he could be a Balzac to the Mississippi but by yarning with all his gusto about an adventure he might have had in the dawn of his days. Although he did not deliberately gather riches, riches came.

—Carl Van Doren, *The American Novel,*
New York: Macmillan, 1921, pp. 170–175

A CONNECTICUT YANKEE IN
KING ARTHUR'S COURT

After *The Adventures of Huckleberry Finn*, Twain returned with character-istic perversity to an English, historical subject. After a few years, and before *A Connecticut Yankee* was even completed, he would try to write *Huck and Tom Among the Indians*, but this proposed work was never finished. *Tom Sawyer Abroad* would be finished and published in 1894, and *Tom Sawyer, Detective* would follow in 1896. Neither book did well. Twain's moving between different tried and proven genres reflects an ongoing need for remuneration more than it does any balanced, consid-ered aesthetic.

Undaunted by the critical disappointment that surrounded *The Prince and the Pauper*, Twain revisited historical England, this time in the Arthurian legends of the sixth century. Once again, an incongruity formed the pivot of the plot—not the switch of a prince and a pauper but the temporal stranding of a Connecticut Yankee in Arthurian England. Perhaps it was Twain's intention that a Connecticut Yankee would allow for some flashes of contemporary American slang as well as facilitating some light relief. Alternatively, he might have been seeking to replicate the theme of Americans in Old Europe, as he did in *The Innocents Abroad*, this time in fiction. The reaction in England (usually a strong market for Twain, notwithstanding the prickly critics) was abysmal.

Twain was clearly anxious about the English reaction before the novel was published, as is evident in his letter to his English publishers Chatto and Windus. Incredibly, this letter has been strategically edited and rewritten by the editor of Twain's letters, Arthur Bigelow Paine. In the first place, Paine neglects to date the letter. Furthermore, he adds Howells's name to Twain's list of authoritative "critical readers." Howells had not read the manuscript at the time. The context of the letter is important, too, since it emerged spontaneously in a correspondence that was routinely friendly and easygoing. The sudden change of tone is inexplicable. What had happened to Twain to make him so combative?

This same anxiety informs Twain's letter to Andrew Lang. The aggressive tone is gone now, replaced by a pleading one. This letter has been quoted often as Mark Twain's key statement of artistic intent and as such is well worth the perusal of anybody who writes about Mark Twain's literary intentions or theories of art. Certainly, to Lang, the letter is an articulate argument against cultural snobbery and supports the celebration of Twain, by Perry Miller, as the only author able to communicate to the highbrow and the lowbrow. To please the cultivated, Twain writes, "is merely feeding the overfed. . . . It is not that little minority who are already saved that are best worth trying to uplift . . . but the mighty mass of the uncultivated who are underneath."

The modern reader might cringe slightly that Mark Twain—the author of *Huckleberry Finn*, no less—had by this time so lost his sense of self-worth that he identified himself with the hurdy-gurdy and not the opera, the "chromo" reproduction and not the masterpiece. Whether the piece really stands as Twain's most candid statement of artistic intent or is merely rhetoric to convince Andrew Lang to write supportive promotional words for him is unclear. The same question is the one that baffles Perry Miller: "We are all . . . in some doubt about Mark Twain's intellect." Is this letter simply a case of "sour grapes"? Are we to take Twain seriously when he insists that he "never cared what became of the cultured classes" (what, then, of Howells?) and only ever sought to "amuse"? This letter should be read particularly with regard to *A Connecticut Yankee*, since the missive was clearly intended to soften the blows that Twain obviously anticipated.

William Dean Howells dependably supplied a hearty recommendation of the book. Was there ever any doubt? He reviews Twain's book in "The Editor's Study" columns of *Harper's Monthly*, after a consideration of Philip Gilbert Hamerton's "recent essays comparing the *French and English*." The opening comments printed here, then, refer to Hamerton's book, inasmuch as it is comparable to Twain's.

Howells pointedly identifies the author of *A Connecticut Yankee* as "Mr. Clemens," since he feels that Twain (Clemens) has imparted "more of his personal quality than in anything else he has done." Students interested in the dual identity of Clemens/Twain will find Howells's remarks useful. Howells suggests that Twain purposely combined his perceived strengths for writing about the European past and the American present. "The elastic scheme of the romance allows it to play freely . . . between the sixth century and the nineteenth century." That is, *A Connecticut Yankee* crosses *The Innocents Abroad* with *The Prince and the Pauper*.

Howells finds Clemens's glimpses of sixth-century monastic life "true enough," a gloss that breezily overlooks certain errors. Those errors are inevitably picked over venomously by the English reviewers. Having evoked the grisly scene in which a still-nursing mother is hanged (a scene challenged, for historical accuracy, by Desmond O'Brien), Howells blithely reassures the reader that the novel is only "obliquely serious." As such a stark contrast suggests, problems of tone haunt this work as they did others. Twain "passes in a sentence from laughing into raving," O'Brien complains. "His fooling is admirable and his preaching is admirable, but they are mutually destructive," he continues. Twain "preaches . . . from the sawdust of the circus and in the intervals between a couple of jests or a couple of summersaults." Students examining Twain's mixture (willing or otherwise) of tones and genres will find another compelling case alleged here.

Howells, meanwhile, compares Twain to Cervantes, apparently because both men deck their heroes out in armor. The book is dreamlike, he continues,

> the whole story has the lawless operation of a dream; none of its prodigies are accounted for; they take themselves for granted, and neither explain nor justify themselves.

Here faint praise comes perilously close to open criticism. Perhaps in viewing the text as dreamlike, Howells seeks to dispel the diplomatic blunder innate to the text, which the reviewer conspicuously ignores. Other reviewers did not.

The reviewer for *Speaker* comments on Twain's irreverence (a charge familiar from the reviews of *The Innocents Abroad*). The *Telegraph*'s writer positively explodes at a novel "that tries to deface our moral and literal currency by bruising and soiling the image of King ARTHUR, as left to us by legend and consecrated by poetry." He treats Arthur with almost religious reverence, as variously "an ideal of kingship and knighthood" and indeed a "shrine in human souls" that "has fired the thoughts and purified the imagination of millions of men and women for many generations." Twain's book flings mud on its very altar. The insult is taken on a national level, as well: America is "a land where commercial fraud and industrial adulteration are fine arts," its presses "based to a great extent on scandalous personalities." The tirade descends into absurdity, with a fantasy of King Arthur on Wall Street and a revisionist account of the Civil War in which Britain came to the rescue of the Union. The reviewer tartly asks: "Where was Mark Twain then?"

The reviewer is, of course, the English equivalent of the Concord library committee and its supporters; nevertheless the review is useful to students of the novel's reception, as well as those looking into Twain's complex relationship with England. While the *Telegraph* review shows little critical detachment, it abundantly demonstrates the level of ire provoked by Twain's latest work.

—◦◦◦—   —◦◦◦—   —◦◦◦—

MARK TWAIN (1889)

GENTLEMEN,—Concerning The Yankee, I have already revised the story twice; and it has been read critically by W. D. Howells and Edmund Clarence Stedman, and my wife has caused me to strike out several passages that have been brought to her attention, and to soften others. Furthermore, I have read chapters of the book in public where Englishmen were present and have profited by their suggestions.

Now, mind you, I have taken all this pains because I wanted to say a Yankee mechanic's say against monarchy and its several natural props, and yet make a book which you would be willing to print exactly as it comes to you, without altering a word.

We are spoken of (by Englishmen) as a thin-skinned people. It is you who are thin-skinned. An Englishman may write with the most brutal frankness about any man or institution among us and we republish him without dreaming of altering a line or a word. But England cannot stand that kind of a book written about herself. It is England that is thin-skinned. It causeth me to smile when I read the modifications of my language which have been made in my English editions to fit them for the sensitive English palate.

Now, as I say, I have taken laborious pains to so trim this book of offense that you might not lack the nerve to print it just as it stands. I am going to get the proofs to you just as early as I can. I want you to read it carefully. If you can publish it without altering a single word, go ahead. Otherwise, please hand it to J. R. Osgood in time for him to have it published at my expense.

This is important, for the reason that the book was not written for America; it was written for England. So many Englishmen have done their sincerest best to teach us something for our betterment that it seems to me high time that some of us should substantially recognize the good intent by trying to pry up the English nation to a little higher level of manhood in turn.

Very truly yours,
S. L. CLEMENS.

—Mark Twain, letter to his English publishers,
July 16, 1889, from *Mark Twain's Letters,*
Paine, ed., New York: Harper and Brothers,
1917, II: pp. 524–525

MARK TWAIN (1889)

They vote but do not print. The head tells you pretty promptly whether the food is satisfactory or not; and everybody hears, and thinks the whole man has spoken. It is a delusion. Only his taste and his smell have been heard from—important, both, in a way, but these do not build up the man; and preserve his life and fortify it.

The little child is permitted to label its drawings "This is a cow—this is a horse," and so on. This protects the child. It saves it from the sorrow and wrong of hearing its cows and its horses criticized as kangaroos and work benches. A man who is white-washing a fence is doing a useful thing, so also is the man who is adorning a rich man's house with costly frescoes; and all of us are sane enough to judge these performances by standards proper to each. Now, then, to be fair, an author ought to be allowed to put upon his book an explanatory line: "This is written for the Head;" "This is written for the Belly and the Members." And the critic ought to hold himself in honor bound to put away from him his ancient habit of judging all books by one standard, and thenceforth follow a fairer course.

The critic assumes, every time, that if a book doesn't meet the cultivated-class standard, it isn't valuable. Let us apply his law all around: for if it is sound in the case of novels, narratives, pictures, and such things, it is certainly sound and applicable to all the steps which lead up to culture and make culture possible. It condemns the spelling book, for a spelling book is of no use to a person of culture; it condemns all school books and all schools which lie between the child's primer and Greek, and between the infant school and the university; it condemns all the rounds of art which lie between the cheap terra cotta groups and the Venus de Medici, and between the chromo and the Transfiguration; it requires Whitcomb Riley to sing no more till he can sing like Shakespeare, and it forbids all amateur music and will grant its sanction to nothing below the "classic."

Is this an extravagant statement? No, it is a mere statement of fact. It is the fact itself that is extravagant and grotesque. And what is the result? This—and it is sufficiently curious: the critic has actually imposed upon the world the superstition that a painting by Raphael is more valuable to the civilizations of the earth than is a chromo; and the august opera than the hurdy-gurdy and the villagers' singing society; and Homer than the little everybody's-poet whose rhymes are in all mouths today and will be in nobody's mouth next generation; and the Latin classics than Kipling's far-reaching bugle-note; and Jonathan Edwards than the Salvation Army; and the Venus de Medici than the plaster-cast peddler; the superstition, in a word, that the vast and awful comet that trails its cold lustre through the remote abysses of space once a century and interests and instructs a cultivated handful of astronomers is worth more to the world than the sun which warms and cheers all the nations every day and makes the crops to grow.

If a critic should start a religion it would not have any object but to convert angels: and they wouldn't need it. The thin top crust of humanity— the cultivated—are worth pacifying, worth pleasing, worth coddling, worth nourishing and preserving with dainties and delicacies, it is true; but to be caterer to that little faction is no very dignified or valuable occupation, it seems to me; it is merely feeding the overfed, and there must be small satisfaction in that. It is not that little minority who are already saved that are best worth trying to uplift, I should think, but the mighty mass of the uncultivated who are underneath. That mass will never see the Old Masters—that sight is for the few; but the chromo maker can lift them all one step upward toward appreciation of art; they cannot have the opera, but the hurdy-gurdy and the singing class lift them a little way toward that far light; they will never know Homer, but the passing rhymester of their day leaves them higher than he found them; they may never even hear of the Latin classics, but they will strike step with Kipling's drum-beat, and they will march; for all Jonathan Edwards's help they would die in their slums, but the Salvation Army will beguile some of them up to pure air and a cleaner life; they know no sculpture, the Venus is not even a name to them, but they are a grade higher in the scale of civilization by the ministrations of the plaster-cast than they were before it took its place upon their mantel and made it beautiful to their unexacting eyes.

Indeed I have been misjudged, from the very first. I have never tried in even one single instance, to help cultivate the cultivated classes. I was not equipped for it, either by native gifts or training. And I never had any ambition in that direction, but always hunted for bigger game—the masses. I have seldom deliberately tried to instruct them, but have done my best to entertain them. To simply amuse them would have satisfied my dearest ambition at any time; for they could get instruction elsewhere, and I had two chances to help to the teacher's one: for amusement is a good preparation for study and a good healer of fatigue after it. My audience is dumb, it has no voice in print, and so I cannot know whether I have won its approbation or only got its censure.

Yes, you see, I have always catered for the Belly and the Members, but have been served like the others—criticized from the culture-standard—to my sorrow and pain; because, honestly, I never cared what became of the cultured classes; they could go to the theatre and the opera—they had no use for me and the melodeon.

And now at last I arrive at my object and tender my petition, making supplication to this effect: that the critics adopt a rule recognizing the Belly and the Members, and formulate a standard whereby work done for them shall be judged. Help me, Mr. Lang; no voice can reach further than yours in a case of this kind, or carry greater weight of authority.

—Mark Twain, letter to Andrew Lang,
1889, from *Mark Twain's Letters,* Paine, ed.,
New York: Harper and Brothers, 1917, II:525–528

WILLIAM DEAN HOWELLS (1890)

The chapter on Purity will most surprise Anglo-Saxon readers; but the chapter on Caste is of even more interest, and it is of almost unique value both in temper and in substance, for it describes without caricature, in a democratic commonwealth, and on the verge of the twentieth century, an ideal of life entirely stupid, useless, and satisfied, and quite that which Mark Twain has been portraying in his wonder-story of *A Connecticut Yankee at the Court of King Arthur.* Mr. Hamerton's French noble of the year 1890 is the same man essentially as any of that group of knights of the Round Table, who struck Mr. Clemens's delightful hero as white Indians. In his circle, achievement, ability, virtue, would find itself at the same disadvantage, without birth, as in that of Sir Launcelot. When you contemplate him in Mr. Hamerton's clear, passionless page, you feel that after all the Terror was perhaps too brief, and you find yourself sympathizing with all Mr. Clemens's robust approval of the Revolution.

Mr. Clemens, we call him, rather than Mark Twain, because we feel that in this book our arch-humorist imparts more of his personal quality than in anything else he has done. Here he is to the full the humorist, as we know him; but he is very much more, and his strong, indignant, often infuriate hate of injustice, and his love of equality, burn hot through the manifold adventures and experiences of the tale. What he thought about prescriptive right and wrong, we had partly learned in *The Prince and the Pauper,* and in *Huckleberry Finn,* but it is this last book which gives his whole mind. The elastic scheme of the romance allows it to play freely back and forward between the sixth century and the nineteenth century; and often while it is working the reader up to a blasting contempt of monarchy and aristocracy in King Arthur's time, the dates are magically shifted under him, and he is confronted with exactly the same principles in Queen Victoria's time. The delicious satire, the marvellous wit, the wild, free, fantastic humor are the colors of the tapestry, while the texture is a humanity that lives in every fibre. At every moment the scene amuses, but it is all the time an object-lesson in democracy. It makes us glad of our republic and our epoch; but it does not flatter us into a fond content with them; there are passages in which we see that the noble of Arthur's day, who fattened on the blood and sweat of his bondmen, is one in essence with the capitalist of Mr. Harrison's day who grows rich on the labor of his underpaid wagemen. Our incomparable humorist, whose sarcasm is so pitiless to the greedy and superstitious clerics of Britain, is in fact of the same spirit and intention as those bishops who, true to their office, wrote the other day from New York to all their churches in the land: "It is a fallacy in social economics, as well as in Christian thinking, to look upon the labor of men and women and children as a commercial commodity, to be bought and sold as an inanimate and irresponsible thing. . . . The heart and soul of a man cannot be bought or hired in any market, and to act as if they were not needed in the doing of the world's vast work is as unchristian as it is unwise."

Mr. Clemens's glimpses of monastic life in Arthur's realm are true enough; and if they are not the whole truth of the matter, one may easily get it in some such book as Mr. Brace's *Gesta Christi*, where the full light of history is thrown upon the transformation of the world, if not the church, under the influence of Christianity. In the mean time, if any one feels that the justice done the churchmen of King Arthur's time is too much of one kind, let him turn to that heart-breaking scene where the brave monk stands with the mother and her babe on the scaffold, and execrates the hideous law which puts her to death for stealing enough to keep her from starving. It is one of many passages in the story where our civilization of to-day sees itself mirrored in the cruel barbarism of the past, the same in principle, and only softened in custom. With shocks of consciousness, one recognizes in such episodes that the laws are still made for the few against the many, and that the preservation of things, not men, is still the ideal of legislation. But we do not wish to leave the reader with the notion that Mr. Clemens's work is otherwise than obliquely serious. Upon the face of it you have a story no more openly didactic than *Don Quixote*, which we found ourselves more than once thinking of, as we read, though always with the sense of the kindlier and truer heart of our time. Never once, we believe, has Mark Twain been funny at the cost of the weak, the unfriended, the helpless; and this is rather more than you can say of Cid Hamet ben Engeli. But the two writers are of the same humorous largeness; and when the Connecticut man rides out at dawn, in a suit of Arthurian armor, and gradually heats up under the mounting sun in what he calls that stove; and a fly gets between the bars of his visor; and he cannot reach his handkerchief in his helmet to wipe the sweat from his streaming face; and at last when he cannot bear it any longer, and dismounts at the side of a brook, and makes the distressed damsel who has been riding behind him take off his helmet, and fill it with water, and pour gallon after gallon down the collar of his wrought-iron cutaway, you have a situation of as huge a grotesqueness as any that Cervantes conceived.

The distressed damsel is the Lady Corisande; he calls her Sandy, and he is troubled in mind at riding about the country with her in that way; for he is not only very doubtful that there is nothing in the castle where she says there are certain princesses imprisoned and persecuted by certain giants, but he feels that it is not quite nice: he is engaged to a young lady in East Hartford, and he finds Sandy a fearful bore at first, though in the end he loves and marries her, finding that he hopelessly antedates the East Hartford young lady by thirteen centuries. How he gets into King Arthur's realm, the author concerns himself as little as any of us do with the mechanism of our dreams. In fact the whole story has the lawless operation of a dream; none of its prodigies are accounted for; they take themselves for granted, and neither explain nor justify themselves. Here he is, that Connecticut man, foreman of one of the shops in Colt's pistol factory, and full to the throat of the invention and the self-satisfaction of the nineteenth century, at the court of the mythic Arthur. He is promptly recognized as a being of extraordinary powers, and becomes the king's right-hand man, with the title of The Boss; but as he has apparently no lineage or blazon, he has no social standing, and the meanest noble has precedence of him, just as would happen in England to-day. The reader may faintly fancy the consequences flowing from this situation, which he will find so vividly fancied for him in the book; but they are simply irreportable. The scheme confesses allegiance to nothing; the incidents, the facts follow as they will. The Boss cannot rest from introducing the apparatus of our time, and he tries to impart its spirit, with a thousand most astonishing effects. He starts a daily paper in Camelot; he torpedoes a holy well; he blows up a party of insolent knights with a dynamite bomb; when he and the king disguise themselves as peasants, in order to learn the real life of the people, and are taken and sold for slaves, and then sent to the gallows for the murder of their master, Launcelot arrives to their rescue with five hundred knights on bicycles. It all ends with the Boss's proclamation of the Republic after Arthur's death, and his destruction of the whole chivalry of England by electricity.

We can give no proper notion of the measureless play of an imagination which has a gigantic jollity in its feats, together with the tenderest sympathy. There are incidents in this wonder-book which wring the heart for what has been of cruelty and wrong in the past, and leave it burning with shame and hate for the conditions which are of like effect in the present. It is one of its magical properties that the fantastic fable of Arthur's far-off time is also too often the sad truth of ours; and the magician who makes us feel in it that we have just begun to know his power, teaches equality and fraternity in every phase of his phantasmagory.

He leaves, to be sure, little of the romance of the olden time, but no one is more alive to the simple, mostly tragic poetry of it; and we do not remember any book which imparts so clear a sense of what was truly heroic in it. With all his scorn of kingcraft, and all his ireful contempt of caste, no one yet has been fairer to the nobility of character which they cost so much too much to develop. The mainly ridiculous Arthur of Mr. Clemens has his moments of being as fine and high as the Arthur of Lord Tennyson; and the keener light which shows his knights and ladies in their childlike simplicity and their innocent coarseness throws all their best qualities into relief. This book is in its last effect the most matter-of-fact narrative, for it is always true to human nature, the only truth possible, the only truth essential, to fiction. The humor of the conception and of the performance is simply immense; but more than ever Mr. Clemens's humor seems the sunny break of his intense conviction. We must all recognize him here as first of those who laugh, not merely because his fun is unrivalled, but because there is a force of right feeling and clear thinking in it that never got into fun before, except in *The Bigelow Papers*. Throughout the text in all its circumstance and meaning is supplemented by the illustrations of an artist who has entered into the wrath and the pathos as well as the fun of the thing, and made them his own.

—William Dean Howells, *Harper's Magazine*, January 1890, pp. 319–321

Desmond O'Brien (1890)

My dear Mr. Wyndham,—It has occurred to a good many prophets since Lord Lytton wrote *The Coming Race,*—

> To dip into the future, far as human eye could see,
> Show the vision of the world, and all the wonders that would be.

but it was reserved, I think, for Mark Twain to put on Hans Andersen's Goloshes of Happiness and go back to the past, carrying with him all the wonders of the present. *A Yankee at the Court of King Arthur* is a bizarre book, full of all kinds of laughable and delightful incongruities—the most striking of its incongruities, however, being unconscious, grim, and disenchanting. For Mark Twain, as he goes on, gets into a fury so ferocious (and natural) with the infernal oppression of the people by the Nobles, the King, and the Church that he passes in a sentence from laughing into raving at the "good old times"; and, like Macbeth at sight of Banquo's ghost, he "displaces the mirth" of the feast he had prepared for us. His fooling is admirable and his preaching is admirable, but they are mutually destructive. In every page he preaches pretty much what Richard Rumbold preached two centuries since—"I never could believe that Providence had sent a few men into the world ready booted and spurred to ride, and millions ready saddled and bridled to be ridden"—but Rumbold preached it from the most commanding of pulpits—the scaffold—whereas Mark Twain preaches it from the sawdust of the circus and in the intervals between a couple of jests or a couple of summersaults. But it is thoroughly sound doctrine, and is needed still so sorely in England and Ireland that it is ungracious to grumble at the mode of its delivery. It will reach a larger audience, and, perhaps, strike many of them more by its grotesque presentation than if the preacher wore a less bizarre garb than motley.

> Ridentem dicere verum
> Quid vetat?

Still, such frightful episodes as that of the woman who was burned to make a fire to warm a slave gang, or that of the hanging of the young mother—wife of the "pressed" man-o'-war's man—with her baby at her breast (an incident, by the way, Mr. Mark Twain, not of the sixth century, but of the beginning of the nineteenth), freeze the laughter on our lips.

—Desmond O'Brien, *Truth* 27,
January 2, 1890, p. 25

Unsigned Review in *Speaker* (1890)

The reviewer for *Speaker* refers to another work being discussed, *Silvie and Bruno* by Lewis Carroll.

Mark Twain is also somewhat affected by the Spirit of his Time, which is didactic; and by the Spirit of his Nation, which is inventive, but not refined. Mr. Lewis Carroll is far beyond Mr. Clemens in points of delicacy and taste; but it may be doubted whether any English author of repute would have tried to win a laugh by an irreverent treatment of the legend of the Holy Grail, as Mr. Clemens has done in *A Yankee at the Court of King Arthur*. It is quite certain that there are few English readers who will care to see the subject begrimed with prime American jests. Mr. Clemens used to be able to make us laugh without resorting to this easy and distressing method; in his last book he fails to make us laugh by any method, even the worst.

But Mr. Clemens is not only dull when he is offensive; he is perhaps even more dull when he is didactic. His views on the peerage, religious tolerance, republics, political economy, and the application of electricity to warfare, may be—some of them are—admirable. But they are out of place in a farcical book: the satire is not fresh; the information is second-hand or inaccurate; and the moral—or immoral, as the case may be—is clumsily enforced and unduly prominent. Tediousness is still further ensured by the length of the book. The joke is a long joke, and the author has not "gompressed him." It would be idle to point out that the book is not a sketch of the sixth century; because Mr. Clemens is careful to remove by a prefatory note any such objection. But he must not think that his confession of incompetence will make him seem any the less incompetent to the intelligent reader.

The illustrations to the book are occasionally allegorical, and remind us of the hieroglyphic which is to be found at the beginning of prophetic almanacks. In one of them the root of a tree is marked Religious Intolerance; but the artist spells quite as well as he draws. They are very badly arranged; they seldom occur at the right place; and they break into text, making the task of reading very difficult. The task was hard enough, too, without that. We hope—we may even believe—that we have seen the artist at his worst; we certainly have not seen the author at his best.

Sometimes we think that we shall never see the author at his best again. American humour depended much upon quaint and happy phrase. When these phrases are repeated *ad nauseam*, their quaintness and happiness seem to disappear. But we have been saddened and depressed by reading two long and humorous books, and are, perhaps unduly inclined to be pessimistic. We had expected to laugh a little; and, instead of that, we have learned much— much that we knew before. And, after all, it must be easy for Mr. Clemens to do better; and we know why it must.

—Unsigned Review in *Speaker* 1, January 11, 1890, pp. 49–50

Unsigned Review in the
Daily Telegraph (1890)

At this holiday season, in books and newspapers, on stage and in drawing-room, the poet and the painter, the author, the actor, and the dramatist compete with one another to bring before young and old scenes and suggestions of beauty, heroism, purity, and truth. One writer is an exception. Mark Twain sets himself to show the seamy side of the legendary Round Table of King Arthur's time. He depicts all the vices of feudalism—the licentiousness of the nobles, their arrogance and insolence to the middle classes, their neglect of the poor, their hours of gluttony and idleness, varied by raids and brawls and riotous disorders. He describes how a Yankee visiting the Court uses modern inventions, defeats the best warriors, and redresses the wrongs of the poor. It is quite possible that a serious purpose underlies what otherwise seems a vulgar travesty. We have every regard for Mark Twain—a writer who has enriched English literature by admirable descriptions of boy life, and who in *The Prince and the Pauper* has given a vivid picture of mediaeval times. A book, however, that tries to deface our moral and literary currency by bruising and soiling the image of King Arthur, as left to us by legend and consecrated by poetry, is a very unworthy production of the great humourist's pen. No doubt there is one element of wit—incongruity—in bringing a Yankee from Connecticut face to face with feudal knights; but sharp contrast between vulgar facts and antique ideas is not the only thing necessary for humour. If it were, then a travelling Cockney putting a flaming tie round the neck of the 'Apollo Belvidere,' or sticking a clay pipe between the lips of the 'Venus de Medici,' would be a matter-of-fact Mark Twain, and as much entitled to respect. Burlesque and travesty are satire brought down to the meanest capacity, and they have their proper province when pretentious falsehoods put on the masks of solemnity and truth. Stilted tragedies, artificial melodramas, unnatural acting, are properly held up to ridicule on the stage or in parodies. The mannerisms of a popular writer like Carlyle, Browning, or even Tennyson, may, through caricature, be good-humouredly exposed; but an attack on the ideals associated with King Arthur is a coarse pandering to that passion for irreverence which is at the basis of a great deal of Yankee wit. To make a jest of facts, phrases, or words—Scriptural, heroic, or legendary—that are held in awe or reverence by other men is the open purpose of every witling on a Western print, who endeavours to follow in the footsteps of Artemus Ward, Bret Harte, and Mark Twain. They may finally be successful enough to destroy their own trade. They now live by shocking decent people who still retain love for the Bible, HOMER, SHAKESPEARE, SCOTT, and TENNYSON; but when they have thoroughly trained a rising generation to respect nothing their irreverence will fall flat.

The stories of King ARTHUR that have come down to us represent in legendary form not any historical fact, but an ideal of kingship and knighthood which had birth in the hearts and aspirations of mediaeval men. This was their ideal of what a King amongst his warriors ought to be, and the beautiful image has fired the thoughts and purified the imagination of millions of men and women for many generations. Will this shrine in human souls be destroyed because a Yankee scribe chooses to fling pellets of mud upon the high altar? The instincts of the past and the genius of TENNYSON have consecrated for ever 'the goodliest fellowship of famous knights Whereof this world holds record.' The Round Table is dissolved, but we can still 'delight our souls with talk of knightly deeds,' as they at Camelot in the storied past. We can still apply the image of the ideal knight as a criterion of modern worth. King ARTHUR swore each of his followers to 'reverence his conscience as his King, To ride abroad redressing human wrongs, To speak no slander, no, nor listen to it, To honour his own word as if his GOD'S, To lead sweet lives in purest chastity. To love one maiden only, cleave to her, And worship her by years of noble deeds.' Such an oath presented to a modern Yankee would seem to convey in almost every phrase a covert insult to American institutions. In a land where commercial fraud and industrial adulteration are fine arts we had better omit appeals to 'conscience.' The United States are not likely to 'ride abroad redressing human wrong'—as they never gave a dollar or a man to help Greece, Poland, Hungary, or Italy in their struggles to be free. 'To speak no slander, no, nor listen to it,' would utterly uproot America's free press—based to a great extent on scandalous personalities. Loving one maiden only and cleaving to her must seem too 'high-toned' in the States, where there are many facilities for ready divorce. So far MARK TWAIN is right as a Western iconoclast to pelt with sarcasm ideals which are not included in the Constitution or customs of the United States. Yet, in spite of all that America has done or can do to deface images of self-sacrifice and beauty, there are chosen souls in her own borders who have fulfilled the heroic ideals of the olden time. The Abolitionists of New England encountered great perils when they first set out to redress the great human wrong of negro slavery, and they fought as noble a contest against organised iniquity as any knight of ARTHUR's Court. They faced political obloquy, mob violence, loss of limb, sometimes of life, and the falling away of friends and relatives, because they had inherited the old instinct of knights, to lead lives of duty to their fellow-men. They were jeered and derided by the MARK TWAINS of the day, but their foresight was proved at the end of the war, when the world recognised the two-fold result, 'a nation saved, a race delivered.' What, too, would have been the fate of the Republic if no ideal image of their country shone before the souls of the men who died to save the Union? Coward souls at the North said, 'It will cost much money and many lives to re-conquer the South: let them go; let the Republic break up; what is a country to us?' but a chivalry that came down from British ancestors animated the men who followed GRANT, and they kept to their high purpose until the field was won. Where was MARK TWAIN then? Why did he not satirise the patriotism that would not let a Republic be mutilated? Why did he not sneer at Yankee reverence for a paper Constitution not a hundred years old? Why did he not sing the glories of trade as better than any preservation of the Union or liberation of negro slaves?

Even if we look at the real feudalism idealised in the legends of King ARTHUR, it was not all evil. No doubt there were licentious nobles at all times, and there were great landlords who were occasionally cruel to the peasants in their fields. The change to modern times, however, is not all a gain. A great lord of old held his possessions by 'suit and service'; he was bound to follow his King to the wars. Now he owns his broad lands free of duty, and may live a life of shameful luxury when he likes. The peasant of the olden times was not always in distress. The country was thinly peopled; he had as much land as he wanted; the woods were full of wild game, the streams of fish; except on occasions of rare famine he was fed well. Such a thing as an eviction was unknown, and for one good reason—the lord was not only bound to serve the King, but to bring men for his army; consequently he had an interest in raising on his estates a body of faithful followers. The modern landlord drives his peasants into the towns, where, uncared for by him, they degenerate and die in slums. We must remember, too, that the vices of the past were characteristic of rough times; they were the sins of brutality, not of fraud. A bad knight of the feudal age wronged a maid or widow, and refused redress; but what are the offences of a commercial age? In America and in England, to a lesser extent, financial swindling is elaborately organised. The wicked man of modern times does not couch his lance against the weak or lowly; he sends out a prospectus. In twelve months the widow and orphan are breadless; the promoter and the financier have added another twenty thousand to their stores. Were King ARTHUR to descend in New York to-morrow he would make for Wall-street, where he would find a host of men whose word is as good, and as bad, as their bond—railway schemers who plunder the shareholders of a continent, and are ever intent by every device of falsehood and of plot to deceive each other and to defraud the public. Talk of the inequality of man! King ARTHUR and the meanest menial in his halls were nearer to each other in conditions of life than the tramp in the slums of New York and the ASTORS, VANDERBILTS, and JAY GOULDS who have piled up millions extracted from the pockets of less successful men. The Republic is a 'land of liberty,' yet its commerce, its railways, and it manufactures are in the hands of a few cliques of almost irresponsible capitalists, who control tariffs, markets, and politics in order that they may be enriched, to the disadvantage of the masses. Which, then, is to be most admired—the supremacy of a knight or the success of a financier? Under which King will the Americans serve—the ideal or the real? Will they own allegiance to King ARTHUR or JAY GOULD?

—Unsigned Review in the *Daily Telegraph*, London, January 13, 1890

HENRY C. VEDDER (1893)

The immediate and permanent popularity of *Innocents Abroad* is not wonderful; it is a book of even greater merit than the public gave it credit for possessing. It was read and enjoyed for its fun, and though nearly twenty-five years have passed it is still a funny book, whether one reads it now for the first or the forty-first time. But underneath the fun was an earnest purpose that the great mass of readers failed to see at the time, and even yet imperfectly appreciate. This purpose was to tell, not how an American ought to feel on seeing the sights of the Old World, but how he actually does feel if he is honest with himself. From time immemorial, books of travel had been written by Americans purporting to record their experiences, but really telling only what the writers thought they might, could, would, or should have experienced. These are the kind of travellers that are seen everywhere in Europe, Murray or Baedeker constantly in hand and carefully conned, lest they dilate with the wrong emotion—or, what is almost as bad, fail to dilate with the proper emotion at the right instant. For sham emotion, sham love of art, sham adventures, Mark Twain had no tolerance, and he gave these shams no quarter in his book. 'Cervantes smiled Spain's chivalry away' is a fine phrase of Byron's, which, like most of Byron's fine phrases, is not true. What Cervantes did was to 'smile away' the ridiculous romances of chivalry—chivalry had been long dead in his day—the impossible tales of knightly adventure, outdoing the deeds of the doughty Baron Munchausen, that were produced in shoals by the penny-a-liners of his time. Not since this feat of Cervantes has a wholesome burst of merriment cleared the air more effectually, or banished a greater humbug from literature than when *The Innocents Abroad* laughed away the sentimental, the romantic book of travels. Mark Twain, perhaps, erred somewhat on the other side. His bump of reverence must be admitted to be practically nonexistent. He sees so clearly the humbug and pretence and superstition beneath things conventionally held to be sacred, that he sometimes fails to see that they are not all sham, and that there is really something sacred there. He was throughout the book too hard-headed, too realistic, too unimpressionable, too frankly Philistine, for entire truthfulness and good taste; but it was necessary to exaggerate something on this side in order to furnish an antidote to mawkish sentimentality. His lesson would have been less effective if it had not been now and then a trifle bitter to the taste. Since that time travellers have actually dared to tell the truth—or shall we say that they have been afraid to scribble lies so recklessly? Whichever way one looks at the matter, there is no doubt that American literature, so far as it has dealt with Europe and things European, has been more natural, wholesome, and self-respecting since the tour of this shrewd innocent.

The same earnestness of purpose underlies much else that Mark Twain has written, especially *The Prince and the Pauper*, and *A Yankee at King Arthur's Court*. The careless reader no doubt sees nothing in the first of these books but a capital tale for boys. He cannot help seeing that, for it is a story of absorbing interest, accurate in its historical setting, and told in remarkably good English. In the latter book he will no doubt discover nothing more than rollicking humor and a burlesque of *Morte d'Arthur*. This is to see only what lies on the surface of these volumes, without comprehending their aim or sympathizing with the spirit. Not the old prophet of Chelsea himself was a more honest and inveterate hater of shams than Mark Twain. Much of the glamor and charm of chivalry is as unreal as the tinsel splendors of the stage—to study history is like going behind the scenes of a theatre, a disenchantment as thorough as it is speedy. *Morte d'Arthur* and Tennyson's *Idylls of the King* present to the unsophisticated a very beautiful, but a very shadowy and unsubstantial picture of Britain thirteen centuries ago. Even in these romances a glimpse of the real sordidness and squalor and poverty of the people may now and then be caught amid all the pomp and circumstance of chivalry. Nobody has had the pitiless courage heretofore to let the full blaze of the sun into these regions where the lime-light of fancy has had full sway, that we might see what the berouged heroes and heroines actually are.

But Mark Twain has one quality to which Carlyle never attained. Joined to his hatred of shams is a hearty and genuine love of liberty. His books could never have been written by one not born in the United States. His love of liberty is characteristic in its manifestation. In a Frenchman it would have found vent in essays on the text of *liberté, fraternité, equalité*, but eloquent writing about abstractions is not the way in which an American finds voice for his sentiments. Mark Twain's love of liberty is shown unostentatiously, incidentally as it were, in his sympathy for, and championship of, the down-trodden and oppressed. He says to us, 'Here, you have been admiring the age of chivalry; this is what your King Arthur, your spotless Galahad, your valiant Launcelot made of the common people. Spending their lives in the righting of imaginary wrongs, they were perpetuating with all their energy a system of the most frightful cruelty and oppression. Cease admiring these heroes, and execrate them as they deserve.' This, to be sure, is a one-sided view, but it is one that we need to take in endeavoring to comprehend the England of King Arthur. There is no danger that we shall overlook the romantic and picturesque view while Malory and Tennyson are read, but it is wholesome for us sometimes to feel the weight of misery that oppressed all beneath the privileged classes of England's days of chivalry.

Except in the two books that may be called historic romances, Mark Twain has been a consistent realist. He was probably as innocent of intent to belong to the realistic school when he began writing as Moliere's old gentleman had all his life been of the intent to talk prose. He was realistic because it came sort o' nateral to him, as a Yankee would say. His first books were the outcome of his personal experiences. These were many and varied, for few men have knocked about the world more and viewed life from so many points. Bret Harte has written of life on the Pacific coast with greater appreciation of its romantic and picturesque features, but one suspects with considerable less truthfulness in detail. The shady heroes and heroines of Bret Harte's tales are of a quality that suggests an amalgam of Byron and Smollett; they smack strongly of Bowery melodrama. Mark Twain's *Roughing It* is a wholesome book, and as accurate in its details as a photograph, but there is nothing romantic or thrilling about it.

It is in the Mississippi Valley, however, that our author finds himself most at home, not only because his knowledge of it is more comprehensive and minutely accurate, but because it is a more congenial field. Mark Twain understands California, admires it even, but he loves the great river and the folk who dwell alongside it. He is especially happy in his delineation of the boy of this region. If ever any writer understood boy nature in general, from A to izzard, the name of that writer is Mark Twain. He has explored all its depths and shallows, and in his characters of Tom Sawyer and Huckleberry Finn he has given us such a study of the American boy as will be sought in vain elsewhere. He has done more than this: he has given us a faithful picture, painfully realistic in details, of the ante-bellum social condition of the Mississippi Valley. The books, considered from any other point of view, are trash or worse. Their realism redeems them from what would otherwise be utter worthlessness, and gives them a certain value.

One ought also to mention the value of this writer's short stories. He has not done as much work in this line as one wishes he had, in view of the great merit of what he has written. Most of these stories are humorous in their fundamental conception, or have a vein of humor running through them, but they are not, for the most part, boisterously funny. They range in style from the avowedly funny tale of 'The Jumping Frog of Calaveras' to the surface sobriety of 'The £1,000,000 Bank Note.' In the composition of the short story, Mark Twain is so evidently perfecting his art, as to warrant one in hazarding the prediction that much of his best work in future is likely to be done along this line.

Even our English cousins—as a rule, not too lenient in their judgments of kin across the sea—admit that American humor has a distinct flavor. Not only so, they also admit that this flavor is delightful. To their tastes there is something wild and gamy about American humor, a 'tang' that is both a new sensation and a continuous source of enjoyment. British commendation of American humor, however, is not always as discriminating as it is hearty. We must allow Englishmen the praise of having been prompt to appreciate the humor of Artemus Ward; but of late years they seem impervious to American humor, except of one type—that which depends for its effect on exaggeration. Exaggeration is, no doubt, one legitimate species of humor. The essence of humor lies in the perception of incongruity, and the effect of incongruity may be produced by exaggeration. This is the more effectively done if the style is 'dry'; the writer must give no sign, until the very end (if even there), that he does not take himself seriously; the narrator must not by a tone of voice or change of facial expression betray any lack of exact veracity in his tale, or the effect is measurably lost. Mark Twain has frequently shown himself to be master of this style of humor. He can invent the most tremendous absurdities, and tell them with such an air of seriousness as must frequently deceive the unwary.

But this is not, as English readers mistakably imagine, the best type of American humor in general, or even the humor in which Mark Twain reaches his highest level. Exaggeration is comparatively cheap humor. Anybody can lie, and the kind of Mark Twain's humor most admired abroad is simply the lie of circumstance minus the intent to deceive. It is morally innocuous, therefore, but it is bad art. No doubt it is frequently successful in provoking laughter, but the quality of humor is not to be gauged by the loudness of the hearers' guffaws. The most delightful fun is that which at most provokes no more than a quiet smile, but is susceptible of repeated enjoyment when the most hilarious joke has become a 'chestnut.' To borrow a metaphor from science, humor is the electricity of literature, but in its finest manifestation it is not static but dynamic. The permanent charm of humorous writing is generally in inverse ratio to its power to incite boisterous merriment when first read. The joker who gives one a pain in the side soon induces 'that tired feeling' that is fatal to continued interest. It is Mark Twain's misfortune at present to be appreciated abroad mainly for that which is ephemeral in his writings. His broad humanity, his gift of seeing far below the surface of life, his subtle comprehension of human nature, and his realistic method, are but dimly apprehended by those Britons who go off in convulsions of laughter the moment his name is mentioned. A false standard of what is truly 'American' has been set up abroad, and only what conforms to that standard wins admiration. For that reason British readers have gone wild over Bret Harte and Joaquin Miller, while they neglected Bryant and Holmes, and for a time even Lowell, on the ground that the latter were 'really more English than American, you know.' Their own countrymen have a juster notion of the relative standing of American authors. In the case of Mark Twain they do not believe that he is rated too high by foreign critics and readers, but that his true merits are very imperfectly comprehended.

—Henry C. Vedder, New York
Examiner, April 6, 1893

WILLIAM DEAN HOWELLS "MY FAVORITE NOVELIST AND HIS BEST BOOK" (1897)

To say something concerning novels, and particularly of my favorite among them? That is a difficult thing to do, for one's point of view changes so much from youth to middle age. One's favorite at twenty would not be one's favorite later; but I am pretty sure that throughout my life there has been an increasing preference for what seems to me *real* in fiction as against what seems to me *factitious*; and whilst I have been very fond, from time to time, of the pure romance, I have never cared for the romantic novel, since I was very young. . . .

I am just now reading over again some stories of Mark Twain. There are no better books in their way than "Tom Sawyer" and "Huckleberry Finn." They are about the honestest boys' books I know; and "A Connecticut Yankee at King Arthur's Court" is delicious. I was thinking this morning that one of the differences between the romantic and realistic was that the realistic finds a man's true character under all accidents and under all circumstances, while romanticism, even when it takes ordinary circumstances, seems to miss character; and in reading this romance of Mark Twain's—it is a pure romance—the "Connecticut Yankee," I feel under all its impossibilities that it is true to the character of that man and true to all the conditions. You know how he imagines him—a Yankee from East Hartford, who finds himself, by some witchery, in the England of King Arthur's time. He always distinctly belongs to this period, and the Arthurian people are always their own kind of Britons. The book is not consecrated by time or by consensus of the world's liking, as "Don Quixote" is, but in its imaginative quality I find the two curiously equal. The scheme of carrying a contemporary Yankee into the age of chivalry is just as delightful as Cervantes' conception of bringing a knight errant into his own period. In fact, it merely reverses the process. . . .

—If I must return to the question of my favorites in fiction, "The Damnation of Theron Ware" is just now my favorite, and so is "The Connecticut Yankee." So, for that matter, are Miss Furman's "Stories of a Sanctified Town." So is Stephen Crane's "Maggie," so is Abraham Cahan's "Yekl," so is Miss Jewett's "Country of the Pointed Firs." But I change, or else it is the books that change, and I cannot say what my favorite will be tomorrow.

—William Dean Howells, "My Favorite
Novelist and His Best Book,"
Munsey's Magazine, April 1897

THE TRAGEDY OF PUDD'NHEAD WILSON

Writing *The Tragedy of Pudd'nhead Wilson* in 1892–93, it was evident enough to Twain what his critics had been saying for years: that his control of the lighthearted and the grave was poor. What he started writing as a comedy based on his experience of seeing Siamese twins turned in its execution into something different, a weird mixture (preaching, again, from the circus sawdust). Perhaps trained by now by the reviews, Twain extricated the comic material from the text and published it separately but alongside the now-serious novel, published as *The Tragedy of Puddʹnhead Wilson and the Comedy* [of] *Those Extraordinary Twins*. Twain's own preface to what he calls "The Suppressed Farce" features his own painstaking explanation of how the rupture (the splitting of the twain) took place. He begins thus: "A man who is not born with the novel-writing gift has a troublesome time of it when he tries to build a novel."

Any students interested in Twain's writing process, in particular the seeming spontaneity of it, will find much here. Students curious about how Twain (at least as a novelist) flitted habitually and helplessly between tragedy and comedy will find a rare insight from the author himself here. Twain acknowledges this shortcoming, well documented by the critics:

> It was so in the case of a magazine sketch which I once started to write—a funny and fantastic sketch about a prince and a pauper; it presently assumed a grave cast of its own accord, and in that new shape spread itself out into a book.

This confession, with his solution of drowning all the extraneous characters in a well, establishes two points: first that Twain was a grievously poor planner of novels and admitted it; second, that he was instinctively and effortlessly a brilliant humorist.

It might be asked, looking over Twain's previous books, how frequently he had been writing "two stories in one" before but had failed in those instances to notice. Students interested in themes of twins, doubles, and impostors in Twain's work will find this meditation particularly fascinating as well.

Twain's decision to separate the twin texts worked for some reviewers—William Livingstone Alden praised the novel as "In point of construction . . . much the best story that Mark Twain has written."

Puddnʹhead Wilson has come under greater critical scrutiny and into greater praise in the last twenty years than it ever formally enjoyed. The themes that Twain explores—identity and its subversion, race, miscegenation, the sexual politics of slavery, blacks "passing" as whites, gender and class, for a start—enjoy great prominence in present-day literary studies. The somewhat bland and muted response of Twain's own contemporaries (at least in the North) tends to suggest that he was well ahead of his time. Indeed, aspects of the plot and many of the themes of *Puddʹnhead Wilson* would crop up later in its modernist doppelgänger, William Faulkner's *Absalom, Absalom!* (1936). These tributes notwithstanding, to the reviewer for *The Critic*, Twain's grotesqueness and funniness, while they revel and sparkle, "cannot be called in any sense *literature*." Mark Twain is treated as a noble savage, while James Russell Lowell is venerated for his "university traditions" which were "very strong." These assessments would change in due course, and students of Twain's protean reputation in colleges and universities should mark *The Critic*'s condescension well. This review is best countered by F.R. Leavis's superior essay which vaunts Twain's "use of popular modes—of the sensational and the melodramatic—for the purposes of significant art."

Slavery (particularly sexual relations between slaves and their masters), race, and miscegenation were still awkward topics in 1894, and most critics are merely contented to be bemused by Twain's tale. The *Athenaeum* reviewer finds Roxana the novel's "best thing" because she is "very human," while he finds the son (Chambers) "artificial and forced." This is hardly astute literary criticism. Unsurprisingly, the most scathing review comes from the reviewer for *Fetter's Southern Magazine*. The reviewer, a southerner named Martha McCulloch Williams, has her inevitable ax to grind. Her review veers willy-nilly between pedantic challenges regarding English usage and a passionate defense of the high-born Virginia male as an ideal. The reader is reminded of the *Telegraph* man's scarcely coherent defense of Arthurian legend in his review of *A Connecticut Yankee*. Such responses are significant to students in that they demonstrate the level of feeling associated with Twain's subjects. It is well worth contemplating whether Twain chose the subjects because they might inflame the bourgeoisie.

Williams's essay on *Pudd'nhead Wilson* supplies the student with evidence that Twain's work actually had a social purpose, and excited a dialogue that is uncomfortable but revelatory. Thus Williams grouses bitterly that, to Twain, "the only man worth either saving or damning in all the South country is the black man." She speaks authoritatively of slaves, distinguishing herself and her milieu as "us who owned them." Nostalgically, clinging to the "Myth of the Lost Cause," she recalls how the slaveholders (that is, "us who owned them") retain "lively memories of their pride in [slaves'] surnames; and how tenaciously, after freedom came, [the slaves] clung to the appellations whereunto they felt themselves born."

While it is easy to read a doomed, irrelevant folly in Williams's review itself, some of her scattershot barbs recall the critiques of cooler heads. That Twain follows the money in choosing his subjects ("He has found out the sort of book that sells best") finds its echo in Van Wyck Brooks's *The Ordeal of Mark Twain*: "It is not the artist but the salesman that speaks here, the salesman with an infallible finger for the public pulse" (Brooks, 1920, p. 97). Furthermore, Williams's criticism of Twain's dramatic employment of the ubiquitous folktale about half a dog (from which Wilson derives his nickname) has some validity. Would anybody at all throughout the South have been unfamiliar with this rote quip? Perhaps Twain had been too long in Europe and Connecticut, and his folk materials were rusty.

F.R. Leavis's analysis of *Pudd'nhead Wilson* is among the first major reconsiderations and rehabilitations of Twain's novel. It is distinguished from its predecessors by its dry sophistication. By the time Leavis, a hugely influential English critic and lecturer at Cambridge University, wrote this piece, *Huckleberry Finn* had been accepted fully into the canon of "classic" American literature. Leavis, after discoursing on Huck, endeavors to plead for similar treatment of *Pudd'nhead Wilson*.

Students comparing *Huckleberry Finn* and *Pudd'nhead Wilson* can find a good foundation in Leavis. "*Pudd'nhead Wilson* is so very unlike *Huckleberry Finn*," he remarks; but within the same paragraph he also notes that "it bears a very close relation to *Huckleberry Finn*." Leavis delivers a long overdue rebuttal to Arnold Bennett's remark, often cited by critics of Twain, that Twain was a "divine amateur." "If Mark Twain lacked art in Arnold Bennett's sense," Leavis reflects,

> that only shows how little art in Arnold Bennett's sense matters in comparison with art that is the answer of creative genius to the pressure of a profoundly felt and complex experience.

In contrast to Bennett, Leavis argues that in *Huckleberry Finn* and *Pudd'nhead Wilson* Twain "did achieve a wholeness." Students examining Twain's use of structure will find Leavis a powerful voice in favor of Twain's competence. His argument seems to go against Twain's own frank admission in the preface to "Those Extraordinary Twins." To this Leavis retorts, quoting D.H. Lawrence, "Never trust the artist; trust the tale."

Leavis challenges one of the commonplaces of American studies, the eidolon (the word is Bernard DeVoto's) of the frontier. Leavis finds there is a tendency "to suggest that the beginnings of the truly American in literary tradition come from the frontier and the West." Leavis argues that any culture wholly separated (or "disinherited") from Europe could not "replace the heritage lost." Twain retains a debt to England and Europe.

Leavis continues by challenging representations of the frontier as utterly feral, citing a description of the protosuburban houses and gardens (in 1830 Missouri) as "outward signs of an inward grace ... a civilized community." Students interested in Twain's representation of the frontier—and the idea of the frontier, both in literature and in criticism generally—will find Leavis's challenge to convention refreshing and provocative. Leavis examines the novel's "complexity of ethical background," which he views as Twain's "central preoccupation." In this regard Leavis examines Twain's attitude to his various characters. Twain "unmistakably admires Judge Driscoll and Pembroke Howard." Twain, he reckons, "set[s] a high value on the human qualities fostered by the aristocratic code" of the duello. Nevertheless, Wilson, who endorses the code, "is not ... to be identified with" Twain. Roxy, meanwhile, "plainly bodies forth the qualities that Mark Twain, in his whole being, most values." Leavis lauds, following DeVoto, Roxy as a "frank and unembarrassed recognition of the actuality of sex," a recognition that occurs nowhere else in Twain's (widely published) work. (Leavis was evidently unfamiliar with *1601*, or Twain's address to the "Stomach Club.")

When Leavis's essay was first published (1956), the level of subtle attention given to these characters was unprecedented (as Perry Miller remarks, "nothing would more surprise Mark Twain ... than to perceive the amount of portentous, solemn critical analysis which has been devoted to expose the hidden meanings of *Huck Finn*"). Students examining the depth of Twain's characterization, as well as the moral dimension of his work, will find a trove of speculation here by Leavis. Arguably every critic has his or her own "Mark Twain"—most obviously, Van Wyck Brooks's Twain clashes utterly with DeVoto's version—and Leavis's Twain may seem rather alien to American eyes, viewed as he is from the quadrangle at Cambridge.

⸻ ⸻ ⸻

MARK TWAIN "THOSE EXTRAORDINARY TWINS" (1894)

A man who is not born with the novel-writing gift has a troublesome time of it when he tries to build a novel. I know this from experience. He has no clear idea of his story; in fact he has no story. He merely has some people in his mind, and an incident or two, also a locality, and he trusts he can plunge those people into those incidents with interesting results. So he goes to work. To write a novel? No—that is a thought which comes later; in the beginning he is only proposing to tell a little tale, a very little tale, a six-page tale. But as it is a tale which he is not acquainted with, and can only find out what it is by listening as it goes along telling itself, it is more than apt to go on and on and on till it spreads itself into a book. I know about this, because it has happened to me so many times.

And I have noticed another thing: that as the short tale grows into the long tale, the original intention (or motif) is apt to get abolished and find itself superseded by a quite different one. It was so in the case of a magazine sketch which I once started to write—a funny and fantastic sketch about a prince and a pauper; it presently assumed a grave cast of its own accord, and in that new shape spread itself out into a book. Much the same thing happened with "Pudd'nhead Wilson." I had a sufficiently hard time with that tale, because it changed itself from a farce to a tragedy while I was going along with it—a most embarrassing circumstance. But what was a great deal worse was, that it was not one story, but two stories tangled together; and they obstructed and interrupted each other at every turn and created no end of confusion and annoyance. I could not offer the book for publication, for I was afraid it would unseat the reader's reason. I did not know what was the matter with it, for I had not noticed, as yet, that it was two stories in one. It took me months to make that discovery. I carried the manuscript back and forth across the Atlantic two or three times, and read it and studied over it on shipboard; and at last I saw where the difficulty lay. I had no further trouble. I pulled one of the stories out by the roots, and left the other—a kind of literary Caesarean operation.

Would the reader care to know something about the story which I pulled out? He has been told many a time how the trained novelist works; won't he let me round and complete his knowledge by telling him how the jack-leg does it?

Originally the story was called "Those Extraordinary Twins." I meant to make it very short. I had seen a picture of a youthful Italian "freak"— or "freaks"—which was—or which were—on exhibition in our cities—a combination consisting of two heads and four arms joined to a single body and a single pair of legs—and I thought I would write an extravagantly fantastic little story with this freak of nature for hero—or heroes—a silly young miss for heroine, and two old ladies and two boys for the minor parts. I lavishly elaborated these people and their doings, of course. But the tale kept spreading along and spreading along, and other people got to intruding themselves and taking up more and more room with their talk and their affairs. Among them came a stranger named Pudd'nhead Wilson, and a woman named Roxana; and presently the doings of these two pushed up into prominence a young fellow named Tom Driscoll, whose proper place was away in the obscure background. Before the book was half finished those three were taking things almost entirely into their own hands and working the whole tale as a private venture of their own—a tale which they had nothing at all to do with, by rights.

When the book was finished and I came to look around to see what had become of the team I had originally started out with—Aunt Patsy Cooper, Aunt Betsy Hale, and two boys, and Rowena the lightweight heroine—they were nowhere to be seen; they had disappeared from the story some time or other. I hunted about and found them—found them stranded, idle, forgotten, and permanently useless. It was very awkward. It was awkward all around, but more particularly in the case of Rowena, because there was a love match on, between her and one of the twins that constituted the freak, and I had worked it up to a blistering heat and thrown in a quite dramatic love quarrel, wherein Rowena scathingly denounced her betrothed for getting drunk, and scoffed at his explanation of how it had happened, and wouldn't listen to it, and had driven him from her in the usual "forever" way; and now here she sat crying and brokenhearted; for she had found that he had spoken only the truth; that it was not he, but the other of the freak that had drunk the liquor that made him drunk; that her half was a prohibitionist and had never drunk a drop in his life, and altogether tight as a brick three days in the week, was wholly innocent of blame; and indeed, when sober, was constantly doing all he could to reform his brother, the other half, who never got any satisfaction out of drinking, anyway, because liquor never affected him. Yes, here she was, stranded with that deep injustice of hers torturing her poor torn heart.

I didn't know what to do with her. I was as sorry for her as anybody could be, but the campaign was over, the book was finished, she was sidetracked, and there was no possible way of crowding her in, anywhere. I could not leave her there, of course; it would not do. After spreading her out so, and making such a to-do over her affairs, it would be absolutely necessary to account to the reader for her. I thought and thought and studied and studied; but I arrived at nothing. I finally saw plainly that there was really no way but one—I must simply give her the grand bounce. It grieved me to do it, for after associating with her so much I had come to kind of like her after a fashion, notwithstanding she was such an ass and said such stupid, irritating things and was so nauseatingly sentimental. Still it had to be done. So at the top of Chapter XVII, I put a "Calendar" remark concerning July the Fourth, and began the chapter with this statistic:

"Rowena went out in the backyard after supper to see the fireworks and fell down the well and got drowned."

It seemed abrupt, but I thought maybe the reader wouldn't notice it, because I changed the subject right away to something else. Anyway it loosened up Rowena from where she was stuck and got her out of the way, and that was the main thing. It seemed a prompt good way of weeding out people that had got stalled, and a plenty good enough way for those others; so I hunted up the two boys and said, "They went out back one night to stone the cat and fell down the well and got drowned." Next I searched around and found old Aunt Patsy and Aunt Betsy Hale where they were around, and said, "They went out back one night to visit the sick and fell down the well and got drowned." I was going to drown some others, but I gave up the idea, partly because I believed that if I kept that up it would arouse attention, and perhaps sympathy with those people, and partly because it was not a large well and would not hold any more anyway.

Still the story was unsatisfactory. Here was a set of new characters who were become inordinately prominent and who persisted in remaining so to the end; and back yonder was an older set who made a large noise and a great to-do for a little while and then suddenly played out utterly and fell down the well. There was a radical defect somewhere, and I must search it out and cure it.

The defect turned out to be the one already spoken of—two stories in one, a farce and a tragedy. So I pulled out the farce and left the tragedy. This left the original team in, but only as mere names, not as characters. Their prominence was wholly gone; they were not even worth drowning; so I removed that detail. Also I took the twins apart and made two separate men of them. They had no occasion to have foreign names now, but it was too much trouble to remove them all through, so I left them christened as they were and made no explanation.

—Mark Twain, "Those Extraordinary Twins,"
preface to *The Tragedy of Pudd'nhead Wilson*,
Hartford, CT: American Book Company, 1894,
pp. 309–315

William Livingston Alden (1894)

Puddenhead Wilson, Mark Twain's latest story, is the work of a novelist, rather than of a "funny man." There is plenty of humour in it of the genuine Mark

Twain brand, but it is as a carefully painted picture of life in a Mississippi town in the days of slavery that its chief merit lies. In point of construction it is much the best story that Mark Twain has written, and of men and women in the book at least four are undeniably creations, and not one of them is overdrawn or caricatured, as are some of the most popular of the author's lay figures. There is but one false note in the picture, and that is the introduction of the two alleged Italian noblemen. These two young men are as little like Italians as they are like Apaches. When challenged to fight a duel, one of them, having the choice of weapons, chooses revolvers instead of swords. This incident alone is sufficient to show how little Italian blood there is in Mark Twain's Italians. But this is a small blemish, and if Mark Twain, in his future novels, can maintain the proportion of only two lay figures to four living characters, he will do better than most novelists. The extracts from "Puddenhead Wilson's Almanac," which are prefixed to each chapter of the book, simply "pizon us for more," to use Huck Finn's forcible metaphor. Let us hope that a complete edition of that unrivalled almanac will be issued at no distant day.

—William Livingston Alden, *The Idler* 6, August 1894, pp. 222–223

Unsigned Review in the *Athenaeum* (1895)

The best thing in *Pudd'nhead Wilson*, by Mark Twain (Chatto & Windus), is the picture of the negro slave Roxana, the cause of all the trouble which gives scope to Mr. Wilson's ingenious discovery about finger-marks. Her gusts of passion or of despair, her vanity, her motherly love, and the glimpses of nobler feelings that are occasionally seen in her elementary code of morals, make her very human, and create a sympathy for her in spite of her unscrupulous actions. But hers is the only character that is really striking. Her son is a poor creature, as he is meant to be, but he does not arrest the reader with the same unmistakable reality: his actions are what might be expected, but his conversations, especially with Wilson and the Twins, seem artificial and forced. Wilson, the nominal hero, appears to most advantage in the extracts from his calendar which head the chapters, but as a personage he is rather too shadowy for a hero. And what has to be said about the book must be chiefly about the individuals in it, for the story in itself is not much credit to Mark Twain's skill as a novelist. The idea of the change of babies is happy, and the final trial scene is a good piece of effect; but the story at times rambles on in an almost incomprehensible way. Why drag in, for example, all the business about the election, which is quite irrelevant? and the Twins altogether seem to have very little *raison d'être* in the book. Of course there are some funny things in the story, it would not be by Mark Twain if there were not, but the humour of the preface might very well be spared; it is in bad taste. Still, if the preface be skipped the book well repays reading just for the really excellent picture of Roxana.

—Unsigned Review in the *Athenaeum*
3508, January 19, 1895, pp. 83–84

UNSIGNED REVIEW IN *THE CRITIC* (1895)

The literary critic is often puzzled how to classify the intellectual phenomena that come within his ken. His business is of course primarily with *literature*. A work may be infinitely amusing, it may abound even with flashes and touches of genius, and yet the form in which it comes into the world may be so crude, so coarse, so erring from the ways of true classicism, so offensive to immemorial canons of taste, that the critic, in spite of his enjoyment and wonder, puts it reluctantly down in the category of unclassifiable literary things only to take it up and enjoy it again!

Of such is *Pudd'nhead Wilson*, and, for that matter, Mark Twain in general. The author is a signal example of sheer genius, without training or culture in the university sense, setting forth to conquer the world with laughter whether it will or no, and to get himself thereby acknowledged to be the typical writer of the West. He is the most successful of a class of American humorists whose impulse to write off their rush of animal spirits is irresistible, and who snatch at the first pen within reach as the conductor of their animal electricity. If we look at other national humorists, like Aristophanes, Cervantes, Molière or Swift, we find their humor expressed in an exquisite literary form, in which a certain polish tempers the extravagance, and annoying metrical (or it may be imaginative) difficulties have been overcome. What wonderful bird-rhythms and wasp melodies and cloud-architecture, so to speak, emerge from the marvellous choral interludes of the Greek comedian; what suave literary graces enclose the gaunt outlines of Don Quixote; in what honeyed verse are Alceste and Tartuffe entangled, and what new, nervous, powerful prose describes the adventures of Gulliver! When we turn our eyes westward we encounter Judge Haliburton, Hosea Biglow, Uncle Remus, Mark Twain—an absolutely new *genre* distinct from what we had previously studied in the line of originalities. The one accomplished artist among these is Lowell, whose university traditions were very strong and controlled his bubbling humor. The others are pure "naturalists"—men of instinctive genius, who have relied on their own conscious strength to produce delight in the reader, irrespective of classicity of form, *literary* grace or any other of the beloved conventions on which literature as literature has hitherto depended. This is true in a less degree of Uncle Remus than of Judge Haliburton and Mark Twain.

Pudd'nhead Wilson is no exception to the rule. It is a Missouri tale of changelings "befo' the wah," admirable in atmosphere, local color and dialect, a drama in its way, full of powerful situations, thrilling even; but it cannot be called in any sense *literature*. In it Mark Twain's brightness and grotesqueness and funniness revel and sparkle, and in the absurd extravaganza, "Those Extraordinary Twins," all these comicalities reach the buffoon point; one is amused and laughs unrestrainedly but then the irksome question comes up: What *is* this? is it literature? is Mr. Clemens a "writer" at all? must he not after all be described as an admirable after-dinner storyteller—humorous, imaginative, dramatic, like Dickens—who in an evil moment, urged by admiring friends, has put pen to paper and written down his stories? Adapted to the stage and played by Frank Mayo, the thing has met with immediate success.

—Unsigned Review in *The Critic* 26,
May 11, 1895, pp. 338–339

Martha McCulloch Williams "In Re 'Pudd'nhead Wilson'" (1894)

A better title, perhaps, would be "The Decline and Fall of Mark Twain;" for, looking at it solely as a piece of literature, there is no denying, that his much-advertised serial is tremendously stupid. If it were nothing more, the reading, even the critical, world could afford to receive it in the charity of silence, remembering the merry heart it has had these twenty years past whenever it pleased Mr. Clemens to amuse it.

"Pudd'nhead Wilson" is more than stupid. So far as it has appeared—to the end of the second installment, that is—it is at once malicious and misleading. So much so, indeed, that involuntarily one recalls the gentleman who, it was said, "went to his memory for his wit, and his imagination for his facts."

It certainly seems to me that Mr. Clemens must have imagined all the local color of his tale. It has to do with Dawson's Landing, a small Missouri town on the Mississippi, populated largely with F. F. V's [First Families of Virginia], all of whom are slaveholders, as are the rest of the inhabitants. Right here I wish to ask why it is that the Southern man who has an honest and decent pride in the fact that he comes of good stock fares so ill at the hands of certain literary gentlemen? Bret Harte gives us Colonel Starbottle as his type. Mr. Cable has won fame and fortune and the heart of the whole North by demonstrating to its entire satisfaction how heartlessly and continually all his well-born gentlemen overstep the color line. Last of all, Mark Twain has set himself the task of showing how impossible it is for a man to have a great-grandfather and, at the same time, any regard for the Decalogue.

Perhaps the gentlemen are bent on gleaning the full harvest of "Uncle Tom's Cabin." Perhaps, too, they are wise in so doing. In my seven years North, I have more than once been asked by people who regarded themselves as very well informed "if there were still in the South any pure blacks at all, or any pure-blooded whites?" At first such questioning made me angry. Later, I have come to recognize it as the legitimate outcome of the deliverances of Mr. Cable and his school. Now that Mark Twain has come under their banner, the impression will doubtless become more than ever current. For he has—and has deserved—the widest public of any living American writer. And it is a melancholy fact that the sheep instinct of humanity is so strong as to make it follow *en masse* into any pasture of opinion where he may lead. A still more melancholy fact is the inability of many folk to judge a thing with eyes blinded by the glamour of a great reputation.

Otherwise, I think, some one would have risen ere this to protest against some of Mr. Clemens' gentle idiosyncrasies displayed in the first installment. For instance, the character of Pembroke Howard, introduced solely that the author might tell us that Howard, too, was an F. F. V., also that "he was popular with the people"—and that the story has no sort of concern with him. A while later he is permitted to die. At least there is a line to that effect. What I want to know, and would like to ask Mr. Clemens, is how a man can be "popular with the people," since popular means of, by, or with the people. It does assuredly seem to me pretty queer usage for a man who was so lately toasted and feted by the Lotos Club, as the leading exponent of literary art.

That is by no means a solitary gem of its kind. Careful reading shows the like upon almost every page. It is not too much to say, in fact, that there is slovenly construction in every other paragraph. But the manner is a trifling burden compared with the matter of it. First to last, the writer seemed to feel his burden of humor-with-malice-aforethought. He had chosen his place, his people. If the facts about them are not humorous, so much the worse for facts.

Witness the naming of the hero. He had come out of Western New York to practice law in the Missouri town. One day, hearing a dog bark, he indulges in the Joe-Millerism of wishing he owned half the dog so he might make an end of it. Thereupon the bystanders "fell away from him as something uncanny, and went into privacy to discuss him." One said:

> "Pears to be a fool."
>
> "Pears?" said another. "*Is*, I reckon. Said he wished he owned half the dog." "The idiot," said a third. "What did he reckon would become of the other half if he killed his half? Do you reckon he thought it would live?"
>
> "In my opinion he ain't got any mind."
>
> No. 3 said: "Well, he's a lummox, anyway."
>
> "That's what he is," said No. 4.
>
> "He's a labrick; just a Simon pure labrick if ever there was one."
>
> "Yes, sir, he's a damn fool, that's the way I put him up," said No. 5. "Anybody can think different that wants to, but those are my sentiments."
>
> "I am with you gentlemen," said No. 6. "Perfect jackass—yes, and it ain't going too far to say he is a pudd'nhead. If he ain't a pudd'nhead, I ain't no judge, that's all."
>
> Mr. Wilson stood elected. The incident was told all over town and gravely discussed by everybody. Within a week he had lost his first name. Pudd'nhead took its place.

This is humor, as the great editors understand it. To one a little bit conversant with the folk who are supposed to be humorous, it seems, contrariwise, something cheap and thin. Throughout the Southwest, for at least seventy five years, "I'd like to own that dog—and kill my half" has been a cant saying so commonly current that it is laughed at only out of compliment to the user of it. The men who should now perpetrate it as original would perhaps be called something worse than a "pudd'nhead," but very certainly nobody—not the most ignorant—would find in it a suggestion of uncanniness. For the thing is so common and proverbial that little children make use of it, or rather of its implication. More than one small lad has told me, rejoicing, "Ma has stopped her half of me from going to school." And one shrewd young person within my knowledge bought half of a coveted dolly, then insisted on a property-right to play with it all the time.

So, too, of Mr. Clemens' young man who went away East to college, and came back with "Eastern polish," whatever that may be—perhaps perfect fitting clothes and a habit of wearing gloves. His old friends overlooked the polish of the clothes, but could not forgive the glove habit, so he was left solitary. This is some more, doubtless, of Mr. Clemens' very peculiar humor. He ought, however, to have stated the fact in a footnote. He might have been at the same pains about the reception to the Brothers Capollo. His account of the honors thrust upon them is doubtless a sly revenge upon the misguided Southern communities, which have stretched out admiring hands to Mr. Clemens when he would rather they did not.

So much for the accidentals of the tale. To deal adequately with the story itself, either in motif or atmosphere, would require more time and space than I, at present, command. It is built around the exchange of two children, born the same day, to one father. One his wife's son; the other, his slave's. The wife dies; the slave mother, who has sixteen parts of white blood to one of black, has sole charge of both babies. After a while, her master (as is the custom of Virginia gentlemen in the hands of high literary persons), for some trifling fault, sells all the other house servants, though as a mark of magnanimity he sells them at home instead of sending them down the river. The life-likeness of this part will be apparent to every ex-slave owner, especially to such as remember how far beyond rubies was in those days the price of a thoroughly excellent servant. Setting wholly aside the human affection that often subsisted between white and black, few men were so foolish as to inconvenience themselves by entire change of *menage*, without the most imperative necessity for such a proceeding. All that is, however, beside the mark. This sale goes forward, and as a result, Roxy, the white slave, puts her son in his half-brother's place to save him from the possibility of such a fate.

She also puts her creator—Mark Twain—in rather a hard dilemma. To his mind the only man worth either saving or damning in all the South country is the black man. The exigencies of fiction, however, make it necessary that the slave baby, who normally would grow up a pin-feathered angel, shall, as his own young master, grow up a pretty respectable devil. Similarly, the white child must be, by the change of position, endowed with all the virtue and grace of the subject race. Anybody can see that it is hard lines for the writer. One can fancy him apologizing beforehand to the little negro for the violence he is compelled to do his character. He makes the plunge and the double transformation boldly. It is more than a little amusing, though, to one who knows experimentally the autocracy of a "black mammy," to read how Roxy, after the exchange, was surprised to see how steadily and surely the awe which had kept her tongue reverent, her manner humble towards her young master, was transferring itself to her speech and manner toward the usurper. Roxy must have been a mighty exceptional character if she did not spank her charges with natural and noble impartiality, whether they were white or black.

She had christened her own child "Valet de Chambre—no surname. Slaves hadn't the privilege." That is some more news to us who owned them, and who keep lively memories of their pride in their surnames; and how tenaciously, after freedom came, they clung to the appellations whereunto they felt themselves born. In founding their families under the new conditions, it was often laughable to see the leaning to aristocracy. In more than one case within my own knowledge, negroes abandoned the names of the living masters, in favor of that of the master's grandfather from whom they were inherited and to whose family they leaned because of its greater distinction. Truly, if they had had no privilege of surnames, there must have been confusion worse confounded in the era '65.

Time and patience fail alike in bringing to book all such matters here set down. Suffice it to say that, first to last, the whole recital is unveracious. If it is meant for caricature, the result is the same as would come from exaggerating the ear, nose, and coat-tails of a Bowery tough, and labelling the picture "Ward McAllister." So far as I know, all that the South, either "Old" or "New," has ever done to Mr. Clemens has been to buy his books, when it had precious little money to buy anything, and to set him upon a pedestal as the very prince of humorists. Wherefore, I quite fail to comprehend why it pleases him to villify us as he is doing in this book.

Let me add that I am no bigot in behalf of mine own people. Some have foibles, faults galore, even sins of deepest dye. There are knaves and fools among them—uncouth fellows not a few. So much I readily grant. I will go further and admit that there is that in the social constitution which, rightly handled, might give a humorist scope to add largely to the gaiety of nations. But take them by little and large, they are neither sordid nor stolid, nor lacking in the finer parts of humanity. All this Mr. Clemens makes them out to be. And because he is who he is, a large part of our common country will take his circus-posters for accurate photographs of life and people in the South. Solely for that reason, I make, here and now, my protest against this injustice. I can not comfort myself with the belief that he has sinned ignorantly against half his countrymen. His experience has been too wide, his intelligence is too keen, for that. He is, it seems to me, thus unveracious for revenue only. He has found out the sort of book that sells best. It is not that which speaks the truth as it is, but as the reader wishes to believe it to be. Beside, it is only against a background so lurid as the one he manufactured that the action of his story could possibly take place. As an occasional dabbler in fiction, I recognize the strength of that necessity. But I can not hold that it is sufficient to justify the falsification of all historic conditions. A long time ago, I read a speech of Mr. Clemens in which he said, at the outset, that he had chosen something he knew nothing whatever about so as to be quite unhampered by facts. To judge from "Pudd'nhead Wilson," he has contracted a habit of being unhampered by facts—a habit which seems to grow stronger with age.

—Martha McCulloch Williams, "In Re 'Pudd'nhead Wilson,'" *Fetter's Southern Magazine* 4, 1894, pp. 99–102

Chronology

1835 Samuel Langhorne Clemens is born November 30 in Florida, Missouri, to John Marshall Clemens and Jane Lampton Clemens.

1839 The Clemens family moves to Hannibal, Missouri.

1847 John Marshall Clemens dies; Samuel leaves school and begins career as a printer.

1853–56 Clemens travels as a journeyman printer to St. Louis, New York, Philadelphia, and Iowa.

1857 Samuel is apprenticed to a Mississippi River steamboat pilot.

1858 Samuel's youngest brother, Henry Clemens, dies in an explosion on the steamboat *Pennsylvania.*

1859 Clemens becomes a fully licensed riverboat pilot; he is steadily employed on the Mississippi River.

1861 The Civil War begins, ending regular riverboat travel. Samuel serves briefly in a volunteer Confederate battalion but leaves after a few weeks. Heads for Carson City, Nevada, with his brother Orion, seeking fortune in mining.

1862 Works as a miner and reporter. Adopts the pen name Mark Twain.

1864 Travels to San Francisco, where he continues working as a reporter.

1865 "Jim Smiley and His Jumping Frog" is published and brings him recognition.

1866 Serves as a correspondent for the *Sacramento Daily Union* in Hawaiian Islands. Begins career as a lecturer. Leaves California for New York.

1867	Publication of *The Celebrated Jumping Frog of Calaveras County and Other Sketches*. Works as a correspondent in Europe.
1869	Publishes *The Innocents Abroad*. Travels in California and Nevada and moves to New York.
1869–71	Writes for the *Buffalo Express*.
1870	Marries Olivia Langdon, lives in Buffalo, New York. A son, Langdon, is born on November 7; he dies in infancy.
1871	Moves to Hartford, Connecticut, where he lives and writes for the next sixteen years. Embarks on several business ventures and accumulates debts.
1872	Daughter Susy Clemens is born. *Roughing It* is published, securing his reputation as the leading humorist in the United States. Travels to England.
1873	*The Gilded Age* (co-authored with Charles Dudley Warner) is published.
1874	Daughter Clara Clemens is born.
1876	*The Adventures of Tom Sawyer* is published.
1878–79	Travels through Europe with his family.
1880	Daughter Jean Clemens is born. *A Tramp Abroad* is published.
1881	*The Prince and the Pauper* is published.
1882	Travels along the Mississippi River.
1883	*Life on the Mississippi* is published.
1884	*Adventures of Huckleberry Finn* is published.
1889	*A Connecticut Yankee in King Arthur's Court* is published.
1890	His mother dies.
1891	Leaves Hartford for a decade, travels through Europe with his family.
1892	*The American Claimant* is published. Disastrous investment in a typesetting scheme.
1894	*Pudd'nhead Wilson* is published.
1895–96	Twain files for bankruptcy and departs on a worldwide lecture tour to pay off debts.
1896	Daughter Susy dies of meningitis. *Personal Recollections of Joan of Arc* is published.
1897	*Following the Equator* is published.
1898	Finishes paying off his debts.
1899	"The Man That Corrupted Hadleyburg" is published.
1900	Moves to New York City; publicly opposes imperialism.

1901	Receives an honorary doctorate from Yale University.
1902	Receives an honorary doctorate from the University of Missouri.
1903	Sails for Florence, Italy, with Olivia.
1904	Olivia dies in Florence. Twain returns to New York.
1906	Begins working on his autobiography. Publishes *What Is Man?* privately and anonymously.
1907	Receives an honorary degree from Oxford University.
1908	Moves to last home, "Stormfield" in Redding, Connecticut.
1909	Daughter Jean dies.
1910	Twain dies on April 21, leaving many unpublished papers, among them the incomplete drafts of "The Mysterious Stranger."

Index